Lecture Notes in Artificial Intelligence   11117

Subseries of Lecture Notes in Computer Science

LNAI Series Editors

Randy Goebel
  University of Alberta, Edmonton, Canada
Yuzuru Tanaka
  Hokkaido University, Sapporo, Japan
Wolfgang Wahlster
  DFKI and Saarland University, Saarbrücken, Germany

LNAI Founding Series Editor

Joerg Siekmann
  DFKI and Saarland University, Saarbrücken, Germany

More information about this series at http://www.springer.com/series/1244

Frank Trollmann · Anni-Yasmin Turhan (Eds.)

KI 2018: Advances in Artificial Intelligence

41st German Conference on AI
Berlin, Germany, September 24–28, 2018
Proceedings

 Springer

Editors
Frank Trollmann
TU Berlin
Berlin
Germany

Anni-Yasmin Turhan
TU Dresden
Dresden
Germany

ISSN 0302-9743   ISSN 1611-3349   (electronic)
Lecture Notes in Artificial Intelligence
ISBN 978-3-030-00110-0   ISBN 978-3-030-00111-7   (eBook)
https://doi.org/10.1007/978-3-030-00111-7

Library of Congress Control Number: 2018953026

LNCS Sublibrary: SL7 – Artificial Intelligence

This Springer imprint is published by the registered company Springer Nature Switzerland AG
The registered company address is: Gewerbestrasse 11, 6330 Cham, Switzerland

Preface

The German conference on Artificial Intelligence (abbreviated KI for "Künstliche Intelligenz") has developed from a series of inofficial meetings and workshops, organized by the German "Gesellschaft für Informatik" (association for computer science, GI), into an annual conference series dedicated to research on theory and applications of intelligent system technology. While KI is primarily attended by researchers from Germany and neighboring countries, it is open to international participation and continues to draw various submissions from the international research community.

This volume contains the papers presented at KI2018, which was held on September 24–28, 2018 in Berlin. In response to the call for papers, we received 65 submissions reporting on original research. Despite its focus on Germany, KI 2018 received submissions from over 20 countries. Each of the submitted papers was reviewed and discussed by at least three members of the Program Committee, who decided to accept 23 papers for presentation at the conference. Due to the unusually high number of good-quality submissions, 11 additional papers were selected for poster presentation, accompanied by a short paper in the proceedings. Prominent research topics of this year's conference were Machine Learning, Multi-Agent Systems, and Belief Revision. Overall, KI 2018 offered a broad overview of current research topics in AI.

As is customary for the KI conference series, there were awards for the best paper and the best student paper. This year's award winners were selected based on the reviews supplied by the PC members. The paper chosen for the best paper award is *Preference-Based Monte Carlo Tree Search* by Tobias Joppen, Christian Wirth, and Johannes Fürnkranz. The paper chosen for the best student paper award is *Model Checking for Coalition Announcement Logic* by Rustam Galimullin, Natasha Alechina, and Hans van Ditmarsch.

Besides the technical contributions, KI 2018 had more to offer. First of all, it was a joint event with the conference INFORMATIK 2018, which is the annual conference of the Gesellschaft für Informatik. Both conferences shared a reception event and an exciting keynote by Catrin Misselhorn on *Machine Ethics and Artificial Morality*. The other invited talks of KI 2018 were by Dietmar Jannach on *Session-Based Recommendation—Challenges and Recent Advances* and by Sami Haddadin on Robotics.

As KI is the premier forum for AI researchers in Germany, there were also several co-located events. The conference week started with a collection of workshops dedicated to diverse topics such as processing web data or formal and cognitive aspects of reasoning. In addition, tutorials on Statistical Relational AI (StarAI, organized by Tanya Braun, Kristian Kersting, and Ralf Möller) and Real-Time Recommenations with Streamed Data (organized by Andreas Lommatzsch, Benjamin Kille, Frank Hopfgartner, and Torben Brodt) where offered. Furthermore, a doctoral consortium was organized by Johannes Fähndrich to support PhD students in the field of AI.

A lot of people contributed to the success of KI 2018. First of all, we would like to thank the authors, the members of the Program Committee, and their appointed reviewers for contributing to the scientific quality of KI 2018. In particular we would like to thank the following reviewers who supplied emergency reviews for some of KI 2018's submissions: Sebastian Ahrndt, Andreas Ecke, Johannes Fähndrich, Ulrich Furbach, Brijnesh Jain, Tobias Küster, Craig Macdonald, and Pavlos Marantidis. We also want to thank all local organizers, especially the local chairs, Sebastian Ahrndt and Elif Eryilmaz, and the team of volunteers, who worked tirelessly to make KI 2018 possible. In addition, we would like to thank TU Berlin for supporting KI 2018 and its collocated events with organization and infrastructure. The AI chapter of the Gesellschaft für Informatik as well as Springer receive our special thanks for their financial support of the conference. The process of submitting and reviewing papers and the production of these very proceedings where greatly facilitated by an old friend: the EasyChair system.

July 2018   Frank Trollman
Anni-Yasmin Turhan

Organization

Program Committee

Sebastian Ahrndt	TU Berlin, Germany
Isabelle Augenstein	University College London, UK
Franz Baader	TU Dresden, Germany
Christian Bauckhage	Fraunhofer, Germany
Christoph Beierle	University of Hagen, Germany
Ralph Bergmann	University of Trier, Germany
Leopoldo Bertossi	Carleton University, Canada
Ulf Brefeld	Leuphana University of Lüneburg, Germany
Gerhard Brewka	Leipzig University, Germany
Philipp Cimiano	Bielefeld University, Germany
Jesse Davis	Katholieke Universiteit Leuven, Belgium
Juergen Dix	Clausthal University of Technology, Germany
Igor Douven	Paris-Sorbonne University, France
Didier Dubois	Informatics Research Institute of Toulouse, France
Johannes Fähndrich	German-Turkish Advanced Research Centre for ICT, Germany
Holger Giese	Hasso Plattner Institute, University of Potsdam, Germany
Fabian Gieseke	University of Copenhagen, Denmark
Carsten Gips	Bielefeld University of Applied Sciences, Germany
Lars Grunske	Humboldt University Berlin, Germany
Malte Helmert	University of Basel, Switzerland
Leonhard Hennig	German Research Center for Artificial Intelligence (DFKI), Germany
Joerg Hoffmann	Saarland University, Germany
Steffen Hölldobler	TU Dresden, Germany
Brijnesh Jain	TU Berlin, Germany
Jean Christoph Jung	University of Bremen, Germany
Gabriele Kern-Isberner	Technische Universität Dortmund, Germany
Kristian Kersting	TU Darmstadt, Germany
Roman Klinger	University of Stuttgart, Germany
Oliver Kramer	Universität Oldenburg, Germany
Ralf Krestel	Hasso Plattner Institute, University of Potsdam, Germany
Torsten Kroeger	KIT, Germany
Lars Kunze	University of Oxford, UK
Gerhard Lakemeyer	RWTH Aachen University, Germany
Thomas Lukasiewicz	University of Oxford, UK

Till Mossakowski	University of Magdeburg, Germany
Eirini Ntoutsi	Leibniz University of Hanover, Germany
Ingrid Nunes	Universidade Federal do Rio Grande do Sul (UFRGS), Brazil
Maurice Pagnucco	The University of New South Wales, Australia
Heiko Paulheim	University of Mannheim, Germany
Rafael Peñaloza	Free University of Bozen-Bolzano, Italy
Guenter Rudolph	Technische Universität Dortmund, Germany
Sebastian Rudolph	TU Dresden, Germany
Gabriele Röger	University of Basel, Switzerland
Klaus-Dieter Schewe	Software Competence Center Hagenberg, Austria
Ute Schmid	University of Bamberg, Germany
Lars Schmidt-Thieme	University of Hildesheim, Germany
Lutz Schröder	Friedrich-Alexander-Universität Erlangen-Nürnberg, Germany
Daniel Sonntag	German Research Center for Artificial Intelligence (DFKI), Germany
Steffen Staab	University of Southampton, UK
Heiner Stuckenschmidt	University of Mannheim, Germany
Matthias Thimm	Universität Koblenz-Landau, Germany
Paul Thorn	Heinrich-Heine-Universität Düsseldorf, Germany
Sabine Timpf	University of Augsburg, Germany
Frank Trollman (Chair)	TU Berlin, Germany
Anni-Yasmin Turhan (Chair)	TU Dresden, Germany
Toby Walsh	The University of New South Wales, Australia
Stefan Woltran	Vienna University of Technology, Austria

Additional Reviewers

Ahlbrecht, Tobias
Berscheid, Lars
Boubekki, Ahcène
Brand, Thomas
Ceylan, Ismail Ilkan
Chekol, Melisachew
Wudage
Dick, Uwe
Diete, Alexander
Ecke, Andreas
Euzenat, Jérôme
Ferber, Patrick
Ferrarotti, Flavio

Fiekas, Niklas
Furbach, Ulrich
González, Senén
Haret, Adrian
Hänsel, Joachim
Keller, Thomas
Kutsch, Steven
Küster, Tobias
Macdonald, Craig
Mair, Sebastian
Marantidis, Pavlos
Medeiros Adriano,
Christian

Meier, Almuth
Meißner, Pascal
Morak, Michael
Neuhaus, Fabian
Ollinger, Stefan
Pommerening, Florian
Rashed, Ahmed
Siebers, Michael
Steinmetz, Marcel
Tavakol, Maryam
Wang, Qing

Machine Ethics and Artificial Morality
(Abstract of Keynote Talk)

Catrin Misselhorn

Universität Stuttgart, Stuttgart, Germany

Abstract. Machine ethics explores whether and how artificial systems can be furnished with moral capacities, i.e., whether there cannot just be artificial intelligence, but artificial morality. This question becomes more and more pressing since the development of increasingly intelligent and autonomous technologies will eventually lead to these systems having to face morally problematic situations. Much discussed examples are autonomous driving, health care systems and war robots. Since these technologies will have a deep impact on our lives it is important for machine ethics to discuss the possibility of artificial morality and its implications for individuals and society. Starting with some examples of artificial morality, the talk turns to conceptual issues in machine ethics that are important for delineating the possibility and scope of artificial morality, in particular, what an artificial moral agent is; how morality should be understood in the context of artificial morality; and how human and artificial morality compare. It will be outlined in some detail how moral capacities can be implemented in artificial systems. On the basis of these findings some of the arguments that can be found in public discourse about artificial morality will be reviewed and the prospects and challenges of artificial morality are going to be discussed with regard to different areas of application.

Contents

Robotics

Learning

Planning

Context Aware Systems

Cognitive Approach

Keynote Talk

Keynote Talk

Keynote: Session-Based Recommendation – Challenges and Recent Advances

Dietmar Jannach$^{(\boxtimes)}$

AAU Klagenfurt, 9020 Klagenfurt, Austria
dietmar.jannach@aau.at

Abstract. In many applications of recommender systems, the system's suggestions cannot be based on individual long-term preference profiles, because a large fraction of the user population are either first-time users or returning users who are not logged in when they use the service. Instead, the recommendations have to be determined based on the observed short-term behavior of the users during an ongoing session. Due to the high practical relevance of such session-based recommendation scenarios, different proposals were made in recent years to deal with the particular challenges of the problem setting.

In this talk, we will first characterize the session-based recommendation problem and its position within the family of sequence-aware recommendation. Then, we will review algorithmic proposals for next-item prediction in the context of an ongoing user session and report the results of a recent in-depth comparative evaluation. The evaluation, to some surprise, reveals that conceptually simple prediction schemes are often able to outperform more advanced techniques based on deep learning. In the final part of the talk, we will focus on the e-commerce domain. We will report recent insights regarding the consideration of short-term user intents, the importance of considering community trends, the role of reminders, and the recommendation of discounted items.

Keywords: Recommender systems · Session-based recommendation

1 Introduction

Recommender systems (RS) are tools that help users find items of interest within large collections of objects. They are omnipresent in today's online world, and many online sites nowadays feature functionalities like Amazon's "Customers who bought ... also bought" recommendations.

Historically, the recommendation problem is often abstracted to a matrix-completion task, see [8] for a brief historical overview. In such a setting, the goal is to make preference or rating predictions, given a set of preference statements of users toward items. These statements are usually collected over longer periods of time. In many real-world applications, however, such long-term profiles often do not exist or cannot be used because website visitors are first-time users, are

© Springer Nature Switzerland AG 2018
F. Trollmann and A.-Y. Turhan (Eds.): KI 2018, LNAI 11117, pp. 3–7, 2018.
https://doi.org/10.1007/978-3-030-00111-7_1

not logged in, or take measures to avoid system-side tracking. These scenarios lead to what is often termed a *session-based recommendation* problem in the literature. The specific problem in these scenarios therefore is to make helpful recommendations based only on information derived from the ongoing session, i.e., from a very limited set of recent user interactions.

While the matrix completion problem formulation still dominates the academic research landscape, in recent years, increasing research interest can be observed for session-based recommendation problems. This interest is increased not only due to the high practical relevance of the problem, but also due to the availability of new research datasets and the recent development of sophisticated prediction models based on deep neural networks [2,3,13].

In this talk, we will first characterize session-based recommendation problems as part of the more general family of *sequence-aware* recommendation tasks. Next, we will briefly review existing algorithmic techniques for "next-item" prediction and discuss the results of a recent comparative evaluation of different algorithm families. In the final part of the talk, we will then take a closer look at the e-commerce domain. Specifically, we will report results from an in-depth study, which explored practical questions regarding the importance of short-term user intents, the use of recommendations as reminders, the role of community trends, and the recommendation of items that are on sale.

2   Sequence-Aware Recommender Systems

In [12], session-based recommendation is considered one main computational task of what is called *sequence-aware* recommender systems. Differently from traditional setups, the input to a sequence-aware recommendation problem is not a matrix of user-item preference statements, but a sequential log of past user interactions. Such logs, which are typically collected by today's e-commerce sites, can contain user interactions of various types such as item view events, purchases, or add-to-cart events (Fig. 1).

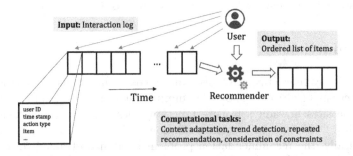

Fig. 1. Overview of the sequence-aware recommendation problem, adapted from [12].

Given such a log, various computational tasks can be defined. The most well-researched task in the literature is termed "context adaptation" in [12], where the goal is to create recommendations that suit the user's assumed short-term intents or contextual situation. Here, we can further discriminate between session-*based* and session-*aware* recommendation. In session-based scenarios, only the last few user interactions are known; in session-aware settings, in contrast, also past sessions of the current user might be available.

The sequential logs of sequence-aware recommender systems can however also be used for other types of computations, including the repeated recommendation of items, the detection of global trends in community, or the consideration of order constraints. These aspects are described in more detail in [12].

3   Session-Based Recommendation

3.1   Algorithmic Approaches

A variety of algorithmic approaches have been proposed over the years for session-based recommendation scenarios. The conceptually most simple techniques rely on the detection of co-occurrence patterns in the recorded data. Recommendations of the form "Customers who bought ... also bought", as a simple form of session-based recommendation, can, for example, be determined by computing pairwise item co-occurrences or association rules of size two [1]. This concept can be extended to co-occurrence patterns that consider also the order of the events, e.g., in terms of simple Markov Chains or Sequential Patterns [11]. This latter approach falls into the category of *sequence learning* approaches [12], and a number of more advanced techniques based on Markov Decision Processes, Reinforcement Learning, and Recurrent Neural Networks were proposed in the literature [3,13,15]. In addition, distributional embeddings were explored to model user sessions in different domains. Finally, different hybrid approaches were investigated recently, which, for example, combine latent factor models with sequential information [14].

3.2   Evaluation Aspects: Recent Insights

Differently from the matrix completion problem formulation, no standards exist yet in the community for the comparative evaluation of session-based recommendation approaches, despite the existence of some proposals [5]. As a result, researchers use a variety of evaluation protocols and baselines in their experiments, which makes it difficult to assess the true value of new methods.

In [6,10], recently, an in-depth comparison of a variety of techniques for session-based recommendation was made. The comparison, which was based on datasets from several domains, included both conceptually simple techniques as well as the most recent algorithms based on Recurrent Neural Networks. To some surprise, it turned out that in almost all configurations, simple methods, e.g., based on the nearest-neighbor principle [6], where able to outperform the more complex ones. This, as a result, means that there is substantial room for improvement for more advanced machine learning techniques for the given problem setting.

4   On Short-Term Intents, Reminders, Trends, and Discounts in E-Commerce

In many session-based and session-aware recommendation problems in practice, a number of additional considerations can be made which are barely addressed in the academic literature. In [7], an in-depth analysis of various practical aspects was presented based on a large e-commerce dataset from the fashion domain.

The Role of Short-Term Intents. One first question relates to the *relative* importance of long-term preference models with respect to short-term user intents. The results presented, for example, in [5,7] indicate that being able to estimate short-term intents is often much more important than further optimizing long-term preference models based, e.g., on matrix factorization techniques. One main challenge therefore lies in the proper estimation of the visitor's immediate shopping goal based only on a small set of interactions.

Recommendations as Reminders. While recommender systems in practice are often designed to also (repeatedly) recommend items that the user has inspected before, little research on the use of recommendations as reminders and navigation shortcuts exists so far. Recent research results however show that including reminders can have significant business value.

Trends and Discounts. A deeper analysis of a real-world dataset from the fashion domain in [7] furthermore reveals that recommending items that were recently popular, e.g., during the last day, is highly effective. At the same time, recommending items that are currently on sale leads to high click-to-purchase conversion, at least in the examined domain.

Learning Recommendations Success Factors from Log Data. A specific characteristic of the e-commerce dataset used in [7] is that it contains a detailed log of the items that were recommended to users along with information about clicks on such recommendations and subsequent purchases. Based on these logs, it is not only possible to analyze under which circumstances a recommendation was successful. We can also build predictive models based on these learned features, which at the end lead to more effective recommendation algorithms.

4.1   Challenges

Despite recent progress in the field, a variety of challenges remain to be further explored. Besides the development of more sophisticated algorithms for the next-item prediction problem, the open challenges, for example, include better mechanisms for combining long-term preference models with short-term user intents and to detect interest drifts. Furthermore, techniques can also be envisioned that are able to detect interest changes at the micro-level, i.e., during an individual session. In particular for the first few events in a new session, alternative approaches are needed to reliably estimate the user's short-term intent, based, e.g., on contextual information, global trends, meta-data, automatically extracted content-features, or from sensor information.

From a research perspective, the development of agreed-upon evaluation protocols and metrics are desirable, and more research is required to understand in which situation certain algorithms are advantageous. In addition, more user-oriented evaluations, as done in [9] for the music domain, are needed to better understand the utility of recommenders in different application scenarios.

From a more practical perspective, session-based recommendation can serve different purposes, e.g., they can be designed to either show alternatives options or complementary items. To be able to better assess the utility of the recommendations made by an algorithm for different stakeholders, purpose-oriented [4] and multi-metric evaluation approaches are required that go beyond the prediction of the next hidden item in offline experiments based on historical data.

References

1. Agrawal, R., Imieliński, T., Swami, A.: Mining association rules between sets of items in large databases. In: SIGMOD 1993, pp. 207–216 (1993)
2. Ben-Shimon, D., Tsikinovsky, A., Friedmann, M., Shapira, B., Rokach, L., Hoerle, J.: RecSys challenge 2015 and the YOOCHOOSE dataset. In: ACM RecSys 2015, pp. 357–358 (2015)
3. Hidasi, B., Karatzoglou, A., Baltrunas, L., Tikk, D.: Session-based recommendations with recurrent neural networks. In: ICLR 2016 (2016)
4. Jannach, D., Adomavicius, G.: Recommendations with a purpose. In: RecSys 2016, pp. 7–10 (2016)
5. Jannach, D., Lerche, L., Jugovac, M.: Adaptation and evaluation of recommendations for short-term shopping goals. In: RecSys 2015, pp. 211–218 (2015)
6. Jannach, D., Ludewig, M.: When recurrent neural networks meet the neighborhood for session-based recommendation. In: RecSys 2017, pp. 306–310 (2017)
7. Jannach, D., Ludewig, M., Lerche, L.: Session-based item recommendation in e-commerce: on short-term intents, reminders, trends, and discounts. User-Model. User-Adap. Interact. 27(3–5), 351–392 (2017)
8. Jannach, D., Resnick, P., Tuzhilin, A., Zanker, M.: Recommender systems - beyond matrix completion. Commun. ACM 59(11), 94–102 (2016)
9. Kamehkhosh, I., Jannach, D.: User perception of next-track music recommendations. In: UMAP 2017, pp. 113–121 (2017)
10. Ludewig, M., Jannach, D.: Evaluation of session-based recommendation algorithms (2018). https://arxiv.org/abs/1803.09587
11. Mobasher, B., Dai, H., Luo, T., Nakagawa, M.: Using sequential and non-sequential patterns in predictive web usage mining tasks. In: ICDM 2003, pp. 669–672 (2002)
12. Quadrana, M., Cremonesi, P., Jannach, D.: Sequence-aware recommender systems. ACM Comput. Surv. 51(4), 1–36 (2018)
13. Quadrana, M., Karatzoglou, A., Hidasi, B., Cremonesi, P.: Personalizing session-based recommendations with hierarchical recurrent neural networks. In: RecSys 2017, pp. 130–137 (2017)
14. Rendle, S., Freudenthaler, C., Schmidt-Thieme, L.: Factorizing personalized Markov chains for next-basket recommendation. In: WWW 2010, pp. 811–820 (2010)
15. Shani, G., Heckerman, D., Brafman, R.I.: An MDP-based recommender system. J. Mach. Learn. Res. 6, 1265–1295 (2005)

Reasoning

Model Checking for Coalition Announcement Logic

Rustam Galimullin[1(✉)], Natasha Alechina[1], and Hans van Ditmarsch[2]

[1] University of Nottingham, Nottingham, UK
{rustam.galimullin,natasha.alechina}@nottingham.ac.uk
[2] CNRS, LORIA, Univ. of Lorraine, France & ReLaX, Chennai, India
hans.van-ditmarsch@loria.fr

Abstract. Coalition Announcement Logic (CAL) studies how a group of agents can enforce a certain outcome by making a joint announcement, regardless of any announcements made simultaneously by the opponents. The logic is useful to model imperfect information games with simultaneous moves. We propose a model checking algorithm for CAL and show that the model checking problem for CAL is PSPACE-complete. We also consider a special positive case for which the model checking problem is in P. We compare these results to those for other logics with quantification over information change.

Keywords: Model checking · Coalition announcement logic
Dynamic epistemic logic

1 Introduction

In the multi-agent logic of knowledge we investigate what agents know about their factual environment and what they know about knowledge of each other [14]. (Truthful) Public announcement logic (PAL) is an extension of the multi-agent logic of knowledge with modalities for public announcements. Such modalities model the event of incorporating trusted information that is similarly observed by all agents [17]. The 'truthful' part relates to the trusted aspect of the information: we assume that the novel information is true.

In [2] the authors propose two generalisations of public announcement logic, GAL (group announcement logic) and CAL (coalition announcement logic). These logics allow for quantification over public announcements made by agents modelled in the system. In particular, the GAL quantifier $\langle G \rangle \varphi$ (parametrised by a subset G of the set of all agents A) says 'there is a truthful announcement made by the agents in G, after which φ (holds)'. Here, the truthful aspect means that the agents in G only announce what they *know*: if a in G announces φ_a, this is interpreted as a public announcement $K_a \varphi_a$ such that a truthful announcement by agents in G is a conjunction of such known announcements. The CAL quantifier $[\![G]\!]\varphi$ is motivated by game logic [15,16] and van Benthem's playability operator [8]. Here, the modality means 'there is a truthful announcement

© Springer Nature Switzerland AG 2018
F. Trollmann and A.-Y. Turhan (Eds.): KI 2018, LNAI 11117, pp. 11–23, 2018.
https://doi.org/10.1007/978-3-030-00111-7_2

made by the agents in G such that no matter what the agents not in G simultaneously announce, φ holds afterwards'. In [2] it is, for example, shown that this subsumes game logic.

CAL has been far less investigated than other logics of quantified announcements – APAL [6] and GAL – although some combined results have been achieved [4]. In particular, model checking for CAL has not been studied. Model checking for CAL has potential practical implications. In CAL, it is possible to express that a group of agents (for example, a subset of bidders in an auction) can make an announcement such that no matter what other agents announce simultaneously, after this announcement certain knowledge is increased (all agents know that G have won the bid) but certain ignorance also remains (for example, the maximal amount of money G could have offered). Our model-checking algorithm may be easily modified to return not just 'true' but the actual announcement that G can make to achieve their objective. The algorithm and the proof of PSPACE-completeness build on those for GAL [1], but the CAL algorithm requires some non-trivial modifications. We show that for the general case, model checking CAL is in PSPACE, and also describe an efficient (PTIME) special case.

2   Background

2.1   Introductory Example

Two agents, a and b, want to buy the same item, and whoever offers the greatest sum, gets it. Agents may have 5, 10, or 15 pounds, and they do not know which sum the opponent has. Let agent a have 15 pounds, and agent b have 5 pounds. This situation is presented in Fig. 1.

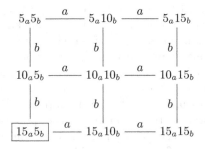

Fig. 1. Initial model $(M, 15_a5_b)$

In this model (let us call it M), state names denote money distribution. Thus, 10_a5_b means that agent a has 10 pounds, and agent b has 5 pounds. Labelled edges connect the states that a corresponding agent cannot distinguish. For example, in the actual state (boxed), agent a knows that she has 15 pounds, but she does not know how much money agent b has. Formally, $(M, 15_a5_b) \models$

$K_a 15_a \wedge \neg(K_a 5_b \vee K_a 10_b \vee K_a 15_b)$ (which mean $(M, 15_a 5_b)$ satisfies the formula, where $K_i \varphi$ stands for 'agent i knows that φ', $\wedge$ is logical and, $\neg$ is not, and $\vee$ is or). Note that edges represent equivalence relations, and in the figure we omit transitive and reflexive transitions.

Next, suppose that agents bid in order to buy the item. Once one of the agents, let us say a, announces her bid, she also wants the other agent to remain ignorant of the total sum at her disposal. Formally, we can express this goal as formula $\varphi ::= K_b(10_a \vee 15_a) \wedge \neg(K_b 10_a \vee K_b 15_a)$ (for bid 10 by agent a). Informally, if a commits to pay 10 pounds, agent b knows that a has 10 or more pounds, but b does not know the exact amount. If agent b does not participate in announcing (bidding), a can achieve the target formula φ by announcing $K_a 10_a \vee K_a 15_a$. In other words, agent a commits to pay 10 pounds, which denotes that she has at least that sum at her disposal. In general, this means that there is an announcement by a such that after this announcements φ holds. Formally, $(M, 15_a 5_b) \models \langle a \rangle \varphi$. The updated model $(M, 15_a 5_b)^{K_a 10_a \vee K_a 15_a}$, which is, essentially, a restriction of the original model to the states where $K_a 10_a \vee K_a 15_a$ holds, is presented in Fig. 2.

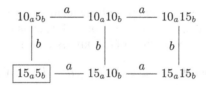

Fig. 2. Updated model $(M, 15_a 5_b)^{K_a 10_a \vee K_a 15_a}$

Indeed, in the updated model agent b knows that a has at least 10 pounds, but not the exact sum. The same holds if agent b announces her bid simultaneously with a in the initial situation. Moreover, a can achieve φ no matter what agent b announces, since b can only truthfully announce $K_b 5_b$, i.e. that she has only 5 pounds at her disposal. Formally, $(M, 15_a 5_b) \models \langle\!\langle a \rangle\!\rangle \varphi$.

2.2   Syntax and Semantics of CAL

Let A denote a finite set of agents, and P denote a countable set of propositional variables.

Definition 1. *The language of coalition announcement logic $\mathcal{L}_{CAL}$ is defined by the following BNF:*

$$\varphi, \psi ::= p \mid \neg\varphi \mid (\varphi \wedge \psi) \mid K_a \varphi \mid [\psi]\varphi \mid [\![G]\!]\varphi,$$

where $p \in P$, $a \in A$, $G \subseteq A$, and all the usual abbreviations of propositional logic and conventions for deleting parentheses hold. The dual operators are defined as follows: $\widehat{K}_a\varphi ::= \neg K_a\neg\varphi$, $\langle\psi\rangle\varphi ::= \neg[\psi]\neg\varphi$, and $\langle\!\langle G\rangle\!\rangle\varphi ::= \neg[\![G]\!]\neg\varphi$. Language $\mathcal{L}_{PAL}$ is the language without the operator $[\![G]\!]\varphi$, and $\mathcal{L}_{EL}$ is the pure epistemic language without the operators $[\psi]\varphi$ and $[\![G]\!]\varphi$.

Formulas of CAL are interpreted in epistemic models.

Definition 2. *An* epistemic model *is a triple* $M = (W, \sim, V)$, *where* W *is a non-empty set of states,* $\sim: A \to \mathcal{P}(W \times W)$ *assigns an equivalence relation to each agent, and* $V : P \to \mathcal{P}(W)$ *assigns a set of states to each propositional variable.* M *is called* finite *if* W *is finite. A pair* (M, w) *with* $w \in W$ *is called a* pointed model. *Also, we write* $M_1 \subseteq M_2$ *if* $W_1 \subseteq W_2$, $\sim_1$ *and* V_1 *are restrictions of* $\sim_2$ *and* V_2 *to* W_1, *and call* M_1 *a* submodel *of* M_2.

Definition 3. *For a pointed model* (M, w) *and* $\varphi \in \mathcal{L}_{EL}$, *an* updated model $(M, w)^\varphi$ *is a restriction of the original model to the states where* φ *holds and to corresponding relations. Let* $[\![\varphi]\!]_M = \{w : (M, w) \models \varphi\}$ *where* $\models$ *is defined below. Then* $W^\varphi = [\![\varphi]\!]_M$, $\sim_a^\varphi = \sim_a \cap ([\![\varphi]\!]_M \times [\![\varphi]\!]_M)$ *for all* $a \in A$, *and* $V^\varphi(p) = V(p) \cap [\![\varphi]\!]_M$. *A model which results in subsequent updates of* (M, w) *with formulas* $\varphi_1, \dots, \varphi_n$ *is denoted* $(M, w)^{\varphi_1, \dots, \varphi_n}$.

Let $\mathcal{L}_{EL}^G$ denote the set of formulas of the form $\bigwedge_{a \in G} K_a\varphi_a$, where for every $a \in G$ it holds that $\varphi_a \in \mathcal{L}_{EL}$. In other words, formulas of $\mathcal{L}_{EL}^G$ are of the type 'for all agents a from group\coalition G, a knows a corresponding φ_a.'

Definition 4. *Let a pointed model* (M, w) *with* $M = (W, \sim, V)$, $a \in A$, *and formulas* φ *and* ψ *be given.*[1]

$$
\begin{aligned}
&(M, w) \models p &&\text{iff } w \in V(p) \\
&(M, w) \models \neg\varphi &&\text{iff } (M, w) \not\models \varphi \\
&(M, w) \models \varphi \wedge \psi &&\text{iff } (M, w) \models \varphi \text{ and } (M, w) \models \psi \\
&(M, w) \models K_a\varphi &&\text{iff } \forall v \in W : w \sim_a v \text{ implies } (M, v) \models \varphi \\
&(M, w) \models [\varphi]\psi &&\text{iff } (M, w) \models \varphi \text{ implies } (M, w)^\varphi \models \psi \\
&(M, w) \models [\![G]\!]\varphi &&\text{iff } \forall\psi \in \mathcal{L}_{EL}^G \; \exists\chi \in \mathcal{L}_{EL}^{A\setminus G} : (M, w) \models \psi \to \langle\psi \wedge \chi\rangle\varphi
\end{aligned}
$$

The operator for coalition announcements $[\![G]\!]\varphi$ is read as 'whatever agents from G announce, there is a simultaneous announcement by agents from $A \setminus G$ such that φ holds.'

The semantics for the 'diamond' version of coalition announcement operators is as follows:

$$(M, w) \models \langle\!\langle G\rangle\!\rangle\varphi \text{ iff } \exists\psi \in \mathcal{L}_{EL}^G \forall\chi \in \mathcal{L}_{EL}^{A\setminus G} : (M, w) \models \psi \wedge [\psi \wedge \chi]\varphi$$

---

[1] For comparison, semantics for group announcement operator of the logic GAL mentioned in the introduction is $(M, w) \models [G]\varphi$ iff $\forall\psi \in \mathcal{L}_{EL}^G : (M, w) \models [\psi]\varphi$ and $(M, w) \models \langle G\rangle\varphi$ iff $\exists\psi \in \mathcal{L}_{EL}^G : (M, w) \models \langle\psi\rangle\varphi$.

Definition 5. *We call formula φ valid if and only if for any pointed model (M, w) it holds that $(M, w) \models \varphi$. And φ is called satisfiable if and only if there is some (M, w) such that $(M, w) \models \varphi$.*

Note that following [1, 6] we restrict formulas that agents in a group or coalition can announce to formulas of $\mathcal{L}_{EL}$. This allows us to avoid circularity in Definition 4.

2.3   Bisimulation

The basic notion of similarity in modal logic is bisimulation [9, Sect. 3].

Definition 6. *Let two models $M = (W, \sim V)$ and $M' = (W', \sim', V')$ be given. A non-empty binary relation $Z \subseteq W \times W'$ is called a bisimulation if and only if for all $w \in W$ and $w' \in W'$ with $(w, w') \in Z$:*

- *w and w' satisfy the same propositional variables;*
- *for all $a \in A$ and all $v \in W$: if $w \sim_a v$, then there is a v' such that $w' \sim_a v'$ and $(v, v') \in Z$;*
- *for all $a \in A$ and all $v' \in W'$: if $w' \sim_a v'$, then there is a v such that $w \sim_a v$ and $(v, v') \in Z$.*

If there is a bisimulation between models M and M' linking states w and w', we say that (M, w) and (M', w') are bisimilar.

Note that any union of bisimulations between two models is a bisimulation, and the union of all bisimulations is a maximal bisimulation.

Definition 7. *Let model M be given. The quotient model of M with respect to some relation R is $M^R = (W^R, \sim^R, V^R)$, where $W^R = \{[w] \mid w \in W\}$ and $[w] = \{v \mid wRv\}$, $[w] \sim_a^R [v]$ iff $\exists w' \in [w]$, $\exists v' \in [v]$ such that $w' \sim_a v'$ in M, and $[w] \in V^R(p)$ iff $\exists w' \in [w]$ such that $w' \in V(p)$.*

Definition 8. *Let model M be given. Bisimulation contraction of M (written $\|M\|$) is the quotient model of M with respect to the maximal bisimulation of M with itself. Such a maximal bisimulation is an equivalence relation.*

Informally, bisimulation contraction is the minimal representation of M.

Definition 9. *A model M is bisimulation contracted if M is isomorphic to $\|M\|$.*

Proposition 1. *$(\|M\|, w) \models \varphi$ iff $(M, w) \models \varphi$ for all $\varphi \in \mathcal{L}_{CAL}$.*

Proof. By a straightforward induction on φ using the following facts: bisimulation contraction of a model is bisimilar to the model, bismilar models satisfy the same formulas of $\mathcal{L}_{EL}$, and public announcements preserve bisimulation [12]. □

3   Strategies of Groups of Agents on Finite Models

3.1   Distinguishing Formulas

In this section we introduce distinguishing formulas that are satisfied in only one (up to bisimulation) state in a finite model (see [10] for details). Although agents know and can possibly announce an infinite number of formulas, using distinguishing formulas allows us to consider only finitely many different announcements. This is done by associating strategies of agents with corresponding distinguishing formulas. Here and subsequently, all epistemic models are *finite* and *bisimulation contracted*. Also, without loss of generality, we assume that the set of propositional variables P is finite.

Definition 10. *Let a finite epistemic model M be given. Formula $\delta_{S,S'}$ is called distinguishing for $S, S' \subseteq W$ if $S \subseteq [\![\delta_{S,S'}]\!]_M$ and $S' \cap [\![\delta_{S,S'}]\!]_M = \emptyset$. If a formula distinguishes state w from all other non-bismilar states in M, we write δ_w.*

Proposition 2 ([10]). *Let a finite epistemic model M be given. Every pointed model (M, w) is distinguished from all other non-bisimilar pointed models (M, v) by some distinguishing formula $\delta_w \in \mathcal{L}_{EL}$.*

Given a finite model (M, w), distinguishing formula δ_w is constructed recursively as follows:

$$\delta_w^{k+1} ::= \delta_w^0 \wedge \bigwedge_{a \in A} (\bigwedge_{w \sim_a v} \widehat{K}_a \delta_v^k \wedge K_a \bigvee_{w \sim_a v} \delta_v^k),$$

where $0 \leq k < |W|$, and δ_w^0 is the conjunction of all literals that are true in w, i.e. $\delta_w^0 ::= \bigwedge_{w \in V(p)} p \wedge \bigwedge_{w \notin V(p)} \neg p$.

Having defined distinguishing formulas for states, we can define distinguishing formulas for sets of states:

Definition 11. *Let some finite and bisimulation contracted model (M, w), and a set S of states in M be given. A distinguishing formula for S is*

$$\delta_S ::= \bigvee_{w \in S} \delta_w.$$

3.2   Strategies

In this section we introduce strategies, and connect them to possible announcements using distinguishing formulas.

Definition 12. *Let $M/a = \{[w_1]_a, \ldots, [w_n]_a\}$ be the set of a-equivalence classes in M. A strategy X_a for an agent a in a finite model (M, w) is a union of equivalence classes of a including $[w]_a$. The set of all available strategies of a is $S(a, w) = \{[w]_a \cup X_a : X_a \subseteq \bigcup M/a\}$. Group strategy X_G is defined as $\bigcap_{a \in G} X_a$ for all $a \in G$. The set of available strategies for a group of agents G is $S(G, w) = \{\bigcap_{a \in G} X_a : X_a \in S(a, w)\}$.*

Note, that for any (M, w) and $G \subseteq A$, $S(G, w)$ is not empty, since the trivial strategy that includes all the states of the current model is available to all agents.

Proposition 3. *In a finite model* (M, w), *for any* $G \subseteq A$, $S(G, w)$ *is finite.*

Proof. Due to the fact that in a finite model there is a finite number of equivalence classes for each agent.   □

Thus, in Fig. 1 of Sect. 2.1 there are three a-equivalence classes: $\{15_a5_b, 15_a10_b, 15_a15_b\}$, $\{10_a5_b, 10_a10_b, 10_a15_b\}$, and $\{5_a5_b, 5_a10_b, 5_a15_b\}$. Let us designate them by the first element of a corresponding set, i.e. 15_a5_b, 10_a5_b, and 5_a5_b. The set of all available strategies of agent a in $(M, 15_a5_b)$ is $\{15_a5_b, 15_a5_b \cup 10_a5_b, 15_a5_b \cup 5_a5_b, 15_a5_b \cup 10_a5_b \cup 5_a5_b\}$. Similarly, the set of all available strategies of agent b in $(M, 15_a5_b)$: $\{15_a5_b, 15_a5_b \cup 15_a10_b, 15_a5_b \cup 15_a15_b, 15_a5_b \cup 15_a10_b \cup 15_a15_b\}$. Finally, there is a group strategy for agents a and b that contains only two states – 15_a5_b and 10_a5_b. This strategy is an intersection of a's $15_a5_b \cup 10_a5_b$ and b's 15_a5_b, that is $\{15_a5_b, 15_a10_b, 15_a15_b, 10_a5_b, 10_a10_b, 10_a15_b\} \cap \{15_a5_b, 10_a5_b, 5_a5_b\}$.

Now we tie together announcements and strategies. Each of infinitely many possible announcements in a finite model corresponds to a set of states where it is true (a strategy). In a finite bisimulation contracted model, each strategy is definable by a distinguishing formula, hence it corresponds to an announcement. This allows us to consider finitely many strategies instead of considering infinitely many possible announcements: there are only finitely many non-equivalent announcements for each finite model, and each of them is equivalent to a distinguishing formula of some strategy.

Given a finite and bisimulation contracted model (M, w) and strategy X_G, a distinguishing formula δ_{X_G} for X_G can be obtained from Definition 11 as $\bigvee_{w \in X_G} \delta_w$.

Next, we show that agents know their strategies and thus can make corresponding announcements.

Proposition 4. *Let agent* a *have strategy* X_a *in some finite bisimulation contracted* (M, w). *Then* $(M, w) \models K_a \delta_{X_a}$. *Also, let* $X_G ::= X_a \cap \ldots \cap X_b$ *be a strategy, then* $(M, w) \models K_a \delta_{X_a} \wedge \ldots \wedge K_b \delta_{X_b}$, *where* $a, \ldots, b \in G$.

Proof. We show just the first part of the proposition, since the second part follows easily. By the definition of a strategy, $X_a = [w_1]_a \cup \ldots \cup [w_n]_a$ for some $[w_1]_a, \ldots, [w_n]_a \in M/a$. For every equivalence class $[w_i]_a$ there is a corresponding distinguishing formula $\delta_{[w_i]_a}$. Since for all $v \in [w_i]_a$, $(M, v) \models \delta_{[w_i]_a}$ (by Proposition 2), we have that $(M, v) \models K_a \delta_{[w_i]_a}$. The same holds for other equivalence classes of a including the one with w, and we have $(M, w) \models K_a \delta_{X_a}$.   □

The following proposition (which follows from Propositions 2 and 4) states that given a strategy, corresponding public announcement yields exactly the model with states specified by the strategy.

Proposition 5. *Given a finite bisimulation contracted model $M = (W, \sim, V)$ and a strategy X_a, $W^{K_a \delta X_a} = X_a$. More generally, $W^{K_a \delta X_a \wedge \ldots \wedge K_b \delta X_b} = X_G$, where $a, \ldots, b \in G$.*

So, we have tied together announcements and strategies via distinguishing formulas. From now on, we may abuse notation and write M^{X_G}, meaning that M^{X_G} is an update of model M by a joint announcement of agents G that corresponds to strategy X_G.

Now, let us reformulate semantics for group and coalition announcement operators in terms of strategies.

Proposition 6. *For a finite bisimulation contracted model (M, w) we have that*

$$(M, w) \models \langle\!\langle G \rangle\!\rangle \varphi \text{ iff } \exists X_G \in S(G, w) \ \forall X_{A \backslash G} \in S(A \backslash G, w) : (M, w)^{X_G \cap X_{A \backslash G}} \models \varphi.$$

Proof. By Propositions 4 and 5, each strategy corresponds to an announcement. Each true announcement is a formula of the form $K_a \psi_a \wedge \ldots \wedge K_b \psi_b$ where ψ_a is a formula which is true in every state of some union of a-equivalence classes and corresponds to a strategy. Similarly for announcements by groups. Hence we can substitute quantification over formulas with quantification over strategies in the truth definitions.   □

Definition 13. *Let some finite bisimulation contracted model (M, w) and G be given. A* maximally informative announcement *is a formula $\psi \in \mathcal{L}_{EL}^G$ such that $w \in W^\psi$ and for all $\psi' \in \mathcal{L}_{EL}^G$ such that $w \in W^{\psi'}$ it holds that $W^\psi \subseteq W^{\psi'}$. For finite models such an announcement always exists [3]. We will call the corresponding strategy X_G the* strongest strategy *on a given model.*

Intuitively, the strongest strategy is the smallest available strategy. Note that in a bisimulation contracted model (M, w), the strongest strategy of agents G is $X_G = [w]_a \cap \ldots \cap [w]_b$ for $a, \ldots, b \in G$, that is agents' strategies consist of the single equivalence classes that include the current state.

4   Model Checking for CAL

Employing strategies allows for a rather simple model checking algorithm for CAL. We switch from quantification over infinite number of epistemic formulas, to quantification over a finite set of strategies (Sect. 4.1). Moreover, we show that if the target formula is a positive PAL formula, then model checking is even more effective (Sect. 4.2).

4.1   General Case

First, let us define the model checking problem.

Definition 14. *Let some model (M, w) and some formula φ be given. The* model checking problem *is the problem to determine whether φ is satisfied in (M, w).*

Algorithm 1 takes a finite model M, a state w of the model, and some $\varphi_0 \in \mathcal{L}_{CAL}$ as an input, and returns $true$ if φ_0 is satisfiable in the model, and $false$ otherwise.

Algorithm 1. $mc(M, w, \varphi_0)$

1: **case** φ_0:
2:     p : **if** $w \in V(p)$ **then return** $true$ **else return** $false$;
3:     $\neg\varphi$: **if** $mc(M, w, \varphi)$ **then return** $false$ **else return** $true$;
4:     $\varphi \wedge \psi$: **if** $mc(M, w, \varphi) \wedge mc(M, w, \psi)$ **then return** $true$ **else return** $false$;
5:     $K_a\varphi$:

        $check = true$
        for all v such that $w \sim_a v$
           if $\neg mc(M, v, \varphi)$ **then** $check = false$
        return $check$
6:     $[\psi]\varphi$: compute the ψ-submodel M^ψ of M
        if $w \in W^\psi$ **then return** $mc(M^\psi, w, \varphi)$ **else return** $true$;
7:     $\langle\!\langle G \rangle\!\rangle\varphi$: compute $(\|M\|, w)$ and sets of strategies $S(G, w)$ and $S(A \setminus G, w)$
        for all $X_G \in S(G, w)$
           $check = true$
           for all $X_{A\setminus G} \in S(A \setminus G, w)$
               if $\neg mc(\|M\|^{X_G \cap X_{A\setminus G}}, w, \varphi)$ **then** $check = false$
           if $check$ **then return** $true$
        return $false$.

Now, we show correctness of the algorithm.

Proposition 7. *Let (M, w) and $\varphi \in \mathcal{L}_{CAL}$ be given. Algorithm $mc(M, w, \varphi)$ returns* true *iff* $(M, w) \models \varphi$.

Proof. By a straightforward induction on the complexity of φ. We use Proposition 6 to prove the case for $\langle\!\langle G \rangle\!\rangle$:
$\Rightarrow$: Suppose $mc(M, w, \langle\!\langle G \rangle\!\rangle\varphi)$ returns $true$. By line 7 this means that for some strategy X_G and all strategies $X_{A\setminus G}$, $mc(\|M\|^{X_G \cap X_{A\setminus G}}, w, \varphi)$ returns $true$. By the induction hypothesis, $(\|M\|, w)^{X_G \cap X_{A\setminus G}} \models \varphi$ for some X_G and all $X_{A\setminus G}$, and $(\|M\|, w) \models \langle\!\langle G \rangle\!\rangle\varphi$ by the semantics.
$\Leftarrow$: Let $(\|M\|, w) \models \langle\!\langle G \rangle\!\rangle\varphi$, which means that there is some strategy X_G such that for all $X_{A\setminus G}$, $(\|M\|, w)^{X_G \cap X_{A\setminus G}} \models \varphi$. By the induction hypothesis, the latter holds iff for some X_G and for all $X_{A\setminus G}$, $mc(\|M\|^{X_G \cap X_{A\setminus G}}, w, \varphi)$ returns $true$. By line 7, we have that $mc(\|M\|, w, \langle\!\langle G \rangle\!\rangle\varphi)$ returns $true$.

Proposition 8. *Model checking for CAL is PSPACE-complete.*

Proof. All the cases of the model checking algorithm apart from the case for $\langle\!\langle G \rangle\!\rangle$ require polynomial time (and polynomial space as a consequence). The case for $\langle\!\langle G \rangle\!\rangle$ iterates over exponentially many strategies. However each iteration can be computed using only polynomial amount of space to represent $(\|M\|, w)$ (which contains at most the same number of states as the input model M) and the result of the update (which is a submodel of $(\|M\|, w)$) and make a recursive call to check whether φ holds in the update. By reusing space for each iteration, we can compute the case for $\langle\!\langle G \rangle\!\rangle$ using only polynomial amount of space.

Hardness can be obtained by a slight modification of the proof of PSPACE-hardness of the model-checking problem for GAL in [1]. The proof encodes satisfiability of a quantified boolean formula as a problem whether a particular GAL formula is true in a model corresponding to the QBF formula. Since the encoding uses only two agents: an omniscient g and a universal i, we can replace $[g]$ and $\langle g \rangle$ with $[\![g]\!]$ and $\langle\!\langle g \rangle\!\rangle$ (since i's only strategy is equivalent to $\top$) and obtain a CAL encoding. $\qquad\square$

4.2 Positive Case

In this section we demonstrate the following result: if in a given formula of $\mathcal{L}_{CAL}$ subformulas within scopes of coalition announcement operators are positive PAL formulas, then complexity of model checking is polynomial.

Allowing coalition announcement modalities to bind only positive formulas is a natural restriction. Positive formulas have a special property: if the sum of of knowledge of agents in G (their distributed knowledge) includes a positive formula φ, then φ can be made common knowledge by a group or coalition announcement by G. Formally, for a positive φ, $(M, w) \models D_G\varphi$ implies $(M, w) \models \langle\!\langle G \rangle\!\rangle C_G\varphi$, where D_G stands for distributed knowledge which is interpreted by the intersection of all $\sim_a$ relations, and C_G stands for common knowledge which is interpreted by the transitive and reflexive closure of the union of all $\sim_a$ relations. See [11,13], and also [5] where this is called *resolving* distributed knowledge. In other words, positive epistemic formulas can always be resolved by cooperative communication. Negative formulas do not have this property. For example, it can be distributed knowledge of agents a and b that p and $\neg K_b p$: $D_{\{a,b\}}(p \wedge \neg K_b p)$. However it is impossible to achieve common knowledge of this formula: $C_{\{a,b\}}(p \wedge \neg K_b p)$ is inconsistent, since it implies both $K_b p$ and $\neg K_b p$. Going back to the example in Sect. 2.1, it is distributed knowledge of a and b that $K_a 15_a$ and $K_b 5_b$. Both formulas are positive and can be made common knowledge if a and b honestly report the amount of money they have. However it is also distributed knowledge that $\neg K_a 5_b$ and $\neg K_b 15_a$. The conjunction

$$K_a 15_a \wedge K_b 5_b \wedge \neg K_a 5_b \wedge \neg K_b 15_a$$

is distributed knowledge, but it cannot be made common knowledge for the same reasons as above.

Definition 15. *The language* $\mathcal{L}_{PAL+}$ *of the positive fragment of public announcement logic PAL is defined by the following BNF:*

$$\varphi, \psi ::= p \mid \neg p \mid (\varphi \wedge \psi) \mid (\varphi \vee \psi) \mid K_a\varphi \mid [\neg\psi]\varphi,$$

where $p \in P$ *and* $a \in A$.

Definition 16. *Formula φ is* preserved under submodels *if for any models M_1 and M_2, $M_2 \subseteq M_1$ and $(M_1, w) \models \varphi$ implies $(M_2, w) \models \varphi$.*

A known result that we use in this section states that formulas of $\mathcal{L}_{PAL+}$ are preserved under submodels [13]. We also need the following special fact:

Proposition 9. $\langle\!\langle G \rangle\!\rangle \varphi \leftrightarrow [\![A \setminus G]\!] \varphi$ *is valid for positive φ on finite bisimulation contracted models.*

Proof. The left-to-right direction is generally valid and we omit the proof. Suppose that $(M, w) \models [\![A \setminus G]\!] \varphi$. By Proposition 6, we have that for all $X_{A \setminus G}$, there is some X_G such that $(M, w)^{X_{A \setminus G} \cap X_G} \models \varphi$. This implies that $(M, w)^{\top_{A \setminus G} \cap X_G} \models \varphi$ for the trivial strategy $\top_{A \setminus G}$ and some X_G. The latter is equivalent to $(M, w)^{X_G} \models \varphi$. Since φ is positive (and hence preserved under submodels), $(M, w)^{X'_G} \models \varphi$, where X'_G is the strongest strategy of G. The latter implies (again, due to the fact that φ is positive) that for all updates of the form $X'_G \cap X_{A \setminus G}$ (since they generate a submodel of $(M, w)^{X'_G}$), we also have $(M, w)^{X'_G \cap X_{A \setminus G}} \models \varphi$. And this is $(M, w) \models \langle\!\langle G \rangle\!\rangle \varphi$ by Proposition 6. $\qquad\square$

Now we are ready to deal with model checking for the positive case.

Proposition 10. *Let $\varphi \in \mathcal{L}_{CAL}$ be a formula such that all its subformulas ψ that are within scopes of $\langle\!\langle G \rangle\!\rangle$ belong to fragment $\mathcal{L}_{PAL+}$. Then the model checking problem for CAL is in P.*

Proof. For this particular case we modify Algorithm 1 by inserting the following instead of the case on line 7:

$\langle\!\langle G \rangle\!\rangle \varphi$: compute $(\|M\|, w)$ and $(\|M\|^{X_G}, w)$, where X_G corresponds to the strongest strategy of G,

   if $mc(\|M\|^{X_G}, w, \varphi)$ **then return** *true* **else return** *false*.

For all subformulas of φ_0, the algorithm calls are in P. Consider the modified call for $\langle\!\langle G \rangle\!\rangle \varphi$. It requires constructing a single update model given a specified strategy, which is a simple case of restricting the input model to the set of states in the strategy. This can be done in polynomial time. Then we call the algorithm on the updated model for φ, which by assumption requires polynomial time. $\qquad\square$

Now, let us show that the algorithm is correct.

Proposition 11. *Let (M, w) and $\varphi \in \mathcal{L}_{PAL+}$ be given. The modified algorithm $mc(M, w, \varphi)$ returns true iff $(M, w) \models \varphi$.*

Proof. By induction on φ. We show the case for $\langle\!\langle G\rangle\!\rangle\varphi$:

$\Rightarrow$: Suppose that $mc(M, w, \langle\!\langle G\rangle\!\rangle\varphi)$ returns *true*. This means that $mc(\|M\|^{X_G}, w, \varphi)$ returns *true*, where X_G is the strongest strategy of G. By the induction hypothesis, we have that $(\|M\|, w)^{X_G} \models \varphi$. Since φ is positive, for all stronger updates $X_G \cap X_{A\setminus G}$ it holds that $(\|M\|, w)^{X_G \cap X_{A\setminus G}} \models \varphi$, which is $(\|M\|, w) \models \langle\!\langle G\rangle\!\rangle\varphi$ by Proposition 6. Finally, the latter model is bisimilar to (M, w) and hence $(M, w) \models \langle\!\langle G\rangle\!\rangle\varphi$.

$\Leftarrow$: Let $(M, w) \models \langle\!\langle G\rangle\!\rangle\varphi$. By Proposition 6 this means that there is some X_G such that for all $X_{A\setminus G}$: $(M, w)^{X_G \cap X_{A\setminus G}} \models \varphi$. Set of all $X_{A\setminus G}$'s also includes the trivial strategy $\top_{A\setminus G}$, and we have $(M, w)^{X_G \cap \top_{A\setminus G}} \models \varphi$, which is equivalent to $(M, w)^{X_G} \models \varphi$. Since φ is positive and hence preserved under submodels, $(M, w)^{X'_G} \models \varphi$, where X'_G is the strongest strategy of G. By the induction hypothesis, we have that $mc(\|M\|^{X'_G}, w, \varphi)$ returns *true*. And by line 7 of the modified algorithm, we conclude that $mc(\|M\|, w, \langle\!\langle G\rangle\!\rangle\varphi)$ returns *true*. $\square$

The case of $[\![G]\!]\varphi$ is resolved by translating the formula into $\langle\!\langle A\setminus G\rangle\!\rangle\varphi$, which is allowed by Proposition 9.

5   Concluding Remarks

We have shown that the model checking problem for CAL is PSPACE-complete, just like the one for GAL [1] and APAL [6]. However, in a special case when formulas within scopes of coalition modalities are positive PAL formulas, the model checking problem is in P. The same result would apply to GAL and APAL; in fact, in those cases the formulas in the scope of group and arbitrary announcement modalities can belong to a larger positive fragment (the positive fragment of GAL and of APAL, respectively, rather than of PAL). The latter is due to the fact that GAL and APAL operators are purely universal, while CAL operators combine universal and existential quantification, and CAL does not appear to have a non-trivial positive fragment extending that of PAL.

There are several interesting open questions. For example, the relative expressivity of GAL and CAL is still an open question. It is also not known what is the model checking complexity for coalition logics with more powerful actions like private announcements [7].

Acknowledgements. We thank anonymous IJCAI 2018 and KI 2018 referees for constructive comments, and IJCAI 2018 referees for finding an error in the earlier version of this paper.

References

1. Ågotnes, T., Balbiani, P., van Ditmarsch, H., Seban, P.: Group announcement logic. J. Appl. Logic **8**(1), 62–81 (2010). https://doi.org/10.1016/j.jal.2008.12.002

2. Ågotnes, T., van Ditmarsch, H.: Coalitions and announcements. In: Padgham, L., Parkes, D.C., Müller, J.P., Parsons, S. (eds.) 7th International Joint Conference on Autonomous Agents and Multiagent Systems (AAMAS 2008), Estoril, Portugal, 12–16 May 2008, vol. 2, pp. 673–680. IFAAMAS (2008). https://doi.org/10.1145/1402298.1402318

3. Ågotnes, T., van Ditmarsch, H.: What will they say? - public announcement games. Synthese **179**(Suppl.-1), 57–85 (2011). https://doi.org/10.1007/s11229-010-9838-8

4. Ågotnes, T., van Ditmarsch, H., French, T.S.: The undecidability of quantified announcements. Studia Logica **104**(4), 597–640 (2016). https://doi.org/10.1007/s11225-016-9657-0

5. Ågotnes, T., Wáng, Y.N.: Resolving distributed knowledge. Artif. Intell. **252**, 1–21 (2017). https://doi.org/10.1016/j.artint.2017.07.002

6. Balbiani, P., Baltag, A., van Ditmarsch, H., Herzig, A., Hoshi, T., de Lima, T.: 'Knowable' as 'known after an announcement'. Rev. Symb. Logic **1**(3), 305–334 (2008). https://doi.org/10.1017/S1755020308080210

7. Baltag, A., Moss, L.S., Solecki, S.: The logic of public announcements and common knowledge and private suspicions. In: Proceedings of the 7th Conference on Theoretical Aspects of Rationality and Knowledge (TARK 1998), Evanston, IL, USA, 22–24 July 1998, pp. 43–56 (1998)

8. van Benthem, J.: Logic in Games. MIT Press, Cambridge (2014)

9. Blackburn, P., van Benthem, J.: Modal logic: a semantic perspective. In: Blackburn, P., van Benthem, J., Wolter, F. (eds.) Handbook of Modal Logic, pp. 1–84. Elsevier, New York (2006)

10. van Ditmarsch, H., Fernández-Duque, D., van der Hoek, W.: On the definability of simulation and bisimulation in epistemic logic. J. Logic Comput. **24**(6), 1209–1227 (2014). https://doi.org/10.1093/logcom/exs058

11. van Ditmarsch, H., French, T., Hales, J.: Positive announcements. CoRR abs/1803.01696 (2018). http://arxiv.org/abs/1803.01696

12. van Ditmarsch, H., van der Hoek, W., Kooi, B.: Dynamic Epistemic Logic. Synthese Library, vol. 337. Springer, Dordrecht (2008). https://doi.org/10.1007/978-1-4020-5839-4

13. van Ditmarsch, H., Kooi, B.: The secret of my success. Synthese **153**(2), 339–339 (2006). https://doi.org/10.1007/s11229-006-8493-6

14. Hintikka, J.: Knowledge and Belief. An Introduction to the Logic of the Two Notions. Cornell University Press, Ithaca (1962)

15. Parikh, R.: The logic of games and its applications. In: Karplnski, M., van Leeuwen, J. (eds.) Topics in the Theory of Computation, Annals of Discrete Mathematics, vol. 24, pp. 111–139. Elsevier Science, Amsterdam (1985). https://doi.org/10.1016/S0304-0208(08)73078-0

16. Pauly, M.: A modal logic for coalitional power in games. J. Logic Comput. **12**(1), 149–166 (2002). https://doi.org/10.1093/logcom/12.1.149

17. Plaza, J.: Logics of public communications (reprint of 1989's paper). Synthese **158**(2), 165–179 (2007). https://doi.org/10.1007/s11229-007-9168-7

Fusing First-Order Knowledge Compilation and the Lifted Junction Tree Algorithm

Tanya Braun$^{(\boxtimes)}$ and Ralf Möller

University of Lübeck, Lübeck, Germany
{braun,moeller}@ifis.uni-luebeck.de

Abstract. Standard approaches for inference in probabilistic formalisms with first-order constructs include lifted variable elimination (LVE) for single queries as well as first-order knowledge compilation (FOKC) based on weighted model counting. To handle multiple queries efficiently, the lifted junction tree algorithm (LJT) uses a first-order cluster representation of a model and LVE as a subroutine in its computations. For certain inputs, the implementation of LVE and, as a result, LJT ground parts of a model where FOKC runs without groundings. The purpose of this paper is to prepare LJT as a backbone for lifted query answering and to use any exact inference algorithm as subroutine. Fusing LJT and FOKC, by setting FOKC as a subroutine, allows us to compute answers faster than FOKC alone and LJT with LVE for certain inputs.

Keywords: Lifting · Probabilistic logical models
Variable elimination · Weighted model counting

1 Introduction

AI areas such as natural language understanding and machine learning need efficient inference algorithms. Modeling realistic scenarios yields large probabilistic models, requiring reasoning about sets of individuals. Lifting uses symmetries in a model to speed up reasoning with known domain objects. We study probabilistic inference in large models that exhibit symmetries with queries for probability distributions of random variables (randvars).

In the last two decades, researchers have advanced probabilistic inference significantly. Propositional formalisms benefit from variable elimination (VE), which decomposes a model into subproblems and evaluates them in an efficient order [28]. Lifted VE (LVE), introduced in [21] and expanded in [19, 22, 25], saves computations by reusing intermediate results for isomorphic subproblems. Taghipour et al. formalise LVE by defining lifting operators while decoupling the constraint language from the operators [26]. The lifted junction tree algorithm (LJT) sets up a first-order junction tree (FO jtree) to handle multiple queries

© Springer Nature Switzerland AG 2018
F. Trollmann and A.-Y. Turhan (Eds.): KI 2018, LNAI 11117, pp. 24–37, 2018.
https://doi.org/10.1007/978-3-030-00111-7_3

efficiently [4], using LVE as a subroutine. LJT is based on the propositional junction tree algorithm [18], which includes a junction tree (jtree) and a reasoning algorithm for efficient handling of multiple queries. Approximate lifted inference often uses lifting in conjunction with belief propagation [1,15,24]. To scale lifting, Das et al. use graph databases storing compiled models to count faster [14]. Other areas incorporate lifting to enhance efficiency, e.g., in continuous or dynamic models [12,27], logic programming [3], and theorem proving [16].

Logical methods for probabilistic inference are often based on weighted model counting (WMC) [11]. Propositional knowledge compilation (KC) compiles a weighted model into a deterministic decomposable negation normal form (d-DNNF) circuit for probabilistic inference [13]. Chavira and Darwiche combine VE and KC as well as algebraic decision diagrams for local symmetries to further optimise inference runtimes [10]. Van den Broeck et al. apply lifting to KC and WMC, introducing weighted first-order model counting (WFOMC) and a first-order d-DNNF [7,9], with newer work on asymmetrical models [8].

For certain inputs, LVE, LJT, and FOKC start to struggle either due to model structure or size. The implementations of LVE and, as a consequence, LJT ground parts of a model if randvars of the form $Q(X), Q(Y), X \neq Y$ appear, where parameters X and Y have the same domain, even though in theory, LVE handles those occurrences of just-different randvars [2]. While FOKC does not ground in the presence of such constructs in general, it can struggle if the model size increases. The purpose of this paper is to prepare LJT as a backbone for lifted query answering (QA) to use any exact inference algorithm as a subroutine. Using FOKC and LVE as subroutines, we fuse LJT, LVE, and FOKC to compute answers faster than LJT, LVE, and FOKC alone for the inputs described above.

The remainder of this paper is structured as follows: First, we introduce notations and FO jtrees and recap LJT. Then, we present conditions for subroutines of LJT, discuss how LVE works in this context and FOKC as a candidate, before fusing LJT, LVE, and FOKC. We conclude with future work.

2   Preliminaries

This section introduces notations and recap LJT. We specify a version of the smokers example (e.g., [9]), where two friends are more likely to both smoke and smokers are more likely to have cancer or asthma. Parameters allow for representing people, avoiding explicit randvars for each individual.

Parameterised Models. To compactly represent models with first-order constructs, parameterised models use logical variables (logvars) to parameterise randvars, abbreviated PRVs. They are based on work by Poole [20].

Definition 1. *Let* **L***,* Φ*, and* **R** *be sets of logvar, factor, and randvar names respectively. A PRV* $R(L_1, \ldots, L_n)$*,* $n \geq 0$*, is a syntactical construct with* $R \in \mathbf{R}$ *and* $L_1, \ldots, L_n \in \mathbf{L}$ *to represent a set of randvars. For PRV* A*, the term* $range(A)$ *denotes possible values. A logvar* L *has a domain* $\mathcal{D}(L)$*. A constraint* $(\mathbf{X}, C_{\mathbf{X}})$ *is a tuple with a sequence of logvars* $\mathbf{X} = (X_1, \ldots, X_n)$ *and a set*

$C_{\mathbf{X}} \subseteq \times_{i=1}^{n} \mathcal{D}(X_i)$ *restricting logvars to given values. The symbol* $\top$ *marks that no restrictions apply and may be omitted. For some P, the term* $lv(P)$ *refers to its logvars,* $rv(P)$ *to its PRVs with constraints, and* $gr(P)$ *to all instances of P grounded w.r.t. its constraints.*

For the smoker example, let $\mathbf{L} = \{X, Y\}$ and $\mathbf{R} = \{Smokes, Friends\}$ to build boolean PRVs $Smokes(X)$, $Smokes(Y)$, and $Friends(X, Y)$. We denote $A = true$ by a and $A = false$ by $\neg a$. Both logvar domains are $\{alice, eve, bob\}$. An inequality $X \neq Y$ yields a constraint $C = ((X, Y), \{(alice, eve),$ $(alice, bob), (eve, alice), (eve, bob), (bob, alice), (bob, eve)\})$. $gr(Friends(X, Y)|C)$ refers to all propositional randvars that result from replacing X, Y with the tuples in C. Parametric factors (parfactors) combine PRVs as arguments. A parfactor describes a function, identical for all argument groundings, that maps argument values to the reals (potentials), of which at least one is non-zero.

Definition 2. *Let* $\mathbf{X} \subseteq \mathbf{L}$ *be a set of logvars,* $\mathcal{A} = (A_1, \dots, A_n)$ *a sequence of PRVs, each built from* $\mathbf{R}$ *and possibly* $\mathbf{X}$, $\phi : \times_{i=1}^{n} range(A_i) \mapsto \mathbb{R}^+$ *a function,* $\phi \in \Phi$, *and* C *a constraint* $(\mathbf{X}, C_{\mathbf{X}})$. *We denote a parfactor* g *by* $\forall \mathbf{X} : \phi(\mathcal{A})|C$. *We omit* $(\forall \mathbf{X} :)$ *if* $\mathbf{X} = lv(\mathcal{A})$. *A set of parfactors forms a model* $G := \{g_i\}_{i=1}^{n}$.

We define a model G_{ex} for the smoker example, adding the binary PRVs $Cancer(X)$ and $Asthma(X)$ to the ones above. The model reads $G_{ex} = \{g_i\}_{i=0}^{5}$, $g_0 = \phi_0(Friends(X, Y), Smokes(X), Smokes(Y))|C$, $g_1 = \phi_1(Friends(X, Y))|C$, $g_2 = \phi_2(Smokes(X))|\top$, $g_3 = \phi_3(Cancer(X))|\top$, $g_4 = \phi_5(Smokes(X), Asthma(X))|\top$, and $g_5 = \phi_4(Smokes(X), Cancer(X))|\top$. g_0 has eight, g_1 to g_3 have two, and g_4 and g_5 four input-output pairs (omitted here). Constraint C refers to the constraint given above. The other constraints are $\top$. Figure 1 depicts G_{ex} as a graph with five variable nodes and six factor nodes for the PRVs and parfactors with edges to arguments.

The *semantics* of a model G is given by grounding and building a full joint distribution. With Z as the normalisation constant, G represents the full joint probability distribution $P_G = \frac{1}{Z} \prod_{f \in gr(G)} f$. The QA problem asks for a likelihood of an event, a marginal distribution of some randvars, or a conditional distribution given events, all queries boiling down to computing marginals w.r.t. a model's joint distribution. Formally, $P(\mathbf{Q}|\mathbf{E})$ denotes a (conjunctive) query with

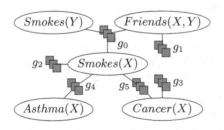

Fig. 1. Parfactor graph for G_{ex}

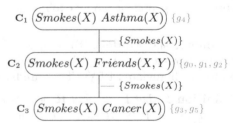

Fig. 2. FO jtree for G_{ex} (local models in grey)

Algorithm 1. Outline of the Lifted Junction Tree Algorithm

> **procedure** LJT(Model G, Queries $\{\mathbf{Q}_j\}_{j=1}^m$, Evidence $\mathbf{E}$)
>
>   Construct FO jtree J for G
>
>   Enter $\mathbf{E}$ into J
>
>   Pass messages on J
>
>   **for** each query $\mathbf{Q}_j$ **do**
>
>   Find subtree J' for $\mathbf{Q}_j$
>
>   Extract submodel G' of local models in J' and outside messages into J'
>
>   Answer $\mathbf{Q}_j$ on G'

$\mathbf{Q}$ a set of grounded PRVs and $\mathbf{E} = \{E_k = e_k\}_k$ a set of events (grounded PRVs with range values). If $\mathbf{E} = \emptyset$, the query is for a conditional distribution. A query for G_{ex} is $P(Cancer(eve)|friends(eve, bob), smokes(bob))$. We call $\mathbf{Q} = \{Q\}$ a singleton query. Lifted QA algorithms seek to avoid grounding and building a full joint distribution. Before looking at lifted QA, we introduce FO jtrees.

First-Order Junction Trees. LJT builds an FO jtree to cluster a model into submodels that contain all information for a query after propagating information. An FO jtree, defined as follows, constitutes a lifted version of a jtree. Its nodes are parameterised clusters (parclusters), i.e., sets of PRVs connected by parfactors.

Definition 3. *Let $\mathbf{X}$ be a set of logvars, $\mathbf{A}$ a set of PRVs with $lv(\mathbf{A}) \subseteq \mathbf{X}$, and C a constraint on $\mathbf{X}$. Then, $\forall \mathbf{X}{:}\mathbf{A}|C$ denotes a* parcluster. *We omit $(\forall \mathbf{X}{:})$ if $\mathbf{X} = lv(\mathbf{A})$. An FO jtree for a model G is a cycle-free graph $J = (V, E)$, where V is the set of nodes (parclusters) and E the set of edges. J must satisfy three properties: (i) $\forall \mathbf{C}_i \in V{:}\ \mathbf{C}_i \subseteq rv(G)$. (ii) $\forall g \in G{:}\ \exists \mathbf{C}_i \in V$ s.t. $rv(g) \subseteq \mathbf{C}_i$. (iii) If $\exists A \in rv(G)$ s.t. $A \in \mathbf{C}_i \wedge A \in \mathbf{C}_j$, then $\forall \mathbf{C}_k$ on the path between $\mathbf{C}_i$ and $\mathbf{C}_j{:}\ A \in \mathbf{C}_k$. The parameterised set $\mathbf{S}_{ij}$, called* separator *of edge $\{i, j\} \in E$, is defined by $\mathbf{C}_i \cap \mathbf{C}_j$. The term $nbs(i)$ refers to the neighbours of node i. Each $\mathbf{C}_i \in V$ has a local model G_i and $\forall g \in G_i{:}\ rv(g) \subseteq \mathbf{C}_i$. The G_i's partition G.*

Figure 2 shows an FO jtree for G_{ex} with the following parclusters, $\mathbf{C}_1 = \forall X : \{Smokes(X), Asthma(X)\}|\top$, $\mathbf{C}_2 = \forall X, Y : \{Smokes(X), Friends(X, Y)\}|C$, and $\mathbf{C}_3 = \forall X : \{Smokes(X), Cancer(X)\}|\top$. Separators are $\mathbf{S}_{12} = \mathbf{S}_{23} = \{Smokes(X)\}$. As $Smokes(X)$ and $Smokes(Y)$ model the same randvars, $\mathbf{C}_2$ names only one. Parfactor g_2 appears at $\mathbf{C}_2$ but could be in any local model as $rv(g_2) = \{Smokes(X)\} \subset \mathbf{C}_i\ \forall\ i \in \{1, 2, 3\}$. [4] details building FO jtrees.

Lifted Junction Tree Algorithm. LJT answers a set of queries efficiently by answering queries on smaller submodels. Algorithm 1 outlines LJT for a set of queries (cf. [4] for details). LJT starts with constructing an FO jtree. It enters evidence for a local model to absorb whenever the evidence randvars appear in a parcluster. Message passing propagates local information through the FO jtree in two passes: LJT sends messages from the periphery towards the center and then back. A message is a set of parfactors over separator PRVs. For a message

m_{ij} from node i to neighbour j, LJT eliminates all PRVs not in separator $\mathbf{S}_{ij}$ from G_i and the messages from other neighbours using LVE. Afterwards, each parcluster holds all information of the model in its local model and received messages. LJT answers a query by finding a subtree whose parclusters cover the query randvars, extracting a submodel of local models and outside messages, and answering the query on the submodel. In the original LJT, LJT eliminates randvars for messages and queries using LVE.

3   LJT as a Backbone for Lifted Inference

LJT provides general steps for efficient QA given a set of queries. It constructs an FO jtree and uses a subroutine to propagate information and answer queries. To ensure a lifted algorithm run without groundings, evidence entering and message passing impose some requirements on the algorithm used as a subroutine. After presenting those requirements, we analyse how LVE matches the requirements and to what extend FOKC can provide the same service.

Requirements. LJT has a domain-lifted complexity, meaning that if a model allows for computing a solution without grounding part of a model, LJT is able to compute the solution without groundings, i.e., has a complexity linear in the domain size of the logvars. Given a model that allows for computing solutions without grounding part of a model, the subroutine must be able to handle message passing and query answering without grounding to maintain the domain-lifted complexity of LJT.

Evidence displays symmetries if observing the same value for n instances of a PRV [26]. Thus, for evidence handling, the algorithm needs to be able to handle a set of observations for some instances of a single PRV in a lifted way. Calculating messages entails that the algorithm is able to calculate a form of parameterised, conjunctive query over the PRVs in the separator. In summary, LJT requires the following:

1. Given evidence in the form of a set of observations for some instances of a single PRV, the subroutine must be able to absorb the evidence independent of the size of the set.
2. Given a parcluster with its local model, messages, and a separator, the subroutine must be able to eliminate all PRVs in the parcluster that do not appear in the separator in a domain-lifted way.

The subroutine also establishes which kind of queries LJT can answer. The expressiveness of the query language for LJT follows from the expressiveness of the inference algorithm used. If an algorithm answers queries of single randvar, LJT answers this type of query. If an algorithm answers maximum a posteriori (MAP) queries, the most likely assignment to a set of randvars, LJT answers MAP queries. Next, we look at how LVE fits into LJT.

Algorithm 2. Outlines of Lifted QA Algorithms

---

function LVE(Model G, Query $\mathbf{Q}$, Evidence $\mathbf{E}$)
    Absorb $\mathbf{E}$ in G
    while G has non-query PRVs **do**
        if PRV A fulfils *sum-out* preconditions **then**
            Eliminate A using *sum-out*
        else
            Apply transformator
    return Multiply parfactors in G ▷ α-normalise

---

procedure FOKC(Model G, Queries $\{Q_j\}_{j=1}^{m}$, Evidence $\mathbf{E}$)
    Reduce G to WFOMC problem with Δ, w_T, w_F
    Compile a circuit $\mathcal{C}_e$ for Δ, $\mathbf{E}$
    for each query Q_j **do**
        Compile a circuit $\mathcal{C}_{qe}$ for Δ, Q_j, $\mathbf{E}$
        Compute $P(Q_j|\mathbf{E})$ through WFOMCs in $\mathcal{C}_{qe}, \mathcal{C}_e$

Lifted Variable Elimination. First, we take a closer look at LVE before analysing it w.r.t. the requirements of LJT. To answer a query, LVE eliminates all non-query randvars. In the process, it computes VE for one case and exponentiates its result for isomorphic instances (lifted summing out). Taghipour implements LVE through an operator suite (see [26] for details). Algorithm 2 shows an outline. All operators have pre- and postconditions to ensure computing a result equivalent to one for $gr(G)$. Its main operator *sum-out* realises lifted summing out. An operator *absorb* handles evidence in a lifted way. The remaining operators (*count-convert, split, expand, count-normalise, multiply, ground-logvar*) aim at enabling lifted summing out, transforming part of a model.

LVE as a subroutine provides lifted absorption for evidence handling. Lifted absorption splits a parfactor into one part, for which evidence exists, and one part without evidence. The part with evidence then absorbs the evidence by absorbing it once and exponentiating the result for all isomorphic instances. For messages, a relaxed QA routine computes answers to parameterised queries without making all instances of query logvars explicit. LVE answers queries for a likelihood of an event, a marginal distribution of a set of randvars, and a conditional distribution of a set of randvars given events. LJT with LVE as a subroutine answers the same queries. Extensions to LJT or LVE enable even more query types, such as queries for a most probable explanation or MAP [5].

First-Order Knowledge Compilation. FOKC aims at solving a WFOMC problem by building FO d-DNNF circuits given a query and evidence and computing WFOMCs on the circuits. Of course, different compilation flavours exist, e.g., compiling into a low-level language [17]. But, we focus on the basic version of FOKC. We briefly take a look at WFOMC problems, FO d-DNNF circuits, and QA with FOKC, before analysing FOKC w.r.t. the LJT requirements. See [9] for details.

Let Δ be a theory of constrained clauses and w_T a positive and w_F a negative weight function. Clauses follow standard notations of (function-free) first-order logic. A constraint expresses, e.g., an (in)equality of two logvars. w_T and w_F assign weights to predicates in Δ. A *WFOMC problem* consists of computing

$$\sum_{I \models \Delta} \prod_{a \in I} w_T(pred(a)) \prod_{a \in HB(T) \setminus I} w_F(pred(a))$$

where I is an interpretation of Δ that satisfies Δ, $HB(T)$ is the Herbrand base and *pred* maps atoms to their predicate. See [6] for a description of how to transform parfactor models into WFOMC problems.

FOKC converts Δ to be in FO d-DNNF, where all conjunctions are decomposable (all pairs of conjuncts independent) and all disjunctions are deterministic (only one disjunct true at a time). The normal form allows for efficient reasoning as computing the probability of a conjunction decomposes into a product of the probabilities of its conjuncts and computing the probability of a disjunction follows from the sum of probabilities of its disjuncts. An *FO d-DNNF circuit* represents such a theory as a directed acyclic graph. Inner nodes are labelled with $\vee$ and $\wedge$. Additionally, set-disjunction and set-conjunction represent isomorphic parts in Δ. Leaf nodes contain atoms from Δ. The process of forming a circuit is called compilation.

Now, we look at how FOKC answers queries. Algorithm 2 shows an outline with input model G, a set of query randvars $\{Q_i\}_{i=1}^m$, and evidence $\mathbf{E}$. FOKC starts with transforming G into a WFOMC problem Δ with weight functions w_T and w_F. It compiles a circuit $\mathcal{C}_e$ for Δ including $\mathbf{E}$. For each query Q_i, FOKC compiles a circuit $\mathcal{C}_{qe}$ for Δ including $\mathbf{E}$ and Q_i. It then computes

$$P(Q_i|\mathbf{E}) = \frac{WFOMC(\mathcal{C}_{qe}, w_T, w_F)}{WFOMC(\mathcal{C}_e, w_T, w_F)} \tag{1}$$

by propagating WFOMCs in $\mathcal{C}_{qe}$ and $\mathcal{C}_e$ based on w_T and w_F. FOKC can reuse the denominator WFOMC for all Q_i.

Regarding the potential of FOKC as a subroutine for LJT, FOKC does not fulfil all requirements. FOKC can handle evidence through conditioning [7]. But, a lifted message passing is not possible in a domain-lifted and exact way without restrictions. FOKC answers queries for a likelihood of an event, a marginal distribution of a single randvar, and a conditional distribution for a single randvar given events. Inherently, conjunctive queries are only possible if the conjuncts are probabilistically independent [13], which is rarely the case for separators. Otherwise, FOKC has to invest more effort to take into account that the probabilities overlap. Thus, the restricted query language means that LJT cannot use FOKC for message calculations in general. Given an FO jtree with singleton separators, message passing with FOKC as a subroutine may be possible. FOKC as such takes ground queries as input or computes answers for random groundings, so FOKC for message passing needs an extension to handle parameterised queries. FOKC may not fulfil all requirements, but we may combine LJT, LVE, and FOKC into one algorithm to answer queries for models where LJT with LVE as a subroutine struggles.

Algorithm 3. Outline of LJTKC

---

  procedure LJTKC(Model G, Queries $\{Q_j\}_{j=1}^m$, Evidence $\mathbf{E}$)
    Construct FO jtree J for G
    Enter $\mathbf{E}$ into J
    Pass messages on J $\triangleright$ LVE as subroutine
    for each parcluster $\mathbf{C}_i$ of J with local model G_i **do**
        Form submodel $G' \leftarrow G_i \cup \bigcup_{j \in nbs(i)} m_{ij}$
        Reduce G' to WFOMC problem with Δ_i, w_T^i, w_F^i
        Compile a circuit $\mathcal{C}_i$ for Δ_i
        Compute $c_i = WFOMC(\mathcal{C}_i, w_T^i, w_F^i)$
    for each query Q_j **do**
        Find parcluster $\mathbf{C}_i$ where $Q_j \in \mathbf{C}_i$
        Compile a circuit $\mathcal{C}_q$ for Δ_i, Q_j
        Compute $c_q = WFOMC(\mathcal{C}_q, w_T^i, w_F^i)$
        Compute $P(Q_j|\mathbf{E}) = c_q/c_i$

---

4   Fusing LJT, LVE, and FOKC

We now use LJT as a backbone and LVE and FOKC as subroutines, fusing all three algorithms. Algorithm 3 shows an outline of the fused algorithm named LJTKC. Inputs are a model G, a set of queries $\{Q_j\}_{j=1}^m$, and evidence $\mathbf{E}$. Each query Q_j has a single query term in contrast to a set of randvars $\mathbf{Q}_j$ in LVE and LJT. The change stems from FOKC to ensure a correct result. As a consequence, LJTKC has the same expressiveness regarding the query language as FOKC.

The first three steps of LJTKC coincide with LJT as specified in Algorithm 2: LJTKC builds an FO jtree J for G, enters $\mathbf{E}$ into J, and passes messages in J using LVE for message calculations. During evidence entering, each local model covering evidence randvars absorbs evidence. LJTKC calculates messages based on local models with absorbed evidence, spreading the evidence information along with other local information. After message passing, each parcluster $\mathbf{C}_i$ contains in its local model and received messages all information from G and $\mathbf{E}$. This information is sufficient to answer queries for randvars contained in $\mathbf{C}_i$ and remains valid as long as G and $\mathbf{E}$ do not change. At this point, FOKC starts to interleave with the original LJT procedure.

LJTKC continues its preprocessing. For each parcluster $\mathbf{C}_i$, LJTKC extracts a submodel G' of local model G_i and all messages received and reduces G' to a WFOMC problem with theory Δ_i and weight functions w_F^i, w_T^i. It does not need to incorporate $\mathbf{E}$ as the information from $\mathbf{E}$ is contained in G' through evidence entering and message passing. LJTKC compiles an FO d-DNNF circuit $\mathcal{C}_i$ for Δ_i and computes a WFOMC c_i on $\mathcal{C}_i$. In precomputing a WFOMC c_i for each parcluster, LJTKC utilises that the denominator of Eq. (1) is identical for varying queries on the same model and evidence. For each query handled at $\mathbf{C}_i$, the submodel consists of G', resulting in the same circuit $\mathcal{C}_i$ and WFOMC c_i.

To answer a query Q_j, LJTKC finds a parcluster $\mathbf{C}_i$ that covers Q_j and compiles an FO d-DNNF circuit $\mathcal{C}_q$ for Δ_i and Q_j. It computes a WFOMC

c_q in $\mathcal{C}_q$ and determines an answer to $P(Q_j|\mathbf{E})$ by dividing the just computed WFOMC c_q by the precomputed WFOMC c_i of this parcluster. LJTKC reuses Δ_i, w_T^i, and w_F^i from preprocessing.

Example Run. For G_{ex}, LJTKC builds an FO jtree as depicted in Fig. 2. Without evidence, message passing commences. LJTKC sends messages from parclusters $\mathbf{C}_1$ and $\mathbf{C}_3$ to parcluster $\mathbf{C}_2$ and back. For message m_{12} from $\mathbf{C}_1$ to $\mathbf{C}_2$, LJTKC eliminates $Asthma(X)$ from G_1 using LVE. For message m_{32} from $\mathbf{C}_3$ to $\mathbf{C}_2$, LJTKC eliminates $Cancer(X)$ from G_3 using LVE. For the messages back, LJTKC eliminates $Friends(X,Y)$ each time, for message m_{21} to $\mathbf{C}_1$ from $G_2 \cup m_{32}$ and for message m_{23} to $\mathbf{C}_3$ from $G_2 \cup m_{12}$. Each parcluster holds all model information encoded in its local model and received messages, which form the submodels for the compilation steps. At $\mathbf{C}_1$, the submodel contains $G_1 = \{g_4\}$ and m_{21}. At $\mathbf{C}_2$, the submodel contains $G_2 = \{g_0, g_1, g_2\}$, m_{12}, and m_{32}. At $\mathbf{C}_3$, the submodel contains $G_3 = \{g_3, g_5\}$ and m_{23}.

For each parcluster, LJTKC reduces the submodel to a WFOMC problem, compiles a circuit for the problem specification, and computes a parcluster WFOMC. Given, e.g., query randvar $Cancer(eve)$, LJTKC takes a parcluster that contains the query randvar, here $\mathbf{C}_3$. It compiles a circuit for the query and Δ_3, computes a query WFOMC c_q, and divides c_q by c_3 to determine $P(cancer(eve))$. Next, we argue why QA with LJTKC is sound.

Theorem 1. *LJTKC is sound, i.e., computes a correct result for a query Q given a model G and evidence $\mathbf{E}$.*

Proof sketch. We assume that LJT is correct, yielding an FO jtree J for model G, which means, J fulfils the three junction tree properties, which allows for local computations based on [23]. Further, we assume that LVE is correct, ensuring correct computations for evidence entering and message passing, and that FOKC is correct, computing correct answers for single term queries.

LJTKC starts with the first three steps of LJT. It constructs an FO jtree for G, allowing for local computations. Then, LJTKC enters $\mathbf{E}$ and calculates messages using LVE, which produces correct results given LVE is correct. After message passing, each parcluster holds all information from G and $\mathbf{E}$ in its local model and received messages, which allows for answering queries for randvars that the parcluster contains. At this point, the FOKC part takes over, taking all information present at a parcluster and compiling a circuit and computing a WFOMC, which produces correct results given FOKC is correct. The same holds for the compilation and computations done for query Q. Thus, LJTKC computes a correct result for Q given G and $\mathbf{E}$. □

Theoretical Discussion. We discuss space and runtime performance of LJT, LVE, FOKC, and LJTKC in comparison with each other.

LJT requires *space* for its FO jtree as well as storing the messages at each parcluster, while FOKC takes up space for storing its circuits. As a combination of LJT and FOKC, LJTKC stores the preprocessing information produced by both LJT and FOKC. Next to the FO jtree structure and messages, LJTKC stores a WFOMC problem specification and a circuit for each parcluster. Since the implementation of LVE for the $X \neq Y$ cases causes LVE (and LJT) to ground, the space requirements during QA are increasing with rising domain sizes. Since LJTKC avoids the groundings using FOKC, the space requirements during QA are smaller than for LJT alone. W.r.t. circuits, LJTKC stores more circuits than FOKC but the individual circuits are smaller and do not require conditioning, which leads to a significant blow-up for the circuits.

LJTKC accomplishes speeding up QA for certain challenging inputs by fusing LJT, LVE, and FOKC. The new algorithm has a faster runtime than LJT, LVE, and FOKC as it is able to precompute reusable parts and provide smaller models for answering a specific query through the underlying FO jtree with its messages and parcluster compilation. In comparison with FOKC, LJTKC speeds up runtimes as answering queries works with smaller models. In comparison with LJT and LVE, LJTKC is faster when avoiding groundings in LVE. Instead of precompiling each parcluster, which adds to its overhead before starting with answering queries, LJTKC could compile on demand. On-demand compilation means less runtime and space required in advance but more time per initial query at a parcluster. One could further optimise LJTKC by speeding up internal computations in LVE or FOKC (e.g., caching for message calculations or pruning circuits using context-specific information).

In terms of *complexity*, LVE and FOKC have a time complexity linear in terms of the domain sizes of the model logvars for models that allow for a lifted solution. LJT with LVE as a subroutine also has a time complexity linear in terms of the domain sizes for query answering. For message passing, a factor of n, which is the number of parclusters, multiplies into the complexity, which basically is the same time complexity as answering a single query with LVE. LJTKC has the same time complexity as LJT for message passing since the algorithms coincide. For query answering, the complexity is determined by the FOKC complexity, which is linear in terms of domain sizes. Therefore, LJTKC has a time complexity linear in terms of the domain sizes. Even though, the original LVE and LJT implementations show a practical problem in translating the theory into an efficient program, the worst case complexity for liftable models is linear in terms of domain sizes.

The next section presents an empirical evaluation, showing how LJTKC speeds up QA compared to FOKC and LJT for challenging inputs.

5 Empirical Evaluation

This evaluation demonstrates the speed up we can achieve for certain inputs when using LJT and FOKC in conjunction. We have implemented a prototype of LJT, named ljt here. Taghipour provides an implementation of LVE (available at https://dtai.cs.kuleuven.be/software/gcfove), named lve. Van den Broeck

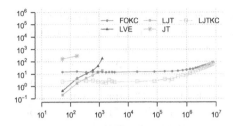 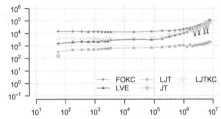

Fig. 3. Runtimes [ms] for G_l; on x-axis: $|gr(G_l)|$ from 52 to 8,010,000

Fig. 4. Runtimes [ms] for G'_l; on x-axis: $|gr(G'_l)|$ from 56 to 8,012,000

provides an implementation of FOKC (available at https://dtai.cs.kuleuven.be/software/wfomc), named `fokc`. For this paper, we integrated `fokc` into `ljt` to compute marginals at parclusters, named `ljtkc`. Unfortunately, the FOKC implementation does not handle evidence in a lifted manner as described in [7]. Therefore, we do not consider evidence as `fokc` runtimes explode. We have also implemented the propositional junction tree algorithm (`jt`).

This evaluation has two parts: First, we test an input model with inequalities to highlight how runtimes of LVE and LJT explode, and how LJTKC provides a speedup. Second, we test a version of the model without inequalities to highlight how runtimes of LVE and LJT compare to FOKC without inequalities.

We compare overall runtimes without input parsing averaged over five runs with a working memory of 16 GB. `lve` eliminates all non-query randvars from its input model for each query, grounding in the process. `ljt` builds an FO jtree for its input model, passes messages, and then answers queries on submodels. `fokc` forms a WFOMC problem for its input model, compiles a model circuit, compiles for each query a query circuit, and computes the marginals of all PRVs in the input model with random groundings. `ljtkc` starts like `ljt` for its input model until answering queries. It then calls `fokc` at each parcluster to compute marginals of parcluster PRVs with random groundings. `jt` receives the grounded input models and otherwise proceeds like `ljt`.

Inputs with Inequalities. For the first part of this evaluation, we test a slightly larger model G_l that is an extension of G_{ex}. G_l has two more logvars, each with its own domain, and eight additional PRVs with one or two parameters. The PRVs are arguments to twenty parfactors, each parfactor with one to three inputs. The FO jtree for G_l has six parclusters, the largest one containing five PRVs. We vary the domain sizes from 2 to 1000, resulting in $|gr(G_l)|$ from 52 to 8,010,000. We query each PRV with random groundings, leading to 12 queries, respectively, among them $Smokes(p_1)$, where p_1 stands for a domain value of X. Figure 3 shows for G_l runtimes in milliseconds [ms] with increasing $|gr(G_l)|$ on log-scaled axes, marked as follows (points are connected for readability): `fokc`: circle, orange, `jt`: star, turquoise, `ljt`: filled square, turquoise, `ljtkc`: hollow square, light turquoise, and `lve`: triangle, dark orange.

The jt runtimes are much longer with the first setting than the other runtimes. Up to the third setting, lve and ljt perform better than fokc with ljt being faster than lve. From the seventh setting on, memory errors occur for both lve and ljt. ljtkc performs best from the third setting onwards. ljtkc and fokc show the same steady increase in runtimes. ljtkc runtimes have a speedup of a factor from 0.13 to 0.76 for G_l compared to fokc. Up to a domain size of 100 ($|gr(G_l)| = 81,000$), ljtkc saves around one order of magnitude.

For small domain sizes, ljtkc and fokc perform worst. With increasing domain sizes, they outperform the other programs. Though not part of the numbers in this evaluation, with an increasing number of parfactors, ljtkc promises to outperform fokc even more, especially with smaller domain sizes.   ·

Inputs without Inequalities. For the second part of this evaluation, we test an input model G_l', that is the model from the first part but with Y receiving an own domain as large as X, making the inequality superfluous. Domain sizes vary from 2 to 1000, resulting in $|gr(G_l')|$ from 56 to 8,012,000. Each PRV is a query with random groundings again (without a Y grounding). Figure 4 shows for G_l' runtimes in milliseconds [ms] with increasing $|gr(G)|$, marked as before. Both axes are log-scaled. Points are connected for readability.

jt is the fastest for the first setting. With the following settings, jt runs into memory problems while runtimes explode. lve and ljt do not exhibit the runtime explosion without inequalities. lve has a steadily increasing runtime for most parts, though a few settings lead to shorter runtimes with higher domain sizes. We could not find an explanation for the decrease in runtime for those handful of settings. Overall, lve runtimes rise more than the other runtimes apart from jt. ljtkc exhibits an unsteady runtime performance on the smaller model, though again, we could not find an explanation for the jumps between various sizes. With the larger model, ljtkc shows a more steady performance that is better than the one of fokc. ljtkc is a factor of 0.2 to 0.8 faster. fokc and ljt runtimes steadily increase with rising $|gr(G)|$. ljt gains over an order of magnitude compared to fokc. In the larger model, ljt is a factor of 0.02 to 0.06 than fokc over all domain sizes. ljtkc does not perform best as the overhead introduced by FOKC does not pay off as much for this model without inequalities. In fact, ljt performs best in almost all cases.

In summary, without inequalities ljt performs best on our input models, being faster by over an order of magnitude compared to fokc. Though, ljtkc does not perform worst, ljt performs better and steadier. With inequalities, ljtkc shows promise in speeding up performance.

6   Conclusion

We present a combination of FOKC and LJT to speed up inference. For certain inputs, LJT (with LVE as a subroutine) and FOKC start to struggle either due to model structure or size. LJT provides a means to cluster a model into submodels, on which any exact lifted inference algorithm can answer queries given the algorithm can handle evidence and messages in a lifted way. FOKC fused with LJT and LVE can handle larger models more easily. In turn, FOKC boosts LJT by avoiding groundings in certain cases. The fused algorithm enables us to compute answers faster than LJT with LVE for certain inputs and LVE and FOKC alone.

We currently work on incorporating FOKC into message passing for cases where an problematic elimination occurs during message calculation, which includes adapting an FO jtree accordingly. We also work on learning lifted models to use as inputs for LJT. Moreover, we look into constraint handling, possibly realising it with answer-set programming. Other interesting algorithm features include parallelisation and caching as a means to speed up runtime.

References

1. Ahmadi, B., Kersting, K., Mladenov, M., Natarajan, S.: Exploiting symmetries for scaling loopy belief propagation and relational training. Mach. Learn. **92**(1), 91–132 (2013)
2. Apsel, U., Brafman, R.I.: Extended lifted inference with joint formulas. In: Proceedings of the 27th Conference on Uncertainty in Artificial Intelligence, UAI 2011 (2011)
3. Bellodi, E., Lamma, E., Riguzzi, F., Costa, V.S., Zese, R.: Lifted variable elimination for probabilistic logic programming. Theory Pract. Logic Program. **14**(4–5), 681–695 (2014)
4. Braun, T., Möller, R.: Lifted junction tree algorithm. In: Friedrich, G., Helmert, M., Wotawa, F. (eds.) KI 2016. LNCS (LNAI), vol. 9904, pp. 30–42. Springer, Cham (2016). https://doi.org/10.1007/978-3-319-46073-4_3
5. Braun, T., Möller, R.: Lifted most probable explanation. In: Chapman, P., Endres, D., Pernelle, N. (eds.) ICCS 2018. LNCS (LNAI), vol. 10872, pp. 39–54. Springer, Cham (2018). https://doi.org/10.1007/978-3-319-91379-7_4
6. van den Broeck, G.: Lifted inference and learning in statistical relational models. Ph.D. thesis, KU Leuven (2013)
7. van den Broeck, G., Davis, J.: Conditioning in first-order knowledge compilation and lifted probabilistic inference. In: Proceedings of the 26th AAAI Conference on Artificial Intelligence, pp. 1961–1967 (2012)
8. van den Broeck, G., Niepert, M.: Lifted probabilistic inference for asymmetric graphical models. In: Proceedings of the 29th Conference on Artificial Intelligence, AAAI 2015, pp. 3599–3605 (2015)
9. van den Broeck, G., Taghipour, N., Meert, W., Davis, J., Raedt, L.D.: Lifted probabilistic inference by first-order knowledge compilation. In: Proceedings of the 22nd International Joint Conference on Artificial Intelligence, IJCAI 2011 (2011)
10. Chavira, M., Darwiche, A.: Compiling Bayesian networks using variable elimination. In: Proceedings of the 20th International Joint Conference on Artificial Intelligence, IJCAI 2007, pp. 2443–2449 (2007)
11. Chavira, M., Darwiche, A.: On probabilistic inference by weighted model counting. Artif. Intell. **172**(6–7), 772–799 (2008)
12. Choi, J., Amir, E., Hill, D.J.: Lifted inference for relational continuous models. In: Proceedings of the 26th Conference on Uncertainty in Artificial Intelligence, UAI 2010, pp. 13–18 (2010)

13. Darwiche, A., Marquis, P.: A knowledge compilation map. J. Artif. Intell. Res. **17**(1), 229–264 (2002)
14. Das, M., Wu, Y., Khot, T., Kersting, K., Natarajan, S.: Scaling lifted probabilistic inference and learning via graph databases. In: Proceedings of the SIAM International Conference on Data Mining, pp. 738–746 (2016)
15. Gogate, V., Domingos, P.: Exploiting logical structure in lifted probabilistic inference. In: Working Note of the Workshop on Statistical Relational Artificial Intelligence at the 24th Conference on Artificial Intelligence, pp. 19–25 (2010)
16. Gogate, V., Domingos, P.: Probabilistic theorem proving. In: Proceedings of the 27th Conference on Uncertainty in Artificial Intelligence, UAI 2011, pp. 256–265 (2011)
17. Kazemi, S.M., Poole, D.: Why is compiling lifted inference into a low-level language so effective? In: Statistical Relational AI Workshop, IJCAI 2016 (2016)
18. Lauritzen, S.L., Spiegelhalter, D.J.: Local computations with probabilities on graphical structures and their application to expert systems. J. R. Stat. Soc. Ser. B: Methodol. **50**, 157–224 (1988)
19. Milch, B., Zettlemoyer, L.S., Kersting, K., Haimes, M., Kaelbling, L.P.: Lifted probabilistic inference with counting formulas. In: Proceedings of the 23rd Conference on Artificial Intelligence, AAAI 2008, pp. 1062–1068 (2008)
20. Poole, D.: First-order probabilistic inference. In: Proceedings of the 18th International Joint Conference on Artificial Intelligence, IJCAI 2003 (2003)
21. Poole, D., Zhang, N.L.: Exploiting contextual independence in probabilistic inference. J. Artif. Intell. **18**, 263–313 (2003)
22. de Salvo Braz, R.: Lifted first-order probabilistic inference. Ph.D. thesis, University of Illinois at Urbana Champaign (2007)
23. Shenoy, P.P., Shafer, G.R.: Axioms for probability and belief-function propagation. Uncertain. Artif. Intell. **4**(9), 169–198 (1990)
24. Singla, P., Domingos, P.: Lifted first-order belief propagation. In: Proceedings of the 23rd Conference on Artificial Intelligence, AAAI 2008, pp. 1094–1099 (2008)
25. Taghipour, N., Davis, J.: Generalized counting for lifted variable elimination. In: Proceedings of the 2nd International Workshop on Statistical Relational AI, pp. 1–8 (2012)
26. Taghipour, N., Fierens, D., Davis, J., Blockeel, H.: Lifted variable elimination: decoupling the operators from the constraint language. J. Artif. Intell. Res. **47**(1), 393–439 (2013)
27. Vlasselaer, J., Meert, W., van den Broeck, G., Raedt, L.D.: Exploiting local and repeated structure in dynamic Baysian networks. Artif. Intell. **232**, 43–53 (2016)
28. Zhang, N.L., Poole, D.: A simple approach to Bayesian network computations. In: Proceedings of the 10th Canadian Conference on Artificial Intelligence, pp. 171–178 (1994)

Towards Preventing Unnecessary Groundings in the Lifted Dynamic Junction Tree Algorithm

Marcel Gehrke[✉], Tanya Braun, and Ralf Möller

Institute of Information Systems, University of Lübeck, Lübeck, Germany
{gehrke,braun,moeller}@ifis.uni-luebeck.de

Abstract. The lifted dynamic junction tree algorithm (LDJT) answers
filtering and prediction queries efficiently for probabilistic relational temporal models by building and then reusing a first-order cluster representation of a knowledge base for multiple queries and time steps. Unfortunately, a non-ideal elimination order can lead to unnecessary groundings.

1 Introduction

Areas like healthcare, logistics or even scientific publishing deal with probabilistic
data with relational and temporal aspects and need efficient exact inference algorithms. These areas involve many objects in relation to each other with changes
over time and uncertainties about object existence, attribute value assignments,
or relations between objects. More specifically, publishing involves publications
(relational) for many authors (objects), streams of papers over time (temporal),
and uncertainties for example due to missing information. For query answering,
our approach performs deductive reasoning by computing marginal distributions
at discrete time steps. In this paper, we study the problem of exact inference and
investigate unnecessary groundings can occur in temporal probabilistic models.

We propose parameterised probabilistic dynamic models (PDMs) to represent probabilistic relational temporal behaviour and introduce the lifted dynamic
junction tree algorithm (LDJT) to exactly answer multiple filtering and prediction queries for multiple time steps efficiently [5]. LDJT combines the advantages
of the interface algorithm [10] and the lifted junction tree algorithm (LJT) [2].
Poole [12] introduces parametric factor graphs as relational models and proposes
lifted variable elimination (LVE) as an exact inference algorithm on relational
models. Further, de Salvo Braz [14], Milch et al. [8], and Taghipour et al. [15]
extend LVE to its current form. Lauritzen and Spiegelhalter [7] introduce the
junction tree algorithm. To benefit from the ideas of the junction tree algorithm
and LVE, Braun and Möller [2] present LJT, which efficiently performs exact
first-order probabilistic inference on relational models given a set of queries.

This research originated from the Big Data project being part of Joint Lab 1, funded
by Cisco Systems Germany, at the centre COPICOH, University of Lübeck.

F. Trollmann and A.-Y. Turhan (Eds.): KI 2018, LNAI 11117, pp. 38–45, 2018.
https://doi.org/10.1007/978-3-030-00111-7_4

Specifically, this paper shows that a non-ideal elimination order can lead to groundings even though a lifted run is possible for a model. LDJT reuses an first-order junction tree (FO jtree) structure to answer multiple queries and reuses the structure to answer queries for all time steps $t > 0$. Unfortunately, due to a non-ideal elimination order unnecessary groundings can occur.

Most inference approaches for relational temporal models are approximative. Additional to being approximative, these approaches involve unnecessary groundings or are only designed to handle single queries efficiently. Ahmadi et al. [1] propose lifted (loopy) belief propagation. From a factor graph, they build a compressed factor graph and apply lifted belief propagation with the idea of the factored frontier algorithm [9], which is an approximate counterpart to the interface algorithm. Thon et al. [16] introduce CPT-L, a probabilistic model for sequences of relational state descriptions with a partially lifted inference algorithm. Geier and Biundo [6] present an online interface algorithm for dynamic Markov logic networks (DMLNs), similar to the work of Papai et al. [11]. Both approaches slice DMLNs to run well-studied static MLN [13] inference algorithms on each slice individually. Vlasselaer et al. [17,18] introduce an exact approach, which involves computing probabilities of each possible interface assignment.

The remainder of this paper has the following structure: We introduce PDMs as a representation for relational temporal probabilistic models and present LDJT, an efficient reasoning algorithm for PDMs. Afterwards, we show how unnecessary groundings can occur and conclude by looking at extensions.

2   Parameterised Probabilistic Dynamic Models

Parameterised probabilistic models (PMs) combine first-order logic, using logical variables (logvars) as parameters, with probabilistic models [4].

Definition 1. *Let $\mathbf{L}$ be a set of logvar names, Φ a set of factor names, and $\mathbf{R}$ a set of factor names names. A parameterised randvar (PRV) $A = P(X^1, ..., X^n)$ represents a set of randvars behaving identically by combining a randvar $P \in \mathbf{R}$ with $X^1, ..., X^n \in \mathbf{L}$. If $n = 0$, the PRV is parameterless. The domain of a logvar L is denoted by $\mathcal{D}(L)$. The term $range(A)$ provides possible values of a PRV A. Constraint $(\mathbf{X}, C_{\mathbf{X}})$ allows to restrict logvars to certain domain values and is a tuple with a sequence of logvars $\mathbf{X} = (X^1, ..., X^n)$ and a set $C_{\mathbf{X}} \subseteq \times_{i=1}^{n} \mathcal{D}(X^i)$. $\top$ denotes that no restrictions apply and may be omitted. The term $lv(Y)$ refers to the logvars in some element Y. The term $gr(Y)$ denotes the set of instances of Y with all logvars in Y grounded w.r.t. constraints.*

Let us set up a PM for publications on some topic. We model that the topic may be hot, conferences are attractive, people do research, and publish in publications. From $\mathbf{R} = \{Hot, DoR\}$ and $\mathbf{L} = \{A, P, X\}$ with $\mathcal{D}(A) = \{a_1, a_2\}$, $\mathcal{D}(P) = \{p_1, p_2\}$, and $\mathcal{D}(X) = \{x_1, x_2, x_3\}$, we build the boolean PRVs Hot and $DoR(X)$. With $C = (X, \{x_1, x_2\})$, $gr(DoR(X)|C) = \{DoR(x_1), DoR(x_2)\}$.

Definition 2. *We denote a parametric factor (parfactor) g with $\forall \mathbf{X} : \phi(\mathcal{A}) \, |C$. $\mathbf{X} \subseteq \mathbf{L}$ being a set of logvars over which the factor generalises and $\mathcal{A} =$*

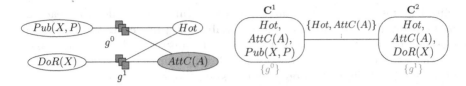

Fig. 1. Parfactor graph for G^{ex}

Fig. 2. FO jtree for G^{ex} (local models in grey)

$(A^1, ..., A^n)$ *a sequence of PRVs. We omit* $(\forall \mathbf{X} :)$ *if* $\mathbf{X} = lv(\mathcal{A})$. *A function* $\phi : \times_{i=1}^n range(A^i) \mapsto \mathbb{R}^+$ *with name* $\phi \in \Phi$ *is defined identically for all grounded instances of* $\mathcal{A}$. *A list of all input-output values is the complete specification for* ϕ. *C is a constraint on* $\mathbf{X}$. *A PM* $G := \{g^i\}_{i=0}^{n-1}$ *is a set of parfactors and semantically represents the full joint probability distribution* $P_G = \frac{1}{Z} \prod_{f \in gr(G)} f$ *where Z is a normalisation constant.*

Adding boolean PRVs $Pub(X, P)$ and $AttC(A)$, $G_{ex} = \{g^i\}_{i=0}^1$, $g^0 = \phi^0(Pub(X, P), AttC(A), Hot) \mid \top$, $g^1 = \phi^1(DoR(X), AttC(A), Hot) \mid \top$ forms a model. All parfactors have eight input-output pairs (omitted). Figure 1 depicts G^{ex} with four variable nodes for the PRVs and two factor nodes for g^0 and g^1 with edges to the PRVs involved. Additionally, we can observe the attractiveness of conferences. The remaining PRVs are latent.

The semantics of a model is given by grounding and building a full joint distribution. In general, queries ask for a probability distribution of a randvar using a model's full joint distribution and fixed events as evidence.

Definition 3. *Given a PM G, a ground PRV Q and grounded PRVs with fixed range values* $\mathbf{E} = \{E^i = e^i\}_i$, *the expression* $P(Q|\mathbf{E})$ *denotes a query w.r.t.* P_G.

To define PDMs, we use PMs and the idea of how Bayesian networks give rise to Bayesian networks [5]. We define PDMs based on the first-order Markov assumption. Further, the underlying process is stationary.

Definition 4. *A PDM is a pair of PMs* $(G_0, G_\rightarrow)$ *where* G_0 *is a PM representing the first time step and* $G_\rightarrow$ *is a two-slice temporal parameterised model representing* $\mathbf{A}_{t-1}$ *and* $\mathbf{A}_t$ *where* $\mathbf{A}_\pi$ *is a set of PRVs from time slice* π.

Figure 3 shows how the model G^{ex} behaves over time. $G^{ex}_\rightarrow$ consists of G^{ex} for time step $t-1$ and for time step t with inter-slice parfactor for the behaviour over time. In this example, the parfactor g^H is the inter-slice parfactors.

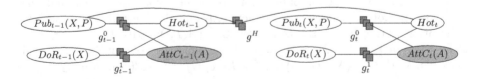

Fig. 3. $G^{ex}_\rightarrow$ the two-slice temporal parfactor graph for model G^{ex}

Definition 5. *Given a PDM G, a ground PRV Q_t and grounded PRVs with fixed range values $\mathbf{E}_{0:t} = \{E_t^i = e_t^i\}_{i,t}$, $P(Q_t|\mathbf{E}_{0:t})$ denotes a query w.r.t. P_G.*

The problem of answering a marginal distribution query $P(A_\pi^i|\mathbf{E}_{0:t})$ w.r.t. the model is called *prediction* for $\pi > t$ and *filtering* for $\pi = t$.

3 Lifted Dynamic Junction Tree Algorithm

To provide means to answer queries for PMs, we introduce LJT, mainly based on [3]. Afterwards, we present LDJT [5] consisting of FO jtree constructions for a PDM and a *filtering* and *prediction* algorithm.

3.1 Lifted Junction Tree Algorithm

LJT provides efficient means to answer queries $P(\mathbf{Q}|\mathbf{E})$, with a set of query terms, given a PM G and evidence $\mathbf{E}$, by performing the following steps: (i) Construct an FO jtree J for G. (ii) Enter $\mathbf{E}$ in J. (iii) Pass messages. (iv) Compute answer for each query $Q^i \in \mathbf{Q}$. We first define an FO jtree and then go through each step. To define an FO jtree, we need to define parameterised clusters (parclusters), the nodes of an FO jtree.

Definition 6. *A parcluster $\mathbf{C}$ is defined by $\forall \mathbf{L} : A|C$. $\mathbf{L}$ is a set of logvars, $\mathbf{A}$ is a set of PRVs with $lv(\mathbf{A}) \subseteq \mathbf{L}$, and C a constraint on $\mathbf{L}$. We omit $(\forall \mathbf{L} :)$ if $\mathbf{L} = lv(\mathbf{A})$. A parcluster $\mathbf{C}^i$ can have parfactors $\phi(\mathcal{A}^\phi)|C^\phi$ assigned given that (i) $\mathcal{A}^\phi \subseteq \mathbf{A}$, (ii) $lv(\mathcal{A}^\phi) \subseteq \mathbf{L}$, and (iii) $C^\phi \subseteq C$ holds. We call the set of assigned parfactors a local model G^i.*

An FO jtree for a model G is $J = (\mathbf{V}, \mathbf{E})$ where J is a cycle-free graph, the nodes $\mathbf{V}$ denote a set of parcluster, and the set $\mathbf{E}$ edges between parclusters. An FO jtree must satisfy the following properties: (i) A parcluster $\mathbf{C}^i$ is a set of PRVs from G. (ii) For each parfactor $\phi(\mathcal{A})|C$ in G, $\mathcal{A}$ must appear in some parcluster $\mathbf{C}^i$. (iii) If a PRV from G appears in two parclusters $\mathbf{C}^i$ and $\mathbf{C}^j$, it must also appear in every parcluster $\mathbf{C}^k$ on the path connecting nodes i and j in J. The separator $\mathbf{S}^{ij}$ of edge $i - j$ is given by $\mathbf{C}^i \cap \mathbf{C}^j$ containing shared PRVs.

LJT constructs an FO jtree using a first-order decomposition tree (FO dtree), enters evidence in the FO jtree, and passes messages through an *inbound* and an *outbound* pass, to distribute local information of the nodes through the FO jtree. To compute a message, LJT eliminates all non-seperator PRVs from the parcluster's local model and received messages. After message passing, LJT answers queries. For each query, LJT finds a parcluster containing the query term and sums out all non-query terms in its local model and received messages.

Figure 2 shows an FO jtree of G^{ex} with the local models of the parclusters and the separators as labels of edges. During the *inbound* phase of message passing, LJT sends messages from $\mathbf{C}^1$ to $\mathbf{C}^2$ and for the *outbound* phase a message from $\mathbf{C}^2$ to $\mathbf{C}^1$. If we want to know whether Hot holds, we query for $P(Hot)$ for which LJT can use either parcluster $\mathbf{C}^1$ or $\mathbf{C}^2$. Thus, LJT can sum out $AttC(A)$ and $DoR(X)$ from $\mathbf{C}^2$'s local model G^2, $\{g^1\}$, combined with the received messages.

3.2   LDJT: Overview

LDJT efficiently answers queries $P(\mathbf{Q}_t|\mathbf{E}_{0:t})$, with a set of query terms $\{\mathbf{Q}_t\}_{t=0}^T$, given a PDM G and evidence $\{\mathbf{E}_t\}_{t=0}^T$, by performing the following steps: (i) Construct offline two FO jtrees J_0 and J_t with *in-* and *out-clusters* from G. (ii) For $t = 0$, using J_0 to enter $\mathbf{E}_0$, pass messages, answer each query term $Q_\pi^i \in \mathbf{Q}_0$, and preserve the state. (iii) For $t > 0$, instantiate J_t for the current time step t, recover the previous state, enter $\mathbf{E}_t$ in J_t, pass messages, answer each query term $Q_\pi^i \in \mathbf{Q}_t$, and preserve the state.

Next, we show how LDJT constructs the FO jtrees J_0 and J_t with *in-* and *out-clusters*, which contain a minimal set of PRVs to m-separate the FO jtrees. M-separation means that information about these PRVs make FO jtrees independent from each other. Afterwards, we present how LDJT connects the FO jtrees for reasoning to solve the *filtering* and *prediction* problems efficiently.

3.3   LDJT: FO Jtree Construction for PDMs

LDJT constructs FO jtrees for G_0 and $G_\rightarrow$, both with an incoming and outgoing interface. To be able to construct the interfaces in the FO jtrees, LDJT uses the PDM G to identify the interface PRVs $\mathbf{I}_t$ for a time slice t.

Definition 7. *The forward interface is defined as* $\mathbf{I}_t = \{A_t^i \mid \exists \phi(\mathcal{A})|C \in G : A_t^i \in \mathcal{A} \wedge \exists A_{t+1}^j \in \mathcal{A}\}$, *i.e., the PRVs which have successors in the next slice*.

For $G_\rightarrow^{ex}$, which is shown in Fig. 3, PRVs Hot_{t-1} and $Pub_{t-1}(X, P)$ have successors in the next time slice, making up $\mathbf{I}_{t-1}$. To ensure interface PRVs $\mathbf{I}$ ending up in a single parcluster, LDJT adds a parfactor g^I over the interface to the model. Thus, LDJT adds a parfactor g_0^I over $\mathbf{I}_0$ to G_0, builds an FO jtree J_0 and labels the parcluster with g_0^I from J_0 as *in-* and *out-cluster*. For $G_\rightarrow$, LDJT removes all non-interface PRVs from time slice $t - 1$, adds parfactors g_{t-1}^I and g_t^I, constructs J_t, and labels the parcluster containing g_{t-1}^I as *in-cluster* and the parcluster containing g_t^I as *out-cluster*.

The interface PRVs are a minimal required set to m-separate the FO jtrees. LDJT uses these PRVs as separator to connect the *out-cluster* of J_{t-1} with the *in-cluster* of J_t, allowing to reusing the structure of J_t for all $t > 0$.

3.4   LDJT: Proceeding in Time with the FO Jtree Structures

Since J_0 and J_t are static, LDJT uses LJT as a subroutine by passing on a constructed FO jtree, queries, and evidence for step t to handle evidence entering, message passing, and query answering using the FO jtree. Further, for proceeding to the next time step, LDJT calculates an α_t message over the interface PRVs using the *out-cluster* to preserve the information about the current state. Afterwards, LDJT increases t by one, instantiates J_t, and adds α_{t-1} to the *in-cluster* of J_t. During message passing, α_{t-1} is distributed through J_t.

Figure 4 depicts how LDJT uses the interface message passing between time step three to four. First, LDJT sums out the non-interface PRV $AttC_3(A)$ from

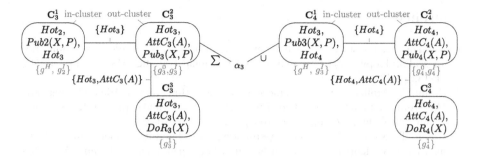

Fig. 4. Forward pass of LDJT (local models and labeling in grey)

$\mathbf{C}_3^2$'s local model and the received messages and saves the result in message α_3. After increasing t by one, LDJT adds α_3 to the *in-cluster* of J_4, $\mathbf{C}_4^1$. α_3 is then distributed by message passing and accounted for during calculating α_4.

4 Unnecessary Groundings in LDJT

Unnecessary groundings have a huge impact on temporal models, as groundings during message passing can propagate through the complete model. LDJT has an intra and inter FO jtree message passing phase. Intra FO jtree message passing takes place inside of an FO jtree for one time step. Inter FO jtree message passing takes place between two FO jtrees. To prevent groundings during intra FO jtree message passing, LJT successfully proposes to fuse parclusters [3]. Unfortunately, having two FO jtrees, LDJT cannot fuse parclusters from different FO jtrees. Hence, LDJT requires a different approach to prevent unnecessary groundings during inter FO jtree message passing.

Let us now have a look at Fig. 4 to understand inter FO jtree message pass can induce unnecessary groundings due to the elimination order. Figure 4 shows J_t instantiated for time step 3 and 4. To compute α_3, LDJT eliminates $AttC_3(A)$ from $\mathbf{C}_3^2$'s local model. The elimination of $AttC_3(A)$ leads to groundings, as $AttC_3(A)$ does not contain all logvars, X and P are missing. Additionally, $AttC_3(A)$ is not count-convertible. Assuming $AttC_3(A)$ would also be included in the parcluster $\mathbf{C}_4^1$, LDJT would not need to eliminate $AttC_3(A)$ in $\mathbf{C}_3^2$ anymore and therefore calculating α_3 would not lead to groundings. Therefore, the elimination order can lead to unnecessary groundings.

5 Conclusion

We present the need to prevent unnecessary groundings in LDJT by changing the elimination order. We currently work on an approach to prevent unnecessary groundings, as well as extending LDJT to also calculate the most probable explanation. Other interesting future work includes a tailored automatic learning for PDMs, parallelisation of LJT, and improved evidence entering.

References

1. Ahmadi, B., Kersting, K., Mladenov, M., Natarajan, S.: Exploiting symmetries for scaling loopy belief propagation and relational training. Mach. Learn. **92**(1), 91–132 (2013)
2. Braun, T., Möller, R.: Lifted junction tree algorithm. In: Friedrich, G., Helmert, M., Wotawa, F. (eds.) KI 2016. LNCS (LNAI), vol. 9904, pp. 30–42. Springer, Cham (2016). https://doi.org/10.1007/978-3-319-46073-4_3
3. Braun, T., Möller, R.: Preventing groundings and handling evidence in the lifted junction tree algorithm. In: Kern-Isberner, G., Fürnkranz, J., Thimm, M. (eds.) KI 2017. LNCS (LNAI), vol. 10505, pp. 85–98. Springer, Cham (2017). https://doi.org/10.1007/978-3-319-67190-1_7
4. Braun, T., Möller, R.: Counting and conjunctive queries in the lifted junction tree algorithm. In: Croitoru, M., Marquis, P., Rudolph, S., Stapleton, G. (eds.) GKR 2017. LNCS (LNAI), vol. 10775, pp. 54–72. Springer, Cham (2018). https://doi.org/10.1007/978-3-319-78102-0_3
5. Gehrke, M., Braun, T., Möller, R.: Lifted dynamic junction tree algorithm. In: Chapman, P., Endres, D., Pernelle, N. (eds.) ICCS 2018. LNCS (LNAI), vol. 10872, pp. 55–69. Springer, Cham (2018). https://doi.org/10.1007/978-3-319-91379-7_5
6. Geier, T., Biundo, S.: Approximate online inference for dynamic Markov logic networks. In: Proceedings of the 23rd IEEE International Conference on Tools with Artificial Intelligence (ICTAI), pp. 764–768. IEEE (2011)
7. Lauritzen, S.L., Spiegelhalter, D.J.: Local computations with probabilities on graphical structures and their application to expert systems. J. R. Stat. Soc. Ser. B (Methodol.) **50**, 157–224 (1988)
8. Milch, B., Zettlemoyer, L.S., Kersting, K., Haimes, M., Kaelbling, L.P.: Lifted probabilistic inference with counting formulas. In: Proceedings of AAAI, vol. 8, pp. 1062–1068 (2008)
9. Murphy, K., Weiss, Y.: The factored frontier algorithm for approximate inference in DBNs. In: Proceedings of the Seventeenth Conference on Uncertainty in Artificial Intelligence, pp. 378–385. Morgan Kaufmann Publishers Inc. (2001)
10. Murphy, K.P.: Dynamic Bayesian networks: representation, inference and learning. Ph.D. thesis, University of California, Berkeley (2002)
11. Papai, T., Kautz, H., Stefankovic, D.: Slice normalized dynamic Markov logic networks. In: Proceedings of the Advances in Neural Information Processing Systems, pp. 1907–1915 (2012)
12. Poole, D.: First-order probabilistic inference. In: Proceedings of IJCAI, vol. 3, pp. 985–991 (2003)
13. Richardson, M., Domingos, P.: Markov logic networks. Mach. Learn. **62**(1), 107–136 (2006)
14. de Salvo Braz, R.: Lifted first-order probabilistic inference. Ph.D. thesis, Ph.D. dissertation, University of Illinois at Urbana Champaign (2007)
15. Taghipour, N., Fierens, D., Davis, J., Blockeel, H.: Lifted variable elimination: decoupling the operators from the constraint language. J. Artif. Intell. Res. **47**(1), 393–439 (2013)
16. Thon, I., Landwehr, N., De Raedt, L.: Stochastic relational processes: efficient inference and applications. Mach. Learn. **82**(2), 239–272 (2011)
17. Vlasselaer, J., Van den Broeck, G., Kimmig, A., Meert, W., De Raedt, L.: TP-compilation for inference in probabilistic logic programs. Int. J. Approx. Reason. **78**, 15–32 (2016)

18. Vlasselaer, J., Meert, W., Van den Broeck, G., De Raedt, L.: Efficient probabilistic inference for dynamic relational models. In: Proceedings of the 13th AAAI Conference on Statistical Relational AI, pp. 131–132. AAAIWS'14-13, AAAI Press (2014)

Acquisition of Terminological Knowledge in Probabilistic Description Logic

Francesco Kriegel[✉] [iD]

Institute of Theoretical Computer Science, Technische Universität Dresden,
Dresden, Germany
`francesco.kriegel@tu-dresden.de`

Abstract. For a probabilistic extension of the description logic $\mathcal{EL}^{\perp}$, we consider the task of automatic acquisition of terminological knowledge from a given probabilistic interpretation. Basically, such a probabilistic interpretation is a family of directed graphs the vertices and edges of which are labeled, and where a discrete probability measure on this graph family is present. The goal is to derive so-called concept inclusions which are expressible in the considered probabilistic description logic and which hold true in the given probabilistic interpretation. A procedure for an appropriate axiomatization of such graph families is proposed and its soundness and completeness is justified.

Keywords: Data mining · Knowledge acquisition
Probabilistic description logic · Knowledge base
Probabilistic interpretation · Concept inclusion

1 Introduction

Description Logics (abbrv. DLs) [2] are frequently used knowledge representation and reasoning formalisms with a strong logical foundation. In particular, these provide their users with automated inference services that can derive implicit knowledge from the explicitly represented knowledge. Decidability and computational complexity of common reasoning tasks have been widely explored for most DLs. Besides being used in various application domains, their most notable success is the fact that DLs constitute the logical underpinning of the *Web Ontology Language* (abbrv. OWL) and many of its profiles.

DLs in its standard form only allow for representing and reasoning with *crisp* knowledge without any degree of *uncertainty*. Of course, this is a serious shortcoming for use cases where it is impossible to perfectly determine the truth of a statement. For resolving this expressivity restriction, probabilistic variants of DLs [5] have been introduced. Their model-theoretic semantics is built upon so-called probabilistic interpretations, that is, families of directed graphs the vertices and edges of which are labeled and for which there exists a probability measure on this graph family.

© Springer Nature Switzerland AG 2018
F. Trollmann and A.-Y. Turhan (Eds.): KI 2018, LNAI 11117, pp. 46–53, 2018.
https://doi.org/10.1007/978-3-030-00111-7_5

Results of scientific experiments, e.g., in medicine, psychology, or biology, that are repeated several times can induce probabilistic interpretations in a natural way. In this document, we shall develop a suitable axiomatization technique for deducing terminological knowledge from the assertional data given in such probabilistic interpretations. More specifically, we consider a probabilistic variant $\mathcal{P}_1^> \mathcal{EL}^\perp$ of the description logic $\mathcal{EL}^\perp$, show that reasoning in $\mathcal{P}_1^> \mathcal{EL}^\perp$ is **ExpTime**-complete, and provide a method for constructing a set of rules, so-called concept inclusions, from probabilistic interpretations in a sound and complete manner.

This document also resolves an issue found by Franz Baader with the techniques described by the author in [6, Sects. 5 and 6]. In particular, the concept inclusion base proposed therein in Proposition 2 is only complete with respect to those probabilistic interpretations that are also quasi-uniform with a probability ε of each world. Herein, we describe a more sophisticated axiomatization technique of not necessarily quasi-uniform probabilistic interpretations and that ensures completeness of the constructed concept inclusion base with respect to *all* probabilistic interpretations, but which, however, disallows nesting of probability restrictions. It is not hard to generalize the following results to a more expressive probabilistic description logic, for example to a probabilistic variant $\mathcal{P}_1^> \mathcal{M}$ of the description logic $\mathcal{M}$, for which an axiomatization technique is available [8]. That way, we can regain the same, or even a greater, expressivity as the author has tried to have tackled in [6], but without the possibility to nest probability restrictions.

Due to space restrictions, all proofs as well as a toy example have been moved to a technical report [9].

2   The Probabilistic Description Logic $\mathcal{P}_1^> \mathcal{EL}^\perp$

The probabilistic description logic $\mathcal{P}_1^> \mathcal{EL}^\perp$ extends the light-weight description logic $\mathcal{EL}^\perp$ [2] by means for expressing and reasoning with probabilities. Put simply, it is a variant of the logic Prob-$\mathcal{EL}$ introduced by Gutiérrez-Basulto, Jung, Lutz, and Schröder in [5] where nesting of probabilistic quantifiers is disallowed, only the relation symbols $>$ and $\geq$ are available for the probability restrictions, and further the bottom concept description $\perp$ is present. We introduce its syntax and semantics as follows.

Fix some *signature* Σ, which is a disjoint union of a set Σ_C of *concept names* and a set Σ_R of *role names*. Then, $\mathcal{P}_1^> \mathcal{EL}^\perp$ *concept descriptions* C over Σ may be constructed by means of the following inductive rules (where $A \in \Sigma_C$, $r \in \Sigma_R$, $\gtrless \in \{\geq, >\}$ and $p \in [0,1] \cap \mathbb{Q}$).[1]

$$C ::= \perp \mid \top \mid A \mid C \sqcap C \mid \exists r.C \mid \mathsf{d} \gtrless p.D$$
$$D ::= \perp \mid \top \mid A \mid D \sqcap D \mid \exists r.D$$

---

[1] If we treat these two rules as the production rules of a BNF grammar, C is its start symbol.

We denote the set of all $\mathcal{P}_1^{>}\mathcal{EL}^{\perp}$ concept descriptions over Σ by $\mathcal{P}_1^{>}\mathcal{EL}^{\perp}(\Sigma)$. An $\mathcal{EL}^{\perp}$ *concept description* is a $\mathcal{P}_1^{>}\mathcal{EL}^{\perp}$ concept description not containing any subconcept of the form $\mathsf{d} > p.\,C$, and we shall write $\mathcal{EL}^{\perp}(\Sigma)$ for the set of all $\mathcal{EL}^{\perp}$ concept descriptions over Σ. A *concept inclusion* (abbrv. CI) is an expression of the form $C \sqsubseteq D$, and a *concept equivalence* (abbrv. CE) is of the form $C \equiv D$, where both C and D are concept descriptions. A *terminological box* (abbrv. TBox) is a finite set of CIs and CEs. Furthermore, we also allow for so-called *wildcard concept inclusions* of the form $\mathsf{d} >_1 p_1.\,* \sqsubseteq \mathsf{d} >_2 p_2.\,*$ that, basically, are abbreviations for the set $\{\,\mathsf{d} >_1 p_1.\,C \sqsubseteq \mathsf{d} >_2 p_2.\,C \mid C \in \mathcal{EL}^{\perp}(\Sigma)\,\}$.

A *probabilistic interpretation* over Σ is a tuple $\mathcal{I} := (\Delta^{\mathcal{I}}, \Omega^{\mathcal{I}}, \cdot^{\mathcal{I}}, \mathbb{P}^{\mathcal{I}})$ consisting of a non-empty set $\Delta^{\mathcal{I}}$ of *objects*, called the *domain*, a non-empty, countable set $\Omega^{\mathcal{I}}$ of *worlds*, a discrete probability measure $\mathbb{P}^{\mathcal{I}}$ on $\Omega^{\mathcal{I}}$, and an *extension function* $\cdot^{\mathcal{I}}$ such that, for each world $\omega \in \Omega^{\mathcal{I}}$, any concept name $A \in \Sigma_{\mathsf{C}}$ is mapped to a subset $A^{\mathcal{I}(\omega)} \subseteq \Delta^{\mathcal{I}}$ and each role name $r \in \Sigma_{\mathsf{R}}$ is mapped to a binary relation $r^{\mathcal{I}(\omega)} \subseteq \Delta^{\mathcal{I}} \times \Delta^{\mathcal{I}}$. Note that $\mathbb{P}^{\mathcal{I}} \colon \wp(\Omega^{\mathcal{I}}) \to [0,1]$ is a mapping which satisfies $\mathbb{P}^{\mathcal{I}}(\emptyset) = 0$ and $\mathbb{P}^{\mathcal{I}}(\Omega^{\mathcal{I}}) = 1$, and is σ-*additive*, that is, for all countable families $(\,U_n \mid n \in \mathbb{N}\,)$ of pairwise disjoint sets $U_n \subseteq \Omega^{\mathcal{I}}$ it holds true that $\mathbb{P}^{\mathcal{I}}(\bigcup\{\,U_n \mid n \in \mathbb{N}\,\}) = \sum(\,\mathbb{P}^{\mathcal{I}}(U_n) \mid n \in \mathbb{N}\,)$. In particular, we follow the assumption in [5, Sect. 2.6] and consider only probabilistic interpretations without any infinitely improbable worlds, i.e., without any worlds $\omega \in \Omega^{\mathcal{I}}$ such that $\mathbb{P}^{\mathcal{I}}\{\omega\} = 0$. We call a probabilistic interpretation *finitely representable* if $\Delta^{\mathcal{I}}$ is finite, $\Omega^{\mathcal{I}}$ is finite, the *active signature* $\Sigma^{\mathcal{I}} := \{\,\sigma \mid \sigma \in \Sigma \text{ and } \sigma^{\mathcal{I}(\omega)} \neq \emptyset \text{ for some } \omega \in \Omega^{\mathcal{I}}\,\}$ is finite, and if $\mathbb{P}^{\mathcal{I}}$ has only rational values. In the sequel of this document we will also utilize the notion of *interpretations*, which are the models upon which the semantics of $\mathcal{EL}^{\perp}$ is built; these are, basically, probabilistic interpretations with only one world, that is, these are tuples $\mathcal{I} := (\Delta^{\mathcal{I}}, \cdot^{\mathcal{I}})$ where $\Delta^{\mathcal{I}}$ is a non-empty set of *objects*, called *domain*, and where $\cdot^{\mathcal{I}}$ is an *extension function* that maps concept names $A \in \Sigma_{\mathsf{C}}$ to subsets $A^{\mathcal{I}} \subseteq \Delta^{\mathcal{I}}$ and maps role names $r \in \Sigma_{\mathsf{R}}$ to binary relations $r^{\mathcal{I}} \subseteq \Delta^{\mathcal{I}} \times \Delta^{\mathcal{I}}$.

Fix some probabilistic interpretation $\mathcal{I}$. The *extension* $C^{\mathcal{I}(\omega)}$ of a $\mathcal{P}_1^{>}\mathcal{EL}^{\perp}$ concept description C in a world ω of $\mathcal{I}$ is defined by means of the following recursive formulae.

$$\perp^{\mathcal{I}(\omega)} := \emptyset \qquad \top^{\mathcal{I}(\omega)} := \Delta^{\mathcal{I}} \qquad (C \sqcap D)^{\mathcal{I}(\omega)} := C^{\mathcal{I}(\omega)} \cap D^{\mathcal{I}(\omega)}$$

$$(\exists r.\,C)^{\mathcal{I}(\omega)} := \{\,\delta \mid \delta \in \Delta^{\mathcal{I}}, (\delta, \epsilon) \in r^{\mathcal{I}(\omega)}, \text{ and } \epsilon \in C^{\mathcal{I}(\omega)} \text{ for some } \epsilon \in \Delta^{\mathcal{I}}\,\}$$

$$(\mathsf{d} > p.\,C)^{\mathcal{I}(\omega)} := \{\,\delta \mid \delta \in \Delta^{\mathcal{I}} \text{ and } \mathbb{P}^{\mathcal{I}}\{\delta \in C^{\mathcal{I}}\} > p\,\}$$

Please note that we use the abbreviation $\{\delta \in C^{\mathcal{I}}\} := \{\,\omega \mid \omega \in \Omega^{\mathcal{I}} \text{ and } \delta \in C^{\mathcal{I}(\omega)}\,\}$. All but the last formula can be used similarly to recursively define the *extension* $C^{\mathcal{I}}$ of an $\mathcal{EL}^{\perp}$ concept description C in an interpretation $\mathcal{I}$.

A concept inclusion $C \sqsubseteq D$ or a concept equivalence $C \equiv D$ is *valid* in a probabilistic interpretation $\mathcal{I}$ if $C^{\mathcal{I}(\omega)} \subseteq D^{\mathcal{I}(\omega)}$ or $C^{\mathcal{I}(\omega)} = D^{\mathcal{I}(\omega)}$, respectively, is satisfied for all worlds $\omega \in \Omega^{\mathcal{I}}$, and we shall then write $\mathcal{I} \models C \sqsubseteq D$ or $\mathcal{I} \models C \equiv D$, respectively. A wildcard CI $\mathsf{d} >_1 p_1.\,* \sqsubseteq \mathsf{d} >_2 p_2.\,*$ is *valid* in $\mathcal{I}$, written $\mathcal{I} \models \mathsf{d} >_1 p_1.\,* \sqsubseteq \mathsf{d} >_2 p_2.\,*$, if, for each $\mathcal{EL}^{\perp}$ concept description C, the

CI $\mathsf{d} >_1 p_1. C \sqsubseteq \mathsf{d} >_2 p_2. C$ is valid in $\mathcal{I}$. Furthermore, $\mathcal{I}$ is a *model* of a TBox $\mathcal{T}$, denoted as $\mathcal{I} \models \mathcal{T}$, if each concept inclusion in $\mathcal{T}$ is valid in $\mathcal{I}$. A TBox $\mathcal{T}$ *entails* a concept inclusion $C \sqsubseteq D$, symbolized by $\mathcal{T} \models C \sqsubseteq D$, if $C \sqsubseteq D$ is valid in every model of $\mathcal{T}$. In the sequel of this document, we may also use the denotation $C \leq_{\mathcal{Y}} D$ instead of $\mathcal{Y} \models C \leq D$ where $\mathcal{Y}$ is either an interpretation or a terminological box and $\leq$ is a suitable relation symbol, e.g., one of $\sqsubseteq$, $\equiv$, $\sqsupseteq$, and we may analogously write $C \not\leq_{\mathcal{Y}} D$ for $\mathcal{Y} \not\models C \leq D$.

Proposition 1. *In $\mathcal{P}_1^{>} \mathcal{EL}^{\perp}$, the problem of deciding whether a terminological box entails a concept inclusion is* **ExpTime**-*complete.*

In the next section, we will use techniques for axiomatizing concept inclusions in $\mathcal{EL}^{\perp}$ as developed by Baader and Distel in [1,4] for greatest fixed-point semantics, and as adjusted by Borchmann, Distel, and the author in [3] for the role-depth-bounded case. A brief introduction is as follows. A *concept inclusion base* for an interpretation $\mathcal{I}$ is a TBox $\mathcal{T}$ such that, for each concept inclusion $C \sqsubseteq D$, it holds true that $\mathcal{I} \models C \sqsubseteq D$ if, and only if, $\mathcal{T} \models C \sqsubseteq D$. For each finite interpretation $\mathcal{I}$ with finite active signature, there is a *canonical base* $\mathsf{Can}(\mathcal{I})$ with respect to greatest fixed-point semantics, which has minimal cardinality among all concept inclusion bases for $\mathcal{I}$, cf. [4, Corollary 5.13 and Theorem 5.18], and similarly there is a minimal *canonical base* $\mathsf{Can}(\mathcal{I}, d)$ with respect to an upper bound $d \in \mathbb{N}$ on the role depths, cf. [3, Theorem 4.32]. The construction of both canonical bases is built upon the notion of a *model-based most specific concept description*, which, for an interpretation $\mathcal{I}$ and a subset $X \subseteq \Delta^{\mathcal{I}}$, is a concept description C such that $X \subseteq C^{\mathcal{I}}$ and, for each concept description D, it holds true that $X \subseteq D^{\mathcal{I}}$ implies $\emptyset \models C \sqsubseteq D$. These exist either if greatest fixed-point semantics is applied (in order to be able to express cycles present in $\mathcal{I}$) or if the role depth of C is bounded by some $d \in \mathbb{N}$, and these are then denoted as $X^{\mathcal{I}}$ or $X^{\mathcal{I}_d}$, respectively. This mapping $\cdot^{\mathcal{I}} \colon \wp(\Delta^{\mathcal{I}}) \to \mathcal{EL}^{\perp}(\Sigma)$ is the adjoint of the extension function $\cdot^{\mathcal{I}} \colon \mathcal{EL}^{\perp}(\Sigma) \to \wp(\Delta^{\mathcal{I}})$, and the pair of both constitutes a *Galois connection*, cf. [4, Lemma 4.1] and [3, Lemmas 4.3 and 4.4], respectively.

As a variant of these two approaches, the author presented in [7] a method for constructing canonical bases relative to an existing terminological box. If $\mathcal{I}$ is an interpretation and $\mathcal{B}$ is a terminological box such that $\mathcal{I} \models \mathcal{B}$, then a *concept inclusion base* for $\mathcal{I}$ *relative to* $\mathcal{B}$ is a terminological box $\mathcal{T}$ such that, for each concept inclusion $C \sqsubseteq D$, it holds true that $\mathcal{I} \models C \sqsubseteq D$ if, and only if, $\mathcal{T} \cup \mathcal{B} \models C \sqsubseteq D$. The appropriate *canonical base* is denoted by $\mathsf{Can}(\mathcal{I}, \mathcal{B})$, cf. [7, Theorem 1].

3   Axiomatization of Concept Inclusions in $\mathcal{P}_1^{>} \mathcal{EL}^{\perp}$

In this section, we shall develop an effective method for axiomatizing $\mathcal{P}_1^{>} \mathcal{EL}^{\perp}$ concept inclusions which are valid in a given finitely representable probabilistic interpretation. After defining the appropriate notion of a *concept inclusion base*, we show how this problem can be tackled using the aforementioned existing results on computing concept inclusion bases in $\mathcal{EL}^{\perp}$. More specifically, we devise an extension of the given signature by finitely many probability restrictions $\mathsf{d} \gg p.\, C$ that are treated as additional concept names, and we define a so-called *probabilistic scaling* $\mathcal{I}_\mathsf{d}$ of the input probabilistic interpretation $\mathcal{I}$ which is a (single-world) interpretation that suitably interprets these new concept names and, furthermore, such that there is a correspondence between CIs valid in $\mathcal{I}$ and CIs valid in $\mathcal{I}_\mathsf{d}$. This correspondence makes it possible to utilize the above mentioned techniques for axiomatizing CIs in $\mathcal{EL}^\perp$.

Definition 2. *A* concept inclusion base *for a probabilistic interpretation $\mathcal{I}$ is a terminological box $\mathcal{T}$ which is* sound *for $\mathcal{I}$, that is, $\mathcal{T} \models C \sqsubseteq D$ implies $\mathcal{I} \models C \sqsubseteq D$ for each concept inclusion $C \sqsubseteq D$,[2] and which is* complete *for $\mathcal{I}$, that is, $\mathcal{I} \models C \sqsubseteq D$ only if $\mathcal{T} \models C \sqsubseteq D$ for any concept inclusion $C \sqsubseteq D$.*

A first important step is to significantly reduce the possibilities of concept descriptions occuring as a filler in the probability restrictions, that is, of fillers C in expressions $\mathsf{d} \gg p.\, C$. As it turns out, it suffices to consider only those fillers that are model-based most specific concept descriptions of some suitable *scaling* of the given probabilistic interpretation $\mathcal{I}$.

Definition 3. *Let $\mathcal{I}$ be a probabilistic interpretation $\mathcal{I}$ over some signature Σ. Then, its* almost certain scaling *is defined as the interpretation $\mathcal{I}_\times$ over Σ with the following components.*

$$\Delta^{\mathcal{I}_\times} := \Delta^{\mathcal{I}} \times \Omega^{\mathcal{I}}$$

$$\cdot^{\mathcal{I}_\times} : \begin{cases} A \mapsto \{\, (\delta, \omega) \mid \delta \in A^{\mathcal{I}(\omega)} \,\} & \text{for each } A \in \Sigma_\mathsf{C} \\ r \mapsto \{\, ((\delta, \omega), (\epsilon, \omega)) \mid (\delta, \epsilon) \in r^{\mathcal{I}(\omega)} \,\} & \text{for each } r \in \Sigma_\mathsf{R} \end{cases}$$

Lemma 4. *Consider a probabilistic interpretation $\mathcal{I}$ and a concept description $\mathsf{d} \gg p.\, C$. Then, the concept equivalence $\mathsf{d} \gg p.\, C \equiv \mathsf{d} \gg p.\, C^{\mathcal{I}_\times \mathcal{I}_\times}$ is valid in $\mathcal{I}$.*

As next step, we restrict the probability bounds p occuring in probability restrictions $\mathsf{d} \gg p.\, C$. Apparently, it is sufficient to consider only those values p that can occur when evaluating the extension of $\mathcal{P}_1^{\geq} \mathcal{EL}^\perp$ concept descriptions in $\mathcal{I}$, which, obviously, are the values $\mathbb{P}^{\mathcal{I}}\{\delta \in C^{\mathcal{I}}\}$ for any $\delta \in \Delta^{\mathcal{I}}$ and any $C \in \mathcal{EL}^\perp(\Sigma)$. Denote the set of all these probability values as $P(\mathcal{I})$. Of course, we have that $\{0, 1\} \subseteq P(\mathcal{I})$. If $\mathcal{I}$ is finitely representable, then $P(\mathcal{I})$ is finite too, it holds true that $P(\mathcal{I}) \subseteq \mathbb{Q}$, and the following equation is satisfied, which can be demonstrated using arguments from the proof of Lemma 4.

$$P(\mathcal{I}) = \{\, \mathbb{P}^{\mathcal{I}}\{\delta \in X^{\mathcal{I}_\times \mathcal{I}}\} \mid \delta \in \Delta^{\mathcal{I}} \text{ and } X \subseteq \Delta^{\mathcal{I}} \times \Omega^{\mathcal{I}} \,\}$$

For each $p \in [0, 1)$, we define $(p)^+_{\mathcal{I}}$ as the next value in $P(\mathcal{I})$ above p, that is, we set

$$(p)^+_{\mathcal{I}} := \bigwedge\{\, q \mid q \in P(\mathcal{I}) \text{ and } q > p \,\}.$$

---

[2] Of course, soundness is equivalent to $\mathcal{I} \models \mathcal{T}$.

If the considered probabilistic interpretation $\mathcal{I}$ is clear from the context, then we may also write p^+ instead of $(p)_{\mathcal{I}}^+$. To prevent a loss of information due to only considering probabilities in $P(\mathcal{I})$, we shall use the wildcard concept inclusions $\mathsf{d} > p. * \sqsubseteq \mathsf{d} \geq p^+. *$ for $p \in P(\mathcal{I}) \setminus \{1\}$.

Having found a finite number of representatives for probability bounds as well as a finite number of fillers to be used in probability restrictions, we now show that we can treat these finitely many concept descriptions as concept names of a signature Γ extending Σ in a way such that a concept inclusion is valid in $\mathcal{I}$ if, and only if, the concept inclusion projected onto this extended signature Γ is valid in a suitable *scaling* of $\mathcal{I}$ that interprets Γ.

Definition 5. *Assume that $\mathcal{I}$ is a probabilistic interpretation over a signature Σ. Then, the signature Γ is defined as follows.*

$$\Gamma_{\mathsf{C}} := \Sigma_{\mathsf{C}} \cup \{\, \mathsf{d} \geq p. X^{\mathcal{I}_\times} \mid p \in P(\mathcal{I}) \setminus \{0\}, \ X \subseteq \Delta^{\mathcal{I}} \times \Omega^{\mathcal{I}}, \ and \ \bot \not\equiv_\emptyset X^{\mathcal{I}_\times} \not\equiv_\emptyset \top \,\}$$
$$\Gamma_{\mathsf{R}} := \Sigma_{\mathsf{R}}$$

The probabilistic scaling *of $\mathcal{I}$ is defined as the interpretation $\mathcal{I}_\mathsf{d}$ over Γ that has the following components.*

$$\Delta^{\mathcal{I}_\mathsf{d}} := \Delta^{\mathcal{I}} \times \Omega^{\mathcal{I}}$$

$$\cdot^{\mathcal{I}_\mathsf{d}} : \begin{cases} A \mapsto \{\, (\delta, \omega) \mid \delta \in A^{\mathcal{I}(\omega)} \,\} & \text{for each } A \in \Gamma_{\mathsf{C}} \\ r \mapsto \{\, ((\delta, \omega), (\epsilon, \omega)) \mid (\delta, \epsilon) \in r^{\mathcal{I}(\omega)} \,\} & \text{for each } r \in \Gamma_{\mathsf{R}} \end{cases}$$

Note that $\mathcal{I}_\mathsf{d}$ extends $\mathcal{I}_\times$ by also interpreting the new concept names in $\Gamma_{\mathsf{C}} \setminus \Sigma_{\mathsf{C}}$, that is, the restriction $\mathcal{I}_\mathsf{d}|_\Sigma$ equals $\mathcal{I}_\times$.

Definition 6. *The* projection $\pi_{\mathcal{I}}(C)$ *of a $\mathcal{P}_1^{\geq} \mathcal{EL}^\bot$ concept description C with respect to some probabilistic interpretation $\mathcal{I}$ is obtained from C by replacing each subconcept of the form $\mathsf{d} > p. D$ with suitable elements from $\Gamma_{\mathsf{C}} \setminus \Sigma_{\mathsf{C}}$, and, more specifically, we recursively define it as follows.*

$$\pi_{\mathcal{I}}(A) := A \qquad\qquad\qquad if \ A \in \Sigma_{\mathsf{C}} \cup \{\bot, \top\}$$
$$\pi_{\mathcal{I}}(C \sqcap D) := \pi_{\mathcal{I}}(C) \sqcap \pi_{\mathcal{I}}(D)$$
$$\pi_{\mathcal{I}}(\exists r. C) := \exists r. \pi_{\mathcal{I}}(C)$$

$$\pi_{\mathcal{I}}(\mathsf{d} > p. C) := \begin{cases} \bot & if \ > p \ = \ > 1 \\ \top & otherwise \ if \ > p \ = \ \geq 0 \\ \bot & otherwise \ if \ C^{\mathcal{I}_\times \mathcal{I}_\times} \equiv_\emptyset \bot \\ \top & otherwise \ if \ C^{\mathcal{I}_\times \mathcal{I}_\times} \equiv_\emptyset \top \\ \mathsf{d} \geq p. C^{\mathcal{I}_\times \mathcal{I}_\times} & otherwise \ if \ > \ = \ \geq \ and \ p \in P(\mathcal{I}) \\ \mathsf{d} \geq p^+. C^{\mathcal{I}_\times \mathcal{I}_\times} & otherwise \end{cases}$$

Lemma 7. *A $\mathcal{P}_1^{\geq} \mathcal{EL}^\bot$ concept inclusion $C \sqsubseteq D$ is valid in some probabilistic interpretation $\mathcal{I}$ if, and only if, the projected CI $\pi_{\mathcal{I}}(C) \sqsubseteq \pi_{\mathcal{I}}(D)$ is valid in $\mathcal{I}_\mathsf{d}$.*

As final step, we show that each concept inclusion base of the probabilistic scaling $\mathcal{I}_\mathsf{d}$ induces a concept inclusion base of $\mathcal{I}$. While soundness is easily verified, completeness follows from the fact that $C \sqsubseteq_{\mathcal{T}} \pi_{\mathcal{I}}(C) \sqsubseteq_{\mathcal{T}} \pi_{\mathcal{I}}(D) \sqsubseteq_{\emptyset} D$ holds true for every valid CI $C \sqsubseteq D$ of $\mathcal{I}$.

Theorem 8. *Fix some finitely representable probabilistic interpretation $\mathcal{I}$. If $\mathcal{T}_\mathsf{d}$ is a concept inclusion base for the probabilistic scaling $\mathcal{I}_\mathsf{d}$ (with respect to the set $\mathcal{B}$ of all tautological $\mathcal{P}_1^{>}\mathcal{EL}^{\perp}$ concept inclusions used as background knowledge), then the following terminological box $\mathcal{T}$ is a concept inclusion base for $\mathcal{I}$.*

$$\mathcal{T} := \mathcal{T}_\mathsf{d} \cup \{\, \mathsf{d} > p.* \sqsubseteq \mathsf{d} \geq p^{+}.* \mid p \in P(\mathcal{I}) \setminus \{1\} \,\}$$

Note that, according to the proof of Theorem 8, we can expand the above TBox $\mathcal{T}$ to a finite TBox that does not contain wildcard CIs and is still a CI base for $\mathcal{I}$ by replacing each wildcard CI $\mathsf{d} > p.* \sqsubseteq \mathsf{d} \geq q.*$ with the CIs $\mathsf{d} > p.X^{\mathcal{I}\times} \sqsubseteq \mathsf{d} \geq q.X^{\mathcal{I}\times}$ where $X \subseteq \Delta^{\mathcal{I}} \times \Omega^{\mathcal{I}}$ such that $\perp \not\equiv_{\emptyset} X^{\mathcal{I}\times} \not\equiv_{\emptyset} \top$. The same hint applies to the following canonical base.

Corollary 9. *Let $\mathcal{I}$ be a finitely representable probabilistic interpretation, and let $\mathcal{B}$ denote the set of all $\mathcal{EL}^{\perp}$ concept inclusions over Γ that are tautological with respect to probabilistic entailment, i.e., are valid in every probabilistic interpretation. Then, the canonical base for $\mathcal{I}$ that is defined as*

$$\mathsf{Can}(\mathcal{I}) := \mathsf{Can}(\mathcal{I}_\mathsf{d}, \mathcal{B}) \cup \{\, \mathsf{d} > p.* \sqsubseteq \mathsf{d} \geq p^{+}.* \mid p \in P(\mathcal{I}) \setminus \{1\} \,\}$$

is a concept inclusion base for $\mathcal{I}$, and it can be computed effectively.

Acknowledgements. The author gratefully thanks Franz Baader for drawing attention to the issue in [6], and furthermore thanks the anonymous reviewers for their constructive hints and helpful remarks.

References

1. Baader, F., Distel, F.: A finite basis for the set of $\mathcal{EL}$-implications holding in a finite model. In: Medina, R., Obiedkov, S. (eds.) ICFCA 2008. LNCS (LNAI), vol. 4933, pp. 46–61. Springer, Heidelberg (2008). https://doi.org/10.1007/978-3-540-78137-0_4
2. Baader, F., Horrocks, I., Lutz, C., Sattler, U.: An Introduction to Description Logic. Cambridge University Press, Cambridge (2017)
3. Borchmann, D., Distel, F., Kriegel, F.: Axiomatisation of general concept inclusions from finite interpretations. J. Appl. Non-Class. Logics **26**(1), 1–46 (2016)
4. Distel, F.: Learning description logic knowledge bases from data using methods from formal concept analysis. Doctoral thesis, Technische Universität Dresden (2011)
5. Gutiérrez-Basulto, V., Jung, J.C., Lutz, C., Schröder, L.: Probabilistic description logics for subjective uncertainty. J. Artif. Intell. Res. **58**, 1–66 (2017)
6. Kriegel, F.: Axiomatization of general concept inclusions in probabilistic description logics. In: Hölldobler, S., Krötzsch, M., Peñaloza, R., Rudolph, S. (eds.) KI 2015. LNCS (LNAI), vol. 9324, pp. 124–136. Springer, Cham (2015). https://doi.org/10.1007/978-3-319-24489-1_10

7. Kriegel, F.: Incremental learning of TBoxes from interpretation sequences with methods of formal concept analysis. In: Calvanese, D., Konev, B. (eds.) Proceedings of the 28th International Workshop on Description Logics, Athens, Greece, 7–10 June 2015. CEUR Workshop Proceedings, vol. 1350. CEUR-WS.org (2015)
8. Kriegel, F.: Acquisition of terminological knowledge from social networks in description logic. In: Missaoui, R., Kuznetsov, S.O., Obiedkov, S. (eds.) Formal Concept Analysis of Social Networks. LNSN, pp. 97–142. Springer, Cham (2017). https://doi.org/10.1007/978-3-319-64167-6_5
9. Kriegel, F.: Terminological knowledge acquisition in probabilistic description logic. LTCS-Report 18–03, Chair of Automata Theory, Institute of Theoretical Computer Science, Technische Universität Dresden, Dresden, Germany (2018)

Multi-agent Systems

Group Envy Freeness and Group Pareto Efficiency in Fair Division with Indivisible Items

Martin Aleksandrov$^{(\boxtimes)}$ and Toby Walsh$^{(\boxtimes)}$

Technical University of Berlin, Berlin, Germany
{martin.aleksandrov,toby.walsh}@tu-berlin.de

Abstract. We study the fair division of items to agents supposing that agents can form groups. We thus give natural generalizations of popular concepts such as envy-freeness and Pareto efficiency to groups of fixed sizes. *Group envy-freeness* requires that no group envies another group. *Group Pareto efficiency* requires that no group can be made better off without another group be made worse off. We study these new group properties from an axiomatic viewpoint. We thus propose new fairness taxonomies that generalize existing taxonomies. We further study *near* versions of these group properties as allocations for some of them may not exist. We finally give three prices of *group* fairness between group properties for three common social welfares (i.e. utilitarian, egalitarian and Nash).

Keywords: Multi-agent systems · Social choice · Group Fair Division

1 Introduction

Fair divisions become more and more challenging in the present world due to the ever-increasing demand for resources. This pressure forces us to achieve more complex allocations with less available resources. An especially challenging case of fair division deals with the allocation of *free-of-charge* and *indivisible* items (i.e. items cannot be divided, items cannot be purchased) to agents cooperating in *groups* (i.e. each agent maximizes multiple objectives) in the absence of information about these groups and their group preferences. For example, food banks in Australia give away perishable food products to charities that feed different *groups* of the community (e.g. Muslims) [18,20]. As a second example, social services in Germany provide medical benefits, donated food and affordable education to thousands of refugees and their *families*. We often do not know the group members or how they share group preferences for resources. Some other examples are the allocations of office rooms to research groups [12], cake to groups of guests [16,33], land to families [26], hospital rooms to medical teams [35] and memory to computer networks [31].

In this paper, we consider the fair division of items to agents under several assumptions. For example, the collection of items can be a mixture of goods and bads (e.g. meals, chores) [6,10,28]. We thus assume that each agent has

© Springer Nature Switzerland AG 2018
F. Trollmann and A.-Y. Turhan (Eds.): KI 2018, LNAI 11117, pp. 57–72, 2018.
https://doi.org/10.1007/978-3-030-00111-7_6

some aggregate utility for a given bundle of items of another agent. However, these utilities can be shared arbitrarily among the sub-bundles of the bundle (e.g. monotonically, additively, modularly, etc.). As another example, the agents can form groups in an arbitrarily manner. We thus assume that each group has some aggregate utility for a given bundle of items of another group. As in [33], we consider arithmetic-mean group utilities. We study this problem for five main reasons. First, people form groups naturally in practice (e.g. families, teams, countries). Second, group preferences are more expressive than individual preferences but also more complex (e.g. complementarities, substitutabilities). Third, we seek new group properties as many existing ones may be too demanding (e.g. coalitional fairness). Fourth, the principles in which groups form are normally not known. Fifth, with arithmetic-mean group utilities, we generalize existing fairness taxonomies [4,5] and characterization results for Pareto efficiency [9].

Two of the most important criteria in fair division are envy-freeness (i.e. no agent envies another agent) and Pareto efficiency (i.e. no agent can be made better off without another agent be made worse off) [14,15,17,43]. We propose *new* generalizations of these concepts for groups of fixed sizes. *Group envy-freeness* requires that no group envies another group. *Group Pareto efficiency* requires that no group can be made better off without another group be made worse off. We thus construct new sets of fairness properties, that let us interpolate between envy-freeness and proportionality (i.e. each agent gets $1/n$ their total utility for bundles), and utilitarian efficiency (i.e. the sum of agent's utilities is maximized) and Pareto efficiency. There is a reason why we focus on these two common properties and say not on other attractive properties such as group strategy-proofness. Group strategy-proofness may not be achievable with limited knowledge of the groups [3]. By comparison, both group envy-freeness and group Pareto efficiency are achievable. For example, the allocation of each bundle uniformly at random among agents is group envy-free, and the allocation of each bundle to a given agent is group Pareto efficient. This example further motivates why we study these two properties in isolation. In some instances, no allocation satisfies them in combination.

Common computational problems about group envy-freeness and group Pareto efficiency are inherently intractable even for problems of relatively small sizes [8,13,25]. For this reason, we focus on the axiomatic analysis of these properties. We propose a taxonomy of n layers of group envy-freeness properties such that group envy-freeness at layer k implies (in a logical sense) group envy-freeness at layer $k + 1$. This is perhaps a good news because envy-free allocations often do *not* exist and, as we show, allocations satisfying some properties in our taxonomy *always* exist. We propose another taxonomy of n layers of group Pareto efficiency properties such that group Pareto efficiency at layer $k+1$ implies group Pareto efficiency at layer k. Nevertheless, it is not harder to achieve group Pareto efficiency than Pareto efficiency and such allocations still *always* exists. We also consider α-taxonomies of *near* group envy-freeness and *near* group Pareto efficiency properties for each $\alpha \in [0, 1]$. We finally use prices of *group* fairness to measure the "loss" in welfare efficiency between group properties.

Our paper is organized as follows. We next discuss related work and define our notions. We then present our taxonomy for group envy-freeness in the cases in which agents might be envy of groups (Theorem 1), groups might be envy of agents (Theorem 2) and groups might be envy of groups (Theorem 3). We continue with our taxonomy for group Pareto efficiency (Theorem 4) and generalize an important result from Pareto efficiency to group Pareto efficiency (Theorem 5). Further, we propose taxonomies of properties approximating group envy-freeness and group Pareto efficiency. Finally, we give the prices of group fairness (Theorem 6) and conclude our work.

2   Related Work

Group fairness has been studied in the literature. Some notions compare the bundle of each group of agents to the bundle of any other group of agents based on Pareto dominance (i.e. all agents are weakly happier, and some agents are strictly happier) preference relations (e.g. coalitional fairness, strict fairness) [19, 23, 27, 32, 41, 42, 45]. Coalitional fairness implies both envy-freeness and Pareto efficiency. Perhaps this might be too demanding in practice as very often such allocations do not exist. For example, for a given allocation, it requires complete knowledge of agents' utilities for any bundles of items of any size in the allocation, whereas our notions require *only* knowledge of agents' utilities for their own bundles and the bundles of other agents in the allocation. Other group fairness notions are based on the idea that the bundle of each group should be perceived as fair by as many agents in the group as possible (e.g. unanimously envy-freeness, h-democratic fairness, majority envy-freeness) [34, 39]. The authors suppose that the groups are disjoint and known (e.g. families), and the utilities of agents for items are known, whereas we suppose that the groups are *unknown*, thus possibly *overlap*, and the utilities of agents are in a *bundle* form.

More group fairness notions have been studied in the context of cake-cutting (e.g. arithmetic-mean-proportionality, geometric-mean-proportionality, minimum-proporti-onality, median-proportionality) [33]. These notions compare the aggregate bundle of each group of agents to their proportional (wrt the number of groups) aggregate bundle of all items. *Unlike* us, the authors assume that the group members and their monotonic valuations are part of the common knowledge. Group envy-freeness notions are also already used in combinatorial auctions with additive quasi-linear utilities and monetary transfers (e.g. envy-freeness of an individual towards a group, envy-freeness of a group towards a group) [40]. The authors assume that the agents' utilities for items and item prices are known. Conceptually, our notions of group envy-freeness resemble these notions but they do *not* use prices. We additionally study notions of near group fairness. Our near group fairness notions for groups of agents are inspired by α-fairness for individual agents [11, 21, 22, 36, 37].

Most of these existing works consider allocating divisible resources (e.g. land, cake) with money (e.g. exchange economies), whereas we consider allocating *indivisible* items *without* money. We further *cannot* directly apply most of these existing properties to our setting with unknown groups, bundle utilities and priceless items. As a result, we *cannot* directly inherit any of the existing results. In contrast, we can apply our group properties in settings in which the group members and their preferences are actually known. Therefore, our results are valid in some existing settings. Our properties are *new* and cannot be defined using the existing fairness framework proposed in [4]. Moreover, existing works are somehow related to our properties of group envy-freeness. However, we additionally propose properties of group Pareto efficiency. Also, most existing properties may *not* be guaranteed even with a single indivisible item (e.g. coalitional fairness). By comparison, *many* of our group envy-freeness properties and *all* of our group Pareto efficiency properties can be guaranteed. Furthermore, we use *new* prices of fairness for our group properties similarly as for other properties in other settings [2,7,24,30]. Finally, several related models are studied in [29,38,44]. However, none of these focuses on axiomatic properties such as ours.

3 Preliminaries

We consider a set $N = \{a_1, \ldots, a_n\}$ of agents and a set $O = \{o_1, \ldots, o_m\}$ of indivisible items. We write $\pi = (\pi_1, \ldots, \pi_n)$ for an *allocation* of the items from O to the agents from N with (1) $\cup_{a \in N}^n \pi_a = O$ and (2) $\forall a, b \in N, a \neq b : \pi_a \cap \pi_b = \emptyset$, where π_a, π_b denote the bundles of items of agents $a, b \in N$ in π. We suppose that agents form groups. We thus write π_G for the bundle $\cup_{a \in G} \pi_a$ of items of group G, and $u_G(\pi_H)$ for the *utility* of G for the bundle π_H of items of group H. We assume *arithmetic-mean* group utilities. That is, $u_G(\pi_G) = \frac{1}{k} \cdot \sum_{a \in G} u_a(\pi_a)$ and $u_G(\pi_H) = \frac{1}{k \cdot h} \cdot \sum_{a \in G} \sum_{b \in H} u_a(\pi_b)$, where the group G has k agents, the group H has h agents and the utility $u_a(\pi_b) \in \mathbb{R}^{\geq 0}$ can be arbitrary for any agents $a, b \in N$ (i.e. monotonic, additive, modular, etc.).

We next define our group fairness properties. Group envy-freeness captures the envy of a group towards another group. Group Pareto efficiency captures the fact that we cannot make each group weakly better off, and some group strictly better off. These properties strictly generalize envy-freeness and Pareto efficiency whenever the group sizes are fixed. Near group fairness is a relaxation of group fairness.

Definition 1 (group envy-freeness). *For $k, h \in \{1, \ldots, n\}$, an allocation π is (k, h)-group envy-free (or simply $\text{GEF}_{k,h}$) iff, for each group G of k agents and each group H of h agents, $u_G(\pi_G) \geq u_G(\pi_H)$ holds.*

Definition 2 (group Pareto efficiency). *For $k \in \{1, \ldots, n\}$, an allocation π is k-group Pareto efficient (or simply GPE_k) iff, there is no other allocation π' such that $u_G(\pi'_G) \geq u_G(\pi_G)$ holds for each group G of k agents, and $u_H(\pi'_H) > u_H(\pi_H)$ holds for some group H of k agents.*

Definition 3 (near group envy-freeness). *For $k, h \in \{1, \ldots, n\}$ and $\alpha \in \mathbb{R}^{[0,1]}$, an allocation π is near (k, h)-group envy-free wrt α (or simply $\text{GEF}_{k,h}^{\alpha}$) iff, for each group G of k agents and each group H of h agents, $u_G(\pi_G) \geq \alpha \cdot u_G(\pi_H)$ holds.*

Definition 4 (near group Pareto efficiency). *For $k \in \{1, \ldots, n\}$ and $\alpha \in \mathbb{R}^{[0,1]}$, an allocation π is near k-group Pareto efficient wrt α (or simply GPE_k^{α}) iff, there is no other allocation π' such that $\alpha \cdot u_G(\pi'_G) \geq u_G(\pi_G)$ holds for each group G of k agents, and $\alpha \cdot u_H(\pi'_H) > u_H(\pi_H)$ holds for some group H of k agents.*

We use prices to measure the "loss" in the welfare $w(\pi)$ between these properties in a given allocation π. The *price of group envy-freeness* p_{GEF}^w is $\max_{k,h} \frac{\max_{\pi_1} w(\pi_1)}{\min_{\pi_2} w(\pi_2)}$ where π_1 is a (h, h)-group envy-free and π_2 is a (k, k)-group envy-free with $h \leq k$. The *price of group Pareto efficiency* p_{GPE}^w is $\max_{k,h} \frac{\max_{\pi_1} w(\pi_1)}{\min_{\pi_2} w(\pi_2)}$ where π_1 is a h-group Pareto efficient and π_2 is a k-group Pareto efficient with $h \geq k$. The *price of group fairness* p_{FAIR}^w is $\max_k \frac{\max_{\pi_1} w(\pi_1)}{\min_{\pi_2} w(\pi_2)}$ where π_1 is a (k, k)-group envy-free and π_2 is a k-group Pareto efficient. We consider these prices for common welfares such as the utilitarian welfare $u(\pi) = \sum_{a \in N} u_a(\pi_a)$, the egalitarian welfare $e(\pi) = \min_{a \in N} u_a(\pi_a)$ and the Nash welfare $n(\pi) = \prod_{a \in N} u_a(\pi_a)$.

Finally, we write Π_H for the *expected allocation* of group H that assigns a probability value to each bundle of items, and $\overline{u}_G(\Pi_H)$ for the *expected utility* of group G for Π_H. We observe that we can define our group properties in terms of expected utilities of groups for expected allocations of groups.

4   Group Envy Freeness

We start with group envy-freeness for arithmetic-mean group utilities. Our first main result is to give a taxonomy of strict implications between group envy-freeness notions for groups of fixed sizes (i.e. $\text{GEF}_{k,h}$ for fixed $k, h \in [1, n)$). We present the taxonomy in Fig. 1.

$$\begin{array}{ccc} \text{GEF}_{k,h} & \Rightarrow & \text{GEF}_{k,h+1} \\ \Downarrow & & \Downarrow \\ \text{GEF}_{k+1,h} & \Rightarrow & \text{GEF}_{k+1,h+1} \end{array}$$

Fig. 1. A taxonomy of group envy-freeness properties for fixed $k, h \in [1, n)$.

Our taxonomy contains n^2 group envy-freeness axiomatic properties. By definition, we observe that $(1, 1)$-group envy-freeness is equivalent to envy-freeness (or simply EF) and $(1, n)$-group envy-freeness is equivalent to proportionality (or simply PROP). Moreover, we observe that $(n, 1)$-group envy-freeness captures the envy of the group of all agents towards each agent. We call this property *grand envy-freeness* (or simply gEF). (n, n)-group envy-freeness is trivially satisfied by any allocation. In our taxonomy, we can interpolate between envy-freeness and proportionality, and even beyond. From this perspective, our taxonomy generalizes existing taxonomies of fairness concepts for individual agents with additive utilities [4,5]. We next prove the implications in our taxonomy. For this purpose, we distinguish between *agent-group* properties (i.e. $(1, h)$-group envy-freeness), *group-agent* properties (i.e. $(k, 1)$-group envy-freeness) and *group-group* properties (i.e. (k, h)-group envy-freeness) for $k \in [1, n]$ and $h \in [1, n]$.

Agent-Group Envy-Freeness. We now consider n properties for agent-group envy-freeness of actual allocations that capture the envy an individual agent might have towards a group of other agents. These properties let us move from envy-freeness to proportionality (i.e. there is $h \in [1, n]$ such that "EF $\Rightarrow$ GEF$_{1,h}$ $\Rightarrow$ PROP"). If an agent is envy-free of a group of $h \in [1, n]$ agents, then they are envy-free of a group of $q \geq h$ agents.

Theorem 1. *For $h \in [1, n]$, $q \in [h, n]$ and arithmetic-mean group utilities, we have that* GEF$_{1,h}$ *implies* GEF$_{1,q}$.

Proof. Let us pick an allocation π. We show the result by induction on $i \in [h, q]$. In the base case, let i be equal to h. The result follows trivially in this case. In the induction hypothesis, suppose that π is $(1, i)$-group envy-free for $i < q$. In the step case, let i be equal to q. By the hypothesis, we know that π is $(1, q - 1)$-group envy-free. For the sake of contradiction, let us suppose that π is not $(1, q)$-group envy-free. Consequently, there is a group of q agents and an agent, say $G = \{a_1, \ldots, a_q\}$ and $a \notin G$, such that inequality (1) holds for G and a, and inequality (2) holds for G, a and each agent $a_j \in G$.

$$u_a(\pi_a) < u_a(\pi_G) = \frac{1}{q} \cdot \sum_{b \in G} u_a(\pi_b) \tag{1}$$

$$u_a(\pi_a) \geq u_a(\pi_{G \setminus \{a_j\}}) = \frac{1}{(q-1)} \cdot \sum_{b \in G \setminus \{a_j\}} u_a(\pi_b) \tag{2}$$

We derive $u_a(\pi_a) < u_a(\pi_{a_j})$ for each $a_j \in G$. Let us now form a group of $(q - 1)$ agents from G, say $G \setminus \{a_q\}$. Agent a assigns arithmetic-mean value to the allocation of this group that is larger than the value they assign to their own allocation. This contradicts with the induction hypothesis. Hence, π is $(1, q)$-group envy-free. The result follows.   □

By Theorem 1, we conclude that $(1, h)$-group envy-freeness implies $(1, h+1)$-group envy-freeness for $h \in [1, n)$. The opposite direction does not hold. Indeed, $(1, q)$-group envy-freeness is a weaker property than $(1, h)$-group envy-freeness for $q > h$. We illustrate this in Example 1.

Example 1. *Let us consider the fair division of 3 items o_1, o_2, o_3 between 3 agents a_1, a_2, a_3. Further, let the utilities of agent a_1 for the items be 1, 3/2 and 2, those of agent a_2 be 3/2, 2, and 1, and the ones of agent a_3 be 2, 1 and 3/2* *respectively. Now, consider the allocation π that gives o_2 to a_1, o_1 to a_2 and o_3 to a_3. Each agent receives in π utility 3/2. Hence, this allocation is not $(1,1)$-group envy-free (i.e. envy-free) as each agent assigns in it utility 2 to one of the other agents. In contrast, they assign in π utility 3/2 to the group of all agents. We conclude that π is $(1,3)$-group envy-free (i.e. proportional).*   □

The result in Example 1 crucially depends on the fact that there are 3 agents in the problem. With 2 agents, agent-group envy-freeness is equivalent to envy-freeness which itself is equivalent to proportionality. Finally, Theorem 1 and Example 1 hold for expected allocations as well.

Group-Agent Envy-Freeness. We next consider n properties for group-agent envy-freeness of actual allocations that capture the envy a group of agents might have towards an individual agent outside the group. These properties let us move from envy-freeness to grand envy-freeness (i.e. there is $k \in [1, n]$ such that "EF $\Rightarrow$ GEF$_{k,1}$ $\Rightarrow$ gEF"). If a group of $k \in [1, n]$ agents is envy-free of a given agent, then a group of $p \geq k$ agents is envy-free of this agent.

Theorem 2. *For $k \in [1, n]$, $p \in [k, n]$ and arithmetic-mean group utilities, we have that GEF$_{k,1}$ implies GEF$_{p,1}$.*

Proof. Let us pick an allocation π. As in the proof of Theorem 1, we show the result by induction on $i \in [k, p]$. The most interesting case is the step case. Let i be equal to p and suppose that π is $(p-1, 1)$-group envy-free. For the sake of contradiction, let us suppose that π is not $(p, 1)$-group envy-free. Consequently, there is a group of p agents and an agent, say $G = \{a_1, \ldots, a_p\}$ and $a \notin G$, such that inequality (3) holds for G and a, and inequality (4) holds for G, a and each $a_j \in G$.

$$p \cdot u_G(\pi_G) = \sum_{b \in G} u_b(\pi_b) < \sum_{b \in G} u_b(\pi_a) \tag{3}$$

$$(p-1) \cdot u_{G \setminus \{a_j\}}(\pi_{G \setminus \{a_j\}}) = \sum_{b \in G \setminus \{a_j\}} u_b(\pi_b) \geq \sum_{b \in G \setminus \{a_j\}} u_b(\pi_a) \tag{4}$$

We derive $u_{a_j}(\pi_{a_j}) < u_{a_j}(\pi_a)$ for each $a_j \in G$. Let us now form a group of $(p-1)$ agents from G, say $G \setminus \{a_p\}$. This group assigns arithmetic-mean value to the allocation of agent a that is larger than the arithmetic-mean value they assign to their own allocation. This contradicts with the fact that π is $(p-1, 1)$-group envy-free. We therefore conclude that π is $(p, 1)$-group envy-free.   □

By Theorem 2, we conclude that $(k, 1)$-group envy-freeness implies $(k+1, 1)$-group envy-freeness for $k \in [1, n]$. However, $(p, 1)$-group envy-freeness is a weaker property than $(k, 1)$-group envy-freeness for $p > k$. We illustrate this in Example 2.

Example 2. *Let us consider again the instance in Example 1 and the allocation π that gives to each agent the item they value with 3/2. We confirmed that π is not $(1,1)$-group envy-free (i.e. envy-free). However, π is $(3,1)$-group envy-free (i.e. grand envy-free) because the group of all agents assigns in π utility 3/2 to their own allocation and utility 3/2 to the allocation of each other agent.*   □

The choice of 3 agents in the problem in Example 2 is again crucial. With 2 agents, group-agent envy-freeness is equivalent to envy-freeness and proportionality. Finally, Theorem 2 and Example 2 hold for expected allocations as well.

Group-Group Envy-Freeness. We finally consider n^2 properties for group-group envy-freeness of actual allocations that captures the envy of a group of k agents towards another group of h agents. Similarly, we prove a number of implications between such properties for fixed parameters k, h and $p \geq k$, $q \geq h$.

Theorem 3. For $k \in [1, n]$, $p \in [k, n]$, $h \in [1, n]$, $q \in [h, n]$ and arithmetic-mean group utilities, we have that $\text{GEF}_{k,h}$ implies $\text{GEF}_{p,q}$.

Proof. We prove by inductions that (1) (p, h)-group envy-freeness implies (p, q)-group envy-freeness for any $p \in [1, n]$, and that (2) (k, h)-group envy-freeness implies (p, h)-group-envy freeness for any $h \in [1, n]$. We can then immediately conclude the result. For $p = 1$ in (1) and $h = 1$ in (2), the base cases of the inductions follow from Theorems 1 and 2. We start with (1). We consider only the step case. That is, let π be an allocation that is $(p, q - 1)$-group envy-free but not (p, q)-group envy-free. Hence, there are groups $G = \{a_1, \ldots, a_p\}$ and $H = \{b_1, \ldots, b_q\}$ such that inequality (5) holds for G and H, and inequality (6) holds for G, H and each $b_j \in H$.

$$\sum_{a \in G} u_a(\pi_a) < \frac{1}{q} \cdot \sum_{a \in G} \sum_{b \in H} u_a(\pi_b) \tag{5}$$

$$\sum_{a \in G} u_a(\pi_a) \geq \frac{1}{(q-1)} \cdot \sum_{a \in G} \sum_{b \in H \setminus \{b_j\}} u_a(\pi_b) \tag{6}$$

We derive $\sum_{a \in G} u_a(\pi_a) < \sum_{a \in G} u_a(\pi_{b_j})$ for each $b_j \in H$ which leads to a contradiction with the $(p, q - 1)$-group envy-freeness of π. We next prove (2) for $h = q$ in a similar fashion. Again, we consider only the step case. That is, let π be an allocation that is $(p - 1, q)$-group envy-free but not (p, q)-group envy-free. Hence, there are groups $G = \{a_1, \ldots, a_p\}$ and $H = \{b_1, \ldots, b_q\}$ such that inequality (5) holds for G and H, and inequality (7) holds for G, H and each $a_j \in G$.

$$\sum_{a \in G \setminus \{a_j\}} u_a(\pi_a) \geq \frac{1}{q} \cdot \sum_{a \in G \setminus \{a_j\}} \sum_{b \in H} u_a(\pi_b) \tag{7}$$

We obtain that $q \cdot u_{a_j}(\pi_{a_j}) < \sum_{b \in H} u_{a_j}(\pi_b)$ holds for each $a_j \in G$. Finally, this conclusion leads to a contradiction with the $(p - 1, q)$-group envy-freeness of π. The result follows.   □

By Examples 1 and 2, the opposite direction of the implication in Theorem 3 does not hold with 3 or more agents. With 2 agents, group-group envy-freeness is also equivalent to envy-freeness and proportionality. Finally, Theorem 3 also holds for expected allocations.

5   Group Pareto Efficiency

We continue with group Pareto efficiency properties for arithmetic-mean group utilities. Our second main result is to give a taxonomy of strict implications between group Pareto efficiency notions for groups of fixed sizes (i.e. GPE_k for fixed $k \in [1, n)$). We present the taxonomy in Fig. 2.

$$\text{GPE}_{k+1} \Rightarrow \text{GPE}_k$$

Fig. 2. A taxonomy of group Pareto efficiency properties for fixed $k \in [1, n)$.

Our taxonomy contains n group Pareto efficient axiomatic properties. By definition, we observe that 1-group Pareto efficiency is equivalent to Pareto efficiency, and n-group Pareto efficiency to utilitarian efficiency. In fact, we next prove that the kth layer of properties in our taxonomy is exactly between the $(k-1)$th and $(k+1)$th layers. It then follows that k-group Pareto efficiency implies j-group Pareto efficiency for any $k \in [1, n]$ and $j \in [1, k]$. We now show this result for actual allocations.

Theorem 4. *For* $k \in [1, n]$, $j \in [1, k]$ *and arithmetic-mean group utilities, we have that* GPE_k *implies* GPE_j.

Proof. The proof is by backward induction on $h \in [j, k]$ for a given allocation π. For $h = k$, the proof is trivial. For $h > j$, suppose that π is h-group Pareto efficient. For $h = j$, let us assume that π is not j-group Pareto efficient. We write G_j for the fact that group G has j agents. We derive that there is π' such that both inequalities (8) and (9) hold.

$$\forall G_j : \sum_{a \in G_j} u_a(\pi'_a) \geq \sum_{a \in G_j} u_a(\pi_a) \tag{8}$$

$$\exists H_j : \sum_{b \in H_j} u_b(\pi'_b) > \sum_{b \in H_j} u_b(\pi_b) \tag{9}$$

We next show that π' dominates π in a $(j+1)$-group Pareto sense. That is, we show that inequalities (10) and (11) hold.

$$\forall G_{(j+1)} : \sum_{a \in G_{(j+1)}} u_a(\pi'_a) \geq \sum_{a \in G_{(j+1)}} u_a(\pi_a) \tag{10}$$

$$\exists H_{(j+1)} : \sum_{b \in H_{(j+1)}} u_b(\pi'_b) > \sum_{b \in H_{(j+1)}} u_b(\pi_b) \tag{11}$$

We start with inequality (10). Let $G_{(j+1)}$ be a group of $(j+1)$ agents for which inequality (10) does not hold. Further, let $G_j^a = G_{(j+1)} \setminus \{a\}$ be a group of j agents obtained from $G_{(j+1)}$ by excluding agent $a \in G_{(j+1)}$. By the fact that inequality (8) holds for G_j^a, we conclude that $u_a(\pi_a') < u_a(\pi_a)$ holds for each $a \in G_{(j+1)}$. We can now form a set of j agents such that inequality (8) is violated for π'. Hence, inequality (10) must hold. We next show that inequality (11) holds as well. Let $H_{(j+1)}$ be an arbitrary group of $(j+1)$ agents for which inequality (11) does not hold. By inequality (8), we derive $u_b(\pi_b') \leq u_b(\pi_b)$ for each $b \in H_{(j+1)}$. There cannot exist a group of j agents for which inequality (9) holds for π'. Hence, inequality (11) must hold. Finally, as both inequalities (10) and (11) hold, π is not $(j+1)$-group Pareto efficient. This is a contradiction. $\square$

The implication in Theorem 4 does not reverse. Indeed, an allocation that is 1-group Pareto efficient might not be k-group Pareto efficient even for $k = 2$ and 2 agents. We illustrate this in Example 3.

Example 3. *Let us consider the fair division of 2 items o_1, o_2 between 2 agents a_1, a_2. Further, suppose that a_1 likes o_1 with 1 and o_2 with 2, whilst a_2 likes o_1 with 2 and o_2 with 1. The allocation π_1 that gives both items to a_1 is 1-group Pareto efficient (i.e. Pareto efficient) but not 2-group Pareto efficient (i.e. utilitarian efficient). To see this, note that π_1 is 2-group Pareto dominated by another allocation π_2 that gives o_2 to a_1 and o_1 to a_2. The utility of the group of two agents is 3/2 in π_1 and 2 in π_2.* $\square$

We next consider expected allocations. We know that an expected allocation that is Pareto efficient can be represented as a convex combination over actual allocations that are Pareto efficient [9] (cited by 502 other papers in Google Scholar). This result holds for actual allocations as well. We generalize this result to our setting with groups of agents and bundles of items. That is, we show that a k-group Pareto efficient expected allocation can be represented as a combination over k-group Pareto efficient actual allocations. We believe that our result is much more general than the existing one because it holds for arbitrary groups and bundle utilities (e.g. monotone, additive, modular, etc.). In contrast, not each convex combination over Pareto efficient actual allocations represents an expected allocation that is Pareto efficient [9]. This observation holds in our setting as well.

Theorem 5. *For $k \in [1, n]$, a k-group Pareto efficient expected allocation can be represented as a convex combination over k-group Pareto efficient actual allocations.*

Proof. Let Π_1 denote an expected allocation that is k-group Pareto efficient and c_1 be a convex combination over group Pareto efficient allocations that represents Π_1. Further, let us assume that Π_1 cannot be represented as a convex combination over k-group Pareto efficient allocations. Therefore, there are two types of allocations in c_1: (1) allocations that are j-group Pareto efficient for some $j \geq k$ and (2) allocations that are j-group Pareto efficient ex post for some $j < k$. By Theorem 4, allocations of type (1) are k-group Pareto efficient. And, by assumption, allocations of type (2) are not g-group Pareto efficient for any $g > j$. Let us consider such an allocation π in c_1 of type (2) that is not

k-group Pareto efficient. Hence, π can be k-group Pareto improved by some other allocation π'. We can replace π with π' in c_1 and thus construct a new convex combination $c_{1,\pi}$. We can repeat this for some other allocation in $c_{1,\pi}$ of type (2) that is not k-group Pareto efficient. We thus eventually can construct a convex combination c_2 over k-group Pareto efficient ex post allocations with the following properties: (1) there is an allocation π_2 in c_2 for each allocation π_1 in c_1 and (2) the weight of π_2 in c_2 is equal to the weight of π_1 in c_1. Let Π_2 denote the allocation represented by c_2.

Let c_1 be over π_1 to π_h such that π_1 to π_i are k-group Pareto efficient and π_{i+1} to π_h are not group k-Pareto efficient. Further, by construction, let c_2 be over π_1 to π_i and π'_{i+1} to π'_h such that π'_g k-group Pareto dominates π_g for each $g \in [i+1, h]$. We derive $\sum_{a_l \in G}(u_{a_l}(\pi'_g) - u_{a_l}(\pi_g)) \geq 0$ for each group G of k agents and $\sum_{a_l \in H}(u_{a_l}(\pi'_g) - u_{a_l}(\pi_g)) > 0$ for some group H of k agents. The expected utility $\overline{u}_{a_l}(\Pi_1)$ of agent a_l in combination c_1 is equal to $\sum_{g \in [1,i]} w(\pi_g) \cdot u_{a_l}(\pi_g) + \sum_{g \in [i+1,h]} w(\pi_g) \cdot u_{a_l}(\pi_g)$. The expected utility $\overline{u}_{a_l}(\Pi_2)$ of agent a_l in combination c_2 is equal to $\sum_{g \in [1,i]} w(\pi_g) \cdot u_{a_l}(\pi_g) + \sum_{g \in [i+1,h]} w(\pi_g) \cdot u_{a_l}(\pi'_g)$. Therefore, $\sum_{a_l \in G}(\overline{u}_{a_l}(\Pi_2) - \overline{u}_{a_l}(\Pi_1)) \geq 0$ holds for each group G of k agents and $\sum_{a_l \in H}(\overline{u}_{a_l}(\Pi_2) - \overline{u}_{a_l}(\Pi_1)) > 0$ holds for some group H of k agents. Hence, Π_2 k-group Pareto dominates Π_1. This is a contradiction with the k-group Pareto efficiency of Π_1.   □

Theorem 5 suggests that there are fewer k-group Pareto efficient allocations than j-group Pareto efficient allocations for $j \in [1, k]$. In fact, there can be substantially fewer such allocations even with 2 agents. We illustrate this in Example 4.

Example 4. *Let us consider again the instance in Example 3. Further, consider the expected allocation Π_ϵ in which agent a_1 receives item o_1 with probability 1 and item o_2 with probability $1 - \epsilon$, and agent a_2 receives item o_2 with probability ϵ. In Π_ϵ, a_1 receives expected utility $3 - 2\epsilon$ and a_2 receives expected utility ϵ. For each fixed $\epsilon \in [0, 1/2)$, Π_ϵ is 1-group Pareto efficient (i.e. Pareto efficient). Hence, there are infinitely many such allocations. By comparison, there is just one 2-group Pareto efficient (i.e. utilitarian efficient) allocation that gives to each agent the item they like with 2.*   □

Interestingly, for an n-group Pareto efficient expected allocation, we can show both directions in Theorem 5. By definition, such allocations maximize the utilitarian welfare. We, therefore, conclude that an expected allocation is n-group Pareto efficient iff it can be represented as a convex combination over actual allocations that maximize the utilitarian welfare. Finally, Theorem 4 and Example 3 also hold for expected allocations and Theorem 5 and Example 4 also hold (trivially) for actual allocations.

6   Near Group Fairness

Near group fairness relaxes group fairness. Our near notions are inspired by α-fairness proposed in [11]. Let $k \in [1, n]$, $h \in [1, n]$ and $\alpha \in [0, 1]$. We start with near group envy-freeness (i.e. $\text{GEF}^\alpha_{k,h}$). For given k and h, we can always find a sufficiently small value for α such that a given allocation satisfies $\text{GEF}^\alpha_{k,h}$. Consequently, for given k and h, there is *always* some α such that at least one allocation is $\text{GEF}^\alpha_{k,h}$. By comparison, for given k and h, allocations that satisfy $\text{GEF}_{k,h}$ may *not* exist. Therefore, for given k, h and α, allocations that satisfy $\text{GEF}^\alpha_{k,h}$ may also *not* exist. For example, note that $\text{GEF}_{k,h}$ is equivalent to $\text{GEF}^\alpha_{k,h}$ for each k, h and $\alpha = 1$. Moreover, for given k, h and α, we have that $\text{GEF}_{k,h}$ implies $\text{GEF}^\alpha_{k,h}$ holds. However, there might be allocations that are near (k, h)-group envy-free with respect to α but not (k, h)-group envy-free. We illustrate this for actual allocations in Example 5.

Example 5. *Let us consider again the instance in Example 1 and the allocation π that gives to each agent the item they like with $3/2$. Recall that π is not $(1, 1)$-group envy-free (i.e. envy-free). Each agent assigns in π utility 2 to one of the other agents and 1 to the other one. For $\alpha = 3/4$, they assign in π reduced utilities 2α, α to these agents. We conclude that π is near $(1, 1)$-group envy-free wrt α (i.e. $3/4$-envy-free).* □

For a given α, we can show that Theorems 1, 2 and 3 hold for the notions $\text{GEF}^\alpha_{k,h}$ with any k and h. We can thus construct an α-taxonomy of near group envy-freeness concepts for each fixed α. Moreover, for $\alpha_1, \alpha_2 \in [0, 1]$ with $\alpha_2 \geq \alpha_1$, we observe that an allocation satisfies an α_2-property in the α_2-taxonomy only if the allocation satisfies the corresponding α_1-property in the corresponding α_1-taxonomy. We further note that $\text{GEF}^{\alpha_2}_{k,h}$ implies $\text{GEF}^{\alpha_1}_{k,h}$. By Example 5, this implication does not reverse.

We proceed with near group Pareto efficiency (i.e. GPE^α_k). For a given k, allocations satisfying GPE_k *always* exists. For given k and α, we immediately conclude that allocations satisfying GPE^α_k also *always* exists. Similarly as for near group envy-freeness, GPE_k is equivalent to GPE^α_k for each k and $\alpha = 1$, and GPE_k implies GPE^α_k for each k and α. However, there might be allocations that are near k-group Pareto efficient with respect to α but not k-group Pareto efficient. We illustrate this for actual allocations in Example 6.

Example 6. *Let us consider again the instance in Example 3 and the allocation π that gives to each agent the item they like with 1. This allocation is not 1-group Pareto efficient (i.e. Pareto efficient) because each agent receives utility 2 if they swap items in π. For $\alpha = 1/2$, π is not α-Pareto dominated by the allocation in which the items are swapped. Moreover, π is not α-Pareto dominated by any other allocation. We conclude that π is near 1-group Pareto efficient wrt α (i.e. $1/2$-Pareto efficient).* □

For a given α, we can also show that Theorem 4 holds for the notions GPE_k^{α} with any k. We can thus construct an α-taxonomy of near group Pareto efficiency properties for each fixed α. In contrast to near group envy-freeness, allocations that satisfy an α-property in an α-taxonomy always exists. Also, for $\alpha_1, \alpha_2 \in [0, 1]$ with $\alpha_2 \geq \alpha_1$, we observe that $\text{GPE}_k^{\alpha_2}$ implies $\text{GEF}_k^{\alpha_1}$ holds. By Example 6, we confirm that this is a strict implication. Theorem 5 further holds for near k-group Pareto efficiency. Finally, Examples 5 and 6 hold for expected allocations as well.

7 Prices of Group Fairness

We use *prices of group fairness* and measure the "loss" in social welfare efficiency between different "layers" in our taxonomies. Our prices are inspired by the price of fairness proposed in [7]. Prices of fairness are normally measured in the worst-case scenario. We proceed similarly and prove only the lower bounds of our prices for the *u*tilitarian, the *e*galitarian and the *n*ash welfares in actual allocations.

Theorem 6. *The prices p_{GEF}^u, p_{GPE}^u, p_{FAIR}^u are all at least the number n of agents, whereas the prices p_{GEF}^e, p_{GPE}^e, p_{FAIR}^e and p_{GEF}^n, p_{GPE}^n, p_{FAIR}^n are all unbounded.*

Proof. Let us consider the fair division of n items to n agents. Swelfares in actual allocations uppose that agent a_i likes item o_i with 1, and each other item with ϵ for some small $\epsilon \in (0, 1)$. For $k \in [1, n]$, let π_k denote an allocation in which k agents receive items valued with 1 and $(n - k)$ agents receive items valued with ϵ. By Theorem 3, π_n is k-group envy-free as each agent receives their most valued item. By Theorem 4, π_n is also k-group Pareto efficient. Further, for a fixed k, it is easy to check that π_k is also k-group envy-free and k-group Pareto efficient. We start with the utilitarian prices. The utilitarian welfare in π_n is n whereas the one in π_k is k as ϵ goes to 0. Consequently, the corresponding ratios for "layer" k in each taxonomy all go to n/k. Therefore, the corresponding prices go to n as k goes to 1. We next give the egalitarian and Nash prices. The egalitarian and Nash welfares in π_n are both equal to 1. These welfares in π_k are equal to ϵ and $\epsilon^{(n-k)}$ respectively. The corresponding ratios for "layer" k in each taxonomy are then equal to $1/\epsilon$ and $1/\epsilon^{(n-k)}$. Consequently, the corresponding prices go to ∞ as ϵ goes to 0. $\square$

Theorem 6 holds for expected allocations as well. Finally, it also holds for near group fair allocations.

8 Conclusions

We studied the fair division of items to agents supposing agents can form groups. We thus proposed new group fairness axiomatic properties. Group envy-freeness requires that no group envies another group. Group Pareto efficiency requires that no group can be made better off without another group be made worse off. We analyzed the relations between these properties and several existing properties such as envy-freeness and proportionality. We generalized an important result from Pareto efficiency to group Pareto efficiency. We moreover considered near group fairness properties. We finally computed three prices of group fairness between such properties for three common social welfares: the utilitarian welfare, the egalitarian welfare and the Nash welfare.

In future, we will study more group aggregators. For example, our results hold for arithmetic-mean group utilities (i.e. Theorems 1–6). We can however also show them for *geometric-mean, minimum,* or *maximum* group utilities (i.e. the root of the product over agents' utilities for the bundle, the minimum over agents' utilities for the bundle, the maximum over agents' utilities for the bundle). We will also study the relations of our group properties to other fairness properties for individual agents such as *min-max fair share, max-min fair share* and *graph envy-freeness.* Finally, we submit that it is also worth adapting our group properties to other fair division settings as well [1].

References

1. Aleksandrov, M., Aziz, H., Gaspers, S., Walsh, T.: Online fair division: analysing a food bank problem. In: Proceedings of the Twenty-Fourth IJCAI 2015, Buenos Aires, Argentina, 25–31 July 2015, pp. 2540–2546 (2015)
2. Aleksandrov, M., Walsh, T.: Most competitive mechanisms in online fair division. In: Kern-Isberner, G., Fürnkranz, J., Thimm, M. (eds.) KI 2017. LNCS (LNAI), vol. 10505, pp. 44–57. Springer, Cham (2017)
3. Aleksandrov, M., Walsh, T.: Pure Nash equilibria in online fair division. In: Sierra, C. (ed.) Proceedings of the Twenty-Sixth IJCAI 2017, Melbourne, Australia, pp. 42–48 (2017)
4. Aziz, H., Bouveret, S., Caragiannis, I., Giagkousi, I., Lang, J.: Knowledge, fairness, and social constraints. In: Proceedings of the Thirty-Second AAAI 2018, New Orleans, Louisiana, USA, 2–7 February 2018. AAAI Press (2018)
5. Aziz, H., Mackenzie, S., Xia, L., Ye, C.: Ex post efficiency of random assignments. In: Proceedings of the 2015 International AAMAS Conference, Istanbul, Turkey, 4–8 May 2015, pp. 1639–1640. IFAAMAS (2015)
6. Aziz, H., Rauchecker, G., Schryen, G., Walsh, T.: Algorithms for max-min share fair allocation of indivisible chores. In: Proceedings of the Thirty-First AAAI 2017, San Francisco, California, USA, 4–9 February 2017, pp. 335–341. AAAI Press (2017)
7. Bertsimas, D., Farias, V.F., Trichakis, N.: The price of fairness. Operations Research 59(1), 17–31 (2011)
8. Bliem, B., Bredereck, R., Niedermeier, R.: Complexity of efficient and envy-free resource allocation: few agents, resources, or utility levels. In: Proceedings of the Twenty-Fifth IJCAI 2016, New York, NY, USA, 9–15 July 2016, pp. 102–108 (2016)
9. Bogomolnaia, A., Moulin, H.: A new solution to the random assignment problem. Journal of Economic Theory 100(2), 295–328 (2001)
10. Bogomolnaia, A., Moulin, H., Sandomirskiy, F., Yanovskaya, E.: Dividing goods and bads under additive utilities. CoRR abs/1610.03745 (2016)
11. Borsuk, K.: Drei Stze über die n-dimensionale euklidische Sphäre. Fundamenta Mathematicae 20(1), 177–190 (1933)

12. Bouveret, S., Cechlárová, K., Elkind, E., Igarashi, A., Peters, D.: Fair division of a graph. In: Proceedings of the Twenty-Sixth IJCAI 2017, 19–25 August 2017, pp. 135–141 (2017)
13. Bouveret, S., Lang, J.: Efficiency and envy-freeness in fair division of indivisible goods: logical representation and complexity. Journal of AI Research (JAIR) **32**, 525–564 (2008)
14. Brams, S.J., Fishburn, P.C.: Fair division of indivisible items between two people with identical preferences: envy-freeness, pareto-optimality, and equity. Social Choice and Welfare **17**(2), 247–267 (2000)
15. Brams, S.J., King, D.L.: Efficient fair division: help the worst off or avoid envy? Rationality and Society **17**(4), 387–421 (2005)
16. Brams, S.J., Taylor, A.D.: Fair Division - From Cake-cutting to Dispute Resolution. Cambridge University Press, Cambridge (1996)
17. de Clippel, G.: Equity, envy and efficiency under asymmetric information. Economics Letters **99**(2), 265–267 (2008)
18. Davidson, P., Evans, R.: Poverty in Australia. ACOSS (2014)
19. Debreu, G.: Preference functions on measure spaces of economic agents. Econometrica **35**(1), 111–122 (1967)
20. Dorsch, P., Phillips, J., Crowe, C.: Poverty in Australia. ACOSS (2016)
21. Dubins, L.E., Spanier, E.H.: How to cut a cake fairly. The American Mathematical Monthly **68**(1), 1–17 (1961)
22. Hill, T.P.: Determining a fair border. The American Mathematical Monthly **90**(7), 438–442 (1983)
23. Husseinov, F.: A theory of a heterogeneous divisible commodity exchange economy. Journal of Mathematical Economics **47**(1), 54–59 (2011)
24. Kaleta, M.: Price of fairness on networked auctions. Journal of Applied Mathematics **2014**, 1–7 (2014)
25. de Keijzer, B., Bouveret, S., Klos, T., Zhang, Y.: On the complexity of efficiency and envy-freeness in fair division of indivisible goods with additive preferences. In: Rossi, F., Tsoukias, A. (eds.) ADT 2009. LNCS (LNAI), vol. 5783, pp. 98–110. Springer, Heidelberg (2009)
26. Kokoye, S.E.H., Tovignan, S.D., Yabi, J.A., Yegbemey, R.N.: Econometric modeling of farm household land allocation in the municipality of Banikoara in northern Benin. Land Use Policy **34**, 72–79 (2013)
27. Lahaie, S., Parkes, D.C.: Fair package assignment. In: Auctions, Market Mechanisms and Their Applications, First International ICST Conference, AMMA 2009, Boston, MA, USA, 8–9 May 2009, Revised Selected Papers, p. 92 (2009)
28. Lumet, C., Bouveret, S., Lemaître, M.: Fair division of indivisible goods under risk. In: ECAI. Frontiers in AI and Applications, vol. 242, pp. 564–569. IOS Press (2012)
29. Manurangsi, P., Suksompong, W.: Computing an approximately optimal agreeable set of items. In: Proceedings of the Twenty-Sixth IJCAI 2017, Melbourne, Australia, 19–25 August 2017, pp. 338–344 (2017)
30. Nicosia, G., Pacifici, A., Pferschy, U.: Price of fairness for allocating a bounded resource. European Journal of Operational Research **257**(3), 933–943 (2017)
31. Parkes, D.C., Procaccia, A.D., Shah, N.: Beyond dominant resource fairness: extensions, limitations, and indivisibilities. ACM Transactions **3**(1), 1–22 (2015)
32. Schmeidler, D., Vind, K.: Fair net trades. Econometrica **40**(4), 637–642 (1972)
33. Segal-Halevi, E., Nitzan, S.: Fair cake-cutting among groups. CoRR abs/1510.03903 (2015)

34. Segal-Halevi, E., Suksompong, W.: Democratic fair division of indivisible goods. In: Proceedings of the Twenty-Seventh IJCAI-ECAI 2018, Stockholm, Sweden, 13–19 July 2018 (2018)
35. Smet, P.: Nurse rostering: models and algorithms for theory, practice and integration with other problems. 4OR **14**(3), 327–328 (2016)
36. Steinhaus, H.: The problem of fair division. Econometrica **16**(1), 101–104 (1948)
37. Stone, A.H., Tukey, J.W.: Generalized sandwich theorems. Duke Mathematical Journal **9**(2), 356–359 (1942)
38. Suksompong, W.: Assigning a small agreeable set of indivisible items to multiple players. In: Proceedings of the Twenty-Fifth IJCAI 2016, New York, NY, USA, 9–15 July 2016, pp. 489–495. IJCAI/AAAI Press (2016)
39. Suksompong, W.: Approximate maximin shares for groups of agents. Mathematical Social Sciences **92**, 40–47 (2018)
40. Todo, T., Li, R., Hu, X., Mouri, T., Iwasaki, A., Yokoo, M.: Generalizing envy-freeness toward group of agents. In: Proceedings of the Twenty-Second IJCAI 2011, Barcelona, Catalonia, Spain, 16–22 July 2011, pp. 386–392 (2011)
41. Varian, H.R.: Equity, envy, and efficiency. Journal of Economic Theory **9**(1), 63–91 (1974)
42. Vind, K.: Edgeworth-allocations in an exchange economy with many traders. International Economic Review **5**(2), 165–177 (1964)
43. Weller, D.: Fair division of a measurable space. Journal of Mathematical Economics **14**(1), 5–17 (1985)
44. Yokoo, M.: Characterization of strategy/false-name proof combinatorial auction protocols: price-oriented, rationing-free protocol. In: Proceedings of the Eighteenth IJCAI 2003, Acapulco, Mexico, 9–15 August 2003, pp. 733–742 (2003)
45. Zhou, L.: Strictly fair allocations in large exchange economies. Journal of Economic Theory **57**(1), 158–175 (1992)

Approximate Probabilistic Parallel Multiset Rewriting Using MCMC

Stefan Lüdtke$^{(\boxtimes)}$, Max Schröder, and Thomas Kirste

Institute of Computer Science, University of Rostock, Rostock, Germany
{stefan.luedtke2,max.schroeder,thomas.kirste}@uni-rostock.de

Abstract. Probabilistic parallel multiset rewriting systems (PPMRS) model probabilistic, dynamic systems consisting of multiple, (inter-) acting agents and objects (entities), where multiple individual actions can be performed in parallel. The main computational challenge in these approaches is computing the distribution of parallel actions (*compound actions*), that can be formulated as a constraint satisfaction problem (CSP). Unfortunately, computing the partition function for this distribution exactly is infeasible, as it requires to enumerate all solutions of the CSP, which are subject to a combinatorial explosion.

The central technical contribution of this paper is an efficient Markov Chain Monte Carlo (MCMC)-based algorithm to approximate the partition function, and thus the compound action distribution. The proposal function works by performing backtracking in the CSP search tree, and then sampling a solution of the remaining, partially solved CSP.

We demonstrate our approach on a Lotka-Volterra system with PPMRS semantics, where exact compound action computation is infeasible. Our approach allows to perform simulation studies and Bayesian filtering with PPMRS semantics in scenarios where this was previously infeasible.

Keywords: Bayesian filtering
Probabilistic multiset rewriting system
Metropolis-Hastings algorithm · Markov chain monte carlo
Constraint satisfaction problem

1   Introduction

Modelling dynamic systems is fundamental for a variety of AI tasks. Multiset Rewriting Systems (MRSs) provide a convenient mechanism to represent dynamic systems that consist of multiple (inter-)acting entities where the system dynamics can be described in terms of *rewriting rules* (also called actions). Typically, MRS are used for simulation studies, e.g. in chemistry [2], systems biology [13] or ecology [16].

Recently, *Lifted Marginal Filtering* (LiMa) [12,18] was proposed, an approach that uses a MRS to describe the state dynamics and maintains the *state*

© Springer Nature Switzerland AG 2018
F. Trollmann and A.-Y. Turhan (Eds.): KI 2018, LNAI 11117, pp. 73–85, 2018.
https://doi.org/10.1007/978-3-030-00111-7_7

distribution over time, which is repeatedly updated based on observations (i.e. it performs Bayesian filtering). More specifically, the transition model of LiMa is described in terms of a *probabilistic parallel MRS* (PPMRS) [1], a specific class of MRSs that model systems where multiple entities act in parallel. This allows to perform Bayesian filtering in scenarios where multiple entities can simultaneously perform activities between consecutive observations, but the order of actions between observations is not relevant.

A multiset of actions that is executed in parallel is called *compound action*. In PPRMS, each state s defines a distribution of compound actions k, $p(k|s)$. This distribution defines the transition distribution $p(s'|s)$, where s' is the result of applying k to s (called *transition model* in the Bayesian filtering context).

One of the computational challenges in probabilistic parallel MRSs is the computation of $p(k|s)$: This distribution is calculated as the normalized *weight* $v_s(k)$ of the compound actions: $p(k|s) = v_s(k)/\sum_{k_i} v_s(k_i)$. To compute this normalization factor (called partition function) exactly, it is necessary to sum over all compound actions. Unfortunately, the number of compound actions can be very large, due to the large number of combinations of actions that can be applied in parallel to a state. Thus, in general, complete enumeration is infeasible. Therefore, we are concerned with methods for approximating this distribution.

A problem closely related to computing the value of the partition function is *weighted model counting* (WMC), where the goal is to find the summed weight of all models of a weighted propositional theory (W-SAT). Exact [4] and approximate [7,19] algorithms for WMC have been proposed. However, our approach requires to sample from the distribution $p(k|s)$, not just compute its partition function. For W-SAT, a method was proposed [3] to sample solutions, based on partitioning the set of satisfying assignments into "cells", containing equal numbers of satisfying assignments. The main reason why these approaches cannot be used directly for our domain is that they assume a specific structure of the weights (weights factorize into weights of literals), whereas in our domain, only weights $v(k)$ of complete samples k are available. Another related line of research is efficiently sampling from distributions with many zeros (hard constraints) [9], which can also be achieved by a combination of sampling and backtracking. However, they assume that the distribution to sample from is given in factorized form (e.g. as a graphical model).

The main technical contribution of this paper is a sampling approach for compound actions, based on the Metropolis-Hastings algorithm. Compound action computation can be formulated as a constraint satisfaction problem (CSP), where each compound action is a solution of the CSP. The algorithm works by iteratively proposing new CSP solutions, based on backtracking of the current solution (i.e. compound action).

We will proceed as follows. In Sect. 2, we introduce probabilistic parallel MRSs in more detail. The exact and approximate algorithms for computing the compound action distribution are presented in Sect. 3. We present an empirical evaluation of our approach in Sect. 4, showing that the transition model can be approximated accurately for situations with thousands of entities, where the exact algorithm is infeasible.

2 Probabilistic Parallel Multiset Rewriting

In the following, we introduce probabilistic parallel multiset rewriting systems (PPMRSs), and show how such a system defines the state transition distribution (also called *transition model*) $p(S_{t+1}|S_t)$.

Such systems have previously been investigated in the context of P Systems [15], a biologically inspired formalism based on parallel multiset rewriting across different regions (separated by *membranes*). Several probabilistic variants of P Systems have been proposed [1,5,16]. We present a slightly different variant here, that does not use membranes, but structured entities (the variant that is used in LiMa [12,18]).

Let $\mathcal{E}$ be a set of entities. A **multiset** over $\mathcal{E}$ is a map $s : \mathcal{E} \to \mathbb{N}$ from entities to multiplicities. We denote a multiset of entities $e_1, \ldots, e_i$ and their multiplicities $n_1, \ldots, n_i$ as $[\![n_1\, e_1, \ldots, n_i\, e_i]\!]$, and define multiset union $s \uplus s'$, multiset difference $s \uplus s'$, and multiset subsets $s \sqsubseteq s'$ in the obvious way. In MRSs, multisets of entities are used to represent the state of a dynamic system. Thus, in the following, we use the terms *state* and *multiset of entities* interchangeably.

Typically, MRSs consider only *flat* (unstructured) entities. Here, we use *structured* entities: Each entity is a map of property names $\mathcal{K}$ to values $\mathcal{V}$, i.e. a partial function $\mathcal{E} = \mathcal{K} \nrightarrow \mathcal{V}$. Structured entities are necessary for the scenarios we are considering, as they contain entities with multiple, possibly continuous, properties.

For example, consider the following multiset, that describes a situation in a predator-prey model, with ten predators and six prey, each entity having a specific age[1]:

$$[\![6\langle \text{T: Prey, A: 2}\rangle, \ 3\langle \text{T: Pred, A: 3}\rangle, \ 7\langle \text{T: Pred, A: 5}\rangle]\!] \tag{1}$$

In [12], a factorized representation of such states is devised, that allows to represent state distributions more compactly. We note that the concepts presented in the following also apply to the factorized representation, but we omit it here for readability.

The general concept of a multiset rewriting system (MRS) is to model the system dynamics by **actions** (also known as rewriting rules) that describe preconditions and effects of the possible behaviors of the entities. An action is a triple (c, e, w) consisting of a precondition list $c \in \mathcal{C}$, an effect function $e \in \mathcal{F}$ and a weight $w \in \mathbb{R}$. In conventional MRSs (e.g. in the context of P Systems [1,5,16]), the preconditions are typically a multiset or a list of (flat) entities. However, when using structured entities, preconditions can be described much more concisely as *constraints* on entities, i.e. as a list of boolean functions: $\mathcal{C} = [\mathcal{E} \to \{\top, \bot\}]$.

---

[1] We use $\langle \cdot \rangle$ to denote partial functions.

For example, consider an action *reproduce*, that can be performed by any entity with Age > 3, regardless of other properties of the entity, which is naturally and concisely represented as a constraint.

The idea of applying an action to a state is to *bind* entities to the preconditions. Specifically, one entity is bound to each element in the precondition list, and entities can only be bound when they satisfy the corresponding constraint. The effect function then manipulates the state based on the bound entities (by inserting, removing, or manipulating entities).We call such a binding **action instance** $(a, i) \in \mathcal{I}$, i.e. a pair consisting of an action and a list of entities. We write $a(i)$ for an action instance consisting of an action a and bound entities i. Note that we use *positional* preconditions, i.e. the action instances eat(x,y) and eat(y,x) are different – either x or y is eaten.

A Compound Action $k \in \mathcal{K}$ is a multiset of action istances. It is applied to a state by composing the effects of the individual action instances. The compound action k is *applicable* in a state s if all of the bound entities are present in s, and it is *maximal* with respect to s if all entities in s are bound in k. Thus, a compound action is applicable and maximal when the multiset of all the bound entities is exactly the state s, i.e. $\biguplus_{a(x) \in k} x = s$. In the following, we are only concerned with applicable maximal compound action (AMCAs), which define the transition model. Scenarios where agents can also choose to not participate in any action can be modelled by introducing explicit "no-op" actions.

Compound Action Probabilities: Our system is probabilistic, which means that each AMCA is assigned a probability. In general, any function from the AMCAs to the positive real numbers which integrates to one is a valid definition of these probabilities, that might be plausible for different domains. Here, we use the probabilities that arise when each entity independently chooses which action to participate in (which is the intended semantics for the scenarios we are concerned with). To calculate this probability, we count the number of ways specific entities from a state s can be chosen to be assigned to the action instances in the compound action. This concept to calculate probabilities is closesly related to [1] – except that due to the fact that we use positional preconditions, the counting process is slightly different.

The *multiplicity* $\mu_s(k)$ of a compound action k with respect to a state s is the number of ways the entities in k can be chosen from s. See Example 1 below for an illustration of the calculation of the multiplicity.

The weight $v_s(k)$ of a compound action is the product of its multiplicity and the actions' weights:

$$v_s(k) = \mu_s(k) * \Pi_i w_i^{n_i} \tag{2}$$

Here, n_i is the number of action instances ai_i present in k. The probability of a compound action in a state s is its normalized weight:

$$p(k|s) = v_s(k) / \sum_{k_i} v_s(k_i) \tag{3}$$

Transition Model: The distribution of the AMCAs define the distribution of successor states, i.e. the *transition model*. The successor states of s are obtained by applying all AMCAs to s. The probability of each successor state s' is the sum of the probabilities of all AMCAs leading to s':

$$p(S'=s'|S=s) = \sum_{\{k\,|\,apply(k,s)=s'\}} p(k|s) \tag{4}$$

Finally, the posterior state distribution is obtained by applying the transition model to the prior state distribution, and marginalizing s (this is the standard predict step of Bayesian filtering):

$$p(S'=s') = \sum_s p(S=s)\,p(S'=s'|S=s) \tag{5}$$

Example 1: *In a simplified population model, two types of entities exist: Prey $x = \langle Type = X \rangle$ and predators $y = \langle Type = Y \rangle$. Predators can eat other animals (prey or other predators, action e), and all animals can reproduce (action r). Reproduction is 4 times as likely as consumption, i.e. action e has weight 1, and r has weight 4.*

For a state $s = [\![1x, 2y]\!]$, the following applicable action instances exist: $r(y)$, $r(x)$, $e(y,x)$, $e(y,y)$. The resulting applicable maximal compound actions are: $k_1 = [\![2r(y), 1r(x)]\!]$, $k_2 = [\![1e(y,y), 1r(x)]\!]$ and $k_3 = [\![1e(y,x), 1r(y)]\!]$. Applying these compound actions (assuming that they have the obvious effects) to the initial state s yields the three successor states $s_1' = [\![4y, 2x]\!]$, $s_2' = [\![1y, 2x]\!]$ and $s_3' = [\![2y]\!]$. The multiplicities of the compound actions are $\mu_s(k_1) = 1$, $\mu_s(k_2) = 2$, $\mu_s(k_3) = 2$ and their weights are $v_s(k_1) = 1 * 4^3 = 64$, $v_s(k_2) = 2 * 1 * 4 = 8$ and $v_s(k_3) = 2 * 1 * 4 = 8$.

3   Efficient Implementation

In this section, we present the main contribution of this paper: An efficient approximate algorithm for computing the posterior state distribution (Eq. 5).

Given a prior state distribution $p(S)$ and a set of actions A, the following steps need to be performed for each s with $p(S=s) > 0$ to obtain the posterior state distribution:

(i) Compute all action instances of each action $a \in A$, given s.
(ii) Compute all AMCAs and their probabilities (Eq. 3).
(iii) Calculate the probabilities of the resulting successor states s', i.e. $p(s'|s)$, by applying all AMCAs to s (Eq. 4).

Afterwards, the posterior state distribution $p(s')$ is obtained by weighting $p(s'|s)$ with the prior $p(s)$ and marginalizing s (Eq. 5). In the following, we discuss efficient implementations for each of these steps.

Step (i) requires, for each action $(c, e, w) = a \in A$, to enumerate all bindings (lists of entities) that satisfy the precondition list $c = [c_1, \ldots, c_n]$ of this action, i.e. the set $\{[e_1, \ldots, e_n] \mid c_1(e_1) \wedge \cdots \wedge c_n(e_n)\}$. This is straightforward, as for each constraint, we can enumerate the satisfying entities independently. In the scenarios we are considering, the number of actions, as well as the number of *different* entities in each state is small (see Example 1). Furthermore, we only consider constraints that can be decided in constant time (e.g. comparisons with constants). Thus, we expect this step to be sufficiently fast.

Steps (ii) and (iii) are, however, computationally demanding, due to the large number of compound actions: Given a state s, let n be the total number of entities in s and i be the number of action instances. The number of possible compound actions is at most the multiset coefficient $\left(\!\!\binom{i}{n}\!\!\right) = \frac{(i+n-1)!}{n!\,(i-1)!}$.

Therefore, in the following, we focus on the efficient computation of $p(K|s)$. We start with an exact algorithm that enumerates all AMCAs, and, based on that, derive a sampling-based algorithm that approximates $p(K|s)$.

In the context of other PPMRSs, efficient implementations for computing $p(K|s)$ have not been discussed. Either, they use a semantics that allows to sample a compound action by sequentially sampling the individual actions[2] [16], or they use a semantics similar to ours (requiring to enumerate all compound actions), but are not concerned with an efficient implementation [1,5].

3.1   Exact Algorithm

The task we have to solve is the following: Given a set of action instances $(a, i) \in I$ and a state s, compute the distribution $p(K|s)$ of the compound actions that are applicable and maximal with respect to s (the AMCAs), as shown in Eq. 3. To compute the partition function of this distribution exactly, it is necessary enumerate all AMCAs and their weights. Thus, the exact algorithm works as follows: First, all AMCAs are enumerated, which then allows to compute the partition function and thus $p(K|s)$.

In the following, we show how the AMCA calculation problem can be transformed into a constraint satisfaction problem (CSP) Γ, such that each solution of the CSP is an AMCA, and vice versa. Then, we only need to compute all solutions of Γ, e.g. by exhaustive search.

A CSP Γ is a triple (X, D, C) where X is a set of variables, D is a set of domains (one for each variable), and C is a set of constraints, i.e. boolean functions of subsets of X. Given action instances I and a state s, a CSP Γ is constructed as follows:

- For each action instance $(a, i) \in I$, there is a variable $x \in X$. The domain of x is $\{0, \ldots, \min_{e \in i}(n_e)\}$, where n_e is the multiplicity of entity e in s.
- For each entity $e \in s$ with multiplicity n_e in s, there is a constraint $c \in C$ on all variables x_i whose corresponding action instances a_i bind e. Let $m_{i,e}$ the number of times the action instance a_i binds e. The constraint then is $\sum_i m_{e,i} = n_e$. This models the applicability and maximality of the compound actions.

---

[2] Due to the sequential sampling process, the probability of a compound action is higher when there are more possible permutations of the individual actions, which is explicitly avoided by our approach.

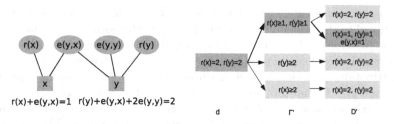

Fig. 1. Left: The CSP for Example 1. Circles represent variables, rectangles represent constraints. Right: Illustration of the proposal function, using the CSP of Fig. 1 and the solution $d = (r(x) = 2, r(y) = 2)$. Equalities represent assignments in the solution, and inequalities represent constraints. Assignments and constraints with 0 are not shown.

Note that the constraint language consists only of summation and equality, independently of the constraint language of action preconditions (which have been resolved before, when computing action instances).

A solution σ of Γ is an assignment of all variables in X that satisfies all constraints. Each solution σ of Γ corresponds to a compound action k: The value $\sigma(x)$ of a variable x indicates the multiplicity of the corresponding action instance (a, i) in k. Each solution σ corresponds to an *applicable* and *maximal* compound action (as this is directly enforced by the constraints of Γ), and each AMCA is a solution of Γ. Figure 1 (left) shows the CSP corresponding to Example 1.

We use standard backtracking to enumerate all solutions of the CSP[3]. Afterwards, the weight of each solution (and thus the partition function) can be calculated.

Note that the CSP we are considering is *not* an instance of a *valued* (or *weighted*) CSP [6,17]: They assume that each satisfied constraint has a value, and the goal is to find the *optimal* variable assignment, whereas in our proposal, only *solutions* have a value, and we are interested the *distribution* of solutions.

3.2 Approximate Algorithm

The exact algorithm has a linear time complexity in the number of AMCAs (i.e. solutions of Γ). However, due to the potentially very large number of AMCAs, enumerating all solutions of Γ is infeasible in many scenarios.

We propose to solve this problem by *sampling* CSP solutions instead of enumerating all of them. However, sampling directly is difficult: To compute the probability of a solution (Eq. 3), we first need to compute the partition function, which requires a complete enumeration of the solutions.

Metropolis-Hastings-Algorithm: Markov chain Monte Carlo (MCMC) algorithms like the Metropolis-Hastings algorithm provide an efficient sampling

---

[3] This is sufficient, as the problem here is not that *finding* each solution is difficult, but that there are factorially many solutions.

mechanism for such cases, where we can directly calculate a value $v(k)$ that is proportional to the probability of k, but obtaining the normalization factor (the partition function) is difficult. The Metropolis-Hastings algorithm works by constructing a Markov chain of samples $\mathcal{M} = k_0, k_1, \ldots$ that has $p(K)$ as its stationary distribution. The samples are produced iteratively by employing a *proposal distribution* $g(k'|k)$ that proposes a move to the next sample k', given the current sample k. The proposed sample is either *accepted* and used as the current sample for the next iteration, or rejected and the previous sample is kept. The *acceptance probability* is calculated as $A(k, k') = \min\{1, (v(k')\, g(k|k'))/(v(k)\, g(k'|k))\}$. It can be shown that the Markov chain constructed this way does indeed have the target distribution $p(K)$ (Eq. 3) as its stationary distribution [10]. The Metropolis-Hastings algorithm thus is a random walk in the sample space (in our case, the space of AMCAs, or equivalently, solutions of Γ) with the property that each sample is visited with a frequency relative to its probability. The Metropolis-Hastings sampler performs the following steps at time $t + 1$:

1. Propose a new sample k' by sampling from $g(k'|k_t)$.
2. Let $k_{t+1} = k'$ with probability $A(k', k_t)$.
3. Otherwise, let $k_{t+1} = k_t$.

Proposal Function: In the following, we present a proposal function of compound actions. The idea is to perform *local* moves in the space of the compound actions as follows: The proposal function $g(k'|k)$ proposes k' by randomly selecting n action instances to delete from k, and sample one of the possible completions of the remaining (non-maximal) compound action. This means the proposal makes small changes to k for proposing k', while ensuring that k' is applicable and maximal.

The proposal function can be formulated equivalently when viewing compound actions as CSP solutions. For a CSP solution σ, "removing" a single action instance is done by removing the assignment of the corresponding variable in σ, and "remembering" the previous value of the variable as a constraint, relaxed by 1: Suppose that we want to remove an action instance corresponding to the CSP variable x, and the solution contains the assignment $x = v$. We do this by removing the assignment, and adding $x \geq v - 1$ as a constraint. This is done randomly for n variables of the CSP. Similarly, for all other variables, we add constraints $x \geq v$ to capture the fact that the remaining CSP can have solutions where these variables have a higher value. In Algorithm 1, a procedure is shown that enumerates all CSPs that can be obtained this way. From the resulting CSPs, one CSP Γ' is sampled uniformly, and then a solution σ' of Γ' is sampled (also uniformly). Notice that each of these CSPs is much easier to solve by backtracking search than the original CSP, as the solution space is much smaller. The proposal function is shown in Algorithm 1.

For example, consider the CSP corresponding to Example 1 (Fig. 1 left) and the solution $d = (r(x) = 2, r(y) = 2, e(y, y) = 0, e(y, x) = 0)$. Suppose we want to remove $n = 2$ action instances. This results in three possible reduced CSPs: Either two r(x), two r(y) or one r(x) and one r(y) are removed. The CSPs, and the possible solutions of each CSP are shown in Fig. 1 (right).

Algorithm 1. Proposal function

1: **function** G(Γ,σ,n)
2:      $\Gamma' \leftarrow$ uniform(REDUCEDCSPs(Γ,σ,n))
3:      $\sigma' \leftarrow$ uniform(ENUMSOLUTIONS(Γ'))   ▷ Enumerate solutions of Γ', sample one
4:      **return** σ'
5: **end function**
6: **function** REDUCEDCSPs($\Gamma = (X, D, C)$,σ,n)
7:      for each x_i, add constraint $x_i \geq d_i$ to C
8:      $R \leftarrow$ set of all combinations with repetitions of variables in X with exactly n
         elements, where x_i occurs at most $\sigma(x_i)$ times
9:      **for** $r \in R$ **do**
10:         $C' \leftarrow$ same constraints as in C, but $\forall x \in X$: replace $x \geq v$ by $x \geq v - x\#r$[a]
11:         $G \leftarrow G \cup (X, D, C')$ ▷ Collect all reduced CSPs
12:     **end for**
13:     **return** (G)
14: **end function**

---

[a] $x\#r$ denotes the number occurences of x in r

Algorithm 2. Probability of a step of the proposal function

1: **function** GPROB(σ',σ,Γ,n)
2:      $\forall x : rem(x) \leftarrow \max(0, \sigma'(x) - \sigma(x))$ ▷ Variable assignments that need to be
         reduced to get from σ to σ'.
3:      $G \leftarrow \{\Gamma' \in$ REDUCEDCSPs(Γ, σ, n) | reductions that reduce each variable x at
         least $rem(x)$ times}   ▷ Reduced CSPs that have d' as a solution
4:      $\forall \Gamma' \in G : n_{\Gamma'} \leftarrow |$ ENUMCSP(Γ') | ▷ Number of CSP solutions for each Γ'
5:      $t \leftarrow |$ REDUCEDCSPs(Γ, σ, n) | ▷ Total number of ways to reduce the CSP
6:      $p \leftarrow 1/t \sum_{\Gamma' \in R} 1/n_{\Gamma'}$ ▷ Calculate probability that σ' is sampled
7:      **return** p
8: **end function**

Probability of a Step: We do not only need to sample a value from g, given σ (as implemented in Algorithm 1), but for the acceptance probability, we also need to calculate the probability of $g(\sigma'|\sigma)$, given σ' and σ. This is implemented by Algorithm 2. The general idea is to follow all possible choices of removed action instances, and count the number of choices that lead to σ'. In Algorithm 1, two random choices are performed: (i) Choosing one of the reduced CSPs Γ', and (ii) choosing one of the solutions of Γ'. In both cases, a uniform distribution is used. Therefore, it is sufficient to know the *number* of elements to choose from. Furthermore, only need to compute the solutions for those CSPs Γ' where σ' can be reached. Both considerations are exploited by Algorithm 2, leading to an increased efficiency.

Figure 1 (right) illustrates these ideas. Suppose the dark grey path has been chosen by the proposal function. The function $gProb(\sigma', \sigma, \Gamma, 2)$ then only has to compute the solutions of the single CSP Γ' in the dark grey path, as it is the only

CSP that has σ' as a solution. The probability is calculated as $gProb(\sigma', \sigma, \Gamma, 2) = 1/3 * 1/2 = 1/6$.

4   Experimental Evaluation

In this section, we investigate the performance of the approximate compound action computation algorithm in terms of computation time and accuracy by simulating a variant of a probabilistic Lotka-Volterra model that has a compound action semantics.

4.1   Experimental Design

The Lotka-Volterra model is originally a pair of nonlinear differential equations describing the population dynamics of predator (y) and prey (x) populations [11]. Such predator-prey systems can be modeled as a MRS [8, 16].

In contrast to previous approaches, we use a *maximally parallel* MRS to model the system, i.e. in our approach, multiple actions (reproduction and consumption) can occur between consecutive time steps. We introduce explicit no-op actions to allow entities to not participate in any action. Modeling the system like this can, for example, be beneficial for Bayesian filtering, where between observations (e.g. a survey of population numbers), a large number of actions can occur, but their order is not relevant. Figure 2 (left) shows an example of the development of the system over time, as modeled by our approach. It shows the expected behavior of stochastic Lotka-Volterra systems: Oscillations that become larger over time [14].

We compare the exact and approximate algorithms by computing the compound action distribution for a single state s of the predator-prey model, i.e. $p(K|s)$. We vary the number of predator and prey entities in s (2, 3, 5, 7, 15, 20, 25, 30, 40, 50, 60, 70) as well as the number of samples drawn by the approximate algorithm (1, ..., 30000).

The convergence of the approximate algorithm is assessed using the *total variation distance* (TVD). Let p be the true distribution, and let q_n be the distribution of the approximate algorithm after drawing n samples. The TVD is then

$$\Delta(n) = 1/2 \sum_s | p(s) - q_n(s) |$$

The *mixing time* $\tau(\epsilon)$ measures how many samples need to be drawn until the TVD falls below a threshold ϵ:

$$\tau(\epsilon) = \min\{t \mid \Delta(n) \le \epsilon \text{ for all } n \ge t\}$$

We assess the TVD and mixing time of (i) the compound action distribution, and (ii) of the state transition distribution. The rationale here is that ultimately, only the successor state distribution is relevant, but assessing the TVD and mixing time of the compound action distribution allows further insight into the algorithm.

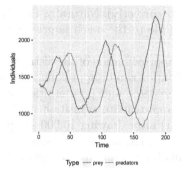
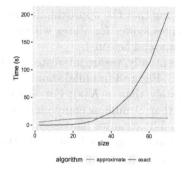

Fig. 2. Left: Sample trajectory, each state transition is obtained by calculating the compound action distribution using the approximate algorithm with 10,000 samples, and then sampling and executing one of the compound actions. Right: Runtime of the algorithms, using constant number of 10,000 samples.

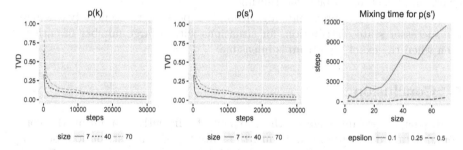

Fig. 3. TVD of $p(K|s)$ (left) and $p(S'|s)$ (middle) for different numbers of samples and for states with different number of entities. Right: Empirical mixing time of $p(S'|s)$, indicating that a linear increase in samples (and thus, runtime) of the approximate algorithm is sufficient to achieve the same approximation quality.

4.2 Results

Figure 2 (right) shows the runtime of the exact and approximate algorithm (with a fixed number of 10,000 samples) for different numbers of entities in s. The exact algorithm is faster for states with only few entities, as solutions of only a single CSP are enumerated, whereas the approximate algorithm enumerates solutions for 10,000 CSPs (although each of those CSPs has only few solutions). However, the runtime of the approximate algorithm does not depend on the number of entities in s at all, as long as the number of samples stays constant (but approximation quality will decrease, as investigated later). In our scenario, the approximate algorithm is faster for states consisting of 40 or more predator and prey entities.

The difference between the exact and approximate compound action distribution $p(K|s)$ in terms of TVD is shown in Fig. 3 (left). When more samples are drawn by the approximate algorithm, the TVD converges to zero, as expected (implying that the approximate algorithm works correctly). Naturally, the TVD converges slower for states with more entities (due to the much larger number of compound actions).

Eventually, we are interested in an accurate approximation of the distribution $p(S'|s)$. Figure 3 (middle) shows that this distribution can be approximated more accurately than $p(K|s)$: For a state with 70 predator and prey entities (with more than 9 million compound actions), the approximate transition model is reasonably accurate (successor state $TVD < 0.1$) after drawing 10,000 samples. Even more, Fig. 2 (left) suggests that this approximation is still reasonable for states with more than 2,000 entities – as we still observe the expected qualitative behavior.

Figure 3 (right) shows the empirical mixing time of $p(S'|s)$. The mixing time grows approximately linear in the number of entities in the state. This suggests that to achieve the same accuracy of the approximation, the runtime of the approximate algorithm only has to grow linearly – as compared to the exact algorithm, which has a factorial runtime.

Thus, using the approximate algorithm, it is possible to accurately calculate the successor state distribution, for situations with a large number of entities, even when the exact algorithm is infeasible.

5   Conclusion

In this paper, we investigated the problem of efficiently computing the compound action distribution (and thus, the state transition distribution, or transition model) of a probabilistic parallel Multiset Rewriting System (PPMRS) – which is required when performing Bayesian filtering (BF) in PPMRSs. We showed that computing the transition model exactly is infeasible in general (due to the factorial number of compound actions), and provided an approximation algorithm based on MCMC methods. This strategy allows to *sample* from the compound action distribution, and is therefore also useful for simulation studies that employ PPMRSs. Our empirical results show that the approach allows BF in cases where computing the exact transition model is infeasible – where the state contains thousands of entities.

Future work includes applying the approach to BF tasks with real-world sensor data, e.g. for human activity recognition. It may also be worthwhile to further investigate the general framework developed in this paper – approximating the solution distribution of a CSP that has probabilistic (or weighted) solutions – and see whether it is useful for other problems beyond compound action computation.

References

1. Barbuti, R., Levi, F., Milazzo, P., Scatena, G.: Maximally parallel probabilistic semantics for multiset rewriting. Fundam. Inform. **112**(1), 1–17 (2011)
2. Berry, G., Boudol, G.: The chemical abstract machine. Theor. Comput. Sci. **96**(1), 217–248 (1992). http://portal.acm.org/citation.cfm?doid=96709.96717

3. Chakraborty, S., Fremont, D.J., Meel, K.S., Seshia, S.A., Vardi, M.Y.: Distribution-aware sampling and weighted model counting for sat. In: AAAI, vol. 14, pp. 1722–1730 (2014)
4. Chavira, M., Darwiche, A.: On probabilistic inference by weighted model counting. Artif. Intell. **172**(6–7), 772–799 (2008)
5. Ciobanu, G., Cornacel, L.: Probabilistic transitions for P systems. Prog. Nat. Sci. **17**(4), 432–441 (2007)
6. Cooper, M., de Givry, S., Sanchez, M., Schiex, T., Zytnicki, M., Werner, T.: Soft arc consistency revisited. Artif. Intell. **174**, 449–478 (2010). http://linkinghub.elsevier.com/retrieve/pii/S0004370210000147
7. Ermon, S., Gomes, C., Sabharwal, A., Selman, B.: Taming the curse of dimensionality: discrete integration by hashing and optimization. In: International Conference on Machine Learning, pp. 334–342 (2013)
8. Giavitto, J.L., Michel, O.: MGS: a rule-based programming language for complex objects and collections. Electron. Notes Theor. Comput. Sci. **59**(4), 286–304 (2001)
9. Gogate, V., Dechter, R.: Samplesearch: importance sampling in presence of determinism. Artif. Intell. **175**(2), 694–729 (2011)
10. Häggström, O.: Finite Markov Chains and Algorithmic Applications, vol. 52. Cambridge University Press, Cambridge (2002)
11. Lotka, A.J.: Analytical Theory of Biological Populations. Springer, New York (1998). https://doi.org/10.1007/978-1-4757-9176-1
12. Lüdtke, S., Schröder, M., Bader, S., Kersting, K., Kirste, T.: Lifted Filtering via Exchangeable Decomposition. arXiv e-prints (2018). https://arxiv.org/abs/1801.10495
13. Oury, N., Plotkin, G.: Multi-level modelling via stochastic multi-level multiset rewriting. Math. Struct. Comput. Sci. **23**, 471–503 (2013)
14. Parker, M., Kamenev, A.: Extinction in the Lotka-Volterra model. Phys. Rev. E **80**(2) (2009). https://link.aps.org/doi/10.1103/PhysRevE.80.021129
15. Paun, G.: Membrane Computing: An Introduction. Springer, Heidelberg (2012). https://doi.org/10.1007/978-3-642-56196-2
16. Pescini, D., Besozzi, D., Mauri, G., Zandron, C.: Dynamical probabilistic P systems. Int. J. Found. Comput. Sci. **17**(01), 183–204 (2006)
17. Schiex, T., Fargier, H., Verfaillie, G.: Valued constraint satisfaction problems: hard and easy problems. In: Proceedings of the International Joint Conference on Artificial Intelligence (1995)
18. Schröder, M., Lüdtke, S., Bader, S., Krüger, F., Kirste, T.: LiMa: sequential lifted marginal filtering on multiset state descriptions. In: Kern-Isberner, G., Fürnkranz, J., Thimm, M. (eds.) KI 2017. LNCS (LNAI), vol. 10505, pp. 222–235. Springer, Cham (2017). https://doi.org/10.1007/978-3-319-67190-1_17
19. Wei, W., Selman, B.: A new approach to model counting. In: Bacchus, F., Walsh, T. (eds.) SAT 2005. LNCS, vol. 3569, pp. 324–339. Springer, Heidelberg (2005). https://doi.org/10.1007/11499107_24

Efficient Auction Based Coordination for Distributed Multi-agent Planning in Temporal Domains Using Resource Abstraction

Andreas Hertle$^{(\boxtimes)}$ and Bernhard Nebel

Department of Computer Science, University of Freiburg, 79110 Freiburg, Germany
`hertle@informatik.uni-freiburg.de`

Abstract. Recent advances in mobile robotics and AI promise to revolutionize industrial production. As autonomous robots are able to solve more complex tasks, the difficulty of integrating various robot skills and coordinating groups of robots increases dramatically. Domain independent planning promises a possible solution. For single robot systems a number of successful demonstrations can be found in scientific literature. However our experiences at the RoboCup Logistics League in 2017 highlighted a severe lack in plan quality when coordinating multiple robots. In this work we demonstrate how out of the box temporal planning systems can be employed to increase plan quality for temporal multi-robot tasks. An abstract plan is generated first and sub-tasks in the plan are auctioned off to robots, which in turn employ planning to solve these tasks and compute bids. We evaluate our approach on two planning domains and find significant improvements in solution coverage and plan quality.

1 Introduction

Recent advances in robotics and AI promise to revolutionize industrial production. Gone will be static assembly lines and hardwired robots. Instead autonomous mobile robots will transport parts for assembly to the right workstation at the right time to assemble an individualized product for a specific customer. At least that is the dream of various manufacturing companies around the globe. To ensure that production runs without interruptions around the clock, these robots will need strong planning capabilities. The challenges for such a planning system stem from making plans with concurrent processes and multiple agents, deadlines and external events.

The Planning and Execution Competition for Logistics Robots in Simulation (PExC) [6] addresses these problems and provide a test-bed for for experimenting with different methods for solving these problems, abstracting away from real

B. Nebel—This work was supported by the PACMAN project within the HYBRIS research group (NE 623/13-1). This work was also supported by the DFG grant EXC1086 BrainLinks-BrainTools to the University of Freiburg, Germany.

F. Trollmann and A.-Y. Turhan (Eds.): KI 2018, LNAI 11117, pp. 86–98, 2018.
https://doi.org/10.1007/978-3-030-00111-7_8

robots. It is a simulation environment based on the RoboCup Logistics League (see Fig. 1).

Our aim was to demonstrate that current planner technology is mature enough to be used in such an environment. As it turned, however, this is far from the the truth. We employed the temporal planners POPF [1] and TFD [2], which seem like a good fit for these kinds of planning tasks, as time and duration of processes are modeled explicitly. It turned out that it is not possible to use them in reliable way. While they both can plan for one robot, two or more robots are beyond the reach. If one requires optimality in makespan, then the planners took too long, meaning using up much of the time reserved for planning and execution. If one chooses to use greedy plan generation, then the plans result often in assigning most of the work to just one robot.

In this paper we show how planning in temporal domains with multiple agents can be improved to find plans with lower makespan and find solutions for bigger problems. The key is to abstract resources, in this case robots, away, and plan for the simplified instance. After that the plan is refined using a contract-net protocol approach for the planning agents.

The rest of the paper is structured as follows: After giving some background information in Sect. 2, we present our approach in Sect. 3. The experimental evaluation can be found in Sect. 4. Section 5 discusses related work.

2 Temporal PDDL

The planning domain definition language (PDDL) was developed as an attempt to standardize Artificial Intelligence Planning. Since its inception in 1998 more features were added to represent planning tasks with numerical functions, non-deterministic outcomes and temporal actions. Due to international planning competitions a number of well tested planning systems are available. We are interested in finding plans for multiple physical robots or systems. Any number of processes could be happening simultaneous and considering various duration

Finals 2017 (1)   Simcomp 2017 (2)

Fig. 1. In the RoboCup Logistics League competition three autonomous robots must coordinate efficiently to solve production tasks. On the left (1): finals of the RCLL competition in 2017 between teams Carologistics and GRIPS. On the right (2): planning track of the simulation competition.

during the planning process is crucial to finding good plans. For this reason we require a planning system capable of temporal planning as defined in PDDL 2.1.

In PDDL a planning task is defined by a domain and a problem file. The domain defines what types, predicates and actions are possible and how they interact. The actions in a domain describe how the state can transition during planning. Each actions has typed arguments that specify which objects are relevant for this action. For temporal planning actions have a start event and an end event separated by the duration of the action. The conditions of an action determine when an action is *applicable* and the effects how the state changes when the action is *applied*. Conditions can refer either to the start, the end or the open interval between them. Effects take place either at the start or the end of an action.

The problem specifies the current situation and the goal condition. The current situation is specified as a set of objects and initial values for relations between them. For temporal planning future events can be specified as *timed initial literals*. These events encode a value change for a predicate or function to happen at a specific time in the future. Our approach makes extensive use of timed initial literals as way to integrate actions from previous plans into the planning process.

Solutions to temporal planning tasks are temporal plans consisting of a list of actions, where each action starts at a certain timestamp and has a specific duration.

3   Task Auction Planning

Our goals are twofold: we want to reduce complexity during the planning process, thus increasing the chance to find a valid plan, and we want to minimize makespans of plans by achieving a better plan parallelization when planning for multiple agents. Our approach decomposes a planning task for multiple agents into multiple simpler planning tasks for each agent. First we solve an abstract planning problem by removing agents form the planning problem and hiding some complex interactions in the planning domain. Once an abstract plan is found, a central agent acts as auctioneer in order to distribute tasks between the other agents, where a task is derived from an action in the abstract plan. Each agent can compute plans for offered tasks and submit bids based on the time it takes this agent to achieve the task goal. The auctioneer chooses from the valid plans for each task and continues to offer the next set of tasks until all tasks have valid plans from one agent.

Another way to look at this is to consider the resources used by the agents. The abstract plan coordinates shared resources between the agents. Each agent in turn uses its own resources to achieve a single step of the abstract plan, while unaware of the other agents and their resources. Our approach is applicable in planning domains that do not require concurrency to be solved. Usually problems in such domains could be solved by a single agent without help. However efficiency can be greatly increased when multiple agents participate.

3.1   PDDL Domain Creation

In this section we show how to convert an existing temporal PDDL domain to
a task- and an agent domain. To ensure compatibility between the domains,
we make no changes to types, predicates or functions, but focus solely on the
actions. We expect the temporal domain to be modeled in the following way: A
certain type represents the agents, the *agent-type*. Some actions in the domain
are modeled to represent activities performed by the agents, we call them the
agent-actions. They can be recognized by having an *agent-type* as parameter.
Other actions represent processes in the environment and are not specific to
an agent, we call them the *environment-actions*. Those do not have *agent-type*
objects as parameter.

First we discuss how to construct the *task-domain*. The intend is to identify
typical sequences of actions that are performed by the same single agent. That
chain of actions could to be replaced with a single macro action. This reduces
the branching factor during planning. A macro can be created by gathering the
effects of each action and either add it to the start or the end effect of the macro
action. Some effects might cancel each other; it is up to the domain designer
to determine which effects are essential for the macro action. The same careful
consideration is necessary to select which action conditions to add to macro
action. In the final step the agent is removed from the macro, meaning the
parameter of *agent-type* and all predicates or functions in the conditions and
effects of the macro that refer to the agent. Once a macro action for each task
is created it is also necessary to add the *environment-actions* from the temporal
domain to ensure that the domain is complete.

Next we discuss the purpose of the *agent-domain*. The agents are supposed
to solve each offered task. However they must not interfere with other unrelated
tasks. For this reason it is helpful to remove all *environment-actions* from the
agent domain. Thus, the agent domain is intentionally incomplete: It is not
possible to solve the whole problem with the agent domain. However it contains
all actions necessary to allow an agent to solve each offered task.

3.2   Combining and Rescheduling Plans

In our approach we combine and reschedule plans. In a *valid* temporal plan each
action is *applicable* at its start time. When looking through effects of previous
actions in the plan we can determine which events made the action applicable.
The action then can be moved to the time of the latest of the events it *depends*
on. If an action does not *depend* on any earlier event it can be moved to the
beginning of the plan. When appending actions from another plan, we insert the
action at the end of the plan (after the last event) and verify applicability. Then
the action can then be rescheduled to the earliest time as described above.

3.3   Solving and Bidding for Sub-tasks

In this section we discuss the planning process from an agent's point of view.
When an agent receives a task offer it needs to find a plan for the task. Once

---

Algorithm 1. Agent: state update and bidding

1: $state \leftarrow state_{init}, Events \leftarrow \varnothing, plan_{agent} \leftarrow \varnothing, Proposals \leftarrow \varnothing$
2: **while** $\top$ **do**
3:      $Assignments, Events_{new}, Tasks \leftarrow$ **receive**()   ▷ Receive from auctioneer
4:      $a \leftarrow$ **find_assigned_to_agent**($Assignments$)
5:      $state, plan_{agent} \leftarrow$ **apply**($Plans[a.task]$)   ▷ Retrieve and apply plan
6:      $Events \leftarrow Events \cup Events_{new}$
7:      **for all** $t \in Tasks$ **do**
8:          $plan \leftarrow$ **make_plan**($state, Events, t$)   ▷ Call PDDL planner
9:          **if** $plan$ solves t **then**
10:             $Plans[t] \leftarrow plan$ ▷ Store plan
11:             **make_bid_and_send**($plan$)   ▷ Send plan to auctioneer
12:         **end if**
13:     **end for**
14: **end while**

---

a plan is found the agent determines the point in time when it could start working on the task and when the task will be finished and submits the plan and those two timestamps as a bid for the task. Then the agent may continue computing solutions for alternative tasks and await the reply from the auctioneer. Algorithm 1 shows a simplified overview of the bidding process. In the actual implementation the communication takes place asynchronously and interrupts the planning process if the situation has changed.

Initially, the agent's current state could be supplied via PDDL file. During the planning process the current state can change from two sources. Once an agent won a bid for a task the current state is updated with the agent's actions by applying the plan that was proposed for the task as showed on line 5. Applying a plan also increases the timestamp of the current state by the makespan of the plan. The other source of changes comes from external events during the planning process, i.e. when other agents interact with the environment as showed on line 6. These external events do not advance the time of the current state. Instead, external events are represented in as timed initial literals, that will happen at a certain time in the future of the current state.

A task is communicated to the agent in the form of a PDDL action definition from the task-domain. The goal for a task can be derived form the effects of the action; this happens in the **make_plan** function on line 8. This is possible because both the tasks- and the agent-domain allow for the same predicates and functions. Thus the effects of the task-action applied to the current state of the agent define the goal for the task. However most planning systems are unable plans for negated goal predicates, so negated effects have to be omitted from the goal conjunction. If necessary complimentary predicates can be added to the PDDL domains such that goals for each possible task are sufficiently specified.

Now that the goal and the current state is known, a temporal planner can search for a solution. If no plan is found the agent is unable to solve this task. If a plan is available the agent can make a bid for the task. The bid consist of the plan and two timestamps. The former indicates when the agent will be able to start working on the task and the latter when the agent will presumably finish the task. The timestamps are useful for the auctioneer to determine which agent to assign a task to.

At some point the auctioneer publishes the next announcement consisting of which agent was assigned which task, what events are going to happen as a consequence and a new set of tasks to solve as showed on line 3. If a task was awarded to the agent, the agent applies the corresponding plan to the current state. The auctioneer also includes a list of future events in the announcement. These events represent the changes to the environment, possibly from actions of other agents. Each event consist of a timestamp and a set of effects. In case their timestamp is earlier than the time of the current state, the events need to be applied in the correct order. Later events are added as timed initial literals to the current state. Once the current state is updated the agent is ready to search for solutions to newly available tasks.

3.4   Decomposing and Auctioning of Sub-tasks

The auctioneer works with two plans: an abstract plan and a combined plan. The abstract plan determines which tasks can be offered to the agents. Once the agents submit bids for some tasks, the auctioneer can chose which bids provide the best value. These plans submitted by the agents are then integrated into the combined plan. This ensures that plans submitted by the agents are free of conflicts. The agents are notified of their assigned tasks. Then the process continues with a search for a new abstract plan. In the end the resulting combined plan is a solution to the original planning problem. Algorithm 2 shows a simplified overview of the process. In the actual implementation the communication takes place asynchronously.

The initial problem could be supplied via PDDL file and with the task-domain a temporal planner can search for the abstract plan as showed in line 3. Once a plan is found, the auctioneer determines which actions in the plan can be offered as tasks to the other agents. As discussed in Sect. 3.1, some actions in the plan are intended as tasks for agents to solve while other model aspects of the environment. The temporal plan needs to be analyzed (line 7) to determine which action depends on previous actions in the plan as discussed in Sect. 3.2. The following rules determine which actions can be offered:

1. A task-action without dependencies can be offered to the agents.
2. An environment-action without dependencies on other actions is *executable*.
3. An environment-action where all dependencies are executable is also executable.
4. A task-action where all dependencies are executable can be offered.

All *executable* environment-actions form the abstract plan are appended to the combined plan as showed on line 8.

In order to solve tasks, the agents need to know what events are scheduled to happen. However they do not need to know the details of the other agents

Algorithm 2. Auctioneer: abstract plan and offering sub-tasks

```
 1: state ← state_init, Events ← ∅, Proposed ← ∅, plan_comb ← ∅
 2: while ⊤ do
 3:     plan_abs ← make_abstract_plan(state, Events)          ▷ Call PDDL planner
 4:     if |plan_abs| = 0 then
 5:         return plan_comb
 6:     end if
 7:     Actions_env, Tasks ← determine_executable_prefix(plan_abs)
 8:     state, plan_comb ← apply(Actions_env)
 9:     Events ← extract_events(plan_comb)
10:     offer_tasks_and_wait(Assignments, Events, Tasks)        ▷ Send to agents
11:     Proposals ← receive()                                  ▷ Receive from agents
12:     Assignments ← assign(Proposals)
13:     for all a ∈ Assignments do
14:         state, plan_comb ← apply(a.plan)
15:     end for
16: end while
```

actions, only the changes they impose on the environment. These events are derived from the effects in the combined plan by removing all agent-specific predicates and functions (line 9).

Once a set of tasks has been offered the auctioneer waits for bids from the agents as showed on line 10. A bid from an agent consist of the plan for the task and the timestamps when the agent will be able to begin and achieve the tasks. An agent can bid on any number of tasks simultaneously. However the agent can only execute one task at a time, thus bidding on multiple tasks provides alternatives for the auctioneer to choose from.

Our approach does not specify or expect a certain number of agents. This offers great flexibility, as agents can join the planning process at any time or leave it provided they completed all tasks they committed to. However when waiting for solutions from agents it is difficult for the auctioneer to determine how long to wait for alternatives. Besides naive greedy strategies we implemented two alternatives:

- *Just-in-time assignment:* The decision is delayed until one the bidding agents needs to start working for this task as indicated by the *starting* timestamp of the bid.
- *Delayed batch assignment:* If there are a lot of simultaneous tasks available, it might take too long to wait for solutions for every task before assigning the winning agents. Once at least one solution is received the auctioneer delays the decision by a fixed duration and then performs a batch assignment.

In the literature the Hungarian method is recommended for optimal assignment of tasks to agents. However, since we do not have a matching problem between robots and tasks, robots can take on more than one task, the method does not work here.

We expect the *Just-in-time assignment* to perform best on physical systems. With this strategy the agents have the maximum amount of time to investigate possible alternative solutions without waiting or delaying the execution of the plan. Also, the agents would be more flexible since they do not commit to certain tasks ahead of time. For benchmark purposes this is impractical however, since the planning process would be prolonged roughly by the makespan of the plan and the planning timeout for our benchmarks is by far lower than the makespans. Thus for the benchmarks in this paper we make assignments based on the *Delayed batch* strategy.

Once an assignment is chosen, the auctioneer integrates the plans submitted by the agents into a combined plan as showed on line 8. Then the auctioneer computes a new abstract plan and continues to offer tasks to agents until an empty abstract plan is found, which signifies that the goal has been achieved.

4 Experimental Evaluation

We evaluated our approach on numerous planning tasks from two domains. Three planner configurations were used for the evaluation:

1. *POPF* is a forwards-chaining temporal planner [1]. Its name is based on the fact that it incorporates ideas from partial-order planning. During search, when applying an action to a state, it seeks to introduce only the ordering constraints needed to resolve threats, rather than insisting the new action occurs after all of those already in the plan. Its implementation is built on that for the planner COLIN, and it retains the ability to handle domains with linear continuous numeric effects.
2. *Temporal Fast Downward* is a temporal planning system that successfully participated in the temporal satisficing track of the 6th International Planning Competition 2008. The algorithms used in TFD are described in the ICAPS 2009 paper [2]. TFD is based on the Fast Downward planning system [3] and uses an adaptation of the context-enhanced additive heuristic to guide the search in the temporal state space induced by the given planning problem.
3. *Temporal Fast Downward Sequential Reschedule*. In this configuration the TFD-SR will search for purely sequential plans without taking advantage of concurrent actions. Once a plan is found it will be rescheduled to take advantage of concurrency. This usually increases planning efficiency allowing to solve bigger planning tasks.

We run each temporal planner configuration as a base line. For our auction based approach we also run all three planner configurations for the auctioneer. For the agents we found that POPF greatly outperformed TFD. The cause for this is likely a costly analysis before the search for a plan starts, where the analysis time is significantly greater than the following search time. For the agents that have to search for many short plans this is highly disadvantageous. Thus for all experiments the agents were planning with POPF. Finally, each plan is validated with *VAL* [4] to verify correctness.

The benchmarks were run on one machine with a Intel Core i7-3930K CPU at 3.2 GHz and 24 GB of memory. The baseline planning configurations run on a single thread, while the auction planning configurations use one thread per agent and one thread for the auctioneer. Each planning instance has a time limit of 15 min. In the results we compare expected execution time, that is makespan of the plan plus time until the first action is known. For the baseline that means total planning time and for our approach that means time until the first round of assignments is announced.

4.1 RoboCup Logistics League Domain

This domain was created for the participation in the planning track of RoboCup Logistics League competition. In the competition, three robots are tasked to assemble a number of products in an automated factory. A product consist of a base, zero to three rings and a cap. Each piece of the product has a certain color and the order of rings does matter. There are six specialized stations each capable of performing a certain step in the assembly. Some assembly steps require additional material that has to be brought to the station before the step can be performed. The robots can transport the workpieces between stations. The exact makeup of the ordered products are not known in advance, instead they are communicated during the production. The decision which products to assemble before the deadline and coordinating the three robots most efficiently is key for performing well in the competition.

In this domain we have modeled most aspects of the competition. However for this benchmark the products to assemble are known at the start and there are no deadlines for finishing them. The agents can perform the following actions: *move* from one station to another, *pickup* a product from a station, *prepare* a station to receive a product and *insert* a product into a station. For the tasks-domain we replaced the agent actions with a number of *task-transport-product* actions;

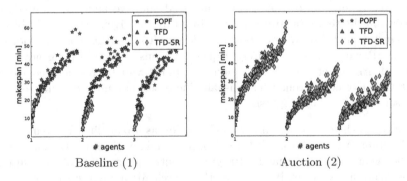

Fig. 2. Benchmark results in the RCLL domain. The problem set is evaluated with one, two and three agents. The lower the makespan, the better the plan result. On the left the baseline is shown. On the right the auction based task assignment is shown.

Table 1. Number of solved instance out of 125 for the RCLL domain with 1–3 agents

# agents	Baseline			Auction		
	1	2	3	1	2	3
POPF	85	90	78	52	40	50
TFD	11	20	12	58	44	47
TFD-SR	17	23	19	123	120	114

one for each station type. Usually the agents find plans in the form *move, pickup, move, prepare, insert* when solving a transport task.

We generated 125 problem instances with five products of varying complexity, the simplest requiring 4 and the most complex 10 production steps. Each problem is solved by one, two and three agents. The results can be seen in Table 1 and Fig. 2.

The baseline results show that both TFD variants can only solve few problems with low complexity. POPF can solve half of the problems, however the makespan for plans for two and three agents are as high as for one agent. Thus POPF is not able take advantage of multiple agents. The auction task assignment results show that TFD-SR is able solve most problems. TFD solves significantly more problems compared to the baseline. POPF solves only one third of the problems, less than in the baseline configuration. In many cases POPF is unable to find an initial plan in the task-domain within the timelimit. For all three planners the makespan for plans with two and three agents is significant lower than with one agent, showing better utilization of multiple agents.

4.2 Transport

For the second experiment we employ the well known transpot domain, where a set of packages need to be delivered to individual destinations by a number of trucks. Trucks can move along a network of roads of different lengths. Each truck can load a certain number of packages at the same time ranging from 2 to 4. Each package is initially found at some location and needs to be transported to its destination location.

The agents can perform the following actions: *move* from one location to a neighbouring location in the road graph, *pick-up* a package at a certain location if below maximum capacity and *drop* a transported package at a certain location. For the task-domain we replaced the agent actions with a *task-pickup-package* and a *task-deliver-package* action. This results in simple task plans, where each package is first picked up at its location and then dropped at its destination. Usually the agents find plans in the form *move, move, ..., move, pickup* for the pickup tasks. Similar plans are found for the drop-tasks, however only the agent that picked up the package before can solve this task. Usually the planner can easily determine whether a deliver-task can be solved. Furthermore, if an agent tries to solve a pickup task while carrying the maximum number of packages, no

Table 2. Number of solved instances out of 13 for the transport domain for 1–5 agents

# agents	Baseline					Auction				
	1	2	3	4	5	1	2	3	4	5
POPF	12	3	2	1	0	13	12	10	9	7
TFD	4	3	4	5	4	12	11	9	8	9
TFD-SR	4	4	5	4	4	3	2	3	2	3

valid plan will be found. It is intended that the agent solves a deliver task for one of the packages it carries. However it is difficult for the planner to determine that a pickup task is impossible, usually the planner searches until timeout. Thus for this domain we use the low planning timeout of 1 second for the agents to reduce time wasted on unsolvable tasks.

We generated a road network for two cities with ten locations each. Travel time within a city is low and travel time between cities is considerably higher. We sampled random locations for between 3 and 40 packages in increments of 3 for a total of 13 problem instances. Each problem is solved by between 1 and 5 agents. The results are shown in Table 2 and Fig. 3.

The baseline results show that both TFD variants can only solve problems with few packages. POPF is able to solve all problems with one agent, but is unable to find plans with multiple agents. The auction task assignment results show that TFD-CR can solve only few problems; in most cases no initial task plan can be found. Since TFD-CR searches for sequential plans, we assume that the search heuristic is confused by the high amount of simultaneous applicable pickup tasks of equal cost. On the other hand POPF and TFD are able to solve most problems with any number of agents.

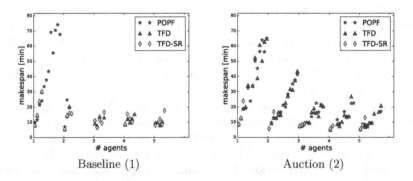

Baseline (1)   Auction (2)

Fig. 3. Benchmark results in the transport domain. The problem set is evaluated with one to five agents. The lower the makespan, the better the plan result. On the left the base line is shown. On the right the auction based task assignment is shown.

5   Related Work

The work closest to ours is the work by Niemüller and colleagues, who describe an architecture based on ASP [8]. They do not use a temporal planner but compile the planning problem into ASP and then only plan a few steps ahead. As they can show, this is an effective and efficient way to address the RCLL planning and execution problem.

Our approach instead is based on abstraction techniques, an approach that goes back a long way [7]. The particular kind of abstraction that we used can be called resource abstraction. This has also been employed before to speed up planning and to increase the number of tasks that could be executed in parallel in the RealPlan system [10]. However, in this case, no temporal planning was involved.

Coordination of agents using announcements and bidding is a technique often used in multi-agent systems [9]. In our context with planning agents, it is very similar to the architecture used in the elevator control designed by Koehler and Ottiger [5].

6   Conclusions

We showed how planning in temporal multi-agent domain can be enhanced by abstracting resource away. A central auctioneer offers tasks related to these resources to agents to be solved individually. The agents propose their solutions and the auctioneer chooses which solutions fit together best and assembles them into a combined plan. Our experiments show that compared to baseline temporal planning our approach can solve bigger problems and the resulting plans have significant lower makespan. The next step in the development will be to deploy our approach on physical robots or in simulations, where plan execution and monitoring could pose additional challenges. In addition, we also aim at automating the process of abstracting the resources away and construct the planning instances for them that are solved individually.

References

1. Coles, A.J., Coles, A.I., Fox, M., Long, D.: Forward-chaining partial-order planning. In: Proceedings of the Twentieth International Conference on Automated Planning and Scheduling (ICAPS 2010), May 2010
2. Eyerich, P., Mattmüller, R., Röger, G.: Using the context-enhanced additive heuristic for temporal and numeric planning. In: Proceedings of the 19th International Conference on Automated Planning and Scheduling, ICAPS 2009, Thessaloniki, Greece, 19–23 September 2009 (2009)
3. Helmert, M.: The fast downward planning system. J. Artif. Intell. Res. 26, 191–246 (2006)
4. Howey, R., Long, D., Fox, M.: Validating plans with exogenous events. In: Proceedings of the 23rd Workshop of the UK Planning and Scheduling Special Interest Group (2004)

5. Koehler, J., Ottiger, D.: An AI-based approach to destination control in elevators. AI Mag. **23**(3), 59–78 (2002)
6. Niemueller, T., Karpas, E., Vaquero, T., Timmons, E.: Planning competition for logistics robots in simulation. In: WS on Planning and Robotics (PlanRob) at International Conference on Automated Planning and Scheduling (ICAPS) (2016)
7. Sacerdoti, E.D.: Planning in a hierarchy of abstraction spaces. Artif. Intell. **5**(2), 115–135 (1974)
8. Schpers, B., Niemueller, T., Lakemeyer, G., Gebser, M., Schaub, T.: ASP-based time-bounded planning for logistics robots. In: Proceedings of the Twenty-Eighth International Conference on Automated Planning and Scheduling (ICAPS 2018) (2018)
9. Smith, R.G.: The contract net protocol: high-level communication and control in a distributed problem solver. IEEE Trans. Comput. **29**(12), 1104–1113 (1980)
10. Srivastava, B., Kambhampati, S., Do, M.B.: Planning the project management way: efficient planning by effective integration of causal and resource reasoning in realplan. Artif. Intell. **131**(1–2), 73–134 (2001)

Maximizing Expected Impact in an Agent Reputation Network

Gavin Rens[1](✉), Abhaya Nayak[2], and Thomas Meyer[1]

[1] Centre for Artificial Intelligence Research - CSIR Meraka,
University of Cape Town, Cape Town, South Africa
{grens,tmeyer}@cs.uct.ac.za
[2] Macquarie University, Sydney, Australia
abhaya.nayak@mq.edu.au

Abstract. We propose a new framework for reasoning about the reputation of multiple agents, based on the partially observable Markov decision process (POMDP). It is general enough for the specification of a variety of stochastic multi-agent system (MAS) domains involving the impact of agents on each other's reputations. Assuming that an agent must maintain a good enough reputation to survive in the system, a method for an agent to select optimal actions is developed.

Keywords: Trust and reputation · Planning · Uncertainty · POMDP

1 Introduction

Autonomous agents need to deal with questions of trust and reputation in diverse domains such as e-commerce platforms, P2P file sharing systems [1,2], and distributed AI/multi-agent systems [3]. However very few computational trust/reputation frameworks can handle uncertainty in actions and observations in a principled way and yet are general enough to be useful in several domains. A partially observable Markov decision process (POMDP) [4,5] is an abstract mathematical model for reasoning about the utility of sequences of actions in stochastic domains. Although its abstract nature allows it to be applied to various domains where sequential decision-making is required, a POMDP is typically used to model a single agent. In this paper we propose to extend it in a way that it can potentially be applied in stochastic multi-agent systems where trust and reputation are an issue. We call the proposed model *Reputation Network POMDP* (*RepNet-POMDP* or simply *RepNet*).

As in the work of Pinyol et al. [6], we distinguish between the *image* of an agent (in the perception of another) and its *reputation* which is akin to a "social image". The unique features of a RepNet are: (i) it distinguishes between undirected (regular) actions and directed actions (towards a particular agent), (ii) besides the regular state transition function, it has a directed transition function for modeling the effects of reputation in interactions and (iii) its definition (and

© Springer Nature Switzerland AG 2018
F. Trollmann and A.-Y. Turhan (Eds.): KI 2018, LNAI 11117, pp. 99–106, 2018.
https://doi.org/10.1007/978-3-030-00111-7_9

usability) is arguably more intuitive than similar frameworks. Furthermore, we suggest methods for updating agents' image of each other, for learning action distributions of other agents, and for determining perceived reputations from images. We present the theory for a planning algorithm for an agent to select optimal actions in a network where reputation makes a difference.

More details can be found in the accompanying report [7].

2   RepNet-POMDP - A Proposal

We shall first introduce the basic structure of a RepNet-POMDP, then discuss matters relating to image and reputation, and finally, develop a definition for computing optimal behaviour in RepNets.

2.1   The Basis

The components of the RepNet structure will first be introduced briefly, followed by a detailed discussion of each component. A RepNet-POMDP is defined as a pair of tuples $\langle System, Agents \rangle$. $System$ specifies the aspects of the network that apply to all agents; global knowledge shared by all agents. $System :=$ $\langle G, S, A, \Omega, I, U \rangle$, where

- G is a finite set of agents $\{g, h, i, \ldots\}$.
- S is a finite set of states.
- A is the union of finite disjoint sets of *directed* actions A^d and *undirected* actions A^u.
- Ω is a finite set of observations.
- $I : G \times S \times G \times S \times A \to [-1, 1]$ is an *impact* function s.t. $I(g, s, h, s', a)$ is the impact on g in s due to h in s' performing action a.
- $U : [0, 1] \times [-1, 1] \times [-1, 1] \to [-1, 1]$ is an *image update* function used by agents when updating their image profiles s.t. $U(\alpha, r, i)$ is the new image level given learning rate α, current image level r and current impact i.

Agents specifies the names and subjective knowledge of the individual agents; individual identifiers and beliefs per agent. *Agents* $:=$ $\langle \{T_g\}, \{DT_g\}, \{O_g\}, \{AD_g^0\}, \{Img_g^0\}, \{B_g^0\} \rangle$, with the understanding that $\{X_g\}$ is shorthand for $\{X_g \mid g \in G\}$ (i.e. there is a function X for each agent in G), where

- $T_g : S \times A^u \times S \to [0, 1]$ is the *transition* function of agent g.
- $DT_g : S \times A^d \times [-1, 1] \times S \to [0, 1]$ is the *directed transition* function of agent g s.t. $DT_g(s, a^h, r, s')$ is the probability that agent g executing an action a^h in state s (directed towards agent h) will take g to state s', while g believes that agent h perceives g's reputation to be at level r. $DT_g(s, a^h, r, s') = P(s' \mid g, s, a^h, r)$, hence $\sum_{s' \in S} DT_g(s, a^h, r, s') = 1$, given some current state s, some reputation level r and some directed action a^h of g.
- O_g is g's observation function s.t. $O_g(a, o, s)$ is the probability that observation o due to action a is perceived by g in s.

- $AD_g^0 : G \times S \to \Delta(A)$ is agent g's initial *action distribution* providing g with a probability distribution over actions for each agent in each state.
- $Img_g^0 : G \times G \to [-1, 1]$ is g's initial image profile. $Img_g(h, i)$ is agent h's image in the eyes of agent i, according to g.
- $B_g^0 : G \to \Delta(S)$ is g's initial mapping from agents to belief states.

The agents in G are thought of as forming a linked group who can influence each other positively or negatively but cannot be influenced by agents outside the network. It is assumed that all action execution is synchronous, that is, one agent executes one action if and only if all agents execute one action. All actions are assumed to have an equal duration and to finish before the next actions are executed. The immediate effects of actions are also assumed to have occurred before the next actions.

All agents have shared knowledge of: the agents in the network, the set of possible states (S), the actions that can possibly be performed (A), impact of actions (I), image update function (U), the set of possible observations (Ω) and the likelihoods of perceiving them in various conditions. Other components of the structure relate to individual agents and how they model some aspect of the network: dynamics of their actions (T_g and DT_g) and observations (O_g), likelihood of actions of other agents (AD_g), beliefs about reputation (Img_g) and their initial belief states (B_g).

In this formalism, only the action distributions (AD_g), image profiles (Img_g) and set of belief states (B_g) change. All other models remain fixed.

An agent should maintain an image profile for all other agents in the network in order to guide its own behaviour. An image profile is an assignment of image levels between every ordered pair of agents. For instance, if (according to g) h's image of i ($Img_g(i, h)$) is, on average, low, g should avoid interactions with i if g has a good image of h ($Img_g(h, g)$ is high). Note that agents' multi-lateral image is not common knowledge in the network. Hence, each agent has only an *opinion* about each pair of agent's image as deemed by each other agent.

$Img_g(h, i)$ changes as agent g learns how agent i 'treats' its network neighbour h. Agent g uses U to manage the update of its levels of reputation as deemed by other agents. An agent needs to have a strategy how to build up its image profile of each other agent. Formally, there is a maximum image level of 1. We decided to define the image update function U common to all agents for the sake of simplicity, while introducing the RepNet-POMDP framework.

Actually, we define directed transitions to be conditioned on reputation (derived from images): Suppose g wants to trade with h. Agent g could perform a `tradeWith_h` action. But if h deems g's reputation to be low, h would not want to trade with g. This is an example where the effect of an action by one agent (g) depends on its level of reputation as perceived by the recipient of the action (h). Note that it does not make sense to condition the transition probability on the reputation level of the recipient as perceived by the actor (h's reputation as perceived by g in this example): The effect of an action by g should have nothing to do with h's image levels, given the *action is already committed to* by g. However, the effect of an action committed to (especially one directed towards a particular agent) may well depend on the actor's (g's) reputation levels; h may react (effect of the action) differently depending on g's reputation.

Continuing with the example, assume s' is a state in which g gets what it wanted out of a trade with h, and s is a state in which g is ready to trade. Then $DT(s, \text{tradeWith\_}h, -0.6, s')$ might equal 0.1 due to h's inferred unwillingness to trade with g due to g's current bad reputation (-0.6) as deemed by h. On the other hand, $DT(s, \text{tradeWith\_}h, 0.6, s')$ might equal 0.9 due to g's high esteem (0.6) as deemed by g and thus inferred willingness to trade with g.

We assume that every agent g has some (probabilistic) idea of what actions its neighbours will perform in a given state. As indicated earlier in Sect. 2.1, $AD_g(h, s)$ is a distribution over the actions in A that h could take when in state s. Every agent thus learns a different action distribution for its neighbours.

The other component of the structure which changes is B_g; every agent (g) maintains a probability distribution over states for every agent in G (including itself). That is, for every agent g, its belief state for every agent h ($B_g(h)$) is maintained and updated. In other words, every agent maintains a belief state representing 'where' it thinks the other agents (incl. itself) are. As actions are performed, every g updates these distributions of itself and its neighbours. In POMDP theory, probability distributions over states are called *belief states*. B_g changes via 'normal' state estimation as in regular POMDP theory.

2.2   Image and Reputation in RepNets

There are many ways in which an agent can compute reputations, given the components of a RepNet-POMDP. In this section, we investigate one approach. Recall that $AD_g(h, s)$ is the probability distribution over actions g believes h executes in s. In other words, $AD_g(h, s)(a)$ is the probability of a being executed by h in s according to g. Recall that B_g is the set of current belief states of all agents in the network, according to g. Hence, $B_g(i)$ is a belief state, and $B_g(i)(s)$ is the probability of i being in s, according to g. For better readability, we might denote $B_g(i)$ as b_i^g. Agent g perceives at some instant that i's image of h is

$$Image_g(h, i, B_g) := \sum_{s^h \in S} b_h^g(s^h) \sum_{s^i \in S} b_i^g(s^i) \sum_{a \in A} \left[\delta AD_g(i, s^i)(a) I(h, s^h, i, s^i, a) \right.$$
$$\left. + (1 - \delta) AD_g(h, s^h)(a) I(i, s^i, h, s^h, a) \right], \tag{1}$$

where $\delta \in [0, 1]$ trades off the importance of the impacts on h and impacts due to h. In (1), the uncertainty of agents h and i's states are taken into account. Note that this perceived image is independent of g's state.

Just as the state estimation function of POMDP theory updates an agent's belief state, the *image expectation* function $IE(g, Img_g, \alpha, B_g) := Img'_g$ updates an agent's image profile. That is, given g's set of belief states B_g, for all $h, i \in G$,

$$Img'_g(h, i) = U(\alpha, Img_g(h, i), Image_g(h, i, B_g)).$$

An agent g could form its opinion about h in at least three ways: (1) by observing how other agents treat h, (2) by observing how h treats other agents and (3) by noting other agents' opinion of h. But g must also consider the reasons for actions and opinions: Agent i might perform an action with a negative impact on h because i believes h has a bad reputation or simply because i is bad. We define reputation as

$$RepOf_g(h) := \frac{1}{|G|}\Big[Img_g(h,g) + \sum_{i\in G, i\neq g} Img_g(h,i) \times Img_g(i,g)\Big].$$

We have assumed that it does not make sense to weight $Img_g(h,g)$ by $Img_g(g,g)$ because it makes no sense to weight one's opinion about h's image by one's opinion of one's own image. Hence, $Img_g(h,g)$ is implicitly weighted by 1.

The simple approach above partly solves the problem of how g gets i's image in two ways. (1) i's reputation is only one of all the reputations considered by g, and g takes the *average* of all agents' opinions of g to come to a conclusion of what to think of h (h's reputation according to g). (2) Reputation is also informed by actual activity, as perceived by each agent g. Hence, every agent forms a more accurate opinion of other agents according to their *activities* (apart from received opinions). Activities inform image and image informs reputation.

2.3   Optimal Behaviour in RepNets

Advancement of an agent in RepNet-POMDPs is measured by the total impact on the agent. An agent might want to maximize the network's (positive) impact on it after several steps in the system. Intuitively, an agent g can choose its next action so as to maximize the total impact all agents will have on it in the future. Then the optimal impact function w.r.t. g over the next k steps is defined as

$$OI(g, AD_g, Img_g, B_g, k) := \max_{a\in A}\Big\{PI_{tot}(g,a,B_g)$$
$$+ \gamma \sum_{o\in\Omega} P(o \mid a, B_g)OI(g, AD_g', Img_g', B_g', k-1)\Big\},$$
$$OI(g, AD_g, Img_g, B_g, 1) := \max_{a\in A}\Big\{PI_{tot}(g,a,B_g)\Big\},$$

where $PI_{tot}(g,a,B_g)$ is the total perceived impact on g (executing a in its belief state $B_g(g)$) by the network, AD_g' is $ADE(g,o,AD_g)$ which is the action distribution expectation function that g uses to learn what actions to expect from other agents, Img_g' is $IE(g,Img_g,\alpha,B_g)$ which is the image expectation function defined above and B_g' is $BSE(g,a,o,B_g)$ which is the belief state estimation function which returns the set of belief states of all agents (from g's perspective) after the next step, determined from the current set of belief states B_g, given agent g executed a and perceived o. The definition above has a very similar form to that of the optimal value function of (regular) POMDP theory.

3 Related Work

Yu and Singh [8] develop an (uncertain) evidential model of reputation management based on the Dempster-Shafer theory. A limitation of this approach is that
it models only the uncertainty in the services received and in the trustworthiness
of neighbours who provide referrals. It does not model dynamical systems, nor
does it allow for stochastic actions and observations. Pinyol et al. [6] propose
an integration of a cognitive reputation model, called *Repage*, into a BDI agent.
With their logic, Pinyol et al. [6] can specify capabilities or services that our
framework cannot. On the other hand, their Repage + BDI architecture cannot
model noisy observations or uncertainty in state (belief states). Regan et al. [9]
aim to construct a principled framework, called *Advisor-POMDP*, for buyers to
choose the best seller based on some measure of reputation in a market consisting
of autonomous agents: a model for collecting and using reputation is developed
using a POMDP. SALE POMDP [10] is an extension of Advisor-POMDP: It
can deal with the seller selection problem by reasoning about advisor quality
and/or trustworthiness and selectively querying for information to finally selects
a seller with high quality. RepNets differ from both: a RepNet has a model for
every agent in the network, and every agent has a (subjective) view on every
other agent's belief state and action likelihood, but Advisor- and SALE POMDP
do not. Decentralized POMDPs (DEC-POMDPs) [11] are concerned more with
effective collaboration in noisy environment than with self-advancement in a
potentially unfriendly network. Interactive POMDPs (I-POMDPs) [12] are for
specifying and reasoning about multiple agents, where willingness to cooperate
is not assumed. Whereas DEC-POMDP agents do not have a model for every
other agent's belief state and action likelihood, I-POMDP agents maintain a
model of *each* agent. I-POMDPs and DEC-POMDPs do not have a notion for
trust, reputation or image. Seymour and Peterson [13] introduce notions of trust
to the I-POMDP, which they call trust-based I-POMDP (TI-POMDP). However,
there are several inconsistencies in the presentation of their framework (which
we cannot discuss due to limited space); it is thus hard to compare RepNets to
TI-POMDPs.

4 Conclusion

This paper presented a new framework, called RepNet-POMDP, for agents in a
network of self-interested agents to make considered decisions. The framework
deals with several kinds of uncertainty and facilitates agents in determining the
reputation of other agents. A method was provided for an agent to look ahead
several steps in order to choose actions in a way that will influence its reputation
so as to maximize the network's positive impact on the agent. We aimed to
make the framework easily understandable and generally applicable in systems
of multiple, self-interested agents where partial observability and stochasticity
of actions are problems.

Clearly, the computation presented here to find the optimal next action $(OI(\ldots))$ is highly intractable. Approximate methods for solving large POMDPs could be looked at to make RepNets practical [10,14].

An implementation and experimental evaluation of RepNet on benchmark problems in the area of trust and reputation is our next task in this work.

Acknowledgements. Gavin Rens was supported by a Clause Leon Foundation post-doctoral fellowship while conducting this research. This research has been partially supported by the Australian Research Council (ARC), Discovery Project: DP150104133 as well a grant from the Faculty of Science and Engineering, Macquarie University. This work is based on research supported in part by the National Research Foundation of South Africa (Grant number UID 98019). Thomas Meyer has received funding from the European Union's Horizon 2020 research and innovation programme under the Marie Sklodowska-Curie grant agr. No. 690974.

References

1. Yu, H., Shen, Z., Leung, C., Miao, C., Lesser, V.: A survey of multi-agent trust management systems. IEEE Access **1**, 35–50 (2013)
2. Pinyol, I., Sabater-Mir, J.: Computational trust and reputation models for open multi-agent systems: a review. Artif. Intell. Rev. **40**, 1–25 (2013)
3. Sabater, J., Sierra, C.: Review on computational trust and reputation models. Artif. Intell. Rev. **24**, 33–60 (2005)
4. Monahan, G.: A survey of partially observable Markov decision processes: theory, models, and algorithms. Manag. Sci. **28**(1), 1–16 (1982)
5. Lovejoy, W.: A survey of algorithmic methods for partially observed Markov decision processes. Ann. Oper. Res. **28**, 47–66 (1991)
6. Pinyol, I., Sabater-Mir, J., Dellunde, P., Paolucci, M.: Reputation-based decisions for logic-based cognitive agents. Auton. Agents Multi-Agent Syst. **24**(1), 175–216 (2012). https://doi.org/10.1007/s10458-010-9149-y
7. Rens, G., Nayak, A., Meyer, T.: Maximizing expected impact in an agent reputation network - technical report. Technical report, University of Cape Town, Cape Town, South Africa (2018). http://arxiv.org/abs/1805.05230
8. Yu, B., Singh, M.: An evidential model of distributed reputation management. In: Proceedings of the First International Conference on Autonomous Agents and Multiagent Systems, AAMAS 2002, pp. 294–301. ACM, New York (2002). http://doi.acm.org/10.1145/544741.544809
9. Regan, K., Cohen, R., Poupart, P.: The advisor-POMDP: a principled approach to trust through reputation in electronic markets. In: Conference on Privacy Security and Trust 1 (2005)
10. Irissappane, A., Oliehoek, F., Zhang, J.: A POMDP based approach to optimally select sellers in electronic marketplaces. In: Proceedings of the Thirteenth International Conference on Autonomous Agents and Multiagent Systems, AAMAS 2014, pp. 1329–1336, International Foundation for Autonomous Agents and Multiagent Systems, Richland (2014). http://dl.acm.org/citation.cfm?id=2615731.2617459
11. Bernstein, D., Zilberstein, S., Immerman, N.: The complexity of decentralized control of Markov decision processes. In: Proceedings of the Sixteenth Conference on Uncertainty in Artificial Intelligence, UAI 2000, pp. 32–37, Morgan Kaufmann Publishers Inc., San Francisco (2000). http://dl.acm.org/citation.cfm?id=2073946.2073951

12. Gmytrasiewicz, P., Doshi, P.: A framework for sequential planning in multi-agent settings. J. Artif. Intell. Res. **24**(1), 49–79 (2005). http://dl.acm.org/citation.cfm?id=1622519.1622521
13. Seymour, R., Peterson, G.: A trust-based multiagent system. In: Proceedings of International Conference on Computational Science and Engineering, pp. 109–116. IEEE (2009)
14. Gmytrasiewicz, P., Doshi, P.: Monte Carlo sampling methods for approximating interactive POMDPs. J. Artif. Intell. Res. **34**, 297–337 (2009)

Developing a Distributed Drone Delivery System with a Hybrid Behavior Planning System

Daniel Krakowczyk, Jannik Wolff, Alexandru Ciobanu, Dennis Julian Meyer, and Christopher-Eyk Hrabia[✉]

DAI-Lab, Technische Universität Berlin,
Ernst-Reuter-Platz 7, 10587 Berlin, Germany
{daniel.krakowczyk,christopher-eyk.hrabia}@dai-labor.de,
{jannik.wolff,alexandru.ciobanu,d.meyer}@campus.tu-berlin.de

Abstract. The demand for fast and reliable parcel shipping is globally rising. Conventional delivery by land requires good infrastructure and causes high costs, especially on the last mile. We present a distributed and scalable drone delivery system based on the contract net protocol for task allocation and the ROS hybrid behaviour planner (RHBP) for goal-oriented task execution. The solution is tested on a modified multi-agent systems simulation platform (MASSIM). Within this environment, the solution scales up well and is profitable across different configurations.

Keywords: Task allocation · Unmanned aerial vehicle (UAV)
Drone delivery · Multi-agent systems · Multi-agent simulation

1 Introduction

Transportation has seen substantial changes in the last decades as electronic commerce has increased the demand for quick and cost-efficient delivery [21]. Unmanned aerial vehicles such as drones could be a promising solution on the last mile. Low dependency on infrastructure constitutes a major benefit compared to conventional transportation by land [9]. Advantages in terms of speed can be exploited for special use cases such as delivery of medical products [25].

Although some drone delivery systems are already tested in the field [24], current applications focus on single or few drones. In this paper we explore a large scale application of drone delivery in a cooperative scenario. For this purpose we deployed our prototype on a modified version of the *multi-agent systems simulation platform* (MASSIM) [1] from the *Multi-Agent Programming Contest 2017 (MAPC)* as other environments focus on different use-cases [12,15]. MASSIM is a discrete and distributed last-mile delivery simulation on top of real *OpenStreetMap* data. In the simulation several teams of independent agents compete by delivering items to storages. Such delivery jobs are randomly generated and split into three categories: *Mission jobs* are compulsorily assigned, *auction jobs*

© Springer Nature Switzerland AG 2018
F. Trollmann and A.-Y. Turhan (Eds.): KI 2018, LNAI 11117, pp. 107–114, 2018.
https://doi.org/10.1007/978-3-030-00111-7_10

are assigned exclusively by prior auction and *regular jobs* are awarded to the first completing it. Jobs might consist of several items that are purchased at shops and stored at warehouses. We adjusted the simulation environment to better resemble last-mile drone delivery: other agent roles (e.g. trucks) and item assembly are neglected; an improved health- and charge-life cycle is introduced.[1]

This paper is structured as follows: The general coordination and decision-making approach is described in Sect. 2. Section 3 describes the implemented application-specific modules. An evaluation and outlook to future work follows in Sect. 4. Finally, Sect. 5 concludes the paper.

2 Approach

Although reinforcement learning promises flexible adaptation to dynamic environments, possible states and actions span an enormous space, suffering the curse of dimensionality. Additionally, the dynamic environment caused by simultaneous agent actions further complicates reinforcement learning. [5] Therefore, reinforcement learning is not considered as we aim for a more light weight solution that scales up more easily.

De Weerdt et al. [7] provide an overview of approaches in *distributed problem solving*. Market-based approaches, which are usually based on auctioning protocols, can govern task allocation [18,26]. *Hierarchical task networks* can be used to decompose tasks [11]. Georgeff [14] introduced the concept of synchronizing plans between agents to decrease dependency problems. Dependencies can also be modeled using prior constraints [16,20]. *Social laws*, which resemble real-world laws such as traffic rules, constitute another coordination technique [13]. Meta-frameworks such as *partial global planning* manage incomplete information by interleaving the stages of distributed problem solving [10].

We decided to use the contract net protocol [6] for task allocation, as this method is well-established, easy to implement, flexible, fast and light-weight. Lacking optimality is put into perspective as task-allocation is usually NP-hard [3]. The method employs negotiation among a group of agents to allocate tasks. A *manager* announces tasks which are evaluated by interested agents and bid on. The manager collects all bids and assigns the task to the winning agent, called the *contractor*. Agents can take both roles simultaneously.

Initiation of communication can be reversed in case of only few idling agents, which then announce availability and receive open tasks [27]. Further extensions focus mostly on a more robust protocol [4] by adding types of messages [2] or services for exception handling [8]. In the *contract net with confirmation protocol* (CNCP), contractors need to send a confirmation to complete the contract [19]. Also, extensions for direct negotiation in case of multiple managers exist [22].

We use the commonly applied *Robot Operating System* (ROS) [23] to simplify possible future migration to a real drone system. The RHBP adds the concept of hybrid behavior networks for decision-making and planning [17]. In RHBP,

---

[1] Modified simulation-source: https://gitlab.tubit.tu-berlin.de/mac17/massim/.

a problem is modeled with behaviors, preconditions, effects and goals, whereby conditions are expressed as a combination of virtual sensors and activation functions. Activation functions allow for a heuristic evaluation of the influence of particular information, which is gathered by a sensor.

The actual operational agent's behavior is modeled and implemented on the foundation of the RHBP base classes. This enables modeling a dependency network of conditions and effects between goals and behaviors of an agent, which results in a behavior network. The activators are applied to interpret the discretized sensor values for decision-making. The symbolic planning is automatically executed by a manager component, after it has compiled a PDDL domain and problem description from the current behavior network representation.

In RHBP, the planner is used to guide the behavior network towards a goal supporting direction instead of forcing the execution of an exact plan. This fosters opportunistic behavior for the agent. Moreover, this results in very adaptive and reactive behavior for individual agents, based on the updated perception.

3   System Design

In this section, we describe the most essential modules of our implementation.

Delivery jobs are decomposed into atomic tasks by the manager. Additionally to the associated action, each task contains a single item type and count, which in sum won't exceed any agent's capacity to ensure that tasks can be executed in a single run. All open tasks are put in a task queue, a collaborating manager-thread processes these tasks consecutively without setting any priorities between delivery tasks. Unassigned tasks are put at the end of the task queue again or are removed if their remaining time is below a threshold.

Jobs are announced sequentially by the manager, agents bid on tasks on sufficient health, energy and cargo capacity. As bid metric the anticipated amount of simulation steps for task fulfillment is used to minimize overall travel distance. The task is assigned to the eligible agent with the lowest bid, and finally acknowledged by this contractor which is in principle an implementation of CNCP [19] without the manager's accept message on agreement.

Specific RHBP behavior models are instantiated on each new assigned delivery task. An agent's goal is the completion of all assigned open delivery tasks. Agents first buy necessary items at the nearest shop and then move to the target destination for delivery. Sufficient vitality attributes (health and charge) are necessary conditions for movement behaviors. In case of failure, agents recognize expired jobs and store already bought items in the closest storage, which makes them available for later reuse. On successful delivery, task- and job-dependent RHBP-models are destructed.

Auction tasks are only announced by the task manager to the other agents if no other delivery task is open to ensure efficient utilization and low opportunity cost. Mission jobs are mandatory and thus preferred, regular jobs are time-sensitive and hence started as soon as possible. Once auctions have been won, the resulting delivery tasks possess the same priority as any other delivery. The

associated bidding behavior after assignment has two stages: start by bidding
the maximal possible amount to ensure profit maximization in scenarios with
no competitors and only bid at a computed threshold if competitors underbid.
If the competitor's bid is below this threshold, agents stop participating in the
auction due to low profitability and send a task-completion message.

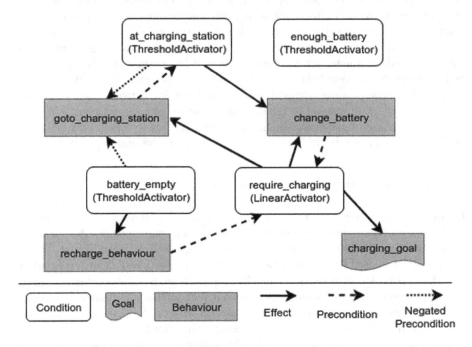

Fig. 1. Simplified RHBP model for charging behavior. Conditions are evaluated by
sensors readings, which are not displayed above for higher clarity. The condition
enough_battery is passed onto other RHBP-models.

Maintaining battery and health is crucial for all drone agents. Figure 1 exemplarily shows the RHBP model for charging behavior. In critical conditions
agents recharge or repair on place without moving to facilities at the expense of
higher costs. In moderate condition, agents move to facilities and charge or repair
until the vitality attribute is sufficient. Activation for such behaviors increases
linearly with decreasing vitality attribute. If two vitality-behaviors are equally
activated, charge-related behavior is prioritized to prevent deadlocks. Charging
using solar-panels is used as idling behavior as it is associated with no additional
costs. Idling occurs when an agent has no assigned and feasible task.

4   Evaluation and Discussion

We conducted the following experiments, each limited to 1000 simulation steps,
which corresponds to the duration in the official MAPC: three runs with team

sizes of 5, 10 and 15, two runs with team size 25 and finally two runs with two (identical and competing) teams, each having 5 agents.

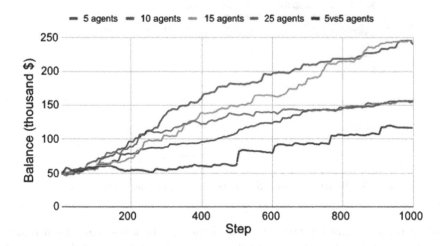

Fig. 2. Team balance in each step for varying amount of operating agents

Figure 2 shows average monetary team balance at each step, which usually consistently increases. Volatility can be explained by the noncontinuous nature of earnings and costs. Increasing the team size results in higher revenue until maximum utilization of limited resources such as jobs and facilities exceeded. In our setting, optimal team sizes lie between 10–15 agents. More drones result in higher costs while earnings remain unchanged. As we find that increasing the number of posted jobs increases optimal team size, the drone system is scalable.

Table 1. Average and standard deviation of profit per step depending on team size

Agents	Avg. ($)	Std. ($)
5	108	550
10	196	820
15	195	1001
25	105	1106
5v5	69	1008

Table 1 shows average and standard deviation of profit per step. We find that all teams in all tested configurations generate profit on average in each step. Standard deviation increases with team size as more operating agents increase overall fluctuation in earnings. Introducing competition lowers average profit per step and increases deviation. Furthermore, agents have no difficulty to stay below the required response time of four seconds, which is fixed by the simulation server. Figure 3 displays the distribution of different actions for varying team size. Recharge and movement are dominant actions. Former mostly resembles idling action and is significantly growing for increased team size.

The contract net protocol introduces some downsides that we plan to address in the future: agents bid on each task independently and currently do not anticipate future states. Therefore, general coherence and compliance with the original

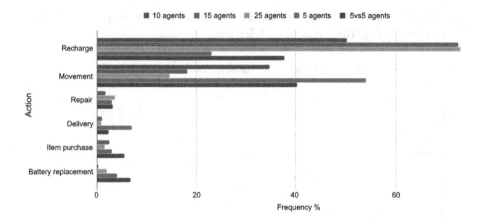

Fig. 3. Distribution of different actions depending on team size

bidding value are not guaranteed. Other issues are task manager concurrency, allocation speed, not modeled conflicts on accessing resources or delegation of tasks in case of failure or inability. Moreover, prioritizing jobs can lead to more profitability per step, especially in scenarios with small team size and many jobs. Job priority could depend on three parameters: remaining time, fee and reward. Additionally, as agents start idling on successful deliveries, clusters of agents frequently appear at targeted storages. Instead, idling agents could be repositioned in close proximity to shops to reduce future job execution time. Furthermore, instantiating job-dependent behavior models on each new task introduces perceptible delays. This can be solved by implementing more elaborate behavior models implemented as singletons. Additionally, agents sometimes turn back or take unfavorable routes for maintaining vitality. Anticipating vitality attributes and actual movement effects could correct those inefficiencies.

5   Conclusion

We developed a distributed and scalable drone system for last mile delivery and tested the implementation in the MASSIM simulation environment. Our solution combines the contract net protocol for task allocation with the RHBP framework for task execution and self maintenance. Our experiments show profitability, robustness and fast agent-response across different configurations, including competition and variable team size. We show scalability by using 25 operating agents per team. Moreover, our approach illustrates how the task-level decision-making and planning framework RHBP can be combined with decentralized task assignment in a scalable setup. Future work might focus on improving the discussed weaknesses.

References

1. MASSim: Multi-agent systems simulation platform. https://github.com/agentcontest/massim/. Accessed 13 May 2018
2. Aknine, S., Pinson, S., Shakun, M.F.: An extended multi-agent negotiation protocol. Auton. Agents Multi-Agent Syst. **8**, 5–45 (2004)
3. Amador, S., Okamoto, S., Zivan, R.: Dynamic multi-agent task allocation with spatial and temporal constraints. In: Proceedings of the 2014 International Conference on Autonomous Agents and Multi-Agent Systems, pp. 1495–1496. International Foundation for Autonomous Agents and Multiagent Systems (2014)
4. Bozdag, E.: A survey of extensions to the contract net protocol. Technical report, CiteSeerX-Scientific Literature Digital Library and Search Engine (2008)
5. Busoniu, L., Babuska, R., De Schutter, B.: A comprehensive survey of multiagent reinforcement learning. IEEE Trans Syst. Man Cybern. Part C **38**(2), 156–172 (2008)
6. Davis, R., Smith, R.G., Erman, L.: Negotiation as a metaphor for distributed problem solving. In: Readings in Distributed Artificial Intelligence, pp. 333–356. Elsevier (1988)
7. De Weerdt, M., Clement, B.: Introduction to planning in multiagent systems. Multiagent Grid Syst. **5**(4), 345–355 (2009)
8. Dellarocas, C., Klein, M., Rodriguez-Aguilar, J.A.: An exception-handling architecture for open electronic marketplaces of contract net software agents. In: Proceedings of the 2nd ACM Conference on Electronic Commerce, pp. 225–232. ACM (2000)
9. Dorling, K., Heinrichs, J., Messier, G.G., Magierowski, S.: Vehicle routing problems for drone delivery. IEEE Trans. Syst. Man Cybern.: Syst. **47**(1), 70–85 (2017)
10. Durfee, E., Lesser, V.: Partial global planning: a coordination framework for distributed hypothesis formation. IEEE Trans. Syst. Man Cybern. **21**(5), 1167–1183 (1991)
11. Erol, K., Hendler, J., Nau, D.S.: HTN planning: complexity and expressivity. In: AAAI, vol. 94, pp. 1123–1128 (1994)
12. Ettlinger, M., Sarp, B., Hrabia, C.E., Albayrak, S.: An evaluation framework for UAV surveillance applications. In: The 31st Annual European Simulation and Modelling Conference 2017, pp. 356–362, October 2017
13. Fitoussi, D., Tennenholtz, M.: Choosing social laws for multi-agent systems: minimality and simplicity. Artif. Intell. **119**(1–2), 61–101 (2000)
14. Georgeff, M.: Communication and interaction in multi-agent planning. In: Proceedings of the National Conference on Artificial Intelligence. Elsevier (1984)
15. Happe, J., Berger, J.: CoUAV: a multi-UAV cooperative search path planning simulation environment. In: Proceedings of the 2010 Summer Computer Simulation Conference, pp. 86–93. Society for Computer Simulation International (2010)
16. Hirayama, K., Yokoo, M.: Distributed partial constraint satisfaction problem. In: Smolka, G. (ed.) CP 1997. LNCS, vol. 1330, pp. 222–236. Springer, Heidelberg (1997). https://doi.org/10.1007/BFb0017442
17. Hrabia, C.E., Wypler, S., Albayrak, S.: Towards goal-driven behaviour control of multi-robot systems. In: 2017 3rd International Conference on Control, Automation and Robotics (ICCAR), pp. 166–173. IEEE (2017)
18. Jones, E.G., Dias, M.B., Stentz, A.: Learning-enhanced market-based task allocation for oversubscribed domains. In: 2007 IEEE/RSJ International Conference on Intelligent Robots and Systems, IROS 2007, pp. 2308–2313. IEEE (2007)

19. Knabe, T., Schillo, M., Fischer, K.: Improvements to the FIPA contract net protocol for performance increase and cascading applications, October 2002
20. Liu, J., Jing, H., Tang, Y.Y.: Multi-agent oriented constraint satisfaction. Artif. Intell. **136**(1), 101–144 (2002)
21. Morganti, E., Seidel, S., Blanquart, C., Dablanc, L., Lenz, B.: The impact of e-commerce on final deliveries: alternative parcel delivery services in France and Germany. Transp. Res. Procedia **4**, 178–190 (2014)
22. Panescu, D., Pascal, C.: An extended contract net protocol with direct negotiation of managers. In: Borangiu, T., Trentesaux, D., Thomas, A. (eds.) Service Orientation in Holonic and Multi-Agent Manufacturing and Robotics. SCI, vol. 544, pp. 81–95. Springer, Cham (2014). https://doi.org/10.1007/978-3-319-04735-5_6
23. Quigley, M., et al.: ROS: an open-source robot operating system. In: ICRA Workshop on Open Source Software, Kobe, Japan, vol. 3, p. 5 (2009)
24. Scott, J., Scott, C.: Drone delivery models for healthcare (2017)
25. Thiels, C.A., Aho, J.M., Zietlow, S.P., Jenkins, D.H.: Use of unmanned aerial vehicles for medical product transport. Air Med. J. **34**(2), 104–108 (2015)
26. Walsh, W.E., Wellman, M.P.: A market protocol for decentralized task allocation. In: 1998 Proceedings of the International Conference on Multi Agent Systems, pp. 325–332. IEEE (1998)
27. Weiss, G.: Multiagent Systems: A Modern Approach to Distributed Artificial Intelligence. MIT Press, Cambridge (1999)

Robotics

A Sequence-Based Neuronal Model
for Mobile Robot Localization

Peer Neubert[1,2]($\boxtimes$), Subutai Ahmad[2], and Peter Protzel[1]

[1] Chemnitz University of Technology, 09126 Chemnitz, Germany
peer.neubert@etit.tu-chemnitz.de
[2] Numenta, Inc., Redwood City, CA, USA

Abstract. Inferring ego position by recognizing previously seen places in the world is an essential capability for autonomous mobile systems. Recent advances have addressed increasingly challenging recognition problems, e.g. long-term vision-based localization despite severe appearance changes induced by changing illumination, weather or season. Since robots typically move continuously through an environment, there is high correlation within consecutive sensory inputs and across similar trajectories. Exploiting this sequential information is a key element of some of the most successful approaches for place recognition in changing environments. We present a novel, neurally inspired approach that uses sequences for mobile robot localization. It builds upon Hierarchical Temporal Memory (HTM), an established neuroscientific model of working principles of the human neocortex. HTM features two properties that are interesting for place recognition applications: (1) It relies on sparse distributed representations, which are known to have high representational capacity and high robustness towards noise. (2) It heavily exploits the sequential structure of incoming sensory data. In this paper, we discuss the importance of sequence information for mobile robot localization, we provide an introduction to HTM, and discuss theoretical analogies between the problem of place recognition and HTM. We then present a novel approach, applying a modified version of HTM's higher order sequence memory to mobile robot localization. Finally we demonstrate the capabilities of the proposed approach on a set of simulation-based experiments.

Keywords: Mobile robot localization
Hierarchical temporal memory · Sequence-based localization

1 Introduction

We describe the application of a biologically detailed model of sequence memory in the human neocortex to mobile robot localization. The goal is to exploit the sequence processing capabilities of the neuronal model and its powerful sparse distributed representations to address particularly challenging localization tasks. Mobile robot localization is the task of determining the current position of the robot relative to its own prior experience or an external reference frame (e.g.

© Springer Nature Switzerland AG 2018
F. Trollmann and A.-Y. Turhan (Eds.): KI 2018, LNAI 11117, pp. 117–130, 2018.
https://doi.org/10.1007/978-3-030-00111-7_11

a map). Due to its fundamental importance for any robot aiming at performing meaningful tasks, mobile robot localization is a long studied problem, going back to visual landmark-based navigation in Shakey the robot in the 1960–80s [1]. Research has progressed rapidly over the last few decades and it has become possible to address increasingly challenging localization tasks. The problem of localization in the context of changing environments, e.g. recognizing a cloudy winter scene which has been seen previously on a sunny summer day, has only recently been studied [2,3]. In most applications, the robot's location changes smoothly and there are no sudden jumps to other places (the famous kidnapped robot problem appears only rarely in practice [4]). Therefore a key element of some of the most successful approaches is to exploit the temporal consistency of observations.

In this paper, we present a localization approach that takes inspiration from sequence processing in Hierarchical Temporal Memory (HTM) [5–7], a model of working principles of the human neocortex. The underlying assumption in HTM is that there is a single cortical learning algorithm that is applied everywhere in the neocortex. Two fundamental working principles of this algorithm are to learn from sequences to predict future neuronal activations and to use sparse distributed representations (SDRs). In Sect. 2 we first provide a short overview of recent methods to exploit sequential information for robot localization. In Sect. 3 we provide an overview of the HTM sequence memory algorithm. In Sect. 4 we show how HTM's higher order sequence memory can be applied to the task of mobile robot place recognition[1]. We identify a weakness of the existing HTM approach for place localization and discuss an extension of the original algorithm. We discuss theoretical analogies of HTM and the problem of place recognition, and finally provide initial experimental results on simulated data in Sect. 5.

2   On the Importance of Sequences for Robot Localization

Mobile robot localization comprises different tasks, ranging from recognizing an already visited place to simultaneously creating a map of an unknown area while localizing in this map (known as SLAM). The former task is known as place recognition problem or loop closure detection. A survey is provided in [8]. A solution to this problem is fundamental for solving the full SLAM problem. The research progress in this area recently reached a level where it is feasible to think about place recognition in environments with significantly changing appearances. For example, camera based place recognition under changing lighting condition, changing weather, and even across different seasons [2,3]. In individual camera images of a scene, the appearance changes can be tremendous. In our own prior work and others, the usage of sophisticated landmark detectors and deep-learning-based descriptors showed to be a partial solution of this task [9]. However, with increasing severity of the appearance changes, making the localization decision purely based on individual images is more and more pushed to its limits.

---

[1] An open source implementation is available:
https://www.tu-chemnitz.de/etit/proaut/seqloc.

The benefit of exploiting sequence information is well accepted in the literature [2, 10–14]. In 2012, Milford et al. [2] presented a simple yet effective way to exploit the sequential character of the percepts of the environment. Given two sequences of images, captured during two traversals through the same environment, the task is to make a decision, which image pairs show the same place. In their experiments one sequence is from a sunny summer day and the other from a stormy winter night. To address this challenging problem, the pairwise similarity of images from the two runs is collected in a matrix. Instead of evaluating each entry individually, Milford et al. [2] propose to search for linear segments of high similarity in this matrix (this also involves a local contrast normalization). This approach significantly improved the state of the art at this time. However, searching for linear segments in this matrix poses important limitations on the data: the data on both environmental traverses has to be captured at the same number of frames per traveled distance. This is usually violated in practice, e.g., if the vehicle's velocity changes. Therefore, several extensions have been proposed. E.g., allowing non-zero acceleration [12] or searching for optimal paths in the similarity matrix using a graph-theoretical max-flow formulation [13]. Localization approaches that include the creation of a map inherently exploit the sequential nature of the data. Simultaneous creation of a map while localizing in this map exploits sequence information by creating a prior for the current position based on the previous data. However, this is equivalent to solving the full SLAM problem and involves maintaining a map of the environments. A particular challenge for SLAM are the consistency of the map after closing long loops and the increasing size and complexity of the map in large environments. One elegant approach to the latter problem is RatSLAM [14]; it uses a finite space representation to encode the pose in an infinite world. The idea is inspired by entorhinal grid cells in the rat's brain. They encode poses similar to a residual number system in math by using the same representatives (i.e. cells) for multiple places in the world. In RatSLAM, grid cells are implemented in form of a three dimensional continuous attractor network (CAN) with wrap-around connections; one dimension for each degree of freedom of the robot. The activity in the CAN is moved based on proprioceptive clues of the robot (e.g. wheel encoders) and new energy is injected by connections from local view cells that encode the current visual input, as well as from previously created experiences. The dynamics of the CAN apply a temporal filter on the sensory data. Only in case of repeated consistent evidence for recognition of a previously seen place, this matching is also established in the CAN representation. Although the complexity and number of parameters of this system prevented a wider application, RatSLAM's exploitation of sequence information allowed to demonstrate impressive navigation results.

3 Introduction to HTM

Hierarchical Temporal Memory (HTM) [7] is a model of working principles of the human neocortex. It builds upon the assumption of a single learning algorithm that is deployed all over the neocortex. The basic theoretical framework builds upon Hawkins' book from 2004 [15]. It is continuously evolving, with the goal to explain more and more aspects of the neocortex as well as extending the range of practical demonstrations and applications. Currently, these applications include anomaly detection, natural language processing and, very recently, object detection [16]. A well maintained implementation is available [17].

Although the system is continuously evolving, there is a set of entrenched fundamental concepts. Two of them are (1) the exploitation of sequence information and (2) the usage of Sparse Distributed Representations (SDRs). The potential benefit of the first concept for mobile robot localization has been elaborated in the previous section. The latter concept, SDRs, also showed to be beneficial in various fields. A SDR is a high dimensional binary vector (e.g. 2,048 dimensional) with very few 1-bits (e.g. 2%). There is evidence that SDRs are a widely used representation in brains due to their representation capacity, robustness to noise and power efficiency [18]. They are a special case of hypervector encodings, which we previously used to learn simple robot behavior by imitation learning [19].

From HTM, we want to exploit the concept of higher order sequence memory for our localization task. It builds on a set of neuronal cells with connection and activation patterns that are closer to the biological paragon than, e.g., a multi-layer perceptron or a convolutional neural network. Nevertheless, for these structures, there are compact and clear algorithmic implementations.

3.1   Mimicking Neuroanatomic Structures

The anatomy of the neocortex obeys a regular structure with several horizontal layers, each composed by vertically arranged minicolumns with multiple cells. In HTM, each cell incorporates dendritic properties of pyramidal cells [20]. Feed-forward inputs (e.g. perception clues) are integrated through proximal dendrites. Basal and apical dendrites provide feedback modulatory input. Feed-forward input can activate cells and modulatory input can predict activations of cells. Physiologically, predicted cells are depolarized and fire sooner than non-depolarized cells. Modulatory dendrites consist of multiple segments. Each segment can connect to a different set of cells and responds to an individual activation pattern. The dendrite becomes active if any of its segments is active. All cells in a minicolumn share the same feed-forward input, thus all cells in an minicolumn become potentially active if the feed-forward connections perceive a matching input pattern. From these potentially active cells, the actual active cells (coined winner cells) are selected based on the modulatory connections. In HTM theory, the modulatory connections provide context information for the current feed-forward input. At each timestep, multiple cells in multiple minicolumns are active and the state of the system is represented by this sparse code. For description of HTM theory and current developments please refer to [15,21].

3.2   Simplified Higher Order Sequence Memory (SHOSM)

In the following, we will give details on a particular algorithm from HTM: higher order sequence memory [5,6]. We will explain a simplified version that we abbreviate SHOSM. For those who are familiar with HTM: the simplifications include the absence of a spatial pooler and segments, the usage of one-shot learning instead of Hebbian-like learning, and SHOSM does not start from a randomly initialized set of minicolumns (whose connections are adapted) but starts from an empty set of minicolumns and increases the number of minicolumns on demand. Goal of the higher order sequence memory is to process an incoming sensor data stream in a way that similar input sequences create similar representations within the network - this matches very well to the sequence-based localization problem formulation. The listing in Algorithm 1 describes the operations:

Algorithm 1. SHOSM - Simplified HTM higher order sequence memory

---

Data: I^t the current input; M a potentially empty set of existing minicolumns; C_{winner}^{t-1} the set of winner cells from the previous time step
Result: M with updated states of all cells; C_{winner}^t

1   $M_{active}^t = match(I^t, M)$ // Find the active minicolumns based on similarity to feed-forward SDR input

// If there are no similar minicolumns: create new minicolumns
2   if $isempty(M_{active}^t)$ then
3      $M_{active}^t = createMinicolumns(I^t)$ // Each new minicolumn samples connections to 1-bits in I^t
4      $M = M \cup M_{active}^t$

// Identify winner cell(s) in each minicolumn based on predictions
5   foreach $m \in M_{active}^t$ do
6      $C_{predicted}^t = getPredictedCells(m)$ // Get set of predicted cells from this active minicolumn m
7      $M = activatePredictions(C_{predicted}^t)$ // Predict for next timestep
8      $C_{winner}^t \mathrel{+}= C_{predicted}^t$ // The predicted cells are also winner cells

// If there are no predicted cells: burst and select new winner
9   if $isempty(C_{predicted}^t)$ then
10         $M = activatePredictions(m)$ // Bursting: Activate all predictions of cells in m for next timestep
11         $C_{winner}^t \mathrel{+}= selectWinner(m)$ // Select cell with the fewest predictive forward connections as winner cell

// Learn predictions: prev. winner cells shall predict current
12   foreach $c \in C_{winner}$ do
13         $learnConnections(c, C_{winner}^{t-1})$ // Given the current winning cell c and the set of previously winning cells C_{winner}^{t-1}: for all cells $c_{winner}^{t-1} \in C_{winner}^{t-1}$ for which there is not already a connection from their minicolumns to the cell c, create the prediction connections $c_{winner}^{t-1} \to c$ (one shot learning)

At each timestep, input is an SDR encoding of the current input (e.g. the current camera image). For details on SDRs and possible encodings please refer to [18,22]. Please keep in mind that all internal representations in Algorithm 1 are SDRs: there are always multiple cells from multiple minicolumns active in parallel. Although the same input is represented by multiple minicolumns, each minicolumn connects only to a fraction of the dimensions of the input SDR and is thus affected differently by noise or errors in the input data. The noise robustness of this system is a statistical property of the underlying SDR representation [18].

In each iteration of SHOSM, a sparse set of winner cells based on the feed-forward SDR input and modulatory input from the previous iteration is computed (lines 8 and 11). Further, the *predicted* attribute of cells is updated to provide the modulatory input for the next iteration (lines 7 and 10). This modulatory prediction is the key element to represent sequences. In case of no predicted cells in an active minicolumn (line 9), all cells activate their predictions and a single winner cell is selected (this mechanism is called *bursting*). This corresponds to current input data that has never been seen in this sequence context before.

This short description of the algorithm lacks many implementation details, e.g. how exactly the connections are sampled or how ties during bursting are resolved. For full details, please refer to the available Matlab source code (cf. Sect. 1) that enables to recreate our results. The following section explains the application and adaptation of this algorithm for mobile robot localization.

4   Using HTM's Higher Order Sequence Memory for Mobile Robot Localization

4.1   Overview

Figure 1 illustrates how HTM's higher order sequence memory is used for place recognition. Let us think of a robot that explores a new environment using a camera. It starts with an empty database and iteratively processes new image data while moving through the world. For each frame (or each n-th frame) it has to decide, whether the currently perceived scene is already in the database or not. This poses a set of binary decision problems, one for each image pair. The similarity matrix on the right side of Fig. 1 illustrates the possible outcome: each entry is the similarity of a current query image to a database image. To obtain binary decisions, a threshold on the similarity can be used. If we think of a continuously moving robot, it is useful to include information of previous frames to create these similarity values (cf. Sect. 2 on sequence-based localization).

On an abstract level, the state of the cells in SHOSM (variable M in Algorithm 1) is an encoding for the current input data in the context of previous observations. In terms of mobile robot localization, it provides an encoding of the currently observed place in the context of the prior trajectory to reach this place. All that remains to be done to use SHOSM for this task is to provide input and output interfaces. SHOSM requires the input to be encoded as sparse distributed representations. For example, we can think of a holistic encoding of the current camera image. More sophisticated encodings could also include local features and their relative arrangement similar to recent developments of

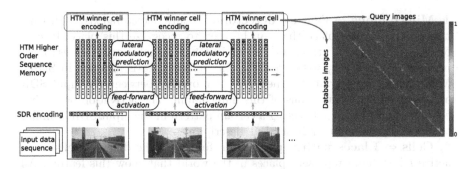

Fig. 1. Place recognition based on SHOSM winner cells. *(left)* Each frame of the input data sequence is encoded in form of a SDR and provides feed-forward input to the minicolumns. Between subsequent frames, active cells predict the activation of cells in the next time step. Output representation is the set of winner cells. *(right)* Example similarity matrix for a place recognition experiment with 4 loops (visible as (minor) diagonals with high similarity). The similarities are obtained from SDR overlap of the sparse vector of winner cells.

HTM theory [16]. For several datatypes there are SDR encoders available [22]. Currently, for complex data like images and point clouds, there are no established SDR encoders, but there are several promising directions, e.g. descriptors based on sparse coding or sparsified descriptors from Convolutional Neural Networks [23]. Moreover, established binary descriptors like BRIEF or BRISK can presumably be sparsified using HTM's spatial pooler algorithm [7].

Output of SHOSM are the states of the cells, in particular a set of current winner cells. This is a high dimensional, sparse, binary code and the decision about place associations can be based on the similarity of these codes (e.g. using overlap of 1-bits [18]). If an input SDR activates existing minicolumns, this corresponds to observing an already known feature. If we also expected to see this feature (i.e. there are predicted cells in the active minicolumn), then this is evidence for revisiting a known place. The activation of the predicted cells yields a similar output code as at the previous visits of this place - this results in a high value in the similarity matrix. If there are no predicted cells, this is evidence for observation of a known feature at a novel place - thus unused (or rarely used) cells in these minicolumns become winner cells (cf. line 11 in Algorithm 1). If there is no active minicolumn, we observe an unseen feature and store this feature in the database by creating a new set of minicolumns.

Using these winner-cell codes instead of the input SDRs directly, incorporates sequence information in the binary decision process. Experimental evidence for the benefit of this information will be provided in Sect. 5.

4.2 Theoretical Analogies of HTM and Place Recognition

This section discusses interesting theoretical association of aspects of HTM theory and the problem of mobile robot localization.

1. Minicolumns ⇔ Feature detectors. Feature detectors extract distinctive properties of a place that can be used to recognize this place. In case of visual localization, this can be, for instance, a holistic CNN descriptor or a set of SIFT keypoints. In HTM, the sensor data is encoded in SDRs. Minicolumns are activated if there is a high overlap between the input SDR and the sampled connections of this minicolumn. The activation of a minicolumn corresponds to detecting a certain pattern in the input SDR - similar to detecting a certain CNN or SIFT descriptor.

2. Cells ⇔ Places with a particular feature. The different cells in an active minicolumn represent places in the world that show this feature. All cells in a minicolumn are potentially activated by the same current SDR input, but in different context. In the above example of input SDR encodings of holistic image descriptors, the context is the sequence of encodings of previously seen images. In the example of local features and iteratively attending to individual features, the context is the sequence of local features.

3. Minicolumn sets ⇔ Ensemble classifier. The combination of information from multiple minicolumns shares similarities to ensemble classifiers. Each minicolumn perceives different information of the input SDR (since they are not fully connected but sample connections) and has an individual set of predictive lateral connections. The resulting set of winner cells combines information from all minicolumns. If the overlap metric (essentially a binary dot product) is used to evaluate this sparse result vector, this corresponds to collecting votes from all winner cells. In particular, minicolumn ensembles share some properties of bagging classifiers [24] which, for instance, can average the outcome of multiple weak classifiers. However, unlike bagging, minicolumn ensembles do not create subsets of the training data with resampling, but use subsets of the input dimensions.

4. Context segments ⇔ Paths to a place. Different context segments correspond to different paths to the same place. In the neurophysiological model, there are multiple lateral context segments for each cell. Each segment represents a certain context that preceded the activation of this cell. Since each place in the database is represented by a set of cells in different minicolumns, the different segments correspond to different paths to this place. If one of the segments is active, the corresponding cell becomes predicted.

5. Feed-forward segments ⇔ Different appearances of a place. Although it is not supported by the neurophysiological model, there is another interesting association: If there were multiple feed-forward segments, they could be used to represent different appearances of the same place. Each feed-forward segment could respond to a certain appearance of the place and the knowledge about context of this place would be shared across all appearances. This is not implemented in the current system.

4.3   rSHOSM: SHOSM with Additional Randomized Connections

Beyond the simplification of the higher order sequence memory described in Sect. 3.2 we propose another beneficial modification of the original algorithm.

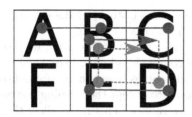 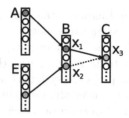

Fig. 2. *(left)* Toy example that motivates rSHOSM. See text for details. *(right)* Illustration of the loss of sequence information in case of multiple lateral connections from different cells x_1, x_2 of one minicolumn representing place B to a cell x_3. If the dotted connection from x_2 to x_3 exists, we can not distinguish the sequences (A, B, C) and (E, B, C) from an activation of x_3. Please keep in mind that in the actual system many parallel active minicolumns contribute to the representation of elements and sequences; for simplification, only a single minicolumn per element is shown. (Color figure online)

The original SHOSM algorithm is designed to provide an individual representation of each element of a sequence dependent on its context. If anything in the context is changed, the representation also changes completely.

Figure 2 illustrates this on a toy grid world with places A-F. What happens if a robot follows the red loopy trajectory $ABCDEBC$? At the first visit of place B, a representation is created that encodes B in the context of the previous observation A, lets write this as B_A. This encoding corresponds to a set of winner cells. At the second visit of place B, there is a different context: the whole previous sequence $ABCDE$, resulting in an encoding B_{ABCDE}. The encodings B_A and B_{ABCDE} share the same set of active minicolumns (those that represent the appearance of place B) but completely different winner cells (since they encode the context). Thus, place B can not be recognized based on winner cells.

Interestingly, the encodings of C_{AB} and C_{ABCDEB} are identical. This is due to the effect of bursting: Since B is not predicted after the sequence $ABCDE$, all cells in minicolumns that correspond to B activate their predictions, including those who predict C (line 10 in Algorithm 1). Thus, the place recognition problem appears only for the first place of such a loopy sequence. Unfortunately, this situation becomes worse if we revisit places multiple times, which is typical for a robot operating over a longer period of time in the same environment. The creation of unwanted unique representations for the same place affects one additional place each iteration through the sequence. For example, if the robot extends its trajectory to the blue path in Fig. 2, there will be a unique (not-recognizable) representation for places B and C at this third revisit. At a fourth revisit, there will be unique representations for B, C and D and so on.

Algorithmically, this is the result from a restriction on the learning of connections in line 14 of Algorithm 1: If the previously active minicolumn already has a connection to the currently active cell, then no new connection is created. Figure 2 illustrates the situation. This behavior is necessary to avoid that two cells x_1, x_2 of a minicolumn predict the same cell x_3 in another minicolumn. If this would happen, the context (i.e., the sequence history) of the cell x_3 could not be distinguished between the contexts from cells x_1 and x_2.

To increase the recognition capabilities in such repeated revisits, we propose to alleviate the restriction on the learning of connections in line 14 of Algorithm 1: Since the proposed systems evaluates place matchings based on an ensemble decision (spread over all minicolumns), we propose to except the learning restriction for a small portion of lateral connections by chance. This is, to allow the creation of an additional new connection from a minicolumn to a cell, e.g., with a 5% probability (i.e., to add the dotted connection from cell x_2 to x_3 in Fig. 2). Thus, some of the cells that contribute to the representation of a sequence element, do not provide a unique context but unify different possible contexts. This increases the similarity of altered sequences at the cost of reducing the amount of contained context. Since creating this connection once, introduces ambiguity for *all* previous context information for this cell, the probability of creating the additional connection should be low. This slightly modified version of the simplified higher order sequence memory is coined rSHOSM. The difference between SHOSM and rSHOSM is experimentally evaluated in the next section.

5   Experimental Results

In this section, we demonstrate the benefit of the additional randomized connections from the previous Sect. 4.3 and compare the presented approach against a baseline algorithm in a set of simulated place recognition experiments. We simulate a traversal through a 2D environment. The robot is equipped with a sensor that provides a 2,048 dimensional SDR for each place in the world; different places are grid-like arranged in the world. Using such a simulated sensor, we circumvent the encoding of typical sensor data (e.g. images or laser scans) and can directly influence the distinctiveness of sensor measurements (place-aliasing: different places share the same SDR) and the amount of noise in each individual measurement (repeated observations of the same place result in somewhat different measurements). Moreover, the simulation provides perfect ground-truth information about place matchings for evaluation using precision-recall curves: Given the overlap of winner cell encodings between all pairings in the trajectory (the similarity matrix of Fig. 1), a set of thresholds is used, each splitting the pairings into matchings and non-matchings. Using the ground-truth information, precision and recall are computed. Each threshold results in one point on the precision-recall curves. For details on this methodology, please refer to [9].

Parameters are set as follows: input SDR size is 2,048; # 1-Bits in input SDR is 40; #cells per minicolumn is 32; #new minicolumns (Algorithm 1, line 3) is 10; connectivity rate input SDR - minicolumn is 50%; and threshold on SDR overlap for active minicolumns is 25%.

5.1   Evaluation of Additional Randomized Connections in rSHOSM

To demonstrate the benefit of the additional randomized connections in rSHOSM, we simulate a robot trajectory with 10 loops (each place in the loop

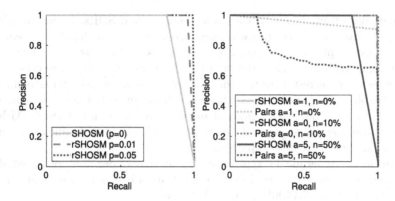

Fig. 3. *(left)* Benefit of the randomized connections in rSHOSM (with probabilities 0.01 and 0.05 of additional connections). This experiment does not involve noise or place-aliasing. *(right)* Comparison of the proposed rSHOSM with a baseline pairwise comparison in three differently challenging experiments. Parameter a is the amount of aliasing (the number of pairs of places with the same SDR representation) and n is the amount of observation noise (percentage of moved 1-bits in the SDR). In both plots, top-right is better. (Color figure online)

is visited 10 times), resulting in a total of 200 observations. In this experiment, there are neither measurement noise nor place-aliasing in the simulated environment. The result can be seen on the left side of Fig. 3. Without the additional randomized connections, recall is reduced since previously seen places get new representations dependent on their context (cf. Sect. 4.3).

5.2 Place Recognition Performance

This section shows results demonstrating the beneficial properties of the presented neurally inspired place recognition approach: increased robustness to place-aliasing and observation noise. Therefore, we compare the results to a simple baseline approach: brute-force pairwise comparison of the input SDR encodings provided by the simulated sensor. The right side of Fig. 3 shows the resulting curves for three experimental setups (each shown in a different color). We use the same trajectory as in the previous section but vary the amount of observation noise and place-aliasing. The noise parameter n controls the ratio of 1-bits that are erroneously moved in the observed SDR. For instance, $n = 50\%$ indicates that 20 of the 40 1-bits in the 2,048 dimensional input vector are moved to a random position. Thus, only 20 of the 2,048 dimensions can contribute to the overlap metric to activate minicolumns. The place-aliasing parameter a counts the number of pairs of places in the world which look exactly the same (except for measurement noise). For instance, $a = 5$ indicates that there are 5 pairs of such places and each of these places is visited 10 times in our 10-loops trajectory.

Without noise and place-aliasing, the baseline approach provides perfect results (not shown). In case of measurement noise (red curves), both approaches are amost not effected, due to the noise robustness of SDRs. In case of place-aliasing (yellow curves), the pairwise comparison can not distinguish the equivalently appearing places resulting in reduced precision. In these two experiments with small disturbances, the presented rSHOSM approach is not affected. The blue curves show the results from a challenging combination of high place-aliasing and severe observation noise - a combination that is expected in challenging real world place recognition tasks. Both algorithms are affected, but rSHOSM benefits from the usage of sequential information and performs significantly better than the baseline pairwise comparison.

In the above experiments, typical processing time of our non-optimized Matlab implementation of rSHOSM for one observation is about 8 ms using a standard laptop with an i7-7500U CPU @ 2.70 GHz.

6   Discussion and Conclusion

The previous sections discussed the usage of HTM's higher order sequence memory for visual place recognition, described the algorithmic implementation and motivated the system with a discussion of theoretical properties and some experimental results where the proposed approach outperformed a baseline place recognition algorithm. However, all experiments used simulated data. The performance on real world data still has to be evaluated. Presumably, the presented benefit above the baseline could also be achieved with other existing techniques (e.g. SeqSLAM). It will be interesting to see, whether the neurally inspired approach can address some of the shortcomings of these alternative approaches (cf. Sect. 2). Such an experimental comparison to other existing place recognition techniques should also include a more in-depth evaluation of the parameter of the presented system. For the presented initial experiments, no parameter optimization was involved. We used default parameters from HTM literature (which in turn are motivated by neurophysiological findings).

The application on real data poses the problem of suitable SDR encoders for typical robot sensors like cameras and laser scanners - an important direction for future work. Based on our previous experience with visual feature detectors and descriptors [3,9,23], we think this is also as a chance to design and learn novel descriptors that exploit the beneficial properties of sparse distributed representations (SDRs). An interesting direction for future work would also be to incorporate recent developments on HTM theory on processing of local features with additional location information - similar in spirit to image keypoints (e.g. SIFT) that are established for various mobile robot navigation tasks.

Although, the presented place recognition approach is inspired by a theory of the neocortex, we do not claim that place recognition in human brains actually uses the presented algorithm. There is plenty of evidence [25] of structures like entorhinal grid cells, place cells, head direction cells, speed cells and so on, that are involved in mammal navigation and are not regarded in this work.

The algorithm itself also has potential theoretical limitations that require further investigation. For example, one simplification from the original HTM higher order sequence memory is the creation of new minicolumns for unseen observation instead of using a fixed set of minicolumns. This allows a simple one-shot learning of associations between places. In a practical system the maximum number of minicolumns should be limited. Presumably, something like the Hebbian-like learning in the original system could be used to resemble existing minicolumns. It would be interesting to evaluate the performance of the system closer to the capacity limit of the representation.

Finally, SDRs provide interesting theoretical regarding runtime and energy efficiency. However, this requires massively parallel implementations on special hardware. Although this is far beyond the scope of this paper, in the future, this might become a unique selling point for deployment of these algorithms on real robots.

References

1. Nilsson, N.J.: Shakey the robot. Technical report 323, AI Center, SRI International, Menlo Park, April 1984
2. Milford, M., Wyeth, G.F.: SeqSLAM: visual route-based navigation for sunny summer days and stormy winter nights. In: Proceedings of International Conference on Robotics and Automation (ICRA), pp. 1643–1649. IEEE (2012)
3. Neubert, P.: Superpixels and their application for visual place recognition in changing environments. Ph.D. thesis, Chemnitz University of Technology (2015). http://nbn-resolving.de/urn:nbn:de:bsz:ch1-qucosa-190241
4. Engelson, S., McDermott, D.: Error correction in mobile robot map-learning. In: International Conference on Robotics and Automation (ICRA), pp. 2555–2560 (1992)
5. Hawkins, J., Ahmad, S.: Why neurons have thousands of synapses, a theory of sequence memory in neocortex. Front. Neural Circuits **10**, 23 (2016). https://www.frontiersin.org/article/10.3389/fncir.2016.00023
6. Cui, Y., Ahmad, S., Hawkins, J.: Continuous online sequence learning with an unsupervised neural network model. Neural Comput. **28**(11), 2474–2504 (2016)
7. Hawkins, J., Ahmad, S., Purdy, S., Lavin, A.: Biological and machine intelligence (BAMI) (2016). https://numenta.com/resources/biological-and-machine-intelligence/. Initial online release 0.4
8. Lowry, S., et al.: Visual place recognition: a survey. Trans. Rob. **32**(1), 1–19 (2016)
9. Neubert, P., Protzel, P.: Beyond holistic descriptors, keypoints, and fixed patches: multiscale superpixel grids for place recognition in changing environments. IEEE Robot. Autom. Lett. **1**(1), 484–491 (2016)
10. Cadena, C., Galvez-López, D., Tardos, J.D., Neira, J.: Robust place recognition with stereo sequences. IEEE Trans. Robot. **28**(4), 871–885 (2012)
11. Ho, K.L., Newman, P.: Detecting loop closure with scene sequences. Int. J. Comput. Vis. **74**(3), 261–286 (2007)
12. Johns, E., Yang, G.: Dynamic scene models for incremental, long-term, appearance-based localisation. In: Proceedings of International Conference on Robotics and Automation (ICRA), pp. 2731–2736. IEEE (2013)
13. Naseer, T., Spinello, L., Burgard, W., Stachniss, C.: Robust visual robot localization across seasons using network flows. In: Proceedings of AAAI Conference on Artificial Intelligence, AAAI 2014, pp. 2564–2570. AAAI Press (2014)

14. Milford, M., Wyeth, G., Prasser, D.: RatSLAM: a hippocampal model for simultaneous localization and mapping. In: Proceedings of International Conference on Robotics and Automation (ICRA), pp. 403–408. IEEE (2004)
15. Hawkins, J.: On Intelligence (with Sandra Blakeslee). Times Books (2004)
16. Hawkins, J., Ahmad, S., Cui, Y.: A theory of how columns in the neocortex enable learning the structure of the world. Front. Neural Circuits **11**, 81 (2017)
17. NuPIC. https://github.com/numenta/nupic. Accessed 09 May 2018
18. Ahmad, S., Hawkins, J.: Properties of sparse distributed representations and their application to hierarchical temporal memory. CoRR abs/1503.07469 (2015)
19. Neubert, P., Schubert, S., Protzel, P.: Learning vector symbolic architectures for reactive robot behaviours. In: Proceedings of International Conference on Intelligent Robots and Systems (IROS) Workshop on Machine Learning Methods for High-Level Cognitive Capabilities in Robotics (2016)
20. Spruston, N.: Pyramidal neurons: dendritic structure and synaptic integration. Nat. Rev. Neurosci. **9**, 206–221 (2008)
21. Numenta. https://numenta.com/. Accessed 09 May 2018
22. Purdy, S.: Encoding data for HTM systems. CoRR abs/1602.05925 (2016)
23. Neubert, P., Protzel, P.: Local region detector + CNN based landmarks for practical place recognition in changing environments. In: Proceedings of European Conference on Mobile Robotics (ECMR), pp. 1–6. IEEE (2015)
24. Breiman, L.: Bagging predictors. Mach. Learn. **24**(2), 123–140 (1996)
25. Grieves, R., Jeffery, K.: The representation of space in the brain. Behav. Process. **135**, 113–131 (2016)

Acquiring Knowledge of Object Arrangements from Human Examples for Household Robots

Lisset Salinas Pinacho[✉], Alexander Wich, Fereshta Yazdani,
and Michael Beetz

Institute for Artificial Intelligence, University Bremen, Bremen, Germany
{salinas,awich,yazdani,beetz}@cs.uni-bremen.de

Abstract. Robots are becoming ever more present in households, interacting more with humans. They are able to perform tasks in an accurate manner, e.g. manipulating objects. However, this manipulation often does not follow the human way to arrange objects. Therefore, robots require semantic knowledge about the environment for executing tasks and satisfying humans' expectations. In this paper, we will introduce a breakfast table setting scenario where a robot acquires information from human demonstrations to arrange objects in a meaningful way. We will show how robots can obtain the necessary amount of knowledge to autonomously perform daily tasks.

1 Introduction

Nowadays, robots are becoming more present and starting to perform household tasks in our everyday life. However, they are not able to perform most of those chores completely alone yet. They still require cognitive capabilities in order to be able to autonomously acquire enough knowledge and produce more flexible, reliable and efficient behavior. Examples are such as analyzing and understanding human activities by understanding his intentions, e.g. which task the human performed, how he did it, and why he performed it like that.

The aim of our work is to support robots in understanding human demonstrations. They should be able to reason and make decisions about human activities to perform actions closer to humans, e.g. "human-like", and, at the same time, to improve their own performance. Our idea is to have robots obtaining and combining the necessary amount of information from different sources in a meaningful way without being remotely controlled or teleoperated [1]. To achieve that, the robot should be able to find answers in a huge amount of structured knowledge and, then, choose the one it needs. In this sense, we present a problem scenario, illustrated in Fig. 1, where a robot asks how to perform the specific task.

In Fig. 1b, we give a proposal to answer those questions where human demonstrations from similar tasks are analyzed. Figure 1a shows the breakfast table setting scenario with a human operator who gives an order, e.g. I'd like to have cereal and juice for breakfast, the robot needs to perform without any further

© Springer Nature Switzerland AG 2018
F. Trollmann and A.-Y. Turhan (Eds.): KI 2018, LNAI 11117, pp. 131–138, 2018.
https://doi.org/10.1007/978-3-030-00111-7_12

(a) Traditionally preprogrammed PR2-robot placing objects on a table by asking how to perform specifics of the task.

(b) Visualization of human performinga table setting in VR. Dots represent sampled locations in other episodes.

Fig. 1. Robot and human performing a breakfast table setting task.

information about how to place the objects. Our research focuses on supporting humans in daily tasks by providing robots tools to obtain appropriate information to fill knowledge gaps in plan descriptions for autonomously performing tasks. We equip robots with commonsense to be able to ask and retrieve the right answers from available knowledge. Unlike traditional planning approaches where robots might only focus on improving the performance of their goal achievements by placing objects based on high success rates or where human executor might additionally consider his psychological comfort during positioning of objects [8]. Nevertheless, robot's planning capabilities could be adapted by the acquired knowledge and, then, increased their performance and flexibility. Furthermore, robots should analyze and understand human actions regarding different contextual relations. For example by grouping objects in categories depending on their location and orientation relations.

In this paper, we propose an architecture, Fig. 2, making use of existing frameworks and extending the planning capabilities. We investigate actions in human demonstrations when arranging objects on tables. We put special attention and deal with the differences in demonstrations, e.g. which different opportunities exist to arrange objects on the dining table. Also, we address the problem by defining a working area and object classification serving for task execution. In this sense, we present a dataset of experiences recorded from humans in virtual reality (VR) and its corresponding queries, the robot can extract and reason about object arrangements on a table setting for breakfast from. The intentions of humans are reflected in the location and orientation of objects.

The rest of this paper is organized as follows: we start with a brief review of existing literature and define the scope of our work. Then, we will briefly introduce our proposed architecture and present our results and conclusions.

2   Related Work

Since humans have a huge amount of knowledge with different levels of expertise to perform tasks, there is an emerging trend to develop robotic systems
autonomously performing actions by analyzing human demonstrations. As the
majority in learning from human demonstrations (LfD) or imitation learning
fields focus on developing systems for directly learning new skills from human
demonstrators [4], we instead propose to reason about human demonstrations
from vitual reality (VR). Similarly to this work, the system presented in [10] uses
VR in a video game. However, they extract manipulations instead of arrangements via logical queries to include semantic descriptions from a physical simulator. Regarding the object arrangement on a kitchen table, Krontiris and
Bekris [9], focus on efficiently solving a general rearrangement of objects. They
obtain the order to move random positioned objects to a grid specific arrangement. Unlike this benchmark, in which objects are arranged in predefined grids,
our work builds those from human demonstrations. In the work presented in
Srivastava et al. [13], they focus on a grasping experiment with obstructions
and the rearrangement of an object by finding small free spots. In our case, the
objects come from a different location, e.g. kitchen counter, and the arrangement
happens in a mostly uncluttered scenario. Also, instead of dealing with a single
target per episode, we deal with two objects in each execution, one per hand.
Furthermore, we are interested in arranging objects depending on their semantic
relation between each other. In this work, we especially contribute to this area
by not only following stability rules but also by taking into account the object
usage and location preferences. Similar to our work, Jiang et al. [8] present object
arrangement preferences by semantically relate objects to human poses in a 3D
environment. In our work, we additionally take into account semantic relations
between objects and actions. The dataset presented in this work includes VR
episodic memories that are richly annotated by relating human logged events in a
KNOWROB ontology format introduced by Haidu and Beetz [7]. These memories
include events in a time-line of execution. However, we still require extra analysis
tools to improve the connection between our virtual environment world and the
robot in order to benefit from this kind of data. In one sense, we give meaning to
an object location based on the context. We also describe a workspace for this
task which is not present in previous work to our knowledge.

3   Description

The architecture, presented in this work, uses different existing frameworks and
some additional analysis and reasoning tools as shown in Fig. 2. KNOWROB
works as a backbone enabling reasoning and answering logical queries about
semantic information in Prolog [3]. OPENEASE works as a cloud system, allowing intuitive analysis of episodes from different experiments and get answers to
queries in a visual environment. Plans are created by CRAM [15] that is able to
extract semantic knowledge from KNOWROB as needed using Lisp programming

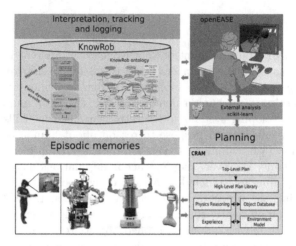

Fig. 2. The proposed architecture comprises existent frameworks.

language. The extension in this work is the use of statistical tools to obtain object arrangements from human demonstrations following certain properties, e.g. having no occlusions between objects.

To give a broader overview of our scenario, the recording is performed in a kitchen environment that includes provisions and kitchenware. From this scenario in a virtual environment, we obtained a dataset of 50 episodic memories where two people performed a breakfast table setting. The instruction was about setting the table for one person breakfast with six predefined objects. First, the task was to pick up and place the objects at different storage places, e.g. fridge and drawers, on the kitchen counter and, then, arrange those objects on the dining table. Then, we accessed the semantically-annotated dataset in OPE-NEASE [2] to retrieve and visualize the distribution of object arrangements on the table and test our proposals. For this, Prolog queries were manually constructed and included in dataset. They are designed to work with a single or multiple recorded episodes, see Sect. 4.

One problem by using human demonstrations is that they don't perform as robots by placing objects in the same location as shown in Fig. 1b and previously studied by Ramirez-Amaro et al. [12]. Furthermore, we present a solution for being able to use this experience, in Sect. 4, by the robot.

4   Experiments and Results

Some relevant information from the robot's perspective is to know where to exactly place objects. Therefore, we designed logical queries and visualized the distribution of object locations in OPENEASE, see Fig. 3.

In our queries the main extracted object properties are location and orientation, dimensions, the time it touched the table at, and the category it belongs to.

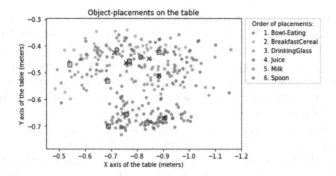

Fig. 3. Distribution of all object placements: centroids are marked by crosses, closest objects to centroids are circled, and final arrangement selections are marked by squares. (Color figure online)

The location and orientation are used to find spatial relationships. The dimension is used to detect object overlaps. The order where objects are placed on the table is reconstructed by using time. The object's category helps grouping object instances, as each of them has its own identifier. Figure 3 displays the exact location objects were placed at on the table for all recorded memories.

To help visualization, object models were replaced by spheres which indicate the final objects' location on the table. The sphere color represents the object category. Some of these objects are placed in a specific region as suggested by the distribution of colors. This distribution is more even to the table's edge, while near the center there is a greater mix of colors. By looking at which objects are placed more likely in a similar area, it can be noted in Fig. 4a that are the bowl and the spoon (purple) closer to the table's edge. Both figures in Fig. 4 are based on the object placements of Fig. 3.

(a) Objects collisions on centroids. (b) Proposed solutions on squares.

Fig. 4. Result for arrangement of objects inside workspace. (Color figure online)

However, objects located more central on the table tend to mix more in the collection of memories (red). A first attempt in proposing an object arrangement is to calculate the object's category centroid and, then, use it as the final location, see Fig. 4a. However, by using this proposal, collisions are present in the back area (red) as objects are too close to each other. The object overlap happens, in particular, between the cereal-box and the milk-box. A robot arranging objects on the table as seen in Fig. 4a would inevitably fail due to collisions. For this reason, a better solution is to select an arrangement from the memories. The arrangements presented in Fig. 4b follow the preference of humans, which might differ from the robot's point of view as objects in the back are more likely to be placed first to avoid collisions. It is important to notice that the numbering in Fig. 3 corresponds to the order which happened more often in the object arrangement. We believe that this order corresponds to the functional relations between each other, e.g. the cereal is related to the bowl as a container.

As mentioned before, some objects seem to follow a defined arrangement while others do not. As an example we can take the red objects in Fig. 4a, which are the cereal, juice and milk boxes, widely spread closer to the central region of the table. In contrast, the bowl and the spoon (purple) have a more defined placement in the arrangement. Therefore, in this work we consider that the spread offers a hint about how strict the placement of a particular object is. For example all the boxes (milk, juice, cereal) seem to have a loose location in the arrangement of a breakfast setting and we can define them as interchangeable, while the bowl and spoon as non-interchangeable.

To overcome the overlap of objects (see Fig. 4a), the robot should take into account possible collisions. It should also consider the priority of a particular object in an arrangement, which plays an important role in the placement's flexibility. Every time objects need to be separated due to overlap the robot is able to move the interchangeable objects to keep the sense of naturalness. Regarding the order of action, the robot places the interchangeable objects first, as they normally come behind the non-interchangeable ones, because they require less accuracy in the location and to avoid collisions. Then, it can place the non-interchangeable objects and be more careful in the placement.

Even further, we define an arrangement-workspace (arrange-space) for the robot in relation to the total area covered by all objects as indicated by the green bounding box. The smallest area required by a breakfast setting is $0.126\,\mathrm{m}^2$, the mean area is $0.188\,\mathrm{m}^2$ and the maximum area is $0.272\,\mathrm{m}^2$. Such information is useful when the robot is looking for a free area in which it could arrange objects when it encounters collisions or a location hard to reach.

5   Conclusions and Future Work

In this work, we showed our proposed architecture is able to reason about and obtain information from human demonstrations in a VR environment. Besides, the planning framework is capable of extracting the right amount of information based on object arrangements. It covers the object arrangements, where their final location and orientation should be related to their function, and the order of actions. This work presents an approach to define a workspace and classification of objects by interchangeable and non-interchangeable. However, we are aware that more work needs to be done in this area and in this work.

Another possible focus is the use of failures. We know that there are failures present in the datasets, e.g. the cereal fell sometimes and was re-placed to have a well-set table. However, it was not analyzed in this work, but we believe it would be interesting for the robot to be able to detect when an object falls after placing it and re-plan the placement as humans do.

Acknowledgements. This work is partially funded by Deutsche Forschungsgemeinschaft (DFG) through the Collaborative Research Center 1320, *EASE*. Lisset Salinas Pinacho and Alexander Wich acknowledge support from the German Academic Exchange Service (DAAD) and the Don Carlos Antonio López (BECAL) PhD scholarships, respectively. We also thank Matthias Schneider for his help in the revision of this work.

References

1. Akgun, B., Subramanian, K.: Robot learning from demonstration: kinesthetic teaching vs. teleoperation (2011)
2. Beetz, M., et al.: Cognition-enabled autonomous robot control for the realization of home chore task intelligence. Proc. IEEE **100**(8), 2454–2471 (2012)
3. Beetz, M., Beßler, D., Haidu, A., Pomarlan, M., Bozcuoglu, A., Bartels, G.: KnowRob 2.0 - a 2nd generation knowledge processing framework for cognition-enabled robotic agents. In: Proceedings of International Conference on Robotics and Automation (ICRA) (2018)
4. Billard, A., Calinon, S., Dillmann, R., Schaal, S.: Robot programming by demonstration. In: Siciliano, B., Khatib, O. (eds.) Springer Handbook of Robotics, pp. 1371–1389. Springer, Heidelberg (2008). https://doi.org/10.1007/978-3-540-30301-5_60. Chap. 59
5. Chernova, S., Thomaz, A.L.: Introduction. In: Robot Learning from Human Teachers, pp. 1–4. Morgan & Claypool (2014). Chap. 1
6. Evrard, R., Gribovskaya, E., Calinon, S., Billard, A., Kheddar, A.: Teaching physical collaborative tasks: object-lifting case study with a humanoid. In: IEEE/RAS International Conference on Humanoid Robots, Humanoids, November 2009
7. Haidu, A., Beetz, M.: Action recognition and interpretation from virtual demonstrations. In: International Conference on Intelligent Robots and Systems (IROS), Daejeon, South Korea, pp. 2833–2838 (2016)
8. Jiang, Y., Saxena, A.: Hallucinating humans for learning robotic placement of objects. In: Desai, J., Dudek, G., Khatib, O., Kumar, V. (eds.) Experimental Robotics, vol. 88, pp. 921–937. Springer, Heidelberg (2013). https://doi.org/10.1007/978-3-319-00065-7_61
9. Krontiris, A., Krontiris, K.E.: Efficiently solving general rearrangement tasks: a fast extension primitive for an incremental sampling-based planner. In: IEEE International Conference on Robotics and Automation (ICRA), pp. 3924–3931, May 2016
10. Kunze, L., Haidu, A., Beetz, M.: Acquiring task models for imitation learning through games with a purpose. In: 2013 IEEE/RSJ International Conference on Intelligent Robots and Systems, pp. 102–107, November 2013
11. Lee, J.: A survey of robot learning from demonstrations for human-robot collaboration. ArXiv e-prints, October 2017

12. Ramirez-Amaro, K., Beetz, M., Cheng, G.: Automatic segmentation and recognition of human activities from observation based on semantic reasoning. In: IEEE/RSJ International Conference on Intelligent Robots and Systems, pp, 5043–5048, September 2014
13. Srivastava, S., Fang, E., Riano, L., Chitnis, R., Russell, S., Abbeel, P.: Combined task and motion planning through an extensible planner-independent interface layer. In: IEEE International Conference on Robotics and Automation (ICRA), pp. 2376–2387, May 2014
14. Tamosiunaite, M., Nemec, B., Ude, A., Wörgötter, F.: Learning to pour with a robot arm combining goal and shape learning for dynamic movement primitives. Robot. Auton. Syst. **59**, 910–922 (2011)
15. Winkler, J., Tenorth, M., Bozcuoğlu, A.K., Beetz, M.: CRAMm - memories for robots performing everyday manipulation activities. Adv. Cogn. Syst. **3**, 47–66 (2014)

Learning

Solver Tuning and Model Configuration

Michael Barry[⊠], Hubert Abgottspon, and René Schumann

Smart Infrastructure Laboratory, Institute of Information Systems,
University of Applied Sciences Western Switzerland (HES-SO) Valais/Wallis,
Rue de Technopole 3, 3960 Sierre, Switzerland
{michael.barry,hubert.abgottspon,rene.schumann}@hevs.ch

Abstract. This paper addresses the problem of tuning parameters of mathematical solvers to increase their performance. We investigate how solvers can be tuned for models that undergo two types of configuration: variable configuration and constraint configuration. For each type, we investigate search algorithms for data generation that emphasizes exploration or exploitation. We show the difficulties for solver tuning in constraint configuration and how data generation methods affects a training sets learning potential.

Keywords: Tuning mathematical solvers · Mathematical solvers
Machine learning · Evolutionary algorithm · Novelty search

1 Introduction

Mathematical solvers, such as CPLEX [7], CONOPT [8], or GUROBI [10], are used to solve mathematical models in varying disciplines. The required runtime for a given model is largely dependent on the complexity of the model, but also on the solver's parameterization. As the solvers have become complex software systems, various parameters can be set to adjust their strategy. Default settings will generally perform well, but can be fine tuned for specific models. The configuration process of the solver's parameters for a specific model is referred to as solver tuning. Solver tuning is often done manually [15], through a mostly trial and error approach, as it is not intuitive how a solver may behave for a specific model. However, the emergence of Machine Learning methods has led to the possibility of automating the process. By using knowledge of previously executed models, a model's runtime with specific solver parameters can be predicted. As a result, a set of parameters can be selected that gives a low predicted runtime. Such systems have been successfully applied to boost the performance of solvers in general, both for a large set of independent models, but also for a single model with different inputs [3]. In the latter case, models are re-run either based on updated information, or to consider different scenarios. Varying the input variables may change the individual data points, while changing constraints may change the mathematical structure of the model. We expect that these two different types require different types of solver configuration. Thus, we

F. Trollmann and A.-Y. Turhan (Eds.): KI 2018, LNAI 11117, pp. 141–154, 2018.
https://doi.org/10.1007/978-3-030-00111-7_13

distinct in the following these two types of configuration: *variable configuration* and *constraint configuration*. As there exist a large set of parameter combinations, and solving mathematical models is a time consuming task, we have to consider a strategy for generating training data for the run time predictor, outlined above. Training data generation strategies define a process of identifying the best training instances and can be described as a search problem. Ideally, we wish to generate a training set that includes instances that represent the entire search space well, but also includes solver parameter settings that result in a low runtime. However, as the search space is not well understood, it is not yet clear which type of search algorithm may be best. In particular, it is not understood whether algorithms that emphasize exploration or exploitation are best suited for this task. Currently, only random selection methods have been investigated. Therefore, we investigate two alternative algorithms based on an Evolutionary Algorithm (EA) that implements exploration and exploitation respectively: Novelty EA and Minimal Runtime EA. We describe each algorithm in detail in Sect. 3.1 and compare results to commonly used random data generation strategies afterwards. In this paper, we will explore the relationship between mathematical solver tuning and the types of configuration of models. Furthermore, we investigate whether algorithms that focus on exploration or exploitation are better suited for finding solver parameters settings resulting in a low runtime. In addition, we analyze how the training data generated by each algorithm performs when used for Machine Learning.

2   State of the Art

The concept of runtime predictions is extensively explored in methods such as surrogate models [25], meta models [23] or empirical performance models [14]. Machine Learning has been applied to solver parameter tuning, e.g. the work of Hutter et al. [12] has been one of the first using the PARAMILS framework. However, the authors stated that the PARAMILS framework may not be the best methodology, as it mainly aims to provide a lower bound on the performance improvements that can be achieved.

Machine Learning methods require inputs that describe the model, so that it can predict the runtime as output. The estimation of a models complexity is known to be difficult [14,18,20,21,27]. Basic representation include counting the number of constraints or variables. However, it is also commonly known that this has a limited use, due to issues such as the easy-hard-easy phenomenon [17].

The work published in [4] indicates that the cost of tuning the parameters, no matter which method, will always outweigh the benefits when considering a single execution of the model. However, it is often justified, as multiple executions of the same model with different inputs may be necessary. If a Machine Learning method can generalize to other model configurations, or possibly even completely different models, it can be worth investing computation effort in the initial training phase to allow faster executions in the future. Furthermore, in addition to our own studies [26], Baz et al. [4] showed there is great potential in using non-default settings for mathematical solvers.

Furthermore, methods exist that use a multi objective approach [4], allowing a user to tune for Time-To-Optimality (runtime), Proven-Gap or Best-Integer-Solution. López and Stützle [24] also make use of an aggregate objective to find the best compromises between solution quality and runtime, to achieve good anytime behavior. Although such approaches have many applications, we will focus on Time-To-Optimality with thresholds given for Proven-Gap and Best-Integer-Solution, which relate more with methods such as [3].

In the following, we focus on tuning a solver for many configurations of the same model. Models are commonly used for a range of inputs that represent either different scenarios, or are simply updated inputs for a new time period.

Training data generation has not been well covered for mathematical solvers. Methods like [12,27] randomly select model and solver configurations to execute and use them as training data. Due to a large number of configurations that are possible and the fact that most solver parameter settings will result in an exceptional high runtime, the sampling space is large and imbalanced. Therefore, random selection has the tendency to produce a dataset where the target set, which has a low runtime, will be underrepresented. Such imbalanced data has been addressed in other fields using data generation strategies [9,11] by searching for the target set.

This forms a search problem that can be addressed using heuristics. However, as the search space is not well understood, it is also not commonly clear what heuristic to be used, i.e. if their emphasis should be given to exploration or exploitation. Which method is more effective depends on the search space, and is not well covered for the trainings data generation for mathematical solvers.

Novelty search has shown its benefits with evolutionary search strategies in some applications [22]. In addition to being an effective search strategy, it has been highly successful [5] in generating training data for Machine Learning techniques in other domains. However, besides the application in [5], there has not been a large body of work applying novelty search for training data generation.

Furthermore, as the algorithms are used to generate the training data, it is important that not only optimal parameter settings are included, but also that the generated training set represents the search space well. If the training set is not a representative sample of the search space, e.g. having a bias towards parameter settings with a high or low runtime, the resulting predictor may over or under estimate the runtime systematically. Therefore, we must consider the effects of the training data generation method on the learning problem.

3 Methodology

The final goal of our method is to reduce the runtime of a mathematical solver. As shown in Fig. 1, we modify the classical approach of how a solver is used, and included a solver configuration phase.

During the solver configuration phase, we take the model instance as an input and consider a variety of solver configurations. Based on the predicted runtimes, we select the best configuration, i.e. the one leading to minimal runtime. To use

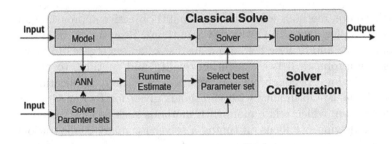

Fig. 1. Graphic showing the process for solving a model.

this solver configuration phase, we must first build a runtime predictor with a potential high accuracy as shown in Fig. 2.

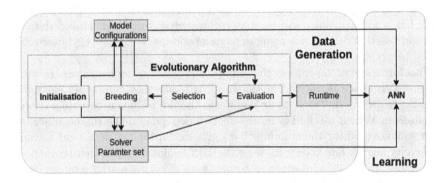

Fig. 2. Graphic showing the data generation and learning phase.

An Evolutionary Algorithm (EA) is used to select instances that consist of a model and solver configuration. These instances are then given to the solver to determine its runtime. The instances are then passed as training data to an Artificial Neural Network (ANN). Once trained, the ANN is used as a predictor during the solver configuration phase described in Fig. 1.

3.1 Evolutionary Algorithm

One aim in our paper is to assess whether an exploration or exploitation method is better suited for finding solver configuration that result in a low runtime. Therefore, we use two different algorithms: minimal runtime EA (MREA) and Novelty EA (NEA). Both algorithms are based on an EA. We use a random initialization, roulette wheel selection and an integer encoding [6]. The encoding is shown in Fig. 3, where each gene in the encoding represents a configuration. For example, the first index for the solver configurations represents the *subalg* solver parameter, where the value 1 represents the variables value (in this case

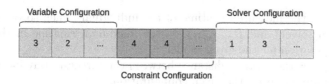

Fig. 3. Graphic showing the individual I in the population as an array of integers. Each integer value corresponds to values for particular settings.

indicating the use of the Primal simplex method). Possible values are shown in [7]. Each input and model configuration referrers to an index, representing the specific model. We use a population size of 100 individuals with a survival rate of 20%. We apply mutation to generate 90% of the new individuals and crossover is applied for the remaining 10%. Parameters were chosen based on initial experiments.

The fitness evaluation in the EA is the computationally most expensive step, as it requires the model to be solved by the mathematical solver based on the individual's model configuration, input configuration and solver parameters. Once the runtime of the individual is determined, its fitness value is assigned.

The difference between the MREA and the NEA is the fitness evaluation. The minimal runtime EA uses an evaluation function that minimizes the runtime, referred to as the *minimal runtime evaluation*. The NEA uses a strategy, referred to as *novelty based evaluation*, that uses Novelty search. Novelty search refers to a strategy that does not consider only the runtime for the fitness evaluation, but also the diversity an individual adds to the population.

Minimal runtime evaluation: The individual fitness is computed as:

$$F_{mr} = \min[R_{real}^{normalized}] \tag{1}$$

$R_{real}^{normalized}$ is the measured runtime of an individual I, which must be obtained by the solver. F_{mr} is the objective based fitness value. To avoid bias towards easier models, we normalize the runtime. For normalization, we use the longest runtime in the subset of all individuals in the current and past population that uses the same model.

Novelty based evaluation. In this approach the fitness of each individual is computed by its novelty. We define novelty as the minimal distance to any other individual in the current and past population. Therefore, the method rewards individuals that behave differently. The fitness is computed as follows, which is also similar to literature, see e.g. [22]:

$$F_{Novelty} = D_{min}/D_{configMax} * 100 \tag{2}$$

D_{min} is the distance between the given individual and the nearest neighbor (in terms of runtime) for the given model configuration. It is given as:

$$D_{min} = \min[|R_{real} - R_{configMax}|] \tag{3}$$

Where R_{real} is the measured runtime of the individual (when solved using the mathematical solver) and $R_{configMax}$ is the maximum runtime in the current and past population for the given model.

$D_{configMax}$ is the runtime distance between the furthest away individuals in the current population for the given configuration:

$$D_{configMax} = |R_{configMax} - R_{configMin}| \tag{4}$$

where $R_{configMin}$ is the minimum runtime in the current population for the given model and input configuration.

Random Algorithm. As stated previously, the current state of the art randomly selects individuals for the training set. To allow for comparison, we use a random algorithm based on the EA described above. We modify the above algorithms so that in each generation we add random individuals to the population instead of evolving individuals from the current population. This allows us to compare different sets of training data of the same size produced by the EA to a random selection.

3.2 ANN

To demonstrate how training sets produced by the various algorithms perform when used to train a predictor, we use a common implementation of an ANN. Although other Machine Learning methods are possible, ANNs have been used in literature [3,14] and cope well for a wide variety of problems. Many ANN architectures and structures are possible, but initial experiments show that a simple multilayer perceptron (MLP) is sufficient. We use a MLP with one hidden layer, using a sigmoid (logistical) activation function [16,19]:

The input and outputs are normalized to values from $[0, 1]$ and the output layer uses a simple linear activation function with only one neuron to output the predicted solver runtime. As an estimate of a models complexity we use four model descriptors consisting of the number of rows, columns, non-zeros and binaries. These are given by the model statistics [7] output in CPLEX, indicating the models complexity and allowing the differentiation between configurations. As noted in Sect. 2, more advanced complexity measurements are available. However, such measurements are computed based on the model descriptors used here. Thus, we consider that adding these additional measures will not provide additional information to the ANN.

The ANN input neurons consist of one neuron per model descriptor and solver parameter. The full list of inputs, as shown in Table 1, were chosen based on literature [13] and initial experiments. The resulting structure consists of 9 input neurons, one hidden layer with 9 neurons and 1 output neuron. For the given input, once the ANN is trained using back propagation, it can predict the runtime for varying configurations.

Table 1. Table showing the inputs to the ANN.

Input name	Type of input	Range
Rows	Model descriptor	$[0 - \infty]$
Columns	Model descriptor	$[0 - \infty]$
Non-zeros	Model descriptor	$[0 - \infty]$
binaries	Model descriptor	$[0 - \infty]$
startalg	Solver parameter	$[0 - 5]$
subalg	Solver parameter	$[0 - 5]$
heurfreq	Solver parameter	$[0 - 2]$
mipsearch	Solver parameter	$[0 - 2]$
cuts	Solver parameter	$[0 - 4]$

3.3 Model Configuration

As described previously, the implications for solver tuning arising from the different types of model configuration are not well studied. For demonstrating such different types of configuration, we use a family of models from the domain of hydropower operation management. The models are used to schedule production, to maximize the profit, selling electric energy to different energy markets. The service can be offered to a permutation of different available markets, considering different market prices and different resulting constraints. As each market is described by a number of constraints, configuring this aspect can be considered to be a *constraint configuration*. *Variable configurations* are applied by modifying variables such as the size of the reservoir, number and capacity of turbines and water inflows. For more details on the hydropower models, we refer to [1,2].

4 Experiment Setup

We show our experiment setup in Fig. 4. This setup is applied for the random algorithm, MRGA and NEA. For every 50 evaluations (or model solves) in any of the three algorithms, an ANN is created and tested. We test the ANN using randomly selected test cases involving two model configurations (and all considered solver configurations), which are hidden during the data generation phase.

As training instances are added (and an ANN trained at intervals) we record:

Training Data Runtime: As we want to analyze how each algorithm performs in finding good solver parameter settings, we record the runtime for each individual in the training set for each algorithm.

ANN Prediction Error: To analyze how well each algorithm performs in creating training data that is effective in training a predictor, we record the prediction error of each ANN trained.

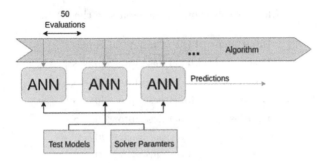

Fig. 4. Graphic showing the experiment setup.

Solver performance: To demonstrate how well each method performs in finally tuning the mathematical solver, we record the runtime for each test case when using the predictors of the ANN to configure the solver. This gives us the final performance of the overall system in tuning the solver.

In addition, as described above, we are going to analyze the effects of different configurations. Therefore, we conduct two experiments. The first experiment considers the effect of variable configurations, while the second consider constraint configurations:

Experiment 1: We keep the constraint configurations constant and consider different variable configurations. In total, we use 9 variable configurations. They consist of 3 different categories of Hydro power stations over 3 time periods. As test data, we select a random category from a 4th time period.

Experiment 2: We keep the variable configurations constant and consider different constraint configurations: In total we use 8 constraint configurations, consisting of various market combinations. As test data we use a randomly selected set of 2 combinations.

Each experiment is repeated 100 times and median values are recorded. The repetition is to cancel any random variance that occur due to the random selection of test data and the non-deterministic algorithms. Furthermore, we are going to analyze the search space, which should be small for an exhaustive search to be performed. Thus, we record the runtime of each individual in the 2 experiments, showing the effects of each type of configuration on a solver's runtime.

The experiments are run on a dedicated server that performs no other tasks. We use our own Java implementation for the individual algorithms and ANN. The hydro model is implemented in GAMS and utilizes CPLEX as the mathematical solver [7]. The model is relatively complex and can have a computation time of around 40 min on default settings. Parallelization is possible, but suffers from high memory usage. For each experiment, we compare the results over time. As a proxy for the time passed we use the measure of the number of unique models solved so far, as it is the computational most expensive aspect. To demonstrate the performance of the solver for a specific configuration and model, we use CPLEX ticks [7]. CPLEX ticks is a measure of how many steps a solver must make to find a solution and is a reliable runtime measurement that cannot be affected by other processes running on the same machine. To avoid any excessive runtime, the solver will abort at a threshold of 4,000,000 CPLEX ticks, which exceeds by far the number of ticks expected for these models.

5   Results and Analysis

It is expected that the space of *good* solver parameter sets differ for the two types of configurations. In particular, some solver configurations are expected to not be suitable at all, while others perform well, but only for specific model configurations. Each data generation method should evolve a population that is representative and includes overall solver parameters sets that result in a low runtime. Furthermore, we expect to see a decrease in prediction errors and resulting runtime (using the predictor's suggestion) as more training instances are added to the training data. Results are compared to the industry standard, which uses the default parameters, and the state of the art, which uses a random data generation strategies. The maximal potential improvement (shown by the results of an exhaustive search) is shown to indicate the maximum potential of solver parameter tuning.

We compare the search space for variable configurations (Experiment 1) in Fig. 5(a) and of constraint configuration (Experiment 2) in Fig. 6(a). We see that for each configuration, we can categorize three types of solver settings: Settings that do not perform well for all models (right), settings that only perform well for some models (center), settings that are stable and perform generally well (left). The potential for using ML in tuning solver parameters can be seen by comparing the lowest runtime of the second and third set. In such a case, it indicates that parameters specialized for particular models can outperform parameter sets that behave best for all. Although only a small increase can be seen, variable configurations is a candidate for Machine Learning. Constraint configuration also indicates this, but only to an extremely small value, indicating that a set that performs well for all model configurations is possible.

Figure 5(b) shows the performances when using the set of data generation methods with an ANNs to predict the runtime and then to tune the mathematical solver for variable configurations. We show in the runtime of individuals in the training sets that MREA initially adds solver parameter sets that generally have a low runtime. However, after finding the small set of solver parameters with a low runtime, less optimal settings are added. The random algorithm maintains a constant median runtime, while the NEA shows a similar but less visible behavior as the MREA. As for the runtime predictions, the error gradually reduces for all algorithms. Although they do not achieve a high prediction accuracy, it is accurate enough to make suggestion for solver tuning. In that respect, we see that MREA performs initially well, as it finds good parameter settings quickly. Nonetheless, as it restricts itself to local optima and gives a less representative training set, it is outperformed in larger training sets by methods that emphasize

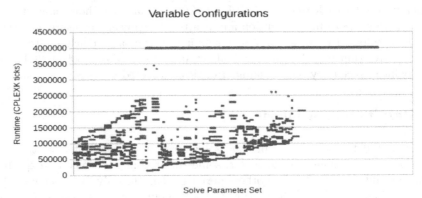

(a) Search space for variable configurations

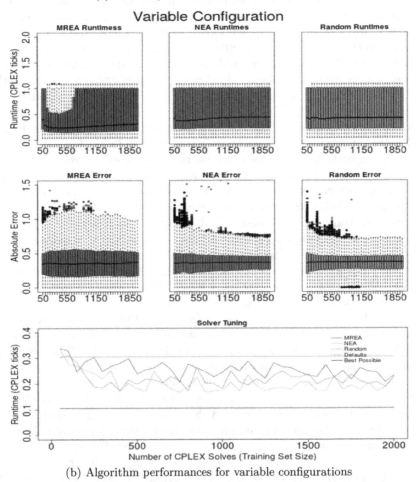

(b) Algorithm performances for variable configurations

Fig. 5. Results from Experiment 1 for variable configurations.

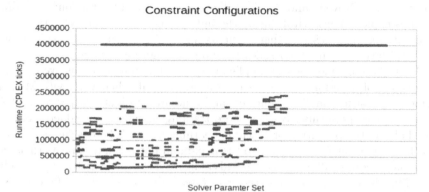

(a) Search space for constraint configurations

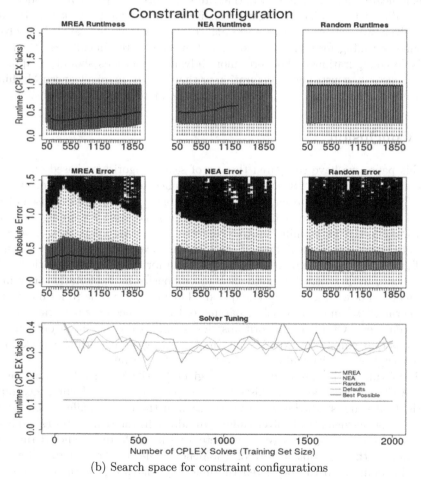

(b) Search space for constraint configurations

Fig. 6. Results from Experiment 2 for constraint configurations

exploration, i.e. Novelty and Random. The performance of the random algorithm indicates exploration is vital during the initial stages. However, Novelty search eventually outperforms all other methods due to its emphasis on exploration, while still favoring parameter sets with uniquely high performance.

When the same methods are applied to constraint configurations, we see that there is less of a performance increase. We see a similar behavior, with MREA performing best for small training sets and random for slightly larger sets. NEA achieves better performance when more training instances are added. As discussed above, the potential for Machine Learning methods here is smaller. However, by comparing performances to the maximum potential, it appears that the performance could still be increased. This indicates that this search space is likely more difficult to learn. Although the error rates indicate not much difference, we notice the large set of outliers in error predictions for constraint configurations. This indicates that parameter sets that are specialized for particular models are more difficult to predict. As these specialized parameter sets are key to tuning the solver, we achieve a lower performance. Overall, this indicates that solver parameter tuning for constraint configuration is a more difficult task than for variable configurations. Therefore, more advanced methods should be applied that focuses on constraint configuration or that utilizes more advanced Machine Learning methods other than ANN to learn the more complex relationship.

6   Conclusion

In this paper we have compared the use of search algorithms based on exploration and exploitation for data generation applied to mathematical solver tuning. Experiments were presented showing that using an exploration based algorithm, namely novelty search, was successful in generating a training data set that was effective for training an ANN. Referring to our results in Sect. 5, we conclude three aspects in our findings. Firstly, solver parameter tuning for constraint configuration presents a more difficult task than for variable configurations.

Second, data generation methods that emphasize on exploitation may find parameter sets with a low runtime quickly, but are susceptible to local optima. Furthermore, when used for solver parameter tuning, they only perform best for small datasets. Otherwise, algorithms that emphasize exploration outperform methods that emphasize exploitation. Implementing an algorithm that exploits the concept of Novelty will achieve best results for learning.

For future work more focus should be given for the Machine Learning methods. Although work already exists that compares different Machine Learning methods, it is not studied how data generation methods would affect them when considering mathematical solver tuning. In addition, the search spaces indicate that simply choosing the solver parameters with the faster predicted runtime may not be the best option. Use of confidence values to choose parameter settings in addition to the predicted runtime may increase performance as miss predictions carry a large penalty.

Acknowledgment. Parts of this work have been funded by the Swiss National Science Foundation as part of the project 407040_153760 *Hydro Power Operation and Economic Performance in a Changing Market Environment.*

References

1. Barry, M., Schillinger, M., Weigt, H., Schumann, R.: Configuration of hydro power plant mathematical models. In: Gottwalt, S., König, L., Schmeck, H. (eds.) EI 2015. LNCS, vol. 9424, pp. 200–207. Springer, Cham (2015). https://doi.org/10.1007/978-3-319-25876-8_17
2. Barry, M., Schumann, R.: Dynamic and configurable mathematical modelling of a hydropower plant research in progress paper. In: Presented at the 29. Workshop "Planen, Scheduling und Konfigurieren, Entwerfen" (PuK 2015), September 2015
3. Baz, M., Hunsaker, B., Brooks, P., Gosavi, A.: Automated tuning of optimization software parameters. Technical Report TR2007-7. University of Pittsburgh, Department of Industrial Engineering (2007)
4. Baz, M., Hunsaker, B., Prokopyev, O.: How much do we "pay" for using default parameters? Comput. Optim. Appl. **48**(1), 91–108 (2011)
5. Boussaa, M., Barais, O., Sunyé, G., Baudry, B.: A novelty search approach for automatic test data generation. In: Proceedings of the Eighth International Workshop on Search-Based Software Testing, pp. 40–43. IEEE Press (2015)
6. Chawdhry, P.K., Roy, R., Pant, R.K.: Soft Computing in Engineering Design and Manufacturing. Springer, London (2012)
7. Cplex, G.: The solver manuals (2014)
8. Drud, A.: Conopt solver manual. ARKI Consulting and Development, Bagsvaerd, Denmark (1996)
9. Guo, H., Viktor, H.L.: Learning from imbalanced data sets with boosting and data generation: the databoost-IM approach. ACM SIGKDD Explor. Newsl. **6**(1), 30–39 (2004)
10. Gurobi Optimization, Inc.: Gurobi optimizer reference manual (2016). http://www.gurobi.com
11. He, H., Garcia, E.A.: Learning from imbalanced data. IEEE Trans. Knowl. Data Eng. **21**(9), 1263–1284 (2009)
12. Hutter, F., Hoos, H.H., Leyton-Brown, K.: Automated configuration of mixed integer programming solvers. In: Lodi, A., Milano, M., Toth, P. (eds.) CPAIOR 2010. LNCS, vol. 6140, pp. 186–202. Springer, Heidelberg (2010). https://doi.org/10.1007/978-3-642-13520-0_23
13. Hutter, F., Hoos, H.H., Leyton-Brown, K., Stützle, T.: Paramils: an automatic algorithm configuration framework. J. Artif. Intell. Res. **36**, 267–306 (2009)
14. Hutter, F., Xu, L., Hoos, H.H., Leyton-Brown, K.: Algorithm runtime prediction: methods & evaluation. Artif. Intell. **206**, 79–111 (2014)
15. IBM: CPLEX Performance Tuning for Mixed Integer Programs (2016). http://www-01.ibm.com/support/docview.wss?uid=swg21400023
16. Jain, A.K., Mao, J., Mohiuddin, K.M.: Artificial neural networks: a tutorial. Computer **29**(3), 31–44 (1996)
17. Juslin, P., Winman, A., Olsson, H.: Naive empiricism and dogmatism in confidence research: a critical examination of the hard-easy effect. Psychol. Rev. **107**(2), 384 (2000)
18. Kadioglu, S., Malitsky, Y., Sellmann, M., Tierney, K.: ISAC-instance-specific algorithm configuration. In: ECAI, vol. 215, pp. 751–756 (2010)

19. Karlik, B., Olgac, A.V.: Performance analysis of various activation functions in generalized MLP architectures of neural networks. Int. J. Artif. Intell. Expert Syst. **1**(4), 111–122 (2011)
20. Knowles, J.: Parego: a hybrid algorithm with on-line landscape approximation for expensive multiobjective optimization problems. IEEE Trans. Evol. Comput. **10**(1), 50–66 (2006)
21. Kotthoff, L.: Algorithm selection for combinatorial search problems: a survey. AI Mag. **35**(3), 48–60 (2014)
22. Lehman, J., Stanley, K.O.: Abandoning objectives: evolution through the search for novelty alone. Evol. Comput. **19**(2), 189–223 (2011)
23. Lehmann, G., Blumendorf, M., Trollmann, F., Albayrak, S.: Meta-modeling runtime models. In: Dingel, J., Solberg, A. (eds.) MODELS 2010. LNCS, vol. 6627, pp. 209–223. Springer, Heidelberg (2011). https://doi.org/10.1007/978-3-642-21210-9_21
24. López-Ibáñez, M., Stützle, T.: Automatically improving the anytime behaviour of optimisation algorithms. Eur. J. Oper. Res. **235**(3), 569–582 (2014)
25. Preuss, M., Rudolph, G., Wessing, S.: Tuning optimization algorithms for real-world problems by means of surrogate modeling. In: Proceedings of the 12th Annual Conference on Genetic and Evolutionary Computation, pp. 401–408. ACM (2010)
26. Stefan Eggenschwiler, R.S.: Parameter tuning for the CPLEX. Bachelor Thesis (2016)
27. Xu, L., Hutter, F., Hoos, H.H., Leyton-Brown, K.: Hydra-MIP: automated algorithm configuration and selection for mixed integer programming. In: RCRA Workshop on Experimental Evaluation of Algorithms for Solving Problems with Combinatorial Explosion at the International Joint Conference on Artificial Intelligence (IJCAI), pp. 16–30 (2011)

Condorcet's Jury Theorem for Consensus Clustering

Brijnesh Jain[(✉)]

Department of Computer Science and Electrical Engineering,
Technical University Berlin, Berlin, Germany
jain@dai-labor.de

Abstract. Condorcet's Jury Theorem has been invoked for ensemble classifiers to indicate that the combination of many classifiers can have better predictive performance than a single classifier. Such a theoretical underpinning is unknown for consensus clustering. This article extends Condorcet's Jury Theorem to the mean partition approach under the additional assumptions that a unique but unknown ground-truth partition exists and sample partitions are drawn from a sufficiently small ball containing the ground-truth.

Keywords: Consensus clustering · Mean partition
Condorcet's Jury Theorem

1 Introduction

Ensemble learning generates multiple models and combines them to a single consensus model to solve a learning problem. The assumption is that a consensus model performs better than an individual model or at least reduces the likelihood of selecting a model with inferior performance [29]. Examples of ensemble learning are classifier ensembles [6,25,31,40] and cluster ensembles (consensus clustering) [14,32,36,39].

The assumptions on ensemble learning follow the idea of *collective wisdom* that many heads are in general better than one. The idea of group intelligence applied to societies can be tracPartition Spacesed back to Aristotle and the philosophers of antiquity (see [37]) and has been recently revived by a number of publications, including James Surowiecki's book *The Wisdom of Crowds* [33].

One theoretical basis for *collective wisdom* can be derived from Condorcet's Jury Theorem [4]. The theorem refers to a jury of n voters that need to reach a decision by majority vote. The assumptions of the simplest version of the theorem are: (1) There are two alternatives; (2) one of both alternatives is correct; (3) voters decide independently; and (4) the probability p of a correct decision is identical for every voter. If the voters are competent, that is $p > 0.5$, then Condorcet's Jury Theorem states that the probability of a correct decision by majority vote tends to one as the number n of voters increases to infinity.

© Springer Nature Switzerland AG 2018
F. Trollmann and A.-Y. Turhan (Eds.): KI 2018, LNAI 11117, pp. 155–168, 2018.
https://doi.org/10.1007/978-3-030-00111-7_14

Condorcet's Jury Theorem has been generalized in several ways, because its assumptions are considered as rather restrictive and partly unrealistic (see e.g. [1] and references therein). Despite its practical limitations, the theorem has been used to indicate a theoretical justification of ensemble classifiers [25,26,31]. In contrast to ensemble classifiers, such a theoretical underpinning is unknown for consensus clustering.

This article extends Condorcet's Jury Theorem to the mean partition approach in consensus clustering [5,7,10,11,15,27,32,34,35]. We consider the special case that the partition space is endowed with a metric induced by the Euclidean norm. Then the proposed theorem draws on the following assumptions: (1) there is a unique but unknown ground-truth partition X_*; and (2) sample partitions are drawn i.i.d. from a sufficiently small ball containing X_*.

The rest of this paper is structured as follows: Sect. 2 introduces background material, Sect. 3 introduces Fréchet functions on partition spaces, Sect. 4 presents Condorcet's Jury Theorem for consensus clustering, Sect. 4.4 proves the proposed theorem, and Sect. 5 concludes.

2   Background and Related Work

2.1   The Mean Partition Approach

The goal is to group a set $\mathcal{Z} = \{z_1, \ldots, z_m\}$ of m data points into ℓ clusters. The mean partition approach first clusters the same data set $\mathcal{Z}$ several times using different settings and strategies of the same or different cluster algorithms. The resulting clusterings form a sample $\mathcal{S}_n = (X_1, \ldots, X_n)$ of n partitions $X_i \in \mathcal{P}$ of data set $\mathcal{Z}$. The mean partition approach aims at finding a consensus clustering that minimizes a sum-of-distances criterion from the sample partitions. In Sect. 3, we specify the underlying partition space and in Sect. 3.3 we present a formal definition of the mean partition approach.

2.2   Context of the Mean Partition Approach

We place the mean partition approach into the broader context of mathematical statistics. The motivation is that mathematical statistics offers a plethora of useful results, the consensus clustering literature seems to be unaware of. For example, the proof of Condorcet's Jury Theorem rests on results from statistical analysis of graphs [21]. These results in turn are rooted on Fréchet's seminal monograph [12] and its follow-up research.

Since a meaningful addition of partitions is unknown, the mean partition approach emulates an averaging procedure by minimizing a sum-of-distances criterion. This idea is not new and has been studied in more general form for almost seven decades. In 1948, Fréchet first generalized the idea of averaging in metric spaces, where a well-defined addition is unknown. He showed that specification of a metric and a probability distribution is sufficient to define a mean element as measure of central tendency. The mean of a sample of elements is any element that minimizes the sum of squared distances from all sample elements. Similarly, the expectation of a probability distribution minimizes an integral of the sum of squared distances from all elements of the entire space.

Since Fréchet's seminal work, mathematical statistics studied asymptotic and other properties of the mean element in abstract metric spaces. Examples include statistical analysis of shapes [2,8,17,24], complex objects [28,38], tree-structured data [9,38], and graphs [13,21].

The partition spaces defined in Sect. 3.2 can be regarded as a special case of graph spaces [18,19]. Consequently, the geometric as well as statistical properties of graph spaces carry over to partition spaces. The proof of the proposed theorem rests on the orbit space framework [18,19], on the mean partition theorem in graph spaces, and on asymptotic properties of the sample mean of graphs [21] that have been adopted to partition spaces [20,23].

3   Fréchet Functions on Partition Spaces

This section first introduces partition spaces endowed with a metric induced by the Euclidean norm. Then we formalize the mean partition approach using Fréchet functions. We assume that $\mathcal{Z} = \{z_1, \ldots, z_m\}$ is a set of m data points to be clustered and $\mathcal{C} = \{c_1, \ldots, c_\ell\}$ is a set of ℓ cluster labels.

3.1   Partitions and Their Representations

Partitions usually occur in two forms, in a labeled and in an unlabeled form, where labeled partitions can be regarded as representations of unlabeled partitions.

We begin with describing labeled partitions. Let $\mathbf{1}_d \in \mathbb{R}^d$ denote the vector of all ones. Consider the set

$$\mathcal{X} = \left\{ \boldsymbol{X} \in [0,1]^{\ell \times m} : \boldsymbol{X}^T \mathbf{1}_\ell = \mathbf{1}_m \right\},$$

of matrices with elements from the unit interval and whose columns sum to one. A matrix $\boldsymbol{X} \in \mathcal{X}$ represents a labeled (soft) partition of $\mathcal{Z}$. The elements x_{kj} of $\boldsymbol{X} = (x_{kj})$ describe the degree of membership of data point z_j to the cluster with label c_k. The columns $\boldsymbol{x}_{:j}$ of $\boldsymbol{X}$ summarize the membership values of the data points z_j across all ℓ clusters. The rows $\boldsymbol{x}_{k:}$ of $\boldsymbol{X}$ represent the clusters c_k.

Next, we describe unlabeled partitions. Observe that the rows of a labeled partition $\boldsymbol{X}$ describe a cluster structure. Permuting the rows of $\boldsymbol{X}$ results in a labeled partition $\boldsymbol{X}'$ with the same cluster structure but with a possibly different labeling of the clusters. In cluster analysis, the particular labeling of the clusters is usually meaningless. What matters is the abstract cluster structure represented by a labeled partition. Since there is no natural labeling of the clusters, we define the corresponding unlabeled partition as the equivalence class of all labeled partitions that can be obtained from one another by relabeling the clusters. Formally, an unlabeled partition is a set of the form

$$X = \{\boldsymbol{P}\boldsymbol{X} \;:\; \boldsymbol{P} \in \Pi^{\ell}\},$$

where Π^{ℓ} is the set of all $(\ell \times \ell)$-permutation matrices.

In the following, we briefly call X a *partition* instead of unlabeled partition. In addition, any labeled partition $\boldsymbol{X}' \in X$ is called a *representation* of partition X. By $\mathcal{P}$ we denote the set of all (unlabeled) partitions with ℓ clusters over m data points. Since some clusters may be empty, the set $\mathcal{P}$ also contains partitions with less than ℓ clusters. Thus, we consider $\ell \leq m$ as the maximum number of clusters we encounter.

A *hard partition* $X \in \mathcal{P}$ is a partition whose matrix representations take only binary membership values from $\{0, 1\}$. By $\mathcal{P}^{+}$ we denote the subset of all hard partitions. Note that the columns of representations of hard partitions are standard basis vectors from $\mathbb{R}^{\ell}$.

Though we are only interested in unlabeled partitions, we need labeled partitions for two reasons: (i) computers can not easily and efficiently cope with unlabeled partitions and (ii) using labeled partitions considerably simplifies derivation of theoretical results.

3.2   Intrinsic Metric

We endow the set $\mathcal{P}$ of partitions with an intrinsic metric δ induced by the Euclidean norm such that $(\mathcal{P}, \delta)$ becomes a geodesic space. The Euclidean norm for matrices $\boldsymbol{X} \in \mathcal{X}$ is defined by

$$\|\boldsymbol{X}\| = \left(\sum_{k=1}^{\ell} \sum_{j=1}^{m} |x_{kj}|^2 \right)^{1/2}.$$

The norm $\|\boldsymbol{X}\|$ is also known as the Frobenius or Schur norm. We call $\|\boldsymbol{X}\|$ Euclidean norm in order to emphasize the geometric properties of the partition space. The Euclidean norm induces the distance function

$$\delta(X, Y) = \min \{\|\boldsymbol{X} - \boldsymbol{Y}\| \;:\; \boldsymbol{X} \in X, \, \boldsymbol{Y} \in Y\}$$

for all partitions $X, Y \in \mathcal{P}$. Then the pair $(\mathcal{P}, \delta)$ is a geodesic metric space [20], Theorem 2.1. Suppose that X and Y are two partitions. Then

$$\delta(X, Y) \leq \|\boldsymbol{X} - \boldsymbol{Y}\| \tag{1}$$

for all representations $\boldsymbol{X} \in X$ and $\boldsymbol{Y} \in Y$. For some pairs of representations $\boldsymbol{X}' \in X$ and $\boldsymbol{Y}' \in Y$ equality holds in Eq. (1). In this case, we say that representations $\boldsymbol{X}'$ and $\boldsymbol{Y}'$ are in *optimal position*. Note that pairs of representations in optimal position are not uniquely determined.

3.3   Fréchet Functions

We first formalize the mean partition approach using Fréchet functions. Then we present the Mean Partition Theorem, which is of pivotal importance for gaining deeper insight into the theory of the mean partition approach [23]. Here, we apply the Mean Partition Theorem to define the concept of majority vote. In addition, the proof of the proposed theorem resorts to the properties stated in the Mean Partition Theorem.

Let $(\mathcal{P}, \delta)$ be a partition space endowed with the metric δ induced by the Euclidean norm. We assume that Q is a probability distribution on $\mathcal{P}$ with support $\mathcal{S}_Q$.[1] Suppose that $\mathcal{S}_n = (X_1, X_2, \ldots, X_n)$ is a sample of n partitions X_i drawn i.i.d. from the probability distribution Q. Then the Fréchet function of $\mathcal{S}_n$ is of the form

$$F_n : \mathcal{P} \to \mathbb{R}, \quad Z \mapsto \frac{1}{n} \sum_{i=1}^{n} \delta(X_i, Z)^2.$$

A mean partition of sample $\mathcal{S}_n$ is any partition $M \in \mathcal{P}$ satisfying

$$F_n(M) = \min_{X \in \mathcal{P}} F_n(X).$$

Note that a mean partition needs not to be a member of the support. In addition, a mean partition exists but is not unique, in general [20].

The Mean Partition Theorem proved in [23] states that any representation $\boldsymbol{M}$ of a local minimum M of F_n is the standard mean of sample representations in optimal position with $\boldsymbol{M}$.

Theorem 1. *Let $\mathcal{S}_n = (X_1, \ldots, X_n) \in \mathcal{P}^n$ be a sample of n partitions. Suppose that $M \in \mathcal{P}$ is a local minimum of the Fréchet function $F_n(Z)$ of $\mathcal{S}_n$. Then every representation $\boldsymbol{M}$ of M is of the form*

$$\boldsymbol{M} = \frac{1}{n} \sum_{i=1}^{n} \boldsymbol{X}_i,$$

where the $\boldsymbol{X}_i \in X_i$ are in optimal position with $\boldsymbol{M}$.

Condorcet's original theorem is an asymptotical statement about the majority vote. To adopt this statement, we introduce the notion of expected partition. An expected partition of probability distribution Q is any partition $M_Q \in \mathcal{P}$ that minimizes the expected Fréchet function

$$F_Q : \mathcal{P} \to \mathbb{R}, \quad Z \mapsto \int_{\mathcal{P}} \delta(X, Z)^2 \, dQ(X).$$

As for the sample Fréchet function F_n, the minimum of the expected Fréchet function F_Q exists but is not unique, in general [20].

---

[1] The support of Q is the smallest closed subset $\mathcal{S}_Q \subseteq \mathcal{P}$ such that $Q(\mathcal{S}_Q) = 1$.

4   Condorcet's Jury Theorem

This section extends Condorcet's Jury Theorem to the partition space defined in Sect. 3.2.

4.1   The General Setting

Theorem 2 extends Condorcet's Jury Theorem for hard partitions. Generalization to arbitrary partitions is out of scope and left for future research.

The general setting of Theorem 2 is as follows: Let $\mathcal{S}_n = (X_1, \ldots, X_n)$ be a sample of n hard partitions $X_i \in \mathcal{P}^+$ drawn i.i.d. from a probability distribution Q. Each of the sample partitions X_i has a vote on a given data point $z \in \mathcal{Z}$ with probability $p_i(z)$ of being correct. The goal is to reach a final decision on data point z by majority vote. Theorem 2 makes an asymptotic statement about the correctness of the majority vote given the probabilities p_i .

To formulate Theorem 2, we need to define the concepts of vote and majority vote. The majority vote is based on the mean partition of a sample and is not necessarily a hard partition. Since the mean partition itself votes, we introduce votes for arbitrary (soft and hard) partitions and later restrict ourselves to samples of hard partitions when defining the majority vote.

Assumption. In the following, we assume existence of an unknown but unique hard ground-truth partition $X_* \in \mathcal{P}^+$. By $\boldsymbol{X}_*$ we denote an arbitrarily selected but fixed representation of X_*.

It is important to note that the unique ground-truth partition is unknown to ensure an unsupervised setting.

4.2   Votes

We model the vote of a partition $X \in \mathcal{P}$ on a given data point $z \in \mathcal{Z}$. The vote of X on z has two possible outcomes: The vote is correct if X agrees on z with the ground-truth X_*, and the vote is wrong otherwise. To model the vote of a partition, we need to specify what we mean by *agreeing on a data-point with the ground-truth.*

An agreement function of representation $\boldsymbol{X}$ of X is a function of the form

$$k_{\boldsymbol{X}} : \mathcal{Z} \rightarrow [0, 1], \quad z_j \mapsto \langle \boldsymbol{x}_{:j}, \boldsymbol{x}_{:j}^* \rangle$$

where $\boldsymbol{x}_{:j}$ and $\boldsymbol{x}_{:j}^*$ are the j-th columns of the representations $\boldsymbol{X}$ and $\boldsymbol{X}_*$, respectively. A column of a matrix represents the membership values of the corresponding data point across all clusters. Then the value $k_{\boldsymbol{X}}(z_j)$ measures how strongly representation $\boldsymbol{X}$ agrees with the ground-truth $\boldsymbol{X}_*$ on data point z_j. If X is a hard partition, then $k_{\boldsymbol{X}}(z) = 1$ if z occurs in the same cluster of $\boldsymbol{X}$ and $\boldsymbol{X}_*$, and $k_{\boldsymbol{X}}(z) = 0$ otherwise.

The vote of representation $\boldsymbol{X}$ of partition X on data point z is defined by

$$V_{\boldsymbol{X}}(z) = \mathbb{I}\{k_{\boldsymbol{X}}(z) > 0.5\},$$

where $\mathbb{I}\{b\}$ is the indicator function that gives 1 if the boolean expression b is true, and 0 otherwise. Observe that $k_X = V_X$ for hard partitions $X \in \mathcal{P}^+$.

Based on the vote of a representation we can define the vote of a partition. The vote of partition is a Bernoulli distributed random variable. We randomly select a representation $\boldsymbol{X}$ of partition X in optimal position with $\boldsymbol{X}_*$. Then the vote $V_X(z)$ of X on data point z is $V_{\boldsymbol{X}}(z)$. By

$$p_X(z) = \mathbb{P}\left(V_X(z) = 1\right).$$

we denote the probability of a correct vote of partition X on data point z. Note that the probability $p_X(z)$ is independent of the particular choice of representation $\boldsymbol{X}_*$ of the ground-truth partition X_*.

4.3 Majority Vote

We assume that $\mathcal{S}_n = (X_1, \ldots, X_n)$ is a sample of n hard partitions $X_i \in \mathcal{P}^+$ drawn i.i.d. from a cluster ensemble. We define a majority vote $V_n(z)$ of sample $\mathcal{S}_n$ on z as follows: First randomly select a mean partition M of $\mathcal{S}_n$. Then set the majority vote $V_n(z)$ on z to the vote $V_M(z)$ of the chosen M.[2]

It remains to show that the vote $V_M(z)$ of any mean partition M of $\mathcal{S}_n$ is indeed a majority vote. To see this, we invoke the Mean Partition Theorem. Any representation $\boldsymbol{M}$ of mean partition M is of the form

$$\boldsymbol{M} = \frac{1}{n} \sum_{i=1}^{n} \boldsymbol{X}_i$$

where $\boldsymbol{X}_i \in X_i$ are representations in optimal position with $\boldsymbol{M}$. For a given data point $z_j \in \mathcal{Z}$, the mean membership values are given by

$$\boldsymbol{m}_{:j} = \frac{1}{n} \sum_{i=1}^{n} \boldsymbol{x}_{:j}^{(i)},$$

where $\boldsymbol{x}_{:j}^{(i)}$ denotes the j-th column of representation $\boldsymbol{X}_i$. Since the columns of $\boldsymbol{x}_{:j}^{(i)}$ are standard basis vectors, the elements m_{kj} of the j-th column $\boldsymbol{m}_{:j}$ contain the relative frequencies with which data point z_j occurs in cluster c_k. Then the vote $V_M(z_j)$ is correct if and only if the agreement function of $\boldsymbol{M}$ satisfies

$$k_M(z_j) = \left\langle \boldsymbol{m}_{:j}, \boldsymbol{x}_{:j}^* \right\rangle > 0.5.$$

This in turn implies that there is a majority $m_{kj} > 0.5$ for some cluster c_k, because X_* is a hard partition by assumption.

---

[2] Recall that a mean partition is not unique in general.

4.4 Condorcet's Jury Theorem

Roughly, Condorcet's Jury Theorem states that the majority vote tends to be correct when the individual voters are independent and competent. In consensus clustering, the majority vote is based on mean partitions. Individual sample partitions X_i are competent on data point $z \in \mathcal{Z}$ if the probability of a correct vote on z is given by $p_i(z) > 0.5$. In the spirit of Condorcet's Jury Theorem, we want to show that the probability $\mathbb{P}(h_n(z) = 1)$ of the majority vote $h_n(z)$ tends to one with increasing sample size n.

In general, mean partitions are neither unique nor converge to a unique expected partition. This in turn may result in a non-convergent sequence $(h_n(z))_{n \in \mathbb{N}}$ of majority votes for a given data points z. In this case, it is not possible to establish convergence in probability to the ground-truth. To cope with this problem, we demand that the sample partitions are all contained in a sufficiently small ball, called asymmetry ball. The *asymmetry ball* $\mathcal{A}_Z$ of partition $Z \in \mathcal{P}$ is the subset of the form

$$\mathcal{A}_Z = \{ X \in \mathcal{P} \, : \, \delta(X, Z) \leq \alpha_Z / 4 \},$$

where α_Z is the *degree of asymmetry* of Z defined by

$$\alpha_Z = \min \{ \| \boldsymbol{Z} - \boldsymbol{PZ} \| \, : \, \boldsymbol{Z} \in Z \text{ and } \boldsymbol{P} \in \Pi \backslash \{ \boldsymbol{I} \} \}.$$

A partition Z is asymmetric if $\alpha_Z > 0$. If $\alpha_Z = 0$ the partition Z is called symmetric. Any partition whose representations have mutually distinct rows is an asymmetric partition. Conversely, a partition is symmetric if it has a representation with at least two identical rows. We refer to [22] for more details on asymmetric partitions.

By $\mathcal{A}_Z^\circ$ we denote the largest open subset of $\mathcal{A}_Z$. If Z is symmetric, then $\mathcal{A}_Z^\circ = \emptyset$ be definition. Thus, a non-empty set $\mathcal{A}_Z^\circ$ entails that Z is symmetric.

A probability distribution Q is *homogeneous* if there is a partition Z such that the support $\mathcal{S}_Q$ of probability distribution Q is contained in the asymmetry ball $\mathcal{A}_Z^\circ$. A sample $\mathcal{S}_n$ is said to be homogeneous if the sample partitions of $\mathcal{S}_n$ are drawn from a homogeneous distribution Q.

Now we are in the position to present Condorcet's Jury Theorem for the mean partition approach under the assumption that there is an unknown ground-truth partition. For a proof we refer to the appendix.

Theorem 2 (Condorcet's Jury Theorem). *Let Q be a probability measure on $\mathcal{P}^+$ with support $\mathcal{S}_Q$. Suppose the following assumptions hold:*

1. *There is a partition $Z \in \mathcal{P}$ such that $X_* \in \mathcal{A}_Z^\circ$ and $\mathcal{S}_Q \subseteq \mathcal{A}_Z^\circ$.*
2. *Hard partitions $X_1, \ldots, X_n \in \mathcal{P}^+$ are drawn i.i.d. according to Q.*
3. *Let $z \in \mathcal{Z}$. Then $p_z = p_X(z)$ is constant for all $X \in \mathcal{S}_Q$.*

Then

$$\lim_{n \to \infty} \mathbb{P}(V_n(z) = 1) = \begin{cases} 1 & : \quad p_z > 0.5 \\ 0 & : \quad p_z < 0.5 \\ 0.5 & : \quad p_z = 0.5 \end{cases} \tag{2}$$

for all $z \in \mathcal{Z}$. If $p_z > 0.5$ for all $z \in \mathcal{Z}$, then we have

$$\lim_{n \to \infty} \mathbb{P}\Big(\delta(M_n, X_*) = 0\Big) = 1, \tag{3}$$

where $(M_n)_{n \in \mathbb{N}}$ is a sequence of mean partitions.

Equation (2) corresponds to Condorcet's original theorem for majority vote on a single data point and Eq. (3) shows that the sequence of mean partitions converges almost surely to the (unknown) ground-truth partition. Observe that almost sure convergence in Eq. (3) also holds when the probabilities p_z differ for different data points $z \in \mathcal{Z}$. From the proof of Condorcet's Jury Theorem follows that the ground-truth partition X_* is an expected partition almost surely and therefore takes the form as described in the Expected Partition Theorem [23].

5   Conclusion

This contribution extends Condorcet's Jury Theorem to partition spaces endowed with a metric induced by the Euclidean norm under the following additional assumptions: (i) existence of a unique hard ground-truth partition, and (ii) all sample partitions and the ground-truth are contained in some asymmetry ball. This result can be regarded as a first step to theoretically justify consensus clustering.

A   Proof of Theorem 2

To prove Theorem 2, it is helpful to use a suitable representation of partitions. We suggest to represent partitions as points of some geometric space, called orbit space [20]. Orbit spaces are well explored, possess a rich geometrical structure and have a natural connection to Euclidean spaces [3, 19, 30].

A.1   Partition Spaces

We denote the natural projection that sends matrices to the partitions they represent by

$$\pi : \mathcal{X} \to \mathcal{P}, \quad \boldsymbol{X} \mapsto \pi(\boldsymbol{X}) = X.$$

The group $\Pi = \Pi^\ell$ of all $(\ell \times \ell)$-of all $(\ell \times \ell)$-permutation matrices is a discontinuous group that acts on $\mathcal{X}$ by matrix multiplication, that is

$$\cdot : \Pi \times \mathcal{X} \to \mathcal{X}, \quad (\boldsymbol{P}, \boldsymbol{X}) \mapsto \boldsymbol{P}\boldsymbol{X}.$$

The orbit of $\boldsymbol{X} \in \mathcal{X}$ is the set $[\boldsymbol{X}] = \{\boldsymbol{P}\boldsymbol{X} : \boldsymbol{P} \in \Pi\}$. The orbit space of partitions is the quotient space $\mathcal{X}/\Pi = \{[\boldsymbol{X}] : \boldsymbol{X} \in \mathcal{X}\}$ obtained by the action of the permutation group Π on the set $\mathcal{X}$. We write $\mathcal{P} = \mathcal{X}/\Pi$ to denote the partition space and $X \in \mathcal{P}$ to denote an orbit $[\boldsymbol{X}] \in \mathcal{X}/\Pi$. The natural projection $\pi : \mathcal{X} \to \mathcal{P}$ sends matrices $\boldsymbol{X}$ to the partitions $\pi(\boldsymbol{X}) = [\boldsymbol{X}]$ they represent. The partition space $\mathcal{P}$ is endowed with the intrinsic metric δ defined by $\delta(X, Y) = \min\{\|\boldsymbol{X} - \boldsymbol{Y}\| : \boldsymbol{X} \in X, \boldsymbol{Y} \in Y\}$.

A.2   Dirichlet Fundamental Domains

We use the following notations: By $\overline{\mathcal{U}}$ we denote the closure of a subset $\mathcal{U} \subseteq \mathcal{X}$, by $\partial \mathcal{U}$ the boundary of $\mathcal{U}$, and by $\mathcal{U}^\circ$ the open subset $\overline{\mathcal{U}} \setminus \partial \mathcal{U}$. The action of permutation $\boldsymbol{P} \in \Pi$ on the subset $\mathcal{U} \subseteq \mathcal{X}$ is the set defined by $\boldsymbol{P}\mathcal{U} = \{\boldsymbol{PX} : \boldsymbol{X} \in \mathcal{U}\}$. By $\Pi^* = \Pi \setminus \{\boldsymbol{I}\}$ we denote the subset of $(\ell \times \ell)$-permutation matrices without identity matrix $\boldsymbol{I}$.

A subset $\mathcal{F}$ of $\mathcal{X}$ is a fundamental set for Π if and only if $\mathcal{F}$ contains exactly one representation $\boldsymbol{X}$ from each orbit $[\boldsymbol{X}] \in \mathcal{X}/\Pi$. A fundamental domain of Π in $\mathcal{X}$ is a closed connected set $\mathcal{F} \subseteq \mathcal{X}$ that satisfies

1. $\mathcal{X} = \bigcup\limits_{\boldsymbol{P} \in \Pi} \boldsymbol{P}\mathcal{F}$
2. $\boldsymbol{P}\mathcal{F}^\circ \cap \mathcal{F}^\circ = \emptyset$ for all $\boldsymbol{P} \in \Pi^*$.

Proposition 1. *Let $\boldsymbol{Z}$ be a representation of an asymmetric partition $Z \in \mathcal{P}$. Then*
$$\mathcal{D}_{\boldsymbol{Z}} = \{\boldsymbol{X} \in \mathcal{X} : \|\boldsymbol{X} - \boldsymbol{Z}\| \leq \|\boldsymbol{X} - \boldsymbol{PZ}\| \text{ for all } \boldsymbol{P} \in \Pi\}$$
is a fundamental domain, called Dirichlet fundamental domain of $\boldsymbol{Z}$.

Proof. [30], Theorem 6.6.13.   □

Lemma 1. *Let $\mathcal{D}_{\boldsymbol{Z}}$ be a Dirichlet fundamental domain of representation $\boldsymbol{Z}$ of an asymmetric partition $Z \in \mathcal{P}$. Suppose that $\boldsymbol{X}$ and $\boldsymbol{X}'$ are two different representations of a partition X such that $\boldsymbol{X}, \boldsymbol{X}' \in \mathcal{D}_{\boldsymbol{Z}}$. Then $\boldsymbol{X}, \boldsymbol{X}' \in \partial \mathcal{D}_{\boldsymbol{Z}}$.*

Proof. [19], Prop. 3.13 and [22], Prop. A.2.   □

A.3   Multiple Alignments

Let $\mathcal{S}_n = (X_1, \ldots, X_n)$ be a sample of n partitions $X_i \in \mathcal{P}$. A multiple alignment of $\mathcal{S}_n$ is an n-tuple $\mathfrak{X} = (\boldsymbol{X}_1, \ldots, \boldsymbol{X}_n)$ consisting of representations $\boldsymbol{X}_i \in X_i$. By
$$\mathcal{A}_n = \{\mathfrak{X} = (\boldsymbol{X}_1, \ldots, \boldsymbol{X}_n) : \boldsymbol{X}_1 \in X_1, \ldots, \boldsymbol{X}_n \in X_n\}$$
we denote the set of all multiple alignments of $\mathcal{S}_n$. A multiple alignment $\mathfrak{X} = (\boldsymbol{X}_1, \ldots, \boldsymbol{X}_n)$ is said to be in optimal position with representation $\boldsymbol{Z}$ of a partition Z, if all representations $\boldsymbol{X}_i$ of $\mathfrak{X}$ are in optimal position with $\boldsymbol{Z}$. The mean of a multiple alignment $\mathfrak{X} = (\boldsymbol{X}_1, \ldots, \boldsymbol{X}_n)$ is denoted by
$$M_{\mathfrak{X}} = \frac{1}{n} \sum_{i=1}^{n} \boldsymbol{X}_i.$$

An optimal multiple alignment is a multiple alignment that minimizes the function
$$f_n(\mathfrak{X}) = \frac{1}{n^2} \sum_{i=1}^{n} \sum_{j=1}^{n} \|\boldsymbol{X}_i - \boldsymbol{X}_j\|^2.$$

The problem of finding an optimal multiple alignment is that of finding a multiple alignment with smallest average pairwise squared distances in $\mathcal{X}$. To show equivalence between mean partitions and an optimal multiple alignments, we introduce the sets of minimizers of the respective functions F_n and f_n:

$$\mathcal{M}(F_n) = \{M \in \mathcal{P} : F_n(M) \leq F_n(Z) \text{ for all } Z \in \mathcal{P}\}$$
$$\mathcal{M}(f_n) = \{\mathfrak{X} \in \mathcal{A}_n : f_n(\mathfrak{X}) \leq f_n(\mathfrak{X}') \text{ for all } \mathfrak{X}' \in \mathcal{A}_n\}$$

For a given sample $\mathcal{S}_n$, the set $\mathcal{M}(F_n)$ is the mean partition set and $\mathcal{M}(f_n)$ is the set of all optimal multiple alignments. The next result shows that any solution of F_n is also a solution of f_n and vice versa.

Theorem 3. *For any sample $\mathcal{S}_n \in \mathcal{P}^n$, the map*

$$\phi : \mathcal{M}(f_n) \to \mathcal{M}(F_n), \quad \mathfrak{X} \mapsto \pi(M_{\mathfrak{X}})$$

is surjective.

Proof. [23], Theorem 4.1.   □

A.4   Proof of Theorem 2

Parts 1–8 show the assertion of Eq. (2) and Part 9 shows the assertion of Eq. (3).

1 Without loss of generality, we pick a representation $\boldsymbol{X}_*$ of the ground-truth partition X_*. Let $\boldsymbol{Z}$ be a representation of Z in optimal position with $\boldsymbol{X}_*$. By

$$\mathcal{A}_{\boldsymbol{Z}} = \{\boldsymbol{X} \in \mathcal{X} : \|\boldsymbol{X} - \boldsymbol{Z}\| \leq \alpha_Z/4\}$$

we denote the asymmetry ball of representation $\boldsymbol{Z}$. By construction, we have $\boldsymbol{X}_* \in \mathcal{A}_{\boldsymbol{Z}}$.

2 Since Π acts discontinuously on $\mathcal{X}$, there is a bijective isometry

$$\phi : \mathcal{A}_{\boldsymbol{Z}} \to \mathcal{A}_{\boldsymbol{Z}}, \quad \boldsymbol{X} \mapsto \pi(\boldsymbol{X})$$

according to [30], Theorem 13.1.1.

3 From [22], Theorem 3.1 follows that the mean partition M of $\mathcal{S}_n$ is unique. We show that $M \in \mathcal{A}_{\boldsymbol{Z}}$. Suppose that $\mathfrak{X} = (\boldsymbol{X}_1, \ldots, \boldsymbol{X}_n)$ is a multiple alignment in optimal position with $\boldsymbol{Z}$. Since $\phi : \mathcal{A}_{\boldsymbol{Z}} \to \mathcal{A}_{\boldsymbol{Z}}$ is a bijective isometry, we have

$$f_n(\mathfrak{X}) = \frac{1}{n^2} \sum_{i=1}^{n} \sum_{j=1}^{n} \|\boldsymbol{X}_i - \boldsymbol{X}_j\|^2 = \frac{1}{n^2} \sum_{i=1}^{n} \sum_{j=1}^{n} \delta(X_i, X_j)^2$$

showing that the multiple alignment $\mathfrak{X}$ is optimal. From Theorem 3 follows that

$$M = M_{\mathfrak{X}} = \frac{1}{n} \sum_{i=1}^{n} \boldsymbol{X}_i$$

is a representation of a mean partition M of $\mathcal{S}_n$. Since $\mathcal{A}_{\boldsymbol{Z}}$ is convex, we find that $\boldsymbol{M} \in \mathcal{A}_{\boldsymbol{Z}}$ and therefore $M \in \mathcal{A}_{\boldsymbol{Z}}$.

4 From Part 1–3 of this proof follows that the multiple alignment $\mathfrak{X}$ is in optimal position with $\boldsymbol{X}_*$. We show that there is no other multiple alignment of $\mathcal{S}_n$ with this property. Observe that $\mathcal{A}_{\boldsymbol{Z}}$ is contained in the Dirichlet fundamental domain $\mathcal{D}_{\boldsymbol{Z}}$ of representation $\boldsymbol{Z}$. Let $\mathcal{S}_{\boldsymbol{Z}} = \phi(\mathcal{S}_Q)$ be a representation of the support in $\mathcal{A}_{\boldsymbol{Z}}^{\circ}$. Then by assumption, we have $\mathcal{S}_{\boldsymbol{Z}} \subseteq \mathcal{A}_{\boldsymbol{Z}}^{\circ} \subset \mathcal{D}_{\boldsymbol{Z}}$ showing that $\mathcal{S}_{\boldsymbol{Z}}$ lies in the interior of $\mathcal{D}_{\boldsymbol{Z}}$. From the definition of a fundamental domain together with Lemma 1 follows that $\mathfrak{X}$ is the unique optimal alignment in optimal position with $\boldsymbol{X}_*$.

5 With the same argumentation as in the previous part of this proof, we find that $\boldsymbol{M}$ is the unique representation of M in optimal position with $\boldsymbol{X}_*$.

6 Let $z \in \mathcal{Z}$ be a data point. Since $\boldsymbol{X}_i \in X_i$ is the unique representation in optimal position with $\boldsymbol{X}_*$, the vote of X_i on data point z is of the form $V_{X_i}(z) = V_{\boldsymbol{X}_i}(z)$ for all $i \in \{1, \ldots, n\}$. With the same argument, we have $V_n(z) = V_M(z) = V_{\boldsymbol{M}}(z)$.

7 By $\boldsymbol{x}^{(i)}(z)$ we denote the column of $\boldsymbol{X}_i$ that represents z. By definition, we have

$$p_z = \mathbb{P}\left(V_{X_i}(z) = 1\right) = \mathbb{P}\left(\left\langle \boldsymbol{x}^{(i)}(z), \boldsymbol{x}^*(z) \right\rangle > 0.5\right)$$

for all $i \in \{1, \ldots, n\}$. Since X_i and X_* are both hard partitions, we find that

$$\left\langle \boldsymbol{x}^{(i)}(z), \boldsymbol{x}^*(z) \right\rangle = \mathbb{I}\left\{ \boldsymbol{x}^{(i)}(z) = \boldsymbol{x}^*(z) \right\},$$

where $\mathbb{I}$ denotes the indicator function.

8 From the Mean Partition Theorem follows that

$$\boldsymbol{m}(z) = \frac{1}{n} \sum_{i=1}^{n} \boldsymbol{x}^{(i)}(z)$$

is the column of $\boldsymbol{M}$ that represents z. Then the agreement of $\boldsymbol{M}$ on z is given by

$$k_M(z) = \langle \boldsymbol{m}(z), \boldsymbol{x}^*(z) \rangle$$
$$= \frac{1}{n} \sum_{i=1}^{n} \left\langle \boldsymbol{x}^{(i)}(z), \boldsymbol{x}^*(z) \right\rangle$$
$$= \frac{1}{n} \sum_{i=1}^{n} \mathbb{I}\left\{ \boldsymbol{x}^{(i)}(z) = \boldsymbol{x}^*(z) \right\}.$$

Thus, the agreement $k_M(z)$ counts the fraction of sample partitions X_i that correctly classify z. Let

$$p_n = \mathbb{P}\left(h_n(z) = 1\right) = \mathbb{P}\left(k_M(z) > 0.5\right)$$

denote the probability that the majority of the sample partitions X_i correctly classifies z. Since the votes of the sample partitions are assumed to be independent, we can compute p_n using the binomial distribution

$$p_n = \sum_{i=r}^{n} \binom{n}{i} p^i (1-p)^{n-i},$$

where $r = \lfloor n/2 \rfloor + 1$ and $\lfloor a \rfloor$ is the largest integer b with $b \le a$. Then the assertion of Eq. (2) follows from [16], Theorem 1.

9 We show the assertion of Eq. (3). By assumption, the support $\mathcal{S}_Q$ is contained in an open subset of the asymmetry ball $\mathcal{A}_Z$. From [22], Theorem 3.1 follows that the expected partition M_Q of Q is unique. Then the sequence $(M_n)_{n \in \mathbb{N}}$ converges almost surely to the expected partition M_Q according to [20], Theorem 3.1 and Theorem 3.3. From the first eight parts of the proof follows that the limit partition M_Q agrees on any data point z almost surely with the ground-truth partition X_*. This shows the assertion.

References

1. Berend, D., Paroush, J.: When is condorcet's jury theorem valid? Soc. Choice Welf. **15**(4), 481–488 (1998)
2. Bhattacharya, A., Bhattacharya, R.: Nonparametric Inference on Manifolds with Applications to Shape Spaces. Cambridge University Press, Cambridge (2012)
3. Bredon, G.E.: Introduction to Compact Transformation Groups. Elsevier, New York City (1972)
4. de Condorcet, N.C.: Essai sur l'application de l'analyse à la probabilité des décisions rendues à la pluralité des voix. Imprimerie Royale, Paris (1785)
5. Dimitriadou, E., Weingessel, A., Hornik, K.: A combination scheme for fuzzy clustering. In: Advances in Soft Computing (2002)
6. Dietterich, T.G.: Ensemble methods in machine learning. In: Kittler, J., Roli, F. (eds.) MCS 2000. LNCS, vol. 1857, pp. 1–15. Springer, Heidelberg (2000). https://doi.org/10.1007/3-540-45014-9_1
7. Domeniconi, C., Al-Razgan, M.: Weighted cluster ensembles: methods and analysis. ACM Trans. Knowl. Discov. Data **2**(4), 1–40 (2009)
8. Dryden, I.L., Mardia, K.V.: Statistical Shape Analysis. Wiley, Hoboken (1998)
9. Feragen, A., Lo, P., De Bruijne, M., Nielsen, M., Lauze, F.: Toward a theory of statistical tree-shape analysis. IEEE Trans. Pattern Anal. Mach. Intell. **35**, 2008–2021 (2013)
10. Filkov, V., Skiena, S.: Integrating microarray data by consensus clustering. Int. J. Artif. Intell. Tools **13**(4), 863–880 (2004)
11. Franek, L., Jiang, X.: Ensemble clustering by means of clustering embedding in vector spaces. Pattern Recognit. **47**(2), 833–842 (2014)
12. Fréchet, M.: Les éléments aléatoires de nature quelconque dans un espace distancié. Annales de l'institut Henri Poincaré **10**, 215–310 (1948)
13. Ginestet, C.E.: Strong Consistency of Fréchet Sample Mean Sets for Graph-Valued Random Variables. arXiv: 1204.3183 (2012)
14. Ghaemi, R., Sulaiman, N., Ibrahim, H., Mustapha, N.: A survey: clustering ensembles techniques. Proc. World Acad. Sci. Eng. Technol. **38**, 644–657 (2009)

15. Gionis, A., Mannila, H., Tsaparas, P.: Clustering aggregation. ACM Trans. Knowl. Discov. Data **1**(1), 341–352 (2007)
16. Grofman, B., Owen, G., Feld, S.L.: Thirteen theorems in search of the truth. Theory Decis. **15**(3), 261–278 (1983)
17. Huckemann, S., Hotz, T., Munk, A.: Intrinsic shape analysis: geodesic PCA for Riemannian manifolds modulo isometric Lie group actions. Statistica Sinica **20**, 1–100 (2010)
18. Jain, B.J., Obermayer, K.: Structure spaces. J. Mach. Learn. Res. **10**, 2667–2714 (2009)
19. Jain, B.J.: Geometry of Graph Edit Distance Spaces. arXiv: 1505.08071 (2015)
20. Jain, B.J.: Asymptotic Behavior of Mean Partitions in Consensus Clustering. arXiv:1512.06061 (2015)
21. Jain, B.J.: Statistical analysis of graphs. Pattern Recognit. **60**, 802–812 (2016)
22. Jain, B.J.: Homogeneity of Cluster Ensembles. arXiv:1602.02543 (2016)
23. Jain, B.J.: The Mean Partition Theorem of Consensus Clustering. arXiv:1604.06626 (2016)
24. Kendall, D.G.: Shape manifolds, procrustean metrics, and complex projective spaces. Bul. Lond. Math. Soc. **16**, 81–121 (1984)
25. Kuncheva, L.I.: Combining Pattern Classifiers: Methods and Algorithms. Wiley, Hoboken (2004)
26. Lam, L., Suen, C.Y.: Application of majority voting to pattern recognition: an analysis of its behavior and performance. IEEE Trans. Syst. Man Cybern.- Part A: Syst. Hum. **27**(5), 553–568 (1997)
27. Li, T., Ding, C., Jordan, M.I.: Solving consensus and semi-supervised clustering problems using nonnegative matrix factorization. In: IEEE International Conference on Data Mining (2007)
28. Marron, J.S., Alonso, A.M.: Overview of object oriented data analysis. Biom. J. **56**(5), 732–753 (2014)
29. Polikar, R.: Ensemble learning. Scholarpedia **4**(1), 2776 (2009)
30. Ratcliffe, J.G.: Foundations of Hyperbolic Manifolds. Springer, New York (2006). https://doi.org/10.1007/978-0-387-47322-2
31. Rokach, L.: Ensemble-based classifiers. Artif. Intell. Rev. **33**(1–2), 1–39 (2010)
32. Strehl, A., Ghosh, J.: Cluster ensembles - a knowledge reuse framework for combining multiple partitions. J. Mach. Learn. Res. **3**, 583–617 (2002)
33. Surowiecki, J.: The Wisdom of Crowds. Anchor, New York City (2005)
34. Topchy, A.P., Jain, A.K., Punch, W.: Clustering ensembles: models of consensus and weak partitions. IEEE Trans. Pattern Anal. Mach. Intell. **27**(12), 1866–1881 (2005)
35. Vega-Pons, S., Correa-Morris, J., Ruiz-Shulcloper, J.: Weighted partition consensus via kernels. Pattern Recognit. **43**(8), 2712–2724 (2010)
36. Vega-Pons, S., Ruiz-Shulcloper, J.: A survey of clustering ensemble algorithms. Int. J. Pattern Recognit. Artif. Intell. **25**(03), 337–372 (2011)
37. Waldron, J.: The wisdom of the multitude: some reflections on Book III chapter 11 of the politics. Polit. Theory **23**, 563–84 (1995)
38. Wang, H., Marron, J.S.: Object oriented data analysis: sets of trees. Ann. Stat. **35**, 1849–1873 (2007)
39. Yang, F., Li, X., Li, Q., Li, T.: Exploring the diversity in cluster ensemble generation: random sampling and random projection. Expert Syst. Appl. **41**(10), 4844–4866 (2014)
40. Zhou, Z.: Ensemble Methods: Foundations and Algorithms. Taylor & Francis Group, LLC, Abingdon (2012)

Sparse Transfer Classification for Text Documents

Christoph Raab[1(✉)] and Frank-Michael Schleif[2]

[1] University for Applied Science Würzburg-Schweinfurt,
Sanderheinrichsleitenweg 20, Würzburg, Germany
`christoph.raab@fhws.de`
[2] School of Computer Science, University of Birmingham,
Edgbaston, Birmingham B15 2TT, UK

Abstract. Transfer learning supports classification in domains varying from the learning domain. Prominent applications can be found
in Wifi-localization, sentiment classification or robotics. A recent study
shows that approximation of training trough test environments is leading to proper performance and out-dates the strategy most transfer
learning approaches pursue. Additionally, sparse transfer learning models are required to address technical limitations and the demand for
interpretability due to recent privacy regulations. In this work, we propose a new transfer learning approach which approximates the learning
environment, combine it with the sparse and interpretable probabilistic
classification vector machine and compare our solution with standard
benchmarks in the field.

Keywords: Transfer learning · Basis-Transfer
Single Value Decomposition · Sparse classification
Probabilistic classification vector machine

1 Introduction

Supervised Classification has a vast range of application and is an important task
in machine learning. Learned models can predict target labels of unseen samples.
The fact that the domain of interest and underlying distribution of training and
test samples must not change is a primer condition to obtain proper predictions.
If the domain is changing to a different but related task, one would like to reuse
already labeled data or available learning models [15].

A practical example is sentiment classification of text documents. First, a
classifier is trained on a collection of text documents concerning a certain topic
which, naturally, has a word distribution according to it. For the test scenario
another topic is chosen which leads to divergences in word distribution concerning the training one. Transfer learning aims, inter alia, to solve these divergences
[13].

Another application of interest is Wifi-localization, which aims to detect user
locations based on recent Wifi-profiles. But, collecting Wifi-localization profiles

F. Trollmann and A.-Y. Turhan (Eds.): KI 2018, LNAI 11117, pp. 169–181, 2018.
https://doi.org/10.1007/978-3-030-00111-7_15

is an expensive process and demands on factors, e.g. time and device. To reduce the re-calibration effort, one wants to adapt previously created profiles (source domain) for new time periods (target domain) or to adapt localization-models to other devices, resulting in a knowledge-transfer problem. [13]

Multiple transfer learning methods have been already proposed, following different strategies and solving various problems [13,15]. The focus of this paper are sparse transfer models which are not yet covered sufficiently by recent approaches.

The *Probabilistic Classification Vector Machine* (PCVM) [1] is a sparse probabilistic kernel classifier, pruning unused basis functions during training. The PCVM is a very successful classification algorithm [1,14] with competitive performance to *Support Vector Machine* (SVM) [2], but is additionally natural sparse and creates interpretable models as needed in many applied domains of transfer learning. The original PCVM is not well suited for transfer learning, because there is no adaption process if test domain distribution is different to train domain distribution.

To tackle this issue, we will propose a new transfer learning method called *Basis-Transfer* (BT) and extend the *probabilistic classification vector machine* with it. The proposed solution is tested against other commonly used transfer learning approaches.

An overview of recent work is provided in Sect. 2. Subsequently, we introduce the used algorithmic concepts in Sects. 3, 4 and 5, followed by an experimental part in Sect. 6, addressing the classification performance and the sparsity of the model. A summary and open issues are provided in the conclusion at the end of the paper.

2 Related Work

Transfer learning is the task of reusing information or trained models in one domain to help to learn a target predictive function in a different domain of interest [13]. For recent surveys and definition see [13,15].

To solve the knowledge transfer issue, a variety of strategies have been proposed. For example *instance-transfer, symmetric-feature transfer, asymmetric-feature transfer, relational-knowledge transfer* and *parameter transfer*.[15]

Summarizing, above strategies may distinguish roughly between following approaches. Let $\mathbf{Z} = \{\mathbf{z}_1, \ldots, \mathbf{z}_N\}$ be training data, sampled from $p(\mathbf{Z})$ in the training domain $\mathcal{Z}$ and $\mathbf{X} = \{\mathbf{x}_1, \ldots, \mathbf{x}_M\}$ a test dataset sampled from $p(\mathbf{X})$ in the test domain $\mathcal{X}$. With $p(\mathbf{Z})$ as marginal probability distribution over all labels. First, aligning divergences in marginal distributions $p(\mathbf{Z}) \approx p(\mathbf{X})$ or, secondly, doing so and simultaneously solve differences in conditional distributions, i.e. $p(\mathbf{Y}|\mathbf{Z}) \approx p(\mathbf{Y}|\mathbf{X})$. With $p(\mathbf{Y}|\mathbf{Z})$ as conditional probability distribution, meaning: '*Probability for label y, given data sample x*'. Here we briefly discuss these techniques and referring to proposed scenarios.

The *instance transfer method* tries to align the marginal distribution by re-weighting some source data. This re-weighted data is then directly used with target data for training. It seems that these type of algorithm works best when the conditional probability is the same in source and the target domain and only aligns marginal distribution divergences [15]. An example is given in [4].

Approaches implementing the *symmetric feature transfer* are trying to find a common latent subspace for source and target domain with the goal to reduce marginal distribution differences, such that the underlying structure of the data is preserved in the subspace. An example of a symmetric feature space transfer method is the *Transfer Component Analysis* (TCA) [12,15].

The *asymmetric feature transfer* learning approach tries to transform the source domain data in the target (subspace) domain. This should be done in a way that the transformed source data will match the target distribution. In comparison to the symmetric feature transfer approaches, there will be no shared subspace, but only the target space [15]. An example is given by the *Joint Distribution Adaptation* (JDA) [8] algorithm, which solves divergences in marginal distributions similar to TCA, but aligning conditional distributions with pseudo-labeling techniques. Pseudo-labeling is performed by assigning labels to unlabeled target data by a baseline classifier, e.g. SVM, resulting in a target conditional distribution, followed by matching it to the source conditional distribution of the ground truth source label [8].

The *relational-knowledge transfer* aims to find some relationship between source and target data commonly in original space [15]. *Transfer Kernel Learning* [9] is a recent approach, which approximates a kernel of training data $K(\mathbf{Z})$ with kernel of test data $K(\mathbf{X})$ via the *Nyström* kernel approximation. It only considers discrepancies in marginal distributions and further claims it is sufficient to approximate a training kernel, i.e. $K(\mathbf{Z}) \approx K(\mathbf{X})$, for effective knowledge transfer [9].

All the considered methods have approximately a complexity of $\mathcal{O}(N^2)$ where N is the largest number of samples concerning test or training [4,8,9,12]. According to the definition of transfer learning [13], these algorithms are doing *transductive* transfer learning, because some *test* data *must* be available at training time. The mentioned solutions do not take the label information into account in solving the transfer learning problem, e.g. to find new feature representations. These solutions can not be directly used as predictors, but rather are wrappers for classification algorithms. The baseline classifier is most often the *Support Vector Machine* (SVM).

3   Probabilistic Classification Vector Learning

According to [1], the SVM has some drawbacks, mainly a rather dense decision function (also in case of so called sparse SVM techniques) and a lack of a mathematically sound *probabilistic* formulation. The *Probabilistic Classification Vector Machine* [1] addressed this issues providing a competitive sparse and probabilistic classification function [1].

It uses a probabilistic kernel regression model:

$$l(\mathbf{x}; \mathbf{w}, b) = \Psi \left(\sum_{i=1}^{N} w_i \phi_i(\mathbf{x}) + b \right) = \Psi \left(\Phi(\mathbf{x})^\top \mathbf{w} + b \right) \tag{1}$$

With a link function $\Psi(\cdot)$, with w_i being the weights of the basis functions $\phi_i(\mathbf{x})$ and b as bias term. In PCVM the basis functions ϕ_i are defined explicitly as part of the model design. In (1) the standard kernel trick can be applied. The implementation of PCVM [1] use the probit link function, i.e.:

$$\Psi(\mathbf{x}) = \int_{-\infty}^{x} \mathcal{N}(t|0, 1) dt \tag{2}$$

where $\Psi(\mathbf{x})$ is the cumulative distribution of the normal distribution $\mathcal{N}(0, 1)$. The PCVM [1] uses the *Expectation-Maximization* algorithm for learning the model. The underlying optimization framework within EM, prunes unused basis functions and, therefore, is a sparse probabilistic learning machine. In PCVM we will use the standard *RBF*-kernel with a *Gaussian* width θ. In [14] a PCVM with linear costs was suggested, which makes use of the *Nyström* approximation and could be used herein as well to improve the run-time/memory complexity. Further details can be found in [1,14].

4   Basis Transfer

The recent *transfer kernel learning* approach [9] from Sect. 2 assumes that there is no need for explicit adjustments of distributions.

A fundamental design choice of the PCVM is that data should distributed as zero-mean *Gaussian*, which is a common choice, but often requires normalization of data, e.g. with z-score. This results in centered and normalized data, i.e. roughly $\mathcal{N}(0, 1)$, and we suggest there is no further need to adjust marginal distributions.

As offered by [9], it is sufficient to approximate some kernel that $K(\mathbf{Z}) \approx K(\mathbf{X})$ for a good transfer approximation. We expand this statement and claim that, naturally, it is sufficient for transfer learning to approximate a training matrix $\mathbf{Z}$ with the use of test samples $\mathbf{X}$, i.e. $\mathbf{Z}_n \approx \mathbf{X}$.

In the following we propose our *Basis-Transfer* approach: Let $\mathbf{Z} = \{\mathbf{z}_1, \ldots, \mathbf{z}_N\}$ be training data, sampled from $p(\mathbf{Z})$ in the training domain $\mathcal{Z}$ and

$\mathbf{X} = \{\mathbf{x}_1, \ldots, \mathbf{x}_M\}$ a test dataset sampled from $p(\mathbf{X})$ in the test domain $\mathcal{X}$. The quality of matrix approximation is measurable with the *Frobenius* norm:

$$E_{BT} = \|\mathbf{Z} - \mathbf{X}\|_F \tag{3}$$

The proposed solution involves *Single-Value-Decomposition* (SVD), which is defined as:

$$\mathbf{X} = \mathbf{U}\Lambda\mathbf{V} \tag{4}$$

Where $\mathbf{U}$ are left-singular vectors, Λ are singular values or square root eigen-values and $\mathbf{V}$ are right-singular vectors. Using SVD we can rewrite our data matrices:

$$\mathbf{Z} = \mathbf{U}_Z \Lambda \mathbf{V}_Z \quad and \quad \mathbf{X} = \mathbf{U}_\mathcal{X} \Gamma \mathbf{V}_\mathcal{X} \tag{5}$$

One can interpret the singular-vector matrices as rotation and singular values as scaling of basis vectors based on underlying data which creates basis vectors.

This assumption is used to approximate training data with test data by using basis information sampled from test domain for row and column span:

$$\mathbf{Z}_n = \mathbf{U}_\mathcal{X} \Lambda \mathbf{V}_\mathcal{X} \tag{6}$$

Where $\mathbf{U}_\mathcal{X}$ and $\mathbf{V}_\mathcal{X}$ are the target singular vectors, expanding singular values Λ from source domain and $\mathbf{Z}_n$ is an approximated transfer matrix, which can be used for learning a classifier-model, e.g. PCVM.

But consider the number of samples from both domains N and M with $N \neq M$. This will cause Eq. (6) to be invalid by definition. Therefore, we model the minor number of examples as topic space with respect to domain and reduce the major topic space to minor resulting in $N = M$.

For now we limit our approach to a *Term-Frequency Inverse-Document-Frequency* (TFIDF) vector space based on text documents or similar. Therefore, reduction of original to topic space is easy to implement via *Latent Semantic Analysis* (LSA)[7], resulting in a reduced matrix $\mathbf{Z}_r$. This validates Eq. (6) and an approximation can be performed.

In Fig. 1, the process of approximation is shown. The figure shows a synthetic dataset, but for the sake of argument suppose the figure shows web pages and domain one are university pages and domain two are news pages. Domain one is labelled as red and magenta and domain two is represented by green and blue. The labels are given by shape x / * identifying positive or negative class. After our *Basis-Transfer* approach, the domains are aligned (e.g. Class * - red/green) and a classifier can be trained on university pages and is able to predict the class of a news page.

The error formulation in Eq. (3) can be rewritten, because the construction of new training data in Eq. (6) relies only on singular values from original training data and singular vectors are taken from test set. Therefore, we can reduce the error to the *Frobenius* Norm between training and test singular values:

$$E_{BT} = \|\mathbf{Z}_n - \mathbf{X}\|_F = \|\mathbf{U}_\mathcal{X} \Lambda \mathbf{V}_\mathcal{X} - \mathbf{U}_\mathcal{X} \Gamma \mathbf{V}_\mathcal{X}\|_F = \|\Lambda - \Gamma\|_F \tag{7}$$

Which is the final approximation error. The computational complexity of this is caused by two SVD's and a eigendecomposition if $N \neq M$. This results in a overall complexity of $\mathcal{O}(3N^2) = \mathcal{O}(N^2)$ where N is the largest number of samples with respect to training and test set. Using a SVD with linear time [5], the complexity is further reduced to $\mathcal{O}(m^2)$, where m are randomly selected *landmarks* with $m \ll N$. This works best when $m = rank(\mathbf{X})$.

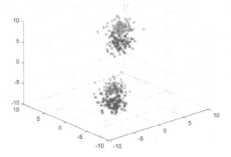

(a) Data unnormalized

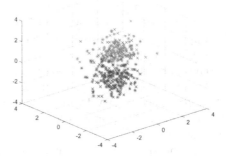

(b) Data after z-Score

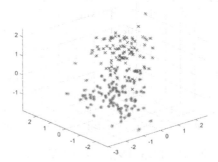

(c) Data after Basis-Transfer

Fig. 1. Process of *Basis-Transfer* with samples from two domains. Class information is given by shape (x,∗) and domain are indicated by colors (domain one - red/green, domain two - magenta/blue). First (a), the unnormalized data with a knowledge gap. Second (b), a normalized feature space. Third (c), *Basis-Transfer* approximation is applied, correcting the samples and training data is usable for learning a classification model for test domain. (Color figure online)

5 Probabilistic Classification Vector Machine with Transfer Learning

As discussed in Sect. 3 the PCVM can solve some drawbacks of the SVM, but is despite the advantages rarely used as baseline algorithm [13,15]. A variety of transfer learning approaches are combined with SVM providing various experimental results (see Sect. 2), however creating non-probabilistic and dense models. To provide a different view on unsupervised transductive transfer learning and being able to provide sparse and probabilistic models, the PCVM is used rather than the SVM. The proposed transfer learning classifier is called Sparse Transfer Vector Machine (STVM).

It combines the proposed transfer learning concept from Sect. 4 and the PCVM formulation [1] or the respective *Nyström* approximated version [14].

The pseudo code of the algorithm is shown in Algorithm 1. Note that for the sake of clarity the decision which domain data must be reduced is omitted and the training matrix is taken instead. This has to be considered when implemented in practice[1]. An advantage of BT is that it has no parameters and, therefore, needs no parameter tuning. The PCVM has the width of the Kernel as tuneable parameter. In the following sections we will validate our approach through a extensive study.

Algorithm 1. Sparse Transfer Vector Machine

Require: $\mathbf{K} = [\mathbf{Z}; \mathbf{X}]$ as N sized training and M sized test set; $\mathbf{Y}$ as N sized training label vector; *ker*; θ as kernel parameter.
Ensure: Weight Vector $\mathbf{w}$; bias b;
1: $\mathbf{Z}_r = LSA(\mathbf{Z})$ $\triangleright$ According to [7]
2: $\Lambda_r = SVD(\mathbf{Z}_r)$;
3: $[\mathbf{U}_{\mathcal{X}}, \mathbf{V}_{\mathcal{X}}] = SVD(\mathbf{X})$
4: $\mathbf{Z}_n = \mathbf{U}_{\mathcal{X}} \Lambda_r \mathbf{V}_{\mathcal{X}}$ $\triangleright$ According to eq. 6
5: $[\mathbf{w}, b] = \text{pcvm\_training}(\mathbf{Z}_n, \mathbf{Y}, ker, \theta)$; $\triangleright$ According to [1]

---

6 Experiments

We follow the experimental design which is typical for transfer learning algorithms [4,6,8,9,13]. A crucial characteristic of the datasets for transfer learning is that domains for training and testing are different but related. This relation exists because train and test classes have the same top category or source. The classes itself are subcategories or subsets.

---

[1] Matlab code of STVM and datasets can be obtained from https://github.com/ChristophRaab/STVM.git.

6.1 Benchmark Datasets

The study consists of twelve benchmark datasets, already preprocessed and taken from [9,10].

Half of them are from *Reuters-21578*[2] and are a collection of *Reuters* news-wire articles assembled in 1987. The text is converted to lower case, words are stemmed and stop-words are removed. With the *Document Frequency* (DF)-Threshold of 3, the numbers of features are cut down. Finally, TFIDF is applied for feature generation [3]. The three top categories *organization (orgs)*, *places* and *people* are used in our experiment.

To create a transfer problem, a classifier is not tested with the same categories as it is trained on, i.e. it is trained on some subcategories of organization and people and tested on others. Therefore, six datasets are used: *orgs vs. places, orgs vs. people, people vs. places, places vs. orgs, people vs. places* and *places vs. people*. They are two-class problems with the top categories as positive and negative class and with subcategories as training and testing examples.

The remaining half are from the *20-Newsgroup*[3] dataset. The original collection has approximately 20000 text documents from 20 newsgroups and is nearly equally distributed in 20 subcategories. The top four categories are *comp, rec, talk* and *sci* and containing four subcategories each. We follow a data sampling scheme introduced by [9] and generate 216 cross domain datasets based on subcategories:

Let C be a top category and $\{C1, C2, C3, C4\} \in C$ are subcategories and K with $\{K1, K2, K3, K4\} \in K$. Select two subcategories each, e.g. C1, C2, K1, and K2, train a classifier, select another four and test the model on it. The top categories are respective classes. Following this, 36 samplings per top category-combinations are possible, which are in total 216 dataset samplings. This is summarized as mean over all test runs as *comp vs rec, comp vs talk, comp vs sci, rec vs sci, rec vs talk* and *sci vs talk*.

This version of *20-Newsgroup* has 25804 TF-IDF features within 15033 documents [9]. The choice of subcategories is the same as in [10]. To reproduce the results below, one should use the linked versions of the datasets.

A summary of all datasets is shown in Table 1.

6.2 Details of Implementation

All algorithms rely on the RBF-kernel. TCA, JDA and TKL are using the SVM as baseline approach, using the *LibSVM* implementation and $C = 10$. TKL has the eigenvalue dumping factor ξ, which is set to 2 for both categories. C and ξ are not optimized via grid search and taken from [9].

---

[2] http://www.daviddlewis.com/resources/testcollections/reuters21578.
[3] http://qwone.com/~jason/20Newsgroups/.

Table 1. Overview of the key figures of 20Newsgroup and Reuters. Choice of subcategories by [9].

Name	#Samples	#Features	#Labels
Comp	4857	25804	2
Rec	3968		
Sci	3946		
Talk	3250		
Orgs	1237	4771	2
People	1208		
Places	1016		

The remaining parameters are optimized on the training data sets wit respect to best performance on it: JDA has two model parameters. First the number of subspace bases k, which is set to 100 and found via grid-search from $k = \{1, 2, 5, 10, 20, \ldots, 100, 200\}$. The regularization parameter λ is set to 1 for both categories, determined by a grid search $\lambda = \{0.1, 0.2, 1, 2, 5, \ldots, 10\}$.

The TCA has also one parameter which gives the subspace dimensions and is determined from $\mu = \{1, 2, 5, 10, 20, \ldots, 100, 200\}$ and finally set to $\mu = 50$ for both. The width of the *Gaussian* kernel is set to one.

6.3 Comparison of Performance

Experimental results are shown in Table 2 as mean errors from a 5 times 2-fold cross-validation schema over six Reuters datasets and the cross-domain sampling for newsgroup which are in total 276 test runs. The standard deviation is shown in brackets. The results are shown for *20Newsgroup* and *Reuters* individually. The proposed STVM classifiers is shown in the third column. The performance of the best classifier is indicated in bold. In Fig. 2, a graph of mean performance and the standard deviation is plotted.

In general, the STVM has a better performance in terms of error than the remaining transfer learning approaches. Comparing STVM to PCVM, the drop in error or improve of performance is significant. The standard deviation of the SVTM is relatively high, especially at *20Newsgroup* dataset. This should be an issue in future work. The performance of PCVM compared to SVM is worse. But, combined with our Basis-Transfer, the PCVM is a sound classifier when it comes to text based knowledge-transfer problems.

The results from Table 2 validate the approach of domain approximation discussed in above sections.

6.4 Comparison of Model Complexity

We measured the model complexity by means of the number of model vectors, e.g. support vectors. The result of model complexity from our experiment

Table 2. Cross-validation comparison of the tested algorithms on twelve domain adaptation datasets by the error and RMSE metrics. Six summarized *20Newsgroup* sets with two classes and six text sets with two classes. Each dataset has two domains. It demonstrates mean of 36 cross domain sampling runs per contrast of *20Newsgroup* and ten runs of cross-validation per dataset of *Reuters* with the standard deviation in brackets. The winner is marked with a bold performance value.

Error 20Newsgroup 2 Domains - 2 Classes	SVM	PCVM	STVM (Our Work)	TCA	JDA	TKL
Comp vs Rec	11.40 (8.16)	17.92 (9.8300)	**1.02** (0.38)	7.74 (7.65)	8.69 (4.84)	4.750 (1.54)
Comp vs Sci	26.31 (4.67)	29.13 (8.4600)	**6.58** (15.06)	30.28 (9.59)	33.01 (10.89)	12.63 (4.66)
Comp vs Talk	6.11 (1.38)	6.15 (0.9700)	9.54(13.90)	**3.33** (0.83)	5.41 (2.14)	3.370 (0.79)
Rec vs Sci	30.45 (9.47)	36.60 (10.1400)	**0.83** (0.27)	22.47 (8.31)	25.86 (8.54)	13.15 (9.58)
Rec vs Talk	18.16 (5.39)	27.79 (11.2000)	**4.56** (3.05)	11.28 (5.87)	15.83 (4.69)	11.41 (7.10)
Sci vs Talk	21.88 (2.58)	31.09 (12.0200)	**9.11** (14.08)	20.01 (2.44)	26.69 (4.77)	14.85 (2.38)
RMSE	19.89 (9.12)	33.11(11.38)	**9.25** (7.63)	17.03 (10.14)	20.14 (11.24)	11.01 (5.39)
Error Reuters 2 Domains - 2 Classes	SVM	PCVM	STVM	TCA	JDA	TKL
Orgs vs People	23.01 (1.58)	26.77 (3.18)	**4.14** (0.51)	22.78 (3.14)	24.88 (2.61)	19.29 (1.73)
People vs Orgs	21.07 (1.72)	27.77 (2.19)	**4.01** (0.64)	19.68 (2.00)	23.23 (1.93)	12.76 (1.16)
Orgs vs Places	30.62 (2.22)	33.42 (6.10)	**8.74** (0.71)	28.38 (3.00)	28.30 (1.51)	22.84 (1.62)
Places vs Orgs	35.45 (2.24)	35.49 (8.19)	**7.87** (0.78)	32.42 (3.91)	35.37 (4.39)	18.33 (3.75)
Places vs People	39.68 (2.35)	41.01 (6.98)	**7.76** (1.21)	40.58 (4.11)	42.41 (2.59)	29.55 (1.46)
People vs Places	41.08 (1.98)	40.69 (5.52)	**11.47** (2.86)	41.39 (3.26)	43.51 (2.23)	33.42 (3.28)
RMSE	32.74 (2.03)	34.65 (4.44)	**7.37** (3.47)	31.94 (3.31)	33.92 (2.70)	23.74 (2.38)

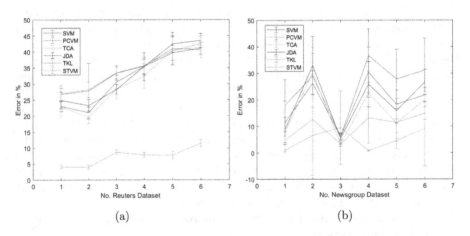

(a)   (b)

Fig. 2. Plot of mean error with standard deviation of the cross-validation/domain test. The left shows the result on *Reuters* and the right shows the result on *20Newsgroup*. A graph shows the error and a vertical bar shows the standard deviation. The number (No.) of datasets are the order of datasets in Table 2. Best viewed in color.

is shown in Table 3. We see that the transfer learning models of the STVM are provide relatively sparse models, while having a very sound performance as shown in Table 2. The difference in the number of model vectors to other transfer learning approaches is significant. The only classifier partly providing less model complexity is PCVM. In Fig. 3, the difference in model complexity is exemplary shown. It demonstrates a sample result of classification of STVM and TKL-SVM on the text dataset *orgs vs people* with the settings from above. The error value of the first is 4% with 47 model vectors and for SVM 22% with 334 support vectors.

Table 3. Mean of model vectors of a classifier for *Reuters* and *20Newsgroup* datasets. The average number of examples in the datasets are shown on the right side of the name.

N. SV.	SVM	PCVM	STVM	TCA	JDA	TKL
Reuters(1154)	482.35	**46.93**	50.4	182.70	220.28	190.73
20Newsgroup(940)	915.03	74.23	**66.02**	215.97	202.93	786.80

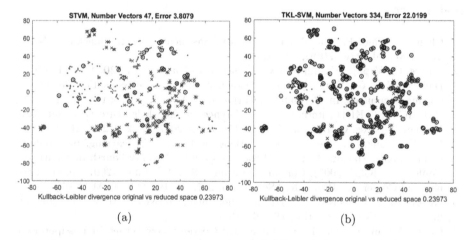

(a)   (b)

Fig. 3. Sample run on *Orgs vs People* (Text dataset). Red colors for the class *orgs* and blue for the class *people*. This plot includes training and testing data. Model complexity of STVM on the left and TKL-SVM on the right. The STVM uses 47 vectors and achieves an error of 4%. The SVM need 334 vectors and has an error of 22%. The black circled points are used model vectors. Reduced with t-SNE [11]. Best viewed in color.

This clearly demonstrates the strength of the STVM in comparison with SVM based transfer learning solutions. STVM achieves *sustain performance* by a *small mode complexity* and provides at least a way to interpret the model. Note that the algorithms are trained in the original feature space and the data and reference/support points of the models are plotted in a reduced space, using the *t-distributed stochastic neighbor embedding algorithm* [11].

7   Conclusions

We proposed a new transfer learning approach and integrated it successfully into the PCVM, resulting in the *Sparse Transfer Vector Machine*. It is based on our unsupervised *Basis-Transfer* approach acting as wrapper to support the PCVM as supervised classification algorithm. The experiments made it clear that approximation of a domain environment is a reliable strategy for transfer problems to achieve very proper classification performance. We showed that the PCVM is able to act as underlying baseline approach for transfer learning situations and still maintain a sparse model competitive to other baseline approaches. Further, the STVM can provide reliable probabilistic outputs, where other transfer learning approach are lacking in. Combining these, the prediction quality of the STVM is charming. The solutions pursues a transductive transfer approach by needing *some unlabeled* target data at training time. Further work should aim to extend Basis-Transfer to other areas of interest, e.g. image classification, multi-class problems and reducing of standard deviation. Besides, applying STVM to practical applications would be of interest.

References

1. Chen, H., Tino, P., Yao, X.: Probabilistic classification vector machines. IEEE Trans. Neural Netw. **20**(6), 901–914 (2009)
2. Cortes, C., Vapnik, V.: Support vector network. Mach. Learn. **20**, 1–20 (1995)
3. Dai, W., Xue, G., Yang, Q., Yu, Y.: Co-clustering based classification for out-of-domain documents. In: Berkhin, P., Caruana, R., Wu, X. (eds.) Proceedings of the 13th ACM SIGKDD International Conference on Knowledge Discovery and Data Mining, San Jose, California, USA, 12–15 August 2007, pp. 210–219. ACM (2007)
4. Dai, W., Yang, Q., Xue, G., Yu, Y.: Boosting for transfer learning. In: Ghahramani, Z. (ed.) Machine Learning, Proceedings of the Twenty-Fourth International Conference (ICML 2007), Corvallis, Oregon, USA, 20–24 June 2007. ACM International Conference Proceeding Series, vol. 227, pp. 193–200. ACM (2007)
5. Gisbrecht, A., Schleif, F.: Metric and non-metric proximity transformations at linear costs. Neurocomputing **167**, 643–657 (2015)
6. Gong, B., Shi, Y., Sha, F., Grauman, K.: Geodesic flow kernel for unsupervised domain adaptation. In: 2012 IEEE Conference on Computer Vision and Pattern Recognition, pp. 2066–2073 (2012)
7. Landauer, T.K., Dumais, S.T.: Latent semantic analysis. Scholarpedia **3**(11), 4356 (2008)
8. Long, M., Wang, J., Ding, G., Sun, J., Yu, P.S.: Transfer feature learning with joint distribution adaptation. In: 2013 IEEE International Conference on Computer Vision, pp. 2200–2207 (2013)
9. Long, M., Wang, J., Sun, J., Yu, P.S.: Domain invariant transfer kernel learning. IEEE Trans. Knowl. Data Eng. **27**(6), 1519–1532 (2015)
10. Long, M., Wang, J., Ding, G., Shen, D., Yang, Q.: Transfer learning with graph co-regularization. IEEE Trans. Knowl. Data Eng. **26**(7), 1805–1818 (2014)
11. van der Maaten, L., Hinton, G.: Visualizing data using t-SNE. J. Mach. Learn. Res. **9**, 2579–2605 (2008)

12. Pan, S.J., Tsang, I.W., Kwok, J.T., Yang, Q.: Domain adaptation via transfer component analysis. IEEE Trans. Neural Netw. **22**(2), 199–210 (2011)
13. Pan, S.J., Yang, Q.: A survey on transfer learning. IEEE Trans. Knowl. Data Eng. **22**(10), 1345–1359 (2010)
14. Schleif, F., Chen, H., Tiño, P.: Incremental probabilistic classification vector machine with linear costs. In: 2015 International Joint Conference on Neural Networks, IJCNN 2015, Killarney, Ireland, 12–17 July 2015, pp. 1–8. IEEE (2015)
15. Weiss, K., Khoshgoftaar, T.M., Wang, D.: A survey of transfer learning. J. Big Data **3**(1), 9 (2016)

Towards Hypervector Representations for Learning and Planning with Schemas

Peer Neubert$^{(\boxtimes)}$ and Peter Protzel

Chemnitz University of Technology, 09126 Chemnitz, Germany
{peer.neubert,peter.protzel}@etit.tu-chemnitz.de

Abstract. The Schema Mechanism is a general learning and concept building framework initially created in the 1980s by Gary Drescher. It was inspired by the constructivist theory of early human cognitive development by Jean Piaget and shares interesting properties with human learning. Recently, Schema Networks were proposed. They combine ideas of the original Schema mechanism, Relational MDPs and planning based on Factor Graph optimization. Schema Networks demonstrated interesting properties for transfer learning, i.e. the ability of zero-shot transfer. However, there are several limitations of this approach. For example, although the Schema Network, in principle, works on an object-level, the original learning and inference algorithms use individual pixels as objects. Also, all types of entities have to share the same set of attributes and the neighborhood for each learned Schema has to be of the same size. In this paper, we discuss these and other limitations of Schema Networks and propose a novel representation based on hypervectors to address some of the limitations. Hypervectors are very high dimensional vectors (e.g. 2,048 dimensional) with useful statistical properties, including high representational capacity and robustness to noise. We present a system based on a Vector Symbolic Architecture (VSA) that uses hypervectors and carefully designed operators to create representations of arbitrary objects with varying number and type of attributes. These representations can be used to encode Schemas on this set of objects in arbitrary neighborhoods. The paper includes first results demonstrating the representational capacity and robustness to noise.

Keywords: Schema mechanism · Hypervectors
Vector Symbolic Architectures · Transfer learning

1 Introduction

The idea to let machines learn like children, in contrast to manually programming all their functionalities, at least goes back to Turing 1946 [1]. Although a comprehensive picture of human learning is still missing, a lot of research has been done. A seminal work is the theory of cognitive development by Jean Piaget [2]. It describes stages and mechanisms that underly the development of children. Two basic concepts are assimilation and accommodation. The first

© Springer Nature Switzerland AG 2018
F. Trollmann and A.-Y. Turhan (Eds.): KI 2018, LNAI 11117, pp. 182–189, 2018.
https://doi.org/10.1007/978-3-030-00111-7_16

describes the process of fitting new information in existing schemas and the latter to adapt existing schemas or create new schemas based on novel experiences. Schemas can be though of as set of rules, mechanisms, or principles, that explain the behaviors of the world. In the 1980s, Gary Drescher developed the Schema Mechanism [3], a "general learning and concept-building mechanism intended to simulate aspects of Piagetian cognitive development during infancy" [3, p. 2]. The Schema Mechanism is a set of computational algorithms to learn schemas of the form $<context, action, result>$ from observations.

Recently, Schema Networks were proposed [4]. They combine inspiration of the Schema Mechanism with concepts of Relational Markov Decision Processes and planning based on Factor Graph optimization. Schema Networks demonstrated promising results on transfer learning. In particular, to learn a set of schemas that resemble the underlying "physic" of a computer game and enable zero-shot transfer to modified versions of this game. Kansky et al. [4] demonstrated these capabilities on variations of the Arcade game Breakout. Previously, Mnih et al. [5] used end-to-end deep reinforcement learning to solve this and other Arcade games. In contrast to this subsymbolic end-to-end approach, Schema Networks operate on objects. However, the algorithms provided in the Schema Network paper require all objects to share the same set of attributes and all schemas to share neighborhoods of the same size. This restricts the application to domains with similar properties of all entities and regular neighborhoods. Thus, the experiments in [4] use again pixels as objects instead of more complex entities (like "brick" and "paddle" in the Breakout game).

In this paper, we present ongoing work on using hypervector representations and Vector Symbolic Architectures to relax the above conditions on the objects. In particular, we describe how objects can be represented as superposition of their attributes based on hypervector representations and how this can be used in a VSA to implement schemas. Similar approaches have previously been successfully applied to fast approximate inference [6] and mobile robot imitation learning [7]. We start with an introduction to the Schema Mechanism, Schema Networks and hyperdimensional computing, followed by a description of the proposed combination of these concepts and initial experimental results.

2   Introduction to the Schema Mechanism

The Schema Mechanism is a general learning and concept-building framework [3]. Schemas are constructed from observation of the world and interaction with the world. They are of the form $<context, action, result>$: Given a certain state of the world (the *context*), if a particular *action* would be performed, the probability of a certain change of the world state (the *result*) would be increased. A schema makes no predication in case of not fulfilled context. Schemas maintain auxiliary data including statistics about their reliability. According to Holmes and Isbell [8, p. 1] they "are probabilistic units of cause and effect reminiscent of STRIPS operators" [9]. In the original Schema Mechanism, the state of the world is a set of binary items. Schema learning is based on *marginal attribution,* involving two steps: discovery and refinement [3]. In the discovery phase, statistics on action-result combinations are used to create context-free schemas. In the refinement phase, context items are added to make the schema more reliable. An important capability of the original Schema Meachanism is to create synthetic item to model non-observable properties of the world [3].

Drescher [3] presented an implementation and results on perception and action planning of a simple simulated agent in a micro-world. Several extensions and applications of this original work have been proposed. For example, Chaput [10] proposed a neural implementation using hierarchies of Self Organizing Maps. This allows to learn schemas with a limited amount of resources. Holmes and Isbell [8] relaxed the condition of binary items and modified the original learning criteria to better handle POMDP domains. They also demonstrated the application to speech modeling. An extension to continuous domains was proposed by Guerin and Starkey [11]. Schemas provide both declarative and procedural meaning. Declarative meaning in form of expectations what happens next and procedural meaning as component in planning. The recently proposed Schema Networks [4] exploit both meanings.

3   Overview of Schema Networks

Schema Networks [4] are an approach to learn generative models from observation of sequential data and interaction with the environment. For action planning, these generative models are combined with Factor Graph optimization. Schema Networks work on entities with binary attributes. For learning, each training sample contains a set of entities with known attributes, a current action of the agent and a resulting state of the world in the next timestep (potentially including rewards). From these samples, a set of ungrounded schemas is learned using LP-relaxation. Ungrounded schemas are similar to templates in Relational MDPs [12,13]. During inference, they are instantiated to grounded schemas with the current data. For each attribute y, there is a set of ungrounded schemas W. The new value of y is computed from its neighborhood:

$$y = \overline{\overline{X}W}\mathbf{1} \tag{1}$$

W is a binary matrix. Each column is an ungrounded schema. X is a binary matrix where each row is the concatenation of attributes of entities in a local neighborhood and a binary encoding of the current action(s). The matrix multiplication in Eq. 1 corresponds to grounding of schemas. If any of the schemas in W is fulfilled, the attribute y is set. For action planning, a Factor Graph is constructed from the schemas. Optimization on this Factor Graph assigns values to variables for each relevant attribute of each relevant entity, the actions and the expected rewards at each timestep in the planning horizon. For more details on this simplified version of schemas, please refer to [4].

Schema Networks showed promising results on learning Arcade games and applying the learned generative model to modified game versions without retraining (zero-shot transfer). However, the description in the paper [4] is rather coarse and not self-contained. Moreover, there are also several theoretical limitations: The perception side is assumed to be solved. Schema Networks work on entities and attributes, not on raw pixel data. In particular, the types of entities and their attributes have to be known in advance and have very large influence on the overall system. The schema learning approach can not deal with stochastic environments, i.e. contradicting (or noisy) observations are not allowed. All items have to be binary. Moreover, all entities have to share the same set of attributes and the neighborhood of all schemas has to be of the same size. This is a consequence of the matrix representation in Eq. 1. Section 5 presents an approach to use hypervector-based VSAs to address these latter two limitations.

4   Properties and Applications of Hypervectors and VSAs

Hypervectors are high dimensional representations (e.g. 2,048 dimensional) with large representational capacity and high robustness to noise, particularly in case of whitened encodings [14,15]. With increasing number of dimensions, the probability of sampling similar vectors by chance deceases rapidly. If the number of dimensions is high enough, randomly sampled vectors are expected to be almost orthogonal. This is exploited in a special type of algorithmic systems: Vector Symbolic Architectures (VSA) [16]. A VSA combines a high dimensional vector space $\mathbb{X}$ with (at least) two binary operators with particular properties: bind $\otimes$ and bundle $\oplus$, both are of the form: $\mathbb{X} \times \mathbb{X} \rightarrow \mathbb{X}$. bind $\otimes$ is an associative operator which is self-inverse, this is $\forall x \in \mathbb{X} : x \otimes x = I$ with I being the identity element. For example in a binary vector space, binding can be implemented by an elementwise XOR. Binding two vectors results in a vector that is not similar to both of the input vectors. However, the results of binding two vectors to the same third vector preserves their distance. In contrast, applying the second bundle $\oplus$ operator creates a result vector that is similar to both input vectors. For more details on these operations, please refer to [17–19].

Hypervectors and VSAs have been applied to various tasks. VSA can implement concepts like role-filler pairs [20] and model high-level cognitive concepts [21]. This has been used to model [22] and learn [7] reactive robot behaviors. Hypervectors and VSAs have also been used to model memory [23], aspects of the human neocortex [24], and approximate inference [6]. An interesting property of VSAs is that all entities (e.g. a program, a variable, a role) are of the same form, a hypervector, independent of their complexity - a property that we want to exploit for representation in schemas in the next section.

5   Combining Hypervectors and Schemas

This section describes an approach to represent context, action and result of a schema based on hypervectors and VSA operators. The goal is to provide a representation for the context that allows to combine objects with varying number and types of attributes and neighborhoods of varying size. The approach is inspired by Predication-based Semantic Indexing (PSI) [6] a VSA-based system

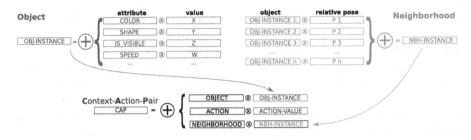

Fig. 1. Hypervector encoding of context-action-pairs (all rectangles are hypervectors).

for fast and robust approximate inference and our previous work on encoding robot behavior using hypervectors [7].

We propose to represent a schema in form of a single condition hypervector and a corresponding result hypervector. The condition hypervector encodes the context-action-pair (CAP) of the schema. To test whether a known schema is applicable for the current context and action, the similarity of the current CAP and the schema's CAP can be used. Figure 1 illustrates the encoding of arbitrary sets of attributes of objects and arbitrary neighborhoods in a single hypervector. We assume that hypervector encoders for basic datatypes like scalars are given (cf. [25]). Objects are encoded as "sum" of their attributes using the VSA bundle operator similar to the PSI system [6]. The more attributes two objects share, the more similar are their hypervector representations. Each attribute is encoded using a role-filler pair. One hypervector is used to represent the type (role) of the attribute and a second (the filler) to encode its value. Filler hypervectors can encode arbitrary datatypes, in particular, it can also be a hypervector representation of an object. The binding of the role and filler hypervectors results again in a hypervector of the same dimensionality. The bundle of all object properties is the hypervector representation of the object. The shape of the representation is independent of the number and complexity of the combined attributes.

Neighborhoods are encoded similarly by encoding the involved objects and binding them to their relative position to the regarded object. Let us consider the very simple example of a 3 × 3 neighborhood in an image. In a hypervector representation of this neighborhood, there are 8 objects surrounding a central object, each object is bound to a pose (i.e., top, top-right,...) and the 8 resulting hypervectors are bundled to a single hypervector. In contrast to the matrix encoding in Schema Networks, the hypervector encoding allows to bundle an arbitrary number of neighbors at arbitrary poses (e.g. at the opposite side of the image). This is due to the fact that the shape of the hypervector bundle is independent of the number of bundled hypervectors (in contrast to the concatenation of the neighbors in Schema Networks) and the explicit encoding of the pose. Thus we can use an individually shaped neighborhood for each schema.

The creation of the CAP is illustrated at the bottom of Fig. 1: object-, action- and neighborhood-hypervector representations are bundled to a single CAP

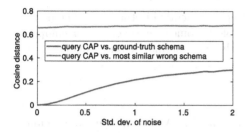

Fig. 2. Distance of noisy query CAP to schema CAPs (averaged over 1000 queries). (Color figure online)

Vectorspace	$[-1,1]^d$
#dimensions d	2,048
VSA bind	elementwise product
VSA bundle	elementwise sum (limited to $[-1,1]$)
Metric	cosine similarity

Fig. 3. Hypervector and VSA parameters used for experiments. For details on the implementation refer to [7].

hypervector. Each of the representations is created by binding the filler encoding to the corresponding role (e.g. filler "OBJ-INSTANCE" to role "OBJECT").

6   Results

The initial goal to allow different attributes in objects and different neighborhoods for schemas is already fulfilled by design. In noiseless environments, recall of a schema based on the similarity of CAP representations is inherently ensured as well (this can also be seen in the later explained Fig. 2 at noise 0). What about finding correct schemas in case of noisy object attributes? We want to demonstrate the robustness of the presented system to noise in the input data. The attributes of the objects that should toggle applicability of schemas are hidden rather deeply in the created CAPs. For application in real world scenarios, a known schema should be applicable to slightly noise-affected observations. If the derivation of the attributes is too large, the schema should become inapplicable. In the presented system, this should manifest in a equivariant relation of change in the input data and the similarity of the resulting CAP to the known schema.

For a preliminary evaluation of this property, we simulate an environment with 5,000 randomly created objects. Each object has 1–30 attributes randomly selected from a set of 100 different attribute types (e.g. color, shape, is-palpable,...). All attribute values are chosen randomly. There are 1,000 a priori known schemas. Each is composed of one of the above objects, one out of 50 randomly chosen actions, a neighborhood of 1–20 other randomly chosen objects, and a randomly chosen result. All random distributions are uniform distributions. These are ad-hoc choices, the results are alike for a wide range of parameters. The properties of the used VSA are provided in Fig. 3. Figure 2 shows the influence of noise on the encoding of the object's attributes on the similarity to the original schema. Noise is induced by adding random samples of a zero-mean Gaussian, drawn independently for each dimension of the hypervector encoding of the object's attribute value encodings. The standard deviation of the noise is varied as shown in Fig. 2. It can be seen that the distance of the noise-affected CAP to the ground-truth schema smoothly increases as desired, although the varied object attribute is deeply embedded in the CAP. The noisier the object attributes are, the less applicable becomes the schema. For comparison, the red curve shows the distance to the most similar wrong schema.

7 Conclusion

We presented a concept to use hypervectors and VSAs for encoding of schemas. This allows to address some limitations of the recently presented Schema Networks. We presented preliminary results on recall of schemas in noisy environments. This is work in progress, there are many open questions. The next steps towards a practical demonstration will in particular address the hypervector encoding of real data and action planning based on the hypervector schemas.

References

1. Carpenter, B.E., Doran, R.W. (eds.): A. M. Turing's ACE Report of 1946 and Other Papers. Massachusetts Institute of Technology, Cambridge (1986)
2. Piaget, J.: The Origins of Intelligence in Children. Routledge & Kegan Paul, London (1936). (French version published in 1936, translation by Margaret Cook published 1952)
3. Drescher, G.: Made-up minds: a constructivist approach to artificial intelligence. Ph.D. thesis, Department of Electrical Engineering and Computer Science, Massachusetts Institute of Technology (1989). http://hdl.handle.net/1721.1/77702
4. Kansky, K., et al.: Schema networks: zero-shot transfer with a generative causal model of intuitive physics. In: Proceedings of Machine Learning Research, ICML, vol. 70, pp. 1809–1818. PMLR (2017)
5. Mnih, V.: Human-level control through deep reinforcement learning. Nature **518**(7540), 529–533 (2015). https://doi.org/10.1038/nature14236
6. Widdows, D., Trevor, C.: Reasoning with vectors: a continuous model for fast robust inference. Log. J. IGPL/Interest Group Pure Appl. Log. **2**, 141–173 (2015)
7. Neubert, P., Schubert, S., Protzel, P.: Learning vector symbolic architectures for reactive robot behaviours. In: Proceedings of International Conference on Intelligent Robots and Systems (IROS) Workshop on Machine Learning Methods for High-Level Cognitive Capabilities in Robotics (2016)
8. Holmes, M.P., Isbell Jr., C.L.: Schema learning: experience-based construction of predictive action models. In: NIPS, pp. 585–592 (2004)
9. Fikes, R.E., Nilsson, N.J.: Strips: A new approach to the application of theorem proving to problem solving. Artificial Intelligence **2**(3), 189–208 (1971). http://www.sciencedirect.com/science/article/pii/0004370271900105
10. Chaput, H.: The constructivist learning architecture: a model of cognitive development for robust autonomous robots. Ph.D. thesis, Computer Science Department, University of Texas at Austin (2004)
11. Guerin, F., Starkey, A.: Applying the schema mechanism in continuous domains. In: Proceedings of the Ninth International Conference on Epigenetic Robotics, pp. 57–64. Lund University Cognitive Studies, Kognitionsforskning, Lunds universitet (2009)

12. Boutilier, C., Reiter, R., Price, B.: Symbolic dynamic programming for first-order MDPs. In: Proceedings of the 17th International Joint Conference on Artificial Intelligence, IJCAI 2001, vol. 1, pp. 690–697. Morgan Kaufmann Publishers Inc., San Francisco (2001). http://dl.acm.org/citation.cfm?id=1642090.1642184

13. Joshi, S., Khardon, R., Tadepalli, P., Fern, A., Raghavan, A.: Relational Markov decision processes: promise and prospects. In: AAAI Workshop: Statistical Relational Artificial Intelligence. AAAI Workshops, vol. WS-13-16. AAAI (2013)

14. Kanerva, P.: Fully distributed representation. In: Proceedings of Real World Computing Symposium, Tokyo, Japan, pp. 358–365 (1997)

15. Ahmad, S., Hawkins, J.: Properties of sparse distributed representations and their application to hierarchical temporal memory. CoRR abs/1503.07469 (2015). http://arxiv.org/abs/1503.07469

16. Levy, S.D., Gayler, R.: Vector symbolic architectures: a new building material for artificial general intelligence. In: Proceedings of Conference on Artificial General Intelligence, pp. 414–418. IOS Press, Amsterdam (2008)

17. Kanerva, P.: Hyperdimensional computing: an introduction to computing in distributed representation with high-dimensional random vectors. Cogn. Comput. **1**(2), 139–159 (2009)

18. Gayler, R.W.: Multiplicative binding, representation operators, and analogy. In: Advances in Analogy Research: Integration of Theory and Data from the Cognitive, Computational, and Neural Sciences, Bulgaria (1998)

19. Plate, T.A.: Distributed representations and nested compositional structure. Ph.D. thesis, Toronto, Ontario, Canada (1994)

20. Smolensky, P.: Tensor product variable binding and the representation of symbolic structures in connectionist systems. Artif. Intell. **46**(1–2), 159–216 (1990)

21. Gayler, R.W.: Vector symbolic architectures answer Jackendoff's challenges for cognitive neuroscience. In: Proceedings of ICCS/ASCS International Conference on Cognitive Science, Sydney, Australia, pp. 133–138 (2003)

22. Levy, S.D., Bajracharya, S., Gayler, R.W.: Learning behavior hierarchies via high-dimensional sensor projection. In: Proceedings of AAAI Conference on Learning Rich Representations from Low-Level Sensors. pp. 25–27. AAAIWS 13-12 (2013)

23. Danihelka, I., Wayne, G., Uria, B., Kalchbrenner, N., Graves, A.: Associative long short-term memory. CoRR abs/1602.03032 (2016). http://arxiv.org/abs/1602.03032

24. Hawkins, J., Ahmad, S.: Why neurons have thousands of synapses, a theory of sequence memory in neocortex. Front. Neural Circuits **10**, 23 (2016). https://www.frontiersin.org/article/10.3389/fncir.2016.00023

25. Purdy, S.: Encoding data for HTM systems. CoRR abs/1602.05925 (2016)

LearnDiag: A Direct Diagnosis Algorithm Based On Learned Heuristics

Seda Polat Erdeniz$^{(\boxtimes)}$, Alexander Felfernig, and Muesluem Atas

Software Technology Institute, Graz University of Technology, Inffeldgasse 16B/2, 8010 Graz, Austria
{spolater,alexander.felfernig,muesluem.atas}@ist.tugraz.at
http://ase.ist.tugraz.at/ASE/

Abstract. Configuration systems must be able to deal with inconsistencies which can occur in different contexts. Especially in interactive settings, where users specify requirements and a constraint solver has to identify solutions, inconsistencies may more often arise. Therefore, diagnosis algorithms are required to find solutions for these *unsolvable problems*. Runtime efficiency of diagnosis is especially crucial in real-time scenarios such as production scheduling, robot control, and communication networks. For such scenarios, diagnosis algorithms should determine solutions within predefined time limits. To provide runtime performance, direct or sequential diagnosis algorithms find diagnoses without the need of calculating conflicts. In this paper, we propose a new direct diagnosis algorithm LearnDiag which uses learned heuristics. It applies supervised learning to calculate constraint ordering heuristics for the diagnostic search. Our evaluations show that LearnDiag improves runtime performance of direct diagnosis besides improving the diagnosis quality in terms of minimality and precision.

Keywords: Constraint satisfaction · Configuration · Diagnosis
Search heuristics · Machine learning · Evolutionary computation

1 Introduction

Configuration systems [8] are used to find solutions for problems which have many variables and constraints. A configuration problem can be defined as a constraint satisfaction problem (CSP) [10]. If constraints of a CSP are inconsistent, no solution can be found. Therefore, diagnosis [1] is required to find at least one solution for this inconsistent CSP. The most widely known algorithm for the identification of minimal diagnoses is *hitting set directed acyclic graph* (HSDAG) [7]. HSDAG is based on conflict-directed hitting set determination and determines diagnoses based on breadth-first search. It computes minimal diagnoses using minimal conflict sets which can be calculated by QuickXplain [4]. The major disadvantage of applying this approach is the need of predetermining minimal conflicts which can deteriorate diagnostic search performance.

© Springer Nature Switzerland AG 2018
F. Trollmann and A.-Y. Turhan (Eds.): KI 2018, LNAI 11117, pp. 190–197, 2018.
https://doi.org/10.1007/978-3-030-00111-7_17

Many different approaches to provide efficient solutions for diagnosis problems are proposed [6]. One approach [14] focuses on improvements of HSDAG. Another approach [13] uses pre-determined set of conflicts based on binary decision diagrams. In diagnosis problem instances where the number of minimal diagnoses and their cardinality is high, the generation of a set of minimum cardinality diagnoses is unfeasible with the standard conflict-based approach. An alternative approach to solve this issue is *direct (sequential) diagnosis* [9] which determines diagnoses by executing a series of queries. These queries check the consistency of the constraint set without the need to identify the corresponding conflict sets.

When diagnoses have to be provided in real-time, response times should be less than a few seconds. For example, in communication networks, efficient diagnosis is crucial to retain the quality of service. To satisfy these real-time diagnosis requirements, FLEXDIAG [2] uses a parametrization that helps to systematically reduce the number of consistency checks (so the runtime) but in the same time the minimality of diagnoses becomes non-guaranteed. Therefore, in FLEXDIAG, there is a tradeoff between diagnosis quality and runtime performance. When the runtime performance (# of diagnoses per second) increases, the quality of diagnosis (degree of minimality) may decrease.

This paper introduces *an efficient direct diagnosis algorithm* (LEARNDIAG) for solving *the quality-runtime performance tradeoff problem* of FLEXDIAG. It learns heuristics (search strategies) [5] to improve runtime performance and quality of diagnosis. Its diagnostic search is based on FLEXDIAG's recursive diagnostic search approach. For evaluations, we used a real dataset collected in one of our user studies and compared LEARNDIAG with FLEXDIAG. Our experiments show that LEARNDIAG outperforms FLEXDIAG in terms of precision, runtime, and minimality.

The remainder of this paper is organized as follows. In Sect. 2, we introduce an example diagnosis problem. Based on this example, in Sect. 3, we show how it is diagnosed by LEARNDIAG. The results of our experiments are presented in Sect. 4. With Sect. 5, we conclude the paper.

2 Working Example

The following (simplified) assortment of digital cameras and given customer requirements will serve as a working example throughout the paper (see Table 1). It is formed as a configuration task [10] on the basis of Definition 1.

Definition 1 *(Configuration Task and Configuration). A configuration task can be defined as a $CSP(V, D, C)$. $V = \{v_1, v_2, ..., v_n\}$ represents a set of finite domain variables. $D = \{dom(v_1), dom(v_2), ... , dom(v_n)\}$ represents a set of variable domains, where $dom(v_k)$ represents the domain of variable v_k. $C = (C_{KB} \cup REQ)$ where $C_{KB} = \{c_1, c_2, ..., c_q\}$ is a set of domain specific constraints (the configuration knowledge base) that restricts the possible combinations of values assigned to the variables in V. $REQ = \{c_{q+1}, c_{q+2}, ..., c_t\}$*

Table 1. An example for a camera configuration problem

V	v1: **effective resolution**, v2: **display**, v3: **touch**, v4: **wifi**, v5: **nfc**, v6: **gps**, v7: **video resolution**, v8: **zoom**, v9: **weight**, v10: **price**
D	dom(v1)={6.1, 6.2, 20.9}, dom(v2)={1.8, 2.2, 2.5, 3.5}, dom(v3)={yes, no}, dom(v4)={yes, no}, dom(v5)={yes, no}, dom(v6)={yes, no}, dom(v7)={4K-UHD/3840 × 2160, Full-HD/1920 × 1080, No-Video-Function}, dom(v8)={3.0, 5.8, 7.8}, dom(v9)={475, 560, 700, 860, 1405}, dom(v10)={189, 469, 659, 2329, 5219}
C_{KB}	c1:{P1∨ P2∨ P3∨ P4∨ P5} where; P1: { v1=20.9 ∧ v2 = 3.5 ∧ v3 = yes ∧ v4 = yes ∧ v5 = no ∧ v6 = yes ∧ v7 = 4K-UHD/3840 × 2160 ∧ v8 = 3.0 ∧ v9 = 475 ∧ v10 = 659}, P2: { v1 = 6.1 ∧ v2 = 2.5 ∧ v3 = yes ∧ v4 = yes ∧ v5 = no ∧ v6 = yes ∧ v7 = 4K-UHD/3840 × 2160 ∧ v8 = 3.0 ∧ v9 = 475 ∧ v10 = 659}, P3: { v1 = 6.1 ∧ v2 = 2.2 ∧ v3 = no ∧ v4 = no ∧ v5 = no ∧ v6 = no ∧ v7 = no-video-function ∧ v8 = 7.8 ∧ v9 = 700 ∧ v10 = 189}, P4: { v1 = 6.2 ∧ v2 = 1.8 ∧ v3 = no ∧ v4 = no ∧ v5 = no ∧ v6 = no ∧ v7 = 4K-UHD/3840, ×2160 ∧ v8 = 5.8 ∧ v9 = 860 ∧ v10 = 2329}, P5: { v1 = 6.2 ∧ v2 = 1.8 ∧ v3 = no ∧ v4 = no ∧ v5 = no ∧ v6 = yes ∧ v7 = Full-HD/1920 × 1080 ∧ v8 = 3.0 ∧ v9 = 560 ∧ v10 = 469}
REQ_new	c2: v1 = 20.9 ∧ c3: v2 = 2.5 ∧ c4: v3 = yes ∧ c5: v4 = yes ∧ c6: v5 = no ∧ c7: v6 = yes ∧ c8: v7 = 4K-UHD/3840 × 2160 ∧ c9: v8 = 5.8 ∧ c10: v9 = 475 ∧ c11: v10 = 659

is a set of customer requirements, which is also represented as constraints. A configuration/solution (S) for a configuration task is a set of assignments $S = \{v_1 = a_1, v_2 = a_2, ..., v_n = a_n\}$ where $a_i \in dom(v_i)$ which is consistent with C.

CSP_new has no solution since the set of customer requirements REQ_new is inconsistent with the product catalog C_{KB}. Therefore, REQ_new needs to be diagnosed. A corresponding *Customer Requirements Diagnosis Problem* and *Diagnosis* can be defined as follows:

Definition 2 (REQ Diagnosis Problem and Diagnosis). *A customer requirements diagnosis problem (REQ diagnosis problem) is defined as a tuple (C_{KB}, REQ) where REQ is the set of given customer requirements and C_{KB} represents the constraints part of the configuration knowledge base. A REQ diagnosis for a REQ diagnosis problem (C_{KB}, REQ) is a set $\Delta \subseteq REQ$, s.t.*

$C_{KB} \cup (REQ - \Delta)$ is consistent. $\Delta = \{c_1, c_2, ..., c_n\}$ is minimal if there does not exist a diagnosis $\Delta' \subset \Delta$, s.t. $C_{KB} \cup (REQ - \Delta')$ is consistent.

3 Direct Diagnosis with LearnDiag

LearnDiag searches for diagnoses for a REQ diagnosis problem using one of the predefined constraint ordering heuristics. Predefined heuristics are calculated by applying supervised learning on a set of inconsistent REQs (Table 2).

Table 2. Inconsistent requirements (REQs) of six past customers

	REQ1	REQ2	REQ3	REQ4	REQ5	REQ6
v1	1	0	1	1	0	0
v2	1	0.23	0.41	0.41	0	0
v3	1	0	1	1	0	0
v4	1	0	1	1	0	0
v5	0	1	0	0	1	1
v6	1	1	1	1	1	0
v7	0	1	0	0	0	0.5
v8	0	0.58	0	0.58	0.58	0
v9	0.09	0.24	0	0	0.41	0.41
v10	0.05	0	0.05	0.09	0	0.05
P	P1	P3	P1	P4	P5	P4

3.1 Clustering

LearnDiag clusters past inconsistent REQs using k-means clustering [3]. *K-means clustering* generates k clusters where it minimizes the sum of squares of distances between cluster elements and the centroids (mean value of cluster elements) of their corresponding clusters. To increase the efficiency of k-means clustering [12], we applied *Min-Max Normalization* on REQs (Table 2).

After k-means clustering is applied with the parameter *number of clusters (k)* = 2, two clusters (κ_1 and κ_2) of REQs are obtained as shown in Table 3. We used $k = 2$ (not a higher value) to demonstrate our example in an understandable way.

Table 3. Clusters of past inconsistent customer requirements

	Cluster elements	Centroid (μ)
κ_1	REQ1, REQ3, REQ4	$\mu_1 : \{1, 0.60, 1, 1, 0, 1, 1, 0.19, 0.03, 0.63\}$
κ_2	REQ2, REQ5, REQ6	$\mu_2 : \{0, 0.07, 0, 0, 1, 0.66, 0.5, 0.38, 0.35, 0.01\}$

3.2   Learning

After clustering is completed, LEARNDIAG runs a genetic algorithm (GA) based
supervised learning [11] to determine constraint ordering heuristics. In our working example, for each cluster (κ_i) four different constraint ordering heuristics
are calculated based on runtime (τ, see Formula (1a)), precision (π, see Formula
(1b)), minimality (Φ, see Formula (1c)) and the combination of them (α, see
Formula (1d)) (Table 4).

$$min(\tau = \sum_{i=1}^{n} runtime(\Delta_i)) \tag{1a}$$

$$max(\pi = \frac{\#(\text{correct predictions})}{\#(\text{predictions})}) \tag{1b}$$

$$max(\Phi = \sum_{i=1}^{n} \frac{|\Delta_{min}|}{|\Delta_i|}) \tag{1c}$$

$$max(\alpha = \frac{1}{\tau} \times \pi \times \Phi) \tag{1d}$$

Table 4. Learned constraint ordering heuristics (H)

$H_1\tau : \{c9, c3, c2, c11, c4, c5, c7, c8, c6, c10\}$	$H_2\tau : \{c6, c9, c7, c11, c10, c5, c2, c8, c4, c3\}$
$H_1\pi : \{c2, c9, c3, c10, c11, c7, c8, c4, c6, c5\}$	$H_2\pi : \{c9, c11, c10, c6, c7, c5, c3, c2, c4, c8\}$
$H_1\Phi : \{c2, c3, c9, c11, c4, c5, c7, c8, c6, c10\}$	$H_2\Phi : \{c6, c7, c9, c11, c10, c5, c2, c8, c4, c3\}$
$H_1\alpha : \{c9, c2, c3, c11, c4, c5, c7, c8, c6, c10\}$	$H_2\alpha : \{c11, c9, c6, c7, c10, c5, c2, c8, c4, c3\}$

3.3   Diagnosis

The diagnosis phase of LEARNDIAG is composed of three steps which are
explained in this section as *finding the closest cluster*, *reordering constraints*
and *diagnostic search*.

Finding the Closest Cluster. LEARNDIAG calculates the distances between
clusters and the new *REQ* using the Euclidean Distance. In our working

example, where the normalized values of REQ_new is $REQ\_new\_norm = \{1, 0.41, 1, 1, 0, 1, 0, 0.58, 0, 0.09\}$, the closest cluster to REQ_new_norm is κ_1.

Reordering Constraints. Learned heuristics (see Table 4) of the closest cluster is applied to the REQ to be diagnosed. Let's use the mixed-performance heuristic ($H_1\alpha$ from Table 4) on the working example. Using the heuristic $H_1\alpha$, constraints of REQ_new are ordered as $REQ\_new\_ordered$: $\{c9, c2, c3, c11, c4, c5, c7, c8, c6, c10\}$.

Diagnostic Search. After calculating the reordered constraints, diagnostic search is done by FLEXDIAG. More details about *DiagnosticSearch* can be found in the corresponding paper [2]. LEARNDIAG helps diagnostic search to decrease the number of consistency checks (which increases the runtime performance).

4   Evaluation

We have collected required (for supervised learning) inconsistent customer requirements and their product purchases, by applying a user study with

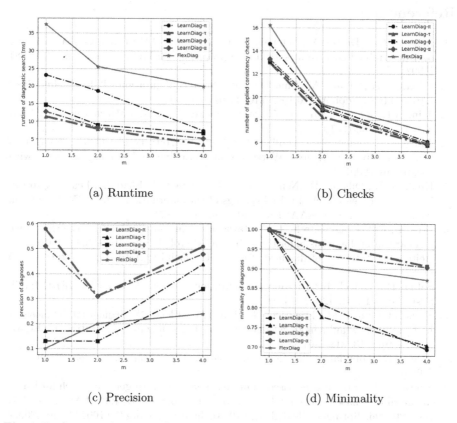

(a) Runtime

(b) Checks

(c) Precision

(d) Minimality

Fig. 1. Performance in terms of runtime, consistency checks, precision, and minimality

$N = 264$ subjects. The study subjects interacted with a web based configurator in order to identify a professional digital camera that best suits their needs.

We observed that LEARNDIAG-α is a solution for solving *the quality-runtime performance tradeoff problem* of FLEXDIAG. As shown in comparison charts of runtime (see Fig. 1(a)), number of consistency checks (see Fig. 1(b)), quality of diagnosis in terms of precision (see Fig. 1(c)) and minimality (see Fig. 1(d)), LEARNDIAG-α always gives better performance results compared to FLEXDIAG.

5   Conclusions

We proposed an out-performing direct diagnosis algorithm LEARNDIAG for solving *the quality-runtime performance tradeoff problem* of FLEXDIAG. According to our experimental results, LEARNDIAG-α solves *the quality-runtime performance tradeoff problem* by improving runtime performance and quality (minimality, precision) of diagnosis at the same time. Besides, if solving the tradeoff problem is not considered, LEARNDIAG performs best in precision with LEARNDIAG-π, in runtime performance with LEARNDIAG-τ and in minimality with LEARNDIAG-Φ.

References

1. Bakker, R.R., Dikker, F., Tempelman, F., Wognum, P.M.: Diagnosing and solving over-determined constraint satisfaction problems. In: IJCAI, vol. 93, pp. 276–281 (1993)
2. Felfernig, A., et al.: Anytime diagnosis for reconfiguration. J. Intell. Inf. Syst. (2018). https://doi.org/10.1007/s10844-017-0492-1
3. Jain, A.K.: Data clustering: 50 years beyond k-means. Pattern Recognit. Lett. **31**(8), 651–666 (2010)
4. Junker, U.: Quickxplain: conflict detection for arbitrary constraint propagation algorithms. In: IJCAI 2001 Workshop on Modelling and Solving problems with constraints (2001)
5. Khalil, E.B., Dilkina, B., Nemhauser, G.L., Ahmed, S., Shao, Y.: Learning to run heuristics in tree search. In: Proceedings of the International Joint Conference on Artificial Intelligence. AAAI Press, Melbourne (2017)
6. Nica, I., Pill, I., Quaritsch, T., Wotawa, F.: The route to success-a performance comparison of diagnosis algorithms. In: IJCAI, vol. 13, pp. 1039–1045 (2013)
7. Reiter, R.: A theory of diagnosis from first principles. Artif. Intell. **32**(1), 57–95 (1987)
8. Sabin, D., Weigel, R.: Product configuration frameworks-a survey. IEEE Intell. Syst. Appl. **13**(4), 42–49 (1998)
9. Shchekotykhin, K.M., Friedrich, G., Rodler, P., Fleiss, P.: Sequential diagnosis of high cardinality faults in knowledge-bases by direct diagnosis generation. In: ECAI, vol. 14, pp. 813–818 (2014)
10. Tsang, E.: Foundations of Constraint Satisfaction. Academic Press, Cambridge (1993)
11. Venturini, G.: SIA: a supervised inductive algorithm with genetic search for learning attributes based concepts. In: Brazdil, P.B. (ed.) ECML 1993. LNCS, vol. 667, pp. 280–296. Springer, Heidelberg (1993). https://doi.org/10.1007/3-540-56602-3_142

12. Visalakshi, N.K., Thangavel, K.: Impact of normalization in distributed k-means clustering. Int. J. Soft Comput. **4**(4), 168–172 (2009)
13. Wang, K., Li, Z., Ai, Y., Zhang, Y.: Computing minimal diagnosis with binary decision diagrams algorithm. In: Sixth International Conference on Fuzzy Systems and Knowledge Discovery, FSKD 2009, vol. 1, pp. 145–149. IEEE (2009)
14. Wotawa, F.: A variant of Reiter's hitting-set algorithm. Inf. Process. Lett. **79**(1), 45–51 (2001)

Planning

Assembly Planning in Cluttered Environments Through Heterogeneous Reasoning

Daniel Beßler[1(⊠)], Mihai Pomarlan[1], Aliakbar Akbari[2], Muhayyuddin[2],
Mohammed Diab[2], Jan Rosell[2], John Bateman[1], and Michael Beetz[1]

[1] Universität Bremen, Bremen, Germany
danielb@cs.uni-bremen.de
[2] Universitat Politècnica de Catalunya, Barcelona, Spain

Abstract. Assembly recipes can elegantly be represented in description logic theories. With such a recipe, the robot can figure out the next assembly step through logical inference. However, before performing an action, the robot needs to ensure various spatial constraints are met, such as that the parts to be put together are reachable, non occluded, etc. Such inferences are very complicated to support in logic theories, but specialized algorithms exist that efficiently compute qualitative spatial relations such as whether an object is reachable. In this work, we combine a logic-based planner for assembly tasks with geometric reasoning capabilities to enable robots to perform their tasks under spatial constraints. The geometric reasoner is integrated into the logic-based reasoning through decision procedures attached to symbols in the ontology.

1 Introduction

Robotic tasks are usually described at a high level of abstraction. Such representations are compact, natural for humans for describing the goals of a task, and at least in principle applicable to variations of the task. An abstract "pick part" action is more generally useful than a more concrete "pick part from position x", as long as the robot can locate the target part and reach it.

Robotics manipulation problems, however, may involve many task constraints related to the geometry of the environment and the robot, constraints which are difficult to represent at a higher level of abstraction. Such constraints are, for example, that there is either no direct collision-free motion path or feasible configuration to grasp an object because of the placement of some other, occluding object. Recently, much research has been centred on solving manipulation problems using geometric reasoning, but there is still a lack of incorporating the geometric information inside higher abstraction levels.

M. Beetz—This work was partially funded by Deutsche Forschungsgemeinschaft (DFG) through the Collaborative Research Center 1320, EASE, and by the Spanish Government through the project DPI2016-80077-R. Aliakbar Akbari is supported by the Spanish Government through the grant FPI 2015.

© Springer Nature Switzerland AG 2018
F. Trollmann and A.-Y. Turhan (Eds.): KI 2018, LNAI 11117, pp. 201–214, 2018.
https://doi.org/10.1007/978-3-030-00111-7_18

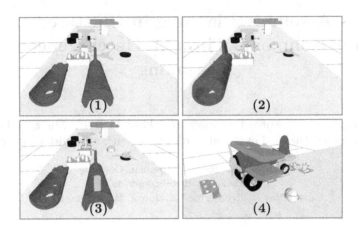

Fig. 1. Different initial workspace configurations of a toy plane assembly (1–3), and the completed plane assembly (4).

In this paper, we look at the task of robotic assembly planning, which we approach, at the higher abstract level, in a knowledge-enabled way. We use an assembly planner based on formal specifications of products to be created, parts they are to be created from, and mechanical connections to be formed between them. At this level we represent what affordances a part must provide, in order for it to be able to enter a particular connection or be grasped in a certain way, as well as model that certain grasps and connections block certain affordances. The planning itself proceeds by comparing individuals in the knowledge base with their terminological model, finding inconsistencies, and producing action items to resolve these. For example, if the asserted type of an entity is "Car", the robot can infer that, to be a car, this entity must have some wheels attached, and if this is not the case, the planner will create action items to add them.

In our previous work, the various geometrically motivated constraints pertaining, for example, what grasps are available on a part depending on what mechanical connections it has to other parts, were modelled symbolically. We added axioms to the knowledge base that assert that a connection of a given type will block certain affordances, thus preventing the part to enter certain other connections and grasps. We also assumed that the workspace of the robot would be sufficiently uncluttered so that abstract actions like "pick part" will succeed. In this paper, we go beyond these limitations and ground geometrically-meaningful symbolic relations through geometric reasoning that can perform collision and reachability checking, and sampling of good placements.

The contributions of this paper are the following ones:

- a framework for assembly planning that allows reasoning about relations that are grounded on demand in results of geometric reasoning procedures, and the definition of procedures that abstract results of the geometric reasoner into symbols of the knowledge base; and

– extensions of the planner that allow switching between different planning strategies with different goal configurations, and the declaration of action pre-conditions and planning strategies for assembly tasks in cluttered scenes.

2   Related Work

Several projects have pursued ontological modelling in robotics. The IEEE-RAS work group ORA [16] aims to create a standard for knowledge representation in robotics. The ORA core ontology has been extended with ontologies for specific industrial tasks [7], such as kitting: the robot places a set of parts on a tray so these may be carried elsewhere. To the best of our knowledge, assembly tasks have not yet been represented in ORA ontologies. Other robotic ontologies are the Affordance Ontology [23] and the open-source KNOWROB ontology [22], the latter of which we use.

Knowledge-enabled approaches have been used for some industrial processes: kitting [3,4,14] and assembly (the EU ROSETTA project [10,12,18]). Logic descriptions have also been used to define a problem for general purpose planners [4,8]. In previously cited papers, knowledge modelling for assembly is either in the form of abstract concepts about sequences of tasks (as in [10]), or about geometric features of atomic parts (as in [13]). The approach we use in this paper builds on our previous work [5], where we generate assembly operations from OWL specifications directly (without using PDDL solvers), and the knowledge modelling includes concepts such as affordances, grasps, mechanical connections, and how grasps and mechanical connections influence which affordances are available. Generating assembly operations from OWL specifications is faster than planning approaches and amenable to frequent customization of assembled products. We improve on our previous work by integrating geometric reasoning about the action execution into the knowledge-based planner.

Different types of geometric reasoning have been considered in manipulation planning. [11] has investigated dynamic interactions between rigid bodies. A general manipulation planning approach using several Probabilistic Roadmaps (PRM) has been developed by [17] that considers multiple possible grasps (usable for re-grasping objects) and stable placements of movable objects. The manipulation problem of Navigation Among Movable Obstacles (NAMO) has been addressed by the work in [20] and [19] using a backward search from the goal in order to move objects out of the way between two robot configurations. The work in [1,2] have extended this work with ontological knowledge by integrating task and motion planning.

3   Assembly Activities in Cluttered Workspaces

Assembly tasks often have a fixed recipe that, if followed correctly, would control an agent such that available parts are transformed into an assembled product. These recipes can elegantly be represented using description logics [5]. But inferring the sequence of assembly actions is not sufficient for robots because actions

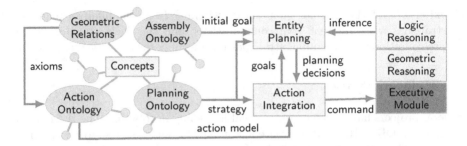

Fig. 2. The architecture of our heterogeneous reasoning system.

may not be performable in the current situation. This is, for example, the case when the robot cannot reach an object because it is occluded. A notion of space, on the other hand, is very complicated in a logic formalism, but specialized methods exist that efficiently compute qualitative spatial relations such as whether objects are occluding each other.

Our solution is depicted in Fig. 2. We build upon an existing planner and extend it with a notion of action, and geometric reasoning capabilities. Actions are represented in terms of the action ontology which also defines action preconditions. Pre-conditions are ensured by running the planner for the action entity. This is used to ensure that the robot can reach an object, or else tries to put away occluding objects. To this end we integrate a geometric reasoner with the knowledge base. The interfaces of the geometric reasoner are hooked into the logic-based reasoning through procedural attachments in the knowledge base.

The planner [5] is an extension of the KNOWROB knowledge base [1] [22]. KNOWROB is a Prolog-based system with Web Ontology Language (OWL) support. OWL semantics is implemented with the closed world assumption through the use of negation as failure in Prolog rules. We use this to identify what information is missing or false about an individual according to OWL entailment rules. Another useful aspect of KNOWROB is that symbols can be grounded through invoking computational procedures such as geometric reasoner.

The geometric reasoner is a module of the Kautham Project [2] [15]. It is a C++ based tool for motion planning that enables to plan under geometric and kinodynamic constraints. It uses the Open Motion Planning Library (OMPL) [21] as a core set of sampling-based planning algorithms. In this work, the RRT-Connect motion planner [9] is used. For the computation of inverse kinematics, the approach developed by [24] is used.

4   Knowledge Representation for Assembly Activities

In our approach, the planner runs within the *perception-action* loop of a robot. The knowledge base maintains a belief state, and entities in it may be referred

---
[1] http://knowrob.org.
[2] https://sir.upc.edu/projects/kautham/.

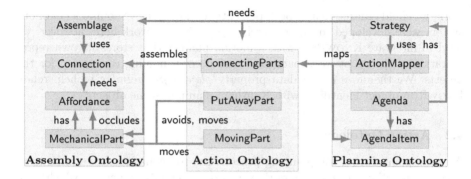

Fig. 3. The interplay of ontologies in our system.

to in planning tasks. In previous work, we have defined an ontology to describe assemblages, and meta knowledge to control the planner [5]. In the following sections, we will briefly review our previous work in assembly modelling and present further additions to it that we implemented for this paper. The interplay between the different ontologies used in our system is depicted in Fig. 3.

4.1 Assembly Ontology

The upper level of the assembly ontology defines general concepts such as *MechanicalPart* and *AssemblyConnection*. Underneath this level there are part ontologies that describe properties of parts such as what connections they may have, and what ways they can be grasped. Finally, assemblage ontologies describe what parts and connections may form an assemblage. This layered organization allows part ontologies to be reused for different assemblies. Also important is the *Affordance* concept. Mechanical parts provide affordances, which are required (and possibly blocked) by grasps and connections. Apart from these very abstract concepts, some common types of affordances and connections are also defined (e.g. screwing, sliding, and snapping connections).

To these, we have added a new relation *occludesAffordance* with domain *AtomicPart* and range *Affordance*. A triple "P occludesAffordance A" means the atomic part P is placed in such a way that it prevents the robot from moving one of its end effectors to the affordance A (belonging to some other part P'). Parts can be said to be graspable if they have at least one non-occluded grasping affordance. The motivation for the addition of this property is that it helps representing spatial constraints in the workspace, a consideration we did not address in our previous work.

Also, in our previous work, the belief state of the robot was stored entirely in the knowledge base. It includes object poses, if and how an object is grasped, mechanical connections between objects, etc. Consistency is easier to maintain for a centralized belief state, but components of the robot control system need to be tightly integrated with the knowledge base for this to work. In our previous work, we could enforce this as both perception and executive components of our system were developed in our research group. For our work here, however, we need to integrate KNOWROB with a motion planner that stores its own representation of the robot workspace, and uses its own naming convention for the objects. We therefore add a data property *planningSceneIndex* to help relate KNOWROB object identifiers with Kautham planning scene objects.

4.2   Action Ontology

At some point during the planning process, the robot has to move its body to perform an action. In previous work, we used action data structures which were passed to the plan executive. The plan executive had to take care that pre-conditions were met, which sub-actions to perform, etc. In this work, explicit action representations are used to ensure that pre-conditions are met before performing an action. The action ontology includes relations to describe objects involved, sub-actions, etc. Here, we focus on the representation of pre-conditions.

Our modelling of action pre-conditions is based on the *preActors* relation which is used to assert axioms about entities involved in the action that must hold before performing it. The upper ontology also defines more specific cases of this relation such as *objectActedOn* that denotes objects that are manipulated, or *toolUsed* that denotes tools which are operated by the robot.

ConnectingParts. The most essential action the robot has to perform during an assembly task is to connect parts with each other. At least one of the parts must be held by the robot and moved in a way that establishes the connection. Performing the action is not directly possible when the part to be moved cannot be grasped. This is the case when a part blocks a required affordance, for example, due to being in the wrong holder, blocked by another part, etc.

First, we define the relations *assemblesPart* $\sqsubseteq$ *objectActedOn*, and *fixedPart* and *mobilePart* $\sqsubseteq$ *assemblesPart*. These denote *MechanicalPart*'s involved in *ConnectingParts* actions, and distinguish between mobile and static parts. We further define the relation *assemblesConnection* that denotes the *AssemblyConnection* the action tries to establish. The *assemblesPart* relation is defined as property chain *assemblesConnection* $\circ$ *hasAtomicPart*, where *hasAtomicPart* denotes the parts linked in an *AssemblyConnection*. This ensures that *assemblesPart* only denotes parts that are required by the connection. Using these relations we assert following axioms for the *ConnectingParts* action:

$$\leq 1 assemblesConnection.\,Thing \wedge\, \geq 1 assemblesConnection.\,Thing \qquad (1)$$

$$\geq 2 assemblesPart.\,Thing \qquad (2)$$

$$\leq 2 mobilePart.\,Thing \wedge\, \geq 1 mobilePart.\,Thing \qquad (3)$$

These axioms define that (1) an action is performed for exactly one assembly connection; (2) at least two parts are involved; and (3) at max two parts are mobile, and at least one mobile part is involved.

Another pre-condition is the graspability of mobile parts. Parts may relate to *GraspingAffordance*'s that describe how the robot should position its gripper, how much force to apply, etc. to grasp the part. We assert the following axioms that ensure each mobile part offers at least one unblocked *GraspingAffordance*:

$$FreeAffordance \equiv (\leq 0 blocksAffordance^-.AssemblyConnection) \qquad (4)$$

$$\forall mobilePart.(\exists hasAffordance.(GraspingAffordance \land FreeAffordance)) \qquad (5)$$

Next, we define a property *partConnectedTo* that relates a part to parts it is connected to. It is sub-property of the property chain *hasAtomicPart⁻* ∘ *hasAtomicPart*. Also, we assert that this relation is transitive such that it holds for parts which are indirectly linked with each other. This is used to assert that fixed parts must be attached to some fixture:

$$\forall fixedPart.(\exists partConnectedTo.Fixture) \qquad (6)$$

Also, parts must be in the correct fixture for the intended connection. To ensure this, we assert that required affordances must be unblocked:

$$\forall assemblesConnection.(\forall usesAffordance.FreeAffordance) \qquad (7)$$

Finally, we define *partOccludedBy* ≡ *hasAffordance* ∘ *occludesAffordance⁻* which relates parts to parts occluding them, and assert that parts cannot be occluded by other parts when the robot intends to put them together:

$$\forall assemblesPart.(\leq 0 partOccludedBy.MechanicalPart) \qquad (8)$$

MovingPart and PutAwayPart. The above statements assert axioms that must be ensured by the planner. These refer to entities in the world and may require certain actions to be performed to destroy or create relations between them. In this work, we focus on ensuring valid spatial arrangement in the scene.

First, the robot should break non permanent connections in case one of the required affordances is blocked. We define this action as *MovingPart* ⊑ *PuttingSomethingSomewhere*. The only pre-actor is the part itself. It is linked to the action via the relation *movesPart* ⊑ *objectActedOn*. We assert that the part must have an unblocked grasping affordance (analogues to axiom (5)).

Further, parts that occlude required parts for an assembly step must be put away. We define this action as *PutAwayPart* ⊑ *PuttingSomethingSomewhere*. This action needs exactly one *movesPart*, and additionally refers to the parts that should be "avoided", which means that the target position should not lie between the robot and avoided parts: ∃*avoidsPart.MechanicalPart*, where *avoidsPart* is another sub-property of *preActors*. Describing possible target positions in detail would be extremely difficult in a logical formalism, and is not considered in the scope of this work.

4.3   Planning Ontology

Our planner is driven by comparing goals, represented in the TBox, with believes, represented in the ABox, and controlled by meta knowledge that we call planning strategy. The planning strategy determines which parts of the ontology are of interest in the current phase, how steps are ordered, and how they are performed in terms of how the knowledge base is to be manipulated. Possible planning decisions are represented in a data structure that we call planning agenda. Planning agendas are ordered sequences of steps that each, when performed, modify the belief state of the robot in some way. The planner succeeds if the belief state is a proper instantiation of the goal description.

Different tasks require different strategies that focus on different parts of the ontology, and that have specialized rules for processing the agenda. The strategy for planning an assemblage, for example, focuses on relations defined in the assembly ontology. Planning to put away parts, on the other hand, is mainly concerned with spatial relations. In previous work, the strategy selection was done externally. Here, we associate strategies to entities that should be planned with them. To this end, we define the relation *needsEntity* that denotes entities that are planned by some strategy. Strategies assert a universal restriction on this relation in order to define what type of entities can be planned with them. For the assemblage planning strategy, for example, we assert the axiom:

$$\forall needsEntity.(Assemblage \lor AssemblyConnection) \tag{9}$$

Planning decisions may not correspond to actions that the robot needs to perform to establish the decisions in its world. Some decisions are purely virtual, or only one missing piece in a set of missing information required to perform an action. The mapping of planning decisions to action entities is performed in a rule-base fashion in our approach. These rules are described using the *AgendaActionMapper* concept, and are linked to the strategy via the relation *usesActionMapper*. Each *AgendaActionMapper* further describes what types of planning decisions should activate it. This is done with agenda item patterns that activate a mapper in case a pattern matches the selected agenda item. These are linked to the *AgendaActionMapper* via the relation *mapsItem*.

Finally, we define the *AgendaActionPerformer* concept which is linked to the strategy via the relation *usesActionPerformer*. *AgendaActionPerformer* provide facilities to perform actions by mapping them to data structures of the plan executive, and invoking an interface for action execution. They are activated based on whether they match a pattern provided for the last agenda item.

5   Reasoning Process Using Knowledge and Geometric Information

Our reasoning system is heterogeneous, which means that different reasoning resources and representations are fused into a coherent picture that covers different aspects. In this section, we will describe the two different reasoning methods used by our system: knowledge-based reasoning and geometric reasoning.

5.1 Knowledge-Based Reasoning

In this project, knowledge-based reasoning refers primarily to checking whether an individual obeys the restrictions imposed on the classes to which it is claimed to belong, identifying an individual based on its relations to others, and identifying a set of individuals linked by certain properties (as done when identifying which parts have been linked, directly or indirectly, via connections). This is done by querying an RDF triple store to check whether appropriate triples have been asserted to it or can be inferred.

KnowRob, however, allows more underlying mechanisms for its reasoning. In particular, decision procedures, which can be arbitrary programs, can be linked to properties. In that case, querying whether an object property holds between individuals is not a matter of testing whether triples have been asserted. Rather, the decision procedure is called, and its result indicates whether the property holds or not. Such properties are referred to as computables, and they offer a way to bring together different reasoning mechanisms into a unified framework of knowledge representation and reasoning.

For this work, we use computables to interface to the geometric reasoner provided by the Kautham Project. The reasoner is called to infer whether the relation *occludesAffordance* holds between some part and an affordance.

5.2 Geometric Reasoning

The main role of geometric reasoning is to evaluate geometric conditions of symbolic actions. Two main geometric reasoning processes are provided:

Reachability Reasoning. A robot can transit to a pose if it has a valid goal configuration. This is inferred by calling an Inverse Kinematic (IK) module and evaluating whether the IK solution is collision-free. The first found collision-free IK solution is returned, and, if any, the associated pose. Failure may occur if either no IK solution exists or if no collision-free IK solution exists.

Spatial Reasoning. We use this module to find a placement for an object within a given region. For the desired object, a pose is sampled that lies in the surface region, and is checked for collisions with other objects, and whether there is enough space to place the object. If the sampled pose is feasible, it is returned. Otherwise, another sample will be tried. If all attempted samples are infeasible, the reasoner reports failure, which can be due to a collision with the objects, or because there is not enough space for the object.

6 OWL Assembly Planning Using the Reasoning Process

We extend the planner for computable relations, and also for being able to generate sub-plans in case some pre-conditions of actions the robot needs to perform are not met. We will explain the changes we made for this paper below.

6.1 Selection of Planning Strategies

The planner is driven by finding differences between a designated goal state and the belief state of a robotic agent. The goal is the classification of an entity as a particular assemblage concept. The initial goal state is part of the meta knowledge supplied to the planner (i.e., knowledge that controls the planning process). Strategies further declare meta knowledge about prioritization of actions, and also allow ignoring certain relations entirely during a particular planning phase.

Strategies are useful because it is often hard to formalize a complete planning domain in a coherent way. One way to approach such problems is decomposition: Planning problems may be separated into different phases that have different planning goals, and that have a low degree of interrelations.

Planning in our approach means to transform an entity in the belief state of the robot with local model violations into one that is in accordance with its model. In our approach, each of the planned entities may use its own planning strategy. The strategy for a planning task is selected based on universal restrictions of the *needsEntity* relation. The selection procedure iterates over all known strategies and checks for each whether the planned entity is a consistent value for the *needsEntity* relation. Only the first matching strategy is selected.

Activating a strategy while another is active pauses the former until the sub-plan finished. In case the sub-plan fails, the parent plan also fails if no other way to achieve the sub-plan goal is known. The meta-knowledge controlling the planner ensures to some extent that the planner does not end up in a bad state where it loops between sequences of decisions that revert each other. In case this happens, the planner will detect the loop and fail.

6.2 Integration with Task Executive

Assembly action commands can be generated whenever an assemblage is entirely specified. This is the case if the assemblage is a proper instance of all its asserted types according to OWL entailment rules including the connection it must establish and the sub-assemblies it must link. Further action commands are generated if a part of interest cannot be grasped because another part is occluding it. To this end, we have extended the planning loop such that it uses a notion of actions, and can reason about which action the robot should perform to establish planning decisions in the belief state.

In each step of the planning loop, the agenda item with top priority is selected for processing. Each item has an associated axiom in the knowledge base that is unsatisfied according to what the robot believes. First, the planner infers a possible domain for the decision. That is, for example, which part it should use to specify a connection. This step is followed by the projection step in which the planner manipulates the knowledge base by asserting or retracting facts about entities. Finally, the item is either deleted if completed, or re-added in case the axiom remains unsatisfied. Also, new items are added to the agenda for all the entities that were linked to the planned entity during the projection step.

We extend this process by the notion of *AgendaActionMapper* and *AgendaActionPerformer* which are used for generating action entities and passing them to an action executive respectively. Their implementation in the knowledge base is very similar. They both restrict relations to describe for which entities they should be activated, and may specify agenda item patterns used for their activation. Matching a pattern means in our framework that the processed agenda item is an instance of the pattern according to OWL entailment rules. Finally, both define hooks to procedures that should be invoked to either generate an action description, or to perform it.

The mapping procedure is invoked after the planner inferred the domain for the currently processed agenda item. The generated action entities must not necessarily satisfy all their pre-conditions. Instead, the planner is called recursively while restricting the planning context to *preActor* axioms. This creates a specific *preActor*-agenda that contains only items corresponding to unsatisfied pre-conditions of the action. The items in the *preActor*-agenda may again be associated to actions that need to be performed to establish the pre-conditions in the belief state, and for which individual planning strategies and agendas are used. Finally, the action entity is passed to the selected action performer. In case the action failed, the agenda item is added to the end of the agenda such that the robot tries again later on, and the planner fails in case it detected a loop.

6.3 Planning with Computable Relations

Computable relations are inferred on demand using decision procedures, and as such are not asserted to the triple store. They often depend on other properties, such as the object locations, and require that the robot performs some action that will change its believes, such as putting the object to some other location.

The planner needs to project its decisions into the belief state for non-computable relations. This step is skipped entirely for computable relations: Only the action handler is called to generate actions that influence the computation. In case the robot was not able to change its believes such that the action pre-conditions are fulfilled, the agenda item is put back at the end of agenda.

In addition, we switched to the computable based reasoning interface offered by KNOWROB. The difference is that it considers computed and asserted triples.

7 Evaluation

We characterize the performance of our work along following dimensions: Variances of spatial configurations our system can handle, and what types of queries can be answered. The planning domain for evaluation is a toy plane assembly targeted at 4 year old children with 21 parts. The plane is part of the YCB Object and Model Set [6]. It uses slide in connections for the parts, and bolts for fixing the parts afterwards. The robot we use is a YuMi. It is simulated in a kinematics simulator and visualized in RViz.

7.1 Simulation

We test our system with different initial spatial configurations, depicted in Fig. 1. The first scene has no occlusions. In the second, the upper part of the plane body is occluding the lower part, and the propeller is occluding the motor grill. Finally, in the third, the chassis is not connected to the holder, and occluded by the upper part of the plane body. We disabled collision checking between the airplane parts to avoid spurious collisions being found at the goal configurations (the connections fit snugly). Geometric reasoning about occlusions allows the robot knowing when it needs to move parts out of the way and change the initial action sequence provided by the OWL planner.

7.2 Querying

In this work, we have extended the robot's reasoning capabilities regarding to geometric relations it can infer, what pre-conditions an action has, and which actions it has to perform to establish planning decisions in its belief state.

The geometric reasoner is integrated through computable geometric relations. The robot can reason about them by asking questions such as *"what are the occluded parts required in a connection?"*:

```
?- holds ( needsAffordance (Connection , Affordance ) ),
   holds ( hasAffordance (Occluded , Affordance ) ),
   holds ( partOccludedBy (Occluded , OccludingPart ) ).
Occluded='PlaneBottomWing1', OccludingPart='PlaneUpperBody1'.
```

The robot can also reason about what action pre-conditions are not fulfilled, and what it can do to fix this. This is done by creating a planning agenda for the action entity that only considers pre-condition axioms of the action:

```
?- entity (Act, [an , action , [type , 'ConnectingParts'] ,
      [assemblesConnection , Connection ]]) ,
   agenda_create (Act , Agenda ),
   agenda_next_item (Agenda , Item ).
Item = "detach _PlaneBottomWing1 _partOccludedBy _PlaneUpperBody1"
```

Finally, the robot can reason about what action it should perform that establishes a planning decision in its belief state. It can, for example, ask what action it should perform to dissolve the *partOccludedBy* relation between parts:

```
?- holds ( usesActionMapper (Strategy , Mapper) ),
   property_range (Mapper , mapsItem , Pattern ),
   individual_of (Item , Pattern ),
   call (Mapper , Item , Action ).
Action = [an , action , [type , 'PutAwayPart'] ,
      [movesPart , 'PlaneUpperBody1'] , ...].
```

8 Conclusion

In this work, we have described how geometric reasoning procedures may be incorporated into logic-based assembly activity planning to account for spatial constraints in the planning process. The ontology used by the logic-based planner serves as an interface to the information provided by the geometric reasoner. Geometric information is computed through decision procedures which are attached to relation symbols in the ontology. Such relations are referred to in action descriptions to make assertions about what should hold for parts involved in the action before performing it. The planner, driven by finding asserted relations that do not hold in the current situation, can also be used for planning how the situation can be changed such that the preconditions become fulfilled. We have demonstrated that this planning framework enables the robot to handle workspace configurations with occlusions between parts, to reason about them, and to plan sub-activities required to achieve its goals.

References

1. Akbari, A., Gillani, M., Rosell, J.: Reasoning-based evaluation of manipulation actions for efficient task planning. Robot 2015: Second Iberian Robotics Conference. AISC, vol. 417, pp. 69–80. Springer, Cham (2016). https://doi.org/10.1007/978-3-319-27146-0_6
2. Akbari, A., Gillani, M., Rosell, J.: Task and motion planning using physics-based reasoning. In: IEEE International Conference on Emerging Technologies and Factory Automation (2015)
3. Balakirsky, S.: Ontology based action planning and verification for agile manufacturing. Robot. Comput.-Integr. Manuf. **33**(Suppl. C), 21–28 (2015). Special Issue on Knowledge Driven Robotics and Manufacturing
4. Balakirsky, S., Kootbally, Z., Kramer, T., Pietromartire, A., Schlenoff, C., Gupta, S.: Knowledge driven robotics for kitting applications. Robot. Auton. Syst. **61**(11), 1205–1214 (2013)
5. Beßler, D., Pomarlan, M., Beetz, M.: OWL-enabled assembly planning for robotic agents. In: Proceedings of the 2018 International Conference on Autonomous Agents, AAMAS 2018 (2018)
6. Çalli, B., Walsman, A., Singh, A., Srinivasa, S., Abbeel, P., Dollar, A.M.: Benchmarking in manipulation research: The YCB object and model set and benchmarking protocols. CoRR abs/1502.03143 (2015)
7. Fiorini, S.R., et al.: Extensions to the core ontology for robotics and automation. Robot. Comput.-Integr. Manuf. **33**(C), 3–11 (2015)
8. Kootbally, Z., Schlenoff, C., Lawler, C., Kramer, T., Gupta, S.: Towards robust assembly with knowledge representation for the planning domain definition language (PDDL). Robot. Comput.-Integr. Manuf. **33**(C), 42–55 (2015)
9. Kuffner, J.J., LaValle, S.M.: RRT-connect: an efficient approach to single-query path planning. In: IEEE International Conference on Robotics and Automation, Proceedings, ICRA 2000, vol. 2, pp. 995–1001. IEEE (2000)
10. Malec, J., Nilsson, K., Bruyninckx, H.: Describing assembly tasks in declarative way. In: IEEE/ICRA Workshop on Semantics (2013)
11. Gillani, M., Akbari, A., Rosell, J.: Ontological physics-based motion planning for manipulation. In: IEEE International Conference on Emerging Technologies and Factory Automation. IEEE (2015)
12. Patel, R., Hedelind, M., Lozan-Villegas, P.: Enabling robots in small-part assembly lines: the "rosetta approach" - an industrial perspective. In: ROBOTIK. VDE-Verlag (2012)

13. Perzylo, A., Somani, N., Profanter, S., Kessler, I., Rickert, M., Knoll, A.: Intuitive instruction of industrial robots: semantic process descriptions for small lot production. In: IEEE/RSJ International Conference on Intelligent Robots and Systems (IROS), pp. 2293–2300 (2016)

14. Polydoros, A.S., Großmann, B., Rovida, F., Nalpantidis, L., Krüger, V.: Accurate and versatile automation of industrial kitting operations with SkiROS. In: Alboul, L., Damian, D., Aitken, J.M.M. (eds.) TAROS 2016. LNCS (LNAI), vol. 9716, pp. 255–268. Springer, Cham (2016). https://doi.org/10.1007/978-3-319-40379-3_26

15. Rosell, J., Pérez, A., Aliakbar, A., Gillani, M., Palomo, L., García, N.: The Kautham project: a teaching and research tool for robot motion planning. In: IEEE International Conference on Emerging Technologies and Factory Automation (2014)

16. Schlenoff, C., et al.: An IEEE standard ontology for robotics and automation. In: 2012 IEEE/RSJ International Conference on Intelligent Robots and Systems (IROS), pp. 1337–1342. IEEE (2012)

17. Siméon, T., Laumond, J.P., Cortés, J., Sahbani, A.: Manipulation planning with probabilistic roadmaps. Int. J. Robot. Res. **23**(7–8), 729–746 (2004)

18. Stenmark, M., Malec, J., Nilsson, K., Robertsson, A.: On distributed knowledge bases for robotized small-batch assembly. IEEE Trans. Autom. Sci. Eng. **12**(2), 519–528 (2015)

19. Stilman, M., Kuffner, J.: Planning among movable obstacles with artificial constraints. Int. J. Robot. Res. **27**(11–12), 1295–1307 (2008)

20. Stilman, M., Schamburek, J.U., Kuffner, J., Asfour, T.: Manipulation planning among movable obstacles. In: 2007 IEEE International Conference on Robotics and Automation, pp. 3327–3332. IEEE (2007)

21. Sucan, I., Moll, M., Kavraki, L.E., et al.: The open motion planning library. IEEE Robot. Autom. Mag. **19**(4), 72–82 (2012)

22. Tenorth, M., Beetz, M.: KnowRob - a knowledge processing infrastructure for cognition-enabled robots. Int. J. Robot. Res. **32**(5), 566–590 (2013)

23. Varadarajan, K.M., Vincze, M.: AfRob: the affordance network ontology for robots. In: 2012 IEEE/RSJ International Conference on Intelligent Robots and Systems (IROS), pp. 1343–1350. IEEE (2012)

24. Zaplana, I., Claret, J., Basañez, L.: Kinematic analysis of redundant robotic manipulators: application to Kuka LWR 4+ and ABB Yumi. Revista Iberoamericana de Automtica e Informtica Industrial (2017, in press)

Extracting Planning Operators
from Instructional Texts for Behaviour
Interpretation

Kristina Yordanova[(✉)] [ID]

University of Rostock, 18059 Rostock, Germany
kristina.yordanova@uni-rostock.de

Abstract. Recent attempts at behaviour understanding through language grounding have shown that it is possible to automatically generate planning models from instructional texts. One drawback of these approaches is that they either do not make use of the semantic structure behind the model elements identified in the text, or they manually incorporate a collection of concepts with semantic relationships between them. To use such models for behaviour understanding, however, the system should also have knowledge of the semantic structure and context behind the planning operators. To address this problem, we propose an approach that automatically generates planning operators from textual instructions. The approach is able to identify various hierarchical, spatial, directional, and causal relations between the model elements. This allows incorporating context knowledge beyond the actions being executed. We evaluated the approach in terms of correctness of the identified elements, model search complexity, model coverage, and similarity to handcrafted models. The results showed that the approach is able to generate models that explain actual tasks executions and the models are comparable to handcrafted models.

Keywords: Planning operators · Behaviour understanding
Natural language processing

1 Introduction

Libraries of plans combined with observations are often used for behaviour understanding [12,18]. Such approaches rely on PDDL-like notations to generate a library of plans and reason about the agent's actions, plans, and goals based on observations. Models describing plan recognition problems for behaviour understanding are typically manually developed [2,18]. The manual modelling is however time consuming and error prone and often requires domain expertise [16]. To reduce the need of domain experts and the time required for building the model, one can substitute them with textual data [17]. As [23] propose, one can utilise the knowledge encoded in instructional texts, such as manuals, recipes, and howto articles, to learn the model structure. Such texts specify tasks for

© Springer Nature Switzerland AG 2018
F. Trollmann and A.-Y. Turhan (Eds.): KI 2018, LNAI 11117, pp. 215–228, 2018.
https://doi.org/10.1007/978-3-030-00111-7_19

achieving a given goal without explicitly stating all the required steps. On the one hand, this makes them a challenging source for learning a model [5]. On the other hand, they are written in imperative form, have a simple sentence structure, and are highly organised. Compared to rich texts, this makes them a better source for identifying the sequence of actions needed for reaching the goal [28].

According to [4], to learn a model for planning problems from textual instructions, the system has to: 1. **extract the actions' semantics** from the text, 2. **learn the model semantics** through language grounding, 3. and finally to **translate it into computational model** for planning problems. In this work we add 4. the **learning of a situation model** as a requirement for learning the model structure. As the name suggests, it provides context information about the situation [24]. It is a collection of concepts with semantic relations between them. In that sense, the situation model plays the role of the common knowledge base shared between different entities. We also add 5. **the need to extract implicit causal relations from the texts** as explicit relations are rarely found in such type of texts.

In previous work we proposed an approach for extracting domain knowledge and generating situation models from textual instructions, based on which simple planning operators can be built [26]. We extend our previous work by proposing a mechanism for generation of rich models from instructional texts and providing a detailed description of the methodology. Further, we show first empirical results that the approach is able to generate planning operators, which capture the behaviour of the user. To evaluate the approach, we examine the correctness of the identified elements, the complexity of the search space, the model coverage, and its similarity to handcrafted models.

The work is structured as follows. Section 2 provides the state of the art in language grounding for behaviour understanding; Sect. 3 provides a formal description of the proposed approach; Sect. 4 contains the empirical evaluation of our approach. The work concludes with discussion of future work (Sect. 5).

2   Related Work

The goal of grounded language acquisition is to learn linguistic analysis from a situated context [22]. This could be done in different ways: through grammatical patterns that are used to map the sentence to a machine understandable model of the sentence [4,13,28]; through machine learning techniques [3,6,8,11,19]; or through reinforcement learning approaches that learn language by interacting with the environment [1,4,5,8,11,22]. Models learned through language grounding have been used for plan generation [4,13,14], for learning the optimal sequence of instruction execution [5], for learning navigational directions [6,22], and for interpreting human instructions for robots to follow them [11,20].

All of the above approaches have two drawbacks. The first problem is the way in which the preconditions and effects for the planning operators are identified. They are learned through explicit causal relations, that are grammatically expressed in the text [13,19]. The existing approaches either rely on initial manual definition to learn these relations [4], or on grammatical patterns and rich texts with complex sentence structure [13]. In contrast, textual instructions usually have a simple sentence structure and grammatical patterns are rarely discovered [25]. The existing approaches do not address the problem of discovering causal relations between sentences, but assume that all causal relations are within the sentence [20]. In contrast, in instructional texts, the elements representing cause and effect are usually found in different sentences [25].

The second problem is that existing approaches either rely on manually defined situation model [4,8,19], or do not use one [5,13,22,28]. Still, one needs a situation model to deal with model generalisation and as a means for expressing the semantic relations between model elements. What is more, the manual definition is time consuming and often requires domain experts. [14] propose dealing with model generalisation by clustering similar actions together. We propose an alternative solution where we exploit the semantic structure of the knowledge present in the text and in language taxonomies.

In previous work, we addressed these two problems by proposing an approach for automatic generation of situation models for planning problems [26]. In this work, we extend the approach to generate rich planning operators and we show first empirical evidence that it is possible to reason about human behaviour based on the generated models. The method adapts an approach proposed by [25] to use time series analysis to identify the causal relations between text elements. We use it to discover implicit causal relations between actions. We also make use of existing language taxonomies and word dependencies to identify hierarchical, spatial and directional relations, as well as relations identifying the means through which an action is accomplished. The situation model is then used to generate planning operators.

3 Approach

3.1 Identifying Elements of Interest

The first step in generating the model is to identify the elements of interest in the text. We consider a text X to be a sequence of sentences $S = \{s_1, s_2, ..., s_n\}$. Each sentence s is represented by a sequence of words $W_s = \{w_{1_s}, w_{2_s}, ..., w_{m_s}\}$, where each word has a tag t_w describing its part of speech (POS) meaning. In a text we have different types of words. We are interested in verbs $v \in V$, $V \subset W$ as they describe the actions that can be executed in the environment. The set of actions $E \subset V$ are verbs in their infinitive form or in present tense, as textual instructions are usually described in imperative form with a missing agent. We are also interested in nouns $n \in$, $N \subset W$ that are related to the verb. One type of nouns are the direct (accusative) objects of the verb $d \in D$, $D \subset N$. These nouns give us the elements of the world with which the agent is interacting (in other words, objects on which the action is executed). We denote the relation between d and e as $dobj(e, d)$. Here a relation r is a function applied to two words a and b. We denote this as $r(a, b)$. Note that $r(a, b) \neq r(b, a)$. An example of such relation can be seen in Fig. 1, where "knife" is the direct object of "take".

Apart from the direct objects, we are also interested in any indirect objects $i \in I$, $I \subset N$ of the action. Namely, any nouns that are connected to the action through a preposition. These nouns give us spacial, locational or directional information about the action being executed, or the means through which the action is executed (e.g. an action is executed "with" the help of an object). More formally, an indirect object $i_p \in I$ of an action e is the noun connected to e through a preposition p. We denote the relation between i_p and e as $p(e, i_p)$. For example, in Fig. 1 "counter" is the indirect object of "take" and its relation is denoted as $from$(take,counter). We define the set $O := D \cup I$ of all relevant objects as the union of all unique direct and indirect objects in a text.

The last type of element is the object's property. A property $c \in C$, $C \subset W$ of an object o is a word that has one of the following relations with the object: $amod(c, o)$, denoting the adjectival modifier or $nsubj(c, o)$, denoting the nominal subject. We denote such relation as $property(c, o)$. For example, in Fig. 1, "clean" is the property of "knife". As in instructions the object is often omitted (e.g. *"Simmer (the sauce) until thickened."*), we also investigate the relation between an action and past tense verbs or adjectives that do not belong to an adjectival modifier or to nominal subject, but that might still describe this relation.

3.2   Building the Initial Situation Model

Given the set of objects O, the goal is to build the initial structure of the situation model. It consists of words, describing the elements of a situation and the relations between these elements. If we think of the words as nodes and the relations as edges, we can represent the situation model as a graph.

Definition 1 *(Situation model).* *Situation model $G := (W, R)$ is a graph consisting of nodes represented through words W and of edges represented through relations R, where for two words $a, b \in W$, there exists a relation $r \in R$ such that $r(a, b)$.*

The initial structure of the situation model is represented through a taxonomy that contains the objects O and their abstracted meaning on different levels of abstraction. To do that, a language taxonomy L containing hyperonymy

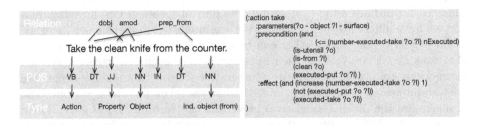

Fig. 1. Elements of a sentence necessary for the model generation and the corresponding PDDL operator. Each sentence is assigned a part of speech tag and the dependencies are annotated. Based on them, the relevant elements are identified. Later, PDDL operators are generated from the identified elements.

relations between the words of the language is used (this is the is-a relation between words). For example, the relation $isa(knife, tool)$ indicates that the concrete object "knife" is of type "tool". To build the initial situation model, we start with the set O as the leaves of the taxonomy and for each object $o \in O$ we recursively search for its hyperonyms. This results in a hierarchy where the bottommost layer consist of the elements in O and the uppermost layer contains the most abstract word, that is the least common parent of all $o \in O$. Here the least common parent $lcp(a,b)$ of two words a and b is the parent on the lowest level in the taxonomy that contains both a and b as children. Then the initial situation model is $G_{init} := (W_{init}, R_{init})$ with $W_{init} = O \cup hyperonyms(O, L)$ and $R_{init} := isa(W_{init})$ where O is the set of objects and L is a language taxonomy. Furthermore, for every two objects $o_i, o_j \in O$, it holds that there exists $l \in L$ such that $l = lcp(o_i, o_j)$. Note that here we use a function $hyperonyms(O,L)$, which returns all hyperonyms of O found in L. The abstraction hierarchy is later used to generalise or specialise the action templates in a planning model.

3.3 Extending the Situation Model

As the initial situation model contains only the abstraction hierarchy of the identified objects, we extend it by first including the list of all actions and properties to the situation model and then adding the relations between actions and indirect objects, actions and direct objects, and properties and objects to the graph. We define the extended situation model as $G_{ext} := (W_{ext}, R_{ext})$, such that $W_{ext} := W_{init} \cup E \cup C$ and $R_{ext} := R_{init} \cup dobj(E,O) \cup p(E,O) \cup property(C,O)$, where E is the set of actions, O is the set of objects, C is the set of properties, and $dobj(E,O)$ and $p(E,O)$ are the direct, respectively indirect, relations between object and action, while $property(C,O)$ is the property - object relation. On the one hand, this step is performed to enrich the semantic structure of the model. On the other hand, it gives the basis for the planning operators as the arguments in an operator are represented by all objects that are related to the action.

3.4 Adding Implicit Causal Relations

The last step is extending the situation model with causal relations. They build up the preconditions and effects in a planning operator. There are two types of predicates that describe the preconditions and effects. The first type is described through the identified properties (e.g. the condition that the knife has the property "clean") and through the indirect object relations (e.g. the counter has the role "from"). The second type of preconditions are based on the assumption that a certain action has to be executed to enable the execution of another action. We call this "predictive causality" [7, p. 254] and the corresponding relations "predictive causal relations" or "implicit causal relations".

    To discover implicit causal relations between actions in the text, we consider two cases: (1) relations between two actions in the text; (2) relations between two action-object pairs in the text. We consider the first case as there are actions that are not related to a specific direct or indirect object but that still are causally related to other actions. We consider the second case because applying one action on an object can cause the execution of another action on the same object. We denote predictive causal relations with $q \in Q$, $Q \subset R$. To discover causal relations between actions, we adapt the algorithm proposed by [25], which makes use of time series analysis. We start by representing each unique action (or each action-object tuple) in a text as a time series. Each element in the series represents the number of occurrences of the action in the sentence. We then make use of the Granger causality test. It is a statistical test for determining whether one time series is useful for forecasting another. It performs statistical significance test for one time series, "causing" the other time series with different time lags using auto-regression [9]. Given two sets of time series x_t and y_t, we can test whether x_t Granger causes y_t with a maximum p time lag. To do that, we estimate the regression $y_t = a_o + a_1 y_{t-1} + ... + a_p y_{t-p} + b_1 x_{t-1} + ... + b_p x_{t-p}$. An F-test is then used to determine whether the lagged x terms are significant[1]. For example, we generate time series for the words "take" and "put" and after applying the Granger test, it concludes that the lagged time series for "take" significantly improve the forecast of the "put" time series, thus we conclude that "take" causes "put".

Now that we have identified the implicit causal relations between actions, we add them in the situation model. The final situation model is $G_{fin} := (W_{fin}, R_{fin})$ such that $W_{fin} := W_{ext}$ and $R_{fin} := R_{ext} \cup Q$, where Q is the set of discovered causal relations, W_{ext} is the set of words and R_{ext} is the set of relations in the extended situation model.

3.5   Generating Planning Operators

The next step is to generate operators based on the situation model. An operator $a := (e, Z, Pr, Fp, Ef, Fe)$ is a tuple, where e is the name of the operator, Z represents the set of arguments with which the operator can be parameterised; Pr, $Ef \subset P$ are the set of precondition, respectively effect, predicates; Fp, $Fe \subset F$ are the set of precondition, respectively effect, functions. The predicates P are boolean functions that provide statements about the model world state. In difference to predicates, functions provide higher-order statements about the model world (e.g. increasing the function value).

Algorithm 1 shows the procedure for generating the operators from the situation model. We take the name e from the set of actions E in the situation model. Then, for each action e, we take the set of arguments Z from the objects O in the situation model that have object-verb relations to the action. The set of precondition predicates Pr is generated from the set of actions, which have implicit

---

[1] Note that regression usually reflects correlation. Granger, however, argued that causality in economics could be tested for by measuring the ability to predict the future values of a time series using prior values of another time series. As the question of "true causality" is philosophical, the Granger causality test assumes that one thing preceding another can be used as evidence of causation.

Algorithm 1. Generating planning operators from the situation model

---

Require: E, C, R, O ▷ actions, properties, relations, objects from G_{fin}
Require: n ▷ number of times an action can be executed
Require: $A := \emptyset$ ▷ empty set of operators
1: **for** e in E **do**   ▷ for each action in E
2:      $(name_{a_e}, Z_{a_e}, Pr_{a_e}, Fp_{a_e}, Ef_{a_e}, Fe_{a_e}) \leftarrow initialise()$
3:      $name_{a_e} \leftarrow e$
4:      **for** o in O **do**
5:          **if** $\exists r := relation(e, o), r \in R_{dobj} \cup R_p$ **then**   ▷ add arguments
6:              $Z_{a_e} \leftarrow add.argument(Z_{a_e}, o)$
7:          **end if**
8:          **if** $\exists r := p(e, o), r \in R_p$ **then**   ▷ add predicates from indirect object relations
9:              $Pr_{a_e} \leftarrow add.predicate(Pr_{a_e}, property\text{-}p(o))$
10:          **end if**
11:      **end for**
12:      $Fp_{a_e} \leftarrow add.function(Fp_{a_e}, (number\text{-}executed\text{-}e(Z) < n))$ ▷ default precondition function
13:      **for** z in Z_{a_e} **do**   ▷ add property predicates
14:          **for** c in C **do**
15:              **if** $\exists r := property(c, z), r \in R$ **then**
16:                  $Pr_{a_e} \leftarrow add.predicate(Pr_{a_e}, property\text{-}c(z))$
17:              **end if**
18:          **end for**
19:      **end for**
20:      **for** y in $E, y \neq e$ **do**
21:          **if** $\exists r := causes(y, e), r \in Q, Q \subset R$ **then**   ▷ add causal predicates to precondition
22:              $Pr_{a_e} \leftarrow add.predicate(Pr_{a_e}, executed(y))$
23:          **end if**
24:          **for** w in $E, w \neq e, w \neq y$ **do**   ▷ remove transitive actions in the precondition
25:              **if** $\exists u := cyclic(y, e) \wedge \exists l := cyclic(w, e) \wedge \exists t := cyclic(y, w), u, l, t \in R$ **then**
26:                  $tmp \leftarrow get.weakest(e, y, w)$ ▷ identify the weakest transitive action
27:                  **if** $tmp \neq e$ **then**
28:                      $Pr_{a_e} \leftarrow remove.predicate(Pr_{a_e}, executed(tmp))$
29:                  **end if**
30:              **end if**
31:          **end for**
32:          **if** $\exists r := cyclic(y, e), r \in R$ **then**   ▷ add predicate for cyclic actions in the effects
33:              $Ef_{a_e} \leftarrow add.predicate(Ef_{a_e}, \neg executed(y))$
34:          **end if**
35:      **end for**
36:      $Fe_{a_e} \leftarrow add.function(Fe_{a_e}, (number\text{-}executed\text{-}e(Z) + 1))$ ▷ increase value of precondition
         function with 1
37:      $Ef_{a_e} \leftarrow add.predicate(Ef_{a_e}, executed(e))$ ▷ mark action as executed
38:      $A \leftarrow add.op(A, (name_{a_e}, Z_{a_e}, Pr_{a_e}, Fp_{a_e}, Ef_{a_e}, Fe_{a_e}))$
39: **end for**
40: **return** $unique(A)$ ▷ return all unique operators

---

causal relation to e, and the set of identified properties, related to the action or its arguments. The set of effects consists of marking the action as executed, increasing the value of the precondition function, and of negating the execution of another action if they are cyclic. Cyclic actions are actions that negate each other's effects. $a, b \in E$ are cyclic, if $causes(a, b)$ and $causes(b, a)$. We denote them as $cyclic(a, b)$. For example, the execution of "put the apple on the table" negates the effect of the action "take the apple". For two operators a and b with cyclic relation, we have to negate the effects of a after executing b and vice versa, otherwise it will not be possible to execute these actions again. Another problem that arises are transitive causal relations. We say that three actions a, b and c are transitive if for $a, b, c \in E$, it holds that $cyclic(a, b)$, $cyclic(b, c)$, and $cyclic(a, c)$. The problem here is that the preconditions and effects of these actions block the execution of at least one of the transitive actions. It no longer suffice to just negate the effects of the cyclic actions, as there is a third action influencing the execution of the two remaining actions. To solve this problem, we follow an approach similar to the one proposed in [21]. We identify any transitive relations an action has, then remove the weakest relation, ending up with only cyclic relations. We find the weakest relation by calculating the frequency of appearance of the relations in the text and removing the one with the lowest frequency. Example operator can be seen in Fig. 1, left.

The target language is the Planning Domain Definition Language (PDDL), which represents the operators through abstracted action templates. To generate templates we replace the operator's arguments with the corresponding hyperonym on level m in the abstraction hierarchy and then removing any repeating abstracted operators. In that manner we control the model specificity. Using hyperonyms on higher abstraction level produces more general models and using those on lower abstraction level produces more specific models.

The planning model M is a tuple (P, F, L, A, Z, x_0, g), where P is a set of predicates, F is a set of functions, L is the language taxonomy (or abstraction hierarchy) from the situation model, A is a set of actions, Z is a set of arguments, x_o is the initial state, and g is the set of goals. The predicates and functions build up the model states $x \in X$, where X is the model state space, which represents a unique combination of the values of all predicates and functions. The initial state x_0 is the state of the world before any action has been executed. To generate x_0, we set all the predicates identifying the execution of a cyclic action to true, add all identified properties, and set all functions to their initial value. Furthermore, we perform analysis based on the action order in the text. We check if the precondition of the first action that requires enabling are initially enabled. In case some predicates cannot be enabled based on the original action order, they are set to true in the initial state description. The rest of the predicates are set to false. The goal states $g \subseteq X$ represent all the predicates that have to hold for the goal to be reached. We generate the goal states by defining that each type of action $a \in A$ has to be executed at least once. The generated operators often have contradicting preconditions and effects. To address this problem, we use a strategy where all ground operators that have impossible preconditions, given the initial state, are removed [10]. The same applies to predicates and functions that are used only in impossible actions. This strategy removes all impossible candidate operators and predicates and returns a model that is causally correct.

4   Evaluation

To evaluate the approach, we used 20 instructional texts, from which we generated planning models. We used an extended version of PDDL [10] as a target format for the planning models. The instructions included cooking recipes (3 instructions), texts from coffee and washing machines manuals (4 instructions), texts from wikiHow[2] (3 instructions), descriptions of the tasks performed in the

---

[2] https://www.wikihow.com/Main-Page.

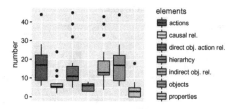

Fig. 2. Median number of elements and relations incorporated in the situation models extracted from 20 instructional texts.

CMU kitchen dataset[3,4] (3 instructions), and descriptions of student exercises for minimally invasive surgery (7 instructions).

The instructions had between 7 and 111 sentences with a mean of 26.5 sentences and a mean sentence length in a text between 5 and 16 words. To obtain the part of speech tags and dependencies between words, we used the Stanford NLP parser. As state of the art parsers have shown to perform poorly with identifying events in instructional texts, we use a postprocessing step, as proposed in [27], to improve the tags accuracy. We used the taxonomy of English language WordNet [15] to obtain the hyperonyms of the identified objects. As some words have different meanings, we took the most frequently used meaning for each object. To generate the PDDL action templates, we used abstraction level of 2. Figure 2 shows the statistics for the extracted from the texts elements that were incorporated in the situation models.

The average number of identified actions in the instructional texts was 17.3 and the average number of objects was 10.2. Relatively small number of properties was discovered (mean of 3.55) with more properties discovered in cooking recipes that use more unstructured language with longer sentences (with maximum number of 18 properties). An average of 7.3 causal relations were discovered in the texts with more causal relations when the texts had more sentences (maximum of 24 relations). This is to be expected, as the time series analysis performs better with longer series. The opposite was observed in discovering semantic relations (i.e. the relations between objects, properties and actions within the sentences). Texts with longer sentence structure but with less sentences tended to have more semantic relations. Finally, the generated abstraction hierarchy (i.e. hyperonyms) had between 3 and 8 levels with an average of 5 levels.

Correctness of the Identified Elements: To evaluate whether the approach is able to correctly identify objects, actions and properties from texts, we asked a human annotator to manually identify these elements in the texts[5]. Figure 3

---

[3] http://kitchen.cs.cmu.edu/.

[4] These descriptions have been generated based on the observed in the video log behaviour.

[5] Note that we did not compare the identified causal relations. This is because implicit causal relations are a subject of interpretation. For that reason, we consider the relations are correctly identified if the model is able to explain the given plan.

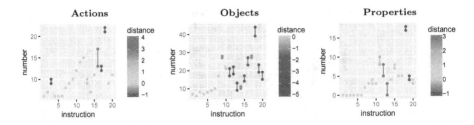

Fig. 3. Difference between automatically discovered elements and manually discovered elements in the 20 instructional texts. Green indicates that the human annotator discovered more elements, red means that our approach discovered false positives, while yellow indicates the same number of elements. (Color figure online)

graphically shows the number of discovered elements and the distance between the number of manually and automatically discovered elements. It can be seen that in the majority of the cases both discovered the same number of elements[6]. Interestingly enough, our approach tended to discover more objects than the human annotator, producing false positives. This can be explained with the fact that it identified abstract concepts such as "level", "time" etc. as objects while the human annotator considered only physical objects.

Complexity of the Model: Figure 4 (left) shows the median number of generated action templates, and the resulting number of grounded operators, predicates, and functions after the pruning phase. A minimum of 7 and a maximum of 57 action templates were generated based on the situation model with a mean of 19.85 templates. The templates resulted in models with 71.5 operators on average, 9.4 predicates, and 64.35 functions. We also applied iterative deepening depth-first search to analyse the state space complexity and branching factor for the resulting models. We limited the search depth to 5 as some of the models had state spaces of hundreds of millions of states. Figure 4 (right) shows the maximum and median branching factors as well as the number of discovered

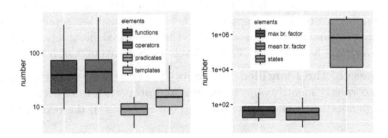

Fig. 4. Median number of action templates, operators, predicates, and functions (left). Median branching factor and states (right).

---

[6] In the case where the number of elements was the same for both the human annotator and our tool, the discovered elements were the same in both cases.

states at a search depth of 5. The branching factor tells us how many states are reachable from any given state in the model. High branching factor indicates that the probability of selecting the actually observed action will be low. The models with small number of operators generated as few as 327 states, while some models had as many as 10 million states at search level 5 (with the search being incomplete at this level). This was also reflected in the branching factor, where a maximum branching factor of 449 was observed. On average, however, the number of reachable states from any given state was 56. This is still a very high number, but with such number plan recognition would still be feasible, especially in the presence of unambiguous observations.

Model Coverage: To evaluate whether a generated model is actually able to explain human behaviour, we used the CMU kitchen dataset. We analysed 15 video logs from the "brownies" dataset and based on the observed execution sequences, we manually generated 15 plans. We then tested a model generated from a text describing the "brownies" dataset. The text was written based on the behaviour observed in the first video log. We expected that the model will be able to better explain the plan corresponding to the first log.

To evaluate the model, we first looked whether the model is able to explain the plans at all (i.e. whether the observed execution sequences are part of the model). The results showed that the model was able to explain all of the 15 plans. We then calculated the final log likelihood of the model. This is the likelihood that tells us how well the model fits to the provided observation sequence (in our case to the plan). The final log likelihood is calculated based on the cumulative action probability of the observed in the plan action, given a model M. This approach is similar to model learning through observations [8].

Figure 5 shows the final log likelihood for the models when explaining the 15 plans and its relation to the length of the executed plan. We fitted a linear model to the results (in blue). It showed that the likelihood of the model (i.e. how well it fits the given plan) is linearly proportional to the length of the plan. This stands to show that the model was able to explain all plans in a similar manner (i.e. it was not overfitted for the first plan).

Similarity to Handcrafted Models: To investigate how a generated model compares to a handcrafted model, we asked experts to develop 3 PDDL models for the "brownies" experiment. We call the generated model $PDDL_g$. We com-

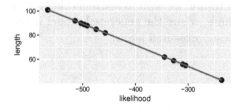

Fig. 5. Negative log likelihood of the model, given a certain plan.

Table 1. Comparison between $PDDL_g$, $PDDL_{h1}$, $PDDL_{h2}$, and $PDDL_{h3}$.

Metrics	$PDDL_g$	$PDDL_{h1}$	$PDDL_{h2}$	$PDDL_{h3}$
Operators	421	1854	1461	257
Predicates	10	1853	424	48
Functions	329	0	0	41
Min/mean/max br.	1/231.19/421	1848/1848/1854	82/117.28/290	5/30.82/55
States (depth 5)	10 000 227	10 000 162	10 000 009	1 785 896

pared $PDDL_g$ to $PDDL_{h1}$, $PDDL_{h2}$, and $PDDL_{h3}$, each of which had increasing complexity in terms of constraints and domain knowledge. $PDDL_{h3}$ was overfitted to explain only the sequences in the "brownies" experiment. Table 1 shows the comparison between the handcrafted models and $PDDL_g$. There the more complex the constraints and context knowledge, the more specific the model becomes, and the search space complexity decreases. In terms of operators and predicates $PDDL_g$ performed more similar to the overfitted $PDDL_{h3}$ with 1.6 more operators than $PDDL_{h3}$. $PDDL_g$ had two times higher branching factor than $PDDL_{h2}$ but it still had 8 times smaller branching factor than $PDDL_{h1}$. This stands to show that the model is comparable to handcrafted models that do not encode implicit common sense knowledge or knowledge used by the system designer to reduce the model state space.

5   Conclusion and Future Work

In this work we showed first empirical results from an approach that generates PDDL models for behaviour understanding from instructional texts. The results showed that the approach is able to identify most of the relevant model elements from textual narratives. In that sense, it performed comparable to human annotator. The approach was also able to generate a model that can explain the actual execution sequences observed in the video logs of the "brownies" dataset from the CMU kitchen activities. Finally, comparing the generated model with handcrafted models, it was shown that the model has better parameters and encodes more context knowledge than a simple handcrafted model but is unable to capture the "common sense" knowledge that is encoded in overfitted handcrafted models. In the future, we plan to address this problem by introducing an additional learning phase, where the generated model is further adjusted based on observations of already executed plans.

References

1. Babeş-Vroman, M., et al.: Learning to interpret natural language instructions. In: Proceedings of the Workshop on Semantic Interpretation in an Actionable Context, Stroudsburg, PA, USA, pp. 1–6 (2012)
2. Baker, C., Saxe, R., Tenenbaum, J.: Action understanding as inverse planning. Cognition 113(3), 329–349 (2009)
3. Benotti, L., Lau, T., Villalba, M.: Interpreting natural language instructions using language, vision, and behavior. ACM Trans. Interact. Intell. Syst. 4(3), 13:1–13:22 (2014)
4. Branavan, S., Kushman, N., Lei, T., Barzilay, R.: Learning high-level planning from text. In: Proceedings of the Annual Meeting of Association for Computational Linguistics, Stroudsburg, PA, USA, pp. 126–135 (2012)
5. Branavan, S., Zettlemoyer, L., Barzilay, R.: Reading between the lines: learning to map high-level instructions to commands. In: Proceedings of the Annual Meeting of Association for Computational Linguistics, Stroudsburg, PA, USA, pp. 1268–1277 (2010)
6. Chen, D., Mooney, R.: Learning to interpret natural language navigation instructions from observations. In: Proceedings of the AAAI Conference on Artificial Intelligence, pp. 859–865, August 2011
7. Diebold, F., Witman, K., Hanseman, D., Lysne, L., Moore, T.: Elements of Forecasting, 2nd edn. Cengage Learning, Boston (2000)
8. Goldwasser, D., Roth, D.: Learning from natural instructions. Mach. Learn. 94(2), 205–232 (2014)
9. Granger, C.: Investigating causal relations by econometric models and cross-spectral methods. Econometrica 37(3), 424–438 (1969)
10. Kirste, T., Krüger, F.: CCBM-a tool for activity recognition using computational causal behavior models. Technical report CS-01-12. Institut für Informatik, Universität Rostock, Rostock, Germany, May 2012
11. Kollar, T., Tellex, S., Roy, D., Roy, N.: Grounding verbs of motion in natural language commands to robots. In: Khatib, O., Kumar, V., Sukhatme, G. (eds.) Experimental Robotics, vol. 79, pp. 31–47. Springer, Heidelberg (2014). https://doi.org/10.1007/978-3-642-28572-1_3
12. Krüger, F., Nyolt, M., Yordanova, K., Hein, A., Kirste, T.: Computational state space models for activity and intention recognition. A feasibility study. PLoS ONE 9(11), e109381 (2014)
13. Li, X., Mao, W., Zeng, D., Wang, F.-Y.: Automatic construction of domain theory for attack planning. In: IEEE International Conference on Intelligence and Security Informatics, pp. 65–70, May 2010
14. Lindsay, A., Read, J., Ferreira, J., Hayton, T., Porteous, J., Gregory, P.: Framer: planning models from natural language action descriptions. In: International Conference on Automated Planning and Scheduling (2017)
15. Miller, G.: WordNet: a lexical database for English. Commun. ACM 38(11), 39–41 (1995)
16. Nguyen, T.A., Kambhampati, S., Do, M.: Synthesizing robust plans under incomplete domain models. In: Advances in Neural Information Processing Systems 26, pp. 2472–2480. Curran Associates Inc. (2013)
17. Philipose, M., Fishkin, K., Perkowitz, M., Patterson, D., Fox, D., Kautz, H., Hahnel, D.: Inferring activities from interactions with objects. IEEE Pervasive Comput. 3(4), 50–57 (2004)

18. Ramirez, M., Geffner, H.: Goal recognition over POMDPs: inferring the intention of a POMDP agent. In: Proceedings of the International Joint Conference on Artificial Intelligence, IJCAI 2011, Barcelona, Spain, vol. 3, pp. 2009–2014 (2011)

19. Sil, A., Yates, A.: Extracting strips representations of actions and events. In: Recent Advances in Natural Language Processing, Hissar, Bulgaria, pp. 1–8, September 2011

20. Tenorth, M., Nyga, D., Beetz, M.: Understanding and executing instructions for everyday manipulation tasks from the world wide web. In: IEEE International Conference on Robotics and Automation, pp. 1486–1491, May 2010

21. Veloso, M., Perez, A., Carbonell, J.: Nonlinear planning with parallel resource allocation. In: Proceedings of the DARPA Workshop of Innovative Approaches to Planning, Scheduling and Control (1990)

22. Vogel, A., Jurafsky, D.: Learning to follow navigational directions. In: Proceedings of the Annual Meeting of Association for Computational Linguistics, Stroudsburg, PA, USA, pp. 806–814 (2010)

23. Webber, B., Badler, N., Eugenio, B., Geib, C., Levison, L., Moore, M.: Instructions, intentions and expectations. Artif. Intell. **73**(1), 253–269 (1995)

24. Ye, J., Dobson, S., McKeever, S.: Situation identification techniques in pervasive computing: a review. Pervasive Mob. Comput. **8**(1), 36–66 (2012)

25. Yordanova, K.: Discovering causal relations in textual instructions. In: Recent Advances in Natural Language Processing, Hissar, Bulgaria, pp. 714–720, September 2015

26. Yordanova, K.: Automatic generation of situation models for plan recognition problems. In: Proceedings of the International Conference Recent Advances in Natural Language Processing, Varna, Bulgaria, pp. 823–830. INCOMA Ltd., September 2017

27. Yordanova, K.: A simple model for improving the performance of the Stanford Parser for action detection in textual instructions. In: Proceedings of the International Conference Recent Advances in Natural Language Processing, Varna, Bulgaria, pp. 831–838. INCOMA Ltd., September 2017

28. Zhang, Z., Webster, P., Uren, V., Varga, A., Ciravegna, F.: Automatically extracting procedural knowledge from instructional texts using natural language processing. In: Proceedings of the International Conference on Language Resources and Evaluation, Istanbul, Turkey, pp. 520–527, May 2012

Risk-Sensitivity in Simulation Based Online Planning

Kyrill Schmid[1(✉)], Lenz Belzner[1], Marie Kiermeier[1], Alexander Neitz[2],
Thomy Phan[1], Thomas Gabor[1], and Claudia Linnhoff[1]

[1] Mobile and Distributed Systems Group, LMU Munich,
Oettingenstr. 67, Munich, Germany
{kyrill.schmid,belzner,marie.kiermeier,thomy.phan,
thomas.gabor,linnhoff}@ifi.lmu.de
http://www.mobile.ifi.lmu.de/
[2] Empirical Inference, Max Planck Institute for Intelligent Systems,
Max-Planck-Ring 4, Tübingen, Germany
alexander.neitz@tuebingen.mpg.de

Abstract. Making decisions under risk is a competence human beings naturally display when being confronted with new and potentially dangerous learning tasks. In an effort to replicate this ability, many approaches have been promoted in different fields of artificial learning and planning. To plan domains with inherent risk in the presence of a simulation model we propose *Risk-Sensitive Online Planning (RISEON)* that extends traditional online planning by using an appropriate risk-aware optimization objective. The objective we use is Conditional Value at Risk (CVaR), where risk-sensitivity can be controlled by setting the quantile size to fit a given risk level. By using CVaR the planner shifts its focus from risk-neutral sample means towards the tail of loss distributions, thus considers an adjustable share of high costs. We evaluate *RISEON* in a smart grid planning scenario and in a continuous control task, where the planner has to steer a vehicle towards risky checkboxes, and empirically show that the proposed algorithm can be used to plan w.r.t. risk-sensitivity.

Keywords: Online planning · Risk-sensitivity · Local planning

1 Introduction

Risk-aware planning and learning approaches come from different fields and deal with risk in multi-armed bandits (MABs) [1], Markov decision processes (MDPs) [2,3] and classification learning [4]. Considerations of risk can be important in domains where free restarts during learning or deployment are prohibitive expensive [5]. Consequently, risk-aware planning is essential for many real-world tasks where expensive hardware is involved like flying a helicopter or steering a vehicle.

Although many approaches have been promoted [6] a great deal of work is suited for discrete state and action spaces whereas many real-world environments

© Springer Nature Switzerland AG 2018
F. Trollmann and A.-Y. Turhan (Eds.): KI 2018, LNAI 11117, pp. 229–240, 2018.
https://doi.org/10.1007/978-3-030-00111-7_20

require both contiunous state and action spaces. An effective approach to handle large spaces is given through simulation based online planning [7]. In this work we extend simulation based online planning to be applicable in domains with inherent risk. We do this by taking a risk-sensitive optimization objective for evaluation of plans. The algorithm we propose is called Risk-Sensitive Online Planning (RISEON). Our contributions are:

- An extension of online planning to plan domains with continuous states and actions in the presence of risk.
- Empirical evidence that the proposed algorithm is an effective means to control risk-sensitivity.

For empirical comparison of risk-sensitive vs. risk-neutral online planning we evaluate RISEON in a smart grid planning scenario where the planning agent needs to solve the trade-off between costly overproduction and fatal shortages of energy supply. The second experiment is a continuous control task, where the planner is in charge of steering a vehicle towards different checkboxes by applying force and torque.

2 Background

This section introduces the necessary material and concepts that build the basis for this work.

2.1 Markov Decision Processes (MDPs)

We assume that an environment can be described by means of a Markov decision process (MDP) [8,9] which is a tuple $(\mathcal{S}, \mathcal{A}, \mathcal{T}, R)$ where $\mathcal{S}$ is the state space, $\mathcal{A}$ is the action space, $\mathcal{T} : \mathcal{S} \times \mathcal{A} \to \mathcal{S}$ is the transition function and $R : \mathcal{S} \times A \times S \to \mathbb{R}$ is the reward function. A policy π is a mapping from states to actions that describes the behavior of an agent. The agent's goal is to find a policy π that maximizes the cumulative, long-term expected return $\mathcal{R}_t := \sum_{t=1}^{\infty} \gamma^{t-1} R_t$ at time t. Learning frameworks such as reinforcement learning (RL) aim at finding a global policy $\pi : \mathcal{S} \to \mathcal{A}$, i.e., after learning for an appropriate number of episodes the policy should cover the whole state space yielding an optimal action for every state. Planning methods are concerned with finding an optimal policy in the policy space. Policies can be evaluated by means of a simulation model $\hat{M}$ which can be everything an agent can use to predict how the environment will behave [10].

2.2 Local Planning

When state and action spaces become large finding a global policy may be intractable or require many training episodes. Local planning mitigates the effects of large spaces by trying to find an optimal policy π for a single state [11,12]. Local planning approaches normally operate with a planning horizion h, i.e., planning is done for h steps into future. One advantage of local planning is that it allows to control planning costs by setting the planning horizon to match a given planning budget.

2.3   Simulation Based Online Planning

Recently, simulation based online planning has been proposed to plan in domains with large state spaces and changing dynamics [7]. Online planning is an iterative process that interleaves planning and execution of actions through three basic steps. Firstly, an agent makes an observation of the current state of the environment. This observation is used to initialize the simulation model $\hat{M}$. The agent then samples plans according to some sampling strategy, e.g., Monte Carlo tree search in case of discrete states and actions. Plans are simulated through rollouts in $\hat{M}$ which provides a next state given an action. After planning for potentially multiple iterations the agent chooses the most promising action to execute in the real environment after which planning restarts.

A simple yet sometimes effective way of planning is vanilla Monte Carlo (VMC) planning [13] which refers to random uniform sampling of actions. A more sophisticated approach to find optimal actions during the planning step in continuous domains is given through cross entropy optimization [11,12,14,15]. Its basic steps are shown in Algorithm 1. Let $\mathcal{A} \subseteq \mathbb{R}$ denote the action space and Φ denote a probability distribution over actions $P(\mathcal{A}) = P(\mathbb{R}^{\mathbb{N}})$. A plan is a vector of actions $\boldsymbol{a} \in \mathcal{A}^{\mathbb{N}}$ and a distribution over plans is a vector of distributions over actions, denoted $\boldsymbol{\phi_a}$.

Cross entropy optimization works by sampling N plans from a plan distribution which gets refined for G generations. Plans are evaluated according to an evaluation function $EVAL$. The current plans and the result from their evaluation is aggregated in the set I which builds the input for the procedure FIT to refine the plan distribution. The plan distribution is fitted to the weighted plans in I by maximum likelihood estimation. In the case of a multivariate gaussian distribution this yields:

$$\phi_a = \langle \boldsymbol{\mu}, \boldsymbol{\Sigma} \rangle \tag{1}$$

$$\mu_t = \frac{\sum_{(a^i, v_i) \in I} v_i \boldsymbol{a}_t^i}{\sum_{(a^j, v_j) \in I} v_j} \tag{2}$$

$$\Sigma_t = \frac{\sum_{(a^i, v_i) \in I} v_i (\boldsymbol{a}_t^i - \mu_t)^T (\boldsymbol{a}_t^i - \mu_t)}{\sum_{(a^j, v_j) \in I} v_j} \tag{3}$$

3   Related Work

Risk-sensitive planning and learning methods come from different fields including approaches for Multi-Armed Bandits (MABs), Markov decision processes (MDPs) and classification learning. This section will give an overview over corresponding approaches.

Algorithm 1. Cross-Entropy Optimization according to [15]

Require: EVAL: $\mathcal{S} \times \mathcal{A}^{\mathrm{N}} \to \mathbb{R}$ ▷ evaluation of plans
Require: FIT: $2^{(\mathcal{A}^{\mathrm{N}} \times \mathbb{R})} \to \varPhi^{\mathrm{N}}$ ▷ refinement of distribution
 1: **function** OPTIMIZE(s, ϕ_a, G, N)
 2:     **for** 0...G **do**
 3:         $I \leftarrow \emptyset$
 4:         **for** 0...N **do**
 5:             $a \sim \phi_a$
 6:             $v \leftarrow EVAL(s, a)$
 7:             $I \leftarrow I \cup (a, v)$
 8:         **end for**
 9:         $\phi_a = FIT(I)$
10:     **end for**
        return ϕ_a ▷ return best plan
11: **end function**

3.1 Multi-armed Bandits

In [1] the authors consider risk as third optimization objective besides the classical exploration vs. exploitation dilemma. They argue that in risky bandits the learned policy should not only minimize regret, but also the incurred risk. Motivated by applications in energy management Galichet et al. proposed the multi-armed risk-aware bandit algorithm (MaRaB) to limit the exploration of risky arms. MaRaB limits exploration of risky arms by taking Conditional Value at Risk as arm quality, thereby reducing risk. In contrast to multi-armed bandits, in this paper we consider state-conditioned, sequential decision making.

3.2 Markov Decision Processes

Risk in MDPs has been analyzed within planning and learning frameworks such as reinforcement learning (RL). Reinforcement learning algorithms traditionally use the expected return to find optimal policies [10]. RL algorithms that transform the optimization criterion to include a notion of risk are known as safe reinforcement learning methods [6].

The notion of risk within MDPs can be broadly categorized into two classes. The first class focusses on the optimization for worst-cases [2]. The other class makes use of utility functions, where utility can reflect the risk-preferences of the planner, i.e., risk-averse, risk-neutral or risk-seeking [3, 16]. Within this class exponential utility functions play an important role, as they have properties which allows efficient Dynamic Programming solutions.

In [2], Heger proposed the worst case criterion also known as minimax to find policies that minimize the worst case total discounted costs. This means, a minimax policy is optimal, if it has the lowest costs in the worst case. As a relaxation of pure worst case optimization, [2] introduced $\hat{Q}$-learning as a counterpart to traditional Q-learning [17], that is related to the minimax criterion. Even if

RISEON uses empirical *CVaR* to account for risk and so in the limit $\alpha \to 0$ is functional equivalent to worst case optimization in contrast to $\hat{Q}$-learning it works in continuous state and action spaces.

Another line of work comprises methods that try to associate the risk with the variance of the return. Normally, these approaches allow to control risk-sensitivity through the presence of a parameter known as the risk-sensitivity parameter. A prominent criterion in this class is given through exponential utility functions, where the return is transformed to reflect subjective measures of utility [18]. Exponential utility functions balance expected return and associated variance, thus deviating from the high restrictiveness incorporated through minimax. Exponential utility functions are the most widely used method and best analyzed concept to deal with risk in finite MDPs [6]. In this sense RISEON is a risk-sensitive approach, as it provides a parameter α through which the risk-level, i.e., the accepted variance of the return can be controlled. In contrast to exponential utility functions, RISEON does not need explicit knowledge of transition probabilities which might be unavailable in many planning tasks.

Moldovan et al. in [5] stressed the importance of risk-awareness to bring RL closer towards real-world learning of dangerous tasks. For many such applications the assumption of consequence-free restarts through which independent and identically distributed versions of the planning scenario are provided has to be drooped. In real-world settings this assumption can often not be fulfilled as restarts might be costly, or hardware can get damaged. As an extension to existing risk-aware objectives Moldovan et al. proposed Chernoff Bounds for MDPs [19]. The main difference to RISEON is that the proposed algorithms in [5] again need MDP transition probabilities to work.

3.3   Classification Learning

To account for risk-sensitivity in classification learning, Kashima proposed in [20] a meta-learning algorithm based on CVaR to extend cost-sensitive algorithms to mitigate risks of huge costs occurring with low probabilities. This approach allows classification that does not primarily minimize the probability of misclassification but rather make decisions based on the potential risk of misclassification and consequent large costs.

4   Risk-Sensitive Online Planning

Risk-sensitive online planning extends simulation based online planning by changing the optimization criterion to evaluate sample plans. That is, evaluation needs to consider associated risk within reward distributions through applying an appropriate risk-metric. The proposed risk-metric is Conditional Value at Risk (CVaR) [21] formally introduced in the following section.

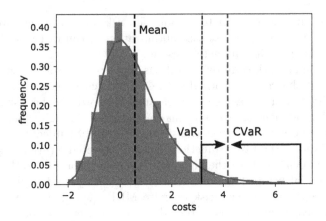

Fig. 1. Value at Risk and Conditional Value at Risk with $\alpha = 0.05$ for costs sampled from a Gumbel distribution with $\mu = 0, \beta = 1$.

4.1 Value at Risk and Conditional Value at Risk

A prominent risk metric from the field of financial engineering is Value at Risk (*VaR*). For a random variable X representing loss, and a parameter α with $0 < \alpha < 1$, *VaR* is defined as the minimum value $c \in \mathbb{R}$ such that with probability α, X will not exceed c [4]:

$$VaR_\alpha(X) := min\{c : P(X \leq c) \geq \alpha\} \tag{4}$$

A disadvantage of VaR_α is that it does not provide any information about potential losses in the $(1 - \alpha) \times 100\%$ worst cases. On the contrary, Conditional Value at Risk (*CVaR*) [21] provides such information. Based on the definition of VaR_α, $CVaR_\alpha$ for a continuous random variable X is defined as the expectation of losses above VaR_α[4]:

$$CVaR_\alpha(X) := \mathbb{E}[X|X > VaR_\alpha(X)] \tag{5}$$

Intuitively, one can interpret $CVaR_\alpha$ as the expected costs in the $(1 - \alpha) \times 100\%$ worst cases. Figure 1 shows exemplarily VaR_α and $CVaR_\alpha$ with $\alpha = 0.05$ for costs sampled from a Gumbel distribution with parameters $\mu = 0, \beta = 1$.

To compute $CVaR_\alpha$ of sample plans during online planning we use a non parametric, consistent estimate denoted $\widehat{CVaR_\alpha}$. Assuming a descendingly ordered list of costs C with length n then $\widehat{CVaR_\alpha}$ is given as [22]:

$$\widehat{CVaR_\alpha}(C) = \frac{1}{k}\sum_{i=1}^{k} c_i, \tag{6}$$

where k is the ceiling integer of $\alpha * n$.

4.2   Plan Evaluation with $CVaR_\alpha$

In order to make simulation based online planning risk-sensitive we propose the procedure $EVAL$ given in Algorithm 2. $EVAL$ takes the current observation and a plan as input. It requires the number of iterations I, the planning horizon H, α to calculate $CVaR_\alpha$ and a discount factor γ. A plan a is executed I times and its accumulated, discounted costs are kept in a list. Subsequently, the list is sorted and $\widehat{CVaR}_\alpha$ is computed according to Eq. 6.

Algorithm 2. Risk-Sensitive Plan Evaluation

Require: $P(\mathcal{S}|\mathcal{S} \times \mathcal{A}), C : \mathcal{S} \to \mathbb{R}$ $\qquad\qquad\qquad$ ▷ transition model, cost function
Require: $I \in \mathbb{N}, H \in \mathbb{N}, \alpha \in \mathbb{R}, \gamma \in \mathbb{R}$
 1: **procedure** EVAL($s \in \mathcal{S}, a \in \mathcal{A}^{\text{N}}$)
 2: $\quad$ $C \leftarrow []$
 3: $\quad$ $c \leftarrow 0$
 4: $\quad$ **for** $i = 0 \to I$ **do**
 5: $\qquad$ **for** $h = 0 \to H$ **do**
 6: $\qquad\quad$ $s \leftarrow P(\cdot|s, a_h)$ $\qquad\qquad\qquad\qquad\qquad$ ▷ execute next action
 7: $\qquad\quad$ $c \leftarrow c + \gamma^h * C(s)$ $\qquad\qquad\qquad\qquad$ ▷ accumulate costs
 8: $\qquad$ **end for**
 9: $\qquad$ $C \leftarrow C \cup c$ $\qquad\qquad\qquad\qquad\qquad$ ▷ append accumulated costs
10: $\quad$ **end for**
11: $\quad$ sort C
$\qquad$ **return** $\widehat{CVaR}_\alpha(C, \alpha)$
12: **end procedure**

---

5   Empirical Results

To evaluate planning w.r.t risk-sensitivity we ran experiments in two planning domains. The first domain is a smart grid setting, where the planner is in charge of satisfying the energy demand. The second domain is called Drift King, a physical environment where the planner controls a vehicle through applying forces and torque to collect different types of checkboxes. In all experiments we use RISEON with different values of α representing different levels of risk-sensitivity. In addition we also plan with *mean* optimization which is equal to RISEON with $\alpha = 1$, i.e., expectation is build upon the whole distribution.

5.1   Smart Grid

This scenario simulates a power supply grid consisting of a consumer and a producer. The planning task is to estimate the optimal power production for the next time step. The consumption behavior c resembles a sinus function with additive noise, i.e., $c(t) = sin(t) + \epsilon$ with $\epsilon \sim \mathcal{N}(0, 0.1)$. The action space in the smart grid domain is $\mathcal{A} \subseteq \mathbb{R}$ and an action describes the change of power production for the next step. Costs arise through differences from actual needed and provided power. Shortages create costs as consumers can not get supplied sufficiently. Ideally, the planner manages to keep the difference of production and consumption as little as possible. This however, can be risky due to the consumer's stochastic behaviour. The different situations create costs C in the form of:

$$C(x) = \begin{cases} |x| + 10, \, x < 0 \\ |x| - 10, \, 0 \le x < 1 \\ |x| \qquad \text{otherwise,} \end{cases} \tag{7}$$

where x is the difference of provided and needed energy. That is, the less surplus is produced the less costs arise. Still, if consumption can not be satisfied, the planner will receive extra costs assuming that shortages are more severe in terms of costs than overshooting. However, to create incentives to reduce the difference of production and consumption the planner receives a bonus if it manages keep the difference under a given threshold ($0 \le x < 1$).

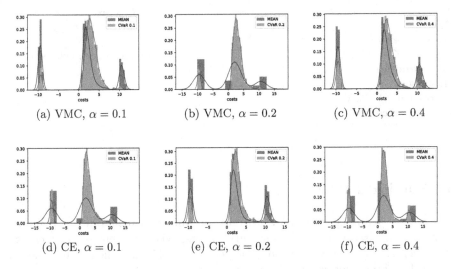

(a) VMC, $\alpha = 0.1$ (b) VMC, $\alpha = 0.2$ (c) VMC, $\alpha = 0.4$

(d) CE, $\alpha = 0.1$ (e) CE, $\alpha = 0.2$ (f) CE, $\alpha = 0.4$

Fig. 2. Histograms of smart grid costs for RISEON with two different planning strategies: vanilla Monte Carlo planning (VMC) and cross entropy planning (CE). Both planners use different levels of α, i.e., $\alpha \in \{0.1, 0.2, 0.4\}$ shown in green. In addition planners also plan with *mean* shown in blue. The planner optimizing for mean is more likely to yield high losses. In contrast, optimizing for CVaR effectively reduces the number of high loss events (best viewed in color). (Color figure online)

Figure 2 shows the produced costs from runs of the smart grid simulation for RISEON with two different planning strategies. The first is plain Vanilla Monte Carlo planning (VMC), the second planner uses Cross Entropy optimization (CE). Planning was done with number of plans, $N = 800$, planning horizon,

$H = 1$ and number of iterations per plan, $I = 20$ in the case of VMC and $N = 200, H = 1, G = 5, I = 20$ for CE.

The results for VMC are shown in Figs. 2a–c and results for CE in Figs. 2d–f. For all planners we used three different values of α, which are $0.1, 0.2, 0.4$. In addition we also used *mean* to represent risk-neutral planning. The results from *CVaR* are marked in green whereas risk-neutral planning i s shown in blue. All runs comprise 1000 steps.

For RISEON with both planning methods we observe a reduction of high costs for all values of α. This can be seen in all plots by a decreased mode of large costs. This goes along with an increased number of costs in the region of 0 to 5 and a reduction of bonus payments (costs beneath -5). In this sense, the planner trades-off the likelihood of encountering large costs by accepting an increased number of average costs. This is the expected reaction from a risk-sensitive planner as it prefers lower variance with reduced expectation over large variance with higher expectation.

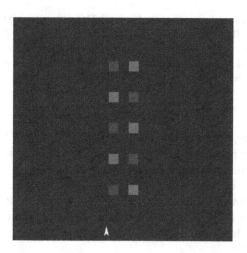

Fig. 3. The Drift King domain confronts the planner with a task of collecting 5 out of 10 checkboxes. Checkboxes provide different rewards, i.e., blue checkboxes give reward $r \sim \mathcal{N}(1.0, 0.001)$ whereas pink checkboxes give reward $r \sim \mathcal{N}(1.0, 1.0)$ (Color figure online)

5.2 Drift King

The second evaluation domain is called Drift King shown in Fig. 3. The agent controls a vehicle (white triangle) by applying forward force and torque, i.e., the action space is $\mathcal{A} \subseteq \mathbb{R}^2$. The goal in Drift King is to collect 5 out of 10 checkboxes, where checkbox rewards come from two different distributions. Blue checkboxes give reward r with $r \sim \mathcal{N}(1, 0.001)$, whereas the pink checkboxes provide rewards according to $r \sim \mathcal{N}(1, 1.0)$. All checkboxes have same expectation, but blue checkboxes have less variance.

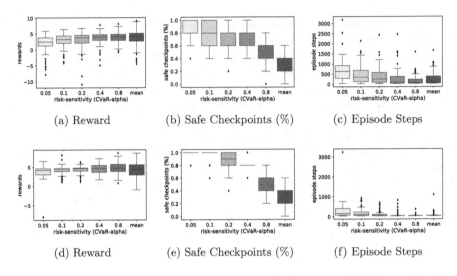

Fig. 4. Drift King results from 90 episodes for VMC planning with different planning budgets, i.e., $N = 20, H = 20, I = 20$ (Figs. 4a–c) and $N = 40, H = 15, I = 20$ (Figs. 4d–f). All runs where conducted with different values for $CVaR_\alpha$ with $\alpha \in \{0.05, 0.1, 0.2, 0.4, 0.8\}$ represented by boxplots 1–5 in each plot. In addition risk-neutral planning was represented through *mean* optimization and is shown in the rightmost boxplot.

In all Drift King experiments we used RISEON with VMC planning with varying budgets for planning. In the first setup the planner was allowed to simulate 8000 steps which were split in number of plans, $N = 20$, planning horizon, $H = 20$ and number of iterations for each plan, $I = 20$. In the second experiment the planner was allowed to simulate 12000 steps with $N = 40$, $H = 15$, $I = 20$. Drift King episodes lasted for a maximum of 5000 steps but an episode ended whenever 5 checkpoints were collected. For each step the planner received a time penalty of 0.004.

To evaluate RISEON in the Drift King domain we consider total episode reward, the percentage of safe checkboxes collected and the number of episode steps. The results from 90 episodes of Drift King are shown in Fig. 4. In Figs. 4a–c are results for RISEON with 8000 simulation steps and Figs. 4d–f show the results for 12000 simulation steps. All Figures show 6 boxplots where boxplots 1–5 represent RISEON with $\alpha \in \{0.05, 0.1, 0.2, 0.4, 0.8\}$ for decreasing consideration of tail-risk and the rightmost boxplot for *mean* optimization.

Over all experiments the variance of rewards correlates with α which can be seen in Figs. 4a and d. Figures 4b and e show the percentage of safe checkpoints that the planner gathered where a value of 1 means that 5 out of 5 collected checkboxes had low variance. This value strongly decreases for growing α and has the lowest expectation for risk-neutral planning with *mean*. The number of episode steps negatively correlates with α, i.e., increasing risk-neutrality goes along with reduced episode duration. A selection of videos from RISEON with different risk-levels can be found at: https://youtu.be/90u1lyPk9tc.

The results from the Drift King environment confirm the smart grid results. Moreover, in the case of Drift King the planner seems to trade-off reward uncertainty for an increased number of episode steps. This is reasonable as a risk-neutral planner can choose the straight way towards the next checkbox disregarding potential reward variance. In contrast a risk-sensitive planner will prefer a longer distance towards a safe checkbox to reduce risk. Again risk-sensitive planning results in lower reward expectation but also significantly reduces the variance. From the variation of α we find that risk-sensitivity can be controlled via a single parameter.

6 Conclusion

In this work we proposed RISEON as an extension of simulation based online planning. Simulation based planning refers to methods which use a model of the environment to simulate actions and gather information about its dynamics. Actions are originated from a given sampling strategy, e.g., vanilla Monte Carlo or cross entropy planning. Through repeatedly simulating actions the agent gains samples of cost distributions. In order to plan w.r.t. to tail risk we use empirical CVaR as optimization criterion. In two different planning scenarios we empirically show the effectiveness of CVaR with respect to risk-awareness. By modifying the α quantiles we demonstrated that risk-sensitivity can be controlled via a single hyper parameter.

References

1. Galichet, N., Sebag, M., Teytaud, O.: Exploration vs exploitation vs safety: risk-aware multi-armed bandits. In: ACML, pp. 245–260 (2013)
2. Heger, M.: Consideration of risk in reinforcement learning. In: Proceedings of the Eleventh International Conference on Machine Learning, pp. 105–111 (1994)
3. Howard, R.A., Matheson, J.E.: Risk-sensitive Markov decision processes. Manag. Sci. 18(7), 356–369 (1972)
4. Kisiala, J.: Conditional value-at-risk: theory and applications. arXiv preprint arXiv:1511.00140 (2015)
5. Moldovan, T.M.: Safety, risk awareness and exploration in reinforcement learning. Ph.D. thesis, University of California, Berkeley (2014)
6. Garcıa, J., Fernández, F.: A comprehensive survey on safe reinforcement learning. J. Mach. Learn. Res. 16(1), 1437–1480 (2015)
7. Belzner, L., Hennicker, R., Wirsing, M.: OnPlan: a framework for simulation-based online planning. In: Braga, C., Ölveczky, P.C. (eds.) FACS 2015. LNCS, vol. 9539, pp. 1–30. Springer, Cham (2016). https://doi.org/10.1007/978-3-319-28934-2_1
8. Howard, R.A.: Dynamic Programming and Markov Processes. Wiley for The Massachusetts Institute of Technology, New York (1964)
9. Puterman, M.L.: Markov Decision Processes: Discrete Stochastic Dynamic Programming. Wiley, Hoboken (2014)

10. Sutton, R.S., Barto, A.G.: Reinforcement Learning: An Introduction, vol. 1. MIT press, Cambridge (1998)
11. Weinstein, A.: Local planning for continuous Markov decision processes. Rutgers The State University of New Jersey-New Brunswick (2014)
12. Weinstein, A., Littman, M.L.: Open-loop planning in large-scale stochastic domains. In: AAAI (2013)
13. Kocsis, L., Szepesvári, C.: Bandit based monte-carlo planning. In: Fürnkranz, J., Scheffer, T., Spiliopoulou, M. (eds.) ECML 2006. LNCS (LNAI), vol. 4212, pp. 282–293. Springer, Heidelberg (2006). https://doi.org/10.1007/11871842_29
14. De Boer, P.T., Kroese, D.P., Mannor, S., Rubinstein, R.Y.: A tutorial on the cross-entropy method. Ann. Oper. Res. 134(1), 19–67 (2005)
15. Belzner, L.: Time-adaptive cross entropy planning. In: Proceedings of the 31st Annual ACM Symposium on Applied Computing, pp. 254–259. ACM (2016)
16. Liu, Y.: Decision-theoretic planning under risk-sensitive planning objectives. Ph.D. thesis, Georgia Institute of Technology (2005)
17. Watkins, C.J., Dayan, P.: Q-learning. Mach. Learn. 8(3–4), 279–292 (1992)
18. Chung, K.J., Sobel, M.J.: Discounted MDP's: distribution functions and exponential utility maximization. SIAM J. Control Optim. 25(1), 49–62 (1987)
19. Moldovan, T.M., Abbeel, P.: Risk aversion in Markov decision processes via near optimal Chernoff bounds. In: NIPS, pp. 3140–3148 (2012)
20. Kashima, H.: Risk-sensitive learning via minimization of empirical conditional value-at-risk. IEICE Trans. Inf. Syst. 90(12), 2043–2052 (2007)
21. Rockafellar, R.T., Uryasev, S., et al.: Optimization of conditional value-at-risk. J. Risk 2, 21–42 (2000)
22. Chen, S.X.: Nonparametric estimation of expected shortfall. J. Financ. Econom. 6(1), 87–107 (2008)

Neural Networks

Evolutionary Structure Minimization of Deep Neural Networks for Motion Sensor Data

Daniel Lückehe[1]([✉]), Sonja Veith[2], and Gabriele von Voigt[1]

[1] Computational Health Informatics, Leibniz University Hanover, Hanover, Germany
lueckehe@chi.uni-hannover.de
[2] Institute for Special Education, Leibniz University Hanover, Hanover, Germany

Abstract. Many Deep Neural Networks (DNNs) are implemented with the single objective to achieve high classification scores. However, there can be additional objectives like the minimization of computational costs. This is especially important in the field of mobile computing where not only the computational power itself is a limiting factor but also each computation consumes energy affecting the battery life. Unfortunately, the determination of minimal structures is not straightforward.

In our paper, we present a new approach to determine DNNs employing reduced structures. The networks are determined by an Evolutionary Algorithm (EA). After the DNN is trained, the EA starts to remove neurons from the network. Thereby, the fitness function of the EA is depending on the accuracy of the DNN. Thus, the EA is able to control the influence of each individual neuron. We introduce our new approach in detail. Thereby, we employ motion data recorded by accelerometer and gyroscope sensors of a mobile device. The data are recorded while drawing Japanese characters in the air in a learning context. The experimental results show that our approach is capable to determine reduced networks with similar performance to the original ones. Additionally, we show that the reduction can improve the accuracy of a network. We analyze the reduction in detail. Further, we present arising structures of the reduced networks.

Keywords: Neuroevolution · Deep learning
Evolutionary Algorithm · Pruning · Motion sensor data
Japanese characters

1 Introduction

In many scenarios, the objective of a DNN [9] is to be as accurate as possible. Thereby, highly complex and computationally expensive networks can arise like GoogLeNet [35] or ResNet [16]. However, there are cases in which not only the accuracy is relevant, e.g., in the field of mobile computing, the computational costs are also very important. These costs affect both, the limited computational

© Springer Nature Switzerland AG 2018
F. Trollmann and A.-Y. Turhan (Eds.): KI 2018, LNAI 11117, pp. 243–257, 2018.
https://doi.org/10.1007/978-3-030-00111-7_21

resources as well as the battery life because each computation consumes energy. Thus, especially for mobile computing, small and efficient networks are required.

A DNN with reduced structures makes it possible to solve classification problems on a mobile device while consuming relatively low energy. An example for such a problem is the classification of Japanese characters which are written by hand in the air. This can support the learning process of a new language. Using body motion for learning is known for being more effective compared to learning without motion [19]. To record the motion, we use the acceleration and gyroscope sensors of a mobile phone which is held in one hand. The developed application was executed on a Google Pixel 2 running Android 8.1. Figure 1(a) shows a screenshot of the application. There are basically two buttons: *record/stop* to start and to stop the recording and by pressing the *paint* button, the user is able to draw virtually in the air. A photo of the setup can be seen in Fig. 1(b).

(a)   (b)

Fig. 1. Setup to log the motion data: (left) the Android application and (right) a photo of the application in usage

Our paper is structured as follows. After the introduction, the foundation is laid. Then, we propose our new approach to determine reduced networks. The experimental results are presented in Sect. 4. Finally, conclusions are drawn.

2 Foundation

In this section, we lay the foundation of our paper. Thereby, we show that learning can benefit from motions, the employed Japanese characters are introduced and related work is presented.

2.1 Learning Using Motions

Enacting or the use of gestures or movements of the body is a long and well known method for improving the success of learning a new language [1]. Since the development of functional magnetic resonance imaging (fMRI), there are several publications which are investigating the connection between the cortical systems for language and the cortical system for action [3,24]. With the help of fMRI, it is possible to detect changes in the blood flow in human brains and thus, to draw conclusions about neural activity in certain areas. The publications found out that combining language learning with enactment results in a more complex network of language regions, sensory and motor cortices. Due to this complexity, it is assumed that language learning with enactment is having a superior retention [24].

The focus of these publications is usually the acquirement of certain vocabulary. But learning a new language can also mean having to learn new characters, e.g., for an Asian language like Japanese. The Japanese writing system consist of three different character types: Kanji, Hiragana and Katakana. Hiragana and Katakana represent syllables and each writing system consists of 48 characters. The origins of Hiragana and Katakana led to a distinction in the application nowadays. Katakana had mainly been used by men and is now usually used for accentuation [10]. In contrast to that Hiragana was originally used by aristocratic women and is now predominantly applied for Japanese texts in combination with Kanji [10]. Kanji are adopted Chinese characters where each symbol represents one word. Because they were originally used for the Chinese language, one Kanji character can be used for different words in Japanese. There is no definite count of Kanji but there is a Japanese Industrial Standard (JIS X 0208) for Kanji which contains 6353 graphic characters [30]. To be able to read a Japanese newspaper, it is required to know the 96 characters of Hiragana and Katakana and also at least 1000 of the logographic Kanji [30]. Learning all these characters takes a lot of effort and time, e.g., Japanese students learn Kanji until the end of high school [36]. In order to make the study of a second language like Japanese for foreigners more successful, it is recommended to use every possible support like learning with enactment to improve the learning process.

2.2 Motion Data of Japanese Characters

In our work, we choose the syllabary Katakana as characters. Katakana consists of rather straight lines with sharp corners compared to Hiragana. From the syllabary Katakana, the following symbols are selected: ア, イ, ウ, エ, オ and カ, キ, ク, ケ, コ. The characters represent the vowels and syllables: a, i, u, e, o and ka, ki, ku, ke, ko. These are the first ten characters of the Katakana syllabary. Katakana is typically used for non-Japanese words or names. When foreigners learn Japanese, it is often the first learning objective in order to be able to write their own name with these characters. Another usage of these characters is to emphasize words like it is done with italics in English or other roman languages.

The motion data are recorded with a sampling rate of 50 Hz. Our mobile device employs an accelerometer which is detecting each acceleration including the gravitational acceleration g. The accelerometer can be combined with the gyroscope which can detect circular motion to exclude the influence to the acceleration due to gravity. Additionally, the remaining small error can be reduced

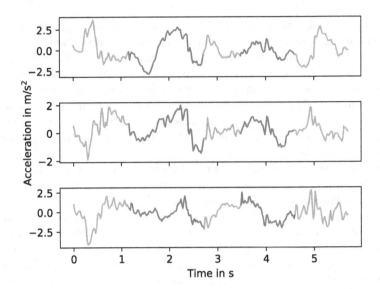

Fig. 2. Acceleration data for each spatial direction of a recorded character ㇵ , latin: *a*. A green line indicates a pushed *paint* button (Color figure online)

by a calibrating measurement before starting the recording. This minimizes the measurement error. However, as we are working with real sensors, there is always a deviation. For this reason, we define that the starting and ending position of each recording have to be at the same location. Using this information and assuming a uniform acceleration deviation makes it possible to improve the data for visualization like in Fig. 3. Thereby, a quadratic relationship between the acceleration a and the position s depending on the time t of $s(t) = 0.5 \cdot a \cdot t^2$ is applied.

The DNN processes the raw acceleration data. An example is shown in Fig. 2. Because the employed Japanese symbols consist of up to four different lines, there is a button *paint* in the application as introduced in Sect. 1. The graph is green for periods where the *paint* button is pressed and gray for the rest of the recorded motion. In the graph, there are changes in the acceleration visible which are typical for each character. However, as this way of representing the motion data is not very intuitive for recognizing the characters by humans, in Fig. 3, we visualize the position data. This visualization uses the improvements introduced in the last paragraph. In the figure, the motion starts with yellow and ends with purple.

Overall, there are ten characters. Each character is recorded 120 times resulting in a data set of more than 1000 recordings. For the experimental results, we employ a 6-point cross-validation using a stratified k-fold cross-validator [29]. This provides 100 patterns per character in the training data and folds which are preserving the percentage of samples for each class.

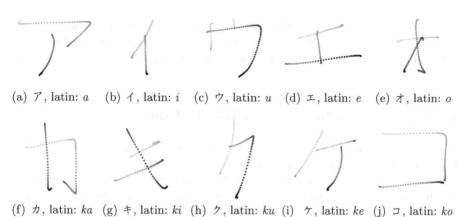

(a) ア, latin: *a*   (b) イ, latin: *i*   (c) ウ, latin: *u*   (d) エ, latin: *e*   (e) オ, latin: *o*

(f) カ, latin: *ka* (g) キ, latin: *ki* (h) ク, latin: *ku* (i) ケ, latin: *ke* (j) コ, latin: *ko*

Fig. 3. The plotted motion data of the Japanese characters

2.3   Related Work

Our work is based on DNNs and EAs. DNNs are feed-forward neural networks with multiple hidden layers [5]. They are mostly used to solve classification problems [15]. In a lot of contests, DNNs showed their superior performance compared to other state-of-the-art methods [31]. An EA is an optimization algorithm which can be applied to various problems [8]. It is stochastic and as it treats its fitness function, which is rating the quality of solutions, as a black-box, EAs can be applied to analytically not solvable problems. Mainly, they are used for highly complex problems in various fields of research [22,23].

Since EAs can handle highly complex optimization problems, they can be applied to optimize DNNs. This line of research is called *neuroevolution*. First approaches occurred in the 1990s [25]. Most approaches from this field can be divided into two main categories: (1) optimizing the structure and hyperparameters of a DNN and (2) finding optimal weights and biases for the artificial neurons. A famous approach from (1) is to evolve neural networks through augmenting topologies [33,34]. The CMA-ES [13] has been used to optimize hyperparameters like number of neurons, parameters of batch normalization, batch sizes, and dropout rates in [21]. But also more simple EAs like a $(1 + 1)$-EA are employed to determine networks [20]. A problem for approaches from (2) is the large amount of data. While gradient based optimizers can cycle through the data, an EA takes all data for each fitness function evaluation into account [27]. Additionally, due to the huge amount of weights, the optimization problems have become very high dimensional. However, [27] indicates that EAs can be an alternative to stochastic gradient descent.

To the best of our knowledge, all approaches from category (1) are not minimizing the structure of DNNs, e.g., in [34] the network is *incrementally growing from minimal structure*. Besides from the field of neuroevolution, there are approaches to minimize DNNs. One reason is to make networks less computational expensive [7,12,26]. As DNNs are usually over-parameterized [6], DNNs can be minimized to reduce network complexity and overfitting [4,14]. Another reason is the memory usage. In [11], pruning, trained quantization and huffman coding are used to minimize the memory usage of DNNs without affecting their accuracy.

3   Evolutionary Structure Minimization

In this section, we introduce our new evolutionary approach to reduce DNNs. A scheme of the approach can be seen in Fig. 4. On the left side of the figure, a DNN is shown. On the right side, the EA is presented from the perspective of solutions as the solutions are controlling the switchable dense layers of the DNN.

The DNN is a typical feed-forward network consisting of five dense layers employing the ReLU activation function [28] followed by a dropout layer [32]

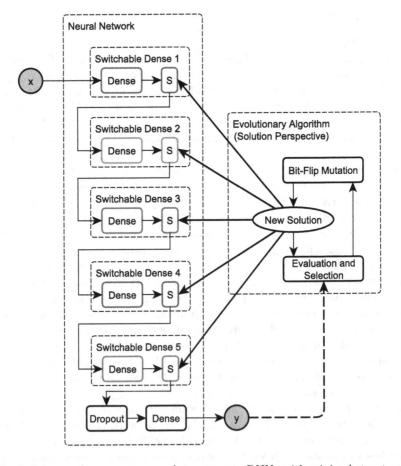

Fig. 4. Scheme of our new approach to compute DNNs with minimal structures.

and an output layer using the softmax activation function [2]. Five layers allow the network to compute complex features while the network complexity stays relatively low. In dense layers, all neurons are connected with every neuron of the following layer. This is different in our network, as there are switch vectors $s_1, \ldots, s_5$ between the dense layers. These vectors consist of zeros and ones. They are multiplied with the outputs of the previous dense layers. Thus, it is possible to let outputs of neurons through, i.e., multiply them by 1, or to stop them, i.e., multiply them by 0. The vectors $s_1, \ldots, s_5$ are configured by the solutions of the EA. This means, the EA is capable to disable the output of each neuron individually. Changes of the network might influence the output y. Therefore, the EA gets a feedback from the network while evaluating its solutions.

A $(1 + 100)$-EA is applied, i.e., in each generation 100 solutions are created and one solution is selected. Due to the 100 solutions, the EA is able to discover the search space relatively broad. On the other hand, the high selection pressure makes our EA also greedy. To create new solutions, we employ the bit flip mutation operator [8], i.e., each value in a vector s is changed independently by the chance of $1/m$ while m is the number of variables. In our case, m is the number of switches which is equal to the number of neurons, i.e., $m = \sum_{i=1}^{5} |s_i|$. If a value v in a vector $s \in \{s_1, \ldots, s_5\}$ should be changed, $v = 1$ becomes $v = 0$ and $v = 0$ becomes $v = 1$.

3.1 Interaction Between Deep Neural Network and Evolutionary Algorithm

First of all, a base configuration c of the DNN is chosen. The configuration $c = (c_1, c_2, c_3, c_4, c_5)$ determines the number of neurons per switchable dense layer. Thus, it applies: $|s_i| = c_i$ for $i = 1, \ldots, 5$. With the initial solution x_{ea}^0 of the EA, the DNN should be able to use all neurons: $x_{ea}^0 = (1, 1, \ldots, 1)$ with $|x_{ea}^0| = m$. With this setting, the DNN is trained by employing the AdamOptimizer [18]. The net is trained for n^e epochs employing a batch size of n^b. After the training, the optimization process of the EA is able to start and x_{ea}^0 becomes x_{ea}. Based on x_{ea}, 100 new solutions are created by the bit flip mutation operator. If the number of ones $ones(\cdots)$ in a new solution x_{ea}' is less or equal to $ones(x_{ea})$, the new solution is added to the population $\mathcal{P}$. Each new solution in $\mathcal{P}$ is used to configure the switches of the DNN. Changing the switches of the DNN influences the output y of the DNN. The differences of the output are rated by the fitness function f of the EA which we introduce in the next subsection. So, each new solution x_{ea}' is evaluated by f and gets a fitness values which expresses the influence of x_{ea}' on the DNN. As x_{ea}' controls the switches $s_1, \ldots, s_5$ which can enable and disable the output of each neuron, the fitness values also expresses the influence of the individual neurons on the DNN. In the selection of the EA, the new solution x_{ea}^* leading to the highest fitness value is determined. If $f(x_{ea}^*) \geq f(x_{ea})$, the solution x_{ea}^* replaces x_{ea} and thus, in the next generation, the 100 new solutions are based on x_{ea}^*. The EA is run for n^g generations.

After the optimization is finished, the reduced net can be determined easily. The reduced net employs dense layers. The number of neurons per layer is the number of ones in the matching vector $s_1, \ldots, s_5$. The neurons get the weights like in the switchable dense layers. Each neuron in the switchable dense layers which is followed by a zero can be removed without any loss as it makes no contribution to the DNN. Figure 5 visualizes the reduction step.

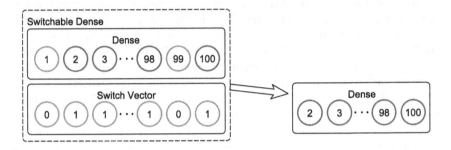

Fig. 5. Scheme of the reduction step

3.2 Fitness Function of Evolutionary Algorithm

The fitness function f of the EA is responsible for evaluating the influence of a solution $\mathbf{x}_{ea}$ to the DNN. As the influence of $\mathbf{x}_{ea}$ is depending on data, f requires data for its evaluation. Like stated in [27], f typically takes the whole training data for its evaluation making the computation very expensive. To reduce the computational costs, we employ batches like in the training of DNNs. The size of the batches is n_{ea}^b. However, different batches lead to different results for the same solution. Thus, it could happen that one solution $\mathbf{x}_{ea}^1$ is rated higher than a different solution $\mathbf{x}_{ea}^2$ just because of a better matching batch. This would make the fitness values incomparable. For this reason, fitness values must use the same batch to be comparable and be usable for the selection of the EA. Therefore, we employ the same batch within each generation. Different generations can use different batches. This also means that the fitness value of the selected solution $\mathbf{x}_{ea}^*$ has to be reevaluated in each generation.

The most simple approach to compute a fitness value for the solution $\mathbf{x}_{ea}$ is the accuracy of the DNN depending on $\mathbf{x}_{ea}$ and the batch. But as each pattern is only rated as correct or false, this approach does not yield much information to the optimization process and would lead to fitness values from $\mathbb{N}$. For this reason, we sum up the output values of the softmax function for each correct label. Thus, there is a smooth transition from a well recognized pattern with a softmax function value of nearly 1 to a not recognized pattern with a softmax function value of nearly 0. This means, for a batch size of n_{ea}^b and a solution $\mathbf{x}_{ea}$, it applies:

$$0 \leq f(\mathbf{x}_{ea}) \leq n_{ea}^b \text{ with } f(\mathbf{x}_{ea}) \in \mathbb{R}. \tag{1}$$

4 Experimental Results

In this section, we show the experimental results of the accuracy, the number of connections, and the development of the accuracy. Then, we point out to possible improvements and analyze arising network structures.

The network structure introduced in the last section is employed with 100 neurons per layer, i.e., $\mathbf{c} = (100, 100, 100, 100, 100)$. As this paper focuses on the analysis of the evolutionary structure minimization (ESM), only one network structure is used. Further research employing different network structures is planned for future work. Especially for advanced structures like long short-term memory networks (LSTMs) [17]. In preliminary experiments, we tested a LSTM employing 100 cells on the data set. The net achieved an accuracy of nearly 100%. However, the execution of the trained net takes on our test system more than 30 ms while the DNN, employed in this work, takes a non-measurable amount of time, i.e., significantly less than 1 ms.

As stated in Sect. 2.2, a 6-fold cross-validation is employed. Each fold is repeated 8 times resulting to nearly 50 experiments. In each experiment, the net is trained for $n^e = 10$ epochs employing a batch size $n^b = 100$, the EA is run for $n^g = 1000$ generations, 100 solutions are created in each generation, and the fitness function uses a batch size $n^b_{EA} = 100$.

Accuracy and Connections. Table 1 presents the accuracy on the test data of the employed DNN. In the first column, the number of generation is shown. Then, in the second column, the mean values and standard deviations of the accuracy are visualized. In the final two columns, the mean values of the number of neurons and connections are presented.

Table 1. Accuracy depending on generation

Generation	Accuracy	Neurons	Connections
0	0.9707 ± 0.0126	500.0	40000.0
5	$\mathbf{0.9714} \pm 0.0125$	494.3	39069.5
10	0.9702 ± 0.0127	488.9	38195.1
25	0.9706 ± 0.0129	473.2	35753.6
50	0.9696 ± 0.0125	447.6	31915.5
100	0.9620 ± 0.0144	395.8	24956.5
200	0.9481 ± 0.0178	315.0	15803.7

In the first row, the results after the training can be seen. There are 100 neurons in each layer. Thus, there are 500 neurons ($5 \cdot 100$) and 40 000 connections ($4 \cdot 100 \cdot 100$) after the training. After 5 generations, the accuracy is slightly improved and there are about 1000 connections less. About 4000 connections are removed after 25 generation while the accuracy is the same as after the training.

Even after 100 generations, the accuracy dropped by less than 1% while the number of connections is reduced by nearly 40%. Then, it can be seen that the accuracy starts to significantly decrease. To better understand the development of the accuracy, we present it in Fig. 6.

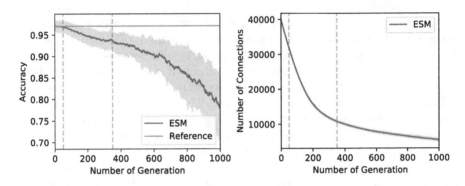

Fig. 6. Development of (left) the accuracy and (right) the number of connections depending on the generation (Color figure online)

Development of Accuracy. On the left side of Fig. 6, the yellow horizontal line represents the initial accuracy. The blue curve show the development of the mean accuracy. Around the curve, the semi-transparent areas indicate the standard deviation. In the right figure, the blue curve shows the development of the number of connections between the neurons. We split the x-axis into three stages by dashed vertical semi-transparent lines at 50 and 350 generations. In the first stage, the accuracy is similar to the initial value. As indicated in Table 1, in this stage there is a potential for small improvements. In the second stage, the accuracy stays relatively stable while the number of connections is significantly decreasing. This stage might be interesting if the computational cost are highly important and slight decreases of the accuracy are acceptable. In the last stage, the accuracy clearly drops. This stage is not interesting as the relation between accuracy and computational costs gets worse. This can also be seen in Fig. 7(a) in which the test error (1 - accuracy) is multiplied with the number of connections and visualized depending on the generation. The product shows a minimum at about 350 generations.

Improving Accuracy. The previous results indicate that it is possible to not only reduce the computational costs of the net but also to improve its accuracy. To show this potential, we take the best test accuracy of each run and compute the mean value. This is only a theoretical value as it is determined by using information from the test data and decisions may only be taken based on the training data. However, if there is a way to determine the information which generation to select from the training data, this accuracy can be achieved. Table 2 presents the results. The test error decreases from 2.93% to 2.40%. A promising approach to achieve the required information from the training data is based on the fitness function value. Figure 7(b) shows the development of f. It can be seen that the value stays constant for slightly less than 100 generations. The best values consists in mean of about 406.7 neurons, see Table 2. Looking at Table 1, 406.7 neurons are matching to the same number: slightly less than 100 generations. Thus, the information which generation to select for the best accuracy might be within the development of f. We will further investigate this point in our future work.

Table 2. Potential accuracy compared to initial accuracy

Generation	Accuracy	Neurons	Connections
0	0.9707 ± 0.0126	500.0	40000.0
Best	**0.9760** ± 0.0125	406.7	27069.3

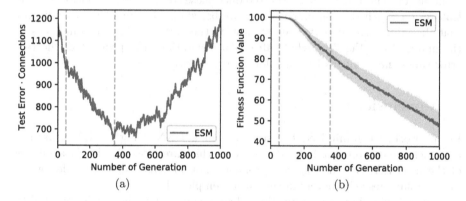

Fig. 7. Development of (left) the test error times the number of connections and (right) the fitness function value depending on the generation

Arising Structure. In the last paragraph of the experimental results, we analyze the structures of the minimized networks. Therefore, in Fig. 8, the mean values of the number of neurons for each layer are visualized depending on the generation.

The number is reduced in each layer but layer 1 consists of the most neurons in each state of the minimization. This makes sense as the inputs of the deeper layers are depending on layer 1 and so, removing a neuron from layer 1 influences each following layer. After 50 generations, the layers are ordered based on their layer number. Thereby, the gap between layer 1 and layer 2 is the largest.

It is interesting to see that after 250 generations, layer 5 is not the layer with the fewest neurons anymore. And after 350 generations, it becomes the

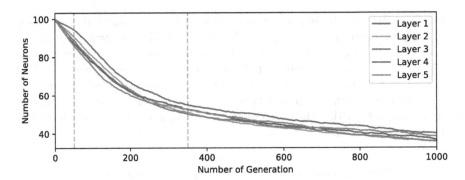

Fig. 8. Comparison of the number of neurons per layer during the optimization process.

layer with the second-most neurons. The extracted features by the network are getting more complex for each layer, e.g., the first layer is only able to separate patterns based on the employed ReLU function. The last layer creates the most complex features which are employed by the output layer to classify patterns. It seems as if the minimization starts to reduce these complex features less than the features on which the complex features are based on, this might be an indicator that the minimization is starting to destroy the network. This also matches to the finding from Fig. 7(a) where after 350 generations the product of the test error times the number of connections starts to rise.

5   Conclusions

In our work, we minimized the structure of a DNN using an EA. Our new approach is based on switchable dense layers which are controlled by the solutions of the used EA. As classification problem, motion sensor data recorded while drawing Japanese characters in the air are employed.

The optimization can be split into three stages. First, there is a potential to improve the accuracy of the network. In the second stage, the accuracy slightly decreases while the computational costs are significantly lower. Finally, the minimization starts to destroy the network. This stage is not interesting. The three stages are well recognizable if looking at the test accuracy. However, it is worthwhile to detect the stages during the optimization applying the training data. Promising approaches are based on the development of the fitness function values and the arising network structures.

In our future work, we plan to transfer the approach to various network structures and advanced networks like LSTMs. For LSTMs, the number of cells could be minimized. Further, we are going to investigate possible improvements of the accuracy in more detail.

References

1. Asher, J.J.: The total physical response approach to second language learning*. Mod. Lang. J. **53**(1), 3–17 (1969)
2. Bishop, C.M.: Pattern Recognition and Machine Learning (Information Science and Statistics). Springer, Heidelberg (2007)
3. Bolger, D.J., Perfetti, C.A., Schneider, W.: Cross-cultural effect on the brain revisited: universal structures plus writing system variation. Hum. Brain Mapp. **25**(1), 92–104 (2005)
4. Cun, Y.L., Denker, J.S., Solla, S.A.: Advances in neural information processing systems. In: Optimal Brain Damage, vol. 2, pp. 598–605. Morgan Kaufmann Publishers Inc., San Francisco (1990)
5. Deng, L., Yu, D.: Deep learning: methods and applications. Found. Trends Signal Process. **7**, 197–387 (2014)
6. Denil, M., Shakibi, B., Dinh, L., Ranzato, M., de Freitas, N.: Predicting parameters in deep learning. In: Proceedings of the 26th International Conference on Neural Information Processing Systems. NIPS 2013, vol. 2, pp. 2148–2156. Curran Associates Inc., New York (2013)
7. Denton, E., Zaremba, W., Bruna, J., LeCun, Y., Fergus, R.: Exploiting linear structure within convolutional networks for efficient evaluation. In: Proceedings of the 27th International Conference on Neural Information Processing Systems. NIPS 2014, vol. 1, pp. 1269–1277. MIT Press, Cambridge (2014)
8. Eiben, A.E., Smith, J.E.: Introduction to Evolutionary Computing. Springer, Heidelberg (2003). https://doi.org/10.1007/978-3-662-05094-1
9. Goodfellow, I., Bengio, Y., Courville, A.: Deep Learning. MIT Press, Cambridge (2016). http://www.deeplearningbook.org
10. Haarmann, H.: Symbolic Values of Foreign Language Use: From the Japanese Case to a General Sociolinguistic Perspective, Contributions to the Sociology of Language, vol. 51. Mouton de Gruyter, Berlin, New York (1989)
11. Han, S., Mao, H., Dally, W.J.: Deep compression: compressing deep neural network with pruning, trained quantization and Huffman coding. CoRR abs/1510.00149 (2015)
12. Han, S., Pool, J., Tran, J., Dally, W.J.: Learning both weights and connections for efficient neural networks. In: Proceedings of the 28th International Conference on Neural Information Processing Systems. NIPS 2015, vol. 1, pp. 1135–1143. MIT Press, Cambridge (2015)
13. Hansen, N.: The CMA evolution strategy: a comparing review. In: Lozano, J., Larranaga, P., Inza, I., Bengoetxea, E. (eds.) Towards a New Evolutionary Computation: Advances on Estimation of Distribution Algorithms, pp. 75–102. Springer, Heidelberg (2006). https://doi.org/10.1007/3-540-32494-1_4
14. Hanson, S.J., Pratt, L.Y.: Comparing biases for minimal network construction with back-propagation. In: Touretzky, D.S. (ed.) Advances in Neural Information Processing Systems, vol. 1, pp. 177–185. Morgan-Kaufmann, San Mateo (1989)
15. Haykin, S.: Neural Networks: A Comprehensive Foundation. Prentice Hall, Upper Saddle River (1999)
16. He, K., Zhang, X., Ren, S., Sun, J.: Deep residual learning for image recognition. CoRR abs/1512.03385 (2015)
17. Hochreiter, S., Schmidhuber, J.: Long short-term memory. Neural Comput. **9**(8), 1735–1780 (1997)

18. Kingma, D.P., Ba, J.: Adam: a method for stochastic optimization. CoRR abs/1412.6980 (2014)
19. Bergmann, K., Macedonia, M.: A virtual agent as vocabulary trainer: iconic gestures help to improve learners' memory performance. In: Aylett, R., Krenn, B., Pelachaud, C., Shimodaira, H. (eds.) IVA 2013. LNCS (LNAI), vol. 8108, pp. 139–148. Springer, Heidelberg (2013). https://doi.org/10.1007/978-3-642-40415-3_12
20. Kramer, O.: Evolution of convolutional highway networks. In: Sim, K., Kaufmann, P. (eds.) EvoApplications 2018. LNCS, vol. 10784, pp. 395–404. Springer, Cham (2018). https://doi.org/10.1007/978-3-319-77538-8_27
21. Loshchilov, I., Hutter, F.: CMA-ES for hyperparameter optimization of deep neural networks. CoRR abs/1604.07269 (2016)
22. Lückehe, D., Kramer, O.: Alternating optimization of unsupervised regression with evolutionary embeddings. In: Mora, A.M., Squillero, G. (eds.) EvoApplications 2015. LNCS, vol. 9028, pp. 471–480. Springer, Cham (2015). https://doi.org/10.1007/978-3-319-16549-3_38
23. Lückehe, D., Wagner, M., Kramer, O.: Constrained evolutionary wind turbine placement with penalty functions. In: IEEE Congress on Evolutionary Computation. CEC, pp. 4903–4910 (2016)
24. Macedonia, M., Mueller, K.: Exploring the neural representation of novel words learned through enactment in a word recognition task. Front. Psychol. **7**, 953 (2016)
25. Mandischer, M.: Representation and evolution of neural networks. In: Albrecht, R.F., Reeves, C.R., Steele, N.C. (eds.) Artificial Neural Nets and Genetic Algorithms, pp. 643–649. Springer, Vienna (1993). https://doi.org/10.1007/978-3-7091-7533-0_93
26. Manessi, F., Rozza, A., Bianco, S., Napoletano, P., Schettini, R.: Automated pruning for deep neural network compression. CoRR abs/1712.01721 (2017)
27. Morse, G., Stanley, K.O.: Simple evolutionary optimization can rival stochastic gradient descent in neural networks. In: Proceedings of the Genetic and Evolutionary Computation Conference 2016. GECCO 2016, pp. 477–484. ACM, New York (2016)
28. Nair, V., Hinton, G.E.: Rectified linear units improve restricted Boltzmann machines. In: Proceedings of the 27th International Conference on International Conference on Machine Learning. ICML2010, pp. 807–814. Omnipress, Madison (2010)
29. Olson, D., Delen, D.: Advanced Data Mining Techniques. Springer, Heidelberg (2008). https://doi.org/10.1007/978-3-540-76917-0
30. Saito, H., Masuda, H., Kawakami, M.: Form and sound similarity effects in kanji recognition. In: Leong, C.K., Tamaoka, K. (eds.) Cognitive Processing of the Chinese and the Japanese languages. Neuropsychology and Cognition, vol. 14, pp. 169–203. Springer, Dordrecht and London (1998). https://doi.org/10.1007/978-94-015-9161-4_9
31. Schmidhuber, J.: Deep learning in neural networks: an overview. CoRR abs/1404.7828 (2014)
32. Srivastava, N., Hinton, G., Krizhevsky, A., Sutskever, I., Salakhutdinov, R.: Dropout: a simple way to prevent neural networks from overfitting. J. Mach. Learn. Res. **15**, 1929–1958 (2014)
33. Stanley, K.O., D'Ambrosio, D.B., Gauci, J.: A hypercube-based encoding for evolving large-scale neural networks. Artif. Life **15**(2), 185–212 (2009)
34. Stanley, K.O., Miikkulainen, R.: Evolving neural networks through augmenting topologies. Evol. Comput. **10**(2), 99–127 (2002)

35. Szegedy, C., et al.: Going deeper with convolutions. In: Computer Vision and Pattern Recognition (CVPR) (2015)
36. van Aacken, S.: What motivates l2 learners in acquisition of kanji using call: a case study. Comput. Assist. Lang. Learn. **12**(2), 113–136 (2010)

Knowledge Sharing for Population Based Neural Network Training

Stefan Oehmcke$^{(\boxtimes)}$ and Oliver Kramer

Computational Intelligence Group, Department of Computing Science,
University Oldenburg, Oldenburg, Germany
{stefan.oehmcke,oliver.kramer}@uni-oldenburg.de

Abstract. Finding good hyper-parameter settings to train neural networks is challenging, as the optimal settings can change during the training phase and also depend on random factors such as weight initialization or random batch sampling. Most state-of-the-art methods for the adaptation of these settings are either static (e.g. learning rate scheduler) or dynamic (e.g ADAM optimizer), but only change some of the hyper-parameters and do not deal with the initialization problem. In this paper, we extend the asynchronous evolutionary algorithm, *population based training*, which modifies all given hyper-parameters during training and inherits weights. We introduce a novel knowledge distilling scheme. Only the best individuals of the population are allowed to share part of their knowledge about the training data with the whole population. This embraces the idea of randomness between the models, rather than avoiding it, because the resulting diversity of models is important for the population's evolution. Our experiments on *MNIST*, *fashionMNIST*, and *EMNIST* (MNIST split) with two classic model architectures show significant improvements to convergence and model accuracy compared to the original algorithm. In addition, we conduct experiments on *EMNIST* (balanced split) employing a ResNet and a WideResNet architecture to include complex architectures and data as well.

Keywords: Asynchronous evolutionary algorithms
Hyper-parameter optimization · Population based training

1 Introduction

The creation of deep neural network models is nowadays much more accessible due to easy-to-use tools and a wide range of architectures. There exist many different architectures to choose from, such as AlexNet [15], ResNet [9], WideResNet [27], or SqueezeNet [12]. But they still require a carefully chosen set of hyper-parameters for the training phase. In contrast to the weight-parameters, which are learned by an optimizer that applies gradient descent, hyper-parameters cannot be included into this optimizer or are part of it, e.g. dropout probability or learning rate. A single set of hyper-parameters can become infeasible in the

© Springer Nature Switzerland AG 2018
F. Trollmann and A.-Y. Turhan (Eds.): KI 2018, LNAI 11117, pp. 258–269, 2018.
https://doi.org/10.1007/978-3-030-00111-7_22

later stages of training, although it was appropriate in the beginning. Further, the weights of a network can develop differently due to factors of randomness, such as initial weights, mini-batch shuffling, etc., even though the same hyper-parameter settings are employed.

Recently, Jaderberg *et al.* [13] proposed a new asynchronous evolutionary algorithm (EA) that creates a population of network models, which passes on their well performing weights and mutates their hyper-parameters. They call this method *population based training* (PBT). Although good models override the weights of badly performing ones, PBT always only inherits the weights of one individual per selection and ignores the knowledge of other individuals in the population. In the worst case, this can lead to a population which has little diversity between its individuals. Without diversity, we can be stuck with sub-optimal weights. To avoid this problem, the population size could be increased, but this also requires more computing resources.

In this work, we present a novel extension to PBT by enabling knowledge sharing across generations. We adapt a knowledge distilling strategy, which is inspired by Hinton *et al.* [10], where the knowledge about the training data of the best individuals is stored separately and fed back to all individuals via the loss function. In an experimental evaluation, we train classic LeNet5 [17] and multi-layer perceptron (MLP) models on *MNIST*, *fashionMNIST*, and the MNIST-split of *EMNIST* using PBT with and without our knowledge sharing algorithm. Additional experiments are conducted on the more complex balanced split of *EMNIST* with either ResNet or WideResNet models. These experiments support our claim that our knowledge sharing algorithm significantly improves the model performance trained with PBT.

This paper is organized as follows. In Sect. 2, we introduce the original algorithm and our knowledge sharing extension. Next, the conducted experiments are described in Sect. 3. Section 4 revises related work about knowledge distilling and hyper-parameter optimization. Finally, in Sect. 5 we draw our conclusions and provide suggestions for future work.

2 Population Based Training with Knowledge Sharing

The original PBT algorithm [13] is described in the following and then extended by our knowledge sharing method afterwards. The complete method is depicted in Algorithm 1.

2.1 Population Based Training

First, we create a population of N individuals and start an asynchronous evolutionary process for each one that runs for G generations. An individual consists of its network weights θ, hyper-parameters $\boldsymbol{h}$, current fitness p, and current update step t. There is a training set $(X_{\text{train}}, Y_{\text{train}}) = \{(\boldsymbol{x}_1, y_1), \ldots, (\boldsymbol{x}_n, y_n)\} \in (\mathbb{R}^d, \{1, \ldots, c\})$ with size n, input dimensions d, and number of classes c. This set is employed to the step-function, where weight θ optimization is performed with

---

Algorithm 1: PBT with knowledge sharing. The extensions to the algorithm are highlighted with green boxes.

---

input: population $\mathcal{P}$, number of generations G, training samples X_{train},
training targets Y_{train}, validation samples X_{val}, validation targets Y_{val}

1   $T \leftarrow$ one-hot encode Y_{train}
2   **for** $(\theta, h, p, t) \in \mathcal{P}$ *(asynchronously in parallel)* **do**
3     $g \leftarrow 0$
4   **while** $g \leq G$ **do**
5       $\theta \leftarrow \text{step}(\theta | h, X_{\text{train}}, Y_{\text{train}}, \boxed{T})$
6       $p \leftarrow \text{eval}(\theta, X_{\text{val}}, Y_{\text{val}})$
7   **if** $ready(p, t, \mathcal{P})$ **then**
8         $h', \theta' \leftarrow \text{exploit}(h, \theta, p, \mathcal{P})$
9   **if** $\theta \neq \theta'$ **then**
10           $h, \theta \leftarrow \text{explore}(h', \theta', \mathcal{P})$
11           $p \leftarrow \text{eval}(\theta, X_{\text{val}}, Y_{\text{val}})$
12   **else**
13           $T \leftarrow \text{teach}(\theta, X_{\text{train}}, Y_{\text{train}}, p, \mathcal{P})$
14       $g \leftarrow g + 1$
15   update $\mathcal{P}$ with new $(\theta, h, p, t + 1)$
16 **return** $\arg\max_{\theta}(p$ *from* $\mathcal{P})$

---

gradient descent depending on the hyper-parameter settings h (Line 5). Then, the `eval`-function assesses the fitness p on a separate validation set $(X_{\text{val}}, Y_{\text{val}})$ (Line 6). If the `ready`-function condition is met, e.g. enough update steps have past, the individual is reevaluated (Line 7). The `exploit`-function chooses the next set of weight and hyper-parameters from the population with a selection operator (Line 8). In our experimental studies we always use truncate selection, which replaces an individual when it occurs in the lower 20% of the fitness-sorted population with a randomly selected individual from the upper 20%. With the `explore`-function we can change the weights and hyper-parameters of an individual (Line 10) and perform another call of `eval` (Line 11). This `explore`-function is equivalent to the mutation operator in classical EAs. The `explore`-function is called perturb, where the hyper-parameters are multiplied by a factor of σ. This factor σ is usually chosen randomly from two values such as 0.9 and 1.1. Finally, the individual is updated in population $\mathcal{P}$. After the last generation, the individual with highest fitness from the population is returned.

2.2   Knowledge Sharing

Next, we explain our extensions to PBT with knowledge distilling. These additions are highlighted with green boxes in Algorithm 1. The teacher output $T = \{t_1, \ldots, t_n\} \in \mathbb{R}^c$ is initialized with the one-hot-encoded class targets of the true training targets Y_{train} (Line 1). During the evolutionary process, the best models are allowed to contribute to T through the `teach`-function (Line 13). We implement this `teach`-function by replacing 20% of the teacher output T

with the predicted probability if the individual is from the upper 20% of the population $\mathcal{P}$ regarding the fitness p. Depending on the population size, we are able to replace the original targets from Y in a few generations and introduce updates from generations continuously. One could adapt this value, but we kept it fixed to reduce the time consumed by reevaluating the training dataset and 20% offered a good-trade-off between introduction of new teacher values and retaining previous values.

While updating the weights through the step-function (Line 5), the output of the teacher is used within the loss function L, which is defined as:

$$L = \underbrace{\alpha \cdot L_{\text{cross}}(y, f(\boldsymbol{x}))}_{\text{cross entropy}} + \underbrace{(1 - \alpha) \cdot D_{\text{KL}}(\boldsymbol{t}, f(\boldsymbol{x}))}_{\text{distance to teacher}}, \tag{1}$$

for a single input image $\boldsymbol{x}$, label y, teacher output $\boldsymbol{t}$, teacher model f, cross entropy loss L_{cross}, Kullback–Leibler divergence D_{KL}, and a trade-off parameter α. This combination of cross entropy and Kullback-Leibler divergence ensures that the models can learn the true labels, while also utilizing the already acquired knowledge of the population. The trade-off parameter α is added to the hyperparameter settings $\boldsymbol{h}$. Hence, no manual tuning is required and the population can self-balance the two loss functions.

To compare the output distributions of the teacher and the individuals, we employ the Kullback–Leibler divergence D_{KL} inspired by other distilling approaches [23]. The one-hot encoding of the true target as initialization results in a loss function equal to only using cross entropy since the Kullback-Leibler divergence is approximately equal to the cross entropy when all-except-one class probabilities are zero. There are similarities to *generative adversarial networks* (GANs) [7], where the generator is similar to the teacher and discriminator is similar to the student. In contrast to knowledge distilling, the generator tries to fool the discriminator. Also, by updating the teacher knowledge iteratively, we elevate the usually static nature of distilling methods to be more dynamic, which is now also similar to GANs.

As an alternative to creating the teacher output ty iteratively, one could also directly use one or more of the models from the population to create a teacher output for the current batch. This has been tried out by Zhang *et al.* [28] and also by Anil *et al.* [1], but without the evolutionary adaption of hyperparameters. The downside of this approach is the increased amount of memory and calculations required, since the teacher models have to be kept to calculate the targets for the same images multiple times and the sharing of models between GPU increases the I/O times.

3   Experiments

In the following, we want to compare the performance of the asynchronous EA with and without knowledge sharing. Each condition is repeated 30 times for reproducible results.

Table 1. The two employed model architectures for ten classes: LeNet5 [17] and a MLP. A dense layer is a fully connected layer with ReLU activation. This activation function is also used by the convolutional layers. The number of neurons and parameters is abbreviated with #neurons and #parameters, respectively.

| | LeNet5 | | | | MLP | |
layer	#neurons	kernel size	#params	layer	#neurons	#params
convolutional	6	5×5	156	dense	256	200 960
max pool	6	2×2	0			
convolutional	16	5×5	2416	dense	128	32 896
max pool	16	2×2	0			
dense	120	–	48 120	dense	64	8256
dense	84	–	10 164			
linear	10	–	850	linear	10	650
total #params			61 706			242 762

3.1 Datasets

We utilize three image datasets with the same amount of data, but with different classification tasks. All contain images of size 28×28 with one grey-channel. We apply normalization to the images as the only data transformation.

The first dataset is *MNIST* [16], which is a classical handwritten digits dataset with the classes being the digits from one to ten. *FashionMNIST* [26] is the second dataset and consists of different fashion articles. The last datasets, *EMNIST* [5], is an extended version of the MNIST dataset with multiple different splits. We decided to use the MNIST split that is similar to MNIST but offers different images. 60 000 images are available for training and validation for each of these three datasets. In our experiments, we use 90% (54 000) for training and 10% (6000) for validation. This validation set is used by PBT to assess a model's fitness. The testing set consists of 10 000 images and is only used for the final performance measurement. There are 10 classes to be predicted in each dataset. These three datasets will from here on referred to as MNIST-like datasets. As an additional, more complex setting, we employ the balanced *EMNIST* split, which encompasses 47 classes (lower/upper case letters and digits) with 112 800 images for training (101 520) and validation (11 280) as well as 18 800 images for validation.

3.2 Model Architectures and PBT Settings

In our experiments on the MNIST-like datasets, we either employ a LeNet5 [17] or a MLP architecture with details in Table 1. Further, we use a ResNet [9] (depth = 14 with 3 blocks) and WideResNet [27] ($k = 2$, depth = 28 with 3 blocks) architecture for the balanced *EMNIST* split. ResNet has 2786 000 and WideResNet 371 620 parameters. Notably, we do not want to compare these

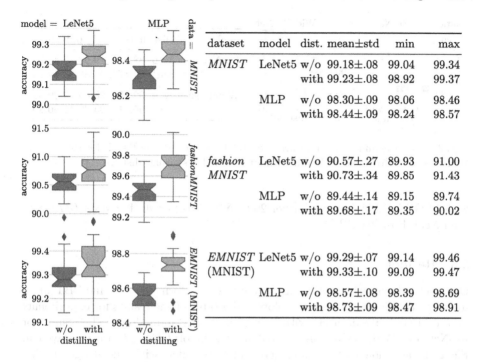

Fig. 1. Box-plots and table of accuracy on the MNIST-like datasets employing LeNet5 or MLP individuals with and without knowledge sharing (distilling).

architecture, but rather compare if better models can be found for an architecture with knowledge sharing.

We employ the cross entropy loss on the validation set as eval-function. The exploit-function is truncate selection and the explore-function is perturb mutation (see Sect. 2). As optimizer, we use stochastic gradient descent with momentum. Hyper-parameters h are learning rate and momentum. For runs with knowledge sharing, the trade-off-parameter α from Eq. 1 is also part of the hyper-parameters. WideResNet individuals also optimize the dropout probabilities for each dropout layer inside the wide-dropout residual blocks as hyper-parameters. For the MNIST-like datasets the population size N is 30, every 250 iterations the ready-function enters the update loop, and the population's life is $G = 40$ generations long, which amounts to ≈ 12 epochs with a batch size of 64. On the balanced *EMNIST* dataset $N = 20$ individuals are employed, within $G = 100$ generations and the ready-function triggers every 317 iterations, which results in ≈ 40 epochs for with batch size of 128.

We implemented the PBT algorithm in Python 3[1] with PyTorch[2] as our deep learning backend. Our experiments ran on a DGX-1, whereby each EA employs its population on 2 (MNIST-like) or 4 (balanced *EMNIST*) Volta NVIDIA GPUs

---

[1] https://www.python.org/.

[2] https://pytorch.org.

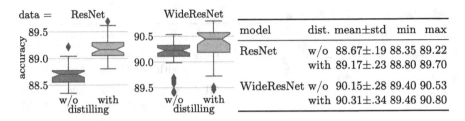

Fig. 2. Box-plots and table of accuracy on the balanced *EMNIST* split for ResNet and WideResNet individuals with and without knowledge sharing (dist.).

with 14 GB VRAM each and either 20 (MNIST-like) or 40 (balanced *EMNIST*) Intel Xeon E5-2698 CPUs.

3.3   Results

Our knowledge sharing extension is able to outperform the baseline PBT in all tested cases. Figure 1 shows box-plots and a table of the results for experiments on the MNIST-like datasets with LeNet5 and MLP individuals. The results for ResNet and WideResNet on the balanced split of *EMNIST* are displayed in Fig. 2. In addition to the convergence of the models with knowledge sharing around a higher mean and median, we observe that the highest achieved performance is also better. Moreover, we apply the Mann-Whitney-U statistical test [20], which confirms that PBT with knowledge sharing significantly surpasses the baseline PBT w.r.t. the test accuracy ($p < 0.05$).

Figure 3 presents the validation loss as well as the test loss and accuracy for one PBT run for WideResNet individuals on balanced *EMNIST* with and without knowledge distilling. Interestingly, both runs show a steady decline in validation loss, but at around 2500 iterations the PBT run without distilling diverges strongly with a lower loss. The best distilling model for this run achieves a test accuracy of 90.47% and a test loss of 0.27, while the validation loss is 0.20. Further, the best model without distilling performs worse on the test set with accuracy (89.67%) and loss (0.33), but the validation loss is 0.11. This is a strong indicator that overfitting to the validation set occurs without distilling and the knowledge sharing method acts as an regularizer. More evidence of this is the slowly increasing test loss for PBT without distilling. The PBT with knowledge sharing also converges faster, as the test loss and accuracy show better values even in early iterations. These effects are similar for the other architectures as well. We discovered that the teacher output usually is not better than the best individuals, which suggests that the different distributions and the resulting diversity are the main advantage of this approach.

In Fig. 4 the lineages of hyper-parameter settings of a WideResNet run with and without knowledge sharing are shown. The learning rate decreases over passing iterations, which is in line with intuition and fixed learning rate schedules. Interestingly, the learning rate for knowledge sharing does not decrease as much

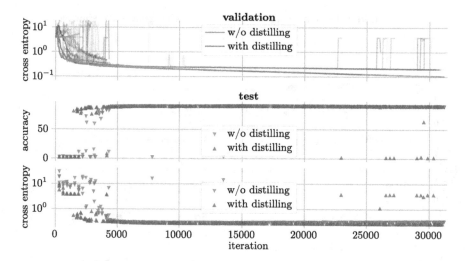

Fig. 3. Validation loss plot of one PBT run with and without distilling on the validation set from *EMNIST* (balanced) with WideResNet individuals. Different color hues depict other individual models from the EA.

and even increases for some models at later iterations. The dropout probabilities also change over time, although with different degrees across the layers and the earlier layers. The trade-off parameter α is steadily increasing to a value between 0.75 and 1, which suggests that the knowledge sharing is especially useful early on, but is also used at all the later iterations. Finally, with knowledge sharing, it requires less iterations until the feasible hyper-parameter search space becomes smaller; from 1300 to 2800 iterations (4 to 8 epochs) instead of 4000 to 4500 iterations (12 to 14 epochs). This means that the selection pressure is higher early on, which could be explained by a faster convergence rate of the models.

4   Related Work

We report related work in distilling knowledge as well as hyper-parameter optimization and differentiate ourselves from these.

4.1   Distilling Knowledge

Hinton *et al.* [10] originally proposed the distilling of knowledge for neural networks. They trained a complex model and let it be the teacher for a simpler model, the student. The student model is then able to achieve nearly the same performance as the complex one, which was not possible when training the simple model without the teacher.

The second iteration of the WaveNet architecture [23] introduced the distilling method called *probability density distillation*. WaveNet is an architecture that generates audio, e.g. for speech synthesis or music generation, proposed by

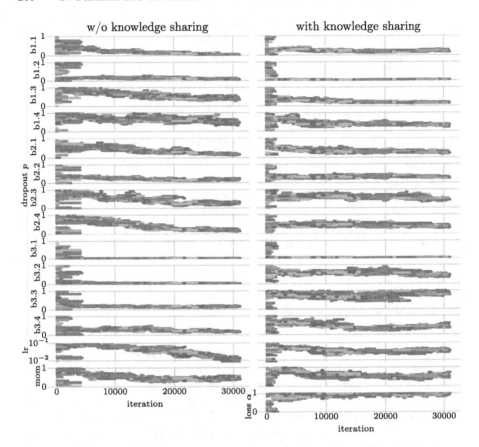

Fig. 4. Exemplary run on *EMNIST* (balanced) with WideResNet individuals showing the hyper-parameter lineage. Models are separated by color. The different dropout probabilities p are depicted for each block and layer within (e.g. block 1 and layer 1 is b1.1). Learning rate is abbreviated to lr and momentum to mom.

Oord *et al.* [22]. The distilling method utilizes the Kullback-Leibler divergence to enable the student network to learn the teacher's output probabilities, which we also employ in our approach.

Various other distilling techniques have been proposed: Mishra and Marr [21] apply it to train models with weights that either have ternary or 4-bit precision. They introduce three different schemes to teach a low precision student with a full-precision teacher that all yield state-of-the-art performance and lower convergence times for these network types. Another form of distillation has been suggested by Radosavovic *et al.* [24], called data distillation for omni-supervised learning. In this special semi-supervised task, unlabeled data is labeled by running the teacher model multiple times on an ensemble of input transformations and the student learns with help of this ensemble prediction. Furthermore, Romero *et al.* [25] additionally utilizes the output of the intermediate layers from the teacher to train deeper, but thinner student networks. A different approach has been submitted by Chen et al. [4]. Their Net2Net approach distills the knowledge through two different network initialization strategies. One strategy increases the width of a layer and the other one increases the depth of the network while preserving the output function of the teacher model.

Our approach differentiates itself from these works since instead of having a fully trained teacher model, our teacher output grows in knowledge alongside the population and is not itself a neural network model. Another key difference is that our student models all use the same architecture and the teacher output is an ensemble of their outputs.

4.2 Hyper-Parameter Optimization

The optimization of hyper-parameters for neural networks is thoroughly researched field. Popular choices are Bayesian optimization methods such as the *tree-structured Parzen estimator approach* [2], or the *sequential model-based algorithm configuration* [11]. Nearly as optimal, but usually much faster is random optimization [3,6]. Further, the *hyperband* algorithm [18] minimizes the time on unfeasible settings and is the current state-of-the-art method. There is also work with EAs, where the *covariance matrix adaptation evolution strategy* (CMA-ES) [8] is used [19].

In contrast to these methods, we do not want to find one optimal set of hyper-parameters, but look at the optimization problem more dynamically and avoid the problem of randomness by training multiple in parallel. This limits the set of available hyper-parameters to those that do not change the network structure, but are important for the training of the network. For example, intuitively the learning rate for a network should decrease over time instead of being fixed to be able to learn fast in the beginning and later only small changes are required to improve the network. This is done in optimizers, such as ADAM [14], but is restricted to a few hyper-parameters and depends on the loss function, whereas PBT can utilize any given fitness function, even if it is non-differentiable.

5   Conclusion

The training of neural networks requires good hyper-parameter settings that can gradually change and are subject to factors of randomness. In this paper, we propose an extension to PBT with knowledge sharing across generations. This approach, based on knowledge distilling, enables the best performing neural networks of a population to contribute to a shared teacher output for the training data that is then reflected within the loss function of all networks in the population. Compared to PBT without our knowledge sharing approach significantly increases the performance on all tested data and architectures.

The approach is limited to computing systems with enough resources to run a population of models. Luckily, powerful hardware and cloud solutions are steadily becoming more accessible and affordable. Further, this work did not include alternative schemes for filling the teacher output, such as averaging or selecting contributers from all individuals. Currently, only classification tasks were considered in our experiments, which could be expanded to reinforcement learning or regression. Although all used datasets consist of image data input, our approach is transferable to other problem scenarios, such as speech recognition or drug discovery.

Future work could include heterogeneous architectures in population that create a more diverse teacher distribution. With diverse networks, it might be feasible to employ ensemble techniques with the best population members instead of only the best individual. Also, it could be explored if the network structure could be adapted as well, e.g. with the `Net2Net` [4] strategies. More general research could evaluate other algorithms for the evolutionary process, such as the CMA-ES and how to incorporate knowledge sharing there. A comparison to traditional hyper-parameter optimization methods could be conducted in the future.

References

1. Anil, R., Pereyra, G., Passos, A., Ormándi, R., Dahl, G.E., Hinton, G.E.: Large scale distributed neural network training through online distillation. CoRR abs/1804.03235 (2018). http://arxiv.org/abs/1804.03235
2. Bergstra, J., Bardenet, R., Bengio, Y., Kégl, B.: Algorithms for hyper-parameter optimization. In: Shawe-Taylor, J., Zemel, R.S., Bartlett, P.L., Pereira, F.C.N., Weinberger, K.Q. (eds.) Annual Conference on Neural Information Processing Systems (NIPS). Advances in Neural Information Processing Systems, pp. 2546–2554 (2011)
3. Bergstra, J., Bengio, Y.: Random search for hyper-parameter optimization. J. Mach. Learn. Res. **13**, 281–305 (2012)
4. Chen, T., Goodfellow, I.J., Shlens, J.: Net2net: Accelerating learning via knowledge transfer. CoRR abs/1511.05641 (2015). http://arxiv.org/abs/1511.05641
5. Cohen, G., Afshar, S., Tapson, J., van Schaik, A.: EMNIST: Extending MNIST to handwritten letters. In: International Joint Conference on Neural Networks (IJCNN), pp. 2921–2926. IEEE (2017)
6. Feurer, M., Klein, A., Eggensperger, K., Springenberg, J.T., Blum, M., Hutter, F.: Efficient and robust automated machine learning. In: Cortes, C., Lawrence, N.D., Lee, D.D., Sugiyama, M., Garnett, R. (eds.) Annual Conference on Neural Information Processing Systems (NIPS). Advances in Neural Information Processing Systems, pp. 2962–2970 (2015)
7. Goodfellow, I., et al.: Generative adversarial nets. In: Annual Conference on Neural Information Processing Systems (NIPS). Advances in Neural Information Processing Systems, pp. 2672–2680. Curran Associates, Inc. (2014). http://papers.nips.cc/paper/5423-generative-adversarial-nets.pdf
8. Hansen, N., Müller, S.D., Koumoutsakos, P.: Reducing the time complexity of the derandomized evolution strategy with covariance matrix adaptation (CMA-ES). Evol. Comput. **11**(1), 1–18 (2003). https://doi.org/10.1162/106365603321828970
9. He, K., Zhang, X., Ren, S., Sun, J.: Deep residual learning for image recognition. In: Conference on Computer Vision and Pattern Recognition (CVPR), pp. 770–778. IEEE (2016). https://doi.org/10.1109/CVPR.2016.90

10. Hinton, G., Vinyals, O., Dean, J.: Distilling the knowledge in a neural network. CoRR http://arxiv.org/abs/1503.02531v1
11. Hutter, F., Hoos, H.H., Leyton-Brown, K.: Sequential model-based optimization for general algorithm configuration. In: Coello, C.A.C. (ed.) LION 2011. LNCS, vol. 6683, pp. 507–523. Springer, Heidelberg (2011). https://doi.org/10.1007/978-3-642-25566-3_40
12. Iandola, F.N., Han, S., Moskewicz, M.W., Ashraf, K., Dally, W.J., Keutzer, K.: Squeezenet: Alexnet-level accuracy with 50x fewer parameters and 0.5 Mb model size. Computing Research Repository (CoRR) abs/1602.07360 (2016). http://arxiv.org/abs/1602.07360
13. Jaderberg, M., et al.: Population based training of neural networks. CoRR abs/1711.09846 (2017). http://arxiv.org/abs/1711.09846
14. Kingma, D.P., Ba, J.: Adam: a method for stochastic optimization. Computing Research Repository (CoRR) abs/1412.6980 (2014). http://arxiv.org/abs/1412.6980
15. Krizhevsky, A., Sutskever, I., Hinton, G.E.: Imagenet classification with deep convolutional neural networks. In: Annual Conference on Neural Information Processing Systems (NIPS). Advances in Neural Information Processing Systems, pp. 1106–1114. Curran Associates (2012)
16. LeCun, Y.: The MNIST database of handwritten digits (1998). http://yann.lecun.com/exdb/mnist/
17. LeCun, Y., Bottou, L., Bengio, Y., Haffner, P.: Gradient-based learning applied to document recognition. Proc. IEEE 86(11), 2278–2324 (1998)
18. Li, L., Jamieson, K., DeSalvo, G., Rostamizadeh, A., Talwalkar, A.: Hyperband: a novel bandit-based approach to hyperparameter optimization. arXiv preprint arXiv:1603.06560 (2016)
19. Loshchilov, I., Hutter, F.: CMA-ES for hyperparameter optimization of deep neural networks. CoRR abs/1604.07269 (2016). http://arxiv.org/abs/1604.07269
20. McKnight, P.E., Najab, J.: Mann-Whitney U Test. Wiley, Hoboken (2010). https://doi.org/10.1002/9780470479216.corpsy0524
21. Mishra, A.K., Marr, D.: Apprentice: using knowledge distillation techniques to improve low-precision network accuracy. CoRR abs/1711.05852 (2017). http://arxiv.org/abs/1711.05852
22. van den Oord, A., et al.: WaveNet: a generative model for raw audio. CoRR abs/1609.03499 (2016). http://arxiv.org/abs/1609.03499
23. van den Oord, A., et al.: Parallel WaveNet: fast high-fidelity speech synthesis. CoRR abs/1711.10433 (2017). http://arxiv.org/abs/1711.10433
24. Radosavovic, I., Dollár, P., Girshick, R.B., Gkioxari, G., He, K.: Data distillation: towards omni-supervised learning. CoRR abs/1712.04440 (2017). http://arxiv.org/abs/1712.04440
25. Romero, A., Ballas, N., Kahou, S.E., Chassang, A., Gatta, C., Bengio, Y.: FitNets: hints for thin deep nets. CoRR abs/1412.6550 (2014). http://arxiv.org/abs/1412.6550
26. Xiao, H., Rasul, K., Vollgraf, R.: Fashion-MNIST: a novel image dataset for benchmarking machine learning algorithms (2017)
27. Zagoruyko, S., Komodakis, N.: Wide residual networks. In: Wilson, R.C., Hancock, E.R., Smith, W.A.P. (eds.) Proceedings of the British Machine Vision Conference (BMVC). BMVA Press (2016). http://www.bmva.org/bmvc/2016/papers/paper087/index.html
28. Zhang, Y., Xiang, T., Hospedales, T.M., Lu, H.: Deep mutual learning. CoRR abs/1706.00384 (2017). http://arxiv.org/abs/1706.00384

Limited Evaluation Evolutionary Optimization of Large Neural Networks

Jonas Prellberg$^{(\boxtimes)}$ and Oliver Kramer

University of Oldenburg, Oldenburg, Germany
{jonas.prellberg,oliver.kramer}@uni-oldenburg.de

Abstract. Stochastic gradient descent is the most prevalent algorithm to train neural networks. However, other approaches such as evolutionary algorithms are also applicable to this task. Evolutionary algorithms bring unique trade-offs that are worth exploring, but computational demands have so far restricted exploration to small networks with few parameters. We implement an evolutionary algorithm that executes entirely on the GPU, which allows to efficiently batch-evaluate a whole population of networks. Within this framework, we explore the limited evaluation evolutionary algorithm for neural network training and find that its batch evaluation idea comes with a large accuracy trade-off. In further experiments, we explore crossover operators and find that unprincipled random uniform crossover performs extremely well. Finally, we train a network with 92k parameters on MNIST using an EA and achieve 97.6% test accuracy compared to 98% test accuracy on the same network trained with Adam. Code is available at https://github.com/jprellberg/gpuea.

1 Introduction

Stochastic gradient descent (SGD) is the leading approach for neural network parameter optimization. Significant research effort has lead to creations such as the Adam [9] optimizer, Batch Normalization [8] or advantageous parameter initializations [7], all of which improve upon the standard SGD training process. Furthermore, efficient libraries with automatic differentiation and GPU support are readily available. It is therefore unsurprising that SGD outperforms all other approaches to neural network training. Still, in this paper we want to examine evolutionary algorithms (EA) for this task.

EAs are powerful black-box function optimizers and one prominent advantage is that they do not need gradient information. While neural networks are usually built so that they are differentiable, this restriction can be lifted when training with EAs. For example, this would allow the direct training of neural networks with binary weights for deployment in low-power embedded devices. Furthermore, the loss function does not need to be differentiable so that it becomes possible to optimize for more complex metrics.

With growing computational resources and algorithmic advances, it is becoming feasible to optimize large, directly encoded neural networks with EAs.

© Springer Nature Switzerland AG 2018
F. Trollmann and A.-Y. Turhan (Eds.): KI 2018, LNAI 11117, pp. 270–283, 2018.
https://doi.org/10.1007/978-3-030-00111-7_23

Recently, the limited evaluation evolutionary algorithm (LEEA) [11] has been introduced, which saves computation by performing the fitness evaluation on small batches of data and smoothing the resulting noise with a fitness inheritance scheme. We create a LEEA implementation that executes entirely on a GPU to facilitate extensive experimentation. The GPU implementation avoids memory bandwidth bottlenecks, reduces latency and, most importantly, allows to efficiently batch the evaluation of multiple network instances with different parameters into a single operation.

Using this framework, we highlight a trade-off between batch size and achievable accuracy and also find the proposed fitness inheritance scheme to be detrimental. Instead, we show how the LEEA can profit from low selective pressure when using small batch sizes. Despite the problems discussed in literature about crossover and neural networks [6,14], we see that basic uniform and arithmetic crossover perform well when paired with an appropriately tuned mutation operator. Finally, we apply the lessons learned to train a neural network with 92k parameters on MNIST using an EA and achieve 97.6% test accuracy. In comparison, training with Adam results in 98% test accuracy. (The network is limited by its size and architecture and cannot achieve state-of-the-art results.)

The remainder of this paper is structured as follows: Sect. 2 presents related work on the application of EAs to neural network training. In Sect. 3, we present our EA in detail and explain the advantages of running it on a GPU. Section 4 covers all experiments and contains the main results of this work. Finally, we conclude the paper in Sect. 5.

2   Related Work

Morse et al. [11] introduced the limited evaluation (LE) evolutionary algorithm for neural network training. It is a modified generational EA, which picks a small batch of training examples at the beginning of every generation and uses it to evaluate the population of neural networks. This idea is conceptually very similar to SGD, which also uses a batch of data for each step. Performing the fitness evaluation on small batches instead of the complete training set massively reduces the required computation, but it also introduces noise into the fitness evaluation. The second component of the LEEA is therefore a fitness inheritance scheme that combines past fitness evaluation results. The algorithm is tested with networks of up to 1500 parameters and achieves results comparable to SGD on small datasets.

Baioletti et al. [1] pick up the LE idea but replace the evolutionary algorithm with differential evolution (DE), which is a very successful optimizer for continuous parameter spaces [3]. The largest network they experiment with employs 7000 parameters. However, there is still a rather large performance gap on the MNIST dataset between their best performing DE algorithm at 85% accuracy and a standard SGD training at 92% accuracy.

Yaman et al. [15] combine the concepts LE, DE and cooperative co-evolution. They consider the pre-synaptic weights of a single neuron a component and evolve many populations of such components in parallel. Complete solutions are created by combining components from different populations to a network. Using this approach, they are able to optimize networks of up to 28k parameters.

Zhang et al. [16] explore neural network training with a natural evolution strategy. This algorithm starts with an initial parameter vector θ and creates many so-called pseudo-offspring parameter vectors by adding random noise to θ. The fitness of all pseudo-offspring is evaluated and used to estimate the gradient at θ. Finally, this gradient approximation is fed to SGD or another optimizer such as Adam to modify θ. Using this approach, they achieve 99% accuracy on MNIST with 50k pseudo-offspring for the gradient approximation.

Neuroevolution, which is the joint optimization of network topology and parameters, is another promising application for EAs. This approach has a long history [5] and works well for small networks up to a few hundred connections. However, scaling this approach to networks with millions of connections remains a challenge. One recent line of work [4,10,12] has taken a hybrid approach where the topology is optimized by an EA but the parameters are still trained with SGD. However, the introduction or removal of parameters by the EA can be problematic. It may leave the network in an unfavorable region of the parameter space, with effects similar to those of a bad initialization at the start of SGD training. Another line of work has focused on indirect encodings to reduce the size of the search space [13]. The difficulty here lies in finding an appropriate mapping from genotype to phenotype.

3   Method

We implement a population-based EA that optimizes the parameters of directly encoded, fixed size neural networks. For performance reasons, the EA is implemented with TensorFlow and executes entirely on the GPU, i.e. the whole population of networks lives in GPU memory and all EA logic is performed on the GPU.

3.1   Evolutionary Algorithm

Algorithm 1 shows our EA in pseudo-code. It is a generational EA extended by the limited evaluation concept. Every generation, the fitness evaluation is performed on a small batch of data that is drawn randomly from the training set. This reduces the computational cost of the fitness evaluation but introduces an increasing amount of noise with smaller batch sizes. To counteract this, Morse et al. [11] propose a fitness inheritance scheme that we implement as well.

The initial population is created by randomly initializing the parameters of λ networks. Then, a total of λ offspring networks are derived from the population P. The hyperparameters p_E, p_C and p_M determine the percentage of offspring created by elite selection, crossover and mutation respectively. First, the $p_E \lambda$ networks with the highest fitness are selected as elites from the population. These elites move into the next generation unchanged and will be evaluated

$P \leftarrow [\theta_1, \theta_2, \ldots, \theta_\lambda \,|\, \theta_i$ randomly initialized]
while termination condition not met **do**

> $x, y \leftarrow$ select random batch from training data
> $P \leftarrow P$ sorted by fitness in descending order
> $E \leftarrow$ select elites $P[:p_E\lambda]$
> $C \leftarrow$ select $p_C\lambda$ parent pairs $(\theta_1, \theta_2) \in P[:\rho\lambda]^2$ uniform at random
> $M \leftarrow$ select $p_M\lambda$ parents $\theta_1 \in P[:\rho\lambda]$ uniform at random
> $C' \leftarrow [\text{crossover}(\theta_1, \theta_2) \,|\, (\theta_1, \theta_2) \in C]$
> $M' \leftarrow [\text{mutation}(\theta_1) \,|\, \theta_1 \in M]$
> $P \leftarrow E \cup C' \cup M'$
> evaluate fitness (θ, x, y) for each individual in $\theta \in P$

end

Algorithm 1: Evolutionary algorithm. Square brackets indicate ordered lists and $L[:k]$ is notation for the list containing the first k elements of L.

again. Even though their parameters did not change, the repeated evaluation is desirable. Because the fitness function is only evaluated on a small batch of data, it is stochastic and repeated evaluations will result in a better estimate of the true fitness when combined with previous fitness evaluation results. Next, $p_C\lambda$ pairs of networks are selected as parents for sexual reproduction (crossover) and finally $p_M\lambda$ networks are selected as parents for asexual reproduction (mutation). The selection procedure in both cases is truncation selection, i.e. parents are drawn uniform at random from the top $\rho\lambda$ of networks sorted by fitness, where $\rho \in [0, 1]$ is the selection proportion.

Due to the stochasticity in the fitness evaluation, it seems advantageous to combine fitness evaluation results from multiple batches. However, simply evaluating every network on multiple batches is no different from using a larger batch size. Therefore, the assumption is made that the fitness of a parent network and its offspring are related. Then, a parent's fitness can be inherited to its offspring as a good initial guess and be refined by the actual fitness evaluation of the offspring. This is done in form of the weighted sum

$$f_{\text{adj}} = (1 - \alpha) \cdot f_{\text{inh}} + \alpha \cdot \text{fitness}(\theta, x, y),$$

where f_{inh} is the fitness value inherited by the parents, fitness (θ, x, y) is the fitness value of the offspring θ on the current batch x, y and $\alpha \in [0, 1]$ is a hyperparameter that controls the strength of the fitness inheritance scheme. Setting α to 1 disables fitness inheritance altogether. During sexual reproduction of two parents with fitness f_1 and f_2 or during asexual reproduction of a single parent with fitness f_3, the inherited fitness values are $f_{\text{inh}} = \frac{1}{2}(f_1 + f_2)$ and $f_{\text{inh}} = f_3$ respectively.

3.2 Crossover and Mutation Operators

Members of the EA population are direct encodings of neural network parameters $\theta \in \mathbb{R}^c$, where c is the total number of parameters in each network. The crossover and mutation operators directly modify this vector representation. An explanation of the crossover and mutation operators that we use in our experiments follows.

Uniform Crossover. The uniform crossover of two parents θ_1 and θ_2 creates offspring θ_u by randomly deciding which element of the offspring's parameter vector is taken from which parent:

$$\theta_{u,i} = \begin{cases} \theta_{1,i} & \text{with probability 0.5} \\ \theta_{2,i} & \text{else} \end{cases}$$

Arithmetic Crossover. Arithmetic crossover creates offspring θ_a from two parents θ_1 and θ_2 by taking the arithmetic mean:

$$\theta_a = \frac{1}{2}(\theta_1 + \theta_2)$$

Mutation. The mutation operator adds random normal noise scaled by a mutation strength σ to a parent θ_1:

$$\theta_m = \theta_1 + \sigma \cdot \mathcal{N}(0,1)$$

The mutation strength σ is an important hyperparameter that can be changed over the course of the EA run if desired. In the simplest case, the mutation strength stays constant over all generations.

We also experiment with deterministic control in the form of an exponentially decaying value. For each generation i, the mutation strength is calculated according to $\sigma_i = \sigma \cdot 0.99^{i/k}$, where σ is the initial mutation strength and the hyperparameter k controls the decay rate in terms of generations.

Finally, we implement self-adaptive control. The mutation strength σ is included as a gene in each individual and each individual is mutated with the σ taken from its own genes. The mutation strength itself is mutated according to $\sigma_{i+1} = \sigma_i e^{\tau \mathcal{N}(0,1)}$ with hyperparameter τ. During crossover, the arithmetic mean of two σ-genes produces the value for the σ-gene in the offspring.

3.3 GPU Implementation

Naively executing thousands of small neural networks on a GPU in parallel incurs significant overhead, since many short-running, parallel operations that compete for resources are launched, each of which also has a startup cost. To efficiently evaluate thousands of network parameter configurations, the computations should be expressed as batch tensor[1] products where possible.

Assume we have input data of dimensionality m and want to apply a fully connected layer with n output units to it. This can naturally be expressed as a product of a parameter and data tensor with shapes $[n, m] \times [m] = [n]$, which in this simple case is just a matrix-vector product. To process a batch of data at once, a batch dimension b is introduced to the data vector. The resulting product has shapes $[n, m] \times [b, m] = [b, n]$. Conceptually, the same product as before is computed for every element in the data tensor's batch dimension. Batching over multiple sets of network parameters follows the same approach and introduces a population dimension p. Obviously, the parameter tensor needs to be extended by this dimension so that it can hold parameters of different networks. However, the data tensor also needs an additional population dimension because the output of each layer will be different for networks with different parameters. The resulting product has shapes $[p, n, m] \times [p, b, m] = [p, b, n]$ and conceptually, the same batch product as before is computed for every element in the population dimension.

In order to exploit this batched evaluation of populations, the whole population lives in GPU memory in the required tensor format. Next to enabling the population batching, this also alleviates the need to copy data between devices, which reduces latency. These advantages apply as long as the networks are small enough. The larger each network, the more computation is necessary to evaluate it, which reduces the gain from batching multiple networks together. Furthermore, combinations of population size, network size and batch size are limited by the available GPU memory. Despite these shortcomings, with 16 GB GPU memory this framework allows us to experiment at reasonably large scales such as a population of 8k networks with 92k parameters each at a batch size of 64.

4 Experiments

We apply the EA from Sect. 3 to optimize a neural network that classifies the MNIST dataset, which is a standard image classification benchmark with 28×28 pixel grayscale inputs and $d = 10$ classes. The training set contains 50k images, which we split into an actual training set of 45k images and a validation set of 5k images. All reported accuracies during experiments are validation set accuracies. The test set of 10k images is only used in the final experiment that compares the EA to SGD. All experiments have been repeated 15 times with different random seeds. When significance levels are mentioned, they have been obtained by performing a one-sided Mann-Whitney-U-Test between the samples of each experiment. The fitness function to be maximized by the EA is defined as the negative, average cross-entropy

$$-\frac{1}{n} \sum_{i=1}^{n} H\left(p_i, q_i\right) = \frac{1}{nd} \sum_{i=1}^{n} \sum_{j=1}^{d} p_{ij} \log\left(q_{ij}\right), \tag{1}$$

---

[1] A tensor is a multi-dimensional array.

where n is the batch size, $p_{ij} \in \{0, 1\}$ is the ground-truth probability and $q_{ij} \in [0, 1]$ is the predicted probability for the jth class in the ith example. Unless otherwise stated, the following hyperparameters are used for experiments:

$$\begin{aligned}
\text{crossover op.} &= \text{uniform} & p_E &= 0.05 & \lambda &= 1000 & \alpha &= 1.00 \\
\text{sigma adapt.} &= \text{constant} & p_C &= 0.50 & \sigma &= 0.001 \\
\text{batch size} &= 512 & p_M &= 0.45 & \rho &= 0.50
\end{aligned}$$

4.1   Neural Network Description

The neural network we use in all our experiments applies 2×2 max-pooling to its inputs, followed by four fully connected layers with 256, 128, 64 and 10 units respectively. Each layer except for the last one is followed by a ReLU non-linearity. Finally, the softmax function is applied to the network output. In total, this network has 92k parameters that need to be trained.

This network is unable to achieve state-of-the-art results even with SGD training but has been chosen due to the following considerations. We wanted to limit the maximum network parameter count to roughly 100k so that it remains possible to experiment with large populations and batch sizes. However, we also wanted to work with a multi-layer network. We deem this aspect important, as there should be additional difficulty in optimizing deeper networks with more interactions between parameters. To avoid concentrating a large part of the parameters in the network's first layer, we downsample the input. This way, it is possible to have a multi-layer network with a significant number of parameters in all layers. Furthermore, we decided against using convolutional layers as our batched implementation of fully connected layers is more efficient than the convolutional counterpart.

All networks for the EA population are initialized using the Glorot-uniform [7] initialization scheme. Even though Glorot-uniform and other neural network initialization schemes were devised to improved SGD performance, we find that the EA also benefits from them. Furthermore, this allows for a comparison to SGD on even footing.

4.2   Tradeoff Between Batch Size and Accuracy

The EA chooses a batch of training data for each generation and uses it to evaluate the population's fitness. A single fitness evaluation is therefore only a noisy estimate of the true fitness. The smaller the batch size, the noisier this estimate becomes because Eq. 1 averages over fewer cross-entropy loss values. A noisy fitness estimate introduces two problems: A good network may receive a low fitness value and be eliminated during selection or a bad network may receive a high fitness value and survive. The fitness inheritance was introduced by Morse et al. [11] with the intent to counteract this noise and allow effective optimization despite noisy fitness values. However, in preliminary experiments fitness inheritance did not seem to have a positive impact on our results, so we performed a systematic experiment to explore the interaction between batch size, fitness inheritance and the resulting network accuracy. The results can be found in Fig. 1. Three key observations can be made:

First of all, the validation set accuracy is positively correlated with the batch size. This relationship holds for all tested settings of λ and α. This means, using larger batch sizes gives better results. Note that the EA was allowed to run for more generations when the batch size was small, so that all runs could converge. In consequence, it is not possible to compensate the accuracy loss incurred by small batch sizes by allowing the EA to perform more iterations.

Second, the validation set accuracy is also positively correlated with α. Especially for small batch sizes, significant increases in validation accuracy can be observed when increasing α. This is surprising as higher values of α reduce the amount of fitness inheritance. Instead, we find that the fitness inheritance either has a harmful or no effect.

Lastly, increasing the population size λ improves the validation accuracy. This is important but unsurprising as increasing the population size is a known way to counteract noise [2].

4.3 Selective Pressure

Having observed that fitness inheritance does not improve results at small batch sizes, we will now show that instead decreasing the selective pressure helps. The selective pressure influences to what degree fitter individuals are favored over less fit individuals during the selection process. Since small batches produce noisy fitness evaluations, a low selective pressure should be helpful because the EA is less likely to eliminate all good solutions based on inaccurate fitness estimates.

We experiment with different settings of the selection proportion ρ, which determines what percentage of the population ordered by fitness is eligible for reproduction. During selection, parents are drawn uniformly at random from this group. Low selection proportions (low values of ρ) lead to high selective pressure because parents are drawn from a smaller group of individuals with high (apparent) fitness. Therefore, we expect high values of ρ to work better with small batches.

Figure 2 shows results for increasing values of ρ at two different batch sizes and two different population sizes. Generally speaking, increasing ρ increases the validation accuracy (up to a certain degree). For a specific ρ it is unfortunately not possible to compare validation accuracies across the four scenarios, because batch size and population size are influencing factors as well. Instead, we treat the relative difference in validation accuracies going from $\rho = 0.1$ to $\rho = 0.2$ as a proxy. Table 1 confirms that decreasing the selective pressure (by increasing ρ) has a positive influence on the validation accuracy.

4.4 Crossover and Mutation Operators

While the previous experiments explored the influence of limited evaluation, another significant factor for good performance are crossover and mutation

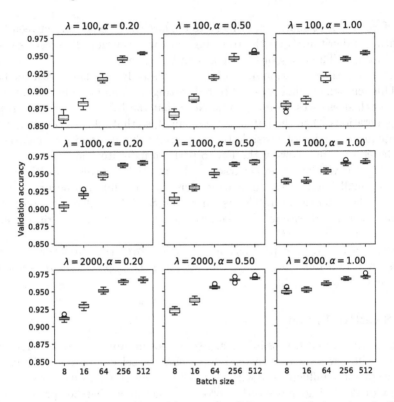

Fig. 1. Validation accuracies of 15 EA runs for different population sizes λ, fitness inheritance strengths α and batch sizes. Looking at the grid of figures, λ increases from top to bottom, while α increases from left to right. A box extends from the lower to upper quartile values of the data, with a line at the median and whiskers that show the range of the data.

Table 1. Relative improvement in validation accuracy when increasing the selection proportion from $\rho = 0.1$ to $\rho = 0.2$ in four different scenarios. Since large population sizes are also an effective countermeasure against noise, the relative improvement decreases with increasing population sizes. The fitness noise column only depends on batch size and is included to highlight the correlation between noise and relative improvement.

Batch size	Fitness noise	Population size	Relative improvement
8	High	100	2.26%
8	High	1000	1.57%
512	Low	100	0.49%
512	Low	1000	0.34%

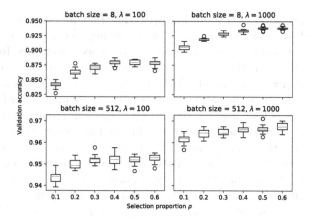

Fig. 2. Validation accuracies of 15 EA runs for different population sizes λ, batch sizes and selection proportions ρ. The first row of figures shows results for small batch sizes, while the second row shows results for large batch sizes.

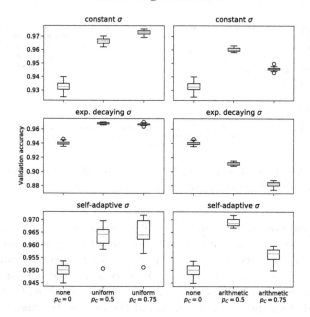

Fig. 3. Validation accuracies of 15 EA runs with different levels of crossover p_C, crossover operators and mutation strength σ adaptation schemes. The left column shows results using uniform crossover, while arithmetic crossover is employed for the right column.

operators that match the optimization problem. Neural networks in particular have problematic redundancy in their search space: Nodes in the network can be reordered without changing the network connectivity. This means, there are multiple equivalent parameter vectors that represent the same function mapping.

Designing crossover and mutation operators that are specifically equipped to deal with these problems seems like a promising research direction, but for now we want to establish baselines with commonly used operators. In particular, these are uniform and arithmetic crossover as well as random normal mutation. It is not obvious if crossover is helpful for optimizing neural networks as there is no clear compositionality in the parameter space. There are many interdependencies between parameters that might be destroyed, e.g. when random parameters are replaced by those from another network during uniform crossover. Therefore, we not only want to compare the uniform and arithmetic crossover operators among themselves, but also test if crossover leads to improvements at all. This can be achieved by varying the EA hyperparameter p_C, which controls the percentage of offspring that are created by the crossover operator. On the other hand, random normal mutation intuitively performs the role of a local search but its usefulness significantly depends on the choice of the mutation strength σ. Therefore, we compare three different adaptation schemes: constant, exponential decay and self-adaptation.

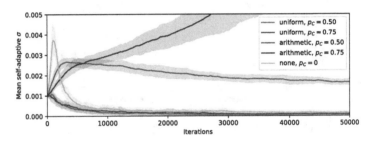

Fig. 4. Population mean of σ from 15 EA runs with self-adaptation turned on. The shaded areas indicate one standard deviation around the mean.

Since crossover operators might need different mutation strengths to operate optimally, we test all combinations and show results in Fig. 3. Using crossover ($p_C > 0$) always results in significantly ($p < 0.01$) higher validation accuracy than not using crossover ($p_C = 0$), except for the case of arithmetic crossover with exponential decay. The reason for this is likely, that arithmetic crossover needs high mutation strengths but the exponential decay decreases σ too fast. This becomes evident when examining the mutation strengths chosen by self-adaptation in Fig. 4. Compared to uniform crossover, the self-adaptation drives σ to much higher values when arithmetic crossover is used. Overall, both crossover operators work well under different circumstances. Uniform crossover at $p_C = 0.75$ with constant σ achieves the highest median validation accuracy of 97.3%, followed by arithmetic crossover at $p_C = 0.5$ with self-adaptive σ at 96.9% validation accuracy. When using uniform crossover at $p_C = 0.75$, a constant mutation strength works significantly ($p < 0.01$) better than the other adaptation schemes. On the other hand, for arithmetic crossover at $p_C = 0.5$, the self-adaptive mutation strength performs significantly ($p < 0.01$) better than the other two tested adaptation schemes. The main drawback of the self-adaptive mutation strength is the additional randomness that leads to high variance in the training results.

4.5   Comparison to SGD

Informed by the other experiments, we want to run the EA with advantageous hyperparameter settings and compare its test set performance to the Adam optimizer. Most importantly, we use a large population, large batch size, no fitness inheritance, and offspring are created by uniform crossover in 75% of all cases:

$$\text{crossover op.} = \text{uniform} \quad p_E = 0.05 \quad \lambda = 2000 \quad \alpha = 1.00$$
$$\text{sigma adapt.} = \text{constant} \quad p_C = 0.75 \quad \sigma = 0.001$$
$$\text{batch size} = 1024 \quad p_M = 0.20 \quad \rho = 0.50$$

Median test accuracies over 15 repetitions are 97.6% for the EA and 98.0% for Adam. Adam still significantly ($p < 0.01$) beats EA performance, but the difference in final test accuracy is rather small. However, training with Adam progresses about 10 times faster so it would be wrong to claim that EAs are competitive for neural network training. Yet, this work is another piece of evidence that EAs have potential for applications in this domain.

5   Conclusion

Efficient batch fitness evaluation of a population of neural networks on GPUs made it feasible to perform extensive experiments with the LEEA. While the idea of using very small batches for fitness evaluation is appealing for computational cost reasons, we find that it comes with the drawback of significantly lower accuracy than with larger batches. Furthermore, the fitness inheritance that is supposed to offset such drawbacks actually has a detrimental effect in our experiments. Instead, we propose to use low selective pressure as an alternative.

We compare uniform and arithmetic crossover in combination with different mutation strength adaptation schemes. Surprisingly, uniform crossover works best among all tested combinations even though it is counter-intuitive that randomly replacing parts of a network's parameters with those of another network is helpful.

Finally, we train a network of 92k parameters on MNIST using an EA and reach an average test accuracy of 97.6%. SGD still achieves higher accuracy at 98% and is remarkably more efficient in doing so. However, having demonstrated that EAs are able to optimize large neural networks, future work may focus on the application to areas such as neuroevolution where EAs may have a bigger edge.

References

1. Baioletti, M., Di Bari, G., Poggioni, V., Tracolli, M.: Can differential evolution be an efficient engine to optimize neural networks? In: Nicosia, G., Pardalos, P., Giuffrida, G., Umeton, R. (eds.) MOD 2017. LNCS, vol. 10710, pp. 401–413. Springer, Cham (2018). https://doi.org/10.1007/978-3-319-72926-8_33
2. Beyer, H.: Evolutionary algorithms in noisy environments: theoretical issues and guidelines for practice. In: Computer Methods in Applied Mechanics and Engineering, pp. 239–267 (1998)
3. Das, S., Mullick, S.S., Suganthan, P.: Recent advances in differential evolution: an updated survey. Swarm Evol. Comput. **27**(Complete), 1–30 (2016). https://doi.org/10.1016/j.swevo.2016.01.004
4. Desell, T.: Large scale evolution of convolutional neural networks using volunteer computing. In: Proceedings of the Genetic and Evolutionary Computation Conference Companion (GECCO 2017), pp. 127–128. ACM, New York (2017). https://doi.org/10.1145/3067695.3076002
5. Floreano, D., Dürr, P., Mattiussi, C.: Neuroevolution: from architectures to learning. Evol. Intell. **1**(1), 47–62 (2008). https://doi.org/10.1007/s12065-007-0002-4
6. García-Pedrajas, N., Ortiz-Boyer, D., Hervás-Martínez, C.: An alternative approach for neural network evolution with a genetic algorithm: crossover by combinatorial optimization. Neural Netw. **19**(4), 514–528 (2006). https://doi.org/10.1016/j.neunet.2005.08.014, http://www.sciencedirect.com/science/article/pii/S0893608005002297
7. Glorot, X., Bengio, Y.: Understanding the difficulty of training deep feedforward neural networks. In: Teh, Y.W., Titterington, M. (eds.) Proceedings of the Thirteenth International Conference on Artificial Intelligence and Statistics. Proceedings of Machine Learning Research. PMLR, vol. 9, pp. 249–256, Chia Laguna Resort, Sardinia, Italy, 13–15 May 2010. http://proceedings.mlr.press/v9/glorot10a.html
8. Ioffe, S., Szegedy, C.: Batch normalization: accelerating deep network training by reducing internal covariate shift. In: Proceedings of the 32nd International Conference on Machine Learning (ICML 2015), Lille, France, pp. 448–456 (2015)
9. Kingma, D.P., Ba, J.: Adam: a method for stochastic optimization. In: The International Conference on Learning Representations (ICLR 2015), December 2015
10. Liu, H., Simonyan, K., Vinyals, O., Fernando, C., Kavukcuoglu, K.: Hierarchical representations for efficient architecture search. In: International Conference on Learning Representations (ICML 2018) abs/1711.00436 (2018). http://arxiv.org/abs/1711.00436
11. Morse, G., Stanley, K.O.: Simple evolutionary optimization can rival stochastic gradient descent in neural networks. In: Proceedings of the Genetic and Evolutionary Computation Conference (GECCO 2016), pp. 477–484. ACM, New York (2016). https://doi.org/10.1145/2908812.2908916
12. Real, E., et al.: Large-scale evolution of image classifiers. In: Proceedings of the 34th International Conference on Machine Learning (ICML 2017) (2017). https://arxiv.org/abs/1703.01041
13. Stanley, K.O., D'Ambrosio, D.B., Gauci, J.: A hypercube-based encoding for evolving large-scale neural networks. Artif. Life **15**(2), 185–212 (2009). https://doi.org/10.1162/artl.2009.15.2.15202
14. Thierens, D.: Non-redundant genetic coding of neural networks. In: Proceedings of IEEE International Conference on Evolutionary Computation, pp. 571–575, May 1996. https://doi.org/10.1109/ICEC.1996.542662

15. Yaman, A., Mocanu, D.C., Iacca, G., Fletcher, G., Pechenizkiy, M.: Limited evaluation cooperative co-evolutionary differential evolution for large-scale neuroevolution. In: Genetic and Evolutionary Computation Conference (GECCO 2018) (2018)
16. Zhang, X., Clune, J., Stanley, K.O.: On the relationship between the OpenAI evolution strategy and stochastic gradient descent. CoRR abs/1712.06564 (2017). http://arxiv.org/abs/1712.06564

Understanding NLP Neural Networks
by the Texts They Generate

Mihai Pomarlan$^{(\boxtimes)}$ and John Bateman

University of Bremen, Bremen, Germany
`pomarlan@uni-bremen.de`

Abstract. Recurrent neural networks have proven useful in natural language processing. For example, they can be trained to predict, and even generate plausible text with few or no spelling and syntax errors. However, it is not clear what grammar a network has learned, or how it keeps track of the syntactic structure of its input. In this paper, we present a new method to extract a finite state machine from a recurrent neural network. A FSM is in principle a more interpretable representation of a grammar than a neural net would be, however the extracted FSMs for realistic neural networks will also be large. Therefore, we also look at ways to group the states and paths through the extracted FSM so as to get a smaller, easier to understand model of the neural network. To illustrate our methods, we use them to investigate how a neural network learns noun-verb agreement from a simple grammar where relative clauses may appear between noun and verb.

Keywords: Recurrent neural networks · Natural language processing
Interpretability

1 Introduction

Neural networks have found uses in a wide variety of domains and are one of the engines of the current ML/AI boom. They can learn complex patterns from real-world noisy data, and perform comparably or better than rival approaches in several applications. However, they are also "opaque": functionality is usually distributed among the connections in a network, making it difficult to interpret what the network has actually learned and how it produces its outputs.

One of the application domains for neural networks is NLP. A recurrent neural network is fed a text (word by word or character by character), and the output may be, e.g., an estimation of the text's sentiment, a translation into a different language, or a probability distribution for what the next word/character will be. The latter type of network is referred to as a "language model", and is

J. Bateman—This work was partially funded by Deutsche Forschungsgemeinschaft (DFG) through the Collaborative Research Center 1320, EASE.

© Springer Nature Switzerland AG 2018
F. Trollmann and A.-Y. Turhan (Eds.): KI 2018, LNAI 11117, pp. 284–296, 2018.
https://doi.org/10.1007/978-3-030-00111-7_24

what we will focus in this paper. Recurrent neural networks trained as language models can also generate text, by choosing the next word/character based on the network's output and feeding it back to the network. They have been shown to generate "plausible" text [11]: meaningless, but syntactically correct. Some neurons in the network turn out to have interpretable functions [12], but in general it is not clear what the learned grammar is.

There are two broad directions to seeking interpretations of a neural network. Recent approaches have mostly focused on finding statistical patterns among neuron activations [12–14]. In this paper however we pursue an older line of research, which is about constructing a (finite state) automaton that approximates the behavior of the network. Grammars can be defined and analyzed in terms of the automata that recognize them, so this representation should be more interpretable than the network itself and, unlike the statistical approaches, produces a (regular) grammar that approximates the network's behavior.

Previous research into grammar inference from neural networks is as old as artificial recurrent neural networks themselves [7], and there are recent examples as well [5]. However, previously published methods have focused on small networks and simple grammars, and do not seem to scale to real-life applications. Also, activation levels of neurons are treated as coordinates in a vector space, and then points from this space, or from a projection to a lower dimension space via tSNE, are clustered using Euclidean distance metrics.

Our method instead consists in constructing a prefix tree automaton from the set of training strings, and merging states in this automaton based on a similarity metric defined by the network's behavior: the most likely suffix (i.e. generated text) from a state. Our method is applicable to any recurrent network architecture, but does need the network to be trained as a language model so that its outputs can be fed back to itself. In future work we will look at an extension to networks trained for other purposes, using a technique from [1]: train a classifier to estimate the next likely word/character based on the network state.

Because previous research into neural grammar inference has used small networks and grammars as examples, it hasn't considered another problem: a model should also be "simple" to be interpretable [16]. A neural network deployed for a realistic application may have a grammar containing thousands of states. It will be very difficult to understand how the network captures syntactic patterns just by looking at the state transition graph of an automaton extracted from it.

We therefore also investigate how to group states and transitions in the automaton so as to produce a simpler model. By necessity, this simpler model will lose information compared to the state machine, and is only intended to capture how a particular syntactic pattern is modelled in the automaton, and hence the network. For our work here, we have chosen noun-verb number agreement as an example, where there are intervening clauses between noun and verb.

Our contributions are then as follows:

– a method to extract a finite state automaton from a recurrent neural network language model, exemplified on character-level LSTM networks

- evaluation of how well the automaton matches the network behavior on new text
- using the automaton to interpret how a language model network understands a particular syntactic pattern.

2   Background: LSTMs and Language Models

Recurrent neural networks have a structure in which previous hidden or output layer activations are fed back as inputs, which allows the network to have a memory. However, it was observed that the error gradient while training simple recurrent networks tends to either explode or vanish. "Long Short-Time Memory", or **LSTM**, were introduced to avoid this problem [8], which they achieve by enforcing a constant error flow through special units. LSTMs can learn very long time dependencies.

A **language model** is some procedure which, when given an input sequence of words or characters, returns a probability distribution on what the next word/character will be. In this paper, we are interested in character-level language models implemented via LSTM networks. The networks themselves are implemented in the Python Keras package, with the TensorFlow backend; the stateful = False flag is used.

To train our language model network, we collect training pairs of (input sequence, output character) from a corpus of text by sliding a window of constant length over each line in the corpus. Padding is added on the left if necessary so that all input sequences have the same length, len_{seq}. We will refer to a sequence of len_{seq} characters as a **prefix**. The output character in a training pair is the next character appearing in the text. Characters, both at the input and output, are encoded in the "one-hot" method.

We will refer to the activation levels of the neurons in the network as the **network activation**, and note that it completely determines the output, and is completely determined by the prefix that was fed into the network. Therefore, we will represent the network activation by the prefix that caused it, rather than as a vector of neuron activation levels. Since it is trivial to extract a prefix automaton from a training text, this offers a simple way to put network activations in correspondence with the states of a prefix automaton. What is not trivial is to further reduce this prefix automaton by merging states in it; we do this based on the behavior of the neural network.

A language model can be used to generate new text. Let p_t be a prefix, after which the network produces an output y_t. One then creates a new prefix $p_{t+1} = p_t[1:] + c_{t+1}$, where $p_t[1:]$ are the last $len_{seq} - 1$ characters from p_t, and c_{t+1} is selected based on the probability distribution y_t. Feeding the p_{t+1} prefix through the network results in a new activation and an output y_{t+1}, and the procedure is repeated as needed to complete the generation of a desired length of text. We refer to text generated in this manner from a prefix p as a **suffix** for p. We will somewhat abuse terminology and define the **most likely suffix** of length l to be a sequence of l characters obtained by at every step selecting the most likely c_{t+1}, when given a distribution y_t (so this is a "greedy", rather than correct, way to search for the most likely suffix).

In general, one can compute the probability of a suffix being generated from a network activation. Let p_t be the prefix that caused the activation, and let the suffix be a sequence $c_0 c_1 \ldots$. Then the probability of the suffix is the product of the probabilities of picking its component characters: $P(c_0|p_t) * P(c_1|p_t[1:], c_0) * \ldots$. An intuitive notion of similarity of two activations is that they deem the same set of suffixes as likely.

3 Extracting a Finite State Machine

Our extraction procedure is conceptually similar to the algorithm for learning a regular language from a stochastic sample presented in [3]: construct a prefix automaton from the network training text, then merge states in it based on their behavior. This implies a tractable upper bound on the number of states in the automaton: at most, the number of distinct states will be the number of distinct prefixes in the text, itself upper bounded by the number of character tokens.

Note, a state in the prefix automaton is a prefix, and a prefix determines a network activation. We can then ask whether two network activations behave the same: if they tend to predict the same characters as we feed new characters to the network, we will say the prefixes corresponding to the similar network activations are the same state in the final extracted automaton.

We approximate this similarity criterion with the following: two network activations, caused by p_t and p_t' respectively, are similar if they produce the same most likely suffix. Algorithm 1 shows the pseudocode for how to obtain the most likely suffix of length "len" when given a neural network "model" and a "prefix". Algorithm 2 gives the pseudocode for how to construct a finite state automaton to approximate the behavior of a neural network "model" on a training text "trainText", where "len" gives the length of the most likely suffixes used for the similarity comparison. The extracted automaton fsm is empty at the start; then for every prefix of every line in the training text we generate the most likely suffix. If no state corresponding to that suffix is in fsm yet, we add it. A transition between two states is added when there are prefixes p, p' generating each state such that $p = p'[1:] + c$ where c is a character. Note that the automaton produced by the method will be nondeterministic. (Here "+" means string concatenation; $[-1]$ means last element, $[1:]$ is all elements except the first.)

In our work, we have set the "len" parameter to equal len_{seq}, which for the networks we trained was 80 and 100. We have observed that, despite there being many possible sequences of 80 or 100 characters, the most likely suffixes were few, and our similarity metric results in non-trivial reductions in size from the prefix automaton to the final extracted one. For example, from a network trained on a text with 60000 distinct prefixes, we extracted an automaton with about 4000 states. Further, the number of automaton states increases sublinearly with the number of prefixes considered (see Sect. 5.2). This gives us confidence that a well trained network will tend to produce only a few most likely suffixes.

Algorithm 1. mlSuffix(model, prefix, len)

```
suffix ← ""
for k upto len do
    c ← argmax(predict(model, prefix))
    suffix ← suffix + c
    prefix ← prefix[1:] + c
end for
return suffix
```

Algorithm 2. getFSM(model, trainText, len)

```
fsm ← {"": {}}
for line in trainText do
    oldState ← ""
    oldPrefix ← ""
    for prefix in line do
        mlSuffix ← mlSuffix(model, prefix, len)
        if mlSuffix not in fsm then
            fsm[mlSuffix] ← {}
        end if
        c ← prefix[-1]
        fsm[oldState][c] ← fsm[oldState][c] ∪ mlSuffix
        oldState ← mlSuffix
        oldPrefix ← prefix
    end for
end for
return fsm
```

3.1 Conceptual Comparison with Previous Approaches

The method in [7] partitions a vector space where the points are network activations, and does not scale well. Even for an extremely coarse partitioning where each neuron gets replaced with a bit, there are still 2^n possible states for a network with n neurons to be in, and neural nets for NLP typically have hundreds of neurons or more. In our attempt at implementing this method, we didn't observe that the set of states accessible from the start states is significantly smaller than 2^n, and we expect this method will not work for realistic applications.

To judge similarity of network activations, methods such as in [5] use Euclidean distance either in a space where the points are network activations, or a lower dimensional projection obtained with tSNE or PCA. These methods have been used to extract only small automata however, and we are unsure how they would scale for more complex ones. In particular, it is not clear to us why Euclidean distance should be a good metric of similarity between network activations, because neural networks contain nonlinearities and therefore points that are close, under a Euclidean metric, may in fact correspond to network activations with very different behaviors.

Our approach instead actually considers the network's behavior to define a locality-sensitive hashing: network activations, represented by prefixes, are hashed to bins represented by their most likely suffixes. Comparing similarity is then linear in the prefix size, which is makes it easier to test and extend our extracted automata if needed. Extending automata obtained by clustering will be quadratic in the number of network activations considered by the clustering: in high dimension spaces, nearest neighbor query structure performance degrades back to quadratic; if instead one uses a tSNE projection, one needs to remake the tSNE model when adding new points.

4   Interpreting the State Machine

Previous investigations into inferring regular grammars from neural networks [5, 7] have looked at very simple grammars, for which recognizer automata can be comprehended "at a glance". It is more likely however that the grammar learned by a more realistic language model network will require thousands of states, and therefore one needs some way of simplifying the automaton further. Interpretable models are simple models [16].

Here we are interested in using the extracted automaton to understand how a neural network captures a particular syntactic pattern (noun-verb number agreement in our case). We show how even a large automaton can be used to obtain an understandable model of how a neural network implements the memory needed to track that syntactic pattern.

Our method proceeds by first **marking** states in the extracted automaton. What is significant to mark, and what markers are available, will depend on the syntactic pattern one wishes to investigate in the automaton. It's possible for a state to have multiple markings, though, depending on their meaning, this may indicate an ambiguity or error, either in the network or the extracted automaton. An **unmarked path** is one that may begin or end at a marked state, but passes through no marked state in between.

Syntactic patterns often require something like a memory to track, so we further define **popping paths** as unmarked paths which begin with one of a set of sequences (typically, sequences related to why states get marked; for example, if a state is marked because suffixes beginning with verbs are likely, then popping paths from that state begin with a verb). **Pushing paths** are unmarked paths that are not popping paths. The significance is the following: in a marked state, the network expects a certain event to happen. A popping path proceeds from that state by first producing the expected event; a pushing path doesn't, so the network must somehow remember that the event is still expected to occur.

We will next show how to apply the above methodology to look for how memory is implemented in the automaton (and hence the network). As an illustration, we use number agreement between nouns and verbs in a sentence. The number of the noun determines what number the verb should have: e.g. "the cow grazes" and "the cows graze" are correct, but "the cow graze" is not. Relative clauses may appear between the noun and verb however (e.g., "the cow, that the

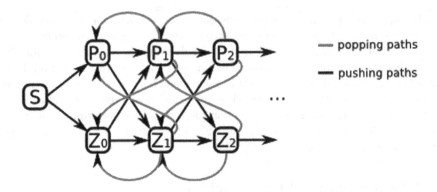

Fig. 1. A potential memory structure: levels of marked states.

dog sees, grazes"), so the network must somehow remember the noun number while it reads the relative clause, which may have its own noun-verb pair and itself contain another relative clause.

In our case, we mark a state in the automaton if its prefix, when fed to the network, results in a network activation from which suffixes that begin with verbs are likely. Essentially, marked states in our example are states in which the network expects a verb (or a sequence of verbs) to follow.

We can then use marked states and the pushing/popping paths between them to define memory structures and look for them in the extracted automaton. One such memory structure is given in Fig. 1. In this structure, all marked states reachable from the start are assigned to a level 0: they correspond to states where the noun of the main clause has been read and a verb is expected: "P" for plural, "Z" for a singular verb. Marked states reachable via pushing paths from level 0 states form the level 1 of marked states; these are states where a noun was read, then a relative clause began and its noun was read, and now the verb in the relative clause is expected. Analogously one can define levels 2 and onwards for marked states. Of course, a popping path from a level k marked state should reach a level k − 1 marked state.

Another possible structure, but one limited to only remembering three verb numbers, is shown in Fig. 2. In this case, states are marked depending on what sequences of three verbs are likely; e.g., a state from which a singular, then two plural verbs are likely would be marked "ZPP". The figure shows the correct transitions via pushing paths between sets of marked states, such that sequences of verbs of length 3 can be remembered. For example, a transition from a "PPP" to a "ZPP" state means the network first expected a sequence of three plural verbs, then encountered a singular noun, and now expects a sequence of a singular verb and two plural verbs.

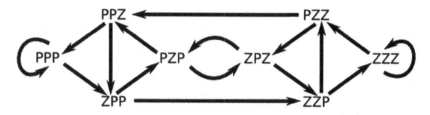

Fig. 2. Another memory structure: remembers sequences of three verb numbers (all transitions are via pushing paths).

5 Evaluation

5.1 Preamble: Grammar and Network Training

To have a better level of control over the complexity of the training and test strings, we define the context free grammar S, given in the listing below. Uppercase names are non-terminal symbols, except for VBZ and VBP. We define the language $S(n)$ as the set of strings S can produce using the REL symbol exactly n times. Every $S(n)$ language is finite, therefore regular and describable by a finite state machine. $S(0)$ contains 60 strings. $S(n+1)$ contains 1800 times more strings than $S(n)$.

```
S  -> SP  |  SZ
SP  -> [ADJ]  NNP  [REL]  VBP
SZ  -> [ADJ]  NNZ  [REL]  VBZ
REL  -> ,  INT  R  ,
R  -> RP  |  RZ
RP  -> [ADJ]  NNP  [REL]  VBP  [ADV]
RZ  -> [ADJ]  NNZ  [REL]  VBZ  [ADV]
ADJ  -> red  |  big  |  spotted  |  cheerful  |  secret
ADV  -> today  |  here  |  there  |  now  |  later
INT  -> that  |  which  |  whom  |  where  |  why
NNP  -> cats  |  dogs  |  magi  |  geese  |  cows
NNZ  -> cat  |  dog  |  magus  |  goose  |  cow
```

We train an LSTM network N1 on a sample containing all the $S(0)$ strings, together with a random collection of 1000 strings from $S(1)$. We train an LSTM network N2 on a sample containing all the $S(0)$ strings, together with a random collection of 1000 strings from $S(1)$ and 1000 strings from $S(2)$. Training for both is done over 150 epochs. The len_{seq} parameter is 80 for N1, and 100 for N2. Training is done as described in Sect. 2. Both N1 and N2 have two LSTM layers of 64 cells each and a dense output layer, with dropout layers in between (dropout set to 0.2).

5.2 Constructing the Finite State Machine

Figure 3 shows how the extracted automata grow as more of the training text is processed by Algorithm 2. While the number of unique prefixes increases steadily

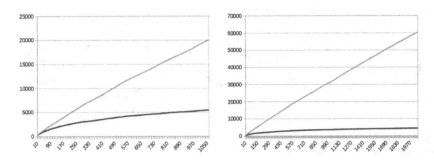

Fig. 3. Unique prefixes (red) and state count of extracted automaton (blue) vs. number of lines of training text. Left: plot for N1 (trained on strings from $S(1)$). Right: plot for N2 (trained on strings from $S(2)$ and $S(1)$).

with the size of the text, the number of states in the automaton increases much more slowly and is near-constant by the end of the extraction process. Final state counts: 5454 states for N1, 4450 states for N2.

In the extracted automata, a transition (from a given source state) is a pair (c, D) containing a character c and a set of destination states D. A transition is deterministic if its D has size 1. For the automata extracted for N1 and N2 respectively, 96% and 89% of transitions are deterministic. The largest destination set for the N2 automaton contains 28 states.

5.3   Comparing Network Behavior to the Extracted Automaton

Next, we want to ascertain how good of a "map" the extracted automata are for their corresponding neural networks. We evaluate this by generating all-new evaluation text. For N1, we generate 200 new sentences in $S(1)$. For N2, we generate 200 new sentences in $S(1)$ and 400 new sentences in $S(2)$.

We first look at how well the networks have learned the target grammars. To observe what the networks do, we feed a sequence of len_{seq} characters (a "prefix", as defined in Sect. 2) from the evaluation text to the network, and see what most likely suffix the network predicts; in particular, we look at whether a verb is predicted to follow at appropriate locations, and if so whether its number is grammatically correct. We observe that N1 is completely accurate on the new text, while N2 mispredicts only 2 verbs in the entire testing corpus. This means the most likely suffixes produced by the networks are not trivial, and appropriate according to the target grammar.

We then look at whether the extracted automata contain "enough" states to account for the network activations caused by new prefixes in the evaluation texts. For each new prefix in the evaluation text, we compute the most likely suffix as predicted by a network using Algorithm 1, and then check whether that suffix already has a state in the extracted automaton by Algorithm 2. We find that less than one in ten new prefixes from the evaluation texts do not have corresponding states in the automata for N1 and N2.

Next, we check whether changes in network activation as we feed consecutive prefixes from the evaluation text match to a transition in the extracted automaton. Ie., for any index b in the evaluation text, given prefixes $p_1 = p[b : b+len_{seq}]$ and $p_2 = p[b+1 : b+1+len_{seq}]$ such that p_1 and p_2 have matching states s_1, s_2 in the extracted automaton, is there a transition from s_1 for character $p[b+len_{seq}]$ whose consecutive prefix pairs fail this s_2. For the automata extracted from N1 and N2, only about 3% of consecutive prefix pairs fail this test.

5.4   Interpreting the Neural Networks

We look for the memory structures described in Sect. 4 in the extracted automata to explain how the trained networks keep track of noun-verb agreement.

We observe that N1 can be explained by the multi-level marked state structure in Fig. 1. We construct the levels of marked states as described in Sect. 4 based on reachability via pushing unmarked paths. There are 49 level-0 states corresponding to main clause verbs and 238 level-1 states corresponding to verbs in the relative clause. Level-0 states can be split based on the verb number they expect in the main clause into 24 "Z" states and 25 "P" states. Level-1 states can further be split based on the verb they expect in the relative clause and the marking of the level-0 states they are reachable from. This split produces 48 "PZ" states (expect a plural verb in the relative clause, only reachable from level-0 "Z" states), 89 "ZZ" states, 46 "PP" states, and 55 "ZP" states. The level-1 states therefore implement a memory of sorts, since a particular level-1 state is reachable only from states of a consistent marking from level 0.

The situation for N2 is different: almost all marked states belong to level 0, of states reachable from the start state via unmarked paths. We then look for the memory structure from Fig. 2. We mark states based on the numbers of the verb triple they expect, and ascertain the connectivity between these sets by Monte Carlo graph traversal: from each marked state, we generate a set of 2000 pushing paths. We then compute "path densities": ratios of how many of the outgoing paths from a set of marked states go to each other marked set.

The graph of paths between marked sets is shown in Fig. 4, where arrow thickness corresponds to path density, red arrows are erroneous connections, and grayed arrows are missing connections. The resulting graph is fairly close to the graph shown in Fig. 2. Some edges are missing because the PZP and ZZP states were only observed near the end of training strings, and so have no pushing paths (were never used to store verbs). The spurious paths, such as the unwanted pushing paths from PZZ to PPP, may be an artifact of our locality-sensitive hashing being too permissive a measure of state similarity.

However, we have also looked at whether we can generate strings on which N2 would mispredict verb numbers, based on the spurious paths observed in the automaton. Note that N2 is very accurate on the testing data: from 200 randomly selected sentences from $S(1)$ and 400 randomly selected sentences from $S(2)$, it only mispredicts 2 verb numbers. Nevertheless, we are able to use the extracted automaton to generate a set of sentences on which N2 makes mistakes.

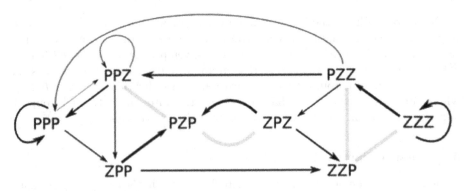

Fig. 4. Pushing path densities between signature subsets for the N2 automaton. Line thickness indicates pushing path density. Grayed lines indicate no pushing path between the subsets; red lines indicate spurious paths. (Color figure online)

We selected an automaton state in the PZZ signature set, and we looked at the subgraph formed by pushing paths from this state to states in PPP. We enumerate strings from this subgraph, resulting in a set of 451 strings. We then feed each of these strings through N2 and observe the predicted sequence of verb numbers. For 24 of the strings, the predicted sequence is incorrect, which suggests, while most of the spurious paths in the automaton are actually artifacts of our permissive state comparison, the automaton is nevertheless a much better way to find difficult strings for the network than random search would be.

6   Related Work

One approach to interpret neural networks uses them in grammar inference. In [7], a simple technique is presented which partitions the continuous state space of a network into discrete "bins". We discuss this technique also in Sect. 3. Very recently, [5] present a technique based on K-means clustering of activation state vectors, but tested it for very simple grammars.

Other research into understanding recurrent networks has used statistical approaches. In [13], networks where cells correspond to dimensions in some word/sentence embedding are visualized to discover patterns of negation and compositionality. Salience is defined as the impact of a cell on the network's final decision. A method to analyze a network via representation erasure is presented in [14]. The method consists in observing what changes in the state or output of a network if features such as word vector representation dimensions, input words, or hidden units are removed. An extensive error analysis for character-level language model LSTMs vs ngram models is presented in [12], which also tracks activation levels for neurons as a sequence is fed into the network. More recent surveys on visualization tools are found in [4,9]. Examples of such tools for recurrent networks are LSTMVis [18] and RNNVis [17], which use Euclidean distance to cluster network activations over many instances of inputs.

The ability of different network architectures and training regimes to capture grammatical aspects, in particular noun-verb agreement, has been investigated in [15]. The paper uses word-level models trained on a corpus of text obtained from wikipedia, and presents an empirical study of the ability of networks to capture grammatical patterns. Another approach to measure the ability of a sentence representation (such as bag of words or LSTM state) to capture grammatical aspects is given in [1], where a representation is deemed good if it is possible to train accurate classifiers for the grammatical aspect in question.

It has been claimed that LSTMs can learn simple context-free and context-sensitive $(a^n b^n c^n)$ grammars [6]. Other neural architectures, augmented with stacks, have also been proposed [10]. We will look at extracting more complex automata from such architectures in the future.

It has been shown that positive samples alone are insufficient to learn regular grammars, but stochastic samples can compensate for a lack of negative samples [2], and polynomial time algorithms to learn a regular grammar from stochastic samples are known [3]; the algorithm also constructs a prefix tree automaton and merges states wherever it can, similar to our Algorithm 2; we however merge states in the prefix tree based on how the neural network behaves, whereas in [3] merging is based on the language sample's statistical properties.

7   Conclusions and Future Work

We have presented a method to extract a finite state machine from a recurrent neural network trained as a language model, in order to explain the network. Our method uses the most likely suffix (i.e. generated text) as a criterion for similarity between network activations, rather than euclidean distance between neuron activation values. An upper bound on the extracted automaton state count is the number of character tokens in the training text. We have tested the method on two networks of realistic size for NLP applications, trained on grammars for which recognizing automata would require a few hundred states.

We observe that for a well trained network, the set of most likely suffixes turns out to be much smaller than the number of characters in the training text, which encourages us to think the method will produce reasonably sized automata even for networks trained on enormous text corpora. However the most likely suffix appears to be a rather permissive similarity metric; an indication of this is the presence of nondeterministic transitions in the extracted automata. We will look at ways to enforce determinism in the future.

The extracted automata have good coverage of network behavior on new text as well: the automata are rich enough to capture distinctions between when the network expects certain sequences to follow (verbs in our example), and when not. Changes in network activation when exposed to new text can be mapped most of the time to states and transitions in the automaton.

We defined sets of marked states and looked at the paths between them to discover how the networks implement memory for syntactic features (noun numbers in our example). Our extracted automata can suggest problematic strings even when the network appears very accurate on a random sample of strings.

The method as presented here is only applicable to language models/sequence predictors, whose output can be used to generate the next timestep input. We will look at adopting a technique from existing literature, which replaces the output layer of a recurrent network with a classifier trained to produce a probability distribution for the next word/character based on the recurrent network state.

References

1. Adi, Y., Kermany, E., Belinkov, Y., Lavi, O., Goldberg, Y.: Fine-grained analysis of sentence embeddings using auxiliary prediction tasks. CoRR abs/1608.04207 (2016)
2. Angluin, D.: Identifying languages from stochastic examples. Technical report, YALEU/DCS/RR-614, Yale University, Department of Computer Science, New Haven, CT (1988)
3. Carrasco, R.C., Oncina, J.: Learning deterministic regular grammars from stochastic samples in polynomial time. ITA **33**(1), 1–20 (1999)
4. Choo, J., Liu, S.: Visual analytics for explainable deep learning. CoRR abs/1804.02527 (2018)
5. Cohen, M., Caciularu, A., Rejwan, I., Berant, J.: Inducing regular grammars using recurrent neural networks. CoRR abs/1710.10453 (2017)
6. Gers, F.A., Schmidhuber, E.: LSTM recurrent networks learn simple context-free and context-sensitive languages. Trans. Neural Netw. **12**(6), 1333–1340 (2001)
7. Giles, C.L., Miller, C.B., Chen, D., Sun, G.Z., Chen, H.H., Lee, Y.C.: Extracting and learning an unknown grammar with recurrent neural networks. In: Proceedings of the 4th International Conference on Neural Information Processing Systems. . NIPS 1991, pp. 317–324. Morgan Kaufmann Publishers Inc., San Francisco (1991)
8. Hochreiter, S., Schmidhuber, J.: Long short-term memory. Neural Comput. **9**(8), 1735–1780 (1997)
9. Hohman, F., Kahng, M., Pienta, R., Chau, D.H.: Visual analytics in deep learning: an interrogative survey for the next frontiers. CoRR abs/1801.06889 (2018)
10. Joulin, A., Mikolov, T.: Inferring algorithmic patterns with stack-augmented recurrent nets. In: Cortes, C., Lawrence, N.D., Lee, D.D., Sugiyama, M., Garnett, R. (eds.) NIPS, pp. 190–198 (2015)
11. Karpathy, A.: The unreasonable effectiveness of recurrent neural networks (2015). http://karpathy.github.io/2015/05/21/rnn-effectiveness/. Accessed 29 Jan 2018
12. Karpathy, A., Johnson, J., Fei-Fei, L.: Visualizing and understanding recurrent networks. CoRR abs/1506.02078 (2015)
13. Li, J., Chen, X., Hovy, E., Jurafsky, D.: Visualizing and understanding neural models in NLP. In: Proceedings of NAACL-HLT, pp. 681–691 (2016)
14. Li, J., Monroe, W., Jurafsky, D.: Understanding neural networks through representation erasure. CoRR abs/1612.08220 (2016)
15. Linzen, T., Dupoux, E., Goldberg, Y.: Assessing the ability of lstms to learn syntax-sensitive dependencies. TACL **4**, 521–535 (2016)
16. Lipton, Z.C.: The mythos of model interpretability. In: 2016 ICML workshop on human interpretability in machine learning. CoRR abs/1606.03490 (2016)
17. Ming, Y., et al.: Understanding hidden memories of recurrent neural networks. CoRR abs/1710.10777 (2017)
18. Strobelt, H., Gehrmann, S., Huber, B., Pfister, H., Rush, A.M.: Visual analysis of hidden state dynamics in recurrent neural networks. CoRR abs/1606.07461 (2016)

Visual Search Target Inference Using Bag of Deep Visual Words

Sven Stauden$^{(\boxtimes)}$, Michael Barz$^{(\boxtimes)}$, and Daniel Sonntag$^{(\boxtimes)}$

German Research Center for Artificial Intelligence (DFKI), Saarbrücken, Germany
{sven.stauden,michael.barz,daniel.sonntag}@dfki.de

Abstract. Visual Search target inference subsumes methods for predicting the target object through eye tracking. A person intents to find an object in a visual scene which we predict based on the fixation behavior. Knowing about the search target can improve intelligent user interaction. In this work, we implement a new feature encoding, the *Bag of Deep Visual Words*, for search target inference using a pre-trained convolutional neural network (CNN). Our work is based on a recent approach from the literature that uses *Bag of Visual Words*, common in computer vision applications. We evaluate our method using a gold standard dataset.

The results show that our new feature encoding outperforms the baseline from the literature, in particular, when excluding fixations on the target.

Keywords: Search target inference · Eye tracking · Visual attention
Deep learning · Intelligent user interfaces

1 Introduction

Human gaze behavior depends on the task in which a user is currently engaged [4,22]; this provides implicit insight into the user's intentions and allows an external observer or intelligent user interface to make predictions about the ongoing activity [1,2,6,8,13]. Predicting the target of a visual search with computational models and the overt gaze signal as input, is commonly referred to as search target inference [3,15,16]. Inferring visual search targets helps to construct and improve intelligent user interfaces in many fields, e.g., robotics [9] or similar to examples in [18]. For example, it allows for a more fine-grained generation of artificial episodic memories for situation-aware assistance of mentally impaired people [17,19]. Recent works investigate algorithmic principles for search target inference on generated dot-like patterns [3], target prediction using *Bag of Visual Words* [15], and target category prediction using a combination of gaze information and CNN-based features [16].

In this work, we extend the idea of using a *Bag of Visual Words* (BoVW) for classifying search targets [15]: we implement a *Bag of Deep Visual Words* model

© Springer Nature Switzerland AG 2018
F. Trollmann and A.-Y. Turhan (Eds.): KI 2018, LNAI 11117, pp. 297–304, 2018.
https://doi.org/10.1007/978-3-030-00111-7_25

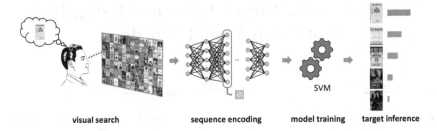

Fig. 1. Search target inference takes a fixation sequence from a visual search as input for target prediction. The pipeline we implement encodes sequences using a *Bag of Words* approach with features from a CNN for model training and inference.

(*BoDVW*), based on image representations from a pre-trained CNN, and investigate its impact on the estimation performance of search target inference (see Fig. 1). First, we reproduce the results of Sattar et al. [15] by re-implementing their method as a baseline and evaluate our novel feature extraction approach using their published *Amazon book cover* dataset[1]. However, the baseline algorithm includes all fixations of the visual search, also the last ones that focus on the target object: the target estimation is reduced to a simpler image comparison task. Other works, including Borji et al. [3] and Zelinsky et al. [23], use fixations on non-target objects only. Consequently, we remove these fixations from the dataset and repeat our experiment with both methods. We implement and evaluate two methods for search target inference based on the *Bag of Words* feature encoding concept: (1) we re-implement the BoVW algorithm by Sattar et al. [15] as a baseline, and (2) we extend their method using *Bag of Deep Visual Words* (BoDVW) based on AlexNet.

2   Related Work

Related work include approaches for inferring targets of a visual search using the fixation signal and image-based features, as well as methods for feature extraction from CNNs.

Wolfe [20] introduces a model for visual search on images that computes an activation map based on the user task. Zelinsky et al. [23] show that objects fixated during a visual search are likely to share similarities with the target. They train a classifier using SIFT features [11] and local color histograms around fixations on distractor objects to infer the actual target. Borji et al. [3] implement algorithms to identify a certain 3×3 sub-pattern in a QR-Code-like image using a simple distance function and a voting-based ranking algorithm with fixated patches. In particular, they investigate the relation between the number of included fixations and the classification accuracy. Sattar et al. [15] consider open and closed world settings for search target inference and use the BoVW method to

---

[1] The *Amazon book cover* dataset from Sattar et al. [15].

encode visual features of fixated image patches. In a follow-up work, Sattar et al. [16] combine the idea of using gaze information and CNN-based features to infer the category of a user's search target instead of a particular object instance or image region. Similar to Sattar et al. [15], we use a *Bag of Words* for search target inference, but using deep visual words from a pre-trained CNN model.

Previous work shows that image representations from hidden layers of CNNs yield promising results for differing tasks, e.g., image clustering. Sharif et al. [12] apply CNN models for scene recognition and object detection using the L2 distance between vector representations. Donahue et al. [5] analyze how image representations generalize to label prediction, when taken from a hidden layer of a network, that was pre-trained on the ImageNet dataset [10]. We use CNN-based image features for encoding the fixation history of a visual search.

3   Visual Search Target Inference Approach

The *Bag of Words* (BoW) algorithm is a vectorization method for encoding sequential data to histogram representations. The BoW encoding is commonly used in natural language processing for, e.g., document classification [7], and was extended to a *Bag of Visual Words* for the computer vision domain for, e.g., scene classification [21]. A BoW is initialized with a limited set of vectors (=codewords) with a fixed size which represent distinguishable features of the data. The method for identifying suitable codewords is an essential part of the setup and influences the performance of classifiers. For encoding a sequence, each sample is assigned to the most similar codeword, resulting in a histogram over all codewords. We implement two methods based on this concept: a BoVW baseline similar to [15] and the CNN-based BoDVW encoding.

3.1   Bag of Visual Words

Sattar et al. [15] use a BoW approach to encode fixation sequences of visual search trials on image collages, e.g., using their publicly available *Amazon book cover* dataset that includes fixation sequences of six participants. They trained a multi-class SVM that predicts the search target from a set of five alternative covers using the encoded histories as input. We re-implement their algorithm for search target inference as a baseline including the BoVW encoding and the SVM target classification. Following their descriptions, we implement methods for image patch extraction from fixation sequences, a BoVW initialization for extracting codewords from these patches, and the histogram generation for a certain sequence. We test our algorithms using their *Amazon book cover* dataset.

3.2   Bag of Deep Visual Words

Our *Bag of Deep Visual Words* approach follows the same concept as in [15], but we encode the RGB patches using a CNN before codeword generation and mapping (see Fig. 2). For this, we feed each image patch to a publicly available

AlexNet model[2] which was trained using the ImageNet dataset [14] for image classification. The flattened activation tensor of a particular hidden layer is used as feature vector of the input image instead of the raw RGB data. We consider the layers `conv1`, `pool2`, `conv4`, `pool5`, `fc6` and `fc8` which represent different stages of the network's layer pipeline. The patch extraction, codeword initialization (clustering) and mapping methods stay the same, but use the flattened tensor as input: the generated codewords are based on the abstract image representations of the deep CNN. Consequently, the fixation sequences get encoded using a histogram over these deep visual codewords.

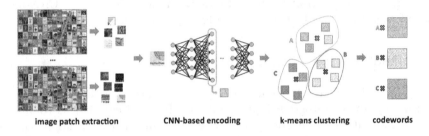

image patch extraction   **CNN-based encoding**   **k-means clustering**   **codewords**

Fig. 2. For initializing the *Bag of Deep Visual Words*, image patches from fixation histories are encoded using a pre-trained CNN. The activations from a certain hidden layer are used for a k-means clustering that identifies deep codewords (cluster centers).

4 Experiment

We conduct a simulation experiment to compare the performance in predicting the search target of a visual search using our re-implementation of Sattar et al. [15]. We investigate the prediction accuracy using their BoVW encoding in comparison to our novel BoDVW encoding. We closely follow the evaluation procedure of Sattar et al. [15] for reproducing their original results using the *Amazon book cover* dataset. For this, fixations of a visual search trial are encoded for model training and target inference, also fixations on the target after it has been found. However, this is in conflict with the goal of actually inferring the search target [3,23]. Therefore, we exclude all fixations at the tail of the signal (target fixations) and repeat the experiment keeping all other parameters constant.

Sattar et al. [15] published a dataset containing eye tracking data of participants performing a search task. They arranged 84 (6 × 14) different book covers from Amazon in collages as visual stimuli. Six participants were asked to find a specific target cover per collage within 20 s after it was displayed for a maximum of 10 s. Fixations were recorded for 100 randomly generated collages in which the target cover appeared exactly once and was taken from a fixed set of 5 covers. Participants were asked to press a key as fast as possible after they found the

---

[2] https://github.com/happynear/caffe-windows/tree/ms/models/bvlc_alexnet.

target. We manually annotated each collage with a bounding box for the target cover.

In our experiment, we compare the target prediction accuracy using the BoVW method against our BoDVW encoding (using different layers). For the BoDVW approaches, we train multiple models, each using a different neural network layer for image patch encoding as stated in Sect. 3.2. First, we use the *Amazon book cover* dataset with all available fixations for training and inference as proposed in [15]. Second, we repeat the experiment without the target fixations at the end of the signal. For each condition, we initialize the respective BoW method using a train set, encode the fixation histories (with or without target fixations) and train a support vector machine for classifying the output label. The codeword initialization and model training is performed, separate for each user (within-user condition), which yielded the best results in Sattar et al. [15]. For initializing the codewords for both approaches, we start with extracting patches around all fixations in the train set. We crop squared fixation patches with an edge length of 80 px and generate $k = 60$ codewords. We train a One-vs-All multiclass SVM with $\lambda = 0.001$ for L1-regularization and feature normalization using Microsoft's Azure Machine Learning Studio[3]. We measure the prediction accuracy using a held-out test set as specified in Sattar et al. [15] (balanced 50/50 split per user).

We hypothesize that, using our *BoVW* implementation, we can reproduce the prediction accuracy of Sattar et al. [15] (H1.1), and that our BoDVW encoding improves the target prediction accuracy concerning the *Amazon book cover* dataset (H1.2). Further, we expect a severe performance drop when excluding target fixations, i.e., when using the filtered *Amazon book cover* dataset (H2.1), whereas the BoDVW encoding still performs better than the BoVW method (H2.2).

4.1 Results

Averaged over all users, our BoVW re-implementation of the method of Sattar et al. [15] achieved a prediction accuracy of 70.67% (20% chance) for search target inference on their *Amazon book cover* dataset with target fixations. We could reproduce their findings, even without an exhaustive parameter optimization. Concerning our *Bag of Deep Visual Words* encoding, applied in the same setting, we observe higher accuracies for all layers. The fc6 layer performed best with an accuracy of 85.33% (see Fig. 3a) which is 14.66% better compared to the baseline. When excluding the target fixations at the tail of the visual search history, the prediction accuracy of both approaches decreases: the BoVW implementation achieves an accuracy of 35.96% and our novel BoDVW encoding achieves a prediction accuracy of 43.56% using the fc8 layer. In this setting, the fc8 layer yields better results than the fc6 layer with 38.26% (see Fig. 3b).

5   Discussion

Our implementation of the BoVW-based search target inference algorithm introduced by Sattar et al. [15] achieves, with a prediction accuracy of 70.67%, a

---

[3] https://studio.azureml.net.

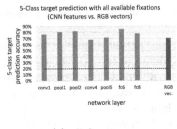
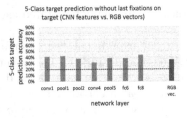

(a) all fixations   (b) filtered target fixations

Fig. 3. Search target inference accuracy of 5-class SVM models using the BoDVW encoding with different layers (orange) and the BoVW encoding (blue) on (a) complete fixation sequences or (b) filtered fixation sequences. (Color figure online)

comparable performance than stated by the authors, for the same settings (confirms H1.1). Our novel BoDVW encoding achieves an improvement of 14.66% with the fc6 layer: an SVM can better distinguish between classes when using CNN features which suggests that H1.2 is correct. In the second part of our experiment, we observed a severe drop in prediction accuracy for both approaches (confirms H2.1). A probable reason is that fixation patches at the end of the search history which show the target object have a vast impact on the prediction performance: the task is simplified to an image comparison. The RGB-based codewords still enable a prediction accuracy above the chance level (20%). Our BoDVW approach performs 7.6% better than this baseline with the fc6 layer (improvement of 21.13%) which suggests that H2.2 is correct. Excluding the target fixations is of particular importance for investigating methods for search target inference due to the introduced bias, hence, the procedure and results of the second part of our experiment should be used as reference for future investigations.

6   Conclusion

We introduced the *Bag of Deep Visual Words* method for integrating learned features for image classification in the popular *Bag of Words* sequence encoding algorithm for the purpose of search target inference. An evaluation showed that our approach performs better than similar approaches from the literature [15], in particular, when excluding fixations on the visual search target. The methods implemented in this work can be used to build intelligent assistance systems by augmenting artificial episodic memories with more specific information about the user's visual attention than possible before [19].

Acknowledgement. This work was funded by the Federal Ministry of Education and Research (BMBF) under grant number 16SV7768 in the Interakt project.

References

1. Akkil, D., Isokoski, P.: Gaze augmentation in egocentric video improves awareness of intention. In: Proceedings of the 2016 CHI Conference on Human Factors in Computing Systems, pp. 1573–1584. ACM Press (2016). http://dl.acm.org/citation.cfm?doid=2858036.2858127

2. Bader, T., Beyerer, J.: Natural gaze behavior as input modality for human-computer interaction. In: Nakano, Y., Conati, C., Bader, T. (eds.) Eye Gaze in Intelligent User Interfaces, pp. 161–183. Springer, London (2013). https://doi.org/10.1007/978-1-4471-4784-8_9

3. Borji, A., Lennartz, A., Pomplun, M.: What do eyes reveal about the mind? Algorithmic inference of search targets from fixations. Neurocomputing 149(PB), 788–799 (2015). https://doi.org/10.1016/j.neucom.2014.07.055

4. DeAngelus, M., Pelz, J.B.: Top-down control of eye movements: Yarbus revisited. Vis. Cognit. 17(6–7), 790–811 (2009). https://doi.org/10.1080/13506280902793843

5. Donahue, J., et al.: DeCAF: A deep convolutional activation feature for generic visual recognition. In: Icml, vol. 32, pp. 647–655 (2014). http://arxiv.org/abs/1310.1531

6. Flanagan, J.R., Johansson, R.S.: Action plans used in action observation. Nature 424(6950), 769–771 (2003). http://www.nature.com/doifinder/10.1038/nature01861

7. Goldberg, Y.: Neural network methods for natural language processing. Synth. Lect. Hum. Lang. Technol. 10(1), 1–309 (2017)

8. Gredeback, G., Falck-Ytter, T.: Eye movements during action observation. Perspect. Psychol. Sci. 10(5), 591–598 (2015). http://pps.sagepub.com/lookup/doi/10.1177/1745691615589103

9. Huang, C.M., Mutlu, B.: Anticipatory robot control for efficient human-robot collaboration. In: 2016 11th ACM/IEEE International Conference on Human-Robot Interaction (HRI), pp. 83–90. IEEE, March 2016. https://doi.org/10.1109/HRI.2016.7451737, http://ieeexplore.ieee.org/document/7451737/

10. Krizhevsky, A., Sutskever, I., Hinton, G.E.: ImageNet classification with deep convolutional neural networks. In: Proceedings of the 25th International Conference on Neural Information Processing Systems - Volume 1, NIPS 2012, pp. 1097–1105. Curran Associates Inc., USA (2012). http://dl.acm.org/citation.cfm?id=2999134.2999257

11. Lowe, D.: Object recognition from local scale-invariant features. In: Proceedings of the Seventh IEEE International Conference on Computer Vision, vol. 2, pp. 1150–1157 (1999). https://doi.org/10.1109/ICCV.1999.790410, http://ieeexplore.ieee.org/document/790410/

12. Razavian, A.S., Azizpour, H., Sullivan, J., Carlsson, S.: CNN features off-the-shelf: an astounding baseline for recognition. In: 2014 IEEE Conference on Computer Vision and Pattern Recognition Workshops, pp. 512–519 (2014). https://doi.org/10.1109/CVPRW.2014.131, http://arxiv.org/abs/1403.6382

13. Rotman, G., Troje, N.F., Johansson, R.S., Flanagan, J.R.: Eye movements when observing predictable and unpredictable actions. J. Neurophysiol. 96(3), 1358–1369 (2006). https://doi.org/10.1152/jn.00227.2006. http://www.ncbi.nlm.nih.gov/pubmed/16687620

14. Russakovsky, O., et al.: ImageNet large scale visual recognition challenge. Int. J. Comput. Vis. (IJCV) 115(3), 211–252 (2015). https://doi.org/10.1007/s11263-015-0816-y

15. Sattar, H., Müller, S., Fritz, M., Bulling, A.: Prediction of search targets from fixations in open-world settings. In: 2015 IEEE Conference on Computer Vision and Pattern Recognition (CVPR), pp. 981–990, June 2015. https://doi.org/10.1109/CVPR.2015.7298700

16. Sattar, H., Bulling, A., Fritz, M.: Predicting the Category and Attributes of Visual Search Targets Using Deep Gaze Pooling (2016). http://arxiv.org/abs/1611.10162

17. Sonntag, D.: Kognit: intelligent cognitive enhancement technology by cognitive models and mixed reality for dementia patients. In: AAAI Fall Symposium Series (2015). https://www.aaai.org/ocs/index.php/FSS/FSS15/paper/view/11702

18. Sonntag, D.: Intelligent user interfaces - A tutorial. CoRR abs/1702.05250 (2017). http://arxiv.org/abs/1702.05250

19. Toyama, T., Sonntag, D.: Towards episodic memory support for dementia patients by recognizing objects, faces and text in eye gaze. In: Hölldobler, S., Krötzsch, M., Peñaloza, R., Rudolph, S. (eds.) KI 2015. LNCS (LNAI), vol. 9324, pp. 316–323. Springer, Cham (2015). https://doi.org/10.1007/978-3-319-24489-1_29

20. Wolfe, J.M.: Guided search 2.0 a revised model of visual search. Psychon. Bull. Rev. 1(2), 202–238 (1994). https://doi.org/10.3758/BF03200774

21. Yang, J., Jiang, Y.G., Hauptmann, A.G., Ngo, C.W.: Evaluating bag-of-visual-words representations in scene classification. In: Proceedings of the International Workshop on Workshop on Multimedia Information Retrieval, MIR 2007, pp. 197–206. ACM, New York (2007). http://doi.acm.org/10.1145/1290082.1290111

22. Yarbus, A.L.: Eye movements and vision. Neuropsychologia 6(4), 222 (1967). https://doi.org/10.1016/0028-3932(68)90012-2

23. Zelinsky, G.J., Peng, Y., Samaras, D.: Eye can read your mind: decoding gaze fixations to reveal categorical search targets. J. Vis. 13(14), 10 (2013). https://doi.org/10.1167/13.14.10. http://www.ncbi.nlm.nih.gov/pubmed/24338446

Analysis and Optimization of Deep Counterfactual Value Networks

Patryk Hopner and Eneldo Loza Mencía$^{(\boxtimes)}$

Knowledge Engineering Group, Technische Universität Darmstadt,
Darmstadt, Germany
eneldo@ke.tu-darmstadt.de

Abstract. Recently a strong poker-playing algorithm called DeepStack was published, which is able to find an approximate Nash equilibrium during gameplay by using heuristic values of future states predicted by deep neural networks. This paper analyzes new ways of encoding the inputs and outputs of DeepStack's deep counterfactual value networks based on traditional abstraction techniques, as well as an unabstracted encoding, which was able to increase the network's accuracy.

Keywords: Poker · Deep neural networks · Game abstractions

1 Introduction

Poker has been an interesting subject for many researchers in the field of machine learning and artificial intelligence over the past decades. Unlike games like chess or checkers it involves imperfect information, making it unsolvable using traditional game solving techniques. For many years the state of the art approach for creating strong agents for the most popular poker variant of No-Limit Hold'em involved computing an approximate Nash equilibrium in a smaller, abstract game, using algorithms like counterfactual regret minimization and then mapping the results back to situations in the real game. However, those abstracted games are several orders of magnitude smaller than the actual game tree of No-Limit Hold'em. Hence, the poker agent has to treat many strategically different situations as if they were the same, potentially resulting in poor performance.

Recently a work was published, combining ideas from traditional poker solving algorithms with ideas from perfect information games, creating the strong poker agent called DeepStack. The algorithm does not need to pre-compute a solution for the whole game tree, instead it computes a solution during game play. In order to make solving the game during game play computationally feasible, DeepStack does not traverse the whole game tree, instead it uses an estimator for values of future states. For that purpose a deep neural network was created, using several million solutions of poker sub-games as training data, which were solved using traditional poker solving algorithms.

It has been proven, that, given a counterfactual value network with perfect accuracy, the solution produced by DeepStack converges to a Nash equilibrium

© Springer Nature Switzerland AG 2018
F. Trollmann and A.-Y. Turhan (Eds.): KI 2018, LNAI 11117, pp. 305–312, 2018.
https://doi.org/10.1007/978-3-030-00111-7_26

of the game. This means on the other hand, that wrong predictions of the network can result in a bad solution. In this paper we will analyze several new ways of encoding the input features of DeepStack's counterfactual value network based on traditional abstraction techniques, as well as an unabstracted encoding, which was able to increase the network's accuracy. A longer version of this paper additionally analyzes the trade-off between the number of training examples and their quality [7] and many more aspects [6].

2   The Poker-Agent DeepStack

In the popular poker variant No-limit Hold'em for two players (Heads-up) each player receives two private cards which can be combined with five public cards [c.f., e.g. 20]. Players are then betting on whose five cards have the highest rank, according to the rules of the game. The *Counterfactual Regret Minimisation* (CFR) algorithm [20] and its variants [4,9,19] are state-of-the-art for finding approximate Nash equilibria [16] in imperfect information games and were the basis for the creation of many strong poker bots [5,11,18,20] such as Libratus [17] which recently won a competition against human professional players. CFR can be used to compute a strategy profile σ and the corresponding *counterfactual values* (CV) at each information set I. The information sets correspond to the nodes in the game tree and the strategy profile assigns a probability to each legal action in an information set. Roughly speaking, the CV $v_i(\sigma, I)$ corresponds to the average utility of player i when both players play according to σ at set I.

Since poker is too large to be solved in an offline manner (the no-limit game tree contains $1.39 \cdot 10^{48}$ information sets) [1,8], CFR is applied to abstracted versions of the game. The *card abstraction* approach groups cards into buckets for which CFR then computes strategies instead. In addition to the usefulness for creating smaller games, card abstractions can also be used to create a feature set for Deep Counterfactual Value Networks (see next), which is the focus of this work.

Depth Limited Continual Resolving. *DeepStack* is a strong poker AI [14] which combines traditional imperfect game solving algorithms, such as CFR and endgame solving, with ideas from perfect information games, while remaining theoretically sound. In contrast to previous approaches using endgame solving [2,3], which use a pre-computed strategy before reaching the endgame, the authors of DeepStack propose to always re-solve the sub-tree, starting from the current state, after every taken action. However, on the early rounds of the game DeepStack does not traverse the full game tree since this would be computationally infeasible. Instead, it uses deep neural networks as an estimator of the expected CV of each hand on future rounds for its re-solving step, resulting in the technique referred to as *depth limited continual resolving*.

Deep Counterfactual Value Networks. DeepStack used a deep neural network to predict the player's counterfactual values on future betting rounds, which

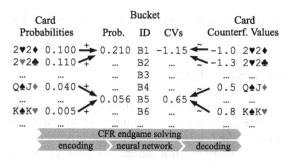

Fig. 1. Diagram depicting the (1) encoding from private cards to buckets (depicted by black arrows) (2) mapping from private card distributions to bucket distributions (the summing of probabilities symbolized by +) (3) mapping from private card counterfactual values to buckets CVs (averaging symbolized by ∼)(4) pipeline of CFR mapping private card distributions to respective CVs (5) replicating DeepStack pipeline consisting of (a) encoding (b) estimating of the buckets' CVs by a neural network (c) decoding back the estimated buckets' CVs to the cards' CVs.

would otherwise be obtained by applying CFR. Consequently, the *deep counterfactual value network* (DCVNN) is trained with examples consisting of representations of poker situations as input and the counterfactual values of CFR as output. More specifically, the network was fed with 10 million random poker situations and the corresponding counterfactual values obtained by applying CFR on the resulting sub-games [15]. For every situation a public board, private card distributions for both players and a pot size were randomly sampled. From this CFR is able to compute two counterfactual value vectors $\mathbf{v}_i = (v_i(j, \sigma))_j$ with $j = 1 \ldots 1326$ for each possible private hand combination and for each player $i = 1, 2$. Note that $I = j$ represents the first level of the game tree starting from the given public board.

The input to the network is given by a representation of the players' private card distributions and the public cards. Hence, before the training of the neural network starts, DeepStack creates a potential aware card abstraction with 1000 buckets (cf. Sect. 3). For each training example the probabilities of holding certain private hands are then mapped to probabilities of holding a certain bucket by accumulating the probabilities of every private hand in said bucket. After the training of the model is completed, the CV for each bucket in a distribution can be mapped back to CV of actual hands by creating a reverse mapping of the used card abstraction. Figure 1 depicts the general process, Sect. 3 describes it in more detail.

DeepStack was able to solve many issues associated with earlier game solving algorithms, such as avoiding the need for explicit card abstraction. However, DCVN introduce their own potential problems. For instance, the incorrect predictions caused by encoding of the player distributions as well as the counterfactual value outputs could potentially result in a highly exploitable strategy. The distributions and outputs are encoded using a potential aware card abstraction, potentially leading to similar problems as traditional card abstraction techniques, which is something we will call *implicit card abstraction*.

3   Distribution Encoding

While DeepStack never uses explicit card abstraction during its re-solving step, the encoding of inputs and outputs of counterfactual value networks is based on a card abstraction, which introduces potential problems. Because the input player distributions get mapped to a number of buckets prior to training, the training algorithm is not aware of the exact hand distributions, but only of the distribution of bucket probabilities. Because this is a many to one mapping, the algorithm might not be able to distinguish different situations, thus not being able to perfectly fit the training set. The second problem stems from the encoding of the output values. Counterfactual values of several hands are aggregated to a counterfactual value of a bucket, potentially losing precision. Both problems are visualized in Fig. 1 which also depicts the basic architecture of DeepStack's counterfactual value estimation.

While the problem is similar for inputs and outputs, we will focus on the loss of accuracy of counterfactual value outputs. We will call the difference between the original counterfactual values of hands, as computed by the CFR solver, and the counterfactual values after an abstraction based encoding was used, the *encoding error*. The difference between the original counterfactual values and the bucket counterfactual values will be measured using the mean squared error as well as the Huber loss (with $\delta = 1$) averaged over all private hands and test examples, as proposed by [14]. For instance, in Fig. 1 we would apply the loss functions on the differences $|-1.0 - (-1.15)|$, $|-1.3 - (-1.15)|$, ...

We will examine three abstraction based encodings, including the potential aware encoding, which was used by DeepStack, as well as an unabstracted encoding. We will then compare the encoding error of each encoding, as well as the accuracy of the resulting networks.

When measuring the accuracy of the model, we have two possible perspectives. The first is to look at the prediction error with both inputs and outputs encoded with a card abstraction. The second way is to map the predictions of buckets back to predicted counterfactual values of private hands and compare them to the unabstracted counterfactual values of the test examples. When measuring the error using encoded inputs and outputs, we will refer to the test set as *abstract test set*. In Fig. 1 this would correspond to the error between the bucket CVs column (after mapping from the actual private privat card CVs) and the predicted bucket CVs. When we are measuring the prediction error for unabstracted private hands, we will call the dataset the *unabstracted test set*, which in Fig. 1 corresponds to comparing to the card CVs column after decoding the predicted bucket CVs. We will use the same logic for the training set.

$E[HS^2]$ **Abstraction.** On the last betting round the *hand strength* (HS) value of a hand is the probability of winning against a uniform opponent hand distribution. On earlier rounds the *expected hand strength squared* ($E[HS^2]$) [11] is calculated by averaging the square of the HS values over all possible card roll outs.

The $E[HS^2]$ abstraction uses the $E[HS^2]$ values in order to group hands into *buckets*. There are several ways to map hands to a bucket, including percentile bucketing, which creates equally sized buckets, clustering of hands with an algorithm such as k-Means [12] or by simply grouping hands together, that differ only by a certain threshold in their $E[HS^2]$ values.

Nested Public Card Abstraction. A *nested public card abstraction* first groups public boards into *public buckets* and those buckets are later subdivided according to some metric which takes private card information into account, such as $E[HS^2]$.

In this work boards were clustered according to two features, the *draw value* and the *highcard value*. The draw value of a turn board was defined as the number of straight and flush combinations, which will be present on the following round. The highcard value is the sum of the ranks of all turn cards, with the lowest card, a deuce, having a rank of zero and an ace having a rank of 12.

Potential Aware Card Abstraction. The *potential aware card abstraction* [10] tries to not only estimate a hand's current strength, but also its potential on future betting rounds. It does that by first creating a probability distribution of future HS values for each hand and then clustering hands using the *k-Means* [12] algorithm and the *earth mover's distance* [10].

Abstraction-Free Direct Encoding. Instead of using a card abstraction in order to aggregate private hand distributions to bucket distributions and private hand CVs to bucket CVs, this encoding uses the private hand data directly. The input distributions are represented as a vector of probabilities of holding one of the 1326 possible card combinations. The boards are represented using one hot encoded vectors where each of the 52 dimensions represents whether a specific card is present on the public board.

4 Evaluation

In order to compare the encodings, first a version of each card abstraction described in the previous section was created. Like in the original DeepStack implementation, the potential aware card abstraction used 1000 buckets. The $E[HS^2]$ abstraction used 1326 buckets based on a equal width partition of the value interval $[0, 1]$. The public nested card abstraction was created by first clustering the public boards into 10 public clusters according to their draw and highcard value and subdividing each public cluster into 100 $E[HS^2]$ buckets, resulting in a total of 1000 buckets. For the analysis of the encoding error, the CVs of each training example were then encoded using each of the three card abstractions, meaning that they were aggregated to a CV of their bucket. Those bucket CVs were then compared with the original CVs of the hands in said bucket and the average error over all available training examples was computed.

Table 1. Encoding error of different encoding schemes on the turn.

Encoding approach	$E[HS^2]$	Public nested	Potential aware
Huber loss	**0.0240**	0.0406	0.0258
MSE	**0.0509**	0.0886	0.0544

Our computational resource only allowed us to create 300,000 endgame solutions instead of the 10 million available to DeepStack. All 300,000 training examples were used for testing the encoding error of each abstraction. For the second comparison the DCVN were trained using each of the 3 abstraction based encodings, as well as the unabstracted encoding. The training set consisted of 80% of the total 300,000 endgame solutions, while the test set consisted of 20%. The networks were trained for 350 epochs using the Adam Gradient descent [13] and the Huber Loss.[1]

Encoding and Prediction Errors. Table 1 shows the encoding error of the abstraction based encodings. Table 2 reports the errors of the trained neural networks. Remember that the abstraction-free encodings do not produce any encoding error, therefore, their performance is also the same on the abstracted and unabstracted sets. Note also that the errors on the abstracted sets are not directly comparable to each other due to the different encoding.

We can observe that the $E[HS^2]$ abstraction introduces a smaller encoding error than the potential aware card abstraction, although not by a big margin. However, it is outperformed in terms of the accuracy of the neural networks. The potential aware abstraction performed better in its own abstraction, as well as after mapping the counterfactual values of buckets back to counterfactual values of cards.

A contrary behaviour can be observed for the public nested encoding. Whereas it has major difficulties in encoding, the resulting encodings carry enough information for the network to predict relatively well on the bucketed CVs. However, mapping the CVs back to the actual hands strongly suffers from the initial encoding problems.

However, the most noteworthy (and surprising) result is the performance of the abstraction-free encoding. Whereas the potential aware encoding was able to produce a lower Huber Loss in its own abstraction, the abstraction-free encoding outperformed the abstraction on the unabstracted training set and the unabstracted test set. The direct encoding was therefore better than the potential aware encoding at predicting counterfactual values of actual hands instead of buckets, which is the most important measure in actual game play. These results suggest that the neural network was able to generalize among the public boards

---

[1] As in DeepStack, the inputs to the networks with 7 layers with 500 nodes each using parametric ReLUs and an outer network ensuring the zero-sum property are the respective encodings.

Table 2. Prediction error of neural network using different input encodings on the abstracted and unabstracted train and test sets, on the turn.

Encoding approach	$E[HS^2]$	Public nested	Potential aware	Abstraction–free
Abstracted train	0.0254	0.0080	**0.0052**	0.0102
Unabstracted train	0.0387	0.0436	0.0267	**0.0102**
Abstracted test	0.0330	0.0161	**0.0102**	0.0143
Unabstracted test	0.0434	0.0478	0.0297	**0.0143**

even though no explicit or implicit support was given in this respect. Note that this was possible even though we only used a small number of training instances compared to DeepStack.

5 Conclusions

In this paper we have analyzed several ways of encoding inputs and outputs of deep counterfactual value networks. We have introduced the concept of the encoding error, which is a result of using an encoding based on lossy card abstractions. An encoding based on card abstraction can lower the accuracy of training data by averaging counterfactual values of multiple private hands, introducing an error before the training of the neural network even started. We have observed that the encoding error can have a substantial impact on the accuracy of the trained network, as observed in the case of the public nested card abstraction which performed well on its abstract test set but lost a lot of accuracy when the counterfactual values of buckets were mapped back to hands.

The potential aware card abstraction produced the best results of all the abstraction based encodings, which corresponds to the results achieved by the abstraction in older algorithms, where it is the most successful abstraction at this point. However, the unabstracted encoding produced the lowest prediction error. While a good result on the training set was expected, it was unclear if the neural network would generalize well to unseen test examples. This result again shows the importance of minimizing the encoding error when designing a deep counterfactual value network.

References

1. Bowling, M., Burch, N., Johanson, M., Tammelin, O.: Heads-up limit hold'em poker is solved. Commun. ACM **60**(11), 81–88 (2017)
2. Burch, N., Bowling, M.: CFR-D: solving imperfect information games using decomposition. CoRR abs/1303.4441 (2013). http://arxiv.org/abs/1303.4441
3. Ganzfried, S., Sandholm, T.: Endgame solving in large imperfect-information games. In: Proceedings of the 2015 International Conference on Autonomous Agents and Multiagent Systems, AAMAS 2015, pp. 37–45, Richland, SC (2015)

4. Gibson, R.: Regret minimization in games and the development of champion multiplayer computer poker-playing agents. Ph.D. thesis, University of Alberta (2014)
5. Gilpin, A., Sandholm, T., Sørensen, T.B.: A heads-up no-limit texas hold'em poker player: discretized betting models and automatically generated equilibrium-finding programs. In: Proceedings of the 7th International Joint Conference on Autonomous Agents and Multiagent Systems - Volume 2, AAMAS 2008, pp. 911–918. International Foundation for Autonomous Agents and Multiagent Systems, Richland, SC (2008)
6. Hopner, P.: Analysis and optimization of deep counterfactual value networks. Bachelor's thesis, Technische Universität Darmstadt (2018). http://www.ke.tu-darmstadt.de/bibtex/publications/show/3078
7. Hopner, P., Loza Mencía, E.: Analysis and optimization of deep counterfactual value networks (2018). http://arxiv.org/abs/1807.00900
8. Johanson, M.: Measuring the size of large no-limit poker games. CoRR abs/1302.7008 (2013). http://arxiv.org/abs/1302.7008
9. Johanson, M., Bard, N., Lanctot, M., Gibson, R., Bowling, M.: Efficient nash equilibrium approximation through Monte Carlo counterfactual regret minimization. In: Proceedings of the 11th International Conference on Autonomous Agents and Multiagent Systems - Volume 2, AAMAS 2012, pp. 837–846. International Foundation for Autonomous Agents and Multiagent Systems, Richland, SC (2012)
10. Johanson, M., Burch, N., Valenzano, R., Bowling, M.: Evaluating state-space abstractions in extensive-form games. In: Proceedings of the 2013 International Conference on Autonomous Agents and Multi-agent Systems, AAMAS 2013, pp. 271–278. International Foundation for Autonomous Agents and Multiagent Systems, Richland, SC (2013)
11. Johanson, M.B.: Robust strategies and counter-strategies: from superhuman to optimal play. Ph.D. thesis, University of Alberta (2016). http://johanson.ca/publications/theses/2016-johanson-phd-thesis/2016-johanson-phd-thesis.pdf
12. Kanungo, T., Mount, D.M., Netanyahu, N.S., Piatko, C.D., Silverman, R., Wu, A.Y.: An efficient k-means clustering algorithm: analysis and implementation. IEEE Trans. Pattern Anal. Mach. Intell. 24(7), 881–892 (2002). https://doi.org/10.1109/TPAMI.2002.1017616
13. Kingma, D.P., Ba, J.: Adam: a method for stochastic optimization. CoRR abs/1412.6980 (2014). http://arxiv.org/abs/1412.6980
14. Moravcík, M., et al.: Deepstack: expert-level artificial intelligence in no-limit poker. CoRR abs/1701.01724 (2017). http://arxiv.org/abs/1701.01724
15. Moravcík, M., et al.: Supplementary materials for deepstack: expert-level artificial intelligence in no-limit poker (2017). https://www.deepstack.ai/
16. Nash, J.: Non-cooperative games. Ann. Math. 54(2), 286–295 (1951)
17. Noam Brown, T.S.: Libratus: the superhuman AI for no-limit poker. In: Proceedings of the Twenty-Sixth International Joint Conference on Artificial Intelligence, IJCAI 2017, pp. 5226–5228 (2017)
18. Schnizlein, D.P.: State translation in no-limit poker. Master's thesis, University of Alberta (2009)
19. Tammelin, O.: Solving large imperfect information games using CFR+. CoRR abs/1407.5042 (2014). http://arxiv.org/abs/1407.5042
20. Zinkevich, M., Johanson, M., Bowling, M., Piccione, C.: Regret minimization in games with incomplete information. In: Platt, J.C., Koller, D., Singer, Y., Roweis, S.T. (eds.) Advances in Neural Information Processing Systems 20, pp. 1729–1736. Curran Associates, Inc. (2008). http://papers.nips.cc/paper/3306-regret-minimization-in-games-with-incomplete-information.pdf

Search

A Variant of Monte-Carlo Tree Search for Referring Expression Generation

Tobias Schwartz and Diedrich Wolter[✉]

University of Bamberg, Bamberg, Germany
diedrich.wolter@uni-bamberg.de

Abstract. In natural language generation, the task of Referring Expression Generation (REG) is to determine a set of features or relations which identify a target object. Referring expressions describe the target object and discriminate it from other objects in a scene. From an algorithmic point of view, REG can be posed as a search problem. Since search space is exponential with respect to the number of features and relations available, efficient search strategies are required. In this paper we investigate variants of Monte-Carlo Tree Search (MCTS) for application in REG. We propose a new variant, called Quasi Best-First MCTS (QBF-MCTS). In an empirical study we compare different MCTS variants to one another, and to classic REG algorithms. The results indicate that QBF-MCTS yields a significantly improved performance with respect to efficiency and quality.

Keywords: Monte-Carlo Tree Search
Referring Expression Generation · Natural language generation

1 Introduction

In situated interaction it is of crucial importance to establish joint reference to objects. For example, a future service robot may need to be instructed which piece of clothing to be taken to the cleaners, or the robot may want to inform its users about some object. When communicating in natural language, the task of generating phrases that refer to objects is known as Referring Expression Generation (REG). It received considerable attention in the field of natural language generation since the seminal works by Dale and Reiter in the early 1990s [10,11]. From a technical point of view, a referring expression like "the green shirt" can be seen as a set of attributes (color, object type) related to values (green, shirt). The REG problem has thus been formulated as the search problem of identifying an appropriate set of attribute-value pairs that yield a distinguishing description [11]. Appropriateness of an description is evaluated using a linguistic model that comprises factors like discriminatory power and acceptability [15]. Knowledgeability of the set of attribute-value pairs that suit a particular object in the scene is usually assumed. Language production is not considered in REG

© Springer Nature Switzerland AG 2018
F. Trollmann and A.-Y. Turhan (Eds.): KI 2018, LNAI 11117, pp. 315–326, 2018.
https://doi.org/10.1007/978-3-030-00111-7_27

since it is not specific to the task. Rather, research has focused on identifying suitable linguistic models and deriving search methods that can efficiently identify adequate referring expressions despite of facing a search space that is exponential with respect to the amount of attribute-value pairs to be considered. For example, the highly successful Incremental Algorithm (IA) [11], for which many extensions have been proposed over the years (for an overview, see [14]) implements a greedy heuristic search. This leads to a trade-off between appropriateness of the referring expression determined and computation time.

In the light of modern search techniques paradigms, in particular Monte-Carlo Tree Search (MCTS), we are motivated to re-visit search algorithms for REG. The contribution of this paper is to propose a new MCTS variant that outperforms other MCTS variants as well as classic REG algorithms regarding computation time and appropriateness with respect to a given linguistic model. The paper is organized as follows. Section 2 introduces the problem of REG in little more detail. We then review relevant approaches to MCTS in Sect. 3. In Sect. 4 we detail a new MCTS variant termed Quasi-Best-First MCTS. Thereafter, we present a comparative evaluation of REG algorithms. The paper concludes with a discussion of the results.

2   Search in Referring Expression Generation

The computational problem of Referring Expression Generation can be defined similar to [11] as follows: Given a set of attributes A, values V and a finite domain of objects O. The set $L = A \times V$ presents all elements that can be employed in a referring expression. Then, given a target object $x \in O$, find a set of attribute-value pairs $D \in 2^L$ whose conjunction describes x, but not any of the distractors $y \in O \setminus \{x\}$. Adequacy of D with respect to x is evaluated by a linguistic model. Different linguistic models have been proposed to identify an appropriate referring expression, ranging from simple Boolean classification to gradual assessment. In our evaluation we adopt a state-of-the-art model based on a probabilistic model [16].

Spatially locative phrases, such as "the green book on the small table", are typically used in referring expressions. They combine the target object with an additional reference object and a spatial preposition. In our example, "the green book" is the target object and "the small table" functions as reference object and "on" is the spatial preposition [2]. Note that above formalization can also encompass locative phrases despite only defining L as set of attribute-value pairs to represent unary features of an object. To make this work, a preposition "on" is modeled as $|O| - 1$ unary features $on_y(x)$, each relating target x to some reference object $y \in O \setminus \{x\}$. This strategy can be generalized to reduce n-ary relations to unary features. In general, using relations in a referring expression requires a recursive invocation of the REG algorithm to identify all reference objects introduced, in our example object y, "the small table". Since considering prepositions would be required for obtaining intuitive referring expressions, search space in REG should be considered to be exponential with respect to $|L|$ as well as to $|O|$. This illustrates the need for efficient algorithms in REG.

Multiple search algorithms have been pursuit for REG so far, most importantly Full Brevity Algorithm (FB), Greedy Heuristic Algorithm (GH), and Incremental Algorithm (IA) [9–11]. FB implements breath-first search, incrementally considering longer descriptions. It will thus always identify the most adequate description, but possibly not within a reasonable amount of time. GH implements a greedy search. In GH, descriptions are build up incrementally by selecting attribute-value pairs that maximally improve assessment according to the linguistic model. IA first sorts attribute-value pairs according to some cognitively motivated preference model and then incrementally selects all pairs which rule out any wrong interpretation according to the linguistic model. The preference model of IA can easily be incorporated into the linguistic model. From a perspective of search, IA then proceeds precisely like GH. However, there exists some evidence that a universal preference order does not exist [19], which means that greedy algorithms are not sufficient for identifying the most adequate description. We are therefore motivated to investigate whether MCTS can provide a viable alternative to performing REG.

3   MCTS Techniques for REG

Monte-Carlo Tree Search (MCTS) [7,8,12] is a best first search based on randomized exploration of the search space. Starting with an empty tree, the algorithm gradually builds up a search tree, repeating the four steps *selection, expansion, simulation* and *backpropagation* until some predefined *computational budget* (typically a time, memory or iteration constraint) is reached. For REG it seems beneficial that every node in the tree represents a specific attribute-value pair $a_i \times v_i \in L$, such that a path in the tree represents a description $D \in 2^L$. The root node of the search tree represents the empty description.

Selection: Starting at the root node of the tree, the algorithm recursively applies a selection strategy until a leaf node is reached. One popular approach is the UCT selection strategy [12], which successfully applies advances from the multi-armed bandit problem with the Upper Confidence Bound (UCB) algorithms [1], in particular UCB1 [1], to MCTS. We also use UCT in our MCTS algorithms.

Expansion: Once a leaf node is reached, an expansion strategy is applied to expand the tree by one or more nodes. A popular approach is to add one node per iteration [8]. Hence, we apply this strategy in our standard implementation of MCTS. In our application domain we observe that adding multiple nodes per iteration yields better outcomes. This approach is followed in our MCTS variant QBF-MCTS.

Simulation: In standard MCTS a simulation strategy is used to choose moves until a terminal node is reached. One of the easiest techniques is to select those moves randomly. In REG, every node corresponds to a possible expression represented by the path to the root node. We therefore consider every node to be a terminal node and compute for every node a score using the linguistic model. Thus, a single simulation in our MCTS realization corresponds to several runs needed in the classic MCTS to estimate one node's value.

Backpropagation: The outcome of the simulation step is now propagated from the leaf node all the way back to the root node, updating all values of every node on its way. This is done according to a specific backpropagation strategy. The arguably most popular and most effective strategy is to use the plain average [5]. While this approach under-estimates the node value, it is significantly better than backing up the maximum, which over-estimates it and thus leads to high instability in the search [8]. We therefore employ the plain average in all our algorithms.

Final Move Selection: Finally, the "best" child from the root node is selected as result of the algorithm. The easiest and most popular approaches are to select the child with the highest value (max child) or with the highest visit count (robust child) [5]. As we use MCTS to find an optimal description and do not encounter any interference (for instance of other players), we believe that it is possible to not only select one node, but instead return the whole path leading to the best description (as also noted in [18]). Therefore, in the standard MCTS we always add the max child to our description, until we reach a leaf node. We observed that this approach not always reveals the best description, although it often contains appropriate attributes. One possibility to overcome this problem could be to restrict node selection to nodes above a certain visit count threshold as proposed by Coulom [8]. Instead, we implemented a variant called Maximum-MCTS (MMCTS) which takes the outcome of the MCTS as input. Since the number of attribute-value pairs contained in this description are usually significantly less than the total number of properties, it is now feasible to determine the best combination of those attribute-value pairs and return the according description.

4   Quasi-Best-First MCTS

Solving the REG problem with MCTS can be modeled similar to a single-player game, for which a MCTS modification called Single-Player Monte-Carlo Tree Search (SP-MCTS) [18] has already been proposed. SP-MCTS employs a variant of the popular UCT algorithm [12] and combines it with a straightforward Meta-Search extension. Meta-Search in general describes a higher level search, which uses other search processes to arrive at an answer [18]. For MCTS applications the often weak simulation strategy can for instance be replaced with an entire MCTS program at lower parts of the search [6]. This idea is also embedded in the Nested Monte-Carlo Search (NMCS) [4], which achieved world records in single-player games. NMCS combines nested calls with randomness in the playouts and memorization of the best sequence of moves. NMCS works as follows. At each step the algorithm tries all possible moves by conducting a lower level NMCS followed said move. The one with the highest NMCS score is memorized. If no score is higher than the current maximum, the best score found so far is returned. The advances of Meta-Search in single-player MCTS were also applied to two-player games in Chaslot's Quasi Best-First (QBF) algorithm [6]. These algorithms formulate the inspiration for our Quasi Best-First Monte-Carlo Tree Search (QBF-MCTS). All steps of the QBF-MCTS are explained in the following, while the pseudo-code is given in Algorithm 1.

Selection: Similar to SP-MCTS [18], we make extensive use of UCT as selection strategy, since it has been proven to maintain a good balance between exploration and exploitation (cf. [3,12]). Additionally, also NMCS [4] improves in combination with UCT [17]. One important parameter of the UCT formula which has to be tuned experimentally is the exploration constant C. It has been shown that a value of $C = \frac{1}{\sqrt{2}}$ satisfies the Hoeffding inequality with rewards in the range of $[0, 1]$ [13]. Since this is exactly the interval we are interested in when using a probabilistic linguistic model, we use this C-value for QBF-MCTS.

Expansion: Instead of adding just one node per iteration, we are following the concept of NMCS [4] by expanding the tree with all available properties, i.e., QBF adds all children to the search tree.

Simulation: As mentioned in Sect. 3, we employ a linguistic model in the simulation step. Thus, we can directly evaluate certain nodes without the need of an approximation from a weak simulation strategy or based on another search framework, as it is done in Meta-Search. This allows for a significant increase in performance. In contrast to QBF [6], which was only used to generate opening books, it is now feasible to perform fast online evaluations of all expanded nodes. This again later allows for a more informed and effective selection and compared to our standard MCTS version vastly reduces the factor of randomness.

Backpropagation: The values from all evaluated nodes are finally propagated back using the plain average, as it is done in our other MCTS variants.

Final Move Selection Strategy: As proposed in all mentioned algorithms (SP-MCTS [18], NMCS [4], QBF [6]), we also memorize the best results. So if the description represented by the path from the root node to a specific leaf node achieves a higher acceptability than the current best description, it is stored as the best description. For the final move selection, we then simply return this description.

It has been noted that by only exploiting the most-promising moves, the algorithm can easily get caught in local maxima [18]. The proposed solution is a straightforward Meta-Search, which simply performs random restarts using a different random seed. Applying this method to our algorithms, we observed no change in performance within the same computational budget. Hence we do not implement this approach. Instead we change the random seed in every iteration.

Algorithm 1. Quasi Best-First Monte-Carlo Tree Search

```
 1: function QBF-MCTS(rootNode)
 2:     bestDescription ← {}
 3:     T ← {rootNode}                                    ▷ T represents search tree
 4:     while not reached computational budget do
 5:         currentNode ← rootNode
 6:         while currentNode ∈ T do
 7:             lastNode ← currentNode
 8:             currentNode ← UCT(currentNode)
 9:         end while                                              ▷ Selection
10:         T ←EXPANDALL(lastNode)                                 ▷ Expansion
11:         result ← Evaluate(lastNode)                            ▷ Simulation
12:         currentNode ← lastNode
13:         while currentNode ∈ T do
14:             Backpropagate(currentNode, result)
15:             currentNode ← Parent(currentNode)
16:         end while                                        ▷ Backpropagation
17:         description ← PathDescription(lastNode)
18:         bestDescription ← max{description, bestDescription}
19:     end while
20:     return bestDescription                            ▷ Final Move Selection
21: end function
```

---

5   Evaluation

With our evaluation we aim to identify the trade-off between efficiency in computing a referring expression and the level of appropriateness reached. Greedy heuristic (GH) and breadth-first full brevity (FB) demarcate extreme cases of classic REG algorithms and thus can serve as reference. GH is most efficient at the cost of not identifying the best referring expression, whereas FB will always find the best expression at the cost of facing combinatorial explosion.

5.1   Implementation Details

In our experiments we employ PRAGR (probabilistic grounding and reference) [15,16] as linguistic model. PRAGR comprises two measures, namely discriminatory power and appropriateness of an attribute-value pair. The optimal description D_x^* of some object x with respect to PRAGR thus jointly maximizes uniqueness of the interpretation (probability of the recipient to identify the target) and appropriateness (probability the recipient will maximizes probability of a recipient to identify object x given description D and to accept D as description of x:

$$D_x^* := \arg \max_{D \subseteq A \times V} (1 - \alpha)P(x|D) + \alpha P(D|x) \qquad (1)$$

Parameter α balances both components and has been chosen as $\alpha = 0.7$. In our evaluation we determine the probabilistic assessment as described in [16], in particular deriving $P(x|D)$ from $P(D|x)$ using Bayes' law, but instead of using attributes grounded in perception we initialize probability distributions randomly.

We have implemented three different MCTS variants in Java as explained above. One standard MCTS algorithm with a whole path final move selection, its improvement called MMCTS, and QBF-MCTS. For reference, we also implemented the REG algorithms FB and GH.

5.2 Analysis of Scene Parameters

We randomly generate scenes containing n objects, select one as target x, and initialize k random distributions for attributes. Then we apply algorithms FB, GH, MCTS, MMCTS, and QBF-MCTS to compute a referring expression and record computation time and PRAGR evaluation relative to the score obtained by FB. In a first evaluation we seek to identify a parameter space with respect to amount of objects n and attributes k that still is feasible for FB with respect to computation time, but already challenging for the MCTS variants with respect to quality. Based on first experiments, we fixed the computational budget of MCTS and MMCTS to 10000 and QBF-MCTS to 1800 iterations. Restarts (as conducted by [18]) did not reveal any performance increase when executed within the same computational budget and thus were not applied. Averaging over 10 scenes per configuration, we obtain the data displayed in Figs. 1 and 3.

Discussion of the Results. The plot in Fig. 1 (left) indicates the combinatorial explosion occurring with FB (blue opaque meshes) if the number of attributes is approaching 20. Since we only employ unary attributes, no dramatic increase of computation time with respect to increasing the amount of objects per scene can be observed. To allow for a comparison between GH and MCTS variants, the right plot in Fig. 1 shows the same data, but without FB compute times. This plot indicates significant differences between GH and all MCTS variants (overlaid, all in red). Looking at the obtained quality relative to FB, Fig. 3 indicates that all algorithms perform nearly optimal in case of few objects and few attributes, but there are significant differences around 15–20 attributes and 15–20 objects. We conclude that consideration of 20 objects and 18 attributes is well-suited to study performance of the algorithms in detail since these parameters are already challenging, yet a comparison with FB is still feasible. These numbers also appear to be reasonable with respect to practical applications.

5.3 Comparison of Algorithms

For comparing MCTS variants against GH and FB we have to fix the computational budget. To determine a suitable budget we randomly generated 200 scenes with 20 object and 18 attributes. Figure 2 shows the quality relative to FB averaged over 200 scenes obtained by all MCTS variants with respect to the number of iterations. As can be seen in the plot, the score of all MCTS variants rises

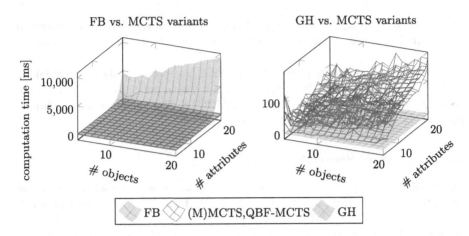

Fig. 1. Average computation time of REG algorithms with respect to scene complexity (Color figure online)

Table 1. Average and median computation time in comparative evaluation. GH executes in less then 1ms, no computation times could be measured.

Algorithm	Avg. computation time [ms]	Std. deviation	Median [ms]
MCTS	98.0	47.3	82
MMCTS	93.5	22.7	83
QBF	90.5	25.5	81
FB	1534.2	187.3	1510

within the first few hundred iterations and levels off after a few thousand iterations. Without empirical evaluation in user studies it is difficult to judge which performance is worth which additional computation time, yet user studies would inevitably be affected by the linguistic model as well as grounding of attribute-value pairs. For comparing obtained quality with respect to our linguistic model we set the computational budget of QBF to 1500 and, to obtain a similar budget in CPU time, to 8500 iterations for (M)MCTS. Figure 4 shows boxplots of the quality relative to FB for all other algorithms. Boxes cover the second and third quartiles, whiskers extend to 1.5 times the difference between second and third quartile. Table 1 shows the average computation times obtained on a 3.4 Ghz Laptop running Windows 8.1 and Java 8. Since times are very similar across all runs, no further statistics are presented.

Discussion of the Results. Figure 4 is most relevant to judge performance of the algorithms. MCTS and MMCTS show the largest spread in quality. From the MCTS variants only the median of QBF-MCTS (1.0, average 0.98) is above that of GH (0.90, average 0.89). MCTS and MMCTS both perform worse than GH with respect to quality and with respect to computation time. This is somewhat

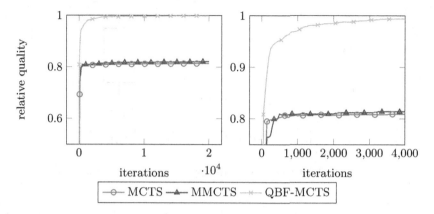

Fig. 2. Effects of computational budget constraints to MCTS performance, right plot shows a magnification.

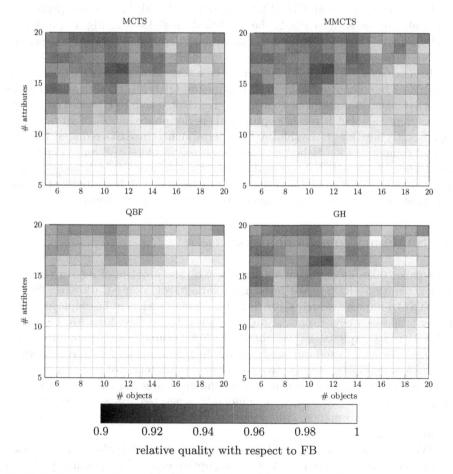

Fig. 3. Relative quality achieved by algorithm, differences to FB are only significant for 15 and more attributes.

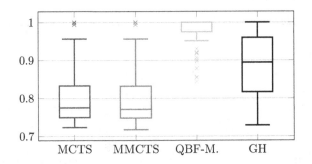

Fig. 4. Relative quality with respect to FB per method.

a surprising observation. While we expected rather greedy search easily to be outperformed by MCTS in a combinatorial optimization problem that exhibits local maxima, application of the reasonable MCTS and MMCTS variants both lead to worse results than GH. While superiority of QBF-MCTS over (M)MCTS could already be seen in Fig. 2, the statistical breakdown in Fig. 4 also reveals that QBF-MCTS performance exhibits the lowest spread in the distribution, i.e., a more or less constant performance.

In conclusion, QBF-MCTS appears to be a new viable alternative to performing REG. The computational budget required for QBF-MCTS with around 83 ms leads to longer computer time than greedy heuristic search (GH) which completes in less than 1ms, but it reaches optimal FB performance in 56% of all runs with significantly less effort. Evaluating the performance in REG required for successful communication is beyond this paper and would significantly depend on the quality of the attribute grounding learnt (in case of PRAGR estimation of $P(D|x)$ and $P(x|D)$ in (1)) and the linguistic model itself, but aiming at finding the most optimal expression avoids introducing further problems.

6   Summary and Conclusion

This paper takes an algorithmic perspective on the problem of referring expression generation (REG). We investigate variants of Monte-Carlo Tree Search (MCTS) to improve search algorithms that have previously be employed. This paper proposes a new variant of MCTS, named Quasi-Best-First MCTS (QBF-MCTS), which exploits the availability of a lower bound heuristics in a UCT-like manner. We have based our study on the linguistic model PRAGR [16] which defines a probabilistic measure to assess the appropriateness of a referring expression candidate. Any assessment of a candidate expression thus yields a lower bound estimate. By evaluation in randomly generated scenes we demonstrate near-optimal performance with respect to the linguistic model at significantly improved efficiency.

While this paper focuses exclusively on application of QBF-MCTS to REG, we expect QBF-MCTS to offer a promising option in a variety of search problems for which a lower bound heuristics is available. In future work we wish to further generalize and improve QBF-MCTS and also test it with other linguistic models for REG.

References

1. Auer, P., Cesa-Bianchi, N., Fischer, P.: Finite-time analysis of the multiarmed bandit problem. Mach. Learn. **47**(2), 235–256 (2002)
2. Barclay, M., Galton, A.: An influence model for reference object selection in spatially locative phrases. In: Freksa, C., Newcombe, N.S., Gärdenfors, P., Wölfl, S. (eds.) Spatial Cognition 2008. LNCS (LNAI), vol. 5248, pp. 216–232. Springer, Heidelberg (2008). https://doi.org/10.1007/978-3-540-87601-4_17
3. Browne, C.B., et al.: A survey of Monte Carlo tree search methods. IEEE Trans. Comput. Intell. AI Games **4**(1), 1–43 (2012)
4. Cazenave, T.: Nested Monte-Carlo search. In: Proceedings of the 21st International Joint Conference on Artifical Intelligence (IJCAI), pp. 456–461. Morgan Kaufmann Publishers Inc. (2009)
5. Chaslot, G.B.: Monte-Carlo Tree Search. Ph.D. thesis, Maastricht University (2010)
6. Chaslot, G.B., Hoock, J.B., Perez, J., Rimmel, A., Teytaud, O., Winands, M.: Meta Monte-Carlo Tree Search for automatic opening book generation. In: Proceedings of the IJCAI 2009 Workshop on General Intelligence in Game Playing Agents, Pasadena, CA, USA, pp. 7–12 (2009)
7. Chaslot, G.B., Saito, J.T., Bouzy, B., Uiterwijk, J., van den Herik, H.J.: Monte-Carlo strategies for computer Go. In: Proceedings of the 18th BeNeLux Conference on Artificial Intelligence, Namur, Belgium, pp. 83–91 (2006)
8. Coulom, R.: Efficient selectivity and backup operators in Monte-Carlo Tree Search. In: van den Herik, H.J., Ciancarini, P., Donkers, H.H.L.M.J. (eds.) CG 2006. LNCS, vol. 4630, pp. 72–83. Springer, Heidelberg (2007). https://doi.org/10.1007/978-3-540-75538-8_7
9. Dale, R.: Cooking up referring expressions. In: Proceedings of the 27th Annual Meeting on Association for Computational Linguistics, pp. 68–75. Association for Computational Linguistics (1989)
10. Dale, R.: Generating Referring Expressions: Building Descriptions in a Domain of Objects and Processes. MIT Press, Cambridge (1992)
11. Dale, R., Reiter, E.: Computational interpretations of the Gricean maxims in the generation of referring expressions. Cogn. Sci. **19**(2), 233–263 (1995)
12. Kocsis, L., Szepesvári, C.: Bandit based Monte-Carlo planning. In: Fürnkranz, J., Scheffer, T., Spiliopoulou, M. (eds.) ECML 2006. LNCS (LNAI), vol. 4212, pp. 282–293. Springer, Heidelberg (2006). https://doi.org/10.1007/11871842_29
13. Kocsis, L., Szepesvári, C., Willemson, J.: Improved Monte-Carlo search. Technical report, University of Tartu, Institute of Computer Science, Tartu, Estonia (2006)
14. Krahmer, E., van Deemter, K.: Computational generation of referring expressions: a survey. Comput. Linguist. **38**(1), 173–218 (2012)
15. Mast, V.: Referring expression generation in situated interaction. Ph.D. thesis, Universität Bremen (2016)
16. Mast, V., Falomir, Z., Wolter, D.: Probabilistic reference and grounding with PRAGR for dialogues with robots. J. Exp. Theor. Artif. Intell. **28**(5), 1–23 (2016)

17. Méhat, J., Cazenave, T.: Combining uct and nested Monte Carlo search for single-player general game playing. IEEE Trans. Comput. Intell. AI Games **2**(4), 271–277 (2010)
18. Schadd, M.P.D., Winands, M.H.M., van den Herik, H.J., Chaslot, G.M.J.-B., Uiterwijk, J.W.H.M.: Single-player Monte-Carlo Tree Search. In: van den Herik, H.J., Xu, X., Ma, Z., Winands, M.H.M. (eds.) CG 2008. LNCS, vol. 5131, pp. 1–12. Springer, Heidelberg (2008). https://doi.org/10.1007/978-3-540-87608-3_1
19. Van Deemter, K., Gatt, A., van der Sluis, I., Power, R.: Generation of referring expressions: assessing the incremental algorithm. Cogn. Sci. **36**, 799–836 (2012)

Preference-Based Monte Carlo Tree Search

Tobias Joppen[✉], Christian Wirth, and Johannes Fürnkranz

Technische Universität Darmstadt, Darmstadt, Germany
{tjoppen,cwirth,juffi}@ke.tu-darmstadt.de

Abstract. Monte Carlo tree search (MCTS) is a popular choice for solving sequential anytime problems. However, it depends on a numeric feedback signal, which can be difficult to define. Real-time MCTS is a variant which may only rarely encounter states with an explicit, extrinsic reward. To deal with such cases, the experimenter has to supply an additional numeric feedback signal in the form of a heuristic, which intrinsically guides the agent. Recent work has shown evidence that in different areas the underlying structure is ordinal and not numerical. Hence erroneous and biased heuristics are inevitable, especially in such domains. In this paper, we propose a MCTS variant which only depends on qualitative feedback, and therefore opens up new applications for MCTS. We also find indications that translating absolute into ordinal feedback may be beneficial. Using a puzzle domain, we show that our preference-based MCTS variant, wich only receives qualitative feedback, is able to reach a performance level comparable to a regular MCTS baseline, which obtains quantitative feedback.

1 Introduction

Many modern AI problems can be described as a Markov decision processes (MDP), where it is required to select the best action in a given state, in order to maximize the expected long-term reward. *Monte Carlo tree search (MCTS)* is a popular technique for determining the best actions in MDPs [3,10], which combines game tree search with bandit learning. It has been particularly successful in game playing, most notably in Computer Go [16], where it was the first algorithm to compete with professional players in this domain [11,17]. MCTS is especially useful if no state features are available and strong time constraints exist, like in general game playing [6] or for opponent modeling in poker [14].

Classic MCTS depends on a numerical feedback or reward signal, as assumed by the MDP framework, where the algorithm tries to maximize the expectation of this reward. However, for humans it is often hard to define or to determine exact numerical feedback signals. Suboptimally defined reward may allow the learner to maximize its rewards without reaching the desired extrinsic goal [1] or may require a predefined trade-off between multiple objectives [9].

This problem is particularly striking in settings where the natural feedback signal is inadequate to steer the learner to the desired goal. For example, if the

© Springer Nature Switzerland AG 2018
F. Trollmann and A.-Y. Turhan (Eds.): KI 2018, LNAI 11117, pp. 327–340, 2018.
https://doi.org/10.1007/978-3-030-00111-7_28

problem is a complex navigation task and a positive reward is only given when the learner arrives in the goal state, the learner may fail because it will never find the way to the goal, and may thus never receive feedback from which it can improve its state estimations.

Real-time MCTS [3,12] is a popular variant of MCTS often used in real-time scenarios, which tries to solve this problem by introducing heuristics to guide the learner. Instead of solely relying on the natural, *extrinsic* feedback from the domain, it assumes an additional *intrinsic* feedback signal, which is comparable to the heuristic functions commonly used in classical problem solving techniques. In this case, the learner may observe intrinsic reward signals for non-terminal states, in addition to the extrinsic reward in the terminal states. Ideally, this intrinsic feedback should be designed to naturally extend the extrinsic feedback, reflecting the expected extrinsic reward in a state, but this is often a hard task. In fact, if perfect intrinsic feedback is available in each state, making optimal decisions would be trivial. Hence heuristics are often error-prone and may lead to suboptimal solutions in that MCTS may get stuck in locally optimal states. Later we introduce heuristic MCTS (H-MCTS), which uses this idea of evaluating non-terminal states with heuristics but is not bound to real-time applications.

On the other hand, humans are often able to provide reliable qualitative feedback. In particular, humans tend to be less competent in providing exact feedback values on a numerical scale than to determine the better of two states in a pairwise comparison [19]. This observation forms the basis of *preference learning*, which is concerned with learning ranking models from such qualitative training information [7]. Recent work has presented and supported the assumption that emotions are by nature relative and similar ideas exist in topics like psychology, philosophy, neuroscience, marketing research and more [22]. Following this idea, extracting preferences from numeric values does not necessarily mean a loss of information (the absolute difference), but a loss of biases caused through absolute annotation [22]. Since many established algorithms like MCTS are not able to work with preferences, modifications of algorithms have been proposed to enable this, like in the realm of reinforcement learning [5,8,21].

In this paper we propose a variant of MCTS which works on ordinal reward MDPs (OMDPs) [20], instead of MDPs. The basic idea behind the resulting preference-based Monte Carlo tree search algorithm is to use the principles of *preference-based* or *dueling bandits* [4,23,24] to replace the *multi-armed bandits* used in classic MCTS. Our work may thus be viewed as either extending the work on preference-based bandits to tree search, or to extend MCTS to allow for preference-based feedback, as illustrated in Fig. 1. Thereby, the tree policy does not select a single path, but a binary tree leading to multiple rollouts per iteration and we obtain pairwise feedback for these rollouts.

We evaluate the performance of this algorithm by comparing it to heuristic MCTS (H-MCTS). Hence, we can determine the effects of approximate, heuristic feedback in relation to the ground truth. We use the 8-puzzle domain since simple but imperfect heuristics already exist for this problem. In the next section, we start the paper with an overview of MDPs, MCTS and preference learning.

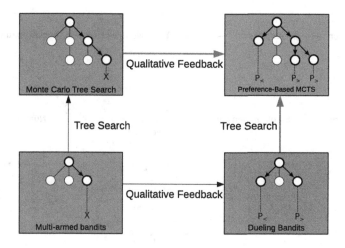

Fig. 1. Research in Monte Carlo methods

2   Foundations

In the following, we review the concepts of *Markov decision processes* (MDP), *heuristic Monte Carlo tree search* (H-MCTS) and *preference-based bandits*, which form the basis of our work. We use an MDP as the formal framework for the problem definition, and H-MCTS is the baseline solution strategy we build upon. We also briefly recapitulate *multi armed bandits* (MAP) as the basis of MCTS and their extension to preference-based bandits.

2.1   Markov Decision Process

A typical Monte Carlo tree search problem can be formalized as a Markov Decision Process (MDP) [15], consisting of a set of *states* S, the set of *actions* A that the agent can perform (where $A(,s) \subset A$ is applicable in state s), a *state transition* function $\delta(s' \mid s, a)$, a *reward function* $r(s) \in \mathbb{R}$ for reaching state s and a distribution $\mu(s) \in [0, 1]$ for starting states. We assume a single *start state* and non-zero rewards only in terminal states.

An Ordinal Reward MDP (OMDP) is similar to MDP but the reward function, which does not lie in $\mathbb{R}$, but is defined over a qualitative scale, such that states can only be compared preference wise.

The task is to learn a *policy* $\pi(a \mid s)$ that defines the probability of selecting an action a in state s. The optimal policy $\pi^*(a \mid s)$ maximizes the expected, cumulative reward [18] (MDP setting), or maximizes the preferential information for each reward in the trajectory [20] (OMDP setting). For finding an optimal policy, one needs to solve the so-called exploration/exploitation problem. The state/action spaces are usually too large to sample exhaustively. Hence, it is required to trade off the improvement of the current, best policy (exploitation) with an exploration of unknown parts of the state/action space.

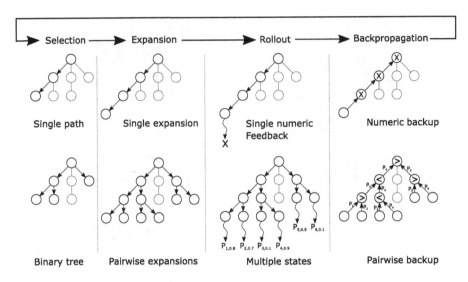

Fig. 2. Comparisons of MCTS (top) and preference-based MCTS (bottom)

2.2 Multi-armed Bandits

Multi-armed bandits (MABs) are a method for identifying the arm (or action) with the highest return by repeatedly pulling one of the possible arms. They may be viewed as an MDP with only one non-terminal state, and the task is to achieve the highest average reward in the limit. Here the exploration/exploitation dilemma is to play the best-known arm often (exploitation) while it is at the same time necessary to search for the best arm (exploration). A well-known technique for resolving this dilemma in bandit problems are *upper confidence bounds* (UCB [2]), which allow to bound the expected reward for a certain arm, and to choose the action with the highest associated upper bound. The bounds are iteratively updated based on the observed outcomes. The simplest UCB policy

$$UCB1 = \bar{X}_j + \sqrt{\frac{2\ln n}{n_j}} \tag{1}$$

adds a bonus of $\sqrt{2\ln n/n_j}$, based on the number of performed trials n and how often an arm was selected (n_j). The first term favors arms with high payoffs, while the second term guarantees exploration [2]. The reward is expected to be bound by $[0, 1]$.

2.3 Monte Carlo Tree Search

Considering not only one but multiple, sequential decisions leads to sequential decision problems. *Monte Carlo tree search* (MCTS) is a method for approximating an optimal policy for a MDP. It builds a partial search tree, guided by the estimates for the encountered actions [10]. The tree expands deeper in parts with the most promising actions and spends less time evaluating less promising action sequences. The algorithm iterates over four steps, illustrated in the upper part of Fig. 2 [3]:

1. *Selection:* Starting from the initial state s_0, a *tree policy* is applied until a state is encountered that has unvisited successor states.
2. *Expansion:* One successor state is added to the tree.
3. *Simulation:* Starting from this state, a *simulation policy* is applied until a terminal state is observed.
4. *Backpropagation:* The reward accumulated during the simulation process is backed up through the selected nodes in tree.

In order to adapt UCB to tree search, it is necessary to consider a bias, which results from the uneven selection of the child nodes, in the tree selection policy. The UCT policy

$$UCT = \bar{X}_j + 2C_p\sqrt{\frac{2\ln n}{n_j}} \tag{2}$$

has been shown to be optimal within the tree search setting up to a constant factor [10].

2.4 Heuristic Monte Carlo Tree Search

In large state/action spaces, rollouts can take many actions until a terminal state is observed. However, long rollouts are subject to high variance due to the stochastic sampling policy. Hence, it can be beneficial to disregard such long rollouts in favor of shorter rollouts with lower variance. *Heuristic MCTS* (H-MCTS) stops rollouts after a fixed number of actions and uses a heuristic evaluation function in case no terminal state was observed [12,13]. The heuristic is assumed to approximate $V(s)$ and can therefore be used to update the expectation.

2.5 Preference-Based Bandits

Preference-based multi-armed bandits (PB-MAB), closely related to *dueling bandits*, are the adaption of multi-armed bandits to preference-based feedback [24]. Here the bandit iteratively chooses two arms that get compared to each other. The result of this comparison is a preference signal that indicates which of two arms a_i and a_j is the better choice ($a_i \succ a_j$) or whether they are equivalent.

The *relative UCB* algorithm (RUCB [25]) allows to compute approximate, optimal policies for PB-MABs by computing the Condorcet winner, i.e., the action that wins all comparisons to all other arms. To this end, RUCB stores the number of times w_{ij} an arm i wins against another arm j and uses this information to calculate an upper confidence bound

$$u_{ij} = \frac{w_{ij}}{w_{ij} + w_{ji}} + \sqrt{\frac{\alpha \ln t}{w_{ij} + w_{ji}}}, \tag{3}$$

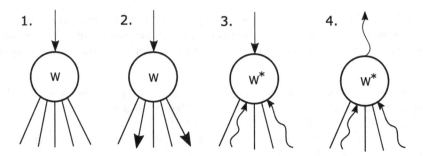

Fig. 3. A local node view of PB-MCTS's iteration:selection; child selection; child backprop and update; backprop one trajectory.

for each pair of arms. $\alpha > \frac{1}{2}$ is a parameter to trade-off exploration and exploitation and t is the number of observed preferences. These bounds are used to maintain a set of possible Condorcet winners. If at least one possible Condorcet winner is detected, it is tested against its hardest competitor.

Several alternatives to RUCB have been investigated in the literature, but most PB-MAB algorithms are "first explore, then exploit" methods. They explore until a pre-defined number of iterations is reached, and start exploiting afterwards. Such techniques are only applicable if it is possible to define the number of iterations in advance. But this is not possible to do for each node. Therefore we use RUCB in the following. For a general overview of PB-MAB algorithms, we refer the reader to [4].

3   Preference-Based Monte Carlo Tree Search

In this section, we introduce a preference-based variant of Monte Carlo tree search (PB-MCTS), as shown in Fig. 1. This work can be viewed as an extension of previous work in two ways: (1) it adapts Monte Carlo tree search to preference-based feedback, comparable to the relation between preference-based bandits and multi-armed bandits, and (2) it generalizes preference-based bandits to sequential decision problems like MCTS generalizes multi-armed bandits.

To this end, we adapt RUCB to a tree-based setting, as shown in Algorithm 1. In contrast to H-MCTS, PB-MCTS works for OMDPs and selects two actions per node in the *selection phase*, as shown in Fig. 3. Since RUCB is used as a tree policy, each node in the tree maintains its own weight matrix $\mathbf{W}$ to store the history of action comparisons in this node. Actions are then selected based on a modified version of the RUCB formula (3)

$$\hat{u}_{ij} = \frac{w_{ij}}{w_{ij} + w_{ji}} + c\sqrt{\frac{\alpha \ln t}{w_{ij} + w_{ji}}}, \qquad (4)$$

$$= \frac{w_{ij}}{w_{ij} + w_{ji}} + \sqrt{\frac{\hat{\alpha} \ln t}{w_{ij} + w_{ji}}},$$

Algorithm 1: One Iteration of PB-MCTS

---

1 **function PB-MCTS** $(T, s, \alpha, \mathbf{W}, B)$;

    Input : A set of explored states $\hat{S}$, the current state s, exploration-factor α,
               matrix of wins $\mathbf{W}$ (per state), list of last Condorcet pick B (per state)

    Output: $[s', \hat{S}, \mathbf{W}, B]$

2   $[a_1, a_2, B] \leftarrow$ SELECTACTIONPAIR$(\mathbf{W}_s, B_s)$;

3   **for** $a \in \{a_1, a_2\}$ **do**

4       $s' \sim \delta(s' \mid s, a)$;

5   **if** $s' \in \hat{S}$ **then**

6          $[sim[a], \hat{S}, \mathbf{W}, B] \leftarrow$ PB-MCTS$(\hat{S}, s', \alpha, \mathbf{W}, B)$;

7   **else**

8          $\hat{S} \leftarrow \hat{S} \cup \{s'\}$;

9          $sim[a] \leftarrow$ SIMULATE(a);

10   **end**

11 **end**

12 $w_{sa_1a_2} \leftarrow w_{sa_1a_2} + 𝟙(sim[a_2] \succ sim[a_1])$
                 $+ \frac{1}{2}𝟙(sim[a_1] \simeq sim[a_2])$;

13 $w_{sa_2a_1} \leftarrow w_{sa_2a_1} + 𝟙(sim[a_1] \succ sim[a_2])$
                 $+ \frac{1}{2}𝟙(sim[a_2] \simeq sim[a_1])$;

14 $s_{return} \leftarrow$ RETURNPOLICY$(s, a_1, a_2, sim[a_1], sim[a_2])$;

15 **return** $[s_{return}, T, \mathbf{W}, B]$;

---

where $\alpha > \frac{1}{2}$, $c > 0$ and $\hat{\alpha} = c^2\alpha > 0$ are the hyperparameters that allow to trade off exploration and exploitation. Therefore, RUCB can be used in trees with the corrected lower bound $0 < \alpha$.

Based on this weight matrix, SELECTACTIONPAIR then selects two actions using the same strategy as in RUCB: If $C \neq \emptyset$, the first action a_1 is chosen among the possible Condorcet winners $C = \{a_c \mid \forall j : u_{cj} \geq 0.5\}$. Typically, the choice among all candidates $c \in C$ is random. However, in case the last selected Condorcet candidate in this node is still in C, it has a 50% chance to be selected again, whereas each of the other candidates can be share the remaining 50% of the probability mass evenly. The second action a_2 is chosen to be a_1's hardest competitor, i.e., the move whose win rate against a_1 has the highest upper bound $a_2 = \arg\max_l u_{la_1}$. Note that, just as in RUCB, the two selected arms need not necessarily be different, i.e., it may happen that $a_1 = a_2$. This is a useful property because once the algorithm has reliably identified the best move in a node, forcing it to play a suboptimal move in order to obtain a new preference would be counter-productive. In this case, only one rollout is created and the node will not receive a preference signal in this node. However, the number of visits to this node are updated, which may lead to a different choice in the next iteration.

The *expansion and simulation phases* are essentially the same as in conventional MCTS except that multiple nodes are expanded in each iteration. SIMULATE executes the *simulation policy* until a terminal state or break condition occurs as explained below. In our experiments the simulation policy performs a random choice among all possible actions. Since two actions per node are selected, one simulation for each action is conducted in each node. Hence, the algorithm traverses a binary subtree of the already explored state space tree before selecting multiple nodes to expand. As a result, the number of rollouts is not constant in each iteration but increases exponential with the tree depth. The preference-based feedback is obtained from a pairwise comparison of the performed rollouts.

In the *backpropagation phase*, the obtained comparisons are propagated up towards the root of the tree. In each node, the **W** matrix is updated by comparing the simulated states of the corresponding actions i and j and updating the entry w_{ij}. Passing both rollouts to the parent in each node would result in a exponential increase of pairwise comparisons, due to the binary tree traversal. Hence, the newest iteration could dominate all previous iterations in terms of the gained information. This is a problem, since the feedback obtained in a single iteration may be noisy and thus yield unreliable estimates. Monte Carlo techniques need to average multiple samples to obtain a sufficient estimate of the expectation. Multiple updates of two actions in a node may cause further problems: The preferences may arise from bad estimates since one action may not be as well explored as the other. It would be unusual for RUCB to select the same two actions multiple times consecutively, since either the first action is no Condorcet candidate anymore or the second candidate, the best competitor, will change. These problems may lead to unbalanced exploration and exploitation terms resulting in overly bad ratings for some actions. Thus, only one of the two states is propagated back to the root node. This way it can be assured that the number of pairwise comparisons in the nodes (and especially in the root node) remains constant ($= 1$) over all iterations, ensuring numerical stability.

For this reason, we need a *return policy* to determine what information is propagated upwards (compare RETURNPOLICY in Algorithm 1). An obvious choice is the *best preference policy* (BPP), which always propagates the preferred alternative upwards, as illustrated in step four of Fig. 3. A random selection is used in case of indifferent actions. We also considered returning the best action according to the node's updated matrix **W**, to make a random selection based on the weights of **W**, and to make a completely random selection. However, preliminary experiments showed a substantial advantage when using BPP.

4   Experimental Setup

We compare PB-MCTS to H-MCTS in the 8-puzzle domain. The 8-puzzle is a move-based deterministic puzzle where the player can move numbers on a grid. It is played on a 3×3 grid where each of the 9 squares is either blank or has a tile with number 1 to 8 on it. A move consists of shifting one of the up to 4 neighboring tiles to the blank square, thereby exchanging the position of the blank and this neighbor. The task is then to find a sequence of moves that lead from a given start state to a known end state (see Fig. 4). The winning

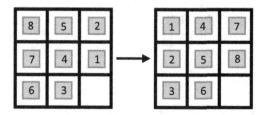

Fig. 4. The start state (left) and end state (right) of the 8-Puzzle. The player can swap the positions of the empty field and one adjacent number.

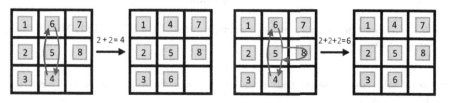

(a) Manhattan distance   (b) Manhattan distance with linear conflict

Fig. 5. The two heuristics used for the 8-puzzle.

state is the only goal state. Since it is not guaranteed to find the goal state, the problem is an infinite horizon problem. However, we terminate the evaluation after 100 time-steps to limit the runtime. Games that are terminated in this way are counted as losses for the agent. The agent is not aware of this maximum.

4.1 Heuristics

As a heuristic for the 8-puzzle, we use the *Manhattan distance with linear conflicts* (MDC), a variant of the *Manhattan distance* (MD). MD is an optimistic estimate for the minimum number of moves required to reach the goal state. It is defined as

$$H_{manhattan}(s) = \sum_{i=0}^{8} |pos(s,i) - goal(i)|, \tag{5}$$

where $pos(s,i)$ is the (x,y) coordinate of number i in game state s, $goal(i)$ is its position in the goal state, and $|\cdot|_1$ refers to the 1-norm or Manhattan-norm.

MDC additionally detects and penalizes linear conflicts. Essentially, a linear conflict occurs if two numbers i and j are on the row where they belong, but on swapped positions. For example, in Fig. 5b, the tiles 4 and 6 are in the right column, but need to pass each other in order to arrive at their right squares. For each such linear conflict, MDC increases the MD estimate by two because in order to resolve such a linear conflict, at least one of the two numbers needs to leave its target row (1st move) to make place for the second number, and later needs to be moved back to this row (2nd move). The resulting heuristic is

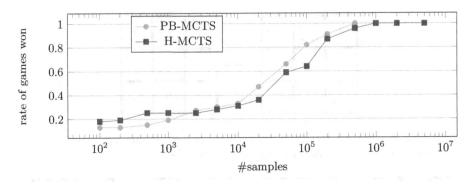

Fig. 6. Using their best hyperparameter configurations, PB-MCTS and H-MCTS reach similar win rates.

still admissible in the sense that it can never over-estimate the actually needed number of moves.

4.2   Preferences

In order to deal with the infinite horizons during the search, both algorithms rely on the same heuristic evaluation function, which is called after the rollouts have reached a given depth limit. For the purpose of comparability, both algorithms use the same heuristic for evaluating non-terminal states, but PB-MCTS does not observe the exact values but only preferences that are derived from the returned values. Comparing arm a_i with a_j leads to terminal or heuristic rewards r_i and r_j, based on the according rollouts. From those reward values, we derive preferences

$$(a_k \succ a_l) \Leftrightarrow (r_k > r_l) \text{ and } (a_k \simeq a_l) \Leftrightarrow (r_k = r_l)$$

which are used as feedback for PB-MCTS. H-MCTS can directly observe the reward values r_i.

4.3   Parameter Settings

Both algorithms H-MCTS and PB-MCTS are subject to the following hyperparameters:

- *Rollout length*: the number of actions performed at most per rollout (tested with: 5, 10, 25, 50).
- *Exploration-exploitation trade-off*: the C parameter for H-MCTS and the α parameter for PB-MCTS (tested with: 0.1 to 1 in 10 steps).
- *Allowed transition-function samples per move (#samples)*: a hardware-independent parameter to limit the time an agent has per move[1] (tested with logarithmic scale from 10^2 to $5 \cdot 10^6$ in 10 steps).

---

[1] Please note that this is a fair comparison between PB-MCTS and H-MCTS: The first uses more #samples per iteration, the latter uses more iterations.

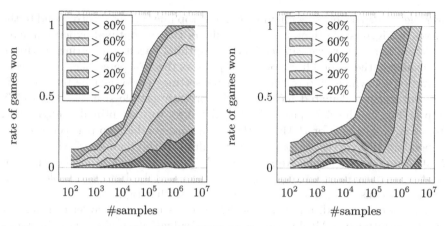

(a) Configuration percentiles of PB-MCTS (b) Configuration percentiles of H-MCTS

Fig. 7. The distribution of hyperparameters to wins is shown in steps of 0.2 percentiles. The amount of wins decreases rapidly for H-MCTS if the parameter setting is not among the best 20%. On the other hand, PB-MCTS shows a more robust curve without such a steep decrease in win rate.

For each combination of parameters 100 runs are executed. We consider #samples to be a parameter of the problem domain, as it relates to the available computational resources. The rollout length and the trade-off parameter are optimized.

5   Results

PB-MCTS seems to work well if tuned, but showing a more steady but slower convergence rate if untuned, which may be due to the exponential growth.

5.1   Tuned: Maximal Performance

Figure 6 shows the maximal win rate over all possible hyperparameter combinations, given a fixed number of transition-function samples per move. One can see that for a lower number of samples (≤ 1000), both algorithms lose most games, but H-MCTS has a somewhat better performance in that region. However, Above that threshold, H-MCTS no longer outperforms PB-MCTS. In contrary, PB-MCTS typically achieves a slightly better win rate than H-MCTS.

5.2   Untuned: More Robust but Slower

We also analyzed the distribution of wins for non-optimal hyper-parameter configurations. Figure 7 shows several curves of win rate over the number of samples, each representing a different percentile of the distribution of the number of wins over the hyperparmenter configurations. The top lines of Fig. 7 correspond to the curves of Fig. 6, since they show the results of the the optimal hyperparameter configuration. Below, we can see how non-optimal parameter settings perform. For example, the second line from the top shows the 80% percentile, i.e. the configuration for which 20% of the parameter settings performed better and 80% perform worse, calculated independently for each sample size. For PB-MCTS (top of Fig. 7), the 80% percentile line lies next to the optimal configuration from Fig. 6, whereas for H-MCTS there is a considerable gap between the corresponding two curves. In particular, the drop in the number of wins around $2 \cdot 10^5$ samples is notable. Apparently, H-MCTS gets stuck in local optima for most hyperparameter settings. PB-MCTS seems to be less susceptible to this problem because its win count does not decrease that rapidly.

On the other hand, untuned PB-MCTS seems to have a slower convergence rate than untuned H-MCTS, as can be seen for high #sample values. This may be due to the exponential growth of trajectories per iteration in PB-MCTS.

6   Conclusion

In this paper, we proposed PB-MCTS, a new variant of Monte Carlo tree search which is able to cope with preference-based feedback. In contrast to conventional MCTS, this algorithm uses relative UCB as its core component. We showed how to use trajectory preferences in a tree search setting by performing multiple rollouts and comparisons per iteration.

Our evaluations in the 8-puzzle domain showed that the performance of H-MCTS and PB-MCTS strongly depends on adequate hyperparameter tuning. PB-MCTS is better able to cope with suboptimal parameter configurations and erroneous heuristics for lower sample sizes, whereas H-MCTS has a better convergence rate for higher values.

One main problem with preference-based tree search is the exponential growth in the number of explored trajectories. Using RUCB grants the possibility to exploit only if both actions to play are the same. This way the exponential growth can be reduced. But nevertheless we are currently working on techniques that allow to prune the binary subtree without changing the feedback obtained in each node. Motivated by alpha-beta pruning and similar techniques in conventional game-tree search, we expect that such techniques can further improve the performance and remove the exponential growth to some degree.

Acknowledgments. This work was supported by the German Research Foundation (DFG project number FU 580/10). We gratefully acknowledge the use of the Lichtenberg high performance computer of the TU Darmstadt for our experiments.

References

1. Amodei, D., Olah, C., Steinhardt, J., Christiano, P., Schulman, J., Mané, D.: Concrete problems in AI safety. CoRR abs/1606.06565 (2016)
2. Auer, P., Cesa-Bianchi, N., Fischer, P.: Finite-time analysis of the multiarmed bandit problem. Mach. Learn. **47**(2–3), 235–256 (2002)
3. Browne, C.B., et al.: A survey of Monte Carlo tree search methods. IEEE Trans. Comput. Intell. AI Games **4**(1), 1–43 (2012)
4. Busa-Fekete, R., Hüllermeier, E.: A survey of preference-based online learning with bandit algorithms. In: Auer, P., Clark, A., Zeugmann, T., Zilles, S. (eds.) ALT 2014. LNCS (LNAI), vol. 8776, pp. 18–39. Springer, Cham (2014). https://doi.org/10.1007/978-3-319-11662-4_3
5. Christiano, P., Leike, J., Brown, T.B., Martic, M., Legg, S., Amodei, D.: Deep reinforcement learning from human preferences. In: Guyon, I., et al. (eds.) Advances in Neural Information Processing Systems 30 (NIPS 2017), Long Beach, CA (2017)
6. Finnsson, H.: Simulation-based general game playing. Ph.D. thesis, Reykjavík University (2012)
7. Fürnkranz, J., Hüllermeier, E. (eds.): Preference Learning. Springer, Heidelberg (2011). https://doi.org/10.1007/978-3-642-14125-6
8. Fürnkranz, J., Hüllermeier, E., Cheng, W., Park, S.H.: Preference-based reinforcement learning: a formal framework and a policy iteration algorithm. Mach. Learn. **89**(1–2), 123–156 (2012). https://doi.org/10.1007/s10994-012-5313-8. Special Issue of Selected Papers from ECML PKDD 2011
9. Knowles, J.D., Watson, R.A., Corne, D.W.: Reducing local optima in single-objective problems by multi-objectivization. In: Zitzler, E., Thiele, L., Deb, K., Coello Coello, C.A., Corne, D. (eds.) EMO 2001. LNCS, vol. 1993, pp. 269–283. Springer, Heidelberg (2001). https://doi.org/10.1007/3-540-44719-9_19
10. Kocsis, L., Szepesvári, C.: Bandit based Monte-Carlo planning. In: Fürnkranz, J., Scheffer, T., Spiliopoulou, M. (eds.) ECML 2006. LNCS (LNAI), vol. 4212, pp. 282–293. Springer, Heidelberg (2006). https://doi.org/10.1007/11871842_29
11. Lee, C.S.: The computational intelligence of MoGo revealed in Taiwan's computer go tournaments. IEEE Trans. Comput. Intell. AI Games **1**, 73–89 (2009)
12. Pepels, T., Winands, M.H., Lanctot, M.: Real-time Monte Carlo tree search in Ms Pac-Man. IEEE Trans. Comput. Intell. AI Games **6**(3), 245–257 (2014)
13. Perez-Liebana, D., Mostaghim, S., Lucas, S.M.: Multi-objective tree search approaches for general video game playing. In: IEEE Congress on Evolutionary Computation (CEC 2016), pp. 624–631. IEEE (2016)
14. Ponsen, M., Gerritsen, G., Chaslot, G.: Integrating opponent models with Monte-Carlo tree search in poker. In: Proceedings of Interactive Decision Theory and Game Theory Workshop at the Twenty-Fourth Conference on Artificial Intelligence (AAAI 2010), AAAI Workshops, vol. WS-10-03, pp. 37–42 (2010)
15. Puterman, M.L.: Markov Decision Processes: Discrete Stochastic Dynamic Programming, 2nd edn. Wiley, Hoboken (2005)
16. Rimmel, A., Teytaud, O., Lee, C.S., Yen, S.J., Wang, M.H., Tsai, S.R.: Current frontiers in computer go. IEEE Trans. Comput. Intell. AI Games **2**(4), 229–238 (2010)
17. Silver, D., et al.: Mastering the game of go without human knowledge. Nature **550**(7676), 354 (2017)
18. Sutton, R.S., Barto, A.: Reinforcement Learning: An Introduction. MIT Press, Cambridge (1998)

19. Thurstone, L.L.: A law of comparative judgement. Psychol. Rev. **34**, 278–286 (1927)
20. Weng, P.: Markov decision processes with ordinal rewards: reference point-based preferences. In: Proceedings of the 21st International Conference on Automated Planning and Scheduling (ICAPS 2011) (2011)
21. Wirth, C., Fürnkranz, J., Neumann, G.: Model-free preference-based reinforcement learning. In: Proceedings of the 30th AAAI Conference on Artificial Intelligence (AAAI 2016), pp. 2222–2228 (2016)
22. Yannakakis, G.N., Cowie, R., Busso, C.: The ordinal nature of emotions. In: Proceedings of the 7th International Conference on Affective Computing and Intelligent Interaction (ACII 2017) (2017)
23. Yue, Y., Broder, J., Kleinberg, R., Joachims, T.: The k-armed dueling bandits problem. J. Comput. Syst. Sci. **78**(5), 1538–1556 (2012). https://doi.org/10.1016/j.jcss.2011.12.028
24. Yue, Y., Joachims, T.: Interactively optimizing information retrieval systems as a dueling bandits problem. In: Proceedings of the 26th Annual International Conference on Machine Learning (ICML 2009), pp. 1201–1208 (2009)
25. Zoghi, M., Whiteson, S., Munos, R., Rijke, M.: Relative upper confidence bound for the k-armed dueling bandit problem. In: Proceedings of the 31st International Conference on Machine Learning (ICML 2014), pp. 10–18 (2014)

Belief Revision

Probabilistic Belief Revision
via Similarity of Worlds Modulo Evidence

Gavin Rens[1]($\boxtimes$), Thomas Meyer[1], Gabriele Kern-Isberner[2],
and Abhaya Nayak[3]

[1] Centre for Artificial Intelligence - CSIR Meraka, University of Cape Town,
Cape Town, South Africa
{grens,tmeyer}@cs.uct.ac.za
[2] Technical University of Dortmund, Dortmund, Germany
gabriele.kern-isberner@cs.tu-dortmund.de
[3] Macquarie University, Sydney, Australia
abhaya.nayak@mq.edu.au

Abstract. Similarity among worlds plays a pivotal role in providing the
semantics for different kinds of belief change. Although similarity is, intuitively, a context-sensitive concept, the accounts of similarity presently
proposed are, by and large, context blind. We propose an account of
similarity that is context sensitive, and when belief change is concerned,
we take it that the epistemic input provides the required context. We
accordingly develop and examine two accounts of probabilistic belief
change that are based on such evidence-sensitive similarity. The first
switches between two extreme behaviors depending on whether or not
the evidence in question is consistent with the current knowledge. The
second gracefully changes its behavior depending on the degree to which
the evidence is consistent with current knowledge. Finally, we analyze
these two belief change operators with respect to a select set of plausible
postulates.

Keywords: Belief revision · Probability · Similarity
Bayesian conditioning · Lewis imaging

1 Introduction

Lewis [1] first proposed *imaging* to analyze conditional reasoning in probabilistic
settings, and it has recently been the focus of several works on probabilistic belief
change [2–5]. Imaging is the approach of moving the belief in worlds at one
moment to similar worlds compatible with evidence (epistemic input) received
at a next moment.

One of the main benefits of imaging is that it overcomes the problem with
Bayesian conditioning, namely, being undefined when evidence is inconsistent
with current beliefs (sometimes called the *zero prior problem*). Gärdenfors [6],
Mishra and Nayak [4] and Rens et al. [5] proposed generalizations of Lewis's

© Springer Nature Switzerland AG 2018
F. Trollmann and A.-Y. Turhan (Eds.): KI 2018, LNAI 11117, pp. 343–356, 2018.
https://doi.org/10.1007/978-3-030-00111-7_29

original definition. Although imaging approaches can deal with the zero prior problem, they could, in principle, be used in nominal cases too.

In this paper we propose a new generalization of imaging – ipso facto a family of imaging-based belief revision operators – and analyze other probabilistic belief revision methods with respect to it. In particular, we propose a version of imaging based on the movement of probability mass weighted by the similarity between possible worlds. Intuitively, the proposed operators use a measure of similarity between worlds to shift probability mass in order to revise according to new information, where the similarity measure is the agent's background knowledge and is informed (parameterized) by what is observed.

Similarity among worlds plays a pivotal role in accounts of belief change – both probabilistic and non-probabilistic. Intuitively, similarity is a context sensitive notion. For instance, Richard is similar to a lion with respect to being brave, not with respect to their food habits, or, if I show you an upholstered chair, the process you use to estimate it similarity to a given bench will likely be different to the process you use to estimate its similarity to a given upholstering fabric. We take that notion seriously, and propose that the account of similarity among worlds should be sensitive to the evidence.

We define the similarity modulo evidence (SME) operator employing a family of similarity functions. SME revision should be viewed as a generalization of probabilistic belief revision. We prove that there is an instantiation of a similarity function for which SME is equivalent to Bayesian conditioning, and we prove that there are versions of SME equivalent to known versions of imaging.

There is a vast amount of literature on similarity between two stimuli, objects, data-points or pieces of information [7,8]. To make a start with this research, we have focused on one measure of similarity. Shepard [9] proposed a "universal generalization law" for converting measures of difference/distance to measures of similarity in an appropriately scaled psychological space. Shepard's approach has been widely adopted in cognitive psychology, and biology (concerning perception) [10,11]. Suppose that the "appropriate scale" is that of probabilities, that is, $[0, 1]$, and that the "psychological space" is the epistemic notion of possible worlds. Shepard's definition of similarity is then easily applied to the possible worlds approach of formal epistemology and seems to fit well into our SME method, which employs the notion of possible worlds. We propose a version of SME based on Shepard's generalization law.

Due to both conditioning and Shepard-based SME revision (SSR) having desirable and undesirable properties, we propose two versions of SME revision which combine the two methods in order to maximize their desirable properties. One of the combination SME revision operators *switches* between BC and SSR depending on whether the new evidence is consistent with the current belief state. The other combination operator varies smoothly between BC and SSR depending on the *degree* to which the new evidence is consistent with the current belief state. Both combination operators satisfy three core rationality postulates, but only the switching operator satisfies all six postulates presented.

Due to space limitations, we only provide proof sketches for some of the less intuitive results.

2 Background and Related Work

We shall work with a finitely generated classical propositional logic. Let $\mathcal{P} = \{q, r, s, \ldots\}$ be a finite set of *atoms*. Formally, a *world* w is a unique assignment of truth values to all the atoms in $\mathcal{P}$. An agent may consider some non-empty subset $W = \{w_1, w_2, \ldots, w_n\}$ of the possible worlds. Let L be all propositional formulae which can be formed from $\mathcal{P}$ and the logical connectives $\wedge$ and $\neg$, with $\top$ abbreviating tautology and $\bot$ abbreviating contradiction. Let α be a sentence in L. The classical notion of satisfaction is used. World w satisfies (is a model of) α is written $w \Vdash \alpha$. $Mod(\alpha)$ denotes the set of models of α, that is, $w \in Mod(\alpha)$ iff $w \Vdash \alpha$. We call w an α-world if $w \in Mod(\alpha)$; α entails β (denoted $\alpha \models \beta$) iff $Mod(\alpha) \subseteq Mod(\beta)$; α is equivalent to β (denoted $\alpha \equiv \beta$) iff $Mod(\alpha) = Mod(\beta)$. In this paper, α and β denote evidence, by default.

Often, in the exposition of this paper, a world will be referred to by its truth vector. For instance, if a two-atom vocabulary is placed in order $\langle q, r \rangle$ and $w \Vdash \neg q \wedge r$, then w may be referred to as 01. We denote the truth assignment of atom q by world w as $w(q)$. For instance, $w(q) = 0$ and $w(r) = 1$.

In this work, the basic semantic element of an agent's beliefs is a probability distribution or a *belief state* $B = \{(w_1, p_1), (w_2, p_2), \ldots, (w_n, p_n)\}$, where p_i is the agent's degree of belief (the probability that she assigns to the assertion) that w_i is the actual world, and $\sum_{(w,p) \in B} p = 1$. For parsimony, let $B = \langle p_1, \ldots, p_n \rangle$ be the probabilities that belief state B assigns to $w_1, \ldots, w_n$ where, for instance, $\langle w_1, w_2, w_3, w_4 \rangle = \langle 11, 10, 01, 00 \rangle$, and $\langle w_1, w_2, \ldots, w_8 \rangle = \langle 111, 110, \ldots, 000 \rangle$. $B(\alpha)$ abbreviates $\sum_{w \in Mod(\alpha)} B(w)$.

Let K be a set of sentences closed under logical consequence. Conventionally, (classical) *expansion* (denoted $+$) is the logical consequences of $K \cup \{\alpha\}$, where α is new information and K is the current belief set. Or if the current beliefs can be captured as a single sentence β, expansion is defined simply as $\beta + \alpha \equiv \beta \wedge \alpha$. One school of thought says that probabilistic expansion (restricted revision) is equivalent to Bayesian conditioning [6] and others have argue that expansion is something else [12,13]. The argument for Bayesian conditioning (BC) is evidenced by it being defined only when $B(\alpha) \neq 0$, thus making BC expansion equivalent to BC revision. In other words, one could define expansion to be

$$B_\alpha^{\mathsf{BC}} := \{(w, p) \mid w \in W, p = B(w \mid \alpha), B(\alpha) \neq 0\},$$

where $B(w \mid \alpha)$ is defined as $B(\phi_w \wedge \alpha)/B(\alpha)$ and ϕ_w is a sentence identifying w (i.e., a complete theory for w).[1] Note that $B_\alpha^{\mathsf{BC}} = \emptyset$ iff $B(\alpha) = 0$. This implies that BC is ill-defined when $B(\alpha) = 0$.

---

[1] In general, we write B_α^* to mean the (the result of) revision of B with α by application of operator $*$.

The technique of *Lewis imaging* for the revision of belief states [1] requires that for each world $w \in W$ there be a unique 'closest' world $w^\alpha \in Mod(\alpha)$ for given evidence α. If we indicate Lewis's original imaging operation with LI, then his definition can be stated as

$$B^{\mathsf{LI}}_\alpha := \{(w,p) \mid w \in W, p = 0 \text{ if } w \not\Vdash \alpha, \text{ else } p = \sum_{\{v \in W \mid v^\alpha = w\}} B(v)\},$$

where v^α is the unique closest α-world to v. He calls B^{LI}_α the image of B on α. In words, $B^{\mathsf{LI}}_\alpha(w)$ is zero if w does not model α, but if it does, then w retains all the probability it had and accrues the probability mass from all the non-α-worlds closest to it. This form of imaging only shifts probabilities around; the probabilities in B^{LI}_α sum to 1 without the need for any normalization.

Every world having a unique closest α-world is quite a strong requirement. We now mention an approach which relaxes the uniqueness requirement. Gärdenfors [6] describes his generalization of Lewis imaging (which he calls *general imaging*) as "... instead of moving all the probability assigned to a world W^i by a probability function P to a unique ("closest") A-world W^j, when imaging on A, one can introduce the weaker requirement that the probability of W^i be distributed among *several* A-worlds (that are "equally close")." Gärdenfors does not provide a constructive method for his approach, but insists that $B^\#_\alpha(\alpha) = 1$, where $B^\#_\alpha$ is the image of B on α. Rens et al. [5] introduced *generalized* imaging via a constructive method. It is a particular instance of Gärdenfors' general imaging. Rens et al. [5] use a pseudo-distance measure between worlds, as defined by Lehmann et al. [14] and adopted by Chhogyal et al. [3].[2]

Definition 1. *A pseudo-distance function $d : W \times W \to \mathbb{Z}$ satisfies the following four conditions: for all worlds $w, w', w'' \in W$,*

1. $d(w, w') \geq 0$ *(Non-negativity)*
2. $d(w, w) = 0$ *(Identity)*
3. $d(w, w') = d(w', w)$ *(Symmetry)*
4. $d(w, w'') \leq d(w, w') + d(w', w'')$ *(Triangle Inequality)*

One may also want to impose a condition on a distance function such that any two distinct worlds must have some distance between them: For all $w, w' \in W$, if $w \neq w'$, then $d(w, w') > 0$. This condition is called *Separability*.[3]

Rens et al. [5] defined $Min(\alpha, w, d)$ to be the set of α-worlds closest to w with respect to pseudo-distance d. Formally,

$$Min(\alpha, w, d) := \{w' \Vdash \alpha \mid \forall w'' \Vdash \alpha, d(w', w) \leq d(w'', w)\},$$

---

[2] Similar axioms of distance have been adopted in mathematics and psychology for a long time.

[3] The term *separability* has been defined differently by different authors.

where $d(\cdot)$ is some pseudo-distance function between worlds (e.g., Hamming or Dalal distance). *Generalized imaging* [5] (denoted GI) is then defined as

$$B_\alpha^{\mathsf{GI}} := \left\{ (w,p) \mid w \in W, p = 0 \text{ if } w \not\Vdash \alpha, \text{ else } p = \sum_{\substack{\{w' \in W \mid \\ w \in Min(\alpha, w', d)\}}} \frac{B(w')}{|Min(\alpha, w', d)|} \right\}.$$

B_α^{GI} is the new belief state produced by taking the generalized image of B on α. In words, the probability mass of non-α-worlds is shifted to their closest α-worlds, such that if a non-α-world $w^\times$ with probability p has n closest α-worlds (equally distant), then each of these closest α-worlds gets p/n mass from $w^\times$.

Recently, Mishra and Nayak [4] proposed an imaging-based expansion operator $\langle prem^{cl} \rangle$ based on the notion of closeness, where closeness between two worlds is defined as "the gap between the distance between them and the maximum distance possible between any two worlds" (in a neighbourhood of relevance). Formally,

$$B \langle prem^{cl} \rangle R := \{(w,p) \mid w \in W, p = B(w) + \sigma^{cl}(w, S, R)\},$$

where R is the set of non-α-worlds (for some observation α), S is the α-worlds and $\sigma^{cl}(w, S, R)$ is the share of the overall probability salvaged from R going to $w \in S$. To re-iterate, $\langle prem^{cl} \rangle$ is an expansion operator; it does not deal with conflicting evidence.

"The most widely adopted function linking distances and similarities is Shepard's (1987) law of generalization, according to which *Similarity* $= e^{-distance}$," [11], where e is Euler's number (≈ 2.71828). (See also, e.g., [10].) Here, *distance* is a term used to refer to the difference in perceived observations (*stimuli* in the jargon of psychology) in an appropriately scaled psychological space. Suppose $\sigma(w, w')$ represents the similarity between worlds w and w'. Then we could define $\sigma(w, w') := e^{-d(w,w')}$. This implies that $d(w, w') = -\ln \sigma(w, w')$.

$$\sigma(w, w'') \geq \sigma(w, w') \cdot \sigma(w', w''). \tag{1}$$

Yearsley et al. [11] derive (1) from the triangle inequality and call it the multiplicative triangle inequality (MTI).

Imaging falls into the class of probabilistic belief change methods that rely on distance or similarity between worlds. There is another class of methods that rely on definitions of distance or similarity between *distributions* over worlds. The most popular of the latter methods employs the notion of (information theoretic) entropy optimization [15–17]. Recently, Beierle et al. [18] presented a knowledge management system with the core belief change method based on entropy optimization. The present work focuses a method that relies on the notion of similarity between *worlds*.

To further contextualize the present work, we do not consider uncertain evidence [19] nor the general case when instead of a single belief state being known, only a *set* of them is known to hold [5, 20, 21]. Other related literature worth mentioning is that of Boutilier [22], Makinson [23], Chhogyal et al. [24] and Zhuang et al. [25]. Space limitations prevent us from relating all these approaches to SME revision.

3   Similarity Modulo Evidence (SME)

Let $\sigma : W \times W \to \mathbb{R}$ be a function signature for a family of *similarity* functions. Let σ_α be a sub-family of similarity function, one sub-family for every $\alpha \in L$. Function $\sigma_\alpha(w, w')$ denotes the similarity between worlds w and w' in the context of evidence α. We consider the following set of arguably plausible properties of a similarity function modulo evidence.

For all $w, w', w'', w''' \in W$ and for all $\alpha, \beta \in L$,

1. $\sigma_\alpha(w, w') = \sigma_\alpha(w', w)$ (Symmetry)
2. $0 \leq \sigma_\alpha(w, w') \leq 1$ (Unit Boundedness)
3. $\sigma_\alpha(w, w) = 1$ (Identity)
4. $\sigma_\alpha(w, w'') \geq \sigma_\alpha(w, w') \cdot \sigma_\alpha(w', w'')$ (MTI)
5. If $w, w' \in Mod(\alpha)$ and $w'' \notin Mod(\alpha)$, then $\sigma_\alpha(w, w') > \sigma_\alpha(w, w'')$ (Model Preference)
6. If $w \neq w'$, then $\sigma_\alpha(w, w') < \sigma_\alpha(w, w)$ (Separability)

A property we assume to be satisfied is, if $\alpha \equiv \beta$, then $\sigma_\alpha(w, w') = \sigma_\beta(w, w')$. Transitivity is not desired for similarity functions: Elephants are similar to wales (large mammals); wales are similar to sharks (sea-dwellers); but elephants are not similar to sharks. We now discuss the listed properties.

1. *Symmetry*: Typically, symmetry of similarity is assumed. However, it is not always the case.
2. *Unit Boundedness*: This is a convention to simplify reasoning.
3. *Identity*: Objects are maximally similar to themselves.
4. *Multiplicative Triangle Inequality (MTI)*: Note that even if a similarity function is not symmetric, it could satisfy MTI (and non-symmetric distance functions could satisfy the (additive) triangle inequality). In general, if one suspects that a similarity function is non-symmetric, one would have to check for every combination of orderings of arguments in the inequality (eight such) to ascertain whether MTI holds.
5. *Model Preference*: Any two worlds which agree on a piece of evidence should be more similar to each other than any two worlds, one of which agrees on that evidence and one which does not.
6. *Separability*: It seems intuitive that non-identical worlds should not be maximally similar. It is, however, conceivable that two non-identical worlds cannot be distinguished, given the evidence, in which case they might be deemed (completely) similar.

Definition 2. *Let B be a belief state, α a new piece of information and σ a similarity function. Then the new belief state changed with α via similarity modulo evidence (SME) is defined as*

$$B_\alpha^{\mathsf{SME}} := \{(w, p) \mid p = 0 \ \text{if} \ w \not\Vdash \alpha, \ \text{else} \ p = \frac{1}{\gamma} \sum_{w' \in W} B(w')\sigma_\alpha(w, w')\},$$

where $\gamma := \sum_{w \in W, w \Vdash \alpha} \sum_{w' \in W} B(w') \sigma_\alpha(w, w')$ is a normalizing factor.

We use some identifier ID to identify a similarity function as a particular instantiation σ^{ID}. By SMEID we mean SME employing σ^{ID}. For any probabilistic belief revision operator $*$, we say that $*$ is SME-compatible iff there exists a similarity function σ^{ID} such that $B^*_\alpha = B^{SMEID}_\alpha$ for all B and α.

An example of revision with SME is provided in Sect. 4.3.

4 Belief Revision Operations via SME

In this section we investigate various probabilistic belief revision operations simulated or defined as SME operations. We simulate Bayesian conditioning, Lewis imaging and generalized imaging via SME. Finally, we present a new SME-based probabilistic belief revision operation with the similarity function based on Shepard's generalization law.

4.1 Bayesian Conditioning via SME

Bayesian conditioning can be simulated as an SME operator. Let σ^{BC} be defined as follows.

$$\sigma^{BC}_\alpha(w, w') := \begin{cases} 1 \text{ if } w = w' \\ 0 \text{ otherwise.} \end{cases}$$

Proposition 1. $B^{BC}_\alpha = B^{SMEBC}_\alpha$ *iff $B(\alpha) > 0$. That is, BC is SME-compatible iff $B(\alpha) > 0$.*

Proof-sketch: σ^{BC}_α acts like an indicator function, picking out only α-worlds; non-α-worlds are also picked but are never considered, that is, are assigned zero probability according to the definition of SME. □

Proposition 2. σ^{BC} *satisfies all the similarity function properties, except Model Preference.*

4.2 Imaging via SME

In this sub-section we show that Lewis and generalized imaging are both SME-compatible, and that their corresponding similarity functions satisfy only four of the similarity function properties.

Let $Max(\alpha, w, \sigma)$ be the set of α-worlds most similar to w with respect to similarity function σ. Formally, $Max(\alpha, w, \sigma) := \{w' \in W \mid w' \Vdash \alpha, \forall w'' \Vdash \alpha, \sigma_\alpha(w', w) \geq \sigma_\alpha(w'', w)\}$.

Lewis imaging can be simulated as an SME operator: Let

$$\sigma^{LI1}_\alpha(w, w') := \begin{cases} 1 \text{ if } Max(\alpha, w', \sigma^L) = \{w\} \\ 0 \text{ otherwise,} \end{cases}$$

where σ^L is defined such that Separability holds and $Max(\alpha, w, \sigma^L)$ is always a singleton, that is, σ^L identifies the unique most similar world to w, for each $w \in W$. Note that due to σ^L being separable, if $w \Vdash \alpha$, then $Max(\alpha, w, \sigma^L) = \{w\}$.

Assume $w \neq w'$, $w \Vdash \alpha$ and $w' \not\Vdash \alpha$. Then $Max(\alpha, w, \sigma^L) = \{w\}$, implying that $\sigma_\alpha^{LI1}(w, w') = 0$. But it could be that $Max(\alpha, w', \sigma^L) = \{w\}$. Then $\sigma_\alpha^{LI1}(w', w) = 1$. Hence, σ^{LI1} does not satisfy Symmetry. To obtain Symmetry, we define σ^{LI2}. Let

$$\sigma_\alpha^{LI2}(w, w') := \begin{cases} 1 \text{ if } w = w' \\ 1 \text{ if } Max(\alpha, w', \sigma^L) = \{w\} \\ 1 \text{ if } Max(\alpha, w, \sigma^L) = \{w'\} \\ 0 \text{ otherwise.} \end{cases}$$

Proposition 3. $B_\alpha^{LI} = B_\alpha^{SME LI1} = B_\alpha^{SME LI2}$. *That is, LI is SME-compatible.*

Proof-sketch:

$$B_\alpha^{LI}(w) = \sum_{\substack{v \in W \\ v = w^\alpha}} B(v) = \sum_{\substack{v \in W \\ Max(\alpha, v, \sigma^L) = \{w\}}} B(v)$$

$$= \sum_{v \in W} B(v) \sigma_\alpha^{LI1}(v, w) = \frac{1}{\gamma} \sum_{v \in W} B(v) \sigma_\alpha^{LI1}(v, w),$$

where $\gamma = 1 = \sum_{w \in W} \sum_{v \in W} B(v) \sigma_\alpha^{LI1}(v, w)$ due to the definition of σ^L.

We then show that $B_\alpha^{SME LI1} = B_\alpha^{SME LI2}$ via the lemma: For all $w \in W$, if $w \Vdash \alpha$, then $\sigma_\alpha^{LI1}(w, w') = \sigma_\alpha^{LI2}(w, w')$.   □

Proposition 4. *Of the similarity function properties, σ^{LI2} satisfies only Symmetry, Unit Boundedness, Identity and MTI.*

Generalized imaging can also be simulated as an SME operator: Let

$$\sigma_\alpha^{GI1}(w, w') := \begin{cases} 1 \text{ if } w \in Min(\alpha, w', d) \\ 0 \text{ otherwise,} \end{cases}$$

where d is a pseudo-distance function defined to allow multiple worlds sharing the status of being most similar to w', for each $w' \in W$, that is, such that $|Min(\alpha, w', d)|$ may be greater than 1.

For similar reasons as for σ^{LI1}, σ^{GI1} does not satisfy Symmetry. To obtain Symmetry, we define σ^{GI2}. Let

$$\sigma_\alpha^{GI2}(w, w') := \begin{cases} 1 \text{ if } w = w' \\ 1 \text{ if } w \in Min(\alpha, w', d) \\ 1 \text{ if } w' \in Min(\alpha, w, d) \\ 0 \text{ otherwise.} \end{cases}$$

Proposition 5. $B_\alpha^{GI} = B_\alpha^{SME GI1} = B_\alpha^{SME GI2}$. *That is, GI is SME-compatible.*

Proof-sketch: The proof follows the same pattern as for Proposition 3, just more complicated due to GI being more general than LI. □

Proposition 6. *Of the similarity function properties, σ^{GI2} satisfies only Symmetry, Unit Boundedness, Identity and MTI.*

4.3 A Similarity Function for SME Based on Shepard's Generalization Law

We now define a model preferred, Shepard-based similarity function:

$$\sigma_\alpha^{Sh}(w, w') := \begin{cases} e^{-d(w,w')} & \text{if } w = w' \text{ or if } w, w' \Vdash \alpha \\ e^{-d(w,w')-d_{max}} & \text{otherwise,} \end{cases}$$

where d is a pseudo-distance function and $d_{max} := \max_{w,w' \in W}\{d(w, w')\}$. Subtracting d_{max} in the second case of the definition of σ^{Sh} is exactly to achieve Model Preference, and the least value to guarantee Model Preference. Note that $\sigma_\alpha^{Sh}(w, w') \in (0, 1]$, for all $w, w' \in W$.

Example 1. Quinton knows only three kinds of birds: quails (q), ravens (r) and swallows (s). Quinton thinks Keaton has only a quail and a raven, but he is unsure whether Keaton has a swallow. Quinton's belief state is represented as $B = \{(111, 0.5), (110, 0.5), (101, 0), \dots, (000, 0)\}$. Now Keaton's sister Cirra tells Quinton that Keaton definitely has no quails, but she has no idea whether Keaton has ravens or swallows. Cirra's information is represented as evidence $\neg q$.

We assume d is Hamming distance. Note that $B^{SMESh}_{\neg q}(w) = 0$ for $w \in Mod(q)$ and that $B^{SMESh}_{\neg q}(w') = \frac{1}{\gamma}[B(111)\sigma_{\neg q}^{Sh}(w', 111) + B(110)\sigma_{\neg q}^{Sh}(w', 110)]$ for $w' \in Mod(\neg q)$. That is, $B^{SMESh}_{\neg q}(w') = \frac{1}{\gamma}0.5[e^{-d(w',111)-d_{max}} + e^{-d(w',110)-d_{max}}] = \frac{0.5}{\gamma}[e^{-d(w',111)-3} + e^{-d(w',110)-3}]$.

For instance, $B^{SMESh}_{\neg q}(011) = \frac{0.5}{\gamma}[e^{-1-3} + e^{-2-3}]$ and γ turns out to be 0.0342. Finally, $B^{SMESh}_{\neg q}$ is calculated as $\langle 0, 0, 0, 0, 0.365, 0.365, 0.135, 0.135 \rangle$. Observe that all $\neg q$-worlds are possible, and that worlds in which Keaton has a raven (but no quail) are more than double as likely than worlds in which Keaton has no raven (and no quail) – due to raven-no-quail-worlds being more similar to Keaton's initially believed worlds than no-raven-no-quail-worlds.

Proposition 7. *Similarity function properties 1 - 4 are satisfied for σ^{Sh}. Model Preference and Separability are satisfied for σ^{Sh} iff d is separable.*

Proof-sketch: The most challenging was to prove that σ^{Sh} satisfies MTI. It was tackled with a lemma stating that $e^{-d(w,w'')-x} \geq e^{-d(w,w')-x} \cdot e^{-d(w',w'')-x} \iff d(w, w'') \leq d(w, w') + d(w', w'')$ for $x \geq 0$, and by considering cases where (i) $w = w''$ (ii) $w \neq w''$, with sub-cases (ii.i) $w = w'$ (or $w' = w''$), and (ii.ii) $w \neq w' \neq w''$, with sub-sub-cases (ii.ii.i) exactly one of w, w' or w'' is in $Mod(\alpha)$, (ii.ii.ii) w, w' and w'' are all in $Mod(\alpha)$, and (ii.ii.iii) exactly one of the three worlds is not in $Mod(\alpha)$. □

4.4   Combined Shepard-Based and Bayesian SME Operators

Suppose that $B(\alpha) > 0$ and $\beta \models \alpha$. Then we would expect the current belief in β (i.e., $B(\beta)$) not to change relative to α due to finding out that α. After all, α tells us nothing new about β; β entails α. We want belief in β to be *stable* w.r.t. α when revising by α (while $B(\alpha) > 0$ and $\beta \models \alpha$).

Definition 3. *Let $B(\alpha) > 0$ and $\beta \models \alpha$, and let $*$ be a probabilistic belief revision operator. We say that $*$ is* stable *iff $B(\beta)/B(\alpha) = B_\alpha^*(\beta)/B_\alpha^*(\alpha)$. We say that $*$ is* inductive *iff there exists a case s.t. $B(\beta)/B(\alpha) > B_\alpha^*(\beta)/B_\alpha^*(\alpha)$*

When belief in β increases relative to α when revising by α, we presume that an *inductive* process is occurring.

Proposition 8. SME*BC* *is stable, and* SME*Sh* *is inductive.*

If we consider stability to be a desirable property, then it should be retained whenever possible, that is, whenever $B(\alpha) > 0$. However, when $B(\alpha) = 0$, an operation other than SME*BC* is required. Moreover, stability is not even defined when $B(\alpha) = 0$. It might, therefore, be desirable to switch between stability and induction. We define an SME revision function which deals with the cases of $B(\alpha) > 0$ and $B(\alpha) = 0$ using SME*BC*, respectively, SME*Sh*:

$$B_\alpha^{\text{SME}Cmb} := \begin{cases} B_\alpha^{\text{SME}BC} & \text{if } B(\alpha) > 0 \\ B_\alpha^{\text{SME}Sh} & \text{otherwise.} \end{cases}$$

Switching is arguably a harsh approach due to its discontinuous behavior. Can we gradually trade off between stability and induction? Let $\tau \in [0,1]$ be the 'degree of stability' desired. Then SME*BC* and SME*Sh* can be linearly combined as SME*BCSh* by defining

$$\sigma_{\alpha,\tau}^{BCSh}(w,w') := \tau \cdot \sigma_\alpha^{BC}(w,w') + (1-\tau)\sigma_\alpha^{Sh}(w,w').$$

We shall write SME*BCSh*(τ) to mean: SME*BCSh* using $\sigma_{\alpha,\tau}^{BCSh}$.

What should τ be? If we use σ_α^{BC} when α is (completely) consistent with B, then we reason that we should use σ_α^{BC} to the *degree* that α is consistent with B. In other words, we set $\tau = B(\alpha)$. We thus instantiate $\sigma_{\alpha,\tau}^{BCSh}$ as

$$\sigma_\alpha^\Theta(w,w') := B(\alpha) \cdot \sigma_\alpha^{BC}(w,w') + (1 - B(\alpha)) \cdot \sigma_\alpha^{Sh}(w,w').$$

We analyze SME*Cmb* and SMEΘ with respect to a set of rationality postulates in the next section.

Conjecture 1. Let $x, y \in [0,1]$ such that $x + y = 1$ and let σ^f and σ^g be similarity functions. If σ^f and σ^g satisfy MTI, then $\sigma_{\alpha,\tau}^{fg}(w,w') := \tau \cdot \sigma_\alpha^f(w,w') + (1-\tau) \cdot \sigma_\alpha^g(w,w')$ satisfies MTI.

In other words, it is unknown at this stage whether σ^Θ satisfies MTI.

Proposition 9. *Similarity function properties 1 - 3 are satisfied for σ^Θ. (i) Separability is satisfied for σ^Θ iff d is separable and (ii) Model Preference is satisfied for σ^Θ iff d is Separable and $B(\alpha) < 1$.*

Proof-sketch: We sketch only the proof of case (ii). If $B(\alpha) = 1$, then $\sigma^\Theta = \sigma^{BC}$, implying that Model Preference fails. Recall that if d is Separable, then σ^{Sh} satisfies Model Preference. If $B(\alpha) < 1$, then $1 - B(\alpha) > 0$, giving σ^{Sh} enough weight in σ^Θ to satisfy Model Preference. □

5   Probabilistic Revision Postulates

We denote the expansion of belief state B with α as B_α^+. Furthermore, we shall equate $+$ with Bayesian conditioning (BC).[4] Let $*$ be a probabilistic belief revision operator. It is assumed that α is logically satisfiable. The probabilistic belief revision postulates are

(P^*1) B_α^* is a belief state
(P^*2) $B_\alpha^*(\alpha) = 1$
(P^*3) If $\alpha \equiv \beta$, then $B_\alpha^* = B_\beta^*$
(P^*4) If $B(\alpha) > 0$, then $B_\alpha^* = B_\alpha^+$
(P^*5) If $B_\alpha^*(\beta) > 0$, then $B_{\alpha \wedge \beta}^* = (B_\alpha^*)_\beta^+$
(P^*6) If $B(\alpha) > 0$ and $\beta \models \alpha$, then $B_\alpha^*(\beta)/B_\alpha^*(\alpha) = B(\beta)/B(\alpha)$

(P^*1) – (P^*5) are adapted from Gärdenfors [6] and written in our notation. (P^*6) is a new postulate. We take (P^*1) – (P^*3) to be self explanatory, and to be the three core postulates. (P^*4) is an interpretation of the AGM postulate [26] which says that if the evidence is consistent with the currently held beliefs, then revision amounts to expansion. (P^*5) says that if β is deemed possible in the belief state revised with α, then expanding the revised belief state with β should be equal to revising the original belief state with the conjunction of α and β; the postulate speaks to the principle of minimal change. (P^*6) states the requirement for stability (cf. Definition 3) as a rationality postulate.

Proposition 10. SME*Cmb* satisfies *(P^*1) – (P^*6).*

Proof-sketch: The most challenging was the proof that SME*Cmb* satisfies (P^*5). The proof depends on the observation that it is known that if $B(\alpha \wedge \beta) > 0$, then $(B_\alpha^{BC})_\beta^{BC} = B_{\alpha \wedge \beta}^{BC}$ and a lemma stating that if $B_\alpha^{SMESh}(\beta) > 0$, then $(B_\alpha^{SMESh})_\beta^{SMEBC} = B_{\alpha \wedge \beta}^{SMESh}$. □

Proposition 11. SMEΘ *satisfies (P^*1) – (P^*3) but not (P^*4) – (P^*6).*

Propositions 10 and 11 make the significant difference between SME*Cmb* and SMEΘ obvious.

---

[4] Other interpretations of expansion in the probabilistic setting may be considered in the future.

6   Concluding Remarks

The key mechanism in SME revision is the weighting of world probabilities by the worlds' similarity to the world whose probability is being revised. SME revision was not developed as a competitor to Bayesian Conditioning; nonetheless, SME is more general and with the availability of a similarity function as a weighting mechanism, it allows for tuning of the 'behavior' of revision. We have defined notions of stability and induction for probabilistic belief change operators, and we proposed that stability is preferred for revision.

SME*Sh* has several advantages over previous operators: It can deal with evidence inconsistent with current beliefs (other imaging methods also have this property), and it is more general than Lewis's original imaging and generalized imaging. Furthermore, σ^{Sh} satisfies most properties one might expect from a similarity measure, notably the multiplicative triangle inequality and model preference. Finally, SME*Cmb* satisfies all the rationality postulates for probabilistic revision investigated in this study.

Another combined belief revision approach was proposed, which allows the user or agent to choose the degree of stability vs. induction. We proposed that the trade-off factor be $B(\alpha)$, the degree to which evidence α is consistent with current beliefs B. We saw, however, that the three non-core rationality postulates are not satisfied. Nonetheless, the idea of trading off between SME*BC* and SME*Sh* via $B(\alpha)$ seems intuitively appealing. But what is the effect of stability versus induction and when is one more appropriate than the other?

Model Preference (MP) is the only similarity function property dependent on evidence. Most operators discussed here do not satisfy MP. The Shepard-based function only satisfies MP because of the d_{max} penalty added specifically to enforce it. One might thus argue to remove MP as a required property. However, MP seems like a very reasonable property to expect, and furthermore, other properties required of a similarity function and which are dependent on evidence might be added in future.

Our view is that when it comes to probabilistic revision, $(P^*4) - (P^*6)$ might be too strong. Perhaps they should be weakened just enough to accommodate SMEΘ. A theorem states that a particular set of rationality postulates identify, characterize or represent a (class of) belief change operator(s), and that the (class of) operator(s) satisfies all the postulates. In general, it would be nice if we could make general statements about the relationships between the revision postulates and the similarity properties. This is left for future work. We acknowledge that representation theorems are desirable, but consider them as a second step after clarifying what properties are adequate for a novel belief revision operator in general. We consider our paper as a first step of presenting and elaborating on a completely novel type of revision operator. The shown relationships to well-known revision operators prove its basic foundation in established traditions of belief change theory.

Acknowledgements. Gavin Rens was supported by a Clause Leon Foundation postdoctoral fellowship while conducting this research. This research has been partially supported by the Australian Research Council (ARC), Discovery Project: DP150104133. This work is based on research supported in part by the National Research Foundation of South Africa (Grant number UID 98019). Thomas Meyer has received funding from the European Union's Horizon 2020 research and innovation programme under the Marie Sklodowska-Curie grant agr. No. 690974.

References

1. Lewis, D.: Probabilities of conditionals and conditional probabilities. Philos. Rev. **85**(3), 297–315 (1976)
2. Ramachandran, R., Nayak, A.C., Orgun, M.A.: Belief erasure using partial imaging. In: Li, J. (ed.) AI 2010. LNCS (LNAI), vol. 6464, pp. 52–61. Springer, Heidelberg (2010). https://doi.org/10.1007/978-3-642-17432-2_6
3. Chhogyal, K., Nayak, A., Schwitter, R., Sattar, A.: Probabilistic belief revision via imaging. In: Pham, D.-N., Park, S.-B. (eds.) PRICAI 2014. LNCS (LNAI), vol. 8862, pp. 694–707. Springer, Cham (2014). https://doi.org/10.1007/978-3-319-13560-1_55
4. Mishra, S., Nayak, A.: Causal basis for probabilistic belief change: distance *vs.* closeness. In: Sombattheera, C., Stolzenburg, F., Lin, F., Nayak, A. (eds.) MIWAI 2016. LNCS (LNAI), vol. 10053, pp. 112–125. Springer, Cham (2016). https://doi.org/10.1007/978-3-319-49397-8_10
5. Rens, G., Meyer, T., Casini, G.: On revision of partially specified convex probabilistic belief bases. In: Kaminka, G., Fox, M., Bouquet, P., Dignum, V., Dignum, F., Van Harmelen, F. (eds.) Proceedings of the Twenty-Second European Conference on Artificial Intelligence (ECAI-2016), The Hague, The Netherlands, pp. 921–929. IOS Press, September 2016
6. Gärdenfors, P.: Knowledge in Flux: Modeling the Dynamics of Epistemic States. MIT Press, Cambridge (1988)
7. Ashby, F.G., Ennis, D.M.: Similarity measures. Scholarpedia **2**(12), 4116 (2007)
8. Choi, S.S., Cha, S.H., Tappert, C.: A survey of binary similarity and distance measures. Syst. Cybern. Inform. **8**(1), 43–48 (2010)
9. Shepard, R.: Toward a universal law of generalization for psychological science. Science **237**(4820), 1317–1323 (1987)
10. Jäkel, F., Schölkopf, B., Wichmann, F.: Similarity, kernels, and the triangle inequality. J. Math. Psychol. **52**(5), 297–303 (2008). http://www.sciencedirect.com/science/article/pii/S0022249608000278
11. Yearsley, J.M., Barque-Duran, A., Scerrati, E., Hampton, J.A., Pothos, E.M.: The triangle inequality constraint in similarity judgments. Prog. Biophys. Mol. Biol. 130(Part A), 26–32 (2017). http://www.sciencedirect.com/science/article/pii/S0079610716301341. Quantum information models in biology: from molecular biology to cognition
12. Dubois, D., Moral, S., Prade, H.: Belief change rules in ordinal and numerical uncertainty theories. In: Dubois, D., Prade, H. (eds.) Belief Change, vol. 3, pp. 311–392. Springer, Dordrecht (1998). https://doi.org/10.1007/978-94-011-5054-5_8
13. Voorbraak, F.: Probabilistic belief change: expansion, conditioning and constraining. In: Proceedings of the Fifteenth Conference on Uncertainty in Artificial Intelligence, UAI 1999, San Francisco, CA, USA, pp. 655–662. Morgan Kaufmann Publishers Inc. (1999). http://dl.acm.org/citation.cfm?id=2073796.2073870
14. Lehmann, D., Magidor, M., Schlechta, K.: Distance semantics for belief revision. J. Symb. Log. **66**(1), 295–317 (2001)

15. Jaynes, E.: Where do we stand on maximum entropy? In: The Maximum Entropy Formalism, pp. 15–118. MIT Press (1978)
16. Paris, J., Vencovská, A.: In defense of the maximum entropy inference process. Int. J. Approx. Reason. **17**(1), 77–103 (1997). http://www.sciencedirect.com/science/article/pii/S0888613X97000145
17. Kern-Isberner, G.: Revising and updating probabilistic beliefs. In: Williams, M.A., Rott, H. (eds.) Frontiers in Belief Revision, Applied Logic Series, vol. 22, pp. 393–408. Kluwer Academic Publishers/Springer, Dordrecht (2001). https://doi.org/10.1007/978-94-015-9817-0_20
18. Beierle, C., Finthammer, M., Potyka, N., Varghese, J., Kern-Isberner, G.: A framework for versatile knowledge and belief management. IFCoLog J. Log. Appl. **4**(7), 2063–2095 (2017)
19. Chan, H., Darwiche, A.: On the revision of probabilistic beliefs using uncertain evidence. Artif. Intell. **163**, 67–90 (2005)
20. Grove, A., Halpern, J.: Updating sets of probabilities. In: Proceedings of the Fourteenth Conference on Uncertainty in Artificial Intelligence, UAI 1998, San Francisco, CA, USA, pp. 173–182. Morgan Kaufmann (1998). http://dl.acm.org/citation.cfm?id=2074094.2074115
21. Mork, J.C.: Uncertainty, credal sets and second order probability. Synthese **190**(3), 353–378 (2013). https://doi.org/10.1007/s11229-011-0042-2
22. Boutilier, C.: On the revision of probabilistic belief states. Notre Dame J. Form. Log. **36**(1), 158–183 (1995)
23. Makinson, D.: Conditional probability in the light of qualitative belief change. Philos. Log. **40**(2), 121–153 (2011)
24. Chhogyal, K., Nayak, A., Sattar, A.: Probabilistic belief contraction: considerations on epistemic entrenchment, probability mixtures and KL divergence. In: Pfahringer, B., Renz, J. (eds.) AI 2015. LNCS (LNAI), vol. 9457, pp. 109–122. Springer, Cham (2015). https://doi.org/10.1007/978-3-319-26350-2_10
25. Zhuang, Z., Delgrande, J., Nayak, A., Sattar, A.: A unifying framework for probabilistic belief revision. In: Bacchus, F. (ed.) Proceedings of the Twenty-fifth International Joint Conference on Artificial Intelligence (IJCAI 2017), pp. 1370–1376. AAAI Press, Menlo Park (2017). https://doi.org/10.24963/ijcai.2017/190
26. Alchourrón, C., Gärdenfors, P., Makinson, D.: On the logic of theory change: partial meet contraction and revision functions. J. Symb. Log. **50**(2), 510–530 (1985)

Intentional Forgetting in Artificial Intelligence Systems: Perspectives and Challenges

Ingo J. Timm[1(✉)], Steffen Staab[2], Michael Siebers[3], Claudia Schon[2],
Ute Schmid[3], Kai Sauerwald[4], Lukas Reuter[1], Marco Ragni[5],
Claudia Niederée[6], Heiko Maus[7], Gabriele Kern-Isberner[8], Christian Jilek[7],
Paulina Friemann[5], Thomas Eiter[9], Andreas Dengel[7], Hannah Dames[5],
Tanja Bock[8], Jan Ole Berndt[1], and Christoph Beierle[4]

[1] Trier University, Trier, Germany
{itimm,reuter,berndt}@uni-trier.de
[2] University Koblenz-Landau, Koblenz, Germany
{staab,schon}@uni-koblenz.de
[3] University of Bamberg, Bamberg, Germany
{michael.siebers,ute.schmid}@uni-bamberg.de
[4] FernUniversität in Hagen, Hagen, Germany
{kai.sauerwald,christoph.beierle}@fernuni-hagen.de
[5] Albert-Ludwigs-Universität Freiburg, Freiburg im Breisgau, Germany
{ragni,friemanp,damesh}@cs.uni-freiburg.de
[6] L3S Research Center Hannover, Hanover, Germany
niederee@l3s.de
[7] German Research Center for Artificial Intelligence (DFKI),
Kaiserslautern, Germany
{christian.jilek,andreas.dengel,heiko.maus}@dfki.de
[8] TU Dortmund, Dortmund, Germany
tanja.bock@tu-dortmund.de,gabriele.kern-isberner@cs.uni-dortmund.de
[9] TU Wien, Vienna, Austria
eiter@kr.tuwien.at

Abstract. Current trends, like digital transformation and ubiquitous computing, yield in massive increase in available data and information. In artificial intelligence (AI) systems, capacity of knowledge bases is limited due to computational complexity of many inference algorithms. Consequently, continuously sampling information and unfiltered storing in knowledge bases does not seem to be a promising or even feasible strategy. In human evolution, learning and forgetting have evolved as advantageous strategies for coping with available information by adding new knowledge to and removing irrelevant information from the human memory. Learning has been adopted in AI systems in various algorithms and applications. Forgetting, however, especially intentional forgetting, has not been sufficiently considered, yet. Thus, the objective of this paper is to discuss intentional forgetting in the context of AI systems as a first step. Starting with the new priority research program on 'Intentional Forgetting' (DFG-SPP 1921), definitions and interpretations of

© Springer Nature Switzerland AG 2018
F. Trollmann and A.-Y. Turhan (Eds.): KI 2018, LNAI 11117, pp. 357–365, 2018.
https://doi.org/10.1007/978-3-030-00111-7_30

intentional forgetting in AI systems from different perspectives (knowledge representation, cognition, ontologies, reasoning, machine learning, self-organization, and distributed AI) are presented and opportunities as well as challenges are derived.

Keywords: Artificial intelligence systems
Capacity and efficiency of knowledge-based systems
(Intentional) forgetting

1   Introduction

Today's enterprises are dealing with massively increasing digitally available data and information. Current technological trends, e.g., Big Data, focus on aggregation, association, and correlation of data as a strategy to handle information overload in decision processes. From a psychological perspective, humans are coping with information overload by selective *forgetting* of knowledge. Forgetting can be defined as non-availability of a previously known certain piece of information in a specific situation [29]. It is an adaptive function to delete, override, suppress, or sort out outdated information [4]. Thus, forgetting is a promising concept of coping with information overload in organizational contexts.

The need for forgetting has already been recognized in computer science [17]. In logics, context-free forgetting operators have been proposed, e.g., [6,30]. While logical forgetting explicitly modifies the knowledge base (KB), various machine learning approaches implicitly forget details by abstracting from their input data. In contrast to logical forgetting, machine learning can be used to reduce complexity by aggregating knowledge instead of changing the size of a KB. As a third approach, distributed AI (DAI) focuses on reducing complexity by distributing knowledge across agents [21]. These agents 'forget' at the individual level while the overall system 'remembers' through their interaction.

For humans, forgetting is *also an intentional mechanism* to support decision-making by focusing on relevant knowledge [4,22]. Consequently, the questions arise when and how humans can intentionally forget and when and how intelligent systems should execute forgetting functions. The new priority research program on "Intentional Forgetting in Organizations" (DFG-SPP 1921) has been initiated to elaborate an interdisciplinary paradigm. Within the program, researchers from computer science and psychology are interdisciplinarily collaborating on different aspects of intentional forgetting in eight tandem projects.[1]

With a strong focus (five projects) on AI systems, multiple perspectives are researched ranging from knowledge representation, cognition, ontologies, reasoning, machine learning, self-organization, and DAI. In this paper we bring together these perspectives as a first building block for establishing a common understanding of intentional forgetting in AI. Contributions of this paper are the identification of AI research fields and their challenges.

---

[1] http://www.spp1921.de/projekte/index.html.de.

2   Knowledge Representation and Cognition: FADE

The goal of FADE (Forgetting through Activation, reDuction and Elimination) is to support the effortful preselection and aggregation of information in information flows, leading to a reduction of the user's workload, by integrating methods from cognitive and computer science: Knowledge structures in organizations and mathematical and psychological modeling approaches of human memory structures in cognitive architectures are analyzed. Functions for priorization and forgetting that may help to compress and reduce the increasing amount of data are designed. Furthermore, a cognitive computational system for forgetting is developed that offers the opportunity to determine and adapt system model parameters systematically and makes them transparent for every single knowledge structure. This model for forgetting is evaluated for its fit to a lean workflow and readjusted in the context of the ITMC of the TU Dortmund.

While forgetting is often attributed negatively in everyday life, forgetting can offer an effective and beneficial reduction process to allow humans to focus on information of higher relevance. Features of the cognitive forgetting process which are crucial to the FADE project work are that information never gets lost but instead has a level of activation [1], and that the relevance of information depends on its connection to other information and its past usage. Moreover, information characteristics require different forms of forgetting; in particular, insights from knowledge representation and reasoning can help to further refine declarative knowledge, and differentiate between assertional knowledge and conceptual knowledge. Finally, it can be expected that cognitive adequacy of forgetting approaches will improve the human-computer interaction significantly.

The project FADE focusses on formal methods that are apt to model the epistemic and subjective aspects of forgetting [3,13]. Here, the wide variety of formalisms of nonmonotonic reasoning and belief revision are extremely helpful [2]. The challenge is to adapt these approaches to model human-like forgetting, and to make them usable in the context of organizations. As a further milestone, these adapted formal methods are integrated into cognitive architectures providing a formal-cognitive frame for forgetting operations [23,24].

3   Ontologies and Reasoning: EVOWIPE

New products are often developed by modifying the model of an already existing product. Assuming that large parts of the product model are represented in a KB, the EVOWIPE project supports this reuse of existing product models by providing methods to intentionally forget aspects from a KB that are not applicable to the new product [14]. E.g., the major part of the product model of the VW e-Golf (with electric motor) is based on the concept of the VW Golf with combustion engine. However, (i) changes, (ii) additions and (iii) forgetting elements of the original product model are necessary, e.g. (i) connecting the engine, (ii) adding a temperature control system for the batteries, and (iii) forgetting the fuel tank, fuel line and exhaust gas treatment. EVOWIPE aims at developing methods to support the product developer in the process of forgetting aspects from product models represented in KBs by developing the following operators for intentional forgetting: *Forgetting of inferred knowledge, restoring forgotten elements, temporary forgetting, representation of place markers in forgetting, cascading forgetting.*

These operators bear similarities to deletion operators known in knowledge representation (cf. Sect. 2). Indeed, we represent knowledge about product models by transforming existing product model data structures into an OWL-based representation and build on existing research that accesses such KBs using SPARQL update queries. These queries allow not only for deleting knowledge but also for inserting new knowledge. Therefore, the interplay of deletion and insertion is investigated in the project as well [25]. To accomplish cascading forgetting, dependencies occurring in the KB have to be specified. They can be added as metaproperties into the KB [10]. These dependencies can be added manually, however the project partners are currently working on methods to automatically extract dependencies from the product model. Dependency-guided semantics for SPARQL update queries use these dependencies to accomplish the desired cascading behavior described above [15]. By developing these operators, the EVOWIPE project extends the product development process to include stringent methods for intentional forgetting, ensuring that the complexity inherent in the product model, the product development process and the forgetting process itself can be mastered by the product developer.

4   Machine Learning: Dare2Del

Dare2Del is a system designed as context-aware cognitive companion [9,26] to support forgetting of digital objects. The companion will help users to delete or archive digital objects which are classified as irrelevant and it will support users to focus on a current task by fading-out or hiding digital information which is irrelevant in a given task context. In collaboration with psychology, it is investigated for which persons and in which situations information hiding can improve task performance and how explanations can establish trust of users in system decisions. The companion is based on inductive logic programming (ILP) [18] – a white-box machine learning approach based on Prolog. ILP allows learning from small sets of training data, a natural combination of reasoning and learning, and the incorporation of background knowledge. ILP has been shown to be able to provide human-understandable classifiers [19].

For Dare2Del to be a cognitive companion, it should be able to explain system decisions to users and be adaptive. Therefore, we currently design an incremental variant of ILP to allow for interactive learning [8]. Dare2Del will take into account explanations given by the user. E.g., if a user decides that an object should not be deleted, he or she can select one or more predicates (presented in natural language) which hold for the object and which are the reason why it should not be deleted. Subsequently, Dare2Del has to adapt its model. As application scenarios for Dare2Del we consider administration as well as connected industry. In the context of administration, users will be supported to delete irrelevant files and Dare2Del will help to focus attention by hiding irrelevant columns in tables. In the context of connected industry, quality engineers are supported in identifying irrelevant measurements and irrelevant data for deletion. Alternatively, measurements and data can be hidden in the context of a given control task. We believe that Dare2Del can be a helpful companion to relieve humans from the cognitive burden of complex decision making which is often involved when we have to decide whether some digital object will be relevant in the future or not.

5   Self-organization: Managed Forgetting

We investigate intentional forgetting in grass-roots (i.e. decentralized and self-organizing) organizational memory, where knowledge acquisition is incorporated into daily activities of knowledge workers. In line with this, we have introduced *Managed Forgetting* (MF) [20] - an evidence-based form of intentional forgetting, where no explicated will is required: what to forget and what to focus on is learned in a self-organizing and decentralized way based on observed evidences.

We consider two forms of MF: *memory buoyancy* empowering forgetful information access and *context-based inhibition* easing context switches. We apply MF in the *Semantic Desktop*, which semantically links information items in a machine understandable way based on a *Personal Information Model* (PIMO) [11]. Shared parts of individual PIMOs form a basis for an Organizational Memory.

As a key concept for this form of MF we have presented *Memory Buoyancy* (MB) [20], which represents an information item's current value for the user. It follows the metaphor of less relevant items "sinking away" from the user, while important ones are pushed closer. MB value computation has been investigated for different types of resources [5,28] and is based on a variety of evidences (e.g. user activities), activation propagation as well as on heuristics. MB values provide the basis for **forgetful access methods** such as hiding or condensation [11], adaptive synchronization and deletion, and forgetful search.

Most knowledge workers experience frequent context switches due to multitasking. Other than the gradual changes of MB in the first form of MF, in the case of context switches, changes are far more abrupt. We, therefore, believe that approaches based on the *concept of inhibition* [16], which temporarily hide resources of other contexts could be employed here, e.g. in a kind of self-tidying and self-(re)organizing context spaces [12]. Our current research focuses on combining both forms of MF.

6   Distributed Artificial Intelligence: AdaptPRO

In DAI, (intelligent) agents encapsulate knowledge which is deeply connected to domain, tasks and action [21]. They are intended to perceive their environment, react to changes, and act autonomously by (social) deliberation. Forgetting is implicitly a subject of research, e.g., Belief Revision (cf. Sect. 2) or possible-worlds semantics [31]. By contrast, the team perspective of forgetting, i.e., change of knowledge distribution, roles, and processes have not been analyzed yet.

In AdaptPRO, we focus on these aspects by adopting intentional forgetting in teams from psychology. We define *intentional forgetting* as the reorganization of knowledge in teams. The organization of human team knowledge is known as team cognition (TC). TC describes the structure in which knowledge is mentally represented, distributed, and anticipated by members to execute actions [7]. The concept of TC can be used to model knowledge distribution in agent systems as well. In terms of knowledge distributions, organization of roles and processes are implemented by allocating, sharing or dividing knowledge. If certain team members are specialized on particular areas, other agents can ignore information related to this area [27]. Especially, when cooperating, it is important for agents to share their knowledge about task- and team-relevant information. Particularly in case of disturbances, redundant knowledge and task competences enable robust teamwork. To strike a balance between sharing and dividing knowledge, i.e., efficient and robust teamwork, AdaptPRO applies an interdisciplinary approach of modeling, analyzing and adapting knowledge structures in teams and measure their implications on individual and team perspective.

7   Challenges and Future Work

We have presented perspectives on intentional forgetting in AI systems. Their key opportunities can be summarized as follows: (a) Establishing guidelines that help to implement human-like forgetting for organizations by bridging Cognition and Organizations with formal AI methods. (b) Mastering information overload by (temporary) forgetting and restoring of knowledge with respect to inferred and cascading knowledge structures. (c) Supporting decision-making of humans by forgetting digital objects with comprehensive knowledge management and machine learning. (d) Assisting organizational knowledge management with intentional forgetting by self-organization and self-tidying. (e) Adapting processes and roles in organizations by reorganization of knowledge distribution. In order to tap into these opportunities, the following challenges must be overcome: (1) Merge concepts of (intentional) forgetting in AI in a common terminology. (2) Formalize kinds of knowledge and forgetting to make prerequisites and aims of forgetting operations transparent and study their formal properties. (3) Investigate whether different forms of knowledge require different techniques of forgetting. (4) Accomplish efficient remembering of knowledge. (5) Develop temporarily forgetting information from a KB. (6) Develop of an incremental probabilistic approach to inductive logic programming which allows interactive learning by mutual explanations. (7) Generate helpful explanations in form of verbal justifications and by providing examples or counterexamples. (8) Develop correct interpretation on user activities, work environment, and information to initiate appropriate forgetting measures. (9) Characterize knowledge in teams and DAI-Systems and develop formal operators for reallocating, extending, and forgetting information.

These challenges foster an important basis for AI research in the next years. Furthermore, intentional forgetting has the potential to evolve to a mandatory function of next generation AI systems, which become capable of coping with our days' complexity and data availability.

Acknowledgments. The authors are indebted to the DFG for funding this research: Dare2Del (SCHM1239/10-1), EVOWIPE (STA572/15-1), FADE (BE 1700/9-1, KE1413/10-1, RA1934/5-1), Managed Forgetting (DE420/19-1, NI1760 1-1), and AdaptPro (TI548/5-1). We would also like to thank our project partners for their fruitful discussion: C. Antoni, T. Ellwart, M. Feuerbach, C. Frings, K. Göbel, P. Kügler, C. Niessen, Y. Runge, T. Tempel, A. Ulfert, S. Wartzack.

References

1. Anderson, J.R.: How Can the Human Mind Occur in the Physical Universe?. Oxford University Press, New York (2007)
2. Beierle, C., Kern-Isberner, G.: Semantical investigations into nonmonotonic and probabilistic logics. Ann. Math. Artif. Intell. **65**(2), 123–158 (2012)
3. Beierle, C., Eichhorn, C., Kern-Isberner, G.: Skeptical inference based on C-representations and its characterization as a constraint satisfaction problem. In: Gyssens, M., Simari, G. (eds.) FoIKS 2016. LNCS, vol. 9616, pp. 65–82. Springer, Cham (2016). https://doi.org/10.1007/978-3-319-30024-5_4
4. Bjork, E.L., Anderson, M.C.: Varieties of goal-directed forgetting. In: Golding, J.M., MacLeod, C. (eds.) Intentional Forgetting: Interdisciplinary Approaches, pp. 103–137. Lawrence Erlbaum, Mahwah (1998)
5. Ceroni, A., Solachidis, V., Niederée, C., Papadopoulou, O., Kanhabua, N., Mezaris, V.: To keep or not to keep: An expectation-oriented photo selection method for personal photo collections. In: Proceedings of the 5th ACM on International Conference on Multimedia Retrieval, Shanghai, China, 23–26 June 2015, pp. 187–194 (2015)
6. Delgrande, J.P.: A knowledge level account of forgetting. J. Artif. Intell. Res. **60**, 1165–1213 (2017)
7. Ellwart, T., Antoni, C.H.: Shared and distributed team cognition and information overload. Evidence and approaches for team adaptation. In: Marques, R.P.F., Batista, J.C.L. (eds.) Information and Communication Overload in the Digital Age, pp. 223–245. IGI Global, Hershey (2017)
8. Fails, J.A., Olsen Jr., D.R.: Interactive machine learning. In: Proceedings of the 8th International Conference on Intelligent User Interfaces, pp. 39–45. ACM (2003)
9. Forbus, K.D., Hinrichs, T.R.: Companion cognitive systems: a step toward human-level AI. AI Mag. **27**(2), 83 (2006)
10. Guarino, N., Welty, C.A.: An overview of ontoclean. In: Staab, S., Studer, R. (eds.) Handbook on Ontologies. IHIS, pp. 201–220. Springer, Heidelberg (2009). https://doi.org/10.1007/978-3-540-92673-3_9
11. Jilek, C., Maus, H., Schwarz, S., Dengel, A.: Diary generation from personal information models to support contextual remembering and reminiscence. In: 2015 IEEE International Conference on Multimedia & Expo Workshops, ICMEW 2015, pp. 1–6 (2015)

12. Jilek, C., Schröder, M., Schwarz, S., Maus, H., Dengel, A.: Context spaces as the cornerstone of a near-transparent and self-reorganizing semantic desktop. In: Gangemi, A. (ed.) ESWC 2018. LNCS, vol. 11155, pp. 89–94. Springer, Cham (2018). https://doi.org/10.1007/978-3-319-98192-5_17

13. Kern-Isberner, G., Bock, T., Sauerwald, K., Beierle, C.: Iterated contraction of propositions and conditionals under the principle of conditional preservation. In: Benzmüller, C., Lisetti, C.L., Theobald, M. (eds.) Proceedings of 3rd Global Conference on Artificial Intelligence, GCAI 2017, EPiC Series in Computing, 18–22 October 2017, Miami, FL, USA, vol. 50, pp. 78–92. EasyChair (2017). http://www.easychair.org/publications/paper/DTmX

14. Kestel, P., Luft, T., Schon, C., Kügler, P., Bayer, T., Schleich, B., Staab, S., Wartzack, S.: Konzept zur zielgerichteten, ontologiebasierten Wiederverwendung von Produktmodellen. In: Krause, D., Paetzold, K., S. Wartzack, S. (eds.) Design for X. Beiträge zum 28. DfX-Symposium, pp. 241–252. TuTech Verlag, Hamburg (2017)

15. Kügler, P., Kestel, P., Schon, C., Marian, M., Schleich, B., Staab, S., Wartzack, S.: Ontology-based approach for the use of intentional forgetting in product development. In: DESIGN Conference Dubrovnik (2018)

16. Levy, B.J., Anderson, M.C.: Inhibitory processes and the control of memory retrieval. Trends Cogn. Sci. 6(7), 299–305 (2002)

17. Markovitch, S., Scott, P.D.: Information filtering: selection mechanisms in learning systems. Mach. Learn. 10(2), 113–151 (1993)

18. Muggleton, S., De Raedt, L.: Inductive logic programming: theory and methods. J. Log. Program. 19, 629–679 (1994)

19. Muggleton, S.H., Schmid, U., Zeller, C., Tamaddoni-Nezhad, A., Besold, T.: Ultrastrong machine learning-comprehensibility of programs learned with ILP. Mach. Learn. 107, 1119–1140 (2018)

20. Niederée, C., Kanhabua, N., Gallo, F., Logie, R.H.: Forgetful digital memory: towards brain-inspired long-term data and information management. SIGMOD Rec. 44(2), 41–46 (2015)

21. O'Hare, G.M.P., Jennings, N.R. (eds.): Foundations of Distributed Artificial Intelligence. Wiley, New York (1996)

22. Payne, B.K., Corrigan, E.: Emotional constraints on intentional forgetting. J. Exp. Soc. Psychol. 43(5), 780–786 (2007)

23. Ragni, M., Sauerwald, K., Bock, T., Kern-Isberner, G., Friemann, P., Beierle, C.: Towards a formal foundation of cognitive architectures. In: Proceedings of the 40th Annual Meeting of the Cognitive Science Society, CogSci 2018, 25–28 July 2018, Madison, US (2018, to appear)

24. Sauerwald, K., Ragni, M., Bock, T., Kern-Isberner, G., Beierle, C.: On a formalization of cognitive architectures. In: Proceedings of the 14th Biannual Conference of the German Cognitive Science Society, Darmstadt (2018, to appear)

25. Schon, C., Staab, S.: Towards SPARQL instance-level update in the presence of OWL-DL tboxes. In: JOWO. CEUR Workshop Proceedings, vol. 2050. CEUR-WS.org (2017)

26. Siebers, M., Göbel, K., Niessen, C., Schmid, U.: Requirements for a companion system to support identifying irrelevancy. In: International Conference on Companion Technology, ICCT 2017, 11–13 September 2017, Ulm, Germany, pp. 1–2. IEEE (2017)

27. Timm, I.J., Berndt, J.O., Reuter, L., Ellwart, T., Antoni, C., Ulfert, A.S.: Towards multiagent-based simulation of knowledge management in teams. In: Leyer, M.,

Richter, A., Vodanovich, S. (eds.) Flexible Knowledge Practices and the Digital Workplace (FKPDW). Workshop within the 9th Conference on Professional Knowledge Management, pp. 25–40. KIT, Karlsruhe (2017)

28. Tran, T., Schwarz, S., Niederée, C., Maus, H., Kanhabua, N.: The forgotten needle in my collections: task-aware ranking of documents in semantic information space. In: CHIIR 2016. ACM Press (2016)

29. Tulving, E.: Cue-dependent forgetting: when we forget something we once knew, it does not necessarily mean that the memory trace has been lost; it may only be inaccessible. Am. Sci. **62**(1), 74–82 (1974)

30. Wang, Z., Wang, K., Topor, R., Pan, J.Z.: Forgetting for knowledge bases in DL-lite. Ann. Math. Artif. Intell. **58**(1), 117–151 (2010)

31. Werner, E.: Logical Foundations of Distributed Artificial Intelligence, pp. 57–117. Wiley, New York (1996)

Kinds and Aspects of Forgetting in Common-Sense Knowledge and Belief Management

Christoph Beierle[1]([✉]), Tanja Bock[2], Gabriele Kern-Isberner[2], Marco Ragni[3], and Kai Sauerwald[1]([iD])

[1] FernUniversität in Hagen, 58084 Hagen, Germany
`christoph.beierle@fernuni-hagen.de`
[2] Technical University Dortmund, 44227 Dortmund, Germany
[3] University of Freiburg, 79110 Freiburg, Germany

Abstract. Knowledge representation and reasoning have a long tradition in the field of artificial intelligence. More recently, the aspect of forgetting, too, has gained increasing attention. Humans have developed extremely effective ways of forgetting e.g. outdated or currently irrelevant information, freeing them to process ever-increasing amounts of data. The purpose of this paper is to present abstract formalizations of forgetting operations in a generic axiomatic style. By illustrating, elaborating, and identifying different kinds and aspects of forgetting from a common-sense perspective, our work may be used to further develop a general view on forgetting in AI and to initiate and enhance the interaction and exchange among research lines dealing with forgetting, both, but not limited to, in computer science and in cognitive psychology.

Keywords: Belief change · Common-sense · Forgetting

1 Introduction

A core requirement for an intelligent agent is the ability to reason about the world the agent is living in. This demands an internal representation of relevant parts of the world, and an epistemic state representing the agent's current beliefs about the world. In an evolving and changing environment, the agent must be able to adapt her world representation and her beliefs about the world according to the changes she observes.

While knowledge representation and inference have been in the focus of many research efforts in Artificial Intelligence and are also core aspects of human reasoning processes, a further vital aspect of human cognitive reasoning has gained much less attention in the AI literature: the aspect of forgetting. Although, in some research contributions, forgetting has been addressed explicitly, e.g. in the context of different logics [4,15], belief revision [1], and in ontologies [16], there seems to be only little interaction among these different approaches to deal with

© Springer Nature Switzerland AG 2018
F. Trollmann and A.-Y. Turhan (Eds.): KI 2018, LNAI 11117, pp. 366–373, 2018.
https://doi.org/10.1007/978-3-030-00111-7_31

forgetting. A uniform or generally accepted notion or theory of forgetting is not available. At the same time, humans have developed extremely effective ways of forgetting e.g. outdated or currently irrelevant information, freeing them to process ever increasing amounts of data. However, quotidian experiences as well as findings in psychology show that, in principle, there is no "absolute" forgetting in the human mind, but that there seems to be some threshold mechanism. Forgotten information falls below a threshold and is no longer available for the current information processing, but specific events can trigger this information and cause it to rise above the threshold again, effectively recovering the information.

The purpose of this short paper is to present abstract formalizations of forgetting operations in an axiomatic style, and to identify, illustrate, and elaborate different kinds and aspects of forgetting on this base. In particular, we will look at knowledge and belief management operations proposed in knowledge representation and reasoning from the point of view of forgetting, employing a high-level common-sense perspective. We will consider change operations both from AI and from cognitive psychology, identify where and how forgetting occurs in these change operations, and provide high-level conceptual formalizations of the different kinds of forgetting. Due to lack of space, a review of forgetting addressed explicitly or implicitly in different areas of AI and computer science (e.g., [4,7,10,11,13,15,17,18]) will be given in an extended version of this paper, as well as a further elaboration of our formalization and classification of forgetting.

2   Forgetting in Knowledge and Belief Changes

We address the notion of forgetting from the technical point of view and as a phenomenon of everyday life. There are situations where we forget to bring milk from the shop, misplace the key of our car or fail to remember the birthday of a good friend. There seems to be a gap between the formally defined notions of forgetting in KR and the common-sense understanding of forgetting. Furthermore, the term forgetting in everyday life, as well as for instance in psychology, might differ substantially from the usage of the notion in KR research. – In the following, we will present several kinds of change which involve forgetting. To make these kinds of change more accessible, we will make use of an abstract models in which an agent is equipped with an epistemic state Ψ (also called *belief state* in this paper) and an inference relation $\approx$. We make no further assumptions about how this belief state is represented, except that Ψ makes use of a language $\mathcal{L}$ over a signature Σ. Thus, the notion of belief state should be understood in a very broad sense only. For instance, Ψ might be a set of logical formulas, a Bayesian network, or a total preorder on possible worlds. The relation $\Psi \approx A$ holds if an agent with belief state Ψ infers A. Thus, depending on Ψ, the relation $\approx$ can be a deductive inference relation, a non-monotonic inference relation based on conditionals, a probabilistic inference relation, etc. When considering different types of changes in the following, Ψ will denote the prior state of the agent and Ψ° the posterior state after the forgetting resp. change operation.

Contraction. The most obvious kind of change that involves forgetting is the direct intention to lose information. For instance, a navigation system might be informed about the (permanent) closure of a street, or laws governing data protection and data security might demand the deletion of information after a given period of time. The operation of contraction is central in the AGM theory of belief change and is parametrized by a parameter A, the element to be contracted with. By the AGM postulates [1], a contraction with A results in not believing A afterwards:

If Ψ is the prior belief state and Ψ° the posterior belief state of a contraction with A, then we have $\Psi^\circ \not\approx A$.

Even further, contraction is an operation which typically results in a consistent belief state [12], a property which also holds for AGM contraction.

Ignorance. While in the case of contraction the agent just gives up belief in a certain information, the agent could alternatively wish to become deliberately unsure about her beliefs. Examples for this kind of forgetting occur in particular in case of conflicting information, e.g., where one is unsure about the status of a person because the person is both a student and staff member. More generally, after becoming ignorant in A, neither A nor the opposite of A is believed:

If Ψ is the prior belief state and Ψ° the posterior belief state of a change, then we have $\Psi^\circ \not\approx A$ and $\Psi^\circ \not\approx \not{A}$.

Note that this formulation is not the only way of understanding ignorance. E.g., in a richer language like a modal logic, one might express ignorance with the agent knowing that she neither believes A nor $\neg A$ [15]. Thus, if Ψ provides a "knowing that" operator $\mathbf{K}$, ignoring A results in $\Psi^\circ \approx \mathbf{K}\,(\neg\mathbf{K}(A) \wedge \neg\mathbf{K}(\neg A))$.

Abstraction. Abstraction could be considered as one of the most powerful change operations both in everyday life and in science. For example, suppose an agent who has built up beliefs about bicycles and keeps rules for inferring whether an object is a bicycle. One rule might say, if an object "has a frame, two wheels, and a bike bell", then this object is a bicycle. Another rule states that if the object "has a frame, two wheels, and there is no bike bell", then this object is a bicycle. Thus, in a deductive way, the agent may abstract a new rule which states: if an object "has a frame and two wheels", then this object is a bicycle. More generally, suppose that for a former belief state Ψ we have $\Psi \approx r_1 : \text{if } (A \text{ and } B) \text{ holds then infer } C$ and $\Psi \approx r_2 : \text{if } (A \text{ and } \neg B) \text{ holds then infer } C$. Then, in a follow-up state Ψ°, the agent might abstract from the rules r_1, r_2:

$$\Psi^\circ \approx r_{\text{new}} : \text{if } A \text{ holds then infer } C$$

Here, a particular kind of forgetting arises on the level of rules: The inference of C from A does not depend on the status of B; thus, in r_{new} the detail B is forgotten. Moreover, the agent might even forget the rules r_1 and r_2.

Another variant of this kind of abstraction corresponds to an inductive inference where rules $r_1, \ldots, r_n$ of the form $\Psi \mathrel{\vnormalapprox} r_i$: *if A and B_i holds then infer C* are abstracted to the rule $\Psi^\circ \mathrel{\vnormalapprox} r_{\text{new}}$: *if A holds then infer C*, thus forgetting the details $B_1, B_2, \ldots, B_n$ and possibly also the rules $r_1, \ldots, r_n$.

Marginalization. The blinding out of information can also be seen as a form of forgetting, and one form of this process is the removal of certain aspects represented in the language. Examples of this marginalization can be found in situations where a decision is made by taking only certain aspects into account. Marginalization is a central technique, most prominently known from probability theory, which reduces the signature in a way that certain signature elements are no longer taken into account. For $\Sigma' \subseteq \Sigma$ with $\Psi|_{\Sigma'}$, we denote the restriction of Ψ such that $\Psi|_{\Sigma'} \mathrel{\vnormalapprox} A$ iff $\Psi \mathrel{\vnormalapprox} A$ for all $A \in \mathcal{L}_{\Sigma'}$. Then, for the marginalization over $\Sigma' \subseteq \Sigma$ we have:

> If Ψ is the prior belief state and Ψ° the posterior belief state of a change, then we have $\Psi^\circ = \Psi|_{\Sigma \setminus \Sigma'}$.

Thus, the forgetting aspect of marginalization is the reduction of the signature, which might be temporal in the most cases of applications. The result of a marginalization in the view of common-sense is the forgetting of details that are determined by some part of the signature.

Focussing. Think about a physician who examines a patient with a rare allergy. The physician has to be careful what medication to administer. This is focussing: the process of (temporal) concentration on relevant aspects of a specific case. The physician, while being focussed on specific evidence, blinds out other treatments being not relevant for the given case. Thus, we can say:

> The operation of focussing on A first determines all irrelevant signature elements $\Sigma' \subseteq \Sigma$ with respect to the objective A of the focus and performs a marginalization to obtain $\Psi^\circ = \Psi|_{\Sigma \setminus \Sigma'}$.

Focussing defined this way is based on marginalization but crucially involves the aspect of relevance. Typically, this change of beliefs of an agent is only temporal.

Tunnel View. Forgetting can also be the result of a temporary restriction to certain beliefs. A tunnel view denotes a change where only certain beliefs are taken into account without respecting their relevance sufficiently. In everyday life, there are many situations where reasoning is restricted by a temporary resource constraint. In such a situation, a tunnel view can enable the agent to react faster due to less information load, but this might lead to non-optimal inferences or conclusions. A realization of tunnel view could make usage of marginalization by marginalizing out the signature elements that are not part of the tunnel. Even more, in a situation of a tunnel view the agent might not be able to make full use of her mental capacities. This can be modelled by restricting the capabilities of the inference relation $\mathrel{\vnormalapprox}$, which we will denote by $\mathrel{\vnormalapprox}^r$. Thus, a tunnel view with the tunnel $T \subseteq \Sigma$ and reasoning limitation r is a change which results in a belief state Ψ° marginalized to T and the agent using the inference relation $\mathrel{\vnormalapprox}^r$:

$$\Psi^\circ \approx A \text{ if and only if } \Psi|_{\Sigma \setminus T} \approx^r A$$

Tunnel view is a kind of change which is only temporal. A specific aspect of tunnel view is that the tunnelled signature elements are selected without sufficient respect to relevance. While tunnel view might be negatively connoted, from a psychological perspective tunnel view can be seen as part of a protection mechanism against information overflow in a stress situation.

Conditionalization. Conditionalization is a change which restricts our beliefs to a specific case or context. For instance, most people might associate the notion of a *tap* with a faucet, but a businessman might think of a government bond, even if they both also know the other meaning. We assume the existence of a conditionalization operator | on Ψ, where $\Psi|A$ has the intended meaning that Ψ should be interpreted under the assumption that A holds. Thus, independently of any particular realization, we may assume that $\Psi|A \approx A$ holds for every A. Then we have:

Let Ψ denote the prior state and Ψ° denote the posterior state of this change, then $\Psi^\circ = \Psi|A$.

Conditionalization is inspired by probabilistic conditionalization where posterior beliefs are determined by conditional probabilities $P(B|A)$, where A represents the evidential knowledge due to this change, i.e. $P^\circ(B) = P(B|A)$. This could be seen as the technical counterpart of eliminating the context from context-dependent beliefs, or shifting our belief in a concrete direction.

Revision/Update. Revising the current belief state Ψ in light of a new information A is the objective of the revision operation. If we do not know the employment status of a person and receive the information that she is a member of staff, we will *revise* our previous knowledge accordingly. If we receive the new information that a person previously known to be a student is a member of staff, we will *update* our previous knowledge accordingly. Note that revision is considered to reflect new information about a static world, whereas update occurs in an evolving world. Also, in revision or update, there is a forgetting aspect because previously held knowledge might no longer be available, e.g., whether a person is a student. Revision is one of the central operations of the AGM theory [6], prioritizing the new information A over the existing beliefs:

If Ψ is the prior belief state and Ψ° the posterior belief state of a change, then we have $\Psi^\circ \approx A$.

Normally, if A is consistent, a revision results in a consistent belief state Ψ° [12].

Fading Out. If we use the PIN code of our credit card rarely, the chances that we will not remember the PIN the next time we need it are much higher than in the case of frequent use. This fading out or decay of knowledge occurs in many everyday life situations, and it depends on a number of parameters, e.g., how often we use this credit card, the amount of time since we last used it, the similarity of the PIN code to some other combination of digits important to us, etc.

In cognitive psychology, fading out is a prominent explanation for forgetting. The first evidences go back to a self-experiment of Ebbinghaus [5], whose results are known today as *forgetting curve*. While this concept strongly influenced cognitive architectures and has been further developed in this area (cf. [2]) there is no approach to model this phenomenon as a variant of belief change in knowledge representation and reasoning. As a step towards modelling this phenomenon we propose to understand fading out as an increasing difficulty to infer the information from the agent's belief state. We associate with inferences an effort or cost function f depending on the current belief state Ψ (cf. the activation function in ACT-R [3] or SOAR [9]). Then, $\Psi \mathrel{\vpalmate} A$ if and only if the activation value $f(A)$ is above a certain threshold, yielding:

> If $\Psi \mathrel{\vpalmate} A$ holds, a fading out of A is given as a sequence of consecutive posterior belief states $\Psi_1^\circ, \Psi_2^\circ, \Psi_3^\circ, \ldots$ such that there is an n with:
> $\Psi_1^\circ \mathrel{\vpalmate} A, \ldots, \Psi_{n-1}^\circ \mathrel{\vpalmate} A$ and $\Psi_n^\circ \mathrel{\not\vpalmate} A$.

A specific difficulty of defining a concrete fading out-operation will be the requirement of the possibility of recovering/remembering the information A again.

3   Aspects of Forgetting and Further Work

As presented before , forgetting occurs in many knowledge and belief change operations. To characterize different forms of forgetting, we identify and distinguish the following aspects:

The aspect of **permanence** describes how long the forgotten information stays forgotten when the agent or the environment undertakes no further intervention to revert the forgetting. For instance, in tunnel view and focussing the forgetting is only temporary. In other operations, like contraction, one would expect that the forgetting is more permanent. The aspect of **duration** describes how long it takes after the initiation of the change for the forgetting to take place. The examples in Sect. 2 make no explicit assertions about the duration of the change, but one would expect that the process of abstraction takes about days to months, whereas a focussing is a change which could have an immediate effect. There are types of changes in which the forgotten entities are selected based on some concept of **relevance**. For instance, a focussing is a change where the kept beliefs are selected due to the relevance to the subject of the focussing, respectively, the forgotten entities are selected based on irrelevance. On the other hand, tunnel view can be a change where tunnelled elements are especially not selected by relevance. With the **subject type** of the forgetting we denote the aspect of forgetting which concerns the type of the beliefs that will be forgotten. For instance, in abstraction, the subject type of the forgetting can be a rule or parts of rules, while the subject type of the forgetting by a contraction or a revision are propositions in classical AGM theory. Another aspect of forgetting is the **awareness** of the forgetting by the agent. For instance, a realization of ignorance in a modal logic is expressive enough to illustrate that the agent is aware of the forgetting.

In future work within the FADE project (cf. [8,14]), we will elaborate more aspects of forgetting and classify different forms of forgetting accordingly. A further major research challenge is the elaboration of formal logical properties of psychologically inspired change operations of tunnel view and fading out.

Acknowledgments. The research reported here was carried out in the FADE project and was supported by the German Research Society (DFG) within the Priority Research Program *Intentional Forgetting in Organisations* (DFG-SPP 1921; grants BE 1700/9-1, KE 1413/10-1, RA 1934/5-1).

References

1. Alchourrón, C.E., Gärdenfors, P., Makinson, D.: On the logic of theory change: partial meet contraction and revision functions. J. Symb. Log. **50**(2), 510–530 (1985)
2. Anderson, J.R.: How Can the Human Mind Occur in the Physical Universe?. Oxford University Press, New York (2007)
3. Anderson, J.R., Byrne, M.D., Douglass, S., Lebiere, C., Qin, Y.: An integrated theory of the mind. Psychol. Rev. **111**(4), 1036–1050 (2004)
4. Delgrande, J.P.: A knowledge level account of forgetting. J. Artif. Intell. Res. **60**, 1165–1213 (2017)
5. Ebbinghaus, H.: Über das Gedächtnis. Untersuchungen zur experimentellen Psychologie. Duncker & Humblot, Leipzig (1885)
6. Gärdenfors, P., Rott, H.: Belief revision. In: Gabbay, D.M., Hogger, C.J., Robinson, J.A. (eds.) Handbook of Logic in Artificial Intelligence and Logic Programming, vol. 4, pp. 35–132. Oxford University Press (1995)
7. Gonçalves, R., Knorr, M., Leite, J.: The ultimate guide to forgetting in answer set programming. In: Baral, C., Delgrande, J.P., Wolter, F. (eds.) Principles of Knowledge Representation and Reasoning: Proceedings of the Fifteenth International Conference, KR 2016, 25–29 April 2016, Cape Town, South Africa, pp. 135–144. AAAI Press (2016)
8. Kern-Isberner, G., Bock, T., Sauerwald, K., Beierle, C.: Iterated contraction of propositions and conditionals under the principle of conditional preservation. In: Benzmüller, C., Lisetti, C.L., Theobald, M. (eds.) 3rd Global Conference on Artificial Intelligence, GCAI 2017, EPiC Series in Computing, 18–22 October 2017, Miami, FL, USA, vol. 50, pp. 78–92. EasyChair (2017)
9. Laird, J.: The Soar Cognitive Architecture. MIT Press, Cambridge (2012)
10. Lang, J., Liberatore, P., Marquis, P.: Propositional independence: formula-variable independence and forgetting. J. Artif. Intell. Res. **18**, 391–443 (2003)
11. Leite, J.: A bird's-eye view of forgetting in answer-set programming. In: Balduccini, M., Janhunen, T. (eds.) LPNMR 2017. LNCS (LNAI), vol. 10377, pp. 10–22. Springer, Cham (2017). https://doi.org/10.1007/978-3-319-61660-5_2
12. Levi, I.: Subjunctives, dispositions and chances. Synthese **34**(4), 423–455 (1977)
13. Lin, F., Reiter, R.: Forget it! In: In Proceedings of the AAAI Fall Symposium on Relevance, pp. 154–159. AAAI Press, Menlo Park (1994)
14. Ragni, M., Sauerwald, K., Bock, T., Kern-Isberner, G., Friemann, P., Beierle, C.: Towards a formal foundation of cognitive architectures. In: Proceedings of the 40th Annual Meeting of the Cognitive Science Society, CogSci 2018, 25–28 July 2018, Madison, US (2018, to appear)

15. van Ditmarsch, H., Herzig, A., Lang, J., Marquis, P.: Introspective forgetting. Synthese **169**(2), 405–423 (2009)
16. Wang, K., Wang, Z., Topor, R., Pan, J.Z., Antoniou, G.: Concept and role forgetting in $\mathcal{ALC}$ ontologies. In: Bernstein, A. (ed.) ISWC 2009. LNCS, vol. 5823, pp. 666–681. Springer, Heidelberg (2009). https://doi.org/10.1007/978-3-642-04930-9_42
17. Zhang, Y., Zhou, Y.: Knowledge forgetting: properties and applications. Artif. Intell. **173**(16), 1525–1537 (2009)
18. Zhou, Y., Zhang, Y.: Bounded forgetting. In: Burgard, W., Roth, D. (eds.) Proceedings of the Twenty-Fifth AAAI Conference on Artificial Intelligence, AAAI 2011, 7–11 August 2011, San Francisco, California, USA. AAAI Press (2011)

Context Aware Systems

Bounded-Memory Stream Processing

Özgür Lütfü Özçep(✉)

Institute of Information Systems (IFIS), University of Lübeck,
Lübeck, Germany
oezcep@ifis.uni-luebeck.de

Abstract. Foundational work on stream processing is relevant for different areas of AI and it becomes even more relevant if the work concerns feasible and scalable stream processing. One facet of feasibility is treated under the term bounded memory. In this paper, streams are represented as finite or infinite words and stream processing is modelled with stream functions, i.e., functions mapping one or more input stream to an output stream. Bounded-memory stream functions can process input streams by using constant space only. The main result of this paper is a syntactical characterization of bounded-memory functions by a form of safe recursion.

Keywords: Streams · Bounded memory · Infinite words · Recursion

1 Introduction

Stream processing has been and is still a highly relevant research topic in computer science and especially in AI. The main aspects of stream processing that one has to consider are illustrated nicely by the titles of some research papers: the ubiquity of streams due to the temporality of most data ("It's a streaming world!", [12]), the potential infinity of streams ("Streams are forever", [13]), or the importance of the order in which data are streamed ("Order matters", [34]).

These aspects are relevant for all levels of stream processing that occur in AI research and AI applications, in particular for stream processing on the sensor-data level, e.g., for agent reasoning on percepts, or on the relational data level, e.g., within data stream management systems. Recent interest on high-level declarative stream processing [6,11,24,28,31] w.r.t. an ontology have lead to additional aspects becoming relevant: The enduser accesses all possibly heterogeneous data sources (static, temporal and streaming) via a declarative query language using the signature of the ontology. The EU funded project CASAM[1], demonstrated how such a uniform ontology interface could be used to realize (abductive) interpretation of multimedia streaming data [18]. The efforts in the EU project OPTIQUE[2] [17] resulted in an extended OBDA system with a flexible, visual interface and mapping management system for accessing static data

---

[1] http://cordis.europa.eu/project/rcn/85475_en.html.
[2] http://optique-project.eu/.

© Springer Nature Switzerland AG 2018
F. Trollmann and A.-Y. Turhan (Eds.): KI 2018, LNAI 11117, pp. 377–390, 2018.
https://doi.org/10.1007/978-3-030-00111-7_32

(wellbore data provided by the industrial partner STATOIL) as well as temporal and streaming data (turbine measurements and event data provided by the industrial partner SIEMENS). This kind of convenience and flexibility for end-users leads to challenges for the designers of the stream engine as they have to guarantee complete and correct transformations of endusers' queries to low-level queries over the backend.

The main challenging fact of stream processing is the potential infinity of the data: It means that one cannot apply a one-shot query-answering procedure, but has to register queries that are evaluated continuously on streams. Independent of the kind of streams (low-level sensor streams or high-level streams of semantically annotated data), the aim is to keep stream processing feasible, in particular by minimizing the space resources required to process the queries. The kind of data structures used to store the relevant bits of information in the so-called synopsis (or summary or sketch [8]) may differ from application to application but sometimes one can describe general connections between the required space and the expressivity of the language for the representation of the stream query.

Bounded-memory queries on streams are allowed to use only constant space to store the relevant bits of informations of the growing stream prefix. This notion depends on the underlying computation model and so bounded-memory computation can be approached from different angles. Bounded-memory stream processing has been in the focus of research in temporal databases [7] under the term "bounded history encoding" and in research on data stream management systems [2,19] but it has been also approached in the area of theoretical informatics in the context of finite-memory automata [23], string-transducers [1,14,15] and from a co-algebraic perspective [32].

In this paper, bounded-memory stream processing is approached in the infinite word perspective of [20]. Streams are represented as finite or infinite words and stream processing is modelled by stream functions/queries, i.e., functions mapping one or more stream to an output stream. The important class of abstract computable functions (AC) are those representable by repeated applications of a kernel, alias window function, on the growing prefix of the input. Various other classes of interesting stream functions, which can be characterized axiomatically (see e.g. [27]), result by considering restrictions on the underlying window functions. The focus of this paper are AC functions with windows computable in bounded memory. The underlying computation model is that of streaming abstract state machines [20].

Though the restriction of constant space for bounded memory functions limits the set of expressible functions, the resulting class of streams functions is still expressive enough to capture interesting information needs over streams. In fact, in this paper it is shown that bounded-memory functions can be constructed using principles of linear primitive recursion. The main idea is to use a form of safe recursion of window function applications. The result is a rule set for inductively building functions on the base of basic functions. In familiar programming speak the paper gives a characterization of stream functions that correspond to programs using linearly bounded for-loops (and not arbitrary while loops).

2   Preliminaries

The following simple definition of streams of words over a finite or infinite alphabet D is used throughout this paper. An alphabet D is also called *domain* here.

Definition 1. *The set of* finite streams *is the set of finite words D^* over the alphabet D. The set of* infinite streams *is the set of ω-words D^ω over D. The set of (all) streams is denoted $D^\infty = D^* \cup D^\omega$.*

The basic definition of streams above is general enough to capture all different forms of streams, in particular those that are considered in the approaches mentioned in Sect. 4 on related work.

$D^{\leq n}$ is the set of words of length maximally n. For any finite stream s the length of s is denoted by $|s|$. For infinite streams s let $|s| = \infty$ for some fixed object $\infty \notin \mathbb{N}$. For $n \in \mathbb{N}$ with $1 \leq n \leq |s|$ let $s^{=n}$ be the n-th element in the stream s. For $n = 0$ let $s^{=n} = \epsilon = $ the empty word. $s^{\leq n}$ denotes the n-prefix of s, $s^{\geq n}$ is the suffix of s s.t. $s^{\leq n-1} \circ s^{\geq n} = s$. For an interval $[j, k]$, with $1 \leq j \leq k$, $s^{[j,k]}$ is the stream of elements of s such that $s = s^{\leq j-1} \circ s^{[j,k]} \circ s^{\geq k+1}$. For a finite stream $w \in D^*$ and a set of streams X the term $w \circ X$ or shorter wX denotes the set of all w-extensions with words from X: $wX = \{s \in D^\infty \mid$ There is $s' \in X$ s.t. $s = w \circ s'\}$. The finite word s is a prefix of a word s', for short $s \sqsubseteq s'$, iff there is a word v such that $s' = s \circ v$. If $s \sqsubseteq s'$, then $s' -_\sqsubseteq s$ is the suffix of s' when deleting its prefix s. If all letters of s occur in s' in the ordering of s (but perhaps not directly next to each other) then s is called a *subsequence* of s'. If $s' = usv$ for $u \in D^*$ and $v \in D^\infty$, then s is called a *subword* of s'. Streams are going to be written in the word notation, sometimes mentioning the concatenation $\circ$ explicitly. For a function $Q : D_1 \longrightarrow D_2$ and $Y \subseteq D_2$ let $Q^{-1}[Y] = Q^{-1}(Y) = \{w \in D_1 \mid Q(w) \in Y\}$ be the preimage of Y under Q.

The very general notion of an *abstract computable* [20] stream function is that of a function which is incrementally computed by calculations of finite prefixes of the stream w.r.t. a function called *kernel*. More concretely, let $K : D^* \longrightarrow D^*$ be a function from finite words to finite words. Then define the *stream query* $Repeat(K) : D^\infty \longrightarrow D^\infty$ induced by kernel K as

$$Repeat(K) : s \mapsto \bigcirc_{j=0}^{|s|} K(s^{\leq j})$$

Definition 2. *A query Q is* abstract computable *(AC) iff there is a kernel such that $Q(s) = Repeat(K)(s)$.*

Using a more familiar speak from the stream processing community, the kernel operator is a *window operator*, more concretely, an unbounded window operator. The "window" terminology is the preferred one in this paper.

That abstract computability is an adequate concept for stream processing can be formally undermined by showing that exactly the AC functions fulfill two fundamental properties: AC functions are prefixed determined (FP$^\infty$) and

they are data-driven in the sense that they map finite streams to finite streams
(F2F).

(FP$^\infty$). For all $s \in D^\infty$ and all $u \in D^*$: If $Q(s) \in uD^\infty$, then there is a $w \in D^*$
s.t. $s \in wD^\infty \subseteq Q^{-1}[uD^\infty]$.
(F2F). For all $s \in D^*$ it holds that: $Q(s) \in D^*$.

The following theorem states the representation result:

Theorem 1 ([20]). *AC queries represent the class of stream queries fulfilling
(F2F) and (FP$^\infty$).*

Multiple (input) streams can be handled in the framework of [20] by attaching
to the domain elements tags with provenance information, in particular information on the stream source from which the element originates. This is the general
strategy in the area of complex event processing (CEP), where there is exactly
one (mega)-stream on which event patterns are evaluated. But this tag-approach
appears in some situation to be too simple as it provides no control on how to
interleave the stream inputs—as it is required, e.g., for state-of-the art stream
query languages following a pipeline architecture. Actually, in this paper the
framework of [20] is generalized to handle functions on multiple streams gen-
uinely as functions of the form $Q : D^\infty \times \cdots \times D^\infty \longrightarrow D^\infty$—similar to the
approach of [35].

3   Bounded-Memory Queries

The notion of abstract computability is very general, even so as to contain also
queries that are not computable by a Turing machine according to the notion of
TTE computability [35]. Hence, the authors of [20] consider the refined notion of
abstract computability modulo a class C meaning that the window K inducing an
abstract computable query has to be in C. In most cases, C stands for a family
of functions of some complexity class. In [20], the authors consider variants
of C based on computations by a machine model called *stream abstract state
machine* (sAsm). In particular, they show that every AC query induced by a
length-bounded window (in particular: each so-called synchronous AC query:
window-length always 1) is computable by an sAsm [20, Corollary 23].
    A particularly interesting class from the perspective of efficient computa-
tion are bounded-memory sAsms because these implement the idea of incrementally maintainable windows requiring only a constant amount of memory.
(For a more general notion of incremental maintainable queries see [29].) Of
course, the space restrictions of bounded-memory sAsms are strong constraints
on the expressiveness of stream functions, e.g., it is not possible to compute
the INTERSECT problem of checking whether prior to some given timepoint
t there were identical elements in two given streams [20, Proposition 26] with
a bounded-memory sAsm. A slightly more general version of bounded-memory
sAMS are o(n)-bitstring sAMS which store, on every stream and every step, only

o(n) bitstrings. (But neither can these compute INTERSECT [20, Proposition 28].)

An sAsm operates on first-order sorted structures with a static part and a dynamic part. The static part contains all functions allowed over the domain of elements D of the streams. The dynamic part consists of functions which may change by transitions in an update process. A set of nullary functions *in* and *out* is pre-defined and are used to describe registers for the input, output data stream elements, resp. Updates are the basic transitions. Based on these, simple programs are defined as finite sequences of rules: The basic rules are updates $f(t_1, \ldots, t_n) := t_0$, meaning that in the running state terms $t_0, t_1, \ldots, t_n$ are evaluated and then used to redefine the (new) value of f. Then, inductively, one is allowed to apply to update rules a parallel execution constructor par that allows parallel firing of the rule; and also, inductively, if rules r_1, r_2 are constructed, then one can build the "if-then-else construct": if Q then r_1 else r_2. Here the if-condition is given by a quantifier free formula Q on the signature of the structure and where the post-conditions are r_1, r_2. For *bounded-memory* sAsm [20, Definition 24] one additionally requires that *out* registers do not occur as arguments to a function, that all dynamic functions are nullary and that non-nullary static functions can be applied only to rules of the form $out := t_0$.

3.1   Constant-Width Windows

In this subsection we are going to consider an even more restricted class of bounded-memory windows, namely those based on constant-width windows. For this, let us recapitulate the definitions (and some result) that were given in [27].

The general notion of an n-kernel which corresponds to the notion of a finite window of width n is defined as follows:

Definition 3. *A function* $K : D^* \longrightarrow D^*$ *that is determined by the n-suffixes* $(n \in \mathbb{N})$, *i.e., a function that fulfills for all words* $w, u \in D^*$ *with* $|w| = n$ *the condition* $K(uw) = K(w)$ *is called an* n-window. *If additionally* $K(s) = \epsilon$, *for all* s *with* $|s| < n$, *then* K *is called a* normal n-window. *The set of stream queries generated by an* n-*window for some* $n \in \mathbb{N}$ *are called* n-window abstract computable *stream queries, for short* n-WAC *operators. The union* WAC $= \bigcup_{n \in \mathbb{N}} n$-WAC *is the set of* window abstract computable *stream queries.*

The class of WAC queries can be characterized by a generalization of a distribution property called (FACTORING-N) that, for each $n \in \mathbb{N}$, captures exactly the n-window stream queries.

(Factoring-n). $\forall s \in D^*$: $Q(s) \in D^*$ and
  1. if $|s| < n$, $Q(s) = \epsilon$ and
  2. if $|s| = n$, for all $s' \in D^\infty$ with $|s'| \geq 1$: $Q(s \circ s') = Q(s) \circ Q((s \circ s')^{\geq 2})$.

Proposition 1 [27]. *For any* $n \in \mathbb{N}$ *with* $n \geq 1$, *a stream query* $Q : D^\infty \longrightarrow D^\infty$ *fulfills* (FACTORING-N) *iff it is induced by a normal* n-*window* K.

Intuitively, the class of WAC stream queries is a proper class of AC stream queries because the former consider only fixed-size finite portions of the input stream whereas for AC stream queries the whole past of an input stream is allowed to be used for the production of the output stream. A simple example for an AC query that is not a WAC query is the parity query PARITY : $\{0,1\}^\infty \longrightarrow$ $\{0,1\}^\infty$ defined as $Repeat(K_{par})$. Here, K_{par} is the parity window function $K :$ $\{0,1\}^* \longrightarrow \{0,1\}$ defined as $K_{par}(s) = 1$, if the number of 1s in s is odd and $K_{par}(s) = 0$ else. The window K_{par} is not very complex, indeed one can show that K_{par} is a bounded-memory function w.r.t. the sAsm model or, simpler, w.r.t. the model of finite automata: It is easy to find a finite automaton with two states that accepts exactly those words with an odd number of 1s and rejects the others. In other words: parity is incrementally maintainable. But finite windows are "stateless", they cannot memorize the actual parity seen so far. Formally, it is easy to show that any constant-width window function is AC^0 computable, i.e., computable by a polynomial number of processors in constant time: For any word length m construct a circuit with m inputs where only the first n of them are actually used: One encodes all the 2^n values of the n-window K in a boolean circuit BC_m, the rest of the m word is ignored. All BC_m have the same size and depth and hence a finite window function is in AC^0. On the other hand it is well known by a classical result [16] that PARITY is not in AC^0.

3.2   A Recursive Characterization of Bounded-Memory Functions

Though the machine-oriented approach for the characterization of bounded-memory stream functions with sAsms is quite universal and fits into the general approach for characterizing computational classes, the following considerations add a simple, straight-forward characterization following the idea of primitive recursion over words [3,22]: Starting from basic functions on finite words, the user is allowed to built further functions by applying composition and simple forms of recursion. In order to guarantee bounded memory, all the construction rules are built with specific window operators, namely $last_n(\cdot)$, which output the n-suffix of the input word. This construction gives the user the ability to built (only) bounded-memory window functions K in a pipeline strategy. The main adaptation of the approach of [20] is adding recursion for n-window kernels. This leads to a more fine-grained approach for kernels K. In particular, now, it is possible to define the PARITY query with n-window Kernels whereas without recursion, as shown in the example before, it is not.

It should be noted that in agent theory usually the processing of streams is described by functions that take an evolvement of states into account: Depending on the current state and the current percept, the agent chooses the next action and the next state. In this paper, a different approach is described which is based on the principle of tail recursion where the accumulators play the role of states.

In order to enable a pipeline-based construction the approach of [20] is further extended by considering multiple streams explicitly as possible arguments for functions with an arbitrary number of arguments. Still, all functions will output a single finite or infinite word—though the approach sketched below can easily be adapted to work for multi-output streams. All of the machinery of Gurevich's framework is easily translated to this multi-argument setting. So, for example the axiom (FP$^\infty$) now reads as follows:

(FP$^\infty$). For all $s_1, \ldots s_n \in D^\infty$, and all $u \in D^*$: If $Q(s_1, \ldots, s_n) \in uD^\infty$, then there are $w_1, \ldots, w_n \in D^*$ such that $s_i \in w_i D^\infty$ for all $i \in [n]$ and $w_1 D^\infty \times \cdots \times w_n D^\infty \subseteq Q^{-1}(uD^\infty)$.

Monotonicity of a function $Q : (D^\infty)^n \longrightarrow D^\infty$ now reads as: For all $(s_1, \ldots, s_n)$ and $(s_1', \ldots, s_n')$ with $s_i \sqsubseteq s_i'$ for all $i \in [n]$: $Q(s_1, \ldots, s_n) \sqsubseteq Q(s_1', \ldots, s_n')$.

The temporal model behind the recursion used in Definition 4 is the following: At every time point one has exactly n elements to consume, exactly one for each of the n input streams. These are thought to appear at the same time. To model also the case where no element arrives in some input stream, a specific symbol $\bot$ can be added to the system. Giving the engine a finite word as input means that the engine gets noticed about the end of the word (when it has read the word). In a real system this can be handled, e.g., the idea of punctuation semantics [33]. Of course, then there is a difference between the finite word abc, where the system can stop listening for the input after 'c' was read in, and the infinite word $abc(\bot)^\omega$, where the system gets notified at every time point that there is no element at the current time.

A further extension of the framework in [20] is that we add to the set of rules a co-recursive/co-inductive rule [32], in order to describe directly bounded-memory queries $Q = Repeat(K)$—instead of only the underlying windows K. This class is denoted MonBmem in Definition 4.

Three types of classes are defined in parallel: classes Accu^n which are intended to model accumulator functions $f : (D^*)^n \longrightarrow D^*$; classes Bmem$^{(n;m)}$ that model incrementally maintainable functions with bounded memory, i.e., window functions that are bounded-memory and have bounded output, and classes MonBmem(n;m) of incrementally maintainable, memory-bounded, and monotonic functions that lead to the definition of monotonic functions on infinite streams. The main idea, similar to that of [3], is to partition the argument functions in two classes, normal and safe arguments. In [3] the normal variables are the ones on which the recursion step happens and which have to be controlled, whereas the safe ones are those in which the growth of the term is not restricted. In the definitions, the growth (the length) of the words is controlled explicitly and the distinction between input and output arguments is used: The input arguments are those where the input may be either a finite or an infinite word. The output variables are the ones in which the accumulation happens. In a function term $f(x_1, \ldots, x_n; y_1, \ldots, y_m)$ the input arguments are the ones before the semicolon ";", here: $x_1, \ldots, x_n$, and the output arguments are the ones after the ";", here: $y_1, \ldots, y_n$.

Using the notation of [22] for my purposes, a function f with n input and m output arguments is denoted $f^{(n;m)}$. Classes Bmem$^{(n;m)}$ and MonBmem$^{(n;m)}$ consist of functions of the form $f^{(n;m)}$. The class MonBmem defined as the union $\bigcup_{n \in \mathbb{N}}$ MonBmem$^{(n;)}$ contains all functions without output variables and is the class of functions which describe the prefix restrictions $Q_{\restriction D^*}$ of stream queries $Q : D^\infty \longrightarrow D^\infty$ that are computable by a bounded-memory sAsm.

Definition 4. *Let $n, m \in \mathbb{N}$ be natural numbers (including zero). The set of bounded n-ary accumulator word functions, for short $\textsc{Accu}^n$, the set of $n + m$-ary bounded-memory incremental functions with n input and m output arguments, for short $\textsc{Bmem}^{(n;m)}$, and the set of monotonic, bounded-memory incremental $n + m$-ary functions with n input and m output arguments, for short $\textsc{MonBmem}^{(n;m)}$, are defined according to the following rules:*

1. $w \in \textsc{Accu}^0$ *for any word* $w \in D^*$ *("Constants")*
2. $last_k(\cdot) \in \textsc{Accu}^1$ *for any* $k \in \mathbb{N}$ *("Suffixes")*
3. $S_k^a(w) = last_k(w) \circ a \in \textsc{Accu}^1$ *for any* $a \in D$ *("Successors")*
4. $P_k(w) = last_{k-1}(w) \in \textsc{Accu}^1$ *("Predecessors")*
5. $cond_{k,l}(w, v, x) = \begin{cases} last_k(v) & \text{if } last_1(w) = 0 \\ last_l(x) & \text{else} \end{cases} \in \textsc{Accu}^3$ *("Conditional")*
6. $\Pi_k^j(w_1, \ldots, w_n) = last_k(w_j) \in \textsc{Accu}^n$ *for any* $k \in \mathbb{N}$ *and* $j \in [n], n \neq 0$.   *("Projections")*
7. $shl(\cdot)^{(1;0)} \in \textsc{MonBmem}$ *with* $shl(aw;) = w$ *and* $shl(\epsilon;) = \epsilon$.   *("Left shift")*
8. *Conditions for Composition*   *("Composition")*
   (a) *If* $f \in \textsc{Accu}^n$ *and, for all* $i \in [n], g_i \in \textsc{Accu}^m$, *then also* $f(g_1, \ldots, g_n) \in \textsc{Accu}^m$; *and:*
   (b) *If* $g^{(m;n)} \in \textsc{MonBmem}^{(m;n)}$ *and, for all* $i \in [m], g_i \in \textsc{Accu}^l$ *and* $h_j^{(k;l)} \in \textsc{MonBmem}^{(k;m)}$ *for* $j \in [n]$, *then* $f^{(k;l)} \in \textsc{MonBmem}^{(k;l)}$ *where using* $\boldsymbol{w} = w_1, \ldots, w_k, \boldsymbol{v} = v_1, \ldots, v_l$

$$f^{(k;l)}(\boldsymbol{w}; \boldsymbol{v}) = g^{(m;n)}(h_1(\boldsymbol{w}; \boldsymbol{v}), \ldots, h_m(\boldsymbol{w}; \boldsymbol{v}); g_1(\boldsymbol{v}), \ldots, g_n(\boldsymbol{v}))$$

   (c) *If* $g^{(m;n)} \in \textsc{Bmem}^{(m;n)}$ *and, for all* $i \in [m], g_i \in \textsc{Accu}^l$ *and* $h_j^{(k;l)} \in \textsc{MonBmem}^{(k;m)}$ *for* $j \in [n]$, *then* $f^{(k;l)} \in \textsc{Bmem}^{(k;l)}$ *where using* $\boldsymbol{w} = w_1, \ldots, w_k, \boldsymbol{v} = v_1, \ldots, v_l$

$$f^{(k;l)}(\boldsymbol{w}; \boldsymbol{v}) = g^{(m;n)}(h_1(\boldsymbol{w}; \boldsymbol{v}), \ldots, h_m(\boldsymbol{w}; \boldsymbol{v}); g_1(\boldsymbol{v}), \ldots, g_n(\boldsymbol{v}))$$

9. *If* $g : (D^*)^n \longrightarrow D^* \in \textsc{Accu}$ *and* $h : (D^*)^{n+3} \longrightarrow D^* \in \textsc{Accu}$ *then also* $f : (D^*)^{n+1} \longrightarrow D^* \in \textsc{Accu}$, *where:*

$$f(\epsilon, v_1, \ldots, v_n) = g(v_1, \ldots, v_n)$$
$$f(wa, v_1, \ldots, v_n) = h(w, a, v_1, \ldots v_n, f(w, v_1, \ldots, v_n))$$

("Accu-Recursion")

10. *If* $g_i : (D^*)^{n+m} \longrightarrow D^* \in \textsc{Accu}$ *for* $i \in [m], g_0 \in \textsc{Accu}$ *then* $k = k^{(n;m)} \in \textsc{Bmem}^{(n;m)}$, *where k is defined using the above abbreviations as follows:*

$$k(\epsilon, \ldots, \epsilon; \boldsymbol{v}) = g_0(\boldsymbol{v})$$
$$k(\boldsymbol{w}; \boldsymbol{v}) = k(shl(\boldsymbol{w}); g_1(\boldsymbol{v}, \boldsymbol{w}^{=1}), \ldots, g_m(\boldsymbol{v}, \boldsymbol{w}^{=1}))$$

("Window-Recursion")

11. *If $g_i : (D^*)^{n+m} \longrightarrow D^* \in$ ACCU for $i \in [m]$, $g_0 \in$ ACCU, then $f = f^{(n;m)} \in$ MONBMEM$^{(n;m)}$, where f is defined using the above abbreviations as follows:*

$$f(\epsilon,\ldots,\epsilon; out, \boldsymbol{v}) = out$$
$$f(\boldsymbol{w}; out, \boldsymbol{v}) = f(shl(\boldsymbol{w}); out \circ g_1(\boldsymbol{v}, \boldsymbol{w}^{=1}), g_1(\boldsymbol{v}, \boldsymbol{w}^{=1}), \ldots, g_m(\boldsymbol{v}, \boldsymbol{w}^{=1}))$$

("Repeat-Recursion")

Let MONBMEM $= \bigcup_{n \in \mathbb{N}}$ MONBMEM$^{(n;)}$.

Within the definition above, three types of recursions occur: the first is a primitive recursion over accumulators. The second, called window-recursion, is a specific form of *tail recursion* which means that the recursively defined function is the last application in the recursive call. As the name indicates, this recursion rule is intended to model the kernel/window functions. The last recursion rule (again in tail form) is intended to mimic the *Repeat* functional.

In the first recursion, the word is consumed from the end: This is possible, as the accumulators are built from left to right during the streaming process. Note, that the length of outputs produced by the accu-recursion rule and the window-recursion rule are length-bounded.

The window-recursion rule and the repeat-recursion rule implement a specific form of tail recursion consuming the input words from the beginning with the left-shift function $shl()$. This is required as the input streams are potentially infinite. Additionally, these two rules implement a form of simultaneous recursion, where all input words are consumed in parallel according to the temporal model mentioned above.

Repeat recursion is illustrated with the following simple example.

Example 1. Consider the window function K_{par} that, for a word w, outputs its parity. The monotonic function $Par(w) = Repeat(K_{par})(w) = \bigcirc_{j=0}^{|w|} K_{par}(w^{\leq j})$ can be modelled as follows. The auxiliary xor function $\oplus$ can be defined with cond because with cond one can define the functionally complete set of junctions $\{\neg, \wedge\}$ with $\neg x := cond_{1,1}(x, 1, 0)$ and $x \wedge y = cond_{1,1}(x, 0, y)$. Using repeat recursion (item 11 in Definition 4) gives the desired function.

$$f(\epsilon; out, v) = out$$
$$f(w; out, v) = f(shl(w); out \circ v \oplus w^{=1}, v \oplus w^{=1})$$
$$Par(w) = f(w; \epsilon, 0)$$

For example, the input word $w = 101$ is consumed as follows:

$$Par(101) = f(101; \epsilon, 0) = f(shl(101); \epsilon \circ 0 \oplus 101^{=1}, 0 \oplus 101^{=1})$$
$$= f(01; \epsilon \circ 0 \oplus 1, 0 \oplus 1) = f(01; 1, 1)$$
$$= f(1; 1 \circ 1 \oplus 0, 1 \oplus 0) = f(1; 1 \circ 1, 1)$$
$$= f(\epsilon; 1 \circ 1 \oplus 1, 1 \oplus 1) = f(\epsilon; 1 \circ 1 \circ 0, 0) = 110$$

The output of the repeat-recursion grows linearly: The whole history is outputted with the help of the concatenation function. Note that the concatenation functions appears only in the repeat-recursion rule and also—in a restricted form—in the successor functions, but there is no concatenation function defined in one of the three classes (as it is not a bounded-memory function). The repeat-recursion function builds the output word by concatenating intermediate results in the out variable. Because of this, it follows that all functions in MONBMEM are monotonic in their input arguments. This is stated in the following proposition:

Proposition 2. *All functions in* MONBMEM *are monotonic.*

Proof (sketch). Let us introduce the notion of a function $f(\boldsymbol{x}; \boldsymbol{y})$ being monotonic w.r.t. its arguments $\boldsymbol{x}$: This is the case if for every $\boldsymbol{y}$ the function $f_{\boldsymbol{y}}(\boldsymbol{x}) = f(\boldsymbol{x}, \boldsymbol{y})$ is monotonic. The functions in MONBMEM are either the left shift function (which is monotonic) or a function constructed with the application of composition, which preserves monotonicity, or by repeat-recursion, which, due to the concatenation in the output position, also guarantees monotonicity. □

The functions in MONBMEM map (vectors of) finite words to finite words. Because of the monotonicity, it is possible to define for each $f \in$ MONBMEM an extension $\tilde{f}$ which maps (vectors) of finite or infinite words to finite or infinite words. If $f^{(n;)} : (D^*)^n \longrightarrow D^*$, then $\tilde{f} : (D^\infty)^n \longrightarrow D^\infty$ is defined as follows: If all $s_i \in D^*$, then $\tilde{f}(s_1, \ldots, s_n) = f(s_1, \ldots, s_n)$. Otherwise, $\tilde{f}(s_1, \ldots, s_n) = sup_{i \in \mathbb{N}} f(s_1^{\leq i}, \ldots, s_n^{\leq i})$ where $sup_{i \in \mathbb{N}} f(s_1^{\leq i}, \ldots, s_n^{\leq i})$ is the unique stream $s \in D^\infty$ such that $f(s_1^{\leq i}, \ldots, s_n^{\leq i}) \sqsubseteq s$ for all i. Let us denote by BMEM-STR those functions Q that can be presented as $Q = \tilde{f}$ for some $f \in$ MONBMEM and call them *bounded-memory* stream queries.

Theorem 2. *A function Q with one argument belongs to* BMEMSTR *iff it is a stream query computable by a bounded-memory* sASM.

Proof (sketch). Clearly, the range of each function f in BMEM is length-bounded, i.e., there is $m \in \mathbb{N}$ such that for all $w \in D^* : |f(w)| \leq m$. But then, according to [20, Proposition 22], f can be computed by a bounded-memory sASM. As the *Repeat* functional does (nearly) nothing else than the repeat-recursion rule, one gets the desired representation.

The other direction is more advanced but can be mimicked as well: All basic rules, i.e. update rules, can be modelled by ACCU functions (as one has to store only one symbol of the alphabet in each register; the update is implemented as accu-recursion). The parallel application is modelled by the parallel recursion principle in window-recursion. The if-construct can be simulated using cond. And the quantifier-free formula in the if construct can also be represented using cond as the latter is functionally complete. □

Note that in a similar way one can model $o(n)$ bitstring bounded sASM: Instead of using constant size windows $last_k(c)$ in the definition of accumulator functions, one uses dynamic windows $last_{f(.)}(\cdot)$, where, for a sublinear function $f \in o(n)$, $last_{f(|w|)}(w)$ denotes the $f(|w|)$ suffix of w.

4   Related Work

The work presented here is based on the foundation of stream processing according to [20] which considers streams as finite or infinite words. The research on streams from the word perspective is quite mature and the literature on infinite words, language characterizations, and associated machine models abounds. The focus in this paper is on bounded-memory functions and their representation by some form of recursion. For all other interesting topics and relevant research papers the reader is referred to [30, 35].

The construction of bounded-memory queries given in this paper are based on the *Repeat* functional applied to a window function. An alternative representation by trees is given in [21]: An (infinite) input word is read as sequence of instructions to follow the tree, 0 for left and 1 for right. The leaves of the tree contain the elements to be outputted. The authors give a characterization for the interesting case where the range of the stream query is a set of infinite words: In this case they have to use non-well-founded trees. Note, that in this type of representation the construction principle becomes relevant. Instead of a simple instantiation with a parameter value, one has to apply an algorithm in order to build the structure (here: the function).

In [20] and in this paper, the underlying alphabet for streams is not necessarily finite. This is similar to the situation in research on data words [5], where the elements of the stream have next to an element from a finite alphabet also an element from an infinite alphabet.

Aspects of performant processing on streams are touched in this paper with the construction of a class of functions capturing exactly those queries computable by an sAsm. This characterization is in the tradition of implicit complexity as developed in the PhD thesis of Bellantoni [4] which is based on work of Leivant [25]. (See also the summary of the thesis in [3] where the main result is the characterization of polynomial time functions by some form of primitive recursion). The main idea of distinguishing between two sorts of variables in my approach comes from [4], the use of constant, $o(n)$ size windows to control the primitive recursion is similar to the approach of [26] used for the rule called "bounded recursion" therein.

The consideration of bounded memory in [2] is couched in the terminology of data-stream management systems. The authors of [2] consider first-order logic (FOL) or rather: (non-recursive) SQL as the language to represent windows. The main result is a syntactical criterion for deciding whether a given FOL formula represents a bounded-memory query. Similar results in the tradition of Büchis result on the equivalence of finite-automata recognizability with definability in second-order logic over the sequential calculus can be shown for streams in the word perspective [1, 14].

An aspect related to bounded memory is that of incremental maintainability as discussed in the area called dynamic complexity [29, 36]. Here the main concern is to break down a query on a static data set into a stream query using simple update operators with small space.

The function-oriented consideration of stream queries along the line of this paper and [20] lends itself to a pipeline-style functional programming language on streams. And indeed, there are some examples, such as [9], that show the practical realizability of such a programming language.

The type of recursion that was used in order to handle infinite streams, namely the rules of window-revision and repeat-revision, uses the consumption of words from the beginning. This is similar to the co-algebraic approach for defining streams and stream functions [32].

5 Conclusion

Based on the foundational stream framework of [20], this paper gives a recursive characterization of bounded-memory functions. Though the achieved results have a foundational character, they are useful for applications relying, say, on the agent paradigm where stream processing plays an important role. The recursive style that was used to define the set of bounded-memory functions can be understood as a formal foundation for a functional style programming language for bounded-memory functions.

The present paper is one step towards axiomatically characterizing practically relevant stream functions for agents [27]. The axiomatic characterizations considered in [27] are on a basic phenomenological level—phenomenological, because only observations regarding the input-output behavior are taken into account, and basic, because no further properties regarding the structure of the data stream elements are presupposed. The overall aim, which motivated the research started in [27] and continued in this paper, is to give a more elaborated characterization of rational agents where also the observable properties of various higher-order streams of states such beliefs or goals are taken into account.

For example, if considering the stream of epistemic states $\Phi_1, \Phi_2, \ldots$ of an agent, an associated observable property is the set of beliefs $Bel(\Phi_i)$ an agent is obliged to believe in its current state Φ_i. The beliefs can be expressed in some logic which comes with an entailment relation $\models$. Using the entailment relation, the idea of a rational change of beliefs of the agent under new information can be made precise. For example, the success axiom expresses an agent's "trust" in the information it receives: If it receives α, then the current state Φ_i is required to develop into state Φ_{i+1} such that $Bel(\Phi_{i+1}) \models \alpha$. The constraining effects that this axiom has on the belief-state change may appear simple but, at least when the new information is not consistent with the current beliefs, it is not clear how the change has to be carried out. Axioms such as the success axiom are one of the main objects of study in the field of belief revision. But what is still missing in current research is the combination of belief-revision axioms (in particular those for iterated belief revision [10]) with axioms expressing basic stream-properties.

References

1. Alur, R., Cerný, P.: Expressiveness of streaming string transducers. In: Lodaya, K., Mahajan, M. (eds.) IARCS Annual Conference on Foundations of Software Technology and Theoretical Computer Science, FSTTCS 2010, Chennai, India, 15–18 December 2010, vol. 8, pp. 1–12 (2010)
2. Arasu, A., Babcock, B., Babu, S., McAlister, J., Widom, J.: Characterizing memory requirements for queries over continuous data streams. ACM Trans. Database Syst. **29**(1), 162–194 (2004)
3. Bellantoni, S., Cook, S.: A new recursion-theoretic characterization of the polytime functions. Comput. Complex. **2**(2), 97–110 (1992)
4. Bellantoni, S.J.: Predicative recursion and computation complexity. Ph.D. thesis, Graduate Department of Computer Science, University of Toronto (1992)
5. Benedikt, M., Ley, C., Puppis, G.: Automata vs. logics on data words. In: Dawar, A., Veith, H. (eds.) CSL 2010. LNCS, vol. 6247, pp. 110–124. Springer, Heidelberg (2010). https://doi.org/10.1007/978-3-642-15205-4_12
6. Calbimonte, J.-P., Mora, J., Corcho, O.: Query rewriting in RDF stream processing. In: Sack, H., Blomqvist, E., d'Aquin, M., Ghidini, C., Ponzetto, S.P., Lange, C. (eds.) ESWC 2016. LNCS, vol. 9678, pp. 486–502. Springer, Cham (2016). https://doi.org/10.1007/978-3-319-34129-3_30
7. Chomicki, J.: Efficient checking of temporal integrity constraints using bounded history encoding. ACM Trans. Database Syst. **20**(2), 149–186 (1995)
8. Cormode, G.: Sketch techniques for approximate query processing. In: Synposes for Approximate Query Processing: Samples, Histograms, Wavelets and Sketches, Foundations and Trends in Databases. NOW Publishers (2011)
9. Cowley, A., Taylor, C.J.: Stream-oriented robotics programming: the design of roshask. In: 2011 IEEE/RSJ International Conference on Intelligent Robots and Systems, pp. 1048–1054, September 2011
10. Darwiche, A., Pearl, J.: On the logic of iterated belief revision. Artif. Intell. **89**, 1–29 (1997)
11. Della Valle, E., Ceri, S., Barbieri, D.F., Braga, D., Campi, A.: A First step towards stream reasoning. In: Domingue, J., Fensel, D., Traverso, P. (eds.) FIS 2008. LNCS, vol. 5468, pp. 72–81. Springer, Heidelberg (2009). https://doi.org/10.1007/978-3-642-00985-3_6
12. Della Valle, E., Ceri, S., van Harmelen, F., Fensel, D.: It's a streaming world! Reasoning upon rapidly changing information. Intell. Syst. IEEE **24**(6), 83–89 (2009)
13. Endrullis, J., Hendriks, D., Klop, J.W.: Streams are forever. Bull. EATCS **109**, 70–106 (2013)
14. Engelfriet, J., Hoogeboom, H.J.: MSO definable string transductions and two-way finite-state transducers. ACM Trans. Comput. Log. **2**(2), 216–254 (2001)
15. Filiot, E.: Logic-automata connections for transformations. In: Banerjee, M., Krishna, S.N. (eds.) ICLA 2015. LNCS, vol. 8923, pp. 30–57. Springer, Heidelberg (2015). https://doi.org/10.1007/978-3-662-45824-2_3
16. Furst, M., Saxe, J.B., Sipser, M.: Parity, circuits, and the polynomial-time hierarchy. Theory Comput. Syst. **17**, 13–27 (1984)
17. Giese, M., et al.: Optique: zooming in on big data. IEEE Comput. **48**(3), 60–67 (2015)
18. Gries, O., Möller, R., Nafissi, A., Rosenfeld, M., Sokolski, K., Wessel, M.: A probabilistic abduction engine for media interpretation based on ontologies. In: Hitzler,

P., Lukasiewicz, T. (eds.) RR 2010. LNCS, vol. 6333, pp. 182–194. Springer, Heidelberg (2010). https://doi.org/10.1007/978-3-642-15918-3_15

19. Grohe, M., Gurevich, Y., Leinders, D., Schweikardt, N., Tyszkiewicz, J., Van den Bussche, J.: Database query processing using finite cursor machines. Theory Comput. Syst. **44**(4), 533–560 (2009)

20. Gurevich, Y., Leinders, D., Van den Bussche, J.: A theory of stream queries. In: Arenas, M., Schwartzbach, M.I. (eds.) DBPL 2007. LNCS, vol. 4797, pp. 153–168. Springer, Heidelberg (2007). https://doi.org/10.1007/978-3-540-75987-4_11

21. Hancock, P., Pattinson, D., Ghani, N.: Representations of stream processors using nested fixed points. Log. Meth. Comput. Sci. **5**(3:9), 1–17 (2009)

22. Handley, W.G., Wainer, S.S.: Complexity of primitive recursion. In: Berger, U., Schwichtenberg, H. (eds.) Computational Logic, vol. 165, pp. 273–300. Springer, Heidelberg (1999). https://doi.org/10.1007/978-3-642-58622-4_8

23. Kaminski, M., Francez, N.: Finite-memory automata. Theor. Comput. Sci. **134**(2), 329–363 (1994)

24. Kharlamov, E., et al.: Semantic access to streaming and static data at siemens. Web Semant. **44**, 54–74 (2017)

25. Leivant, D.: A foundational delineation of poly-time. Inf. Comput. **110**(2), 391–420 (1994)

26. Lind, J., Meyer, A.R.: A characterization of log-space computable functions. SIGACT News **5**(3), 26–29 (1973)

27. Özçep, Ö.L., Möller, R.: Towards foundations of agents reasoning on streams of percepts. In: Proceedings of the 31st International Florida Artificial Intelligence Research Society Conference (FLAIRS 2018) (2018)

28. Özçep, Ö.L., Möller, R., Neuenstadt, C.: A stream-temporal query language for ontology based data access. In: Lutz, C., Thielscher, M. (eds.) KI 2014. LNCS (LNAI), vol. 8736, pp. 183–194. Springer, Cham (2014). https://doi.org/10.1007/978-3-319-11206-0_18

29. Patnaik, S., Immerman, N.: Dyn-Fo: a parallel, dynamic complexity class. J. Comput. Syst. Sci. **55**(2), 199–209 (1997)

30. Perrin, D., Pin, J.: Infinite Words: Automata, Semigroups, Logic and Games. Pure and Applied Mathematics. Elsevier Science, Amsterdam (2004)

31. Le-Phuoc, D., Dao-Tran, M., Xavier Parreira, J., Hauswirth, M.: A Native and adaptive approach for unified processing of linked streams and linked data. ISWC 2011. LNCS, vol. 7031, pp. 370–388. Springer, Heidelberg (2011). https://doi.org/10.1007/978-3-642-25073-6_24

32. Rutten, J.J.M.M.: A coinductive calculus of streams. Math. Struct. Comput. Sci. **15**(1), 93–147 (2005)

33. Tucker, P.A., Maier, D., Sheard, T., Fegaras, L.: Exploiting punctuation semantics in continuous data streams. IEEE Trans. Knowl. Data Eng. **15**(3), 555–568 (2003)

34. Della Valle, E., Schlobach, S., Krötzsch, M., Bozzon, A., Ceri, S., Horrocks, I.: Order matters! Harnessing a world of orderings for reasoning over massive data. Seman. Web **4**(2), 219–231 (2013)

35. Weihrauch, K.: Computable Analysis: An Introduction. Springer, Heidelberg (2000). https://doi.org/10.1007/978-3-642-56999-9

36. Zeume, T., Schwentick, T.: Dynamic conjunctive queries. In: Schweikardt, N., Christophides, V., Leroy, V. (eds.) Proceedings of 17th International Conference on Database Theory (ICDT), 24–28 March 2014, pp. 38–49. OpenProceedings.org (2014)

An Implementation and Evaluation of User-Centered Requirements for Smart In-house Mobility Services

Dorothee Rocznik[1(✉)], Klaus Goffart[1], Manuel Wiesche[2], and Helmut Krcmar[2]

[1] BMW Group, Parkring 19, 85748 Garching, Germany
dorothee.rocznik@bmw.de
[2] Department of Information Systems, Technical University of Munich, Boltzmannstr. 3, 85748 Garching, Germany

Abstract. In smart cities we need innovative mobility solutions. In the near future, most travelers will start their multi-modal journey through a seamlessly connected smart city with intelligent mobility services at home. Nevertheless, there is a lack of well-founded requirements for smart in-house mobility services. In our original journal publication [7] we presented a first step towards a better understanding of the situation in which travelers use digital services at home in order to inform themselves about their mobility options. We reported three main findings, namely (1) the lack of availability of mobility-centered information is the most pressing pain point regarding mobility-centered information at home, (2) most participants report a growing need to access vehicle-centered information at home and a growing interest in using a variety of smart home features and (3) smart in-house mobility services should combine pragmatic (i.e., information-based qualities) and hedonic (i.e., stimulation- and pleasure-oriented) qualities. In the present paper, we now extend our previous work among an implementation and evaluation of our previously gained user insights into a smart mirror prototype. The quantitative evaluation again highlighted the importance of pragmatic and hedonic product qualities for smart in-house mobility services. Since these insights can help practitioners to develop user-centered mobility services for smart homes, our results will help to maximize customer value.

Keywords: Smart home technology · Smart mobility services
User needs

1 Introduction and Theoretical Background

Within the last few years, the interest in smart environments has grown intensely in scientific research (e.g., [1, 2]). With regard to various target groups, smart environments can be seen as a wide field of research addressing any potential location, ranging from public institutions such as hospitals or nursing centers (e.g., [2]) to private smart homes [3]. One topic that is connected to all of these aspects is smart mobility. Since in the morning, most travelers start their daily journey at home, our research focuses on

© Springer Nature Switzerland AG 2018
F. Trollmann and A.-Y. Turhan (Eds.): KI 2018, LNAI 11117, pp. 391–398, 2018.
https://doi.org/10.1007/978-3-030-00111-7_33

easing daily life in smart environments through providing smart mobility services for the traveler's home. Smart in-house mobility services are an interesting field of application because instead of providing one smart and individually tailored service, the market provides a huge list of digital mobility services with different features [4–6]. Through a structured search within app stores and articles from blogs, Schreieck et al. [6] provided an overview of currently existing urban mobility services. This overview includes 59 digital mobility services that can be grouped in six different categories, namely (1) trip planners, (2) car or ride sharing services, (3) navigation, (4) smart logistics, (5) location-based information and (6) parking services (listed in order of decreasing category size). In a deeper analysis, the authors examined, which service modules (i.e., map view, routing, points of interest, location sharing, traffic information, parking information and matching of demand and supply) are integrated in which of the six service categories listed above. Interestingly, the results show a very heterogeneous combination of service modules in digital mobility services. For example, traffic information services are only included in 40% of the digital mobility services that focus on navigation, in 60% of the location-based information services and in none of the other four service categories. The only two service modules that can be found in all of the six categories of digital mobility services are map view and routing. Within the categories, however, these two service modules are not part of every single digital mobility service. Similar to other studies [4, 5], these findings highlight that some features are rarely integrated in smart mobility services, although they might provide a comfort service for the user (e.g., traffic information). Therefore, users have to fall back upon multiple mobility services in order to satisfy their individual need for information sufficiently. The ideal situation, however, would include a smart all-in-one mobility service. Instead of searching for mobility-centered information using different services and putting effort into evaluating and combining the information from different sources, the user's workload should be reduced through providing individually tailored information at the right time proactively. In order to develop this mobility-centered artificial intelligence, we need to understand the current pain points the user faces while using digital mobility services. Moreover, we need to assess the user's mobility-centered pragmatic needs (e.g., time and type of information) and the user's non-mobility-centered additional needs (e.g., leisure time planning), which are associated to the situation in which travelers inform themselves about their mobility options. Therefore, in this paper, we focus on providing an initial step towards formulating requirements for smart mobility services for smart homes as private living spaces. In our original journal publication [7] we focused on mobility-centered needs at home (i.e., pain points, stress level, time and type of information and interest in vehicle-centered information) and non-mobility-centered additional needs (e.g., event recommendations). In our previous work we had three main findings, namely (1) the lack of availability of mobility-centered information is the most pressing pain point regarding mobility-centered information at home, (2) most participants report a growing need to access vehicle-centered information at home and a growing interest in using a variety of smart home features and (3) smart in-house mobility services should combine pragmatic (i.e., information-based qualities) and hedonic qualities (i.e., stimulation- and pleasure-oriented qualities). Now, we extend these existing user insights [7] among the implementation of our findings into a smart mirror prototype and an empirical evaluation of this prototype.

2 Implementation of the Smart Mirror Prototype

This paper aims to extend our previous results [7] among an implementation of the identified user needs into a prototype. In the online survey [7], mobility-centered needs at home (i.e., pain points, stress level, time and type of information and interest in vehicle-centered information) and non-mobility-centered additional needs (e.g., news, preparing grocery shopping) that are associated to the situation in which travelers inform themselves about their mobility options at home were assessed. A detailed description of the results of the online survey can be found in the journal paper on which this paper relays on [7]. Our previous results [7] showed that travelers most suffer from a lack of availability of information about their mobility options. This means that current digital mobility services do not satisfy the users' need for reliable information about different mobility options at home whenever they need them without putting a considerable amount of effort in the search for information. We found that searching for mobility options at home is associated with stress for most users. Proactively presenting the needed information from a reliable data source could reduce the users' stress level because the service would reduce the users' workload for getting mobility-centered information and making mobility-centered decisions. Therefore, we decided to implement our features into a smart mirror on which information can be derived in passing and without actively deriving it (i.e., without starting an application and entering information). The following feature sets were integrated into our prototype. Pictures of each feature of the prototype can be found online [8]:

- **"Agenda":** The service should retrieve the users' personal agenda from their digital calendar. The calendar integration enables the proactive presentation of intelligent information. For example, the digital calendar can tell the service whether it is a working day, weekend or a holiday for the user. Based on this information, the smart in-house mobility service could display the appropriate information for the appropriate kind of day, time and situation.
- **"My Mobility":** Here, the following three sets of features were included: **(1) Vehicle Status:** vehicle-centered information such as tank fill, in-car temperature, and lock status, **(2) Mobility Options:** car sharing, own car, public transport, and walking, **(3) Routing:** departure time, duration, alternative modes of transportation, traffic situation. Our previous results [7] have highlighted that most travelers inform themselves about multiple decision-relevant aspects. Hence, smart mobility services should combine multiple types of information into one service. Thus, travelers can get all the information they need from one service. Moreover, a growing interest in vehicle-centered information was identified [7] and therefore integrated.
- **"Home Status":** This feature is meant to satisfy the identified growing interest in smart home [7]. It includes smart home features like an intelligent security system, home automation, and energy monitoring and management.

- **"Discover & Enjoy"** and **"Family & Friends":** Based on our previous study [7], we combined pragmatic product qualities in form of information-based elements (e.g., multi-modal routing) with hedonic product qualities in our prototype. Within "Discover & Enjoy" a virtual dressing room for online shopping was presented to stimulate the users. Moreover, "Discover & Enjoy" contains the features "Weekend Inspiration" (i.e., event and restaurant recommendations) and "Fitness Inspiration" (i.e., workout videos). Within "Family & Friends" a memo board and a picture board with notifications and pictures from peers was meant to motivate the user hedonically to use the prototype. Moreover, a messaging feature enabled text messaging and video calls.

3   Empirical Evaluation of the Smart Mirror Prototype

In the following paragraphs, we focus on the evaluation of the prototype described above. Since one of the main findings of our previous research [7] is the potential of the combination of pragmatic and hedonic product qualities in smart in-house mobility services, our evaluation concentrates on analyzing the pragmatic and hedonic qualities of our prototype and their interplay in forming the user's overall impression.

3.1   Method

Procedure and Material. The study started with a briefing about the procedure which contained information about the duration (i.e., 20 min presentation of prototype and 15 min questionnaire) and the content of the study (i.e., a prototype and an online questionnaire on a tablet). Then, the investigator presented the smart mirror prototype described above [8]. After the presentation, the participants explored the prototype on their own. Next, the participants filled out an online questionnaire on a tablet. Following acknowledged guidelines for the evaluation of user experiences [9], the questionnaire contained items that assessed (1) the participants' evaluation of the pragmatic and hedonic product qualities of the prototype, (2) their experienced psychological need fulfillment, and (3) their evaluation of the overall appeal of the prototype. Pragmatic quality describes a system that is perceived as clear, supporting and controllable by the user. Hedonic quality describes a system that is perceived as innovative, exciting and exclusive [10]. Hedonic product qualities are closely related to the users' experienced psychological need fulfillment [9] because it "addresses human needs for excitement (novelty/change) and pride (social power, status)" [10] p. 275. Psychological need fulfillment assesses the amount of need fulfillment in terms of stimulation, relatedness, meaning, popularity, competence, security, and autonomy [11] that is experienced by the user. The overall appeal contains the users' overall evaluation of the prototype as a desirable or non-desirable product. The items for need fulfillment were taken from [9]. The items for pragmatic and hedonic product qualities were taken from [12]. The items for overall appeal were taken from [13]. All items were translated into German according to an adaption of Brislin's Translation Model [14] and assessed on a 7-point Likert-Scale ranging from totally agree to not agree at all. The questionnaire also assessed demographic variables (i.e., age, gender and job) and the participants' technological affinity (i.e., ownership and usage intensity of a smartphone).

Participants. We recruited participants in a show room of a German industrial partner [8] in Munich in December 2017. The customers who were visiting the show room could decide voluntarily whether they would like to experience a new smart mirror prototype. In sum, $N = 47$ participants took part in our study voluntarily. Only full data sets were included in the analysis. Among these participants, 61.7% are male ($n = 29$), 38.3% are female ($n = 18$). Their age ranges from 18 to 62 years ($M = 29.6$, $SD =$ 12.4). Most of the participants were working professionals ($n = 26$; 55.32%), 34.04% were students ($n = 16$) and 10.64% ($n = 5$) were in other work situations (e.g., free-lancer). Most of the participants own a car ($n = 37$; 78.72%). All of the participants own a smartphone which they use more than two hours per day.

Statistical Analysis. The analysis was made with RStudio 1.0.153 (2017). A signifi-cance level of $\alpha = .05$ was used as standard. Other significance levels are listed explicitly in the results section. Moreover, the size of effects and relationships are interpreted according to the convention of Cohen [15] (i.e., 0.10 = small; 0.30 = medium; 0.50 = large). The relationship between the dependent variable overall appeal and the independent variables (i.e., pragmatic quality, hedonic quality, need fulfillment) was analyzed with the help of two linear models. The adjusted R^2 was used as an indicator for the amount of explained variance of the two models. The F-ratio was used to compare the specified linear models with the null model. A significant F-ratio shows that the specified model explains significantly more variance than the null model [16]. In order to estimate the effect of pragmatic and hedonic quality with and without the influence of the users' experienced need fulfillment, we calculated two models: Model 1 without need fulfillment and model 2 with need fulfillment as an additional predictor for appeal.

3.2   Results

Table 1 summarizes the results of the descriptive statistics and the parameter estimation for the linear models predicting the prototype's overall appeal. This includes the

Table 1. Descriptive statistics and parameter estimation for the linear models predicting the prototype's overall appeal (***p < .001, **p < .01, *p < .05).

	M	SD	Model 1			Model 2		
			Est.	SE	t	Est.	SE	t
Intercept			−.68	1.24	−.55	.04	1.02	.04
Pragmatic quality	5.43	0.81	.70	.19	3.78***	.44	.16	2.76**
Hedonic quality	5.38	0.78	.43	.19	2.20*	.16	.17	.97
Need fulfillment	4.07	1.27				.52	.11	4.79***
Overall appeal	5.45	1.21						
Adjusted R^2			.34			.56		
F-statistic (df1, df2)			13.07 (2,44)***			20.73 (3,43)***		

estimation of the regression coefficient (Est.), its standard error of estimation (SE) and the t-value (t) for each independent variable. Moreover, the adjusted R^2, F-ratio, and the degrees of freedom (df) for the two specified models are listed.

4 Discussion, Future Research and Conclusion

In sum, our evaluation shows a positive perception of the prototype. Since the means of all indicators are above 4.00 (i.e., indicating agreement) the prototype was perceived as having a high pragmatic and a high hedonic quality. Moreover, the users experienced a positive need fulfillment while interacting with the prototype and evaluated the prototype as a desirable product or rather as having a high overall appeal. The linear models show that both, pragmatic and hedonic elements have a positive effect on the overall evaluation of the prototype. In model one pragmatic quality has a large positive effect and hedonic quality has a medium positive effect on the users' rating of the overall appeal of the prototype. Taken together, in this model pragmatic and hedonic product qualities explain 34% of the variance in the users' judgement of the prototype's overall appeal (see model 1). Integrating need fulfillment into model two results in a reduced effect of pragmatic and hedonic quality on overall appeal and a large positive effect of need fulfillment on overall appeal. In sum, all three predictors explain 56% of the variance in overall appeal (see model 2). Since need fulfillment contains the evaluation of hedonic elements, the positive effect of hedonic elements still remains in this model. The differences in the effects between the two models indicates, however, that need fulfillment mediates the relationship between pragmatic and hedonic quality and the overall evaluation. Summarizing, the prototype lead to a positive user experience that was characterized by both, a fulfillment of pragmatic and hedonic user needs.

These results underlie some restrictions. First, our study gives no insights about how to implement demanded functions such as recommendations on food and drinks. Open questions concerning the technical transfer and the practical implementation (e.g., [17]) should be addressed in future research (e.g., which technical means are used to identify the different context of use and to learn about the user's preferences?). Furthermore, the evaluation should be enlarged among a longitudinal and experimental evaluation. The next step should be that the smart mirror prototype allows users to configure the presented information according to their individual needs and situations. The configurable version should then be used over a period of some weeks and should be evaluated by the users regarding its product qualities and its effect on the users' stress level.

In conclusion, this paper is a first step to formulate user-centered requirements for smart in-house mobility services that combine pragmatic and hedonic product qualities. First of all, we think that different pressing use cases should be bundled in one service so that the service is important in more than one situation. This becomes obvious since user needs differ between workdays and weekends [7] and the service should be of use in most parts of the user's everyday life to facilitate user retention. Hence, in contrast to most mobility services that are currently available [6] smart in-house mobility services should be improved through the combination of multiple functions. This includes the combination of a high pragmatic product quality in form of providing information-based hard facts (e.g., temporally optimized route by car) and a high hedonic product quality in form of more stimulating functions that maximize customer benefit through creating joy of use and a positive user experience (e.g., weekend and fitness inspirations). All information presented should be adjusted to the user's demands. After inferring the user's needs and habits in exchange with connected information technology like the user's digital calendar or wearable fitness application, only individually desired information should be presented proactively in a timely manner. In order to provide sustained customer value it is important to combine pragmatic and hedonic product qualities in everyday information systems.

References

1. Vaidya, B., Park, J.H., Yeo, S.-S., Rodrigues, J.J.P.C.: Robust one-time password authentication scheme using smart card for home network environment. J. Comput. Commun. **34**(3), 326–336 (2011)
2. Virone, G., Noury, N., Demongeot, J.: A system for automatic measurement of circadian activity deviations in telemedicine. IEEE Trans. Biomed. Eng. **49**(12), 1463–1469 (2002)
3. Alam, M.R., Reaz, M.B.I., Ali, M.A.M.: A review of smart homes – past, present, and future. IEEE Trans. Syst. Man Cybern. Part C Appl. Rev. **42**(6), 1190–1203 (2012)
4. Motta, G., Sacco, D., Ma, T., You, L., Liu, K.: Personal mobility service system in urban areas: the IRMA project. In: Proceedings of the IEEE Symposium on Service-Oriented System Engineering, San Francisco, USA, pp. 88–97. IEEE Computer Society (2015)
5. Sassi, A., Mamei, M., Zambonelli, F.: Towards a general infrastructure for location-based smart mobility services. In: Proceedings of the International Conference on High Performance Computing & Simulation (HPCS), Bologna, Italy, pp. 849–856. IEEE (2014)
6. Schreieck, M., Wiesche, M., Krcmar, H.: Modularization of digital services for urban transportation. In: Proceedings of the Twenty-Second Americas Conference on Information Systems, San Diego, USA, pp. 1–10. Association for Information Systems (2016)
7. Rocznik, D., Goffart, K., Wiesche, M., Krcmar, H.: Towards identifying user-centered requirements for smart in-house mobility services. KI – Künstl. Intell. **31**(3), 249–256 (2017)
8. Rocznik, D., Goffart, K., Wiesche, M., Krcmar, H.: Implementation of a smart mirror prototype. Lecture Notes in Artificial Intelligence. SSRN (2018, forthcoming). https://ssrn.com/abstract=3206486
9. Hassenzahl, M., Wiklund-Engblom, A., Bengs, A., Hägglund, S., Diefenbach, S.: Experience-oriented and product-oriented evaluation: psychological need fulfillment, positive affect, and product perception. Int. J. Hum.-Comput. Interact. **31**(8), 530–544 (2015)
10. Hassenzahl, M., Kekez, R., Burmester, M.: The importance of a software's pragmatic quality depends on usage modes. In: Proceedings of the 6th International Conference on Work with Display Units, pp. 275–276. Ergonomic, Institut für Arbeits- und Sozialforschung, Berchtesgaden, Germany (2002)
11. Johnson, M., Bradshaw, J.M., Feltovich, P.J., Jonker, C.M., van Riemsdijk, B., Sierhuis, M.: The fundamental principle of coactive design: interdependence must shape autonomy. In: De Vos, M., Fornara, N., Pitt, J.V., Vouros, G. (eds.) COIN 2010. LNCS (LNAI), vol. 6541, pp. 172–191. Springer, Heidelberg (2011). https://doi.org/10.1007/978-3-642-21268-0_10

12. Hassenzahl, M., Monk, A.: The inference of perceived usability from beauty. Hum.-Comput. Interact. **25**(3), 235–260 (2010)
13. Hassenzahl, M., Platz, A., Burmester, M., Lehner, K.: Hedonic and ergonomic quality aspects determine a software's appeal. In: Proceedings of the SIGCHI Conference on Human Factors in Computing Systems (CHI 2000), pp. 201–208. ACM, New York (2000)
14. Jones, P.S., Lee, J.W., Phillips, L.R., Zhang, X.E., Jaceldo, K.B.: An adaptation of Brislin's translation model for cross-cultural research. Nurs. Res. **50**(5), 300–304 (2001)
15. Cohen, J.: A power primer. Psychol. Bull. **112**(1), 155–159 (1992)
16. Field, A., Miles, J., Field, Z.: Discovering Statistics Using R. Sage Publications, Thousand Oaks (2012)
17. Johnson, M.J., Bradshaw, J.M., Feltovich, P.J., Jonker, C.M., van Riemsdijk, M.B., Sierhui, M.: Coactive design: designing support for interdependence in joint activity. J. Hum. Robot Interact. **3**(1), 43–69 (2014)

Cognitive Approach

Predict the Individual Reasoner: A New Approach

Ilir Kola[1,2(✉)] and Marco Ragni[1]

[1] Cognitive Computation Lab, University of Freiburg, Freiburg, Germany
i.kola@tudelft.nl, ragni@informatik.uni-freiburg.de
[2] Technical University Delft, 2628 CD Delft, The Netherlands

Abstract. Reasoning is a core ability of humans being explored across disciplines during the last millenia. Investigations focused, however, often on identifying general principles of human reasoning or correct reasoning, but less on predicting conclusions for an individual reasoner. It is a desideratum to have artificial agents that can adapt to the individual human reasoner. We present an approach which successfully predicts individual performance across reasoning domains for reasoning about quantified or conditional statements using collaborative filtering techniques. Our proposed models are simple but efficient: they take some answers from a subject, and then build pair-wise similarities and predict missing answers based on what similar reasoners concluded. Our approach has a high accuracy in different data sets, and maintains this accuracy even when more than half of the data is missing. These features suggest that our approach is able to generalize and account for realistic scenarios, making it an adequate tool for artificial reasoning systems for predicting human inferences.

Keywords: Computational reasoning · AI and Psychology
Predictive modeling

1 Introduction

Reasoning problems have been studied in such diverse disciplines as psychology, philosophy, cognitive science, and computer science. From an artificial intelligence perspective, modeling human reasoning is crucial if we want to have artificial agents that can assist us in everyday life.

There are currently at least five theories of reasoning [1,3,5,6,9,11,14,15,21], each of them having principally the potential for predicting individual reasoning. For each domain of reasoning there are about a dozen models which use one of these theories as an underlying principle to model human behavior in different tasks. It is important to notice that these models merely fit the data and attempt to reproduce distributions of answers, rather than generalize to new and untested problems. Furthermore, these models focus on aggregated data and simply account for what the "average" reasoner would do. After more than 50

© Springer Nature Switzerland AG 2018
F. Trollmann and A.-Y. Turhan (Eds.): KI 2018, LNAI 11117, pp. 401–414, 2018.
https://doi.org/10.1007/978-3-030-00111-7_34

years of research, there is still no state-of-the-art model for predicting individual performance in reasoning tasks: even those few models which try to take into consideration individual differences, do so for only one reasoning domain.

Collaborative filtering, a method employed in recommender systems [19], exploits the fact that people's preferences seem to be consistent to successfully recommend them movies or items to buy. We assume that human reasoning, like preferences, is consistent and we show that a single reasoner does not deviate from similar reasoners. Consequently her answers can be predicted based on answers of similar reasoners.

The model we propose takes as input subjects' answers for some tasks, and based on them and on answers given by similar reasoners, it predicts the subjects' answers in the remaining tasks. Since currently there are no models that try to predict human reasoning on an individual level, we compare our approach to the existing cognitive models. As expected, our model clearly outperforms them since it is more adequate in predicting the answers of specific individuals. This approach works independently of the underlying theory of reasoning, which is a great advantage given that it is still unclear what the "correct" underlying theory is. This feature suggests that it would be possible to combine the advantage of our approach, i.e., the fact that it accounts for individuals, with the advantage of the theories of reasoning, i.e., their insight regarding why are certain answers given, to build even better models.

Our approach is not only able to extend for different reasoning tasks, but also exhibits high robustness and performs well even when more than half of the data set is missing. We deleted 8 out of 12 answers for 70% of the subjects, and the prediction accuracy remained the same. Both these points suggest that our approach is not only useful for ideal situations in laboratory settings, but that it can actually generalize to real life scenarios involving different reasoning domains and high amounts of answers to be predicted.

The rest of this article is structured as follows: we start by giving background information about the reasoning tasks as well as collaborative filtering techniques (Sect. 2). In Sect. 3 we explain the experimental setting used to collect the data. Section 4 introduces the model, while results are presented and discussed in Sect. 5. We conclude the paper and outline future work in Sect. 6.

2   State-of-the-Art

2.1   Reasoning Domains

Syllogistic Reasoning. Syllogisms are arguments about properties of entities, consisting of two premises and a conclusion. The first analysis of syllogisms is due to Aristoteles, and throughout history the task has been widely studied both by logicians, and since the past century, also by psychologists. In Aristotles account of syllogisms, the premises can be in four moods:

- Affirmative universal (abbrev. as *A*): *All A are B*
- Affirmative existential (abbrev. as *I*): *Some A are B*

– Negative universal (abbrev. as E): *No A are B*
– Negative existential (abbrev. as O): *Some A are not B*

Furthermore, the terms can be distributed in four possible figures, based on their configuration:

Figure 1	Figure 2	Figure 3	Figure 4
$A - B$	$B - A$	$A - B$	$B - A$
$B - C$	$C - B$	$C - B$	$B - C$

An example of a syllogism is:

> *All Actors are Bloggers*
> *Some Bloggers are Chemists*
> ———————————————
> *Therefore, Some Actors are Chemists*

[12] provides a review of seven theories of syllogistic reasoning. We will describe the ones which perform better in their meta-analysis, and they will be later used as a baseline for the performance of our model. The first theory, *illicit conversions* [2,20], is based on a misinterpretation of the quantifiers, assuming *All B are A* when given *All A are B* and *Some B are not A* when given *Some A are not B*. Both these conversions are logically invalid, and lead to errors such as inferring *All C are A* given the premises *All A are B* and *All C are B*. In order to predict the answers of syllogisms, this theory uses classical logic conversions and operators, as well as the two aforementioned invalid conversions.

The *verbal models* theory [16] claims that reasoners build verbal models from syllogistic premises and then either formulate a conclusion or declare that nothing follows. The model then performs a reencoding of the information based on the assumption that the converse of the quantifiers *Some* and *No* are valid. In another version, the model also reencodes invalid conversions. The authors argue that a crucial part of deduction is the linguistic process of encoding and reencoding the information, rather than looking for counterexamples.

Unlike the previous example, *mental models* (first formulated for syllogisms in [8]) are inspired by the use of counterexamples. The core idea is that individuals understand that a putative conclusion is false if there is a counterexample to it. The theory states that when faced with a premise, individuals build a mental model of it based on meaning and knowledge. E.g., when given the premise All Artists are Beekeepers the following model is built:

> Artist   Beekeeper
> Artist   Beekeeper
> . . .

Each row represents the properties of an individual, and the ellipsis denotes individuals which are not artists. This model can be fleshed out to an explicit model which contains information on all potential individuals, including someone who is a Beekeeper but not an Artist. In a nutshell, the theory states that many individuals simply reach a conclusion based on the first implicit model, which can be wrong (in this case it would give the impression that All Beekeepers are Artists). However, there are individuals who build other alternative models in order to find counterexamples, which usually leads to a logically correct answer.

The Wason Selection Task. The second task we will use is the Wason Selection Task. Since its proposal by the late Wason in 1966 [24], it has led to several hundreds of experiments and articles, as well as to about 15 cognitive theories which try to explain it. In the original version of the task, subjects were shown four randomly selected cards like in Fig. 1. The experimenter explains to the subjects that each card contains a letter on one side, and a number on the other side. Furthermore, the experimenter would add that *if there is a vowel on one side of the card, then there is an even number on the other side.* The subjects' task is to select all those cards, and only those cards, which would have to be turned over in order to discover whether the experimenter was lying in asserting this conditional rule about the four cards.

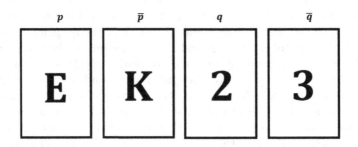

Rule: If a card has a vowel on one side, then it has an even number on the other side

Fig. 1. The cards in the original Wason Selection Task [24], as well as the conditional rule participants were presented with.

The rule can be formalized by classical propositional logic as the material implication *if p, then q*, where p is the antecedent (in this case, the letter) and q is the consequent (in this case, the number). The correct answer, as per classical logic, would be E and 3, since only these cards can prove the rule false (the E card by having an odd number on the other side, and the 3 card by having a vowel on the other side). However, people often err in this task. In an analysis by Wason and Johnson-Laird [26] the results of four experiments give the following distribution:

Patterns	pq	p	$pq\bar{q}$	$p\bar{q}$	Other
	46%	33%	7%	4%	10%

Hence, only 4% of the participants give the logically correct answer.

Different experiments focused on changing the content of the rule, and this had a reliable effect. These rules could have a deontic form, in which subjects are asked to select those cards which could violate the rule, or an everyday generalization form, where subjects have to evaluate whether the rule is true or false. An everyday generalization such as *Every time I go to Manchester, I travel by car* [25] led to 10 out of 16 subjects making only falsifying selections. The first example of a deontic rule was due to Johnson-Laird, Legrenzi and Legrenzi [10] who based their example on the postal regulation. The rule was *if a letter is sealed, then it has a 50 lire stamp on it*, and instead of cards they used actual envelopes. Nearly all of the participants selected the falsifying envelopes, while their performance in the abstract task was poor. This suggested that the content of the rule can facilitate the performance. These are just some important aspects, for an overview of the theories of the selection task please refer to [17].

2.2   Collaborative Filtering

Recommender systems are software tools used to provide suggestions for items which can be useful to users [19]. These recommendations can be used in many domains such as online shopping, website suggestion, music suggestion etc. One of the most common ways in which we get recommendations for products is by asking friends, especially the ones who have similar taste to ours. Collaborative filtering techniques are based exactly on this idea, and the term was first introduced by Goldberg [7]. A collaborative filtering algorithm searches a group of users and finds the ones with a taste similar to yours, and recommends items to you based on the things they like [23]. In a nutshell, collaborative filtering suggests that if Alice likes items 1 and 2, and Bob likes items 1, 2 and 3, then Alice will also probably like item 3. More formally, in collaborative filtering we look for patterns in observed preference behavior, and try to predict new preferences based on those patterns. Users preferences are stored as a matrix, in which each row represents a user and each column represents an item. It is important to notice that the data can be very sparse (i.e., with many missing values), since users might have rated only a subset of the items. There are two main types of collaborative filtering techniques: similarity-based ones (also called "correlation-based") and model-based ones. In this work we will focus on the former.

Similarity-based techniques start by using a similarity measure to build pairwise similarities between users. Then, they perform a weighted voting procedure, and use the simple weighted average to predict the ratings [22]. An immanent problem in this approach is the difficulty of finding the most appropriate similarity measure. A commonly used one is the Pearson correlation, calculated as follows:

$$w_{i,j} = \frac{\sum\limits_{u}(r_{i,u} - \bar{r}_i)(r_{j,u} - \bar{r}_j)}{\sqrt{\sum\limits_{u}(r_{i,u} - \bar{r}_i)^2}\sqrt{\sum\limits_{u}(r_{j,u} - \bar{r}_j)^2}}$$

where the summations are over the items which both the users i and j have rated, and $\bar{r}_i$ and $\bar{r}_j$ are the average ratings on items rated by both users of the i-th and j-th user respectively. Then, the prediction is made by applying the following formula [18]:

$$P_{a,x} = \bar{r}_a + \frac{\sum\limits_{s}(r_{s,x} - \bar{r}_s) \cdot w_{a,s}}{\sum\limits_{s}|w_{a,s}|}$$

where $w_{a,s}$ is the similarity between users a and s (will be introduced in Sect. 4), and $\bar{r}_a$ and $\bar{r}_s$ are the average ratings for users a and s on rated items other than x.

However, this is just one of the different options, and normally the similarity function is based on the domain and type of answers.

3 Experimental Setting

We tested 112 subjects who answered both the syllogistic reasoning task and the Wason Selection Task. Subjects were recruited through an online survey in the Amazon Mechanical Turk[1] webpage. They were from 24 to 58 years old, and their education ranged from high school to doctoral degree level. Subjects received a monetary compensation.

Subjects answered 12 versions of the Wason Selection Task and 12 syllogisms, for a total of 24 tasks. Subjects were given six valid syllogisms and six invalid ones. There were three tasks in Fig. 1, three tasks in Fig. 2, two tasks in Fig. 3 and four tasks in Fig. 4. For each version (valid and invalid) subjects received three tasks with a low difficulty, one task with medium difficulty, and two tasks with a high difficulty. The difficulty was assessed by looking at the percentage of subjects who gave a correct answer to the task in the meta-analysis by Khemlani and Johnson-Laird [12]. Syllogisms for which more than 55% of the subjects gave a correct answer in the meta-analysis were considered to have a low difficulty, from 40% to 50% a medium difficulty, and those with less than 20% a high difficulty. The contents for each pair of premises were common professions, such as *Actors* or *Dentists*, for the end terms, and common hobbies or personal features, such as *Stamp − collectors* or *Vegetarians*, for the middle terms.

In the Wason Selection Task, participant answered four tasks in the abstract version, four tasks in the deontic version and four tasks in the everyday generalization version. The four tasks in each version included negation as following:

True antecedent, true consequent: if p, then q
True antecedent, false consequent: if p, then not q
False antecedent, true consequent: if not p, then q
False antecedent, false consequent: if not p, then not q

The materials for the abstract version were letters and numbers, as in the original version [24] (e.g., *if there is an A on one side of the card, there is a 3 on the other side*), for the deontic version were places where people can go and colors they can wear (e.g., *if you are going to the cinema, you should be wearing something green*), and for the everyday generalization version of the task were food and drinks, inspired by an experiment conducted by Manktelow and Evans [13] (e.g., *every time I eat meat, I drink wine*).

---

[1] http://www.mturk.com/.

4   The Model

We build our model using a similarity-based collaborative filtering approach. The basic idea is to predict answers based on a neighborhood of "similar" subjects.

Our model starts by randomly choosing 10% of the subjects, and for each of these subjects it deletes 25% of their answers. These are the tasks that our model will try to predict. For each missing answer, first of all the model calulates the pairwise similarities between the subject whose answer is missing, and each other subject. Then, a weighted voting procedure occurs: the answer of each subject with a similarity of higher than 0.35 with the subject whose answer is missing is weighted by this similarity measure, and added to the respective option (i.e., the answer given by this subject). At the end of the procedure, the option with the highest vote is recommended as the preferred answer. The procedure is represented in Algorithm 1. This algorithm runs in polynomial time. $T(n) = O(n^2)$ is a function of the number of subjects and the number of tasks.

Algorithm 1. Procedure for the collaborative filtering model

---

  repeat
      $to\_delete.append(random\_element)$ ▷ pick random subjects to delete
  until for 10% of the subjects
  for $subject$ in to_delete **do**
      repeat
         $delete\_random\_task$ ▷ pick random tasks to delete
      until for 25% of the tasks
  end for
  for $missing\_answer$ **do**
      for $other\_subject$ **do**
         $x \leftarrow similarity(subject, other\_subject)$ ▷ use the $sim_{i,j}$ equation
         if $x > 0.35$ **then**
             $value[answer[other\_subject]] + = 1 * x$ ▷ perform weighted aggregation
         end if
      end for
      $missing\_answer \leftarrow key.max(value)$ ▷ select most chosen answer
  end for

Since we need to gauge similarity among subjects, we have to define a similarity function. For the syllogistic task, we count the number of same answers between the two subjects, and divide it by the number of tasks that both subjects answered. Let N be the number of tasks answered by both subject i and j, and $n_{sameAnswers}$ the number of tasks for which subjects i and j gave the same answer, then the similarity between i and j, $sim_{i,j}$ would be calculated as follows:

$$sim_{i,j} = \frac{n_{sameAnswers}}{N}$$

The similarity measure for the Wason Selection Task experiment is slightly different, since in each task subjects have to decide whether or not to turn each of four cards. In this case, $n_{sameAnswers}$ represents the number of cards for which both i and j made the same decision, and N the overall number of cards on which both subjects decided. The intuition behind is fairly simple: suppose we have three subjects (Alice, Bob, and Charlie) answering the abstract version of the task where the cards are A, K, 4, 7. Let us suppose Alice turns only the A card, Bob turns cards K, 4 and 7 and Charlie turns all four cards. With the simple similarity measure, after comparing the answers for this task, all three subjects are equally "un-similar". However, it seems unreasonable to say that Alice and Bob should get the same similarity measure as Bob and Charlie, since in the former case the two take a different decision for each card, while in the latter three out of four decisions are the same.

5   Results and Discussion

We test our model to three different data sets: the first one contains data from the syllogistic reasoning domain, the second from the Wason Selection Task, and the third includes a combination of the first two data sets, with answers from both domains.

5.1   Syllogistic Reasoning

We use accuracy as a measure of evaluation, which means we count the number of correct predictions and divide it with the overall number of predictions. We choose this measure since the predictions can either be correct or incorrect, and not something in between. Let $n_{correct}$ be the number of correct predictions and N the number of overall predictions, we would calculate accuracy using the following formula:

$$accuracy = \frac{n_{correct}}{N}$$

We compare our model with the following existing models or theoretical predictions from the literature: illicit conversions, verbal models, mental models, as well as mReasoner, an implementation of the mental models theory of reasoning. These models are not specifically designed to predict individual answers, they rather try to predict what most people would say in a given task. Consequently, each of them predicts more than one answer for each syllogistic task. For example, a theory can state that given the premises *All A are B* and *Some B are C*, people draw the conclusion *Some A are C*, *Some C are A* or *All A are C*. To make the models comparable, if the model predicts multiple answers we randomly pick one of the predictions and compare it to the true answer. Models have to predict out of 9 possible options, this means that a model which simply guesses would be correct in 11% of the cases. Results are shown in Fig. 2.

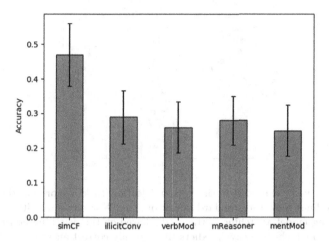

Fig. 2. Accuracy of the model in syllogistic reasoning. We present the average of 500 runs, the lines show the standard deviation. simCF = our similarity-based collaborative filtering model, illicitConv = the model based on the illicit conversions theory, verbMod = the model based on the verbal reasoning theory, mReasoner = the mReasoner model, mentMod = the model based on the mental models theory.

5.2 Wason Selection Task

Since the Wason Selection task is a binary setting as for each card the model has to predict whether it should be turned or not, we use the same formula as for syllogistic reasoning, but we adapt the notation:

$$accuracy = \frac{n_{correct}}{N} = \frac{TP + TN}{TP + FP + TN + FN}$$

where TP refers to turned cards predicted correctly, TN refers to not turned cards predicted correctly, FP refers to not turned cards predicted as turned, and FN refers to turned cards predicted as not turned.

As for syllogisms, we believe it would be useful to compare our models with other theoretical models. However, for the Wason Selection Task this is even more difficult: not only these models do not offer predictions for individuals but rather for answer distributions (a problem which we managed to overcome for syllogistic reasoning), the central conundrum is that they do not differentiate between the several versions of the task, and moreover they rarely offer quantitative predictions. One very simple theory which we can use is matching [4]. This theory predicts that only the cards mentioned in the rule (i.e., p and q) will be turned. We also add the logically correct answer ($p\bar{q}$) to the comparison. Results are reported in Fig. 3.

5.3 Combined Domains

We decided to focus on two reasoning tasks not only because we wanted to validate our model in multiple domains, but also to check whether it still performs

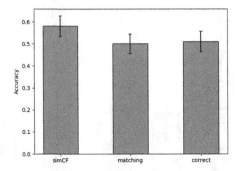

Fig. 3. Accuracy of the models in the Wason Selection Task. We present the average of 500 runs, the lines show the standard deviation. simCF = our similarity-based collaborative filtering model, matching = the model based on the matching heuristic theory, correct = a model which always predicts the logically correct answer.

well when we put these reasoning domains together. Our data set now contains the answers that each subject gave to the Wason Selection Task and to the syllogistic reasoning task.

Depending whether we are dealing with a Wason Selection Task or with a syllogism we use the respective accuracy measure, as previously introduced. In our case, this works since the number of each task is similar,otherwise this could be problematic. We can generalize using the following formula:

$$accuracy = \frac{n_{correctCards} + n_{correctSyllog}}{N_{cards} + N_{syllog}}$$

where $n_{correctCards}$ is the number of correctly predicted cards, $n_{correctSyllog}$ is the number of correctly predicted syllogisms, N_{cards} is the total number of cards to be predicted and N_{syllog} is the total number of syllogisms to be predicted.

Being unable to perform model comparisons, since there is no model that we know of which accounts for both tasks, we simply present the accuracy of our model. In the standard setting with 25% of the tasks deleted for 10% of the subjects, our model achieved a 52% accuracy. This performance is approximately the average of the accuracies achieved in the individual domains. However, it is important to notice that now the similarity between two subjects was measured by taking into account both tasks. This suggests that there is consistency accross reasoning tasks.

5.4 Discussion

As expected, our model outperforms all other models or theoretical predictions in each of the reasoning domains. For syllogistic reasoning it is true that the competitors are penalized by the fact that we randomly pick one of their predictions, however this supports our argument that these models at this stage are not fit to predict individual answers.

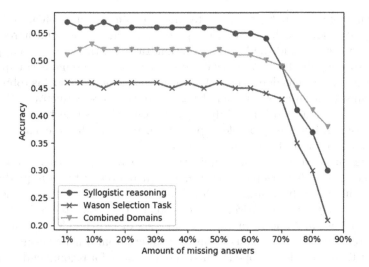

Fig. 4. Accuracy of our model in each application, for different amounts of missing data. E.g., 40% means that the model was built on 60% of the data, and we report the accuracy of prediction for the 40% of the data which is missing.

In order to check whether the model is robust, we gradually increased the amount of deleted data which in turn needs to be predicted. The results in Fig. 4 show that our model deals well with sparse data, as seen by the fact that it maintains its accuracy until 65% of the data is missing. This holds for all three applications of the model, which means this approach works well for different reasoning domains. Both these arguments suggest that using collaborative filtering to predict individual performance in reasoning tasks can be used successfully for real life applications.

Despite comparing our model with predictions from other cognitive models, these results are not well interpretable due to the fact that these other models do not deal specifically with individual answers. For this reason, our results can be considered as a first benchmark in this domain, setting a standard for comparision for future models.

6   Conclusions

So far, there is very little research on modeling individual differences in reasoning tasks. This poses a problem for computer science, since artificial agents will have to deal with people who reason differently. To tackle this, we implemented a model which predicts individual performance in reasoning tasks using collaborative filtering. The idea is simple but efficient: predict missing answers of a subject based on how similar subjects answered those tasks. In a nutshell, the models take some answers from a subject, and given these responses and answers from other subjects, they estimate what would the subject conclude for a different tasks.

This model is the first attempt at tackling human reasoning on an individual level. It outperforms other theoretical predictions on two prominent reasoning domains: syllogisms and the Wason Selection Task. Furthermore, this approach is shown to work also for data sets with answers from both domains, an approach no cognitive theory has done so far. The performance of the model is robust, and it maintains its accuracy even when it has to predict more than 50% of the data. Moreover, the model does not only predict cases when subjects give logically correct answers, but it is also able to predict mistakes. Both these features make the model appropriate for real life situations.

Our results have interesting implications for psychology of reasoning. First of all, they show that people's performance in reasoning tasks is predictable, and more importantly it suggests that their reasoning, even when it does not produce logically correct answers, is consistent. This consistency is shown by the fact that we are able to predict the answers of individuals for tasks across two different reasoning domains by using answers from other reasoners. In the same spirit, this article also opens a new research path for recommender systems techniques like collaborative filtering by showing that they are not only suited to predict people's preferences, but they can also be extended to account for human reasoning.

There are multiple ways in which our approach can be extended. To begin with, we limited ourself to only two tasks both in the domain of deductive reasoning. It would be useful to test whether the same approach can be applied to other reasoning domains. Secondly, there is space for improving the model, for instance the similarity measure can be further refined by using theoretical findings. Furthermore, it would be possible to employ model-based collaborative filtering models for which preliminary results show potential for higher accuracy.

One of the issues that future work will have to tackle is the so-called "cold-start" situation: how to deal with a new reasoner for whom we do not have any data? At this point, we need a minimal amount of answers to be able to account for missing ones, however future models should be able to overcome this weakness. Furthermore, just predicting answers is not the same as understanding reasoning, since it holds no explanatory power. A solution would be to combine our approach with one of the theories of reasoning. This way, we would have on one hand a model which performs well on an individual level, and on the other hand some very useful domain knowledge which might shed light on why certain answers are given, and in turn help predicting future ones. This combination is possible: theories of reasoning argue about potential reasons why individual differences appear, which might be exactly what our model is estimating, so including this information in our model can improve its learning ability. Another interesting contribution would be to link our approach with meta-learning models which learn to infer.

Acknowledgements. This research has been supported by a Heisenberg grant to MR (RA 1934/3-1 and RA 1934/4-1) and RA 1934/2-1. The authors would like to thank the anonymous reviewers for their valuable comments and suggestions.

References

1. Braine, M.D., O'Brien, D.P.: A theory of if: a lexical entry, reasoning program, and pragmatic principles. Psychol. Rev. **98**(2), 182 (1991)
2. Chapman, L.J., Chapman, J.P.: Atmosphere effect re-examined. J. Exp. Psychol. **58**(3), 220 (1959)
3. Cheng, P.W., Holyoak, K.J.: Pragmatic reasoning schemas. Cogn. Psychol. **17**(4), 391–416 (1985)
4. Evans, J.S.B.T., Lynch, J.S.: Matching bias in the selection task. Br. J. Psychol. **64**(3), 391–397 (1973)
5. Evans, J.S.B.T.: In two minds: dual-process accounts of reasoning. Trends Cogn. Sci. **7**(10), 454–459 (2003)
6. Evans, J.S.B.T.: The heuristic-analytic theory of reasoning: extension and evaluation. Psychon. Bull. Rev. **13**(3), 378–395 (2006)
7. Goldberg, D., Nichols, D., Oki, B.M., Terry, D.: Using collaborative filtering to weave an information tapestry. Commun. ACM **35**(12), 61–70 (1992)
8. Johnson-Laird, P.N.: Models of deduction. In: Reasoning: Representation and Process in Children and Adults, pp. 7–54 (1975)
9. Johnson-Laird, P.N.: Mental Models: Towards a Cognitive Science of Language, Inference, and Consciousness, no. 6. Harvard University Press (1983)
10. Johnson-Laird, P.N., Legrenzi, P., Legrenzi, M.S.: Reasoning and a sense of reality. Br. J. Psychol. **63**(3), 395–400 (1972)
11. Johnson-Laird, P.N.: Deductive Reasoning. Wiley Online Library (1991)
12. Khemlani, S., Johnson-Laird, P.N.: Theories of the syllogism: a meta-analysis. Psychol. Bull. **138**(3), 427 (2012)
13. Manktelow, K.I., Evans, J.S.B.T.: Facilitation of reasoning by realism: effect or non-effect? Br. J. Psychol. **70**(4), 477–488 (1979)
14. Oaksford, M., Chater, N.: A rational analysis of the selection task as optimal data selection. Psychol. Rev. **101**(4), 608 (1994)
15. Oaksford, M., Chater, N.: Bayesian Rationality: The Probabilistic Approach to Human Reasoning. Oxford University Press, Oxford (2007)
16. Polk, T.A., Newell, A.: Deduction as verbal reasoning. Psychol. Rev. **102**(3), 533 (1995)
17. Ragni, M., Kola, I., Johnson-Laird, P.N.: On selecting evidence to test hypotheses: a theory of selection tasks. Psychol. Bull. **144**(8), 779 (2018)
18. Resnick, P., Iacovou, N., Suchak, M., Bergstrom, P., Riedl, J.: GroupLens: an open architecture for collaborative filtering of netnews. In: Proceedings of the 1994 ACM Conference on Computer Supported Cooperative Work, pp. 175–186. ACM (1994)
19. Resnick, P., Varian, H.R.: Recommender systems. Commun. ACM **40**(3), 56–58 (1997)
20. Revlis, R.: Two models of syllogistic reasoning: feature selection and conversion. J. Verbal Learn. Verbal Behav. **14**(2), 180–195 (1975)
21. Rips, L.J.: The Psychology of Proof: Deductive Reasoning in Human Thinking. MIT Press, Cambridge (1994)
22. Sarwar, B., Karypis, G., Konstan, J., Riedl, J.: Item-based collaborative filtering recommendation algorithms. In: Proceedings of the 10th International Conference on World Wide Web, pp. 285–295. ACM (2001)
23. Segaran, T.: Programming Collective Intelligence: Building Smart Web 2.0 Applications. O'Reilly Media, Inc., Sebastopol (2007)
24. Wason, P.C.: Reasoning. In: Foss, B. (ed.) New Horizons in Psychology (1966)

25. Wason, P.C., Shapiro, D.: Natural and contrived experience in a reasoning problem. Q. J. Exp. Psychol. **23**(1), 63–71 (1971)
26. Wason, P.C., Johnson-Laird, P.N.: Psychology of Reasoning: Structure and Content, vol. 86. Harvard University Press (1972)

The Predictive Power of Heuristic Portfolios in Human Syllogistic Reasoning

Nicolas Riesterer[1]([✉]), Daniel Brand[2], and Marco Ragni[1]

[1] Cognitive Computation Lab, University of Freiburg, 79110 Freiburg, Germany
{riestern,ragni}@cs.uni-freiburg.de
[2] Center for Cognitive Science, University of Freiburg, 79104 Freiburg, Germany
daniel.brand@cognition.uni-freiburg.de

Abstract. A core method of cognitive science is to investigate cognition by approaching human behavior through model implementations. Recent literature has seen a surge of models which can broadly be classified into detailed theoretical accounts, and fast and frugal heuristics. Being based on simple but general computational principles, these heuristics produce results independent of assumed mental processes.

This paper investigates the potential of heuristic approaches in accounting for behavioral data by adopting a perspective focused on predictive precision. Multiple heuristic accounts are combined to create a portfolio, i.e., a meta-heuristic, capable of achieving state-of-the-art performance in prediction settings. The insights gained from analyzing the portfolio are discussed with respect to the general potential of heuristic approaches.

Keywords: Cognitive modeling · Heuristics · Syllogistic reasoning

1 Introduction

Cognitive modeling is a method that has taken psychological and cognitive research by storm. Nowadays, theories are formalized, evaluated on representative data, and ultimately compared on mathematically motivated common grounds. Especially in cognitive science, modeling has allowed to tackle phenomena from a variety of angles ranging from simple heuristics based on psychological effects (e.g., the *Atmosphere* effect [23]), to regression models of varying complexity (e.g., *Power Law of Practice* [21] or the *Semantic Pointer Architecture Unified Network*, SPAUN [4]).

A recent meta-analysis [12] investigated the state of the art in modeling human syllogistic reasoning. By evaluating a set of twelve models, the authors found that heuristics representing fast and frugal principles perform worse than more elaborate model-based accounts. This is unsurprising considering the simple nature of heuristic models, especially when compared to models attempting to tie into the grand scheme of cognition.

F. Trollmann and A.-Y. Turhan (Eds.): KI 2018, LNAI 11117, pp. 415–421, 2018.
https://doi.org/10.1007/978-3-030-00111-7_35

In this article, we expand upon the work of [12] by revisiting the role of heuristics in modeling human syllogistic reasoning. Instead of treating heuristics as full-fledged cognitive models, we see their purpose in specifying plausible building blocks of the mental processes constituting human reasoning. We evaluate the heuristic models by relying on a *portfolio approach* heavily influenced by recent work in *Artificial Intelligence* (AI) research. This method is based on the idea that a collection of weakly performing models can be turned into strong models by identifying and exploiting strengths while avoiding individual weaknesses. For instance, research on developing improved solving techniques for the *Boolean Satisfiability Problem* (SAT) progressed by intelligently combining different algorithm instances to produce portfolios capable of applying promising candidates specifically selected for the task at hand [8, 24]. In similar spirit, research of classification, especially in the domain of decision trees, found that it is possible to obtain significantly better performing meta-models by combining weak models (Boosting, [6, 7, 18]). By applying similar techniques to human reasoning, we achieve state-of-the-art performance in predicting human reasoning behavior while simultaneously gaining insight into the conceptual properties of the underlying models.

2   Heuristics of the Syllogism

A syllogistic premise consists of a quantified assertion (All, Some, None, Some ... not) about two terms (e.g., A and B). A syllogism is composed of two such premises linked by a common term. Depending on the order of the terms in the premises, the syllogism is in one of four so-called figures. By abbreviating the quantifiers as A, I, E, and O, respectively, and enumerating the figures, syllogisms can be denoted as AA1, AA2, ..., OO4 resulting in 64 distinct syllogistic problems. For example, "All B are A; All B are C" is represented by the identifier AA4. In syllogistic reasoning tasks, participants are instructed to give one of nine possible conclusions relating the non-common terms or to follow "No Valid Conclusion" (NVC). For the example above, [12] reported that the logical conclusion "Some A are C" was responded by 12% whereas "All A are C" and NVC responses were given by 49% and 29%, respectively. This demonstrates the necessity of identifying human reasoning strategies which apparently do not follow classical logics.

The term *heuristic* is pertinent to many fields of research. In computer science and AI, heuristics are commonly applied in complex scenarios such as planning, to obtain fast and frugal approximations without necessitating a comprehensive model (e.g., *Fast-Forward Planning* [10]). In this sense, heuristics are known as "rules of thumb, educated guesses, intuitive judgments or simply common sense. In more precise terms, heuristics stand for strategies using readily accessible though loosely applicable information to control problem-solving processes in human beings and machine." [15, p. vii].

In the domain of cognitive modeling and, more specifically, in human reasoning, the term heuristic is used to represent simple models for behavioral effects not intended to specify a comprehensive theoretical account of the function of the mind. For this paper we extend this notion of heuristics by including models which generally do not consider interactions with related cognitive functions (e.g., memory effects, encoding errors, etc.). Our set of heuristics is composed of non-adaptive, static approaches which produce predictions from their core principles instead of from assumed ties to general underlying cognition. This definition includes logic-based methods such as First-Order Logics with and without existential import (*FOL* and *FOL-Strict*), and the Weak Completion Semantics (*WCS*; [2,11]), as well as well-known models from cognitive science such as the *Atmosphere* [16,19,20,23], *Conversion* [1] and *Matching* Hypotheses [22], the min- and attachment heuristics from the Probability Heuristics Model (*PHM-Min*, *PHM-Min-Att*; [14]), and the Psychology of Proof model (*PSYCOP*; [17]). For an in-depth description of most of the cognitive models see [12].

3 Portfolio Analysis

The following sections give details about defining a portfolio of syllogistic heuristics. The analyses and corresponding results[1] are based on data collected from a web experiment run on Amazon Mechanical Turk[2]. In total, the computations are performed on records of 139 participants providing conclusions to the full set of 64 syllogisms, each. All values and visualizations presented below are based on the mean over 500 iterations of *Repeated Random Subsampling* [9] with 100 participants for training and the remaining 39 for testing purposes.

3.1 Portfolio Construction

At the core of the portfolio approach lies a mechanism to identify the quality of a submodel's prediction given a specific task. In the domain of syllogistic reasoning, this corresponds to an algorithm assigning an individual score per submodel and syllogism. We define this score to be the *Mean Reciprocal Rank* (MRR), a metric commonly used in database and recommender systems incorporating a degree of relevance when comparing a set of conclusions predicted by the model with true data [3]. We use the MRR on the set of model predictions and the list of human responses ranked by their frequencies collected from psychological experiments:

$$MRR_M(A_1, A_2, ..., A_{64}) = \frac{1}{64} \sum_{s=1}^{64} \frac{1}{|P_M(s)|} \sum_{p \in P_M(s)} \frac{1}{r(p, A_s)} \tag{1}$$

where A_s represents the aggregated responses of reasoners to syllogism s ranked by frequency, $P_M(s)$ denotes the set of predictions of model M to syllogism s, and $r(p, A_s)$ is a function to compute the rank of response p in A_s.

Following the score assignment strategy detailed above, we obtain the matrix depicted in Fig. 1. It illustrates that certain modeling approaches appear to be

---

[1] https://github.com/nriesterer/syllogistic-portfolios.
[2] https://www.mturk.com.

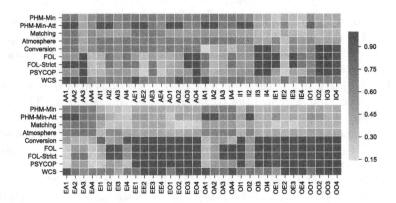

Fig. 1. MRR scores assigned to the set of heuristic models for individual syllogistic tasks. The values are directly used as weights for constructing the portfolio.

associated with good performance for specific regions of the syllogistic problem domain. For instance, theories based on the Atmosphere effect, which is not capable of generating NVC responses, perform well only on valid syllogisms. In contrast, models based on formal logics such as FOL excel on invalid syllogisms but show weaknesses in accounting for illogical human behavior on valid syllogisms. This highlights the potential inherent to portfolio approaches. By only selecting promising models for generating predictions, the performance of the individual submodels can be improved significantly.

3.2   Portfolio Evaluation

In order to define a common ground for evaluation and comparison, different approaches have been pursued in the recent literature. As an example, answer frequencies from human reasoners were dichotomized based on a threshold in order to obtain a vector of representative conclusions which could be compared to the set of predictions given by a model [12]. This metric obfuscates the real-life merit of models by not distinguishing quantitative differences in the answer frequencies. As a result, it allows for a comparison of models, but prevents an intuitive interpretation of the values themselves. We opt for a prediction scenario based on individual responses quantified by precision instead. We define the precision $\mathcal{P}_M$ of model M as the mean over individual task precisions:

$$\mathcal{P}_M(a_1, ..., a_{64}) = \frac{1}{64} \sum_{s=1}^{64} \frac{tp_M(a_s)}{tp_M(a_s) + fp_M(a_s)} \tag{2}$$

where a_s represents the answer of an individual reasoner to syllogism s, and $tp_M(a_s)$ and $fp_M(a_s)$ denote the number of true positives and false positives in the set of predictions generated by model M with respect to the datapoint a_s, respectively.

This precision-based evaluation punishes models producing unranked sets of predictions which generally indicate uncertainty, because only the specific response of a human reasoner is considered correct. Due to the population-based nature of their initial development, this affects all of the psychologically motivated models used for this analysis. Models that are not given the chance to adapt to individual reasoners cannot be expected to perform optimally with respect to precision. However, this adaptive class of models is not considered in current research and subject to future work. Still, the fact that models for all kinds of data levels and complexities can be compared on the same scale is an important advantage of precision.

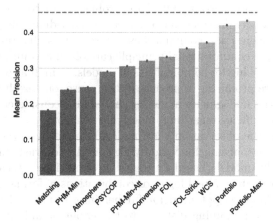

Model	Precision
MFA	0.456
Portfolio-Max	0.433
Portfolio	0.421
WCS	0.372
FOL-Strict	0.355
FOL	0.332
Conversion	0.320
PHM-Min-Att	0.306
PSYCOP	0.290
Atmosphere	0.247
PHM-Min	0.240
Matching	0.182

Fig. 2. Mean precision of the heuristic models as well as the portfolios on the test dataset. The dashed line depicts the upper bound on precision as specified by the *Most Frequent Answer* (MFA).

Figure 2 depicts the results obtained from applying the available models to the test dataset. It shows precision values obtained by the included submodels as well as by two portfolio variants. When being queried for a prediction, the portfolio generates responses based on the individual model's predictions weighted by the corresponding MRR. While *Portfolio* directly generates conclusions on the basis of linear combinations, *Portfolio-Max* only considers the best submodels. Apart from the model performances, the figure additionally includes the precision obtained by following a strategy concluding the *Most Frequent Answer* (MFA). By being defined on the data to be predicted, MFA represents the upper bound of performance models without detailed knowledge about the dataset can hope to achieve.

As expected, the portfolios perform better than the individual submodels. The regular portfolio beats WCS [2] as the best individual model by roughly 5%, arriving at 42%. Portfolio-Max is able to reach 43% pushing near the upper bound of 46% given by MFA. Both portfolios perform significantly better than the best individual model, WCS (Mann-Whitney rank test [13] with $p < .001$ for both, Portfolio and Portfolio-Max).

The fact that Portfolio-Max manages to approach the upper bound of MFA illustrates the fact that in combination, the models are capable of accounting for population-based aggregate data almost optimally. However, without proceeding to the level of modeling individual reasoners, pushing beyond MFA is impossible.

4   General Discussion

Our results demonstrate model differences in accounting for specific parts of the syllogistic problem domain. The portfolio offers novel insight into which strategies reasoners tend to follow for certain syllogistic problems. Its composition identifies clusters of models with distinct performance on individual syllogistic tasks: atmospheric models, logics, and combinations. These results illustrate the unlikeliness of finding a single computational principle capable of accounting for human reasoning. Instead, looking for combinations of models, as in dual-process theories [5], might be a more promising approach. In this sense, our results suggest that the role of heuristics in cognitive modeling should be reconsidered with a stronger focus on their specificity regarding underlying concepts.

Of particular interest is the observation that models inspired by psychological effects are superior in accounting for valid syllogisms. In contrast, invalid syllogisms are dominated by models based on logics. Looking into alternative logics such as nonmonotonic three-valued logics or combinations of formal logics and psychological insight hints at potential for further improvement of single model performance. Still, the remaining distance to the upper bound given by the most frequent answer suggests an approaching saturation of the performance from future models built on the basis of aggregated population data. In order to push the predictive performance even further, models need to start incorporating individual traits in reasoning, e.g., by solving completion tasks where missing data is to be imputed.

By achieving state-of-the-art performance, portfolios can serve as a first step towards finding sets of models optimally accounting for human behavior, either on the basis of individuals or populations. This allows for the assessment of the methodological composition of human reasoning while creating high-performant models. Specific challenges for the future include finding a minimal set of models to optimally account for human behavior and the iterative construction of reasoning theories based on fundamental inference methods. As a particularly beneficial side-effect, subjecting the domain to prediction tasks allows for more competition. By providing a well-defined problem and intuitive methods for evaluation, computer scientists and cognitive scientists alike can compete and collaborate to advance our knowledge about the mind.

Acknowledgements. This paper was supported by DFG grants RA 1934/3-1, RA 1934/2-1 and RA 1934/4-1 to MR.

References

1. Chapman, L.J., Chapman, J.P.: Atmosphere effect re-examined. J. Exp. Psychol. **58**(3), 220 (1959)
2. da Costa, A.O., Saldanha, E.A.D., Hölldobler, S., Ragni, M.: A computational logic approach to human syllogistic reasoning. In: Proceedings of the 39th Annual Conference of the Cognitive Science Society (2017)
3. Craswell, N.: Mean reciprocal rank. In: Liu, L., Özsu, M. (eds.) Encyclopedia of Database Systems. Springer, New York (2016). https://doi.org/10.1007/978-1-4899-7993-3
4. Eliasmith, C., et al.: A large-scale model of the functioning brain. Science **338**(6111), 1202–1205 (2012)
5. Evans, J.S.B.: Heuristic and analytic processes in reasoning. Br. J. Psychol. **75**(4), 451–468 (1984)
6. Freund, Y.: Boosting a weak learning algorithm by majority. Inf. Comput. **121**(2), 256–285 (1995)
7. Freund, Y., Schapire, R.E.: A decision-theoretic generalization of on-line learning and an application to boosting. J. Comput. Syst. Sci. **55**(1), 119–139 (1997)
8. Gomes, C.P., Selman, B.: Algorithm portfolios. Artif. Intell. **126**(1–2), 43–62 (2001)
9. Han, J., Pei, J., Kamber, M.: Data Mining: Concepts and Techniques. Elsevier, New York (2011)
10. Hoffmann, J., Nebel, B.: The FF planning system: fast plan generation through heuristic search. J. Artif. Intell. Res. **14**, 253–302 (2001)
11. Hölldobler, S.: Weak completion semantics and its applications in human reasoning. In: Bridging@ CADE, pp. 2–16 (2015)
12. Khemlani, S., Johnson-Laird, P.N.: Theories of the syllogism: a meta-analysis. Psychol. Bull. **138**(3), 427 (2012)
13. Mann, H.B., Whitney, D.R.: On a test of whether one of two random variables is stochastically larger than the other. Ann. Math. Stat. **18**, 50–60 (1947)
14. Oaksford, M., Chater, N., Larkin, J.: Probabilities and polarity biases in conditional inference. J. Exp. Psychol.: Learn. Mem. Cogn. **26**(4), 883 (2000)
15. Pearl, J.: Heuristics: Intelligent Search Strategies for Computer Problem Solving. Addison-Wesley Publishing Co. Inc., Reading (1984)
16. Revlis, R.: Two models of syllogistic reasoning: feature selection and conversion. J. Verbal Learn. Verbal Behav. **14**(2), 180–195 (1975)
17. Rips, L.J.: The Psychology of Proof: Deductive Reasoning in Human Thinking. MIT Press, Cambridge (1994)
18. Schapire, R.E.: The strength of weak learnability. Mach. Learn. **5**(2), 197–227 (1990)
19. Sells, S.B.: The atmosphere effect: an experimental study of reasoning. Archives of Psychology (Columbia University) (1936)
20. Sells, S.B., Koob, H.F.: A classroom demonstration of "atmosphere effect" in reasoning. J. Educ. Psychol. **28**(7), 514 (1937)
21. Snoddy, G.S.: Learning and stability: a psychophysiological analysis of a case of motor learning with clinical applications. J. Appl. Psychol. **10**(1), 1 (1926)
22. Wetherick, N., Gilhooly, K.: Atmosphere, matching, and logic in syllogistic reasoning. Current Psychology **14**(3), 169–178 (1995)
23. Woodworth, R.S., Sells, S.B.: An atmosphere effect in formal syllogistic reasoning. Journal of Experimental Psychology **18**(4), 451 (1935)
24. Xu, L., Hutter, F., Hoos, H.H., Leyton-Brown, K.: SATzilla: portfolio-based algorithm selection for SAT. Journal of artificial intelligence research **32**, 565–606 (2008)

Author Index

Printed in the United States
By Bookmasters